SOCIALIST CHURCHES

SOCIALIST CHURCHES

RADICAL SECULARIZATION AND THE PRESERVATION OF THE PAST IN PETROGRAD AND LENINGRAD, 1918–1988

CATRIONA KELLY

NIU Press / DeKalb, IL

978-0-87580-743-0 (cloth)
978-1-60909-204-7 (e-book)

Book and cover design by Yuni Dorr

Library of Congress Cataloging-in-Publication Data
Names: Kelly, Catriona, author.
Title: Socialist churches : radical secularization and the preservation of
   the past in Petrograd and Leningrad, 1918–1988 / Catriona Kelly.
Description: DeKalb : Northern Illinois University Press, 2016. | Includes
   bibliographical references and index.
Identifiers: LCCN 2016011327 (print) | LCCN 2016031749 (ebook) | ISBN
   9780875807430 (cloth : alk. paper) | ISBN 9781609092047 (ebook)
Subjects: LCSH: Atheism—Soviet Union. | Church buildings—Soviet Union. |
   Historic buildings—Conservation and restoration—Soviet Union.
Classification: LCC BL2765.S65 K425 2016 (print) | LCC BL2765.S65 (ebook) |
   DDC 322/.109470904—dc23
LC record available at https://lccn.loc.gov/2016011327

To the memory of my parents

Alexander Kelly

(June 30, 1929–October 23, 1996)

Margaret Moncrieff Kelly

(February 6, 1921–November 12, 2008)

Contents

Acknowledgments

The work for this book has been generously supported by large numbers of funding bodies, colleagues, and friends. The project "National Identity in Russia from 1961: Traditions and Deterritorialization," sponsored by the Arts and Humanities Research Councils, allowed me to do preliminary work on preservation in the post-Stalin era. Travel and interviewing costs for the remainder of the project were supported by the Ludwig Fund, New College, and by the John Fell Fund, University of Oxford. Given the controversial nature of religious issues in Russia and beyond, I should emphasize that none of the institutions or individuals whom I mention here should be held to account for matters of fact or opinion in this book, which are entirely my own responsibility.

Interviews carried out for the book are cited with the code Oxf/AHRC, the place code SPb and date (09, etc.), and also a recording number and the initials of the interviewer. My thanks go to the informants and to the interviewers, Alexandra Piir, Veronika Makarova, and Marina Samsonova, who also provided many insights of their own and advice along the way. Alexandra Piir deserves particular gratitude for having suggested the topic to begin with, and for helping with archival work at an early stage. I have benefited a great deal from conversations with leading local historians Aleksandr Margolis, Aleksandr Kobak, and Lev Lur'e. The audience of the "Urban Anthropology" seminar at the European University, St. Petersburg, commented incisively on some of the material when I presented it to their uniquely knowledgeable forum. I am grateful also to the other audiences and readers who have responded to materials in their emerging state, including the members of the Russian History Workshop at Georgetown University, particularly Michael David-Fox, Steven A. Grant, and Eric Lohr; the participants in the conference "Global Transformation and Pastiche Identities" at Queen Mary, University of London; and the workshops, "The State, Nationalism, and Historic Buildings," organized by Mark Thatcher at the European University

Institute, Florence and Bocconi University, Milan; "Science, Religion, and Communism during the Cold War," organized by Paul Betts and Steve Smith at St. Antony's College, Oxford; and "Soviet Traditions: 'Official' vs. 'Unofficial' Reality" at the European University, St. Petersburg. Victoria Arnold's study of "sacred space" in Perm', and Victoria Donovan's work on Vologda, Novgorod, and Pskov were of great help as I was forming my ideas on this topic. I also thank the editors of the journals where some materials have previously appeared in a different form, particularly Mark D. Steinberg, then editor of *Slavic Review*, and Marc Elie and Isabelle Ohayon, guest editors of a special number of *Cahiers du monde russe* on the Brezhnev years.

Information about architecture generally, and church architecture particularly, is scattered in a range of different repositories, and while doing research for this book, I have worked in over twenty libraries and archives. I am deeply grateful to the staffs of all of them, especially Ol'ga I. Khodakovskaia in the St. Petersburg Diocesan Archive; Maria V. Medvedeva in the Scholarly Archive of the Institute of the History of Material Culture, Russian Academy of Sciences; Natalia V. Savinova of the Central State Archive of Historico-Political Documents; Liubov' N. Pyzhova of the Central State Archive of Film, Photographic, and Phonographic Documents; and Mikhail V. Shkarovskii in the Central State Archive of St. Petersburg. I am also very grateful to the many members of the Orthodox clergy who have helped in one way or another, including the late Metropolitan Vladimir of St. Petersburg and Ladoga, who kindly agreed to allow my work in the St. Petersburg Diocesan Archive, and others who prefer to remain anonymous. Canon Michael Bourdeaux generously shared his considerable expertise on Orthodox affairs and was helpful with contacts, as was Professor Vitaly Bezrogov in Moscow. Konstantin Erofeev, a lawyer specializing in church affairs, helped me through some of the complications of the legal measures relating to use of churches for worship. I have also learned much from conversations with friends and colleagues, in particular Al'bert Baiburin, Vadim Bass, Konstantin Bogdanov, Simon Dixon, Al'bin Konechnyi, Jeanne Kormina, Kseniia Kumpan, Stephen Lovell, Aleksandr Panchenko, Andreas Schönle, Sergei Shtyrkov, Steve Smith, Aleksandr Strugach, and Josie von Zitzewitz. Jeanne Kormina was kind enough to read the entire draft, and made numerous helpful suggestions, as did Karl Qualls and another reader for Northern Illinois University Press. Christine Worobec, Amy Farranto, and Nathan Holmes have supported the publication of the book in a great many ways, and Lucy Dunlop was an excellent indexer.

In a book about commemoration, it seems appropriate to pay tribute to my late parents, professional musicians with the artist's sensitivity to beauty of all kinds. My father's architecture walks when my sister and I were children laid the foundation for the structure that is completed here. Both he and my mother firmly believed, like many of the actors in this book, that there is life beyond the material world. I hope they were right. May their memory shine.

List of Abbreviations and Glossary

ansambl': a coordinated set of architectural features or complex of buildings (from the French *ensemble)*, a key term in city planning through the Soviet period.

Antonov and Kobak, *SSPb*: V. V. Antonov and A. V. Kobak, *Sviatyni Sankt-Peterburga: Entsiklopediia khristianskikh khramov*, 3rd ed. (St. Petersburg: Fond Spas, 2010).

ASPbE: Arkhiv Sankt-Peterburgskoi eparkhii (St. Petersburg Diocesan Archive).

ASPbGASU: Archive of SPbGASU (see below).

BAN: Biblioteka Akademii Nauk (Library of the Academy of Sciences, St. Petersburg).

blagolepie: a Church Slavonic term signifying decorum, good order.

chapel (*chasovnia*): a freestanding chapel, e.g., in a street.

Church Council (Vserossiiskii Pomestnyi Sobor): the All-Russian Local (as opposed to Ecumenical) Council of the Orthodox Church held in Moscow from 1917 to 1918.

Coreligionists (*Edinovertsy*): A body of the Orthodox faithful who, while celebrating rites according to the practices of the Old Believers, have since 1800 been in communion with the mainstream Orthodox Church.

diocese (*eparkhiia*): An ecclesiastical territory under the jurisdiction of a bishop or metropolitan (metropolitan bishop). The diocese of which Petrograd/Leningrad was the center was known from August 18, 1914, to June 17, 1917, as the Diocese of Petrograd and Ladoga, from then until January 1924 as the Diocese of Petrograd and Gdov, from 1924 until 1943 as the Diocese of Leningrad and Gdov, from 1943 to 1957 as the Diocese of Leningrad and Novgorod, and from 1957 until 1991 as the Diocese of Leningrad and Ladoga.

It is now the Diocese of St. Petersburg and Ladoga. For the sake of brevity I refer here to "Petrograd diocese" and "Metropolitan of Leningrad," etc.

DSV: *Dekrety sovetskoi vlasti*: (Moscow: Institut marksizma-leninizma, 1957–)

dvadtsatka: The group of at least twenty worshippers forming a congregation or community (*obshchina*) for the purposes of leasing a place of worship and so on under the statute of January 20, 1918, and throughout the Soviet period.

FN: author's field notes.

funerary chapel (*usypal'nitsa*): a memorial structure, e.g., in a cemetery.

GARF: Gosudarstvennyi arkhiv Rossiiskoi Federatsii (State Archive of the Russian Federation)

GMISPb: Gosudarstvennyi muzei istorii Sankt-Peterburga (State Museum of St. Petersburg).

GIOP: Gosudarstvennaia inspektsiia okhrany pamiatnikov (State Inspectorate for the Protection of Monuments)

Gorkom: Gorodskoi komitet Kommunisticheskoi partii Sovetskogo Soiuza (City Committee of the Communist Party), the primary organ of Party rule in Leningrad city, subordinate to the Obkom.

house church (*domovaia tserkov'*): a "chapel" in the sense of an institutional or domestic place of worship, whether inside a building or freestanding.

incumbent (*nastoiatel'*): the senior cleric in a church or cathedral, roughly equivalent to "rector" or "vicar" in the Anglican Church and "parish priest" in the Roman Catholic Church, in the first case, and "dean" in the second.

KG: *Krasnaia gazeta*.

Lengubsovet: Leningradskii gubernskii sovet rabochikh, krest'ianskikh i krasnoarmeiskikh deputatov, the Council of Deputies, or main organ of government for Leningrad Province, 1924–1927.

Lenispolkom: Ispolnitel'nyi sovet Leningradskogo soveta deputatov trudiashchikhsia: the Executive Committee of Lensovet (see below).

Lenoblispolkom: Ispolnitel'nyi komitet Leningradskogo oblastnogo soveta deputatov trudiashchikhsia: the Executive Committee of Lenoblsovet (see below).

Lenoblsovet: Leningradskii oblastnoi sovet rabochikh, krest'ianskikh i krasnoarmeiskikh deputatov (later deputatov trudiashchikhsia and then narodnykh
deputatov), the Council of Deputies, or main organ of government, for
Leningrad Province, 1927–1991.

Lensovet: Leningradskii sovet rabochikh, krest'ianskikh i krasnoarmeiskikh deputatov (later deputatov trudiashchikhsia and then narodnykh deputatov), the
Council of Deputies, or main organ of municipal government, 1924–1991.

liniia: a term occasionally used for streets in St. Petersburg, particularly on
Vasilievskii Island.

LISI: Leningradskii inzhinerno-stroitel'nyi institut (the Leningrad Institute of
Civil Engineering and Construction), previously the Institute of Civil Engineers, founded 1832, the training place for most of Leningrad's planners
from the mid-1930s.

LOSA: Leningradskoe otdelenie Soiuza arkhitektorov (the Leningrad branch of
the Union of Architects).

LP: *Leningradskaia pravda.*

NA UGIOP: Nauchnyi arkhiv Upravleniia Gosudarstvennoi inspektsii okhrany
pamiatnikov (Scholarly Archive of the Board of Management of the State
Inspectorate for the Preservation of Monuments, St. Petersburg).

NEP: Novaia ekonomicheskaia politika (New Economic Policy, or period of limited license for private enterprise, 1921–1928).

Obkom: Oblastnoi komitet Kommunisticheskoi partii Sovetskogo Soiuza (Provincial Committee of the Communist Party), the primary organ of Party
rule at regional level (superior to the Gorkom).

OPIK 1973: Anisimov, G. G., ed. *Okhrana pamiatnikov istorii i kul'tury; Sbornik
dokumentov.* Moscow: Sovetskaia Rossiia, 1973.

OR RNB: Otdel rukopisei Rossiiskoi natsional'noi biblioteki (Manuscript Department of the Russian National Library).

parish (*prikhod*): a territorial subdivision of a diocese; traditionally, the community associated with a church in geographical terms; in the Soviet period,
the members of the "religious society."

pereulok: a side street.

Petrogubsovet: Petrogradskii Gubernskii Sovet rabochikh, krest'ianskikh i soldatskikh deputatov, the highest organ of administration in Petrograd province, 1917–1924.

Petrosovet: Petrogradskii Sovet rabochikh i soldatskikh deputatov (Petrograd City Council), the highest organ of the city administration, 1917–1924.

ploshchad': a city square.

PP: *Petrogradskaia pravda.*

prospekt: avenue, a major street.

PSZ: *Polnoe sobranie zakonov Rossiiskoi Imperii* (St Petersburg: Tipografiia Sobstvennoi Ego Velichestva Kantseliarii, 1830-1884; Gosudarstvennaia tipografiia, 1885–1916).

RA IIMK: Rukopisnyi arkhiv Instituta material'noi kul'tury Rossiiskoi Akademii Nauk (Manuscript Archive of the Institute of Material Culture, Russian Academy of Sciences, St. Petersburg).

RGANI: Rossiiskii gosudarstvennyi arkhiv noveishei istorii (Russian State Archive of Recent History, Moscow).

RGB: Rossiiskaia gosudarstvennaia biblioteka (Russian State Library, former Lenin Library, Moscow).

RNB: Rossiiskaia natsional'naia biblioteka (Russian National Library, former Public Library, St. Petersburg).

RO IRLI RAN: Rukopisnyi otdel Instituta russkoi literatury Rossiiskoi Akademii Nauk (Manuscript Section of the Institute of Russian Literature, Russian Academy of Sciences, St. Petersburg).

RSFSR: Rossiiskaia Sovetskaia Federativnaia Sotsialisticheskaia Respublika (Russian Soviet Federal Socialist Republic), the official title of what is now the Russian Federation under Soviet rule. Unlike the other Soviet republics, the RSFSR did not have a separate government or central committee of the Communist Party, but it did have its own ministries, responsible, among other things, for aspects of conservation policy.

Sovnarkom: Sovet narodnykh komissarov (The Council of People's Commissars), the main government (as opposed to Party) organ of executive government in the USSR (replaced by the Council of Ministers [Sovet ministrov] in 1946).

SPbGASU: Sankt-Peterburgskii gosudarstvennyi arkhitekturno-stroitel'nyi universitet (the St. Petersburg State University of Architecture and Construction) (formerly LISI).

SU: *Sobranie uzakonenii i rasporiazhenii raboche-krest'ianskogo pravitel'stva* (Moscow: Narodnyi komissariat iustizii, 1919–)

TsGA-SPb: Tsentral'nyi gosudarstvennyi arkhiv Sankt-Peterburga (Central State Archive of St. Petersburg).

TsGAIPD-SPb: Tsentral'nyi gosudarstvennyi arkhiv istoriko-politicheskikh dokumentov Sankt-Peterburga (Central State Archive of Historico-Political Documents, St. Petersburg).

TsGAKFFD-SPb: Tsentral'nyi gosudarstvennyi arkhiv kino- foto- fonodokumentov Sankt-Peterburga (State Archive of Film, Photographic, and Phonographic Documents, St. Petersburg).

TsGALI-SPb: Tsentral'nyi gosudarstvennyi arkhiv literatury i iskusstva Sankt-Peterburga (Central State Archive of Literature and Art, St. Petersburg).

TsGANTD-SPb: Tsentral'nyi gosudarstvennyi arkhiv nauchno-tekhnicheskoi dokumentatsii Sankt-Peterburga (Central State Archive of Scientific and Technical Documentation, St. Petersburg).

ulitsa: a street.

VL: *Vechernii Leningrad.*

Note on Translation

The question of whether to translate and/or adapt ecclesiastical terminology when writing in English about the Russian Orthodox Church has no conclusive answer. In this book, the names of saints, prophets, and so on common to both the Eastern and Western churches appear in the forms familiar in the West (Isaac, Elijah, Anne, not Isaak, Il'ia, Anna). However, the names of churchmen appear in the Russian form (Metropolitan Grigorii, rather than Gregory). I have naturalized "eparkhiia" as "diocese" and "blagochinnyi" as "dean," but have retained the alien term "house church" to refer to institutional and domestic chapels, since the status of these in Russian and Soviet history was subject to specific regulation. Equally, I have used Westernized forms of certain major city spaces much mentioned in the book (the Haymarket [later Peace Square], Uprising Square, International Prospect), because this conveys to readers without a thorough knowledge of Russian and local history the discursive transformations that accompanied reshaping of these sites in planning terms. However, most names of streets and public places are left in transliteration (Bol'shoi prospekt, not Big Avenue, ulitsa Pestelia, not Pestel' Street, etc.). I have not rendered *khram* (the high-style word for a church) as the literal "temple": although the Russian word is used for some categories of non-Christian religious buildings (e.g., Buddhist temples), the usage does not suggest that Orthodoxy and other faiths are equivalent or akin. Nor have I attempted to mimic the standard vernacular Russian usage that denotes churches without reference to the word "saint" (Isaac Cathedral, Vladimir Church, etc.), though I have adopted familiar names rather than official titles: Smol'nyi Cathedral rather than the Cathedral of the Resurrection of the Lord at Smol'nyi, St. Isaac's rather than the Cathedral of the Venerable St. Isaac of Dalmatia, and so on. In some cases, the popular title not only abbreviates the official one, but is completely different: thus, the Savior on the Haymarket rather than the Church of the Dormition of the Mother of God.

I have generally used Library of Congress transliteration, with exceptions for surnames, place names, etc., where an alternative spelling is more familiar (Dostoevsky, Alexander Nevsky, Yeltsin).

List of Illustrations

IN ISAAK BABEL'S SHORT story "At St. Walenty's," first published in 1924, a Red Cossack division engaged on the Polish campaign of 1920 reaches the baroque church of Berestechko, formerly in the Western part of the Russian Empire.[1] Liutov, Babel's narrator and alter ego, a political officer with the division, enters "a square annex to the altar" to discover Sashka, a camp follower of the division, rummaging through a heap of rich textiles:

> She had ripped up the vestments and torn the silk off someone's clothes. A deathly smell of brocade, scattered flowers, aromatic rot poured into her trembling nostrils, tickling them and poisoning them. Then into the room came the Cossacks. They guffawed, seized Sasha by one breast and flung her on the rebound on to the mountain of textiles and holy books. The Cossacks laid bare Sashka's body, flowering and stinking like the flesh of a cow just slaughtered, they laid bare her squadron lady's legs, iron-strong and slender, and Kurdiukov, a foolish lad, mounted Sashka and, jerking as though he were in the saddle, affected to be in the act of passion. She threw him off, giving him a crack on the head, and flung herself on her sack. The Cossacks and I had hard work of it to drive her off those silks. She pointed a revolver at us and slunk off, staggering and snarling, like an angry dog, and dragging the sack behind her. She carried off the sack, and only then, walking past the altar, did we enter the church.[2]

The scene in the church itself seems, to Liutov's eyes, more decorous:

> Maddened by recollections of my dream, my dream of Apolek, I did not even notice
> the signs of destruction in the church, or they seemed to amount to little. It was
> only the shrine of St. Walenty that was broken. Scraps of rotten fluff lolled under it,
> along with the ridiculous bones of the saint, more like a chicken's than anything else.
> And Afon'ka Bida was playing the organ. He was drunk, Afon'ka, savage and hacked
> about. Only yesterday he'd come back to us with a horse he'd gotten off some peasant
> men. Afon'ka determinedly picked out a march on the organ, and someone was
> trying to stop him, saying sleepily: "Cut it, Afon'ka, time for some grub."

However, if Liutov is undisturbed by the carnival that he witnesses, the same cannot be said of the bell ringer, Pan Ludomirski, who pronounces anathema upon
the intruders. The outraged congregation, though, is not allowed the last word: at
the end of the narrative, Liutov observes that order has been restored by the Soviet
government itself.

> Having come back to my senses in headquarters, I sent a report to the division com-
> mander about the offense caused to the religious feelings of the local population. An
> order was issued to close the church and for those responsible to be court-martialed
> on disciplinary charges.[3]

Though Babel's story is dated with some precision: "Berestechko, August 1920,"
the incident goes unrecorded in his field diary of 1920 (which, instead, describes
the synagogue at Berestechko). The relationship with fact has been significantly
adjusted. For instance, the name of the church (in reality, dedicated to the Trinity)
has been changed to achieve a symbolic effect: Babel's "St. Valentine" chimes ironically with the obscene mating ritual enacted by Sashka and Kurdiukov. Rather
than meticulous documentation, the aim of the story is a mythic representation
of iconoclasm as a dramatic contest. Pan Ludomirski sees the church mainly as
a place of ritual prohibitions (he cannot put right the damage to the reliquary,
Babel tells us, because "an ordinary person may not touch sacred things").[4] Sashka
and Afon'ka relentlessly pursue their own ends, whether self-enrichment or self-
expression, and the narrator's aestheticizing gaze is gripped from the first by the
theatricality of the building: "The church rose before us, blinding as a stage set."[5]
Equally mythic is the repudiation of wild destructive impulses, and more particularly, the offense to believers, as unworthy of those serving in the Soviet armed

forces—and the fact that the final restoration of order also demands the closure of the church.

Within *Red Cavalry* as a literary text, "At St. Walenty's" has its own logic, expressing the mixture of horror and erotic fascination that the Cossacks inspire in Liutov (and the reader). It also illustrates the interplay of different models of art: the radically innovative religious paintings of Pan Apolek (the protagonist of another, independent story in Babel's cycle); the wild organ-playing of Afon'ka; and the late-baroque beauty of the church itself.

Yet, for all its commitment to mythic rather than literal truth, Babel's portrait of the competition between the different impulses aroused by a historic church at times of social conflict gives a good sense of the actual problems that were negotiated by the central and local administrations of the new Soviet state as they dealt with ecclesiastical buildings that were held to be of historic and artistic value. The desire to destroy; the determination to loot or to appropriate for one's own ends, whether those of personal gain or connoisseurship; the sense of a building's aesthetic integrity; the awareness of the impermissibility of "offense to believers"—all these, or a mixture, were possible responses to the symbols of a religious establishment now toppled from its former domination.

From the point of view of political leaders, action against churches, like that against symbols of the ancien régime generally, was useful where it indicated or encouraged support for the revolutionary government and its ideals, but dangerous where it expressed random hostility to social order of any kind.[6] The leaders, unlike some activists at the grass roots, were also keenly aware of the distinction between anticlerical feeling and the rejection of religious belief and practice. "Superstition" might prove tenacious even where anticlerical feeling was high. How to eradicate it without exacerbating social dislocation was a crucial and difficult question.[7] Though the circumstances of a church in war-torn Berestechko were highly specific, the different attitudes to the building (as work of art, as repository of treasures to be snatched and cashiered, as symbol of the detested old order, and as haven of piety) were to be found in many other places during the early years of Soviet culture—and, indeed, its later phases as well.

So far as secular buildings were concerned, there was a decisive move against random destruction at a very early stage of Soviet history. After the October Revolution, the Winter Palace and other royal residences were extensively looted:

> The picture of rout inside the palace was complete: broken furniture and smashed glass, etc., etc., was lying round everywhere. On further investigation and

checking-over of the property, it emerged that the amount of a fairly small quantity of mostly utilitarian property and decorative items had been stolen. The quarters of the ladies-in-waiting had been plundered completely; the results of looting were also clear in some of the storage rooms. The historical apartments of Alexander II and Nicholas II had also suffered, but in their case insignificantly.[8]

Anatoly Lunacharsky, responsible for cultural policy in his position as commissar of enlightenment, set his face against such acts with the transfer, on November 6, 1917, of the palaces and other property formerly regulated by the Ministry of the Imperial Court to the jurisdiction of the Commissariat of State Property. Within Lunacharsky's education commissariat (Narodnyi komissariat prosvesh-cheniia, familiarly abbreviated to Narkompros) was created a special "Museums Department," responsible also for the protection of monuments. It was headed by Natal'ia Sedova, whose married name, Trotskaia, pointed to her powerful connections at the heart of government. The Museum Department's Restoration Section was led by the painter and director of the Tretyakov Gallery, Igor' Grabar', soon to become one of the leading figures in the Soviet preservation of heritage, and other restorers held positions in the central offices of the Museums Department also.[9]

Lunacharsky's preservationist stance was supported by Vladimir Lenin, who on October 5, 1918, signed into law the first Soviet legislation on the protection of monuments, the "Decree on the Registration, Inventorization, and Protection of Monuments of Art and History. As well as ordaining the registration of "all works of monumental art and objects," the decree initiated a process whereby monuments of significance would be placed on a state inventory, and the sale of these and alteration and repair work to them would be regulated by the Museums Department. Breach of these rules was punishable by confiscation, as was the failure to take due care of a registered monument.[10]

The preservation of heritage was enshrined in the 1922 Criminal Code. Article 102, in the section relating to "counterrevolutionary crimes," outlawed the failure to declare "collections and monuments of history and art requiring restoration, inclusion in official inventories, or transfer to the collections of museums." The maximum sentence was a year's compulsory labor, with confiscation of the items in question.[11] In 1923, the Museums Department proposed to add to Article 102 violation of protection legislation, to be punishable by a fine of up to 500 gold rubles and up to a year's imprisonment.[12]

In 1923–1924, further specific legislation on the protection of monuments was pushed through. These statutes remained on the books for the next sixty-five and more years, and other important legislation expanding monuments protection followed, notably in 1947 and 1966. In 1965 was founded a special broadly based public organization, the All-Russian Society for the Protection of Monuments of History and Culture (VOOPIiK), which became an important lobbying body in the Soviet Union's last decades.[13]

In due course, the preservation of heritage was to become a source of pride to Soviet historians; the country's record was seen as exceptional both in national and international terms.[14] Yet the canonical retrospective discussions of how preservation evolved lend an illusory smoothness to a set of processes that expressed deep political and cultural divisions.[15] Heritage preservation was located at the intersection of several different policy areas—including, but not limited to, aesthetic education, city planning, and the construction of national identity. Institutional fragmentation was also characteristic, with the education and culture ministries, architecture and planning departments of local authorities, architects' professional associations, and building authorities all at some level involved in the regulation of how listed buildings were used—and often at loggerheads with each other also. At some periods of Soviet history, notably 1921–1930 and 1965–1991, public organizations lobbying for heritage protection also entered the area, and tussles proliferated.

While this atomization and conflict characterized other areas of cultural policy too, there was an additional problem where heritage preservation was concerned, in that the extent to which Soviet administrators could draw on, or even react against, prerevolutionary policy was limited. Certainly, legislation to protect historic buildings and monuments went back nearly a century, the first statute having been enacted in 1822. Over the course of the nineteenth century, regulations had proliferated, and the process of agreeing alterations had been professionalized. From March 11, 1889, special committees of the Academy of Sciences and the Academy of Arts were responsible for vetting proposals to carry out work in buildings that were deemed to be of historical and/or artistic value, and on works of monumental art.[16] However, work to draw up an integrated statute on the preservation of monuments ended in stalemate, partly because of the complexities of liaising between the different bureaucracies with an interest in the problem. These included the Ministry of the Court, the Office of the Orthodox Confession, the Ministry of War, the Ministry of Justice, State Chancery, the Ministry of Popular Enlightenment, the Technical and Buildings Committee, the Zemstvo Department, and the General Department, not to speak of professional bodies such as the Archaeological Commission and the Commission on Russian Icon-Painting.[17]

There were no nationwide official lists of legally recognized "monuments of history" (*pamiatniki stariny*), although planning for such lists began in the late nineteenth century, and though heritage issues were regularly discussed at architects' and artists' professional congresses of the day.[18] As with planning issues generally, there was a tense conflict between emerging attention to the rights of property owners and the emphasis on aesthetic standards and pleasing uniformity that was embodied in the Russian term *blagoustroistvo*, or "the good organization of construction." In 1911, at the Fourth Congress of Russian Architects, E. E. Baumgarten and Lev Il'in argued for a crackdown on various types of street signage, including both commercial advertising and government notices, but this type of initiative was, as they noted, unusual even in Russia's main cities.[19]

When it started work in 1918, the Museums Department therefore had no ready-made chain of command, no procedural template, and no inventories of objects deserving protection. An enormous amount of energy, in its first years of existence, went into the exercise of creating these, and particularly the inventories. According to a report dating from 1921, 570 country estates had been surveyed by the Museums Department, and 320 "registered as having artistic and historic interest"; 170 churches and monasteries had also been assessed. However impressive these figures were, they represented only a fraction of the patrimony, and so the next task of the Department was to organize seventy-eight provincial and district sections, which were also charged mainly with continuing the surveying work.[20] This tendency to work on paper—to legislate, survey, and admonish—persisted through the successive decades of heritage protection as well.

At its beginnings, Soviet policy with regard to heritage was essentially reactive: something had to be done to control destruction. As Babel's "At St. Walenty's" shows, the issue was not only that such action threatened art and history; it also smacked of popular misrule.[21] Like all manifestations of "spontaneous" rebellion (as opposed to "conscious" revolutionary struggle), assaults on buildings were suspicious because they suggested potentially uncontrollable, directionless self-assertion by groups that were at best semiliterate in political terms.[22] Added to this, Bolshevik administrators grasped from an early stage that the material heritage had value not just in aesthetic terms, but from other points of view also. Like all cultural forms inherited from the past, it had the potential to aid *vospitanie* (moral and political education).[23] But the material heritage—unlike say literature or music—also had value in a straightforward economic sense.[24] Buildings could be leased out in return for payment, and artworks sold. The best-known cases of such sales took place from 1927 onward, in order to finance the industrialization and urbanization drive initiated by the First Five-Year Plan.[25] But the mechanisms for them were put in place much earlier. A July 13, 1920, decree allowed state agencies to seize precious metals, jewels, private collections with monetary or scientific value, theater sets and costumes, and artworks that had been abandoned, or which were being illegally exported.[26] Natal'ia Sedova-Trotskaia, alongside her leading role at the Museums Department at Narkompros, was also chair of the Commission on the Inventorization and Realization of State Funds of the Council of Labor and Defense. In the latter capacity, she oversaw a sifting of museum stock in 1922–1923 whose purpose was to remove items made of precious metal and gemstones that had "exclusively material value" and those whose "material value predominated over their historical and artistic value."[27] The object of the exercise was to realize the monetary value of the items concerned. This monetization drive ran in direct contradiction to the understanding of architecture and works of art as expressions of timeless spiritual values and appurtenances of the national patrimony (*narodnoe dostoianie*). Even the appropriation into state care of valuable items threatened preservation: on May 26, 1919, the Museums Department in Petrograd reported, "Often the entire setting, not just individual objects, is left broken and damaged, and, where honesty is in abeyance, may even be traded on the black market."[28]

It was not just economic pragmatism that was the enemy of conservation. In ideological terms, fear of endorsing "open season" on radical efforts to overturn the past vied with a fear of the past. There was a good deal of uncertainty about whether old buildings were an asset to Soviet culture or an obstacle to its construction. Definition of "historical and artistic value" was a sensitive issue. If culture could be instrumental to Soviet political ends where it was compatible with these, ideologically suspect forms of culture were held to threaten political purity and Soviet morality. The most famous effect of this binary stance was the creation, from the first months of Bolshevik rule, of a formidable apparatus of print (and later theater and film) censorship.[29] An equally important if less well-known result was the commitment to "purging" parts of the material culture that were associated with negative aspects of the past. Premises that before 1917 had been in the exclusive use of the cultural elite were used to house institutions dedicated to the welfare of the Soviet masses, broadly interpreted (a palace might become a children's home or an educational institution).[30] A more neutral development was the institution of so-called "museums of daily life" that created exhibitions out of dwelling-houses once used by aristocrats and merchants, employing objects for the documentation of history, according to interdisciplinary patterns that drew on local history, ethnography, and history of art.[31] Elite buildings were also used for the dissemination of culture in a broader sense. There was never any doubt that the former court and private theaters (now owned by the state) should continue to be used as theaters, and the conservatories and ballet schools remained in the buildings that had housed them before 1917. The former Assembly of the Nobility in Petrograd was transformed, in 1921, into a concert hall, the official home of the Philharmonic Orchestra, while the Merchants' Club became the home of the Karl Marx Club and the Free Theater.[32]

Conversions of this kind were straightforward in ideological terms. The Communist Party leaders themselves had conservative artistic tastes, and regarded avant-garde directions in art at best ironically. In any case, in the early years of Soviet rule, there was not yet a coherent drive for "new architecture" to challenge the tastes of the past (this movement acquired the necessary political capital only in the second half of the 1920s).[33] Practically speaking, there were few difficulties either. Running a scientific institute in a building that consisted of splendid halls and cramped garrets, and little if anything in between, might present everyday challenges. But those working in such places "got by" (as they did in later periods of Soviet history, and indeed after 1991).[34] From the point of view of central and local government, these arrangements also suited because hand-to-mouth use of existing buildings and furniture was significantly cheaper than building and manufacturing modern alternatives. To shift a building from one secular purpose to another was usually straightforward in conversion terms too. In Petrograd, former ministries became departments of the city administration without the need for replanning or even much rethought of office layouts.[35]

A far more significant problem was what to do with ecclesiastical buildings, which were inimical to the new political system in ideological terms. Before 1917, the preservation of churches had been at the heart of efforts to protect heritage, with some of the earliest legislation relating specifically to them.[36] This was, of course, directly related to the centrality of churches to the official Russian nationalism and imperial legitimacy of the day: successive emperors, beginning with Nicholas I, made excursions in national ecclesiastical architecture the heart of their push to exercise spatial authority.[37] While legislation on the conservation of churches began about two decades later than legislation on the conservation of old buildings in general (1842 rather than 1822), it was in some respects more strict. For example, a synodal decree of 1865 required that not just "ancient" churches be preserved, but those "which are not ancient, but are remarkable in terms of their architecture, or in terms of historical remembrance."[38] Another set of regulations stipulated that churches should be well kept. Indeed, it was requisite to replace churches in poor repair, rather than allow them to linger on as eyesores.[39] The clergy and congregations were generally only too happy to comply with these requirements: one reason for introducing legislation regulating building in historic churches was that valuable artifacts had been lost when those who used them sought to "improve" them.[40] Publications on the special architectural status of medieval Russian churches went back to the mid-nineteenth century (a landmark was Ivan Snegirev's *Russian Antiquity in Monuments of Ecclesiastical and Civic Architecture*, published in 1851). By the end of the 1880s, alterations to historic churches had to be agreed with the Archaeological Commission of the Academy of Sciences, and by the start of the twentieth century, such buildings were attracting interest from tourists, encouraged by guidebooks of the day.[41] Systematic collection of icons and other devotional items began in the mid-nineteenth century, and the Alexander III Museum, founded in 1898, had a resplendent array of church art (over 5,000 items), concentrating particularly on artifacts from northern Russia; in 1915, a special Treasury of Antiquities was opened to house them.[42] At the same time, a major share of the responsibility for regulating the care of churches was assigned to the ecclesiastical authorities, in recognition of the Orthodox Church's status as the state faith.[43] Intense conflicts between parishes (who resented being compelled to maintain old churches that might be in the wrong place or dilapidated, and fragments of wall paintings that time had turned uncanonical), the church hierarchy, and experts, ran through the culture in the late nineteenth century.[44] By the early twentieth century, though, at least some churchmen took their role as conservationists very seriously. In 1916, Grand Duke Nicholas Mikhailovich, the patron of the Society for the Defense and Preservation in Russia of Artistic and Historic Monuments, wrote to the bishop of Novgorod in order to congratulate him on the Great Monastery at Tikhvin's excellent state of preservation.[45] In the same year, Andrei Murav'ev, the elder of a village church in Kursk province as well as master of ceremonies at the Imperial Court, wrote to the Society in order to propose the creation of special diocesan museums to which "dilapidated" icons of historical and artistic value might be transferred, rather than simply discarded or sent for sale in markets.[46] As Murav'ev's letter shows, the rank-and-file clergy might still be far from recognizing the value of "dilapidated" objects, but educated churchmen and laity now had a different view.

The new Soviet state, by contrast, had a hierarchy of historical value that put in the highest place rebels against the prerevolutionary order, including radical atheists as well as republicans and champions of populism.[47] It was also committed to eradicating the influence of religion on modern life. On January 20, 1918 (February 2 New Style), months before the monuments protection decree was passed, Soviet Russia disestablished the Orthodox Church and declared an absolute separation between church and state.[48] The structures used as religious buildings were classed as "cultic buildings," and "cult" had no place in Soviet society.[49] "Religious organizations" were placed in the paradoxical position of quasi-private associations under conditions of total state ownership. Though required to bear contractual obligations, they had no status as juridical subjects (*iuridicheskie litsa*). "Cultic buildings" themselves were state property, used by congregations on a strictly regulated basis. While the legislation applied to all denominations, it had the largest impact on the national church and majority faith. The decree was intended as nothing less than the initial step in the creation of a new social and civic identity, to which religion would be entirely peripheral.[50]

Obviously, churches were the very last type of architecture to have a positive significance in the new state. At the same time, the contract of lease promulgated in 1918 described the "cultic building" as "national patrimony" (*narodnoe dostoianie*), underlining its importance in terms of Soviet culture generally.[51] Soviet perception distinguished between "cultic buildings" as "havens of obscurantism" (*ochagi mrakobesiia*, in a ubiquitous propaganda phrase of the early Soviet period) and "cultic buildings" as works of art.[52] The established usage, "the building of a former church" underlined the gulf between the transcendent identity of the structure and its transient purpose. Legislation on the preservation of monuments, far from excluding "cultic buildings" (as has sometimes been argued since),[53] specifically included them. The architect-conservators responsible for day-to-day practice in the state and municipal authorities assigned to the preservation of heritage were inspired by the ideals of *nauka*, or "science and scholarship," and aimed to enshrine values that were independent of political expediency and the shifts of ideological fashion.[54] But the categories of "ideologically harmful" and "artistically valuable" had permeable boundaries, leading to much argument about which building should be assigned to which. There was little precision from the top here: unlike Nicholas I, Soviet leaders took next to no personal interest in architecture (as opposed to literature, film, or even music). The many legends about how Joseph Stalin himself designed the postwar Moscow skyscrapers and so on should be set against the archival evidence showing that architectural projects were seldom favored in the Stalin prize competition, a much better indication of their perceived importance.[55]

Even in the conditions of "democratic centralism" and across-the-board state ownership and administration, Soviet cultural politics pulled in contradictory directions. Yet the cultural establishment itself—while considerably more power-ful than the weak and vulnerable "religious associations"—was peripheral to the central political interests of successive Party leaders. With increasing commitment to the needs of the "military-industrial bloc" as Stalin entrenched his leadership in the late 1920s, and a more and more ruthless attitude to anything that smacked of political opposition, both religious associations and the cultural establishment found themselves under threat. The Decree on Religious Organizations of April 8, 1929, as well as significantly restricting the activities of believers, enshrined in law the principle that church buildings could be requisitioned if there were pressing economic grounds for so doing. High-profile demolitions of major churches in Moscow—including buildings that had been restored in the foregoing years—suggested a no-compromise policy should be applied to any building that had connections with religious worship.[56]

It was not until the Great Patriotic War that attitudes shifted again. Heritage became more precious once it acquired associations with the despoliation of the Motherland by the Nazi invaders, and Stalin's rapprochement with the Orthodox Church in 1943 put an end to the extreme anticlericalism of the 1930s. All the same, the Soviet state's self-image, and the propaganda image of the "new Soviet man and woman," were so deeply associated with atheistic rationalism that churches remained at the margins of heritage policy. Heritage preservation itself, funded on the "left-over principle" and peripheral to the overwhelming and vocal needs of the armed forces and industrial development, continued to be starved of resources—a few high-profile sites aside.[57] Only when the attitude to religious practice itself fundamentally shifted, in the late 1980s, did churches become fully ensconced as memorial tokens of the national past (though this was also, of course, a form of secularization).[58] Even before that, though, a building constructed by a leading architect might transcend its function as a mere (from the Soviet point of view) church, and become the acknowledged expression of national and indeed international architectural genius.[59] It is these shifts of value and perception, which both imposed meaning on material culture and took meaning from it, that I shall delineate in this book.

•   •   •

In a sense, the subject of "church-monuments" can be described as "hidden in plain view," since it stands at the intersection of two well-known areas of Soviet history that have seldom been placed in conjunction with each other. The for-midable history of direct and indirect control of religious believers under Soviet power has been exhaustively researched, particularly since relatively free access to archives became possible in the late 1980s. We now know much about church-state relations at various levels, and about the experience of ordinary believers, and the stubborn survival of "irrational" beliefs and practices.[60] A specialist litera-ture also deals with the Soviet drive to inculcate rational atheism in its population: through the educational programs in schools and universities, through propa-ganda, and through the activities of public associations such as the League of the Militant Godless and the "Knowledge" society.[61] Another set of studies addresses in detail the Soviet regime's custodianship of the past, including the built envi-ronment.[62] But there has been almost no specific discussion of the history of the "church monument" (tserkov'-pamiatnik) as such. From the late 1980s onward, there was a series of important publications on the history of church buildings under Soviet power.[63] Their primary purpose, though, was to catalogue the out-rages that were perpetrated on ecclesiastical buildings during what are usually described as "the years of savagery." In the words of a recent publication, "A group of political adventurists, headed by Vladimir Lenin [...] skillfully manipulated" the Russian people. As a result, "the desecrated churches, left without pastors, began to be destroyed. Criminals always cover their tracks."[64]

Many of the churches catalogued in these books were not "monuments" in the official sense (i.e., included in lists of official pamiatniki under state protection). However, to point this out is already to adopt a "secular" position. In the eyes of church believers, the whole concept of a "church monument" is tautological: every church is a "monument," since the Eucharist is an act of commemoration, and in addition, churches are likely to be used as burial places, and hence are "monu-ments" in a secondary sense.[65] Old churches, like old icons, may be particularly valuable, because they are namolennye ("much prayed-over"). But beauty and decorum (blagolepie) are not guaranteed by venerability, any more than holiness is.[66] The very suggestion that the secular authorities might decide which churches should be preserved and which should not generates irritation, if not outrage.[67]

The subject of "church monuments" is equally uncongenial to Russian spe-cialists in heritage preservation, who—both before 1991 and after—have tended to take a uniformly positive view of Soviet achievements in this area.[68] If any-thing, this tendency has increased in the recent past, since the at times cavalier attitude to heritage preservation in post-Soviet Russia has made conservators wax nostalgic about the Soviet past.[69] Matters have been further complicated by the vehement debate about whether or not to return churches that are currently used for museum displays to regular use by worshippers. The disagreement pits believers (who resent control by conservators) against the heritage preservation lobby (who fear that church buildings will not be maintained properly if control by the secular authorities is removed).[70] That church buildings formerly suffered from neglect, if not unsympathetic conversion and demolition, is what used in the Soviet period to be called "an objectionable fact" (*vozmutitel'nyi fakt*), best passed over in silence.[71] From this point of view, to attempt a "neutral" study of the historic church buildings after 1917 is difficult, if not impossible.

One fundamental problem is that secular and religious views of the building used for worship are, in Russian tradition, incompatible to a degree that may be difficult to grasp for observers from, say, the evangelical Protestant tradition.[72] In Russian Orthodox practice, as set out in a widely used prerevolutionary manual, Father Petr Nechaev's *A Practical Guide for Priests*, the premises of the church, like the icon, are sacred in an absolute sense, to be preserved, as far as possible, from contact with the sinful world. The church should not be used for activities such as eating, and may not be entered by unclean animals.[73] In medieval and early modern Russia, indeed, churches had to be purified if they were entered by persons not of the Orthodox faith.[74] The idea that a church might simultaneously serve both sacred and secular purposes is, according to this tradition, absurd—as ridiculous as having one's own portrait painted in order to represent the saint whose name one shares, or keeping a copy of the Bible in a lavatory.[75] The ecclesiastical censorship of the Imperial era forbade the performance of sacred and secular music in the same concert, and to this day, some Orthodox priests have doubts about whether any concert performances are appropriate in a church.[76] Pre-1917 legislation also closely regulated decorum in church buildings: talking during Mass was prohibited, and the police were mandated to preserve social order.[77]

Unlike Catholicism, Orthodoxy does not have the tradition of the "house mass." Performance of a full divine service not only requires the possession of the antimins (the altar-cloth signed by a bishop and containing the relic of a saint that is granted to a particular church community to be used for worship), but also transforms a secular building into a sacred one.[78] There was therefore no possible point of mediation between the viewpoint of early Soviet officials, who felt that the best solution for a chapel in a state mental hospital was for the room housing it to become a club, usable on appropriate occasions by all the different denominations with their own portable altars, and the perspective of believers, for whom this amounted to sacrilege at two levels (removing the decoration of an Orthodox church, and forcing the faithful to worship in an unsuitable place).[79] This background explains why the neo-Platonist Father Pavel Florensky could forcefully argue in 1918 that demolition was preferable to partial secularization: "I would understand a fanatical demand, in the name of the religion of socialism, to tear down the Trinity and St. Sergius Monastery stone by stone; but I entirely refuse to comprehend a cultural mission emanating from the *fortuitous* predominance in our age of specialists in the visual arts, rather than in others; which zealously defends the icon, the wall-painting, and the wall [of the church] itself, but is indifferent to other, no less precious achievements of time-hallowed art, and above all ignoring the highest purpose of the arts— their perfect synthesis, as embodied so successfully and uniquely in the ecclesiastical rites of the Trinity and St. Sergius Monastery, and as so tirelessly sought by the late Scriabin."[80] Church tradition allows for the demolition of buildings and destruction of icons, since these are seen as preferable to misuse.[81]

Yet in a situation where misunderstanding is so prevalent, even to constitute difference in a way that attempts to engage with each viewpoint in its own terms may be valuable.[82] From the point of view of Soviet officials, religious believers were not "martyrs," but (at best) groups that required governance under the laws of public assembly, or (at worst) enemies of the new state. Churches and their contents were not "sacred"; they were places and things like any others. Believers, obviously, thought very differently. However, there were other possible perceptions of "cultic buildings" in play as well, and religious communities and state officials engaged in the project of secularization, as well as non-believers more generally, could find some common ground when discussions of the historical and aesthetic significance of these buildings were in process. To recapture this sense of cooperation, given the increasing polarization of Russian society, since the early twenty-first century, between radical anticlericalism and conformist piety, at least makes for discursive diversity.[83] And by placing in the foreground the demolition of buildings, rather the persecution of people, I do not mean to suggest that I think the former is the greater crime, only that some historical subjects themselves believed it was.[84]

Studying the variety of different views that religious buildings inspired can also act as a corrective to unduly simplistic models of secularization, which—despite the fact that the earliest meaning of the word referred to the alienation of religious property[85]—has a ring of neutral abstraction, poorly reflecting the vehement and painful way in which meaning was fought over, sometimes in the literal sense, and the impact of this on materiality. Eastern Europe tended to be treated as insignificant flotsam on the vast wave of secularization theory that rose up in the late 1960s, dominated as this was by the obsession in classical sociology with the rise of Protestantism, and by the concomitant preoccupation of sociologists and historians with northern Europe of the early modern and modern era.[86] Attempts at greater inclusivity in later decades turned secularization into something like the "multi-faith room" of modernization theory, at once encompassing and bland.[87]

Revisions during the 1980s and 1990s of the classical sketch of dissipation and decline were at best partial. If America, with what came to be understood as its lively "market" in different faiths, was widely seen as the stumbling block for classical models of secularization, or at the very least an inconvenient complicating factor, Europe was generally held to bear out the old rules by which religions became "privatized" as they lost state support, accompanied by catastrophic declines in church attendance.[88] Eastern Europe, however, barely mentioned during the socialist years (presumably because it was considered too neat an illustration of the model even to be interesting), suddenly began to figure as an intriguing instance of secularization's non-success.[89] Even commentators championing the classical view of religion's progressive marginalization tended to take this line. Steve Bruce, for example, cited Russia (along with Turkey) as exceptions to the general rule that the separation of religion and the state and privatization of religion are irreversible processes, because in these countries the situation emerged from "a minority coup" (rather than, presumably, from the ineluctable processes of advancing modernism).[90]

Such interpretations, with their reification of "the state," not only simplified the history of belief under Soviet rule, and the transmutations and adjustments that took place, but the part played by distinctive and various groups of what one might term "stakeholders of secularism." Among such were not just self-declared atheists (for example, the League of the Militant Godless), but also the city planners and heritage preservationists on whom I concentrate here.[91] It would be inaccurate to say that architecture was a "substitute religion" for those who tried to find a worldly role for "cultic buildings," though certainly the term "temples of art" did circulate. Rather, one could say that those striving to find a new role were quasi-religious in their commitment to the honor of the past as a supreme virtue.[92] Secularization was a meaningful process for those involved. As David Powell pointed out nearly fifty years ago, the crudity of the anti-church sallies in Soviet official culture might not be effective in deterrent terms, but it could work to cement solidarity: "While atheist propaganda is irrelevant to the believer, it is highly functional to the atheist, and therefore to the Party."[93] Not all restorers were atheists, but over the decades of Soviet power, they did acquire a strong corporate identity that regarded any mere "users" of buildings as potential threats to its fabric and contents. In the post-Soviet period, the view that church architecture was important not primarily for its religious associations, but as an artistic achievement, proved tenacious, as did the belief that believers had no greater right to churches than any other social group. A grasp of the past helps to illuminate the process by which ecclesiastical buildings acquired lasting historical and architectural associations, a process echoed in the ways in which believers themselves perceived these buildings.[94] It is one manner of coming to grips with the intertwined, as well as mutually antagonistic, relations of those who sought to secularize and those who wished to continue worship unmolested.[95] Discussion of this kind can contribute to the current move toward "religious studies," or to "history of religion" that emphasizes contingency and horizontal social relations. The Soviet campaign against religion, as a *project*, had totalizing ambitions—the eradication of belief. It is this history that I have named as "radical secularization" here. As a *process*, however, secularization was non-linear, multi-tracked, and embraced the shifting values and beliefs of secularizers themselves as well as the modifications to religious beliefs and practices.[96] It certainly does not make sense to assume that religion was merely "an imposed set of values," but nor should secularism be seen in this way.[97] Equally, the official evidence of church attendance, closures, reopenings, demolitions, and reconstructions becomes as much a chronicle of ambitions asserted as of aims achieved, "judgments which accrue power—faith-power—in those who collect and wield them."[98]

A microhistory of church preservation and destruction is revealing for a variety of other reasons as well. Analysis of the fate of ecclesiastical buildings contributes to the history of architectural monuments, and more broadly, to the understanding of the link between memory and local identity, and to the history of public spaces and of city planning. If histories of monuments have often seen these as "tokens of exchange"—emperors on horses replaced by Lenin statues replaced by emperors again—focusing on buildings points to deeper process of emotional and indeed practical investment in the urban fabric. Monuments can be ignored; buildings, if not noticed, at least have to be used.[99]

The city variously known as Petrograd, Leningrad, and St. Petersburg is a particularly inviting place for the exploration of this contradictory and intricate history, with its many shifts and reversals. To begin with, the city was enormously important in terms of church culture. The administrative center of the Orthodox Church of Russia prior to November 21, 1917 (the date when the Moscow Patriarchate was restored), it retained a distinctive clerical tradition well into the 1920s, and, arguably, later also.[100] Added to this, records of heritage preservation in the city are unusually complete. Monuments protection was already well established before 1917. Already in 1909, a contributor to a leading antiquarian journal exclaimed, "When on earth is Moscow going to get its own society for the preservation of monuments? After all, the one in Petersburg has been a huge success."[101] Petrograd was one of the first Soviet urban centers to acquire its own branch of the Museums Department, which was functioning energetically at a stage when staff at local museums in some provincial towns were reluctant to regulate heritage preservation at all.[102] By 1936, the city had its own inspectorate of architectural monuments, an institution set up at the national level only during the Second World War. Alongside the local branches of central preservation bodies, there was a Monuments Office in the apparatus of the city soviet.[103] Preservationists were proud of their record, believing it to be better than in Moscow, and perhaps anywhere else in the world as well.[104]

Certainly, there are some frustrating gaps, notably the scarcity of information about many of the officials involved in the regulation of the daily life of "church-monuments."[105] While biographical information about leading specialists in heritage preservation and planning, such as Konstantin Romanov, Lev Il'in, Aleksandr Udalenkov, and Nikolai Belekhov, is relatively easy to find, almost no details can be traced about the rank-and-file employees of local government departments such as the Church Office, the Department of Communal Property Management, the Architectural and Planning Board, the State Inspectorate of Monuments (GIOP), and the many other branches of the bureaucracy that were concerned with regulating the use of historic churches, both by believers and by other members of society. Even information about the stop-and-start history of the agencies themselves can be elusive. The procedural documentation (*delo-proizvodstvo*) relating to monuments protection is largely off-limits to historical researchers, as is the massive quantity of materials relating to control of religious groups' activities held in the archives of the (post-)Soviet political police.[106] I have not been able to trace publicly accessible minutes of the City Planning Council (Gradostroitel'nyi sovet), the advisory body of Lensovet's Directorate of Architecture and Planning (Arkhitekturno-planirovochnoe upravlenie), while holdings relating to the Directorate itself are very limited.[107] The immensely informative and meticulous work of local historians has largely been concerned with the results of planning policy, rather than its procedures.[108] But enough survives relating to the activities of planners, preservationists, and the various voluntary associations dedicated to the local past, to provide both a picture of emerging policy, and—just as significant—its context. Local documents tell their own stories about the motives and personalities of those who wrote them. Their compositional and stylistic texture records with eloquence a multi-voiced debate: from the polysyl-labic courtesies of churchmen and architect-restorers who had been fully edu-cated under the old order to half-literate complaints, laments, and ruminations, from unsolicited autobiography to clumsy efforts at engaging with the political and managerial tropes of the day. By quoting generously from the documents, I have tried to give a sense of their linguistic and generic specificity, and the writ-ers' sensitivity to the temporal currents that swirled around them, and the inter-subjectivity on which the use of churches depended.[109]

As many studies of Leningrad and St. Petersburg have emphasized, study of the city's past began developing vigorously in the late Imperial era, driven by, for example, the work of the Old St. Petersburg Museum, founded in 1907, and of its Society of Friends. From 1921 onward, the Old St. Petersburg Society (renamed the Old St. Petersburg-New Leningrad Society in 1925) continued these efforts.[110] The general assumption has been that in the city often known as the "cultural capi-tal" or "museum city," the preservation of heritage was inevitable and unproblematic. In this sense, academic commentators, both in Russia and outside, have replicated the views of heritage professionals, also focusing on the successful maintenance of an aesthetic going back in an unbroken line to the city's foundation, and dwell-ing on the set pieces of restoration policy, such as the postwar reconstruction of the palaces at Pushkin (Tsarskoe Selo), Pavlovsk, and Petrodvorets (Peterhof) destroyed by enemy action during the Great Patriotic War.[111] Histories of archi-tecture operate according to similar principles, as exemplified, for instance, in the practice of using Soviet-era, or even completely modern, photographs to illustrate the appearance of a given building.[112]

However, the so-called "Leningrad school" of restoration was distinguished, both before and after the war, precisely by its radical intervention into the past (the removal of some buildings that did not suit the conservationists' aesthetic and historical principles, and the remodeling of others in order to strip them back to what was known as the "optimal date"). A good deal of reconstruction also went on at an "everyday" level, for instance, the widespread use of *nadstroika* ("extension upwards," or the construction of additional stories), both as a way of providing accommodation and as a way of leveling out the heights of buildings in a given area.[113] All this suggests that the automatic association of Leningrad culture and conservation of the local past (as opposed to reinterpretation and creative reworking of this past) may need to be reexamined. As in the Soviet cus-todianship of the classical arts generally (painting, music, and ballet were other examples), proclamation of the unchallengeable authority of past masters went alongside remarkably bold intervention into the works created by them.[114]

It would be a mistake to overemphasize the "Soviet" character of all this. Conservation was an area where, even in the 1920s, tolerance of "bourgeois specialists" was higher than in many areas of Soviet culture, partly because, as Alexander Rabinowitch has argued, "Bolshevik leaders had precious little taste for day-to-day municipal administration."[115] There remained a distinction between Party and city officials throughout Soviet history. Of course, many senior officials were members, but their role in the city administration usually came first.[116] Rather than a command of slogans and the "general line," they needed a command of another language of power, with executive force—"we suggest you should" (*predlagaem Vam*) (code for "do it, or else"), "forthwith" (*nemedlenno*), "do not consider possible" (*ne schitaem vozmozhnym*). These were not empty clichés, but instruments of compulsion—exactly in the same way as comparable phrases ("we give notice that if you do not take steps to remove the structure it will be compulsorily demolished") were in Anglophone planning regimes.[117]

Equally, the practices of city planning in Leningrad, at once constructive and destructive, were matched in other major European cities of the twentieth century, which likewise saw simultaneous drives to tear down and to preserve the inherited fabric.[118] The non-transparency of the planning process and the lack of leverage exercised by those affected by it—particularly if they came from socially marginal groups, such as religious believers—were distinguishing factors of the Soviet planning system (indeed, these factors have persisted in Russian city planning up to the present). However, there was a high degree of similarity between the ideals and practices of urban planners themselves across different modern European cultures. While it is tempting to compare this era of Russian history with the "stripping of the altars" that took place during the English Reformation, such a comparison would be misleading, given that the sixteenth and seventeenth centuries had no group analogous to heritage preservationists, for whom sacred vessels and buildings were empty of any mystical significance, whether positive or negative.[119] The carnival upheavals of the French Revolution, rapidly followed by the concordat of Napoleon, are also an awkward comparison.[120] Treatment of churches in the Soviet era has closer analogies to practices in "Western" Europe as it industrialized: one might note the wholesale destruction of "redundant" churches in London during the 1840s (though the Church of England remained the state faith).[121] Certainly, the closure and demolition of ecclesiastical buildings in Petrograd-Leningrad was sometimes egged on by demagogic rhetoric that was specific to the time and place, but some of the ends in view were generically "modern."[122]

Thus, the role of churches in the urban landscape is an area that could be used to supplement recent arguments about the recourse to international techniques of modernizing statecraft under Soviet power.[123] Yet practices relating to planning and heritage preservation in some respects elude a "strategies of power" paradigm. Even in the first two decades of Bolshevik rule, when the "radical" variant of Marxism was most influential, city officials in urban planning often followed alternative currents, including pragmatic approaches as well as "modernizing/ technocratic" Marxism.[124] Put more simply, practical questions—how to provide the many incomers with living space, how to find raw materials and space for enterprises—were at least as important as living up to ideals of atheistic probity. Religious practice was one of the most ideologized areas of Soviet power, yet many officials were considerably more familiar with "the regulations," and above all with the latest command from above, than with "militant godless" rhetoric.[125]

Work on the history of religious belief has understandably tended to take for granted the binary and antagonistic relations of church and state on the one hand, and believers and non-believers on the other. If recent studies have sometimes voiced arguments for the at least partial "Sovietization" of at least some believers, one is still faced with the inalienable fact that religious "cults" were not—even legally—"Soviet" institutions, and that the assimilation of their members to the new ideology and language was at best limited.[126] Unquestionably, believers were marginalized (in Petrograd and Leningrad as anywhere else). However, there were distinctions between the treatment of believers and attitudes to religious buildings, and the handling of the latter points to tensions in preservation policy that have not hitherto been fully registered. By looking at the complicated and often contradictory work of heritage specialists, we can get a sense of how the "socialist city" was shaped not by the "regime" in the abstract, but by different social actors—and also of how culture itself exercised an inalienable influence on the decisions of those who lived alongside it. Following recent work by anthropologists, we can explore "the actual flux of 'objects' in time"—in this case, the contested and changeable meanings of works of architecture.[127] Rather than assume that officials either preserved (or did not) buildings of inalienable architectural merit, we can seek to understand how perceptions of value and significance were created, as well as violated, by their actions, and more generally, by official planning policy. And we can start to understand, as well, the social resonance of their actions, and those of the officials and believers who, rather than being locked in single combat, were part of a wider world of cultural transformation and contestation of values.[128]

FIGURE 1. St Catherine's Orthodox Church, Vasilievskii Island, 1911. (TsGANTD-SPb.)

CHAPTER ONE

"October Has Caught Up with the Church"

The Separation of Church and State, 1918–1923[1]

THE JANUARY 20, 1918, Decree on Freedom of Conscience, Ecclesiastical and Religious Societies (more commonly known as the Decree on the Separation of Church and State) came at a key point in the new Bolshevik government's shift toward tighter political control.[2] With the Decree on the Press of November 9, 1917 (which arraigned "the counterrevolutionary press of various shades") and the suppression of the Constituent Assembly on January 6, 1918, the Bolsheviks had already moved decisively against the political opposition.[3] Religious institutions were next in the line of fire. Hostility to religious belief, viewed in the classical Marxist terms as "opium of the people" (or, as Lenin put it, "a type of booze for the spirit, wherein the slaves of capital drown their human identity and their demands for a life worthy of human beings"), was only one factor.[4] The new leaders also regarded religious groups as forces of political subversion and instruments for the political manipulation of the masses. The issue was not whether religion should vanish, but when.

The foremost adversary was the Orthodox Church, as the majority faith and the official church of the tsarist regime. From the first, the Bolsheviks, unlike the Provisional Government, which had proceeded cautiously where the church was concerned, sought to neutralize its political, economic, and social presence.[5] The Decree on Land, passed on October 26 (November 8), 1917, the day after the Bolsheviks seized power, removed land not only from secular landowners, but also from all churches and monasteries.[6] On November 2 (15), 1917, the Declaration of Rights of the Peoples of Russia made the holders of all religious faiths and none equal before the law, removing the historic primacy of Orthodoxy.[7] In December, civil divorce and marriage were introduced.[8] The new constitution of July 10, 1918, stripped voting rights from "the servants of cults," as from other categories of "former people," the tsarist political and social establishment.[9] In the second half of 1918 and 1919, Bolshevik administrators dissolved most of the country's principal monasteries, as the main stronghold of church power in city and countryside.[10] Yet the practice of religion (including Orthodox Christianity) at the individual level was guaranteed by the 1918 Decree on the Separation of Church and State, which stipulated that "any citizen may confess any religion or none," and permitted the "free execution of religious rites" where this did not "disrupt public order."[11] It was in the contradictory territory shaped by this tendentious and grudging pluralism that religious societies existed from day to day.[12]

Secularization versus Preservation: Divided Objectives

The Orthodox hierarchy was in any case badly weakened by fissures that had started to open well before 1917, though they had been widened by the revolutionary upheavals that year. Dissatisfaction with the official church and its close links with the autocracy had been expressed, from the late nineteenth century, not just in unofficial movements such as the "Religious-Philosophical Society" of St. Petersburg, but in movements within the Orthodox Church for "renovation," in the form of greater democracy and accountability.[13] The election of the clerical leadership and the empowerment of the laity were the twin pillars of the new movement. Monasticism came under attack not only from the godless intelligentsia, but from radical members of the "white clergy" (the priestly rank-and-file) such as Father Aleksandr Vvedenskii, who lambasted the departure of contemporary monks from the ideals of the early Christian era.[14] There were official plans also to devolve power to the parishes, though with significant control still assigned to the church hierarchy, which had jurisdiction over the composition of parish councils.[15]

After the Revolution, the followers of "renovation" were heartened by the uncoupling of the Orthodox Church from the old regime, and looked forward to a new era of social relevance. The All-Russian Local Church Council (Vserossiiskii Pomestnyi Sobor), which began work on August 15, 1917, wholly restructured the former methods of governance. The former "Most Holy Governing Synod" was dissolved, and replaced by an elected body, termed simply "the Holy Synod," which presided over the church alongside the newly elected patriarch, Tikhon.[16] According to the encyclical convening the Council, "The recent coup d'état, which has radically altered the life of our society and state, has also provided the Church with the opportunity for and right to self-determination [*ustroenie*]."[17] At the same time, a resolution passed at the Council on December 2, 1917, while asserting the "freedom and independence of the Orthodox Church in Russia" and its right to "self-definition and self-administration," also demanded concessions by the state, including recognition of Orthodoxy as the primary faith, consultation regarding all laws passed, and the guarantee that church property would be inviolable and that funding from the state budget would be provided.[18]

The mainstream drift in the Orthodox Church, then, was to press for state sponsorship, and the recognition of the church's leading role among faiths in Russia, but also an end to state control. Reforms within the church would be limited to administrative reorganization. But for those who had dreamed of "renovation" before 1917, this was not enough. Among them, the Bolshevik Revolution encouraged radical moods, since the early attacks on superstition and monasticism expressed sentiments that the followers of "renovation" shared.[19] The notional leader of the Orthodox Church, Patriarch Tikhon, himself a member of the "black" (monastic) clergy, and a man with a conciliatory and reticent personality, was in no position to unify these different tendencies.

The Soviet administration did all it could to exploit divisions within the church as part of the fight with religious belief. Yet it too was far from homogeneous. It included, alongside hard-line secularizers, such as Leon Trotsky and the founder of the Cheka, Felix Dzerzhinsky, those who were prepared, in the meantime at least, to take a more pragmatic line. As Lenin had pronounced in 1905, "We do not and should not declare openly our atheism in our party program," nor would Communists "forbid proletarians who have not yet abandoned these or the other relics of archaic superstitions to ally themselves with our party."[20] An editorial in a journal that was the mouthpiece of official policy, *Revolution and the Church*, published in mid-1918, underlined that there was an important difference between active political subversion and mere belief:

> Despite the blatantly counterrevolutionary character of the Church in general, the Soviet government finds it expedient to adopt a defensive position where faith in the narrow sense is concerned. The full force of repression will be unleashed on

churchmen only insofar as they may be involved in counterrevolutionary activity, while the decrees and other measures that the government has propounded have been intended purely to remove the education of the people from the hands of the servants of cult, and to deprive the reactionary classes of the past of the capacity to mobilize and entrench the forces of counterrevolution by exploiting the illiteracy and ignorance of the masses, with the aid of the church apparatchiks left over from the days of autocracy, and the wealth that has been accumulated over the centuries.[21]

The French Revolution had shown that it was a serious mistake to crack down on those who were too backward to live without performers of "magic actions," since this simply added to the allure of such "magic," and was likely to provoke "conflicts between the forward-thinking and backward sections of the working population."[22] In the meantime at least, expediency required restraint.[23]

The policy relating to heritage was also contradictory. Looking after buildings and objects of "artistic and historic value" was, in terms of the Bolshevik government's public proclamations, a laudable and necessary activity. But very little practical support was provided (hence the effort, from the start, to delegate the maintenance of "monuments," where possible, to those who were using them). At the same time, the "hands off" attitude of the state also applied to the classification of monuments (which was left to the discretion of local "museums departments"). No historical or ideological boundaries were set down as to what might or might not be listed.[24] The central Museums Department also avoided detailed regulation of the process of restoration. Buildings dating from 1850 or later might be renovated without a requirement that the users sought permission, and the guiding principle, as articulated in 1923, was "do no harm":

> The restoration of monuments of architecture has as its aim the preservation of the appearance of such monuments in the form in which they were when restoration began, or the reconstruction, in full or in part, of the appearance of the monument when first constructed, on the basis of exact data accumulated by the close study of the monument in its historico-artistic, archaeological, and historical dimensions.[25]

The import of the documentation was that the issue of whether to repair, or to reconstruct, should be taken on a case-by-case basis, and it was "exact data," rather than aesthetic convictions, that were to be the foundation of conservation.[26] There was no prohibition upon the preservation of "cultic buildings," as Soviet usage termed them. Nor was there anything that explicitly discouraged this. An Instruction on the Registration and Protection of Religious Property was issued by Narkompros as early as 1920.[27] Where deemed of historic and architectural interest, ecclesiastical buildings were subject to state protection. Some of the earliest preservation orders in the new Soviet state related to places of worship.[28] Once the Civil War began, efforts were made to evacuate items of especial interest, including the contents of churches.[29] The Museums Department had its own "Churches Section," which in 1923 reported a broad package of activities over the forgoing five years, including the creation of museums and repositories of antiquities in twenty-three different monasteries.[30] Restoration work continued to be done on important sites, including the Cathedral of Christ the Redeemer, Moscow, as well as the Kremlin churches there, into the new era.[31]

That said, there was also no explicit effort to protect "cultic buildings" from the social transformation that was envisaged by the January 20, 1918, decree. It is instructive to contrast the terms of the statute with the December 9, 1905, secularizing law passed in France. The Soviet decree had borrowed from this its guarantee of freedom of conscience and prohibition on religious symbolism in public places (article 28 of the French statute had confined religious symbols to places of worship, cemeteries, and museums).[32] The French statute had anticipated the Soviet one in nationalizing all church buildings constructed prior to the moment of its passing and in prohibiting the use of public money to fund religious activities. But the maintenance of church buildings became a recognized state responsibility, and *associations cultuelles* were allowed to maintain funds of their own, provided that the surplus remained below a stipulated ceiling (at the time the law was passed, 5,000 francs). Added to that, the French statute included a clause requiring an inventory of all ecclesiastical buildings of historic value.[33] In Soviet Russia, by contrast, secularization and preservation were, from the regime's early days, seen as separate activities.

In the first months after the October Revolution, there was a high degree of understanding between the Orthodox Church and restorers. When the Restoration Commission was set up by decree of the Council of People's Commissars in June 1918, Patriarch Tikhon explicitly welcomed the plan set out by its head, Igor' Grabar', to undertake a first-hand study of work by late medieval Russia's most important icon painters, Dionisii (1450–1502) and Andrei Rublev (c. 1370–1428). The conservators' "journey round the holy places of Russia of our Fatherland" was "a useful mission for the Holy Church," and one to which he gave his blessing.[34] In their turn, restorers were sympathetic to religious art. Grabar', director of the Tretyakov Gallery and the author of a major history of Russian art going back to the medieval period, was typical of heritage specialists across the country.[35] At the same time, the preservation bodies had to operate within the constraints of church-state relations, which pitted radical secularism against the Orthodox Church's determination not to acknowledge the authority of the new government.[36] And the 1918 preservation law had given them rather weak powers of regulation. The issuing of "preservation certificates" (*okhrannye svidetel'stva*) and polite requests to local authorities to honor these was not underwritten by powers of sanction; in the case of damage to buildings and artworks, the Museums Department could do no more than send indignant representations further up the line.[37]

Church Property after January 20, 1918: Nationalization or Sacrilege?

The January 20, 1918, decree gave communities of believers that counted at least twenty people among their number the right to apply to use a building for worship.[38] These *dvadtsatki* (from the Russian word for "twenty"), as they came to be known, might use the building free of charge, though members were collectively and individually liable for the safety of its contents, and for keeping these in good repair—a process regulated by an elaborate contract that was countersigned by the state bureaucracy under whose care the building was placed (normally a department of the local district council, *raisovet*).[39] *Dvadtsatki* who applied to use a building that was a registered monument were required to sign a contract containing additional clauses prohibiting alterations of any kind to the fabric or contents without the express permission of the Museums Department. Drawn up in 1920 (two years later than the basic contract), this document also compelled the religious community to report to the Museums Department all cases of damage to the fabric, and to grant free access to its officials in order to carry out such inspections as might be required.[40] Added to this, the July 13, 1920, decree "On the Confiscation of Precious Metals" specifically mentioned that Narkompros officials were empowered to confiscate "objects pertaining to religious cults with historic or artistic significance."[41]

Not just religious buildings, but also their contents, were now state property, loaned to communities of worshippers on sufferance. Members of the *dvadtsatka* took collective and personal responsibility for the "national heritage" in their care.[42] What an instruction issued by the Museum Committee of Narkompros in 1920 termed "all property of an archaeological, historical, and artistic significance used for the execution of religious rites" fell, like buildings of comparable significance, under the jurisdiction of the Museums Department. On the one hand, this meant that other sections of the state bureaucracy had to consult with the Museums Department where such property was concerned, for example, when they carried out the requirements of the August 24, 1918, instruction.[43] However, the Museums Department had the right to remove all such property as it might deem necessary from believers, and transfer it to the holdings of museums. The 1920 instruction required officials of the Department to carry out inventories of all movable church property, and to classify this according to three categories:

1.   Property of a quite exceptional historico-artistic value (unique objects);
2.   Property of high historico-artistic value, with an exemplary and museum significance;
3.   Property of an insignificant historico-artistic value, with no exemplary historico-artistic character, and representing an everyday phenomenon of ecclesiastical life.

Property in the first category, the instruction continued, "comprises the State fund," and "should this be possible and essential, for instance if the conditions in which it is kept are inadequate, or if the plans for museum construction should require this, should be removed and added to the collection of a suitable *central museum*."[44] Property in the second category *"may be removed by the Department for the needs of the State Museums Fund*, with the purpose of distribution to central and provincial museums as planning may dictate." It was only items in the third category—those of no interest to the Department—over which it was prepared to cede control. Certainly, property in any of the three categories could be left in the use of believers, but only if this would not "cause damage to the property concerned."[45]

The considerable powers given to state institutions accorded with the preferences of heritage preservationists themselves. Already in 1917, a statement on "the great heritage of our ancestors" from the Union of Art Activists, a broad front for artists and writers, had argued that, once the separation of church and state took place, ecclesiastical property should be transferred to state ownership. Private ownership was fatal to the preservation of monuments. Allowing to parishes jurisdiction over churches and their contents would leave monuments vulnerable.

> The best decision is the recognition of all buildings and movable property belonging to churches, monasteries, chapels, dioceses, and the vestries and treasuries attached

to these as the property of the state in general [*obshchegosudarstvennaia sobstvennost'*], and what is more, this rule should be extended to all objects, whether they are included in inventories or not, and whether they are currently listed or have been removed from the lists. Any restriction of this rule will mean that a whole series of monuments may perish, often of first-class importance, since not all monuments are currently known, and some of them are to be found on the rubbish dumps of property removed from church inventories.[46]

Prior to 1917, preservationists had routinely lamented that there was no way to stop property owners from mistreating works of architectural importance that they fortuitously happened to own.[47] In a culture where all public organizations were regarded as potentially subversive unless licensed, the efforts to foster a civic movement to protect monuments had placed activists in a "parastatal" position of compromise with official directives and policy.[48] This position was much resented, and heritage protectionists were determined to exercise greater leverage as soon as this appeared to lie in their powers. They welcomed the confiscation of private property—including church property—as a step to the better protection of historic buildings.

Maintaining overall political neutrality did not preclude making allegiances on a strategic basis, as P. P. Veiner, a local historian passionately committed to honoring and conserving Petrograd's past, recollected in the early 1920s:

When, immediately after the October Revolution, we began working for the preservation of monuments of art and history, we did not hesitate to engage in cooperation with a party that was alien to us, since we considered that the demands of the cause lay beyond all politics, and on the other hand, we are well aware that mistakes will never be forgiven; the devastation of the country's economic life can still be put right, but no action of any kind, no efforts, however great, can bring back what has been lost in this area [that is, demolished and destroyed monuments].[49]

The problem was that where religious buildings were concerned, nothing lay "beyond politics." The monasteries, seen by Bolshevik activists (and reforming clergy) as bastions of counterrevolution, were also some of the most important historical and architectural sites in Soviet Russia. But historical value was no impediment to dissolution. As *Revolution and the Church* boasted in 1920, 673 of the 890 monastic foundations existing in 1917 had already been "liquidated," to be replaced by hospitals, sanatoriums, farms, workshops, schools, clinics, orphanages, and "concentration camps."[50] The process of "liquidation" was left to the local soviets, which could decide on the redeployment of monastic territories as they saw fit, though churches were supposed to be made available to groups of believers, should such come forward.[51] A circular issued by the Commissariat of Justice on January 3, 1919, evoked the gleeful iconoclasm with which secularization of former religious buildings sometimes took place. It was quite inappropriate to remove items such as communion vessels, brocade cloths, and the precious metal coverings of icons from ecclesiastical buildings. There had been no order to this effect, to begin with, "and secondly, such actions are counterproductive, since they injure the religious feelings of the citizenry, and in addition to that, destroy and damage the objects themselves, often stripping them of all artistic value. The use of such items to serve as revolutionary emblems, flags, banners etc., is devoid of internal meaning."[52] The conversion of monasteries to museums was an obvious solution in preservation terms, but might also be perceived as "desecration" by those who regarded churches as always and only places of worship.[53]

Equally, the officially sponsored campaign for the exposure of relics resulted both in offense to the "religious feelings" of many ordinary Russians, and damage to the often old and artistically valuable caskets in which the relics were kept.[54] Yet this was not remarked in government circulars, evidently passing for the necessarily collateral to the ideologically valuable attack on "superstition."[55] As the institutional location of heritage preservation—the Commissariat of Enlightenment—suggested, a major argument in favor of caring for monuments was that they had educational value. If the monuments came to be identified with "counterrevolutionary" or "anti-Soviet" forces, this educational value was immediately vitiated. Those striving to preserve heritage had to exercise a delicate balancing act. They were required to appear as Soviet patriots when defending the past in a society that was committed above all to *transforming* the past. Buildings that were associated with negative aspects of the past were always tricky to deal with—and churches in particular.[56]

A second consideration was that the primary loyalty of preservation officials was to the objects and buildings under their care, and not to those who used them. The drive animating them was to bring items of "artistic and historic interest" under the eye of state bodies. This meant, if necessary, removing church goods and buildings and placing them in more reliable, "scientific," care. Indicative was a Narkompros circular published by *Revolution and the Church* at the start of 1919, which instituted special commissions, with representation from the College of Museums and Monument Preservation of Narkompros, the local soviet, and the State Control bureaucracy. Their purpose was to docket information about objects and buildings of value, and in the case of the former, to "identify items that should be immediately removed and transferred to the stores of the State Museum Fund."[57] The spiritual and liturgical meaning of "cultic buildings" and their contents lay outside the purview of architect-restorers, who prided themselves on taking a neutral attitude to buildings and artworks. If a treasured icon was in poor condition, or vestments or a chalice vulnerable to theft, these should be removed, whatever their devotional value to a particular congregation.

Within the church, by contrast, care for ecclesiastical buildings and their contents was universally understood as the responsibility of the Orthodox faithful. The discussions of June and July leading up to the Church Council had given voice to a variety of opinion about how church property should be administered—by the church hierarchy (as before 1917), or by the parishes themselves.[58] The proponents of the former view cited canon law as well as practical fears (that parishes would simply disperse property as and when they felt like), the latter held that only when they had a personal stake in church property would parishes care for it properly.[59] The prospect that property might be nationalized by the state was not entertained at this stage, and the process was universally resented when it did take place. As Patriarch Tikhon put it in 1922, "I cannot manage church property, for it has been removed from me. As you will be pleased to know, the pope considered himself a sovereign without a sovereign state when the Italian government removed his property from him."[60] Patriarch Tikhon was no doubt aware that the 1873 confiscation of church property by the new Italian state had been followed, as in France, by concessions to the church's rights, but the hint was lost on his interlocutors.[61] The double bind of expectations without rights—according to which parishes were merely caretakers for artifacts understood to belong to the state—placed parishes in a situation that was worse than the situation obtaining before 1917. Then, they had been responsible for property to the higher ecclesiastical authorities, which shared many of their values. Now, removal of property could occur on grounds that were meaningless if not offensive in religious terms. If the laicization of church management introduced by the new government had some objective benefits (and achieved some of the aims that the Orthodox faithful had pursued themselves prior to 1917), the ownership of church property opened up a fault line from the time the decree was enacted.[62]

In the immediate period after January 20, 1918, those campaigning for the preservation of heritage were, on the whole, conciliatory toward religious communities—if nothing else, because they hoped that use of buildings for religious purposes would help preserve masterpieces of architecture and decoration. But their assigned (if not always actual) function was to control, rather than to support, the use of the artworks in their care. Regulation by the secular state was far more intrusive than under the heritage regimes of other European countries at this period.[63] Equally importantly (in fact, more so from the point of view of an inward-looking church culture that was little concerned with practices beyond the world of Orthodoxy), no amount of tact could disguise the fact that oversight by the bureaucracy of the secular state had now replaced the oversight by the ecclesiastical bureaucracy that had been the norm before the October Revolution.

Overall, attitudes to "cultic buildings" were shaped by a set of contradictory political and cultural imperatives. The drive to eradicate religious belief was offset by the grudging recognition of the right to worship. The right of believers to use churches and objects of value was established in law, but so was the right of heritage workers to remove these if they felt the interests of the buildings and objects concerned would be better served by professional care.[64] Commitment to preservation of architectural treasures competed with recognition of secularization as an inalienable objective.

These conflicts were deeply entrenched in Petrograd also—indeed, perhaps more than in most places, since the city had a particularly vocal and effective museums lobby and highly articulate and legally aware religious groups, but also a significant body of local officials who were strongly committed to the cause of Sovietization. As the country's biggest city, and a place hit hard by the epidemics, social anomie, and organizational chaos that accompanied world war, revolution, and civil war, Petrograd was also a place where the practical obstacles to heritage preservation were highly significant, since the tasks of day-to-day local administration—for example, managing the city's housing stock—already placed the authorities under considerable stress.[65] And the city was riven by the religious divisions of the period. The "Renovation" movement was particularly well represented in Petrograd, the home city of several leading figures, including Evgenii Belkov, Father Aleksandr Boiarskii, and the church historian Boris Titlinov (a professor at the Theological Academy), as well as Aleksandr Vvedenskii. At the same time, as the official center, before 1917, of the ecclesiastical administration, Petrograd was also the home of many conservative clergy who had warmly supported the ancien regime, and who reacted to the abdication of the tsar and the abolition of the Holy Synod with consternation and disgust.[66] However, recognition of the newly reestablished patriarch as the legitimate inheritor of the mantle of prerevolutionary ecclesiastical authority was made particularly tricky by the fact that the resurrection of the position had brought a relocation of the church elite from Petrograd to Moscow.[67] These rifts, present below the surface during the first years after the Bolshevik Revolution, opened further as Bolshevik hostility to Orthodoxy itself sharpened. At that point, it was precisely ecclesiastical "monuments" (the objects used for ritual and the premises they were housed in) that were to be at the center of conflicts between those pushing forward radical secularization and the preservation lobby, not to speak of religious believers. In the first years after the Revolution, though, the atmosphere was less vexed, and all-out battle lay in the future.

Among churchmen and believers in the months after October 1917, equally contradictory processes were in train. The Parish Charter (*Prikhodskoi ustav*) approved by the Church Council on April 7 (20), 1918, assigned to the parish and to the church itself the status of juridical subjects, and conferred on the parish the right to use several churches and chapels (a cemetery church, for instance), as well as the main one. Control over church buildings and contents was assigned to the local dean (*blagochinnyi*). The church was to press for the restoration of all property that had been removed, and the Orthodox hierarchy reserved the right to close down churches where the local community had engaged in sacrilegious

FIGURE 2. Church of the Annunciation, 8-ia liniia, Vasilievskii Island (1750–1762, architect unknown), photographed c. 1920. (GMISPb.)

practices.[68] Yet the Council also resolved that church buildings might be handed over to the authorities if there was danger of the imminent use of force, and that a community deprived of its church might worship in a private home, using the simplest possible vestments and communion vessels.[69] Some margin of adjustment to the new times had to be set in place.

"Many Petrograd raisovety Simply Do Not Know the Content of the Instruction": Preservation by Default, 1918–1920

A major dilemma for the preservation lobby emerged soon after the January 20, 1918, decree was passed. The instruction of August 24, 1918, issued by the People's Commissariat of Justice, clarified the terms of the original decree: the separation of church and state related not just to political and social practices, but to the spaces in which they were enacted:

> 29. In state and other public and legal buildings of assembly, there is an absolute and categorical prohibition upon:
>
>   a) the execution of religious rites and ceremonies (prayers, funerals, etc.);
>   b) the placing of all and any religious images (icons, pictures, statues of a religious character, etc.).
>
> 30. Soviet local authorities will do everything in their powers to remove and curtail the phenomena mentioned in the preceding articles, and running contrary to the Decree on the Freedom of Conscience.[70]

Not just society, but buildings themselves, were to be made Soviet, to express the values of a radically secular modernity.

An especially tricky question in this context was what to do with the "house churches" (*domovye tserkvi*) that most pre-1917 institutions and public buildings had contained, as a token of the Orthodox Church's position as state faith. These churches, or chapels (Russian employs a separate word, *chasovnia*, for a freestanding ecclesiastical building of small size, but a subdivision of or annexe to a larger building is a "church"), were enclaves of the sacred in the social realm.[71] They testified to the equivalence of spiritual and temporal power, spatially asserted also by the accommodation of the Russian Empire's two executive authorities, the Senate and the Most Holy Governing Synod, in two identical wings of a single building. Ministries, educational institutions, orphanages, hospitals, and clinics were just some of the many public buildings containing "house churches," which were also to be found in many private residences—not only the palaces and mansions at the top of the status hierarchy, but also relatively humble private dwellings.[72] While the category of "house church" could extend to premises used for worship in any denomination or faith (Catholic, Baptist, Lutheran, Jewish, Islamic, Buddhist, etc.), as well as Orthodox Christianity and its various sects (notably the so-called "Old Believers," or groups that had split from established Orthodoxy in the seventeenth century), the vast majority of such structures served the rites and practices of the former state religion—which was in any case the primary target of the new government's secularizing activities. The purging of these particular buildings was therefore a key demonstration of state power.

For the Orthodox faithful, it was equally important to retain a religious presence in public buildings. There was, to be sure, no single legislative act from the Imperial period that required the provision of chapels in all public buildings. Rather, legal instruments had emerged piecemeal, including, for example, churches for border-guards from 1831, and in retirement homes from 1826.[73] But in practice, a great many public buildings had contained such premises. Their existence was, to a large extent, taken for granted within the church. The discussions at the Church Council, for instance, had recognized that reforms would be required exclusively in the case of "house churches" inside former royal palaces. The definition of "house churches" evolved in July 1917 continued to refer to those "intended for the satisfaction of religious requirements by persons linked in one or another way with the building in which the churches are housed, and specifically, persons studying at educational institutions, or serving in ecclesiastical, government, public, and private institutions, or members of families and residents in, and visitors to, the building concerned." Even if the building were closed, the "worshippers and parishioners" would be responsible for "preservation of the sacredness of the premises of the closed church."[74] To move from this perception of the future to a reality where churches could be not simply closed, but also summarily dismantled, generated indignation and shock.

Certainly, the Commissariat of Justice warned in January 1919 that the removal of icons from public places "should not be turned into an antireligious demonstration." Instead, the religious emblems were to be quietly removed outside working hours, and handed over to a local religious society for safekeeping. But it is clear from the very need for the Commissariat's intervention that officials sometimes took a confrontational view.[75] At the same time, the question of what a "house church" actually signified was not straightforward, as a stream of representations to the advice columns of *Revolution and the Church* made clear.[76] The new order sometimes made itself felt by high-handedness, but equally often by inertia and the turning of blind eyes. An article published in the journal of the reformist clergy, *Conciliar Wisdom*, claimed in 1918: "Parishes have gradually won for themselves the right to act as juridical subjects, they have de facto exercised these rights, and no-one has dared challenge these."[77]

If "house churches" were at the center of things for those who wished to transform public space, they were also crucial to heritage preservation in the first years after the Revolution, precisely as a type of "cultic building" that early came under assault. The heritage preservation authorities became third parties as those who wished to "liquidate" them and those who wished to keep them open locked in combat. In turn, the haphazard process by which the fate of the "house churches" was decided laid bare the new order's conflicted priorities: the protection of individual rights versus the creation of a rational new society; and the curatorial stance toward historical objects against the drive to create new kinds of material relations and to transform the public realm.

Petrograd was at the epicenter of these developments, since the former capital had by far the largest concentration across Soviet Russia of "house churches" (a function of its size and of the number of government buildings located there). It was these, rather than monastic foundations or traditional holy sites, or sacral objects such as icons and saints' relics, that formed the main target of the secularizing drive in the period between 1918 and 1923. The campaign to expose relics—which countrywide represented the most significant confrontation between secularizers and the devout—at first made little headway.[78] For the meantime, the Alexander Nevsky Monastery escaped wholesale dissolution, despite efforts by Alexandra Kollontai to requisition the premises even before the Decree on the Separation of Church and State was passed.[79]

In the first years of Soviet power, the Museums Department in Petrograd seems to have adopted a moderate attitude to religious groups. While state intervention in the form of protection orders began quite early—a number of churches that were considered significant were brought under state control as early as 1918—this was not accompanied by all-out meddling in the affairs of the *dvadtsatki*. For example, an inspection in 1919 of the Coreligionists' Church on Nikolaevskaia (now ulitsa Marata), built by A. I. Mel'nikov in 1820–1838, concluded that the roof and other capital parts of the church were in reasonable condition, though some superficial mending and redecoration would do no harm.[80] The 1920 instruction did not generate mass transfers of property from religious buildings to museums, or large-scale termination of contracts to use the religious buildings themselves.

FIGURE 3. Interior of the Nikol'skaia Coreligionists' Church (Avraam Mel'nikov, 1820–1838), photograph c. 1920, from the collection of the Leningrad State Restoration Workshop). (FO NA IIMK RAN, negative no. II 3391, print 0.3569-120, collection no. 16-990.)

But the Museums Department was only one of the departments of state bureaucracy that congregations had to deal with; and carrying the extra financial and
organizational burden of specialist repairs did not give them extra leeway when
it came to other negotiations with the Soviet authorities. From the point of view
of Soviet law and practice, a religious association that happened to be using an
architectural monument was subject to the same controls as any other in terms of
the legislation related to public order, hygiene, and safety, and "counterrevolutionary activity," as well as the legislation specifically related to religious practice. The
bodies that it negotiated with included not just the Churches Office (Tserkovnyi
stol) of the district council (raisovet), but also the office overseeing building control (the Communal Resource Maintenance Section, Otkomkhoz), and the local
branches of the Commissariat of Justice, and the NKVD (Commissariat of the
Interior, responsible for control over public assemblies).[81] All these bodies were in
turn subordinate to the City and Regional Committees of the Communist Party,
which also had specialist departments dealing with matters of faith. Below the
surface, church communities were also regulated by the different branches of
the secret police, with which the Administrative Sections of local and provincial
councils liaised. Secret policemen favored a particularly hard line toward religious
observers, though since they were also responsible for regulating public order,
also counseled against direct confrontation.[82]

It was not the architectural status of a church, but other factors that were of significance when dealing with these bodies. The word "parish" had no validity in Soviet
law, but the closest analogy to the dvadtsatka in traditional Orthodox institutional
practice was in fact the parish (prikhod), though the priest had now been transformed from the administrative as well as spiritual leader of the religious community
to a spiritual figure who was not entitled to any influence in administrative matters.[83]

The continuity between the dvadtsatka and the traditional "parish" meant that
the "cultic buildings" that were most likely to be granted without argument to
religious groups were the former parish churches. At the same time, after the dissolution of monasteries, it was sometimes possible for religious communities to
establish themselves in monastic churches; such communities might even include
former monks and nuns, reclassified as members of a "work commune."[84] When
it came to former "house churches," though, the provisions of the 1918 Decree on
the Separation of Church and State raised certain highly specific ambiguities and
complications. The letter of the law forbade the presence of religious symbols in
Soviet public buildings. But if members of a dvadtsatka applied for use of a former
"house church" in order to practice their beliefs, they were asserting rights that

were supported by the very same Soviet legislation that had declared public build-ings secular places. So far as many Soviet officials were concerned, there seemed to be no automatic reason why a group of coworkers in some Soviet institution or factory should not form a *dvadtsatka* and continue to use the "house church" for religious worship—acting as a non-Soviet presence within a Soviet institution.

Another incentive for the adoption of a conciliatory attitude to the contin-uance of worship in "house churches" came from a different direction. While some institutional and private "house churches" were basic, or, even if elaborate, recently constructed and thus unlikely to be accorded "architectural and historic value," many had been built and arranged by famous architects and contained artworks of the first importance. Often, it was possible to trace the process of commissions and design through archival documentation, and decoration had survived essentially intact and unchanged since the churches were first created, forming what local preservationists referred to as its *ansambl'*, or integral whole.[85] It was notable that the model "record card" published by the Petrograd Museums Department in 1919 selected a "house church"—that in the central post office, created by Giacomo Quarenghi in 1830—to show how the architectural and dec-orative features of ecclesiastical buildings should be recorded.[86] A report on work done in 1918–1921 to preserve Petrograd's architecture stated that thirty-six of fifteen hundred wooden houses had been deemed worthy of protection orders, and three out of twenty-three "artistically outstanding" parish churches. The pro-portion of "house churches" listed was far higher—thirty-one, with two hundred deemed to be of "museum importance."[87]

"House churches" were seen as a priority by heritage preservationists from the moment they began work. But if the law relating to secularization were followed to the letter, then house churches would have to be dismantled and removed, something that would undermine the architect's intentions for the building as a whole, and not just for the church itself. Besides, the limited state funds for res-toration were targeted primarily at secular buildings.[88] If a religious association was in place, the work of restoration could be delegated to its members. From the point of view of preservation, it made sense to be maximally permissive about allowing the conversion of former "house churches" into "parish churches."

Formally speaking, there were obstacles to this process: house churches that were an integral part of buildings were not supposed to be used for worship.[89] In 1920, the Narkompros (NKP) instruction transferring property of historical and artistic value to the Museums Department had emphasized that "house churches attached to public institutions of any kind" were "under no circumstances to be assigned to a Community of Believers for the performance therein of religious rites."[90] But this left room for creative interpretation of the term "attached."[91] In any case, by the time the NKP instruction emerged, many of Petrograd's "house churches" had already been reclassified as parish churches.[92] The Museums Department was far too preoccupied with other commitments to participate in hair-splitting. The registration and disposal of Petrograd's many private collections, not to speak of the administration of the city's museums, took huge amounts of effort.[93] The Department was, in any case, responsible for monuments protection not just in Petrograd, but right across the enormous northwest region, which included a large number of ecclesiastical sites of the first importance—in Pskov and Novgorod, Tikhvin, Kirillovo-Belozersk, Goritsy, Ferapontovo, and Solovki, among many others. Heritage protection officials took their duties here extremely seriously and in the first years after the Revolution, more restoration work was carried out there than in Petrograd itself.[94] While the Museums Department was afforced by the Monuments Department attached to the Petrograd provincial soviet (in full, the Department for the Protection of Monuments of History and Art), the sheer number of the capital's major buildings and statues meant that the cooperation of the maximum possible number of social groups was essential to making heritage policy work.[95]

The other Soviet organizations were in no hurry to close "house churches" either. At this early period of the country's history, many officials had only the haziest notion of the provisions of the statute on the separation of church and state. According to a report dating from late 1918:

> Many Sovdeps [district soviets] are totally uninformed about the publication of the Instruction [on the Separation of Church and State] itself, with the result that they have no idea at all about its contents and the questionnaires issued by the [Museums] Department; all they know about the decree is its name. In this respect, especially striking in terms of overall ignorance is the Sovdep of Spasskii district, despite its central location. The only offices that have more or less been gotten into order in the district Sovdeps are the Departments of Civil Registration, and the arrangements for divorce being handled by the local legal departments.[96]

A year later, on March 27, 1919, the Department of Justice at Petrosovet was still complaining that the vast majority of district soviets simply had no idea what they were doing. Despite the decision at an inter-district meeting on February 26, 1919, to remove documents relating to the registration of christenings and

funerals from churches, and to record the transfer to *dvadtsatki* of church property, in some districts, including both central districts, no progress at all had been
made in the month that had elapsed. Equally slow was the process of closing
"house churches" in institutions such as hospitals. The chaos was augmented by
lack of ideological resolution: "Where the No. 2 Central district is concerned, the
following negative fact must be recorded: the Sovdep has given permission for
the house church of the former Senate, which was closed over a year since, to be
reopened for the Lenten services." Where not lax, officials were illegally draconian.
In some districts, they had even removed the official stamps (an indispensable
tool of bureaucratic procedures) from churches; in others, they had arrogated to
themselves the work of compiling inventories of church property (a task supposed
to be done by representatives of the parish). The Department of Justice expressed
irritation at the deficiencies of local officials' work, including the failure to "shut
down churches while the situation [relating to registration of property, etc.] is
investigated." It stated its own intention of taking measures to right the state of
affairs. However, it also admitted that at least eight extra members of staff would
be needed to work as "executive inspectors" to carry out the necessary investiga-
tions, making clear the large gap that existed between intention and the capacity
to realize this.[97]

Much though the Department of Justice might disapprove of the fact that
"house churches" continued to function, there was little that its officials could
immediately do to stop this, despite measures from central government that
allowed local soviets to requisition church premises if they were required for
living accommodation, medical premises, or the needs of "political and cultural education."[98] By the end of 1919, there were still eight churches belonging
to institutions of higher education left in use, six attached to former ministries,
at least five attached to primary schools, and twenty-nine attached to hospitals.
Fifty-three out of sixty-four churches in former charitable institutions were still
working, and all twelve churches once operated by institutions of religious education, such as temperance societies.[99] By no means all the churches could be
classified as self-contained: for instance, the church of the Kushelev-Bezborodko
Home for Elderly Female Paupers, on the first floor of the main building, was still
in operation, as was the church in the Brunitsyn Refuge, located directly over the
institution's main dining hall.[100]

Certainly, the general trend was toward closure. By the end of 1919, twelve out
of twenty-one churches in places of higher education had closed, twenty out of
fifty in hospitals, thirty-five out of forty-three in secondary schools, eleven out of

eighteen in primary and "incomplete secondary" schools, and nine out of ten in prisons. The type of institution certainly played some role in driving the differences in policy: children and criminals were two key targets of Bolshevik political and moral education (*vospitanie*), and it was therefore especially important that competing systems of *vospitanie*, such as religion, were kept away. At the other end of the scale lay charitable institutions, whose premises (as with monasteries) could be commandeered for living accommodation; in a microenvironment that had a mixed social composition and a range of age groups, the presence of a church was not so inflammatory. But it was not just factors of this kind that were of significance. An important consideration also was whether a particular ecclesiastical building happened to be under a heritage preservation order.

Architectural merit did not always weigh in the favor of believers. The church in the former Ministry of the Court, housed in the former Golitsyn mansion on the Fontanka Embankment, was closed in 1918, at the point when the mansion was taken over by the Monuments Department itself, to be used as accommodation for its officials.[101] But the overwhelming majority of churches in former ministries that remained open after 1919 were structures of acknowledged architectural importance. They included those of the former State Duma in the Tauride Palace, the former Ministry of State Control, the former Holy Synod, the Theater and Ballet School, and the Ministry of the Post and Telegraph.[102]

In the case of Petrograd University, there is direct evidence for the use of the heritage argument, as the head of the General Department for the Separation of Church and State, one Dranitsyn, inarticulate with rage, complained on August 29, 1919:

> The Rector of the University's behavior is extremely odd. He pays no heed to the spirit of the decrees of the worker-peasant government, or simply does not want to know. The liberal bourgeoisie, despite its generally atheistic tendencies, does not even wish to follow the example of, say, its French brothers, such as [Georges] Clemenceau or [Abel] Hermant,[103] who enacted the principle of the state's independence from the church, and caused items of religious cult in state educational institutions to be destroyed.
>
> In order to try and prove the in fact non-existent self-contained character of the church, the university administration asserts that the church is not in direct communication with any of the lecture halls. And this despite the fact that a door from the altar leads directly into a lecture hall, though at the moment it, admittedly, is locked. However, doors from the narthex lead to a landing beside the main ceremonial hall of the University.

Moving to the artistic side of things, I should say that the church has no artistic value at all. On the contrary: the general character of the building housing the
TWELVE COLLEGES, built by the famous architect [Domenico] Trez[z]ini, is
impaired by the fact that under Nicholas I (in 1837), in an effort to create the effect
of ecclesiastical architecture, dome-like recesses were inserted into the ceiling, and
metalworkers from the merchant classes, working to commission, confected some
fake gold gates, which in every respect jar with the existing columns of white artificial marble.[104]

Concluding that in any case the entire edifice was more "a tribute to the building skills of the great Petrine era" than to the work of "Trezini" (*sic*), Dranitsyn
nevertheless argued that it should be preserved "to avoid the horrible error of the
prerevolutionary government, which destroyed Trez[z]ini's most successful building—the old [Vasilievskii Island] Gostinyi dvor [covered market]." Whichever
way, the church, as a later addition, could safely be expunged.[105] This labored and
tendentious sketch of architectural history did not achieve the desired effects. The
University Church, despite the drive to combat religious influence in education,
remained, in the meantime, open.

The actions of the Museums Department were certainly not fortuitous. Leading members of staff had a specialization of one kind or another in church architecture.[106] Konstantin Romanov (1882–1942), a distinguished archaeologist and
medievalist as well as a trained architect, had given lectures on "Christian architecture" at the Imperial Archaeological Institute between 1911 and 1918. His restoration work included St. George's Cathedral in Iur'ev-Pol'skii as well as surveys
of many other ecclesiastical buildings; his publications also focused on churches.
Grigorii Kotov (1859–1942), named in 1922 as the head of the Museums Department's Restoration Section, was the architect of the Russian Embassy church in
Vienna, and had taken part in the restoration of the Cathedral of the Dormition
in Ivanovo-Voznesensk, as well as in work on the Academy of Arts buildings in
St. Petersburg. One of the most active members of the Museums Department's
architectural section from its foundation was Aleksandr Udalenkov (1887–1975).
He, superficially, had a more "Soviet" profile than Romanov or Kotov. Born into
a peasant rather than gentry or merchant family, and from a distant village in
Tver' rather than Tsarskoe Selo (in Romanov's case) or Moscow (in Kotov's),
Udalenkov had worked for a decade as a printer. All the same, he had received
a full professional education before 1917: he was, like the others, a graduate of
the Higher College of Art at the Academy. He too had worked on church sites,

including the Cathedral of the Dormition in the Moscow Kremlin, before 1917, and he continued to undertake restoration of this kind in the Soviet period, including "cultic buildings" in Samarkand as well as Staraia Ladoga, Ferapontovo, and Novgorod.[107] There is no evidence that Romanov, Kotov, and Udalenkov were active churchgoers, or even religious in a loose sense, but they certainly valued church architecture.

Not surprisingly, given this background, believers themselves seem to have perceived officials in the preservation body as likely allies. A case in point was the petition sent to the authorities in late 1921 by worshippers at the Admiralty Cathedral, who claimed that the church's closure had not simply violated the laws on freedom of conscience, but also the regulations relating to heritage protection, since the building had a "certificate of protection" granted in 1919.[108] At this stage of Soviet history, religion and the organs of the state could sometimes make common cause—at least when it came to the interests of historic buildings.

"In View of the Extremity of the Situation, the Resources of the Entire Country Must Be Mobilized": The Sequestration of Church Property[109]

Where Petrograd was concerned, the impact of the January 20, 1918, decree was at best muted. Among the officials applying policy, ignorance of the new regulations, legalistic caution about applying them, and the preservation authorities' perception of religious users as, relatively speaking, allies, all impeded quick implementation. But these factors had weight because antireligious mobilization at the center of Soviet power was still hesitant. Certainly, the clergy were, along with army officers and other "former people," among the key targets of the "Red Terror." In summer 1918, 827 priests were executed, and the following year, another 19.[110] But given that at least 800 people were shot in Petrograd during September 1918 alone, it is hard to argue that the clergy were singled out for judicial murder.[111] Many of the worst atrocities against them took place in areas torn by violence during the Civil War and beyond the reach of central control, sometimes in the spirit of mob rule.[112] There was as yet no coordinated national campaign against religion. Even the exposure of relics, the best-publicized campaign of action, was pushed forward by a highly specific agency, the Eighth Directorate of the Commissariat of Justice, rather than figures in the leadership.[113] Removal of symbolism focused on objects with royal connections, while antireligious initiatives concentrated on the provision of alternative festivals: Union Days, July Days, *subbotniki* (or "clean up the streets" days), as well as the central revolutionary occasions, May 1 (International Labor Day) and November 7 (anniversary of the Great October Socialist Revolution).[114] *Revolution and the Church* might fulminate, but while the Soviet government was preoccupied with imposing its authority in the most basic sense, and with uniting the country in the face of Civil War, large-scale alienation of religious believers was simply not a risk worth taking.

In the course of 1921, however, relations between the hierarchy of the Orthodox Church and the Soviet leadership worsened drastically. The underlying factors included the growth in political confidence among the Bolsheviks as a result of military success, and also the desire to offset the institution of the New Economic Policy (NEP), widely seen by the Party faithful as an act of political betrayal, by manifestations of fidelity to Communist values.[115] But the proximate cause for the conflict was the crisis precipitated by severe famine in the Volga areas of the Russian heartland.[116]

The church had been among many non-Soviet organizations to mount philanthropic drives as a response to the famines. While the acceptance of aid was, practically speaking, essential (the Soviet state did not have the resources to cope with a crisis threatening millions of deaths), charitable activity on the part of religious groups was illegal by the letter of the 1918 Decree on the Separation of Church and State and ideologically invidious; more importantly, it was a threat to Party control.[117] After much hesitation in the late summer and fall of 1921, the Party leadership decided on a strategy intended both to solve the funding crisis and to weaken the church.[118] From late December 1921 a series of measures legalizing the sequestration of church property was set in place. The decree, On Items of Value in Churches and Monasteries, of December 27, 1921, referred to the presence of objects with a "colossal value," which might be, on the one hand, "historical and artistic," and on the other, "purely material." There was also a third class of objects, with no intrinsic value at all. It stipulated that items in the second category were to be "transferred into the State Reserve of Items of Value."[119] On January 2, 1922, a further decree, On the Liquidation of Church Property, ordered the removal of all items of value housed in churches, though it also stated that "ancient churches containing decorative items, iconostases, and icons are to remain untouched."[120]

In Petrograd, activity to implement the measures got underway almost immediately. On January 11, 1922, the chairman of the Parish Council of the Post Office Church wrote, in great alarm, to the Monuments Department in order to emphasize the church's artistic and historic importance. "The Church of the Twelve Apostles at the Main Post Office was constructed by Quarenghi," ran the letter. "It is located in the former palace of Prince Bezborodko, a grandee of the time of Catherine the Great, and together with the vessels and icons by Shamshin, Borispol'ts, Ivanov, Rubens, Raphael, and painters of the Flemish and Bolognese schools, is under Government Protection as a building of exceptional artistic interest in its entirety." But they had recently had a visitation from officials wishing to confiscate objects:

> On January 9 this year, quite unexpectedly for the church in question, two represen- tatives of the Second Central Petrograd District arrived and without consulting the Artistic Commission and in direct contravention of its certificate dated September 16, 1918, No. 394, flagrantly breached the said contract and began to liquidate the given church, despite the fact that the Parish Council had presented them with a written statement to the effect that if no representative of the Artistic Commission was present, liquidation of the church must not take place.

Having cited these legitimating documents, the Parish Council's chairman then continued to iterate the church's historical importance:

> The above church has existed since 1794, a total of 125 years,[121] the entire church premises—its white marble walls and grey marble pillars, its beautifully crafted plasterwork and sculptures to look like wood-carving are products of the human genius and intellect, and the result of the huge effort and meticulous work and colossal patience exerted by the Russian working people, who brought to life human ideas and left to us to preserve and to honor in memory their labor. All of this has been preserved and looked after by the laboring people of the Post and Telegraph Service for more than 125 years, and with its closure, it is all certainly going to collapse, because there isn't enough money in the Department for the Preservation of Monuments of Art and History to keep this church up without any heating and repairs going on, they just don't have the money for the heating and so on.[122]

By early 1922, believers had learned that appeals to monuments protection were potentially a more effective strategy for keeping their particular church open than appeals to freedom of worship (which might be countered by saying they could satisfy their rights and needs in some other "cultic building" nearby). And for the time being, the Post and Telegraph Church escaped.[123] But the momentum behind confiscations was building up. On February 14, 1922, a meeting of the Commis- sion on Removal of Gold from Churches set out the plans for a campaign of public information, which was to concentrate on the famine: this was to be "fused with antireligious propaganda, but the task must be undertaken carefully." After activities at public meetings (both in the Party network itself and at large factories), "a broad agitational campaign is to begin on March 1."[124]

Local preparations were, in the event, overtaken by more decisive action at the center. The Decree on the Stripping of Church Goods (February 16, 1922) announced that religious communities would be required to surrender items of high monetary value, such as utensils composed of gold or silver, or decorated with precious stones, to the local section of Pomgol (Aid to the Starving).[125] On February 28, 1922, Patriarch Tikhon reacted to the decree with a "Call to the Faithful." Here, he commended the idea of donating for this charitable purpose such church valuables as might not have been sanctified, but described as "sacrilege" the removal of church vessels that had been formally consecrated for use, even if believers had agreed to their removal.[126] The foundations had been laid for all-out conflict.

It is notable that the earliest legislative acts related to sequestration referred to the removal of church property into museums. The member of the leadership with primary responsibility for "the unification and expedition of efforts to increase the reserves of hard currency independent of whence those reserves may be derived" was Leon Trotsky.[127] Perhaps Natal'ia Sedova-Trotskaia had been able to use her personal connections, at the early stages of the campaign, to press the importance of preservation. Certainly, the Museums Department continued to push for the exemption of goods of "artistic and historical importance" from the general surge of breaking up and melting down. An instruction issued by the Museums Department on March 4, 1922, citing the January 2, 1922, decree, insisted that no items created earlier than 1725 should be "liquidated" at all, and even fragments of these, such as the decorative trims on icons and enamel plaques, were to be spared destruction. Only "exceptional" items from the period 1725–1835 might be converted into scrap; "objects in the style of Louis XV and XVI and the Empire should on no account be liquidated." From the period 1835 onward, all objects were potentially subject to liquidation, except those of "high artistic value." The instruction also underlined that "ancient churches" should be preserved holistically, with nothing at all removed from the *ansambl'*; and in case of doubt, consultation with experts, as well as specialists from the Museums Department, was essential.[128]

The instruction raised important practical questions. Did the prohibition on destroying items from the era of "Louis XV and XVI and the Empire" extend to Russian-made objects of the same period, a far more likely discovery in most churches? How easy was it to establish dating in an artistic culture where following tradition had always been of central importance? In Petrograd, a Special Commission of the Museums Department met on March 4–5, 1922, directly after the new central instruction appeared, to evolve its own set of regulations for classifying church property. These affirmed still more strongly than the central guidelines the importance not just of individual objects, but of the entire setting in which they were housed:

> Churches both in Petrograd and in the provinces preserve within them a large quantity of monuments that are of exceptional scholarly and artistic value. Given the special degree to which church architecture in Rus[s]ia was developed, ecclesiastical monuments of Art and History have a special interest, and if these perish, irreparable damage will be done to world knowledge of history and art. Therefore, the confiscation of such monuments must be carried out with special care.[129]

But the preservation bodies had an important stumbling block in their way, since the legislation of February 16, 1922, which acted as the main stimulus to the sequestration campaign, gave no direct attention to items of "historical or artistic value."[130] Neither (less surprisingly) did Patriarch Tikhon refer to this issue in his address to the faithful. The result was to initiate a primary conflict between the instrumental and the sacral view of church goods. They were either items of mere monetary value, fit only for melting down; or, on the other hand, sacral objects that could not be assessed on any scale, whether economic, aesthetic, or historic.

This conflict ran through the press coverage of church sequestrations, which was carefully managed so that the practical aim of aid to the starving was always kept in view. An item published in *Petrogradskaia pravda* (Petrograd Truth) on February 14, 1922, referred to the "participation" of the church in the Pomgol campaign, citing a representative of Patriarch Tikhon. In order to reinforce the message, the church hierarchy was separated into sheep and goats. "Progressive" spiritual leaders, in particular Father Aleksandr Vvedenskii, the Church of Renovation's leading local representative, articulated their commitment to the support of the starving above all else. On February 18, 1922, *Petrogradskaia pravda* published an article in which Vvedenskii melodramatically alluded to the starving mothers on the Volga who were reduced to eating their own babies. He called on the Orthodox faithful to sacrifice the "gold, the silver, and the stones that we have transported to the man-made churches of Christ. For now, when the churches not made by human hands, living people, are perishing, should we not turn that gold into bread, in order that we may save them?"[131] An item published on March 14 reported that Vvedenskii had demonstratively handed over his own gold pectoral cross in aid of the starving, and his congregation, emboldened by this, had consented to surrender a number of silver icon cases.[132] Later reports referred to warm support by the clergy for requisitions in some places, and on March 24 appeared the "Declaration of the Progressive Petrograd Group of Clergy," a manifesto for cooperation with the campaign.[133] This was the period of the emergence of "the Church of Renovation" as a major political force; encouraged by contacts in the Soviet security services, prominent figures in the reform movement began to present collaboration with the authorities as the only true pathway to the inner spiritual transformation of Orthodoxy.[134]

Those who resisted the sequestrations, however, were presented as adversaries from the start. On March 21, 1922, *Petrogradskaia pravda* mentioned Metropolitan Veniamin of Petrograd's opposition to the surrender of communion vessels, and asserted, in a passage highlighted in bold print:

> The Petrograd Soviet wishes to make clear: Soviet power respects the religious feelings of the faithful, it will under no circumstances impede anyone from practicing whatever religion he may choose. But Soviet power will not permit a gang of higher representatives of the clergy who have grown used to serving tsars and landowners to subvert the aid to the starving campaign.[135]

Even when Veniamin, in April 1922, modified his earlier opposition, and sanctioned the surrender of most items, including communion vessels, if this avoided open conflict, there was no easing of hostilities.[136] A compromise whereby believers would be able to "buy out" the most precious icons and devotional items by providing an alternative donation of equivalent value was ridiculed the day after it was announced: a prominently published reader's letter mocked the very idea that items made of precious metals might be "sacred." Thus, the message was repeatedly pressed home that church valuables were simply "valuables"—items like any other, whose significance was purely material. And in June 1922 came the trial, and eventual condemnation to death for counterrevolutionary activity, of Metropolitan Veniamin (or "citizen Kazanskii," as the first day's court report had it)—the most senior churchman in Petrograd to fall victim to political terror.[137]

"Who Has Most Right to Such Objects Anyway?" The Fate of Sequestered Church Property

As well as breaking the hold of the Orthodox faithful on the movable objects enshrined in churches, Party, state, and municipal officials also had to decide what to do with the items that had fallen into their hands. Should these be consigned for sale as they stood, melted down, or placed in the care of the state?[138] While church property that was considered to be of "artistic and historical value" was, by the letter of the law, supposed to be ceded to the state museum authority, on the ground, confusion reigned.

At a meeting of the Petrograd Soviet on March 20, 1922, the lead speaker, Comrade Kondrat'ev, referred, in his opening remarks, to plans set up by central government for the protection of artistic works. However, his phrasing was distinctly grudging: "It was directed by the Moscow committee that as far as certain items are concerned that might be of only limited value in terms of price but greater value in the artistic or historic sense, they should be left and replaced with other things, and they said action should be agreed separately in every individual case."[139] After this bald acknowledgment of "artistic and historic value," Kondrat'ev moved on to deal exclusively with the issues raised by the potential purchasing power of the church goods, once realized, and the immediate problems of managing the resistance likely to be mounted by believers. Though conceding that the "fixed ideas of the Russian people" (*kosnost' russkogo naroda*) might be an obstacle, he still insisted that the removal of valuables was essentially a "trivial" business. "Most like there'll be a few tears shed over the removal of church valuables, it'll be like children, when we're dividing up the rations and slice off a pound or two of bread. That don't cause damage to the economy and it won't hurt the Soviet republic neither." Now the moment had come for the Russian people to, as it were, cash in on its own investment: "We know where those valuables came from, and we know they was achieved by the broad masses of the toiling people, we know that they was created out of those pennies that me and you, out of our lack of political consciousness, not just our forefathers but us too, gave to those churches." Though citing causes where resistance had been offered, Kondrat'ev dismissed these as down to "provocation." An incident on Haymarket Square (where a crowd of over 10,000 had emerged to defend the Church of the Savior after rumors that it was going to be stripped) was the result of agitation by reactionary clergy.[140]

That popular opinion was more complicated than Kondrat'ev suggested was made clear even by another speaker at the same meeting. There were precedents, he conceded, for the removal of valuables from churches at moments of national crisis: "Right before the Sebastopol campaign, Nicholas I forced the Kiev Cave Monasteries to hand over 20 million worth of stuff like that." But given the consequences of the Crimean War, though, "it didn't do him no good. The Sebastopol campaign . . ." Here, according to the stenographic record, he was interrupted by uproar ("Shouts of 'Enough!' Loud noise. The chairman rings his bell.") Still the speaker ploughed on, undeterred: "Comrades, I'm telling you the truth. I should firstly say that I'm the son of a former serf, I'm not going against Soviet power, I wish it well, but I keep saying: don't go against God . . ." At this point bedlam broke out in all directions.[141]

For the most part, speakers at the meeting (as the general derision inspired by the reference to God suggests) adopted a radically anticlerical position. Priests in Kronstadt had objected to workers handling ecclesiastical objects with their "grimed horny hands," yet the hands of church prelates were themselves stained with blood. Who had more right to such objects anyway, those who had made and donated them, or "those who pray for eternal rest for their own sinful little souls, so as to fetch up in the heavenly kingdom"? Believers were a counterrevolutionary force, imbued with "Black Hundred" values such as anti-Semitism. The meeting concluded with a unanimous vote to implement the central decree on church valuables.[142]

The policy endorsed by the Party hierarchy aimed to avoid turning the removal of church goods into an open confrontation with religious believers. A secret circular dispatched by Molotov on March 20, 1922, criticized the anticlerical tone of much newspaper reporting, with its "cheery satirical verses directed against priests in general." Rather than tarring all clergy with the same brush, the "political task" was now quite different: to work with the churchmen who were favorably disposed to the sequestrations, and thus to "deepen and sharpen the already existing schism."[143]

This manipulative approach was in any case the preferred method in Petrograd.[144] On March 11, 1922, a secret circular from the highest Party authority, the North-Western Bureau, had advised that it was important to convince believers that the removal of church treasures was not "offensive" when aid to the starving was in question (personal appearances by witnesses of the catastrophe would be useful). Addressees were advised to "create a mood in your agitation and propaganda" that would mean believers themselves put pressure on the clergy. It should be emphasized, the circular went on, that the sequestrations applied to all faiths, and not just Orthodoxy. "Extreme caution" was necessary when carrying out sequestrations: "so-called sacred objects should be replaced with other, less valuable, ones." Destructive acts were to be avoided, partly on pragmatic grounds: "Do not break or tear off decorations that are of inferior value, in case you render the entire object useless," officials were warned.[145] A resolution passed by the Bureau of the Petrograd Provincial Committee of the Communist Party on March 25, 1922, endorsed the policies set out in Molotov's circular, proposing that "the loyal mood among part of the clergy" should be exploited, and contacts with suitable churchmen made. It stated that the Central Committee should be asked for permission to delay expropriations in Petrograd until the second half of April (after the celebration of Orthodox Easter). However, in resolving also to petition the Central Executive Committee for permission to use the death penalty to deal with the "cases of banditry and light-headed behavior bordering on criminality that are being recorded during expropriations," the Party authorities indicated the sheer difficulty of managing the political situation on the ground.[146]

As attitudes on both sides hardened, the full force of animus was directed against monastic foundations. On May 12, 1922, the eighteenth-century silver casket containing the relics of St. Alexander Nevsky enshrined in the Trinity Cathedral of the Lavra was forced open, and the casket removed, stripped of its relics, to the State Museums Fund (it was later placed on display in the Hermitage, where it remains to this day). On November 20, 1922, the relics themselves were removed, and in due course found their way into the collection of Leningrad's Museum of Atheism.[147] Worship in some of the churches on the site, including the Trinity Cathedral, continued into the 1930s, but they were now classed as "parish churches." The city's second most important monastic foundation, the New Maiden Convent, underwent requisitions in May 1922, and was also extensively secularized in 1923, when the local tram depot made a claim on the living accommodation. There were plans to convert the memorial church of Our Lady of Kazan' (1908–1912) into a "theater, auditorium, cinematograph, or suchlike." Yet the building, while not an official monument, was a lavish neo-Byzantine construction by the well-regarded architect Vasilii Kosiakov, decorated with sumptuous mosaics.[148]

Other churches also came under assault. Harassment of worshippers became common. On March 5, 1922, parish councils were required to submit data about all members of the parishes, including sex, occupation, and age, a regulation that the administrators of Petrograd district used as the justification to circulate detailed

questionnaires about personal biographies.[149] Administrators had increasing ammunition at their disposal, since central legislation was tightened up to make protest
more difficult. The edition of the Soviet Criminal Code published on June 1, 1922,
devoted the entirety of its section 3 to "offenses against the regulations on the separation of church and state." Among such "offenses" were "the exploitation of the
religious prejudices of the masses with the aim of overthrowing Soviet power,"
the committal of "acts of deception," and "the religious instruction of the young."
Alongside "the arrogation by religious or church organizations of administrative,
juridical, or other public legal rights" stood "the performance in state institutions
and enterprises of any religious rituals, and equally the placing in these of any religious images." While the Code also forbade "interference in the performance of
religious rites where these do not disrupt public order," its overall function was to
criminalize a broad range of practices whose previous status had been ambiguous.[150]
On August 3, 1922, a Commissariat of Justice and Commissariat of Internal Affairs
decree underlined that it was essential all religious groups should be properly registered, and required delivery of a heap of paperwork to the local authorities.[151]

In the wake of the new regulations, "bald administration" (the issuing of rude
and arbitrary demands) became common. In August 1922, the NKVD put out a
secret circular threatening criminal proceedings against parish councils if copies
of church property inventories relating to liquidated churches and monasteries
were not supplied by them in short order. Officials at the Petrosovet Department
of State Property had to point out to the NKVD that there were no ecclesiastical
buildings in Petrograd in this category, and that "house churches" had never possessed the inventories in question to begin with.[152]

The aggressive attitude to church closures had not just ideological, but practical, roots. It was far easier to remove items from a non-functioning church than
from a working one.[153] As in other parts of the Soviet Union, so in Petrograd,
believers made their opposition felt. In April 1922, parishioners of the Prince
Vladimir Cathedral prevented officials who had arrived to remove church goods
from doing this, or even carrying out an inventory, despite the attempts of the
church's incumbent (*nastoiatel'*) to mediate the situation.[154] In the same month,
officials attempting to confiscate property from the Church of St. Mary Magdalene
in Smol'nyi district were hit by flying stones.[155] Even if not expressing their feelings so directly, members of congregations initiated protests in verbal form. For
example, in June 1922, a meeting to decide the fate of the Cavalry School "house
church" held at the Petrograd Waterworks, whose employees used the church for
their devotions, was attended by nearly 500 people, who protested that its closure

would be an assault on their "proletarian rights," and presented a petition with "hundreds of signatures." As the chair of the executive committee of Smol'nyi district soviet reported to the Management Department of the Petrograd provincial soviet, "We had to nip that discussion in the bud right away."[156]

"Impeding the Due Process of Liquidation": Challenges to Preservation

If representations from believers carried some weight, still more was attached to representations from heritage protection bodies. As officials in the Administrative Section of the Department for the Management of State Property regularly reminded officials in district soviets, "House churches that have been taken under the care of the Museums Department, as monuments of history and art, are not subject to liquidation. If there are churches in a given district where certain cultic objects have been earmarked by the Museums Department and have not yet been transferred to Museums, then you should urge the Museums Department to remove such at the earliest possible opportunity, and then liquidate the premises in the customary manner."[157] In the short term at least, a "certificate of protection" could be effective. For instance, the Church of the Savior on the Waters was certified as a protected monument on October 22, 1919, and it was not stripped of any church property in 1922. As the incumbent priest noted in a report to the city authorities, the representatives of Aid to the Starving had paid a visit during the confiscation campaign, but had brought along "representatives of Monuments Protection." Though the Aid to the Starving officials had talked about returning, in the event they had removed nothing, "maybe because the amount of things you could take away without destroying the whole *ansambl'* of the church would be too insignificant; indeed, anything removable would be of either artistic or historic interest."[158]

There were other cases also where the "representatives of Monuments Protection" were able to discourage mass confiscations.[159] But there were serious difficulties too. Aid to the Starving officials sometimes simply ignored the directives about consultation with "the representatives of Monuments Protection." As Konstantin Romanov recorded in the summer of 1922:

> Unfortunately, in practice, violations of this agreement were encountered; the sequestrations were carried out while experts were not present, and while they were taking place, items of ancient date and of high [artistic and historical] value were badly

damaged. So, for instance, the icon cases in the Sampson Cathedral on Vyborg Side, dating from the eighteenth century, were removed from their places despite expert opinion to the contrary, and then sent off to the repository of Aid to the Starving.

This type of behavior, Romanov continued, had not come to an end after a directive from Mikhail Kalinin issued on April 11, 1922, that reminded local officials of their obligations:

> The directions given by the experts made only a partial impact, and objects were very often removed contrary to their opinion; and moreover, items valuable from a museum perspective were transported off to the repository of Aid to the Starving without being properly packed up, and were removed in ways that damaged them to begin with. Finally, in recent weeks, representatives of the Aid to the Starving Commission have begun to remove all valuables of any kind from churches that are under protection as monuments of outstanding artistic or historic significance, just as they have been doing from churches that are not protected. [. . .] Sequestrations of this kind have taken place in such churches of outstanding historical significance and containing icon cases of the first rank as the Church of the Tauride Palace (dating from the eighteenth century) and the Icon of the Vladimir Mother of God on Vladimirskii prospekt, and the Trinity-Izmailovskii Regiment Cathedral (an iconostasis dating from the time when the church was built).[160]

Romanov's diary for 1922 confirms this account, noting that in the Harbor Trinity Church on Vasilievskii Island, one of Petrograd's two remaining eighteenth-century wooden churches, "triptychs dating back to the reign of Peter I were prized out of their frames [. . .] in order to get at the gold."[161] At the same time, he also expressed dissatisfaction that on occasion Aid to the Starving had permitted "parishes to buy off items of Museum value, a process that transfers these from the category of objects protected by the appropriate authorities to those wholly owned by the parishes."[162] The aim remained that objects of historical and aesthetic significance should be in state hands, not those of believers.

Yet heritage protectionists had at best limited leverage. If the officials carrying out the sequestrations made contact at all, this was often to let them know late in the evening that their presence would be required the morning of the following day. This was what happened in the case of the Kazan' Cathedral in mid-March 1922, for instance.[163] The fact that efforts to protect churches had to be coordinated with the chaos and stress of the requisitions themselves placed a heavy burden on preservation officials. From March 4, 1922, members of the Monuments Office Special Commission on the Sequestration of Church Property worked frantically to try and draw up a list of protected churches, placed in the three agreed categories: those protected in their entirety, those from which property might be removed, but which were not to be liquidated, and those which contained individual items of movable property that were under protection, but which were not deemed worthy of protection overall.[164] At a succession of meetings, the Commission tried to review every single "cultic building" in the city, of which, according to its own records, there were 468. By April 7, 1922, the Commission had managed to review 115 ecclesiastical buildings, of which 89 (44 house churches and 45 parish churches) had been taken under protection—an impressive, but far from exhaustive, tally. During the process of review, decisions were constantly referred back for further information, and items moved up and down on the lists. In the early stages, there was no church in the city that preservationists were without further investigation prepared to categorize as of zero interest (whether architecturally or in terms of its contents).[165] The many lists spawned by the review process were inconclusive and often contradicted each other. Information about protected "house churches" was particularly confusing.[166] It is scarcely surprising that Pomgol and local soviet officials were left at best bewildered, and at worst obdurate—particularly as the instructions from the local soviets themselves about what should happen during liquidations were also far from lucid.[167]

Whatever happened, preservationists could not question the assumptions of the Decree on the Confiscation of Church Property, or do much to cool its ardor. One effect of the Decree was to prompt a far more energetic drive to close "house churches." An instruction issued in February 1922 by the deputy head of the Administrative Section of the Department for the Management of State Property and the head of the Church Office of the Petrograd Provincial Soviet decreed, "Any house churches attached to institutions that may still be functioning are to be closed. The parishioners of such churches may, if they wish, obtain an attachment to the nearest parish church that is still open; church property of a ritual kind is also to be transferred thence." The instruction acknowledged the right of heritage preservation, stating: "The Department for the Preservation of Monuments of History and Art is to be informed concerning the determination and removal of valuables of an archival artistic [sic] kind." But it also added, "If a representative of the Department does not attend, this will be taken to signify the Department's lack of interest, and the liquidation will take place without the participation of its representative"—thus placing the onus on the Monuments Department itself to keep track of the sequestrations.[168] Meanwhile, the Department of Justice of the Petrograd Provincial Soviet, ostensibly responsible for making sure procedures were followed, mainly occupied itself with pressuring district soviets to get on with the closures.[169]

Over the following months, large numbers of "house churches" were scheduled for liquidation. In May 1922, for example, six places of worship in this category in Moskovskii district alone were placed on the list for closure, including the churches at the city's neoclassical abattoir, as well as the Air Balloon Park and the former College of Trades and Crafts. Also among the six places of worship was a house synagogue—in living accommodation, but counted as being sited in "a public place" (since all apartment blocks in cities were now the property of the state).[170] Churches in hospitals—where patients by definition had difficulty in attending places of worship that were not located on the premises—were closed along with the rest, though in some cases officials still expressed a readiness to tolerate the occasional use of a former house church, once liquidated, for religious services.[171]

Preservation officials appear to have continued to assume that churches were better off in regular use for worship. Where possible, they attempted to uphold classification of "house churches" as autonomous structures that did not form an integral part of a public building. On June 15, 1922, a commission including Udalenkov and Romanov adjudicated that the church in the Apraksin Market should remain open for worship:

> The church, both in terms of its external and of its internal features, does not have the character of a house church. [...] The placing of the church at a corner of the block with civic buildings adjoining is quite common in Old Russian architecture, and examples of this disposal of freestanding churches are also very often found in Petrograd.[172]

Often, though, attempts to protect church property ran up against local officials' ingrained suspicion that congregations were concealing valuables from view. On May 10, 1922, the Executive Committee of the Moscow District Soviet recorded in the minutes of its meeting, "It has been established that there were no accurate inventories of church valuables and property in existence. So, for instance, in the New Maiden Convent, the inventories record about 27 poods of silver, but the amount confiscated was actually closer to 40 poods. About 800 precious stones were removed, and 89 poods 48 pounds of precious metals."[173] Clearly, there was a vanishingly small likelihood that officials committed to maximizing quantity of goods removed would carefully review which particular cross or chalice dated from prior to 1725 or might have "high artistic value."[174] Rather than laboriously work through inventories, those carrying out sequestration would be far more inclined to brand these as intrinsically misleading, and carry out confiscations as they saw fit.

Indeed, there was often positive hostility to experts on preservation, who were seen as "fifth columnists" for the Orthodox faithful.[175] In November 1922, the head of the Church Office in Vasilieostrovskii district, together with a colleague from the Administrative Department, wrote with inarticulate irritation to the Church Office of the Executive Committee of the Petrograd Provincial Soviet in order to suggest that the Museums Department was institutionally biased in favor of keeping house churches open:

> Take the church in the Patriotic Institute. [Only] the iconostasis there was found to be artistic, but the entire church is given over to the Museums Department. The Academy of Arts despite the fact that part of the property is definitely not artistic all the same has pretensions to keep it for itself and is making completely unfounded excuses. The Museums Department representative is backing them up and has even refused to inspect the church in question. Something comparable has happened in the Mining Institute, where despite the lack of value in the objects these all the same remained after a submission from the Museums Department representative thanks to a request to him from a representative of the Mining Institute. The same thing happened in the Vera Slutskaia Library, where the entire premises along with the church was given over to the Museums Department. This situation creates abnormalities, on the one hand it removes necessary premises from an institution to create church museums in these and scatters such museums all over the city and inevitably makes them lose their practical value and on the other hand giving over all kinds of things to itself that aren't necessary only leads to excessive burdens both on institutions and on themselves [i.e., the Museums Department], thus impeding the due process of liquidation.[176]

Responding three days later, the Petrograd Directorate of Scientific and Scientific-Artistic Institutions sent a long letter justifying the policy, and the three-category classification applied to house churches. Petrograd was the city where there was the most important eighteenth- and nineteenth-century architecture in the entire country. Yet only 15 percent of house churches were protected at all, though there were almost none in other cities, and certainly not of such quality. In any case, several of the churches mentioned were not protected by the Museums Department; others, such as the Institute of Mines and the Academy of Arts, were of exceptional historical and artistic interest. As soon as funding allowed, the Museums Department was planning to complete the removal of protected objects from the lower-category churches, which were not scheduled for preservation as a whole.[177]

However, there was some substance in the charge that the sheer numbers of empty churches placed impossible burdens on preservation officials. By August 22, 1922, over 160 "house churches" across Petrograd had been closed, including 157 Orthodox ones.[178] The number of liquidations was running so high that local administrators were overwhelmed. On October 25, 1922, the head of the Management Department of the Central district wrote to the Management Department of the Petrograd Provincial Soviet to express bewilderment about what to do with the residuum of church property remaining after liquidation had taken place:

> We offered icons kiots and iconostases free of charge to Parish Councils of Parish churches that are still open but they refused on account of having no spare funds for transport and proper packing. On the basis of the above we request you to issue the appropriate order of what we are to do with the icons and kiots. If we take them into storage then they might as well be firewood or should we sell them to private icon shops or destroy them on the spot.[179]

It was beyond the resources of the Monuments Department even to rescue all the individual items of property that had been classified as worthy of conservation, let alone to turn all the sites of special interest into museums.

Officials responsible for heritage preservation did what they could to mitigate the situation. But staff cuts—from over ninety employees at the start of 1921 to just over thirty in early 1922—had taken their toll.[180] Pressure from district soviet officials, desperate to finish with the liquidations, continued to mount. On December 8, 1922, there was another attack on the institutions of preservation, this time accusing the Monuments Department of unreasonable behavior:

> At the time when liquidation is in process and almost at the very moment when the church property is being removed[,] the parish of the church being liquidated asserts that the property to be removed is artistically and historically valuable, and

the Provincial Department for the Preservation of Monuments of Art and History for its part endorses this assertion without due cause. As for instance in the case of the Community of the Raising of the Cross.[181]

The official added that the Provincial Museums Department representative "did not find anything of historic and artistic value, but nevertheless, decided to leave the church untouched, motivating this decision exclusively by the fact that the pictures in the church (carried out in 1910) are copies of pictures by Vosnetsov [*sic*]."[182] Among other things, the Museums representative had, allegedly, said "the parish deserves some sympathy; why not let them have the church to pray in?" Such behavior on the part of the Provincial Museums Department was, the district official ranted, "completely incomprehensible." "A Soviet organization, it nevertheless obstructs another Soviet organization (the Management Department [of the Moscow District Soviet]) in the execution of the duties assigned to it by the state." The response of the Monuments Department was once again to stress that there might be items of value in a building that was classified as representing little or no interest. But, as the initial reaction from the Moscow District Soviet showed, distinctions of this kind were now treated dismissively to begin with; there was little point in restating them.[183]

In 1923, the mood hardened further. Pressure to register religious groups was stepped up, and an instruction of the Commissariat of Justice and Commissariat of Internal Affairs issued on June 19 underlined that churches required for essential purposes, such as clinics or "places of cultural education," could be removed from believers.[184] By July 1923, a further thirteen "house churches" that were the subject of preservation orders had been closed to worship.[185] "Liquidations" of closed "house churches" now went ahead whatever the architectural status of the structure concerned. On October 4, 1923, the heads of the Section for the Management of State Property and the Administrative Subsection of the Petrograd City Soviet wrote to the Presidium of Petrosovet demanding that the premises of the Royal Stables Church (an architectural monument and also the place where Pushkin's funeral had taken place) should be handed over to the city's mounted police, and that "the Museums Department should immediately remove all the property of museum significance that has been ceded to it, and also the iconostasis."[186] By December 1923, both the Orthodox church of the former Corps des Pages and the famous "Maltese Chapel" in the building had been substantially reconstructed, with items of "museum importance" removed, so that the Petrograd First Military

College now occupying the building could use the premises of the former places of worship for "cultural purposes."[187]

"House churches" were now liable to closure and "liquidation" on a whole range of grounds. Their rich contents made them vulnerable to requisitions. The communities using them did not have the same level of political capital as worshippers at humbler Petrograd churches. (The faithful of St. Pitirim's Church, Kievskaia ulitsa, for instance, were able to assert, "Our church is little, and was made not by the efforts and capital of the *burzhui*, but by our calloused hands alone, and we have collected the essential vessels as and when we could."[188]) Pressure also came from the institutions in which the churches were housed, as the movement to create clubs started to gain momentum. For instance, in 1923 the Komsomol activists belonging to the "Old and New Guard" club reshaped the "house church" of the Trinity monastic legation (*podvor'e*) at 44 Fontanka Embankment (a category two listed monument) into an auditorium for plays and other performances. As *Krasnaia gazeta* (Red Newspaper) reported, the "unwelcoming, gloomy" exterior, with its pictures of saints and crosses, belied the impressions of anyone who actually entered the building. "Inside is our new Soviet life, tempestuous, powerful, and healthy young people." A "laboratory of Soviet science" had been set up:

> The Komsomol had to put huge efforts into destroying the magnificent marble iconostasis. In place of the altar, they constructed a stage, and used church vestments to confect a curtain. In the dome, instead of God of the Sabaoth, was delineated a wonderful image of the emblem of the Communist International of Youth.[189]

Symbolic as well as practical pressures bore down on those who attempted to champion preservation. Soviet propaganda and agitation celebrated innovation, internationalism, and the effacement of the past, spearheaded by the new generation. The "God of the Sabaoth" stood for the old patriarchal order of obscurantist patriotism. Those who wished to tear churches down and destroy religious artifacts could invoke the powerful rhetoric of "scientific atheism," expressed in a rising tide of propaganda and activism. From the carnival looting evoked by Babel in his "At St. Walenty's," the annihilation of religious property had become—in theory at least—a purposive didactic ritual, aimed at the conversion of believers to the new ways. Petrograd was meant to be a center of antireligious activity of a "conscious" kind: the production of brochures, the organization of shows, and the generation of alternative rites of passage such as "red christenings."[190]

With so many voices in favor of closure, the advocacy for preserving "house churches" on architectural grounds was almost inaudible. In any case, simply closing buildings up was not a neutral solution, since extensive damage to church property by theft or vandalism was likely to result. In March 1922, the church of St. Alexander Nevsky in the No. 6 Petrograd Courses for Infantry Commanders (formerly the No. 2 Cadet Corps) was burgled, probably by some students studying at the institution where it was housed. Inspectors from the Museums Department discovered a scene of systematic destruction. Little had been removed, apart from a copper kettle, a mirror, three stools, twelve bentwood chairs, and a few icons.[191] However, damage of a studiedly sacrilegious kind had been done. The inspectors were so shocked that they did not content themselves with simply listing the missing items, but provided a full description:

> The silk curtain from the Royal Gates [of the iconostasis] has been torn down and snatched away. The cloths on the altar and the sanctuary, and the church banners and the epitaphios [cloth with the image of the crucified Christ on it] have been torn to shreds and the tatters are lying on the floor nearby. There is damage to an icon of Christ in the Garden of Gethsemane [*Molenie o chashe*]: a hole has been drilled in the image of the Savior's mouth and a cigarette stuck into it. Between the altar and the sacristy, the floor in one place has been smeared with human ordure.
>
> The whole floor of the vestry is covered with heaps of torn vestments. Many objects, for instance the wedding crowns, the vessels from the sanctuary and so on, have been bent out of shape.[192]

Rather than risk scenes such as this, officials preferred to remove temptation by simply stripping a church, as the commandant of Smol'nyi exhorted the authorities to do in 1923:

> I request your urgent decision about the following—the liquidation of house churches as soon as may be practicable. The aforementioned churches, 6 in number, along with a morgue, have been closed and sealed since 1917. The seals have been torn off or knocked off by small boys and the churches do not have reliable locks. Placing sentries in every church is out of the question. Some churches contain equipment that could be put to use and of which there is currently a shortage, but it is now lying round unused and will certainly deteriorate completely, given the damp.[193]

"The churches have been assigned to the Department for the Protection of Ancient Monuments," the commandant concluded. In the circumstances, it sounded like an accusation.

To the average believer, there was certainly little, if any, difference between unsanctioned vandalism, purposive desecration in the cause of "scientific atheism" (as represented by, say, the breaking open of St. Alexander Nevsky's shrine), and the all-out sequestration during which precious stones were prized out of icon covers, and chalices reduced to heaps of scrap for recycling. But the Petrograd Party and city authorities did attempt to distance themselves from the most vocal and active anticlerical trends of the time. In 1923, a secret Party circular on "Red Easter" relegated antireligious carnivals to "closed premises." It recommended that more decorous forms of agitation should be used for public consumption, such as "debates with members of the clergy," posters, and slide-shows. The circular emphasized once more that "crude offense to religious feelings" should be avoided, "since it can cause embitterment and fanaticism in the broad masses."[194] Yet the efforts to close "house churches" were not scaled back, whatever their likely contribution to "embitterment."

The Monuments Department, far from being able to stop liquidations, lacked the resources even to keep careful track of what was removed. The vast majority of items transferred into museum collections were not accompanied by information about provenance, and no tallies were kept of which items had been transferred where.[195] Some house churches had been spared liquidation, for example, those in the Academy of Arts, the College of Jurisprudence, and the Senate, but as they were now in secular hands, their long-term safety could not be guaranteed.[196] And there was also the issue of what to do with the large amount of valuable church property that was now in the custody of the preservation bureaucracy. In no mood for self-congratulation, heritage officials were faced with the headache of trying to evolve a plan for protecting the interiors that they had "preserved"—but as it turned out, only in the most temporary and contingent sense.[197]

• • •

The January 20, 1918, Decree on the Separation of Church and State, whatever the intentions of its formulators, did not lead to an immediate and tidy division of responsibilities between sacred and secular power. The primary obstacles lay not so much in decisive opposition from the Orthodox Church itself, since many of the clergy and laity saw opportunities as well as problems, but in the requirement for officers of the state to steer between the objective of marginalizing "religious associations" and the objective of retaining social control. In Petrograd, the second objective dominated throughout the period immediately after the Bolsheviks took power. Added to this, there was a great deal of confusion about what the decree actually required in terms of action, particularly as related to former religious spaces in public institutions. In other parts of the former Russian Empire, officials stormed in and closed down "house churches," whatever the rules. But Petrograd officials appear to have been more thoughtful and law-abiding—perhaps because of longer experience in the administration, or perhaps because of higher literacy levels.[198] For their part, specialists in preservation at this period took an extremely permissive attitude to the listing of buildings, issuing "certificates of protection" to large numbers of premises, particularly "house churches."

This situation, however, changed radically in 1922, when the Decree on the Confiscation of Church Property unleashed a frantic scramble to realize the value of ecclesiastical objects, followed by a crackdown on "house churches" that were in use for worship. In the circumstances, the concerns of preservation were at best secondary, certainly from the late spring of 1922. In other Soviet Russian historic cities and towns, it was monasteries and relics that took the brunt of the secularizing drive; in Petrograd, it was "house churches" and their contents. The result was irreparable damage not just to church-state relations, but to the historical fabric of the city, and, indeed, to levels of trust within the new state and municipal agencies, already battered and bewildered by conflicting orders and incessant shifts in policy demands.

FIGURE 4. Interior of Smol'nyi Cathedral (Bartolomeo Rastrelli, 1748–1764), c. 1924. Photograph from the collection of the Leningrad State Restoration Workshop. (FO NA IIMK RAN, negative no. II 3353, collection no. 16-994.)

CHAPTER TWO

Monuments to the Golden Age

The Canons of Preservation, 1924–1928

BY THE START OF 1924, the closures of "house churches" had spread all over Petrograd. Only one attached to a hospital was still functioning—the Church of St. Panteleimon at the No. 2 Psychiatric Hospital in the remote suburb of Udel'naia—as well as two in former church schools, seven churches once operated by religious education societies, and seventeen churches in former charities. Just one former house church was liquidated during 1924—in the former Shcherbakov Rest Home and School, which lay in a working-class area of Vyborg Side distant from the city center.[1]

This highly significant symbolic step in the separation of religion and the state achieved, officials were able to pause for breath. The renaming of Petrograd on January 26, 1924, a mere five days after Lenin had died, attested that the former capital was believed to have triumphed over its dubious past. Such an honor could have been conferred only on a place of complete ideological purity. Key central streets and squares with religious associations had been renamed in 1918, and many others in 1923, and the population was starting to forget their original titles. The writer A. Men'shoi reported that, riding down the former Vladimirskii prospekt (named for the Church of the Vladimir Icon of the Mother of God), now prospekt Nakhimsona, he had heard the tram conductor shout out the next stop as, "Comrade Nakhimson Church!"[2]

With so much achieved in Leningrad, campaigns against the city's prerevolutionary past could be reined in a little. The situation in the country at large was favorable to a remission in other ways also. The process of confiscation in 1922–1923 had achieved its object in terms of smashing the power of the Moscow Patriarchate; Tikhon, who died in 1925, lived out his last years under constant harassment. The Church of Renovation's "Board of Church Management," which had held its Second All-Russian General Synod in 1923, was in the ascendant.[3] Still the largest group of Orthodox believers, the "Tikhonites" had lost any meaningful political leadership. Large numbers of splinter groups ("the Ancient Apostolic Church," "the Laboring Church") appeared.[4] The government had succeeded in containing large-scale rebellion at the grass roots; now the Orthodox community was shattered.

Behind the scenes, jockeying for position preoccupied the political leadership. Antireligious campaigns could, for the time being, be left to public organizations such as the Komsomol and the League of Militant Godless.[5] The new mood had already emerged in the spring of 1923. In the first months of its existence, the Antireligious Commission of the Central Committee, founded in the late fall of 1922, had pursued a hard line, insisting at the end of the year that religious images should be removed from all public places (including those that were privately run).[6] By May 1923, however, it was passing instructions to the political police (GPU) to take action against officials who closed churches without due legal support.[7] A similar spirit of conciliation was expressed, for example, in a decree passed in the summer of 1924, which referred to the continuing delays in registering religious communities "through no fault of their own," and extended the deadline for a further three months.[8]

The ebbing of obvious aggression toward "cults" was reflected in monuments protection statutes too. A list of state-funded public monuments published in the summer of 1923 included seven museums in monastic sites, and four churches (Christ the Redeemer and St. Basil's in Moscow, and St. Isaac's Cathedral and the Cathedral of SS. Peter and Paul in Petrograd).[9] A new decree of January 7, 1924, for the first time expressly forbade "demolition and use of monuments of architecture (civic and defensive structures, the structures of religious cult, etc.) that are registered in the Museums Department" without the "advance agreement of the aforesaid Department." An instruction issued with the decree divided monuments into three categories: those (such as fountains and walls) that despite their "exemplary museum value" might be used for "practical purposes"; those that might be used for the "housing of museum collections"; and those that were to be used "exclusively with an eye to the conservation of their artistic-historic external character [*oblik*], arrangement, and internal decoration." Specifically listed among the last category were not just "museums, palaces, houses, and premises associated with famous people," but "museum-churches and museum-monasteries."[10]

Behind these measures stood awareness that ecclesiastical buildings were likely to be under particular threat.[11] The day-to-day practice of preservation recognized this situation too. As early as February 8, 1923, the staff of the central Museums Department had contacted the Vladimir provincial museum with a request to state "which monasteries should be protected and in general, which monuments of art and history (you should also provide a brief description, with information about when they were built and about the items of artistic value that are located there)."[12] Following the general pattern, the Petrograd Museums Department issued its own "Schema for Monthly Reports," which included a section on "the liquidation of churches and what has been removed from these." Officials were asked to note "steps being taken to preserve artistic and historic churches," and also "house churches that have been liquidated and property removed therefrom (overall nos. of items removed)," not to speak of "contracts with religious communities (and which churches these relate to)."[13]

In 1923–1924, after the reorganization of the Narkompros museums management body under Glavnauka (the Office of Science and Scholarship, set up in 1922), there was also an attempt to increase the autonomy of the monuments protection bodies. The restoration commission was reformed as the State Restoration Workshops and made a department of Glavnauka in its own right, rather than being subordinated to the Museums Department. However, the new structures went with a budget cut, and activities were significantly constricted.[14]

In any case, given the institutional weakness of the Monuments Department (accorded by the law a merely consultative role), the new decree had little impact on day-to-day practicalities. From the start of 1924, buildings that had previously escaped began to come under threat of requisitions, if not actual liquidation. In early March 1924, property at the Church of the Savior on the Waters was inspected by the Office of Registration of Religious Groups. The Office compiled two inventories, one listing objects of artistic and historic value, the other objects without such value. This was followed by dispersal of some of the church's contents: on March 17, 1924, fourteen items were selected for transfer to the State Museums Fund.[15]

The pace of liquidation did not let up either. Indeed, pressure to "liberate" church buildings for "cultural purposes" mounted. At Easter 1924, the Leningrad magazine *The Young Proletarian* published a typical snatch of doggerel evoking the transformation of a church into a club:

> Seven years have passed at quite a rate,
> And god's already liquidated.
> Year eight is with us now: don't shirk,
> Let's make a club out of the church.

A caricature printed alongside showed villagers tearing down the cross on the roof of the church, and hoisting a red flag in its place.[16] Against this vigorous championing of iconoclasm, the calls to preserve churches in their original state could only sound feeble.

A landmark case of iconoclastic transformation in Petrograd itself was the reconstruction, in 1925, of the former church at the Red Putilov Factory into the enterprise's culture club.[17] The work was carried out by Aleksandr Nikol'skii (1884–1953), responsible for some of the most important Constructivist projects of the period, such as the model worker housing on Traktornaia ulitsa. Nikol'skii added an airy glass-and-steel belvedere; a long triangular wind-bay jutted from the façade above the massive entrance, next to hammer-and-sickle motifs and letters reading RED PUTILOVETS CLUB. While not a listed building, the Putilov church was the work of the noted early twentieth-century architect Vasilii Kosiakov (who, in a Oedipal irony, had been Nikol'skii's teacher when the latter was an architecture student working in the arts-and-crafts style, diligently preparing a design for a monastery cathedral as his graduation assignment).[18] In 1925, a report on the churches of the Moskovsko-Narvskii district described the Putilov church as "one of the only monuments of early twentieth-century church architecture in a severe style, which is of artistic and historic interest as a complete *ansambl'*".[19] Nevertheless, the conversion went ahead without impediment. A less dramatic, but also significant, act of architectural interventionism was the construction of the Lenin Stadium on a prominent embankment site, formerly dominated by the domes and bell tower of the Prince Vladimir Cathedral. Rather than being reminded of the soul by the vistas of their city, Leningraders were now prompted to think of the body.[20] And the neat triangulation of the stadium's arcading, designed by the Czech footballer Aloise Wejwoda, gave its architecture an open, light-saturated character that mounted a direct visual challenge to the Cathedral's baroque solidity, suggesting that sport was closer to the heavens than the dark glitter of the Orthodox Church.[21]

"The Most Notable, World-Famous Monuments of Our City": The
Old St. Petersburg Society and the Classification of Architectural and
Artistic Value

As in other areas of Soviet civic activity during the New Economic Policy—the
care of children was a striking example—the deficiencies of work sponsored by
the state were in part made good by voluntary efforts.[22] Central in this respect
was the work of the Old St. Petersburg Society (OSP), an association devoted to
commemorating the history of the city. The Society (which had prerevolutionary
antecedents) had been founded as early as 1921.[23] However, activities in the early
months were mainly organizational: dividing the city into twenty-five different
districts and assigning members to look after them.[24] The following year, practical
work began in earnest.

The remit of the OSP was broad, including the encouragement of research into
local history and the organization of lecture programs and exhibitions. It was an
important catalyst of, and platform for, the development of *kraevedenie*, or "local
studies," in Petrograd and Leningrad.[25] Its activities overlapped with those of the
Museum of the City, and a number of its members were employed there also—
notably the architect Lev Il'in (1880–1942), the museum's first director.

Il'in, born in Tambov, had spent his school years at the Alexander Cadet
Corps, a traditional place for the education of boys from the gentry and nobility,
before entering the prestigious Institute of Civil Engineers in 1897. He had then
undertaken further study at the Academy of Arts before working on a number of
neoclassical projects, including his own mansion on the Pesochnaia Embankment.
He had belonged to the Committee of the Old St. Petersburg Museum from
1909.[26] However, for all these links with the prerevolutionary cult of the past, the
Museum of the City was—unlike the Old St. Petersburg Museum—a center for
urban studies as well as local history. Likewise, from the early days, the Society
aimed to have a role that was not just custodial, but would have a direct impact
upon policy. Members of the OSP busied themselves with discussions about street
renaming and city's memorials, such as the many statues of the Russian emperors.
The Society's active section for the protection of monuments also expended
much effort on surveying the city's architectural heritage and lobbying for its
protection.[27]

In some circumstances, activities of this kind on the part of a voluntary
organization might have had irritant value (in the Brezhnev era, the officials
in Leningrad's State Inspectorate of Monuments regularly accused VOOPIiK

of duplicating their efforts to record historical buildings worthy of listing and to monitor the condition of existing monuments.)[28] However, from the first, cooperation with the Museums Department was close and relations amicable. As early as September 12, 1922, a meeting was held in the Museums Department in order to harmonize the activities of the Department and OSP. It was agreed that delegates from the Department would become full members of the OSP, and that the OSP would send representatives to a number of different departments, including the Surveying Commission of Ecclesiastical and Civic Buildings attached to the Restoration Section of the Museums Department.[29]

Over the next years, the OSP duly worked to complement and reinforce the activities of the Museums Department. The Section (Bureau) for the Preservation of Artistic and Historic Monuments busied itself with numerous "house churches," taking an interest in the fate of listed buildings, such as the Royal Stables Church and the chapels in the men's and the women's sections of the Obukhovo Hospital, and itself organizing inspections of a number of "house churches."[30] The cooperation continued after the State Restoration Workshops had been set up as the body responsible for preservation policy. Members of the OSP were convinced that working with state organizations was the only way forward.[31] In this they resembled large numbers of experts on prerevolutionary St. Petersburg, who allowed themselves to believe that a golden age of custodianship of the past was now on the horizon.[32]

Members of the OSP continued being very active in hands-on preservation work as time passed. In October 1924, for example, they carried out a survey of the former Senate Church, as well as of the funerary chapel of the Vsevolozhskiis (work on transferring the iconostasis of this had begun the previous August).[33] A report composed by the Section for the Preservation of Monuments in mid-1925 was able to boast,

> Moving on to the question of the preservation of the old churches in the city, it is worth remarking that the Section is currently engaged in some extremely interesting work, namely, an exhaustive survey of all the house churches in Leningrad. The questionnaire for this is currently being finalized and the materials that will result will have enormous importance for the future historian of the city.[34]

Other categories of ecclesiastical architecture were not neglected. On October 19, 1923, the OSP began organizing a Museum of the Alexander Nevsky Monastery in the former vestry.[35] The following year, a lengthy jeremiad on the state of the city's monuments singled out, alongside the Winter Palace and the Alexander Column, the St. Isaac's and Smol'nyi Cathedrals (evidently as the start of a push to take these in hand):

> Among the most notable, world-famous monuments of our city, those which constitute its reason to hold its head up high before Europe, it is sufficient to remark the chronically dreadful state of the St. Isaac's Cathedral or Smol'nyi Convent, or the parlous condition of the Winter Palace, as well as the Alexander Column, which in the recent past has attracted so much attention because of the utterly fantastic schemes attached to this construction.[36]

A list of surveying work dating from mid-1924 included a number of "freestanding churches," among others, the Chesme Church, the Suvorov Church on Semenov Platz, the Savior on the Waters, the Cathedral of the Transfiguration, and the Prince Vladimir Cathedral, as well as the iconostases removed from closed churches and the mosaics in St. Isaac's Cathedral.[37] In this period, the OSP was also involved in a large-scale survey of all the working churches in the Moskovsko-Narvskii district, precipitated by the demand from local officials that they should make their interest in any heritage items known within two weeks, or cede the right to consultation.[38]

The work of the OSP was important for policy reasons as well as on practical grounds. The Museums Department regularly evoked "artistic and historic value" in the abstract, but gave little guidance on how to apply these terms in the concrete local context. It was staffed by specialists in architectural restoration and archaeology, many of them (such as Konstantin Romanov and Grigorii Kotov) scholars and academics. The OSP, by contrast, was dominated by more worldly individuals, including the local historian and former radical journalist Petr Stolpianskii (1872–1938) and the teacher, amateur Pushkinist, and bibliophile Sergei Zharnovskii. It had a sprinkling of well-connected artists, among them the composer Boris Asaf'ev and the painter Aleksandr Benua (Alexandre Benois). The academics included such an obvious heavyweight as Sergei Platonov, historian and full member of the Academy of Sciences. Also involved at an early stage was Lev Il'in, a leading figure in the new cultural establishment, since he was director not just of the Museum of the City, but also of the City Bureau, responsible for evolving planning policy.[39] Il'in and his associates saw preservation policy as part of a larger vision of the city, informed both by detailed local history and by a utopian vision of the future that gave much emphasis, for instance, to the development of green space, the preservation and beautification of the Neva embankments, and the clearance from Petrograd of ugly and unsuitable structures, such as the eighteenth-century Gagarin Warehouses on the Petrovskaia Embankment, which were held to "ruin" the perspective of the riverfront.[40]

The OSP was thus concerned not just to celebrate and protect individual buildings, but to regulate entire landscapes. Already in 1923, it deemed that the Department of Communal Property Management (responsible at this period for the city infrastructure) should set up "a commission for the preservation and artistic rebirth [*vozrozhdenie*]" of the city.[41] The center of its vision was the unified, integrated architectural realm (*ansambl'*), not just at the level of a particular room or suite of rooms within a building, or indeed an entire building, but at the level of streets, squares, embankments, districts, and urban panoramas.

While critically inclined toward "capitalist" urban life and the traditions of building and planning associated with it (and especially the social divisions of the city landscape seen as characteristic of the class society), such visions of the new city were respectful to the established aesthetic principles of spatial organization—and especially the balance between water, parkland, and stone. These principles were understood as a logical development of the best achievements of the so-called "Golden Age" of the late eighteenth and early nineteenth centuries, with the buildings and city quarters planned by Carlo Rossi and Giacomo Quarenghi taken as the pinnacle. Neoclassical architecture was the most admired mode. While this perception underlay the work done by the Museums Office too, it was still more entrenched in the OSP. As the society's statutes put it in January 1922, the OSP "pursues the end of the preservation and reconstruction of the character of the city and of new city planning that, in tracing its new path, does not introduce disharmony into the unified *ansambli* of squares, streets, and embankments."[42]

Not all old buildings, in this process of creative preservation and reconstruction, were deemed deserving of survival. A strong influence on the tastes of those who worked in the OSP, the Museum of the City, and the City Bureau was the work of such prerevolutionary city theorists such as Vladimir Kurbatov, who, writing in 1913, had lambasted the work of Nicholas I's favorite architect, Konstantin Ton, as well as the *style russe*.[43] As he put it both these developments had shown "the bourgeois influence," which was "taken to the heights of horror by those working in the 'cockerel style.'"[44] Architects speaking at professional congresses excoriated "architectural vulgarity" and championed work of the eighteenth and early nineteenth centuries. As a resolution put forward by Grigorii Kotov in 1895 expressed it, "Where this has artistic and historic value, it as much deserves preservation as do the monuments of earlier ages."[45] The obvious correlative was that buildings lacking such value did not deserve preservation.

Leningrad intellectuals of the 1920s and 1930s agreed. And if, under the rules obtaining before 1917, churches had merited special treatment as churches, now they were judged by the same exacting standards. The art critic Nikolai Punin, making a rare visit to church in 1923, commented on the "tasteless cathedral" in which the poorly attended service took place.[46] The fact that in the "Petersburg text" of the nineteenth and twentieth centuries, created by classic writers such as Alexander Pushkin, Nikolai Gogol', Fedor Dostoevskii, and Aleksandr Blok, churches mostly figured to satirical ends, increased the sense that such buildings were not really an organic part of the city's landscape.[47] As Boris Eikhenbaum put it in 1917, in Moscow "there are churches on every corner, snuggled down between the houses in a way that's touching to look at, with no sense of apartness; in Petersburg, on the other hand, there aren't any churches, just pompous places of worship that keep their distance from ordinary buildings."[48] This was partly related to the sturdy tradition of anticlericalism in Petersburg: according to Ariadna Tyrkova-Williams, in the late Imperial era, "the only thing that stopped the intelligentsia from storming the Church was police regulations."[49] But it also echoed the international prejudice among modernists against vulgar decoration and elaborate opulence. In his essay "The Old Town of Pskoff," based on his years in Russia between 1902 and 1908, the British writer H. H. Munro ("Saki") had observed:

> After an hour or two spent among these tombs and ikons and memorials of dead Russia, one feels that some time must elapse before one cares to enter again the drearily magnificent holy places of St. Petersburg, with their depressing *nouveau riche* atmosphere, their price-list-tongued attendants, and general lack of historic interest.[50]

OSP's members, for whom *style russe* played the same role as the word "Victorian" in British modernist taste—a catch-all for anything stuffy, hypocritical, over-elaborate and bogus (though with added ancien régime stigma on top)—agreed.[51] They, too, considered that some of the former capital's churches were "*nouveau riche*" and had a "general lack of historic interest," and they unsparingly excluded these from their lists. In November 1922, OSP resolved to undertake an inspection of the chapel at the Conservatoire, which, a month or so later, produced the response that the expert in charge, A. A. Shul'ts, had decreed the architecture to be "uninteresting in an artistic and historical regard." The iconostasis was accordingly dismantled and transferred to the nearby Cathedral of St. Nicholas, apart from five icons, which "because of their memorial connections," were allowed to remain in the Conservatoire itself.[52]

In 1924, the OSP brusquely rebuffed overtures from the religious community at the Trinity-Izmailovskii Regiment Cathedral, whose members had been hoping that their chapel, currently in use for a tobacco kiosk, would be deemed worthy of preservation:

> This chapel represents of itself [*sic*] a copy in miniature of the Cathedral and is valuable in the architectural and archaeological respect, there are icons there that are the work of Professor artists.[53] The Society for the Protection of Historical Monuments "Old Petrograd" has expressed to us its firm intention to take our Cathedral and our chapel under its supervision and protection.[54]

Not only was the chapel of no interest, the OSP's representatives snorted, but the cathedral itself had little appeal in artistic and historical terms.

> [The Society] has no intention of taking the Trinity Cathedral under its supervision and protection, and still less could that apply to the chapel, which was built in 1894–1896, has no architectural connection with the Cathedral and no artistic significance.[55]

FIGURE 5. Bol'shoi prospekt, Vasilievskii Island, showing the Chapel of St Spiridon of Trimythus (S. P. Kondrat'ev, 1903–1904, also the architect of the Trinity-Izmailovskii Regiment Cathedral chapel), 1939.

Such chapels were freely used as kiosks in other places too: a late 1930s panorama of Bol'shoi prospekt, Vasilievskii Island, shows the comparable domed building in use as a photographic studio. Indeed, it was only when they could be converted for such practical uses that freestanding chapels survived. From the hundreds scattered over the city in the early twentieth century, not more than a few dozen survived the architectural purges of Soviet power in its early years.[56]

Of all the churches in the city, only one—the Old Believer Oratory at 19 Volkovskaia ulitsa, next to the Volkovo Cemetery—was in the immediate care of the OSP.[57] A sense of the reasoning behind this is given by the report detailing the transfer of the property to OSP's supervision on November 14, 1922:

> It represents a completely exceptional monument in the sense of the history of everyday life, since it is probably the only example of a secret prayerhouse that has survived in an untouched condition for over 100 years of constant use by the Fedoseevo Concord for their cultic practices, which, as specialists argue, have still to be studied exhaustively. The prayerhouse is maintained in perfect order under the constant care of the Bureau of Protection [of Monuments].[58]

Historically unique, the Oratory could also boast authenticity from the artistic point of view, since it was in an "untouched condition." While not by a major architect, it was in every other way the ideal building—from the right period, aesthetically coherent, and unspoiled by later interventions. It was useful, too, that as a formerly oppressed minority, the Old Believers could be understood as victims, rather than beneficiaries, of the old regime.

"The Entire *ansambl'*, Fortunately, Has Survived to This Day": The Holistic Approach to Preservation

The officials working at Glavnauka's Monuments Office held views that were comparable to those of the OSP (as the harmonious collaboration of the two bodies suggests). Certainly, in the immediate post-revolutionary years, Petrograd conservators trod warily when it came to restoration. In 1919, a major row broke out when the restorer Petr Pokryshkin returned from Novgorod with a report that Aleksandr Anisimov, the Moscow-based restorer leading a team working on important medieval icons, was directing the craftsmen to strip down layers of overpainting. The preferred procedure in Petrograd, vehemently advocated to the Central Restoration Workshops in Moscow, was to place conservation first, and stabilize the entire image, with great attention paid to temperature regulation, and with the use of close-up photography and meticulous written records to chronicle the work that had been done.[59] When discussing the particular care required when historic churches were stripped during the sequestrations of 1922, a Special Commission set up by the Office underlined that not just items relating to the original date when a church was constructed should be preserved in situ, but also items relating to major early alterations. Yet historical inclusivity only went so far. "On the other hand, many churches that are mainly memorials of high artistic worth also contain items that were placed there in later periods, often of considerable material value, but distorting the overall integrity of the monuments. The removal of such items would only increase the scholarly and artistic significance of the churches they are in."[60]

The idea of preservation policy as a refinement of the past became more entrenched as time went on. In the first years after the Revolution, the buildings under the especial care of the Monuments Office in Petrograd had essentially ended up there accidentally. The prerevolutionary Archaeological Commission had been subordinated to the Ministry of the Court. Inheriting the remit of the Archaeological Commission, Glavnauka also inherited the premises that had once been in the care of the Ministry of the Court. The fifty-three buildings in question included not just palaces, court theaters, the royal ballet school, and the grace-and-favor residences of the ministry's officials, but also three churches: the Cathedral in the St. Peter and Paul Fortress, St. Isaac's Cathedral, and the Church of the Savior on the Blood, built by Alfred Parland in 1883–1907.[61] These were three buildings of very different dates and styles, from baroque to the full flowering of *style russe*. But this does not seem to have caused particular soul-searching, since the Monuments Department liberally handed out preservation certificates to a considerable variety of buildings. In the course of the listings process in 1922, churches placed under protection included the church in the Xenia Institute, finished in 1860, with neo-Byzantine wall paintings by Ludwig Thiersch.[62] When the March 4, 1922, instruction was drawn up by the Commission, it listed 1850 as the date before which church property automatically deserved protection. As Konstantin Romanov recalled slightly later, some members of the Commission had favored making that cutoff date 1825.[63] Romanov's own views had carried the day, but dating was, in fact, merely a side issue. It was the principle of the work of architecture's overall integrity that applied, with, for example, the Royal Stables

Church—one in which "the entire *ansambl'*, fortunately, has survived to this day" regarded as "one of the most precious in the city."[64]

Once inventories of protected monuments began, this preference for integrated architecture became more marked. So too did the preference for pre-1825 buildings. A 1923 list of monuments of architecture whose upkeep was funded by Narkompros included both St. Isaac's and St. Peter and Paul's, but not the Savior on the Blood.[65] A list of churches under official protection compiled in the same year further entrenched the preference for baroque and neoclassical architecture. It consisted of forty-three buildings, and included none built later than the mid-nineteenth century.[66] A "List of Architectural (Ecclesiastical) Structures" compiled by the Old St. Petersburg Society (OSP) in 1924 included only two buildings out of forty-five built after 1830.[67] One exception was the Church of the Savior on the Waters (built in 1909, and a creative interpretation by the leading modernist architect Marian Peretiatkovich of the severe "white stone" early medieval "Vladimir-Suzdal'" style that was firmly ensconced in the preservation aesthetic of the time). The other was the Church of the Transfiguration of the Grenadier Guards by Konstantin Ton, built in 1839, a building on a smaller scale and less florid than his other Petersburg churches.[68]

Since the OSP list is not in alphabetical or chronological order, it is logical to assume that it may express an order of priorities. Among the major churches (*sobory*),[69] primacy was given to the Smol'nyi Cathedral (Bartolomeo Rastrelli, 1748–1757). The Cathedral of the Transfiguration of All the Guards (Vasilii Stasov, 1825) and the Trinity Cathedral of the Izmailovskii Regiment (also Vasilii Stasov, 1827) came toward the end of the list. Among parish churches, highly ranked were the Church of SS. Simeon and Anne (Matvei Zemtsov, 1731–1734) on the Mokhovaia; the Prince Vladimir Cathedral (Antonio Rinaldi, 1789); and the Church of the Mother of God Joy of Those Who Grieve (Iosif Sherleman', 1816) on ulitsa Voinova (Shpalernaia). "House churches" were ranked on similar principles: as well as the Oratory of the Fedoseevo Community (bringing up the end of the list), those placed in the first category included the church in the "Palace of Arts" (the Winter Palace), at number one, followed by St. Catherine's in the Widows' Refuge at Smol'nyi, the churches in the Imperial Orphanage (Moika, 48), the Ministry of Foreign Affairs, and the Senate Building, the Royal Stables church, and so on down the list, with the Academy of Arts church at number twenty-four.[70] All these buildings were from the "magic" period of 1750–1830, and had escaped extensive alteration. The vast majority were also by canonical architects.[71] The university church, however, which had undergone alterations in the nineteenth century, was relegated to the second category, despite the importance of the Twelve Colleges in which it was housed. The fact that nearly as many "house churches" were listed as other types of ecclesiastical structure was a token of the esteem in which the OSP, like the Museums Department, held these quintessential *ansambli*.

A report put out by the central Museums Department in 1925 confirmed the narrowing of the process of selection. It claimed that more than 3,500 churches and 30,000 objects of ecclesiastical art were now included in the Department's records, but also observed that "when it came to the countless numbers of *churches and monasteries* with which Old Russia was so richly provided, it took especial efforts to survey them and to select those whose historic value means that they are entitled to preservation by the Soviet state."[72] The highly inclusive approach that had shaped the first period of Soviet preservation practice had been seriously challenged by the requisitions of 1922. In the years that followed, the selectivity imposed on preservationists by force majeure began to be championed as something positive, exemplifying the aesthetic discrimination and scrupulosity of the new Soviet establishment.[73]

Preserving Church Interiors: "The Museum of Dying Cult"

As more and more of the house churches were scheduled for dismantling, the issue of how to save their contents from destruction became ever more pressing. In Moscow, entire complexes of ecclesiastical, in particular monastic, buildings that were designated as particularly significant were converted into museums, with iconostases and other decorations left in place. (The Assumption and Archangel Michael Cathedrals of the Kremlin are present-day examples of the long-term results of this policy.) At first, according to archival records, all of the twenty-three monasteries where curatorial activities took place were either in, or within easy reach of, the new capital.[74] But in due course, the "museum church" movement became widespread in other Old Russian cities also.[75] In Petrograd, by contrast, the "museum church" was not a significant feature of the landscape, the sole notable examples of "cultic buildings" administered by the Museums Department being the Cathedral in the Peter and Paul Fortress and the Cathedral of the Savior on the Blood. Even this was the result of inertia, since when the Department took over the administration of the Ministry of the Court, the churches in the Ministry's care had fallen into its lap.[76] There was no push to add to the tally.

Even the Alexander Nevsky Lavra was not "museified," with efforts limited to helping believers organize a service of watchmen to protect church property from theft and vandalism.[77] In some empty churches such as the Smol'nyi Cathedral, the iconostasis was—at least for the time being—left in place, but without any attempt to "museify" anything else.[78] One of the premier works of ecclesiastical rococo in Russia, the Cathedral of the Savior Not Made by Human Hands in the Winter Palace (built by Bartolomeo Rastrelli, 1752–1763), was used as a hall for temporary exhibits from as early as 1918.[79]

The situation was, in terms of overall preservation policy in the early 1920s, peculiar. This was the heyday of the "museum of daily life," and a whole range of former aristocratic dwellings in Petrograd (including the Anichkov Palace, the Karlova Mansion, and the Sheremet'ev Palace) were turned into such museums.[80] Emphasis on the sacrosanct nature of the *ansambl'* pointed in that direction too. Of course, Petrograd was distinguished from other Russian cities by the sheer number of secular buildings that were considered to be of the first architectural importance.[81] There was no need to showcase religious buildings in order to demonstrate the new regime's sensitivity to culture. And once the city had been renamed as a tribute to the recently dead Lenin, the celebration of religion would have seemed still less appropriate. Added to this, "museum interest," as understood in the early Soviet period, required that what was on display should be not just "remarkable," but beneficial to the cause of education, including aesthetic education.[82] It was considerably easier to emphasize the "educational" impact of religious artifacts by placing them in the setting of an ordinary Soviet museum, rather than by embalming the original context for which the artifacts had been made. In a long article published at the beginning of 1926, Natal'ia Sedova-Trotskaia herself expressed ambivalence about museifying churches. The removal of artifacts from ecclesiastical sites in 1922 had meant the disappearance of "superfluous clutter," with only occasional excesses (such as the scrapping of the silver iconostasis in the Kazan' Cathedral). Such "editing" was positive. At most a few sites deserved the full museum treatment.[83]

Yet it seems that the Museums Department did plan, in 1922, to set up individual "church museums," since this policy was explicitly criticized by local officials who felt it was holding up the confiscations campaign.[84] Whichever way, no such museums ever materialized, and nor did the unified museum that the local officials had seen as a more sensible alternative.[85]

In due course, the vacuum so far as museum display was concerned was filled, not by the Museums Department itself, but by the OSP, which, in 1923, began

organizing, on the basis of the materials that it had been collecting from closed
house churches, the Museum of Daily Life and Church History (*Istoriko-Bytovoi
Tserkovnyi Muzei*).[86] By March 1924, the OSP was arranging to rent a building
at 3 Volkhovskii pereulok on Vasilievskii Island (next door to its original
premises at number one), whence were transferred the interiors of the Royal
Stables church, the church of the Finland Regiment, and others.[87] According
to an outline plan of May 1924, the intention of the museum was to cover "all
ecclesiastical buildings and furnishings in the city of Leningrad created between
1703 and 1917, and reflecting in their stylistic properties the characteristic
features of all the historical eras of Old Petersburg, from Peter I to Nicholas II
inclusive." The material was to be studied in terms of its "purely stylistic and
artistic value," its "historical significance," and its "everyday [*bytovoe*] content."
It was anticipated at this stage that the museum would not include any materials
from churches in category one, "which have a quite exceptional significance and
should be preserved where they were originally constructed." As well as material
exhibits—"architectural constructions," icons, books, and manuscripts, objects,
and so on—it would include displays relating to "everyday life" in the sense of
ritual processes and the process of manufacturing the objects and buildings
showcased by the museum.[88]

Over the next months, collection of items for the Museum continued, now
augmented by objects from category-one churches that the OSP had hoped to
keep in situ. During the autumn of 1924, for example, the iconostasis of the
former church of the Twelve Apostles in the central post office was transferred to
it, as well as the slightly damaged iconostasis of the church of Alexander Nevsky
in the former Senate, from which three icons had been removed for transfer to
another museum collection, but had then been lost.[89]

By 1925, the enterprise, in a significant concession to the changing ideological
climate, had been renamed "The Museum of Dying Cult."[90] (It was also at this
point, and for similar reasons, that the official name of the OSP itself became
"The Old St. Petersburg and New Leningrad Society," though the shorter name
continued to be in general use throughout its later existence.) Excursions around
the collections of church artifacts had now begun, and the transfer of objects
continued. For example, toward the end of 1925, the iconostasis of the house
church in the College of Jurisprudence arrived, along with an iconostasis "painted
on glass" from the former Miatlev Mansion on ulitsa Soiuza Sviazi.[91] A "Report
on the Museum of Dying Cult" from mid-October 1925 recorded the transfer of
"the complete interiors, along with their iconostases, of the Post Office, Senate,

and Office of Military Campaigns" house churches, and "parts of the artistic and artistic and daily life objects from the closed church of the Nicholas Orphanage."[92] In 1926, the OSP started to plan a survey of the church at the Tsaritsa Alexandra Women's Hospital, evidently with a view to removal of its contents.[93]

Where suitable "ensembles" were not in evidence, OSP staff were happy to "cherry-pick" ecclesiastical objects that were felt to be of significant historical interest, for example noting that there were "many objects from an earlier church going back to the reign of Empress Elizabeth" in the otherwise uninteresting house church of the former Yaroslavl Monastic Legation on the Nikol'skaia Embankment.[94]

There remained the thorny issue of how to fund the organization of the permanent exhibition, not to speak of its staff salaries and other running costs. In late 1925, the OSP finally received a small grant toward its work from Narkompros, and in 1926, the Scientific Office took over its financial management.[95] But this was a bad time to press for further expansion. In early 1927 began what was referred to as "a concentration of museums" (kontsentratsiia muzeev), or (to use the modern term) a "rationalization." This was used to justify, for instance, closing the former Stiglitz Museum, the former Royal Mews Museum, and the Palace Museums Directorate. The future of the Stroganov Palace was also raised at this point.[96] Still more devastatingly for the OSP's plans, in 1927, its close ally, the Museum of the City, underwent a wholesale purge in which the place was vilified as not just wasteful in economic terms, but also a subversive nest of "former people," or those belonging to classes that were hostile to Soviet power. Lev Il'in was dismissed from his post as director, and the "everyday life" display in the Karlova Mansion on the Fontanka was closed, and the contents divided up. Some objects were assigned to other museums, such as the Hermitage, some appropriated for use in the offices of the city soviet, and some transferred to hotels; much else appears to have been destroyed or simply disappeared.[97]

In the new circumstances, the "Museum of Dying Cult" was no longer a viable entity, since the Museum of the City had effectively been its guarantor. With a new director committed to a focus on the modern city, the collection of ecclesiastical artifacts was doomed. As the OSP's representatives explained at a meeting with the Scientific Office on October 27, 1927:

> The fact that the organization and opening of the Museum were so long-drawn-out because the Society no longer had sufficient funds to develop it, coupled with the refusal of Glavnauka to grant it any more subsidies, provoked annoyance in the

executive committee of the local soviet which, given the worsening accommodation crisis in Leningrad and the huge amount of space in the buildings assigned to the museum (more than 130 rooms), petitioned the executive committee of the provincial soviet to transfer the aforesaid buildings to the control of the district soviet executive committee in order that they may be used to house the needy worker population of Vasilievskii Island.

The executive committee of the provincial soviet having decided the question without bothering to call in a representative of the OSP, the Society was accordingly forced to transfer its holdings to other museums, and in view of the quite incontestable value of the items that had been collected, the Museum of the City agreed to accept them. But now that the Museum of the City is itself undergoing reorganization, this proposal has run into difficulties.

As a result, the church interiors had all in fact been transferred into the Museums Fund, which was allocating them to the Russian Museum, the Hermitage, and "other organizations." On top of that, the interiors were not even being preserved as unified works of art. "Sometimes the Museums Fund does not hand out iconostases as *ansambli*, but piecemeal, which destroys the integrated character of the monuments, since the bits left behind lose any significance when they are looted in this way. The intentions of great master artists are completely annihilated, as is the meticulous work done by the Society to collect the items for display in the first place."[98]

The protests were in vain, however. The policies behind what the OSP itself called "looting," and the vitiation of its plans for a museum of church history, were outside the control of Glavnauka itself: nothing less than the financing of the industrial and armaments drive of the First Five-Year Plan through a wholesale sell-off of museum goods. The monetization of icons, chalices, and crosses, like the monetization of the china teacups and ormolu knick-knacks removed from the Karlova Mansion, was to be expedited by the storage of valuables in megamuseums, such as the Russian Museum and the Hermitage, whence they could be retrieved for sale more easily than from the collections of atomized "museums of daily life."[99] The sole exception to the general drift was the St. Isaac's Cathedral, which, after its closure in 1928, was assigned to the Scientific Directorate and opened as one of Leningrad's few church-museums, with displays relating to the building's "technology and the economic and social conditions of its construction" as well as to its "political significance under tsarism."[100] But the tolerance of curatorial aspirations was, overall, running out. Across the country, 1927–1928 saw widespread closures of "church-museums," now interpreted, in the ripening technocratic culture, as a waste of money and an ideological distraction, a "specific sort of haven for religious moods."[101]

"The Aforesaid Cathedral Is to Be Closed Immediately": Regulating Parish Churches from 1923

The second half of the 1920s was to see increased interference from the city administration in another area of the preservation bodies' work—control over the churches in Petrograd and Leningrad that were still used by congregations.

This did not happen immediately. Certainly, a new central Museums Department instruction of August 1923 once again underlined that it was essential all major repairs to listed churches should be under the Department's oversight, but the effect of the regulations was to allow a certain degree of autonomy to parishes (these now simply had to agree the plans for repairs with the Department, rather than being required to use certified restorers, and they were entitled to arrange minor repairs, such as repainting, independently). In some respects, requirements had become more fussy: when doing external repainting, parishes were now expected to try and find traces of the original coloring, and to imitate the medium used, if it came to light.[102] But in practice, attitudes in the Museums Department remained relaxed: in 1924, when the Committee on the Repair and Restoration of Monuments of Art, History, and Nature discovered that the parishioners of the Church of St. Simeon and St. Anne would have great difficulty in repainting the church using the original medium (soft distemper) to match early eighteenth-century paint scrapings from the outside wall, it decided to modify its original demands.[103]

A few years later, however, the preservation bodies started to take a more demanding attitude to church congregations. For instance, in 1927, the officials of the State Restoration Workshop got in contact with the Church Office of the central district in order to ask the staff there to insist that the *dvadtsatka* of the Cathedral of the Transfiguration should give priority to the repair and redecoration of the church's façade, rather than the paintings in the interior. The restoration of the latter was unnecessary and in any case it was being done "carelessly and incorrectly," Aleksandr Udalenkov complained.[104]

In the same year, the Leningrad State Restoration Workshop insisted that the parishioners of the St. Andrew's Cathedral on Vasilievskii Island should use lime-based paint for repainting the church, despite the fact that an inspector had originally agreed it would be in order to use oil-based paint. "The order made by the executive committee of the Vasilieostrovskii district soviet runs contrary to [that of] such an organ of the protection of monuments as is the Restoration Workshops, and may have a harmful impact on the business of monument protection," the officials complained in a letter to the executive committee of the provincial soviet. They requested that the *dvadtsatka* should be required to carry out repairs according to the conditions set by the State Restoration Workshops, and that the district soviet should be ordered to cease its interference.[105]

But as the second case also shows, the protection of monuments did not resolve into a straight state-institution-versus-religious-communities conflict. The preservation bodies were as concerned to control the behavior of other Soviet organizations as to regulate the non-Soviet religious organizations. Rather than being hostile on first principles to the religious bodies using "cultic buildings" that were under their care, they were prepared to think flexibly when the welfare of the building demanded it. Thus, in 1927, the Leningrad State Workshops wrote to the Administrative Department of the city soviet to support the application for funds made by the *dvadtsatka* of the Savior on the Waters Church.

> Alongside its artistic significance, this Church-Monument also has an enormous social and political significance as the only token of remembrance to the enormous Russian fleet that was almost totally destroyed as a result of the short-sighted policies of the imperial government, and to the thousands of sailors whose names are engraved on the brass tablets which almost completely cover the middle parts of all the walls. It should be observed that these tablets are the only ones in existence; no copies were cast at the time; further, the tablets include the names of all the fallen, making no difference between admirals and ratings, and even including sailors of all faiths. This is, accordingly, the first case ever when even the names of holders of the Muslim faith have been honored within an Orthodox church.
>
> Glavnauka has no funding to support the upkeep of this Monument, and neither has the *dvadtsatka* of the church. The *dvadtsatka* is already struggling to cover its ordinary costs, and is not even in a position to reconstruct the dome, which, if it should collapse, will bring about the collapse of the entire monument.[106]

It is instructive to contrast the attention to salient political detail (the democratic and internationalist character of this unusual monument of the tsarist era), and the brusque refusal to support the Trinity-Izmailovskii Regiment parish's defense of their tobacco-sullied kiosk back in 1925.

In the event, the OSP's diplomacy got nowhere. The request for special funding was doomed from the outset. By now, the city authorities were starting to take an increasingly tough line with religious communities. One sign of this was an entire series of closures of "cultic buildings" on the grounds that health and safety legislation was being violated. Such closures had occasionally happened in earlier years also. For instance, in December 1922, the authorities had shut down the Church of the Protecting Veil on Novoderevenskaia Embankment, describing it as "being in a dangerous condition both from a technical point of view and in terms of fire safety."[107] But from late 1926, action of this kind became much more common. For example, on October 28, 1926, an inspection of the Prince Vladimir Cathedral concluded that "the exterior of the church is threatening to public safety on account of the possibility that fragments of iron, brick, and plaster may fall, which would cause destruction to load-bearing elements in the construction."

FIGURE 6. The architect Evgenii Katonin (1889–1984) inspecting restoration work inside the cupola of the Trinity Cathedral, Revolution Square   (Domenico Trezzini, 1710–1711), c. 1927. Photograph from the collection of the Leningrad State Restoration Workshops. (FO NA IIMK RAN, negative no. 6381, print 0.3602-20, inventory no. 91319.)

It estimated costs of repairing the damage at 40,000 rubles. "Work will have to be postponed until the warm season," the report continued; all that could be done till then was to underpin one pillar and wire the place off from the public.[108]

The Prince Vladimir Cathedral was only one case where "administrative measures" were applied to a church congregation.[109] In the summer of 1927, pressure over regulations about health and safety started to be applied also to the *dvadtsatka* of the Trinity Cathedral on the Petrogradskaia Embankment, one of the city's oldest churches in terms of its foundation, which went back to the reign of Peter the Great. Devastated by fire in 1913, it was being slowly restored, a process organized and paid for by the parishioners. The Monuments Office had been regulating and supporting this process since the early 1920s.[110]

Now, officials from the Communal Resource Maintenance Section (Otkomkhoz) in the local soviet, who had previously made no effort to police the reconstruction, began to insist that a whole range of measures should be put in place to ensure fire safety, including not just clearing out flammable items, but installing central heating. On top of that, as the *dvadtsatka* complained to the city soviet, the Executive Committee had refused to allow them to recycle materials from the temporary church, including its modern central heating system, but had simply sold these to a contact who had offered to pay slightly more. "Thus, the *dvadtsatka* has not been able to count on any cooperation," the complaint continued.[111]

It is probably no coincidence that the harassment of the Trinity's parishioners occurred immediately after an important event in church-state relations at the center. On July 29, 1927, Metropolitan Sergii (Stratogorodskii), the locum tenens at the Moscow Patriarchate, issued his declaration, "On the Relationship of the Orthodox Church of Russia and the Present Civil Government," emphasizing the loyalty of Orthodoxy to "our Soviet state" in the face of assault "by our foreign enemies": "We wish to be Orthodox and at the same time to recognize the Soviet Union as our civil motherland, whose joys and successes are our joys and successes, and whose misfortunes are our misfortunes," he proclaimed. Unfortunately, the expression of loyalty was seen as an acknowledgment of weakness by the Soviet government, initiating the most aggressive push against the church since 1922–1923.[112]

Certainly, the pressure on the Trinity was only the start of church users' tribulations. In September 1927, a circular of the NKVD initiated a drive to force repairs of churches that were in poor condition with the threat of closing, and if the technical committee so decreed liquidating and demolishing the structure if the work was not done.[113] On October 30, 1927, the Presidium of the City Soviet

FIGURE 7. The Prince Vladimir Cathedral (Antonio Rinaldi and Ivan Starov, 1766–1789). View of the southwest corner of the exterior, showing deterioration to the façade and roofs. Photograph from the collection of Leningrad State Restoration Workshops, 1927. (FO NA IIMK RAN: negative no. II 3272, print 0.3659-14, collection no. 16-863.)

followed through with an order to shut the Prince Vladimir Cathedral forthwith: "The aforesaid cathedral is to be closed immediately, and no assemblies of any kind are to be organized in it until the requisite technical condition has been restored."[114] The Cathedral's congregation was again plunged into a panic-stricken search for funds.

The Prince Vladimir Cathedral was one of a number of churches that had been handed over in 1924 to the Renovationists, but the fact that the worshippers belonged to a "friendly" organization made no difference at all when it came to maintenance.[115] A consideration here may have been that while the Renovationists had vocally supported the secularization of movable church property during 1922, there was no comparable movement to embrace the secularization of church buildings. Certainly, a Church of Renewal leader, Bishop (briefly Metropolitan) Antonin Granovskii, had toyed at his Moscow church with the idea of removing the altar from its traditional place behind the iconostasis to a central position, but this experiment was short-lived, and without broader influence.[116] Some activists in the Church of Renovation pushed for the reform of the liturgy in order to bring it closer to everyday speech, but the church's clergy were as committed to the sacral status and hierarchical layout of the church building as any supporter of the Patriarchate. So far as church use went, there was therefore no "alternative track" for any confession or denomination.

Nor was there necessarily special treatment for listed churches. The September 19, 1927, circular demanding the closure and demolition of dilapidated churches stipulated that staff of Glavnauka should be consulted about all repair work to churches in their care, and that a representative of the local museums authority should be present when a church was liquidated. However, it also introduced an incentive for Glavnauka to agree liquidations, since the agency would now be entitled to claim 60 percent of the proceeds from the disposal of church property for its own purposes. Clearly, support from heritage preservation officials for the retention of interiors and church furnishings that they considered of marginal interest was now a slim possibility, given that it had come to carry "opportunity costs."[117]

Added to this, the influence of the central institutions of education and culture was now significantly on the wane. Once Trotsky was removed from his Party and government positions in 1927, his wife's position as heritage chief became a liability. She was soon forced to stand down, while the commissar of enlightenment himself, Anatoly Lunacharsky, a spent force, barely hung on, eventually quitting his post in 1929.[118]

As "culture" was framed in increasingly ideological terms, a hard-nosed attitude to anything old started to become widespread in Party and administrative circles. A milestone in national terms was the demolition of the Red Gates in Moscow. Igor' Grabar' wrote to Aleksandr Udalenkov on March 7, 1927, describing the crucial meeting to decide the building's fate:

> Despite the fiery defense made by A. V. Lunacharsky (coached by me during a session at his apartment yesterday) and P. G. Smidovich's equally fiery defense, and my own defense toward the end of the discussion, made in the spirit not so much of protection of monuments as of plain common sense, Rogov (the deputy chair of Mossovet) dug his heels in. The order to demolish the Red Gates has gone through.[119]

At this, a back-room campaign to save the Red Gates began, with, for instance, a group of leading figures in the Leningrad cultural establishment, including the director of the Hermitage as well the rector of Leningrad State University and the chairman of the Leningrad Society of Architects, signing a petition to insist on the reversal of the decision to demolish: "We are sure that the traffic problems in the area of the Red Gates can be solved some other way." Nikolai Marr, in his capacity as director of the Academy of the History of Material Culture, sent a telegram of protest on behalf of the entire Academy.[120] The protests, however, were to no avail, and on June 3, 1927, the Red Gates were summarily reduced to rubble.[121]

Where Leningraders were concerned, the shift in the local political elite was of equal if not greater importance to developments at the national level. Zlata Lilina—the wife of Grigory Zinoviev, the Petrograd (later Leningrad) Party leader—was a leading figure in the local administration of Narkompros. While she primarily occupied herself with the educational remit of the commissariat (particularly issues such as nursery education and the administration of children's homes), her political leadership made the city a hospitable place for Glavnauka also. But with the deposal of Zinoviev on March 26, 1926, Leningrad began to be run by a very different figure, Sergei Kirov. Modestly educated, and brought up in the provincial town of Viatka, Kirov lacked the old intelligentsia credentials of Sedova-Trotskaia, Lilina, or Zinoviev himself. As the contents of his apartment—hunting trophies, political books, pipe-smoking paraphernalia, and an enormous, gleaming American refrigerator—suggest, he harbored no piety toward prerevolutionary St. Petersburg, or deep interest in the past.[122] A sense of priorities is given by a 1927 picture of the Church of the Presentation (a listed architectural monument),

FIGURE 8. The Church of the Presentation (Semenovskii Regiment) (Konstantin Ton, 1836–1842), decorated for the fifth anniversary of the founding of the USSR, 1927. (TsGAKFFD-SPb.)

near-hidden by political slogans posted for the fifth anniversary of the founding of the Soviet Union. The slogans walled round the church, protecting passersby from contamination.

With the decline in value of "cultural goods," Leningrad heritage specialists underwent a major loss of confidence. Igor' Grabar', when reporting the original decision on the Red Gates, had also informed Aleksandr Udalenkov, "We have unexpectedly managed to win the battle to save the Grebnevo and Stoleshnikov Churches, with the demolition of parts of the buildings, as we suggested."[123] Grabar' evidently saw this as at least a partial victory; Udalenkov, though, seems to have reacted very differently. The following year, Sergei Oldenburg, the permanent secretary of the Academy of Sciences, made contact with Udalenkov to ask whether it would be worth making a fuss about another planned demolition, this time of the seventeenth-century Church of St. Paraskeva on Okhotnyi Riad, which Oldenburg had read was a building of considerable architectural interest, in part because of its polychrome tiles, rare in a building of that date. Udalenkov's reply was a full and candid statement in favor of tactful expediency. It would not be possible to preserve everything, he contended, and in the circumstances, selectivity was requisite:

> The circumstances [relating to this demolition] became known in due time to the
> Academy of Sciences, and the Academy's opinion led to a revision of the original

plan: the plan for the buildings on the corner was changed so that the Golitsyn and Troekurov houses could be retained, and only the Church of St. Paraskeva demolished, that being a structure that had, because of various alterations over the course of time, lost to a significant degree its interest from a historical and artistic point of view. I am concerned that we may have a repeat of the story with the Red Gates, the demolition of which took place despite all the many protests against it, and mainly because of the Museum Department's own very late decision to sacrifice the Church of the Three Priests in order to save the Red Gates, as the Moscow City Soviet had suggested—the whole issue of the demolition of the Red Gates having turned into an issue of amour-propre.

And so I would see it as essential to avoid any protests this time round and to, as it were, firm up the ground that we will have to stand on when it comes to another, more serious, case. One has to resign oneself to the fact that, in order to save the most valuable monuments of history and art, we will have, and probably on more than one occasion, to sacrifice a whole series of interesting and noteworthy, but still in sum less valuable, ones.[124]

A few months later, Udalenkov himself followed the advice that he had given Oldenburg, sacrificing the "interesting and noteworthy" in favor of the truly outstanding. In November 1928, the Communal Resource Maintenance Section (Otkomkhoz) forwarded to him, with a request for comment, a list of churches that were to be demolished as a supply of recycled brick. The list included three official monuments, among them Smol'nyi Cathedral.[125] In response, Udalenkov commented that two of the churches scheduled to be reused as brick were dispensable: the Annunciation on Labor Square (built by Ton) and the unattributed Harbor Trinity Church, Vasilievskii Island. The State Restoration Workshops simply wished to stake a claim to 60 percent of their realization value. Smol'nyi Cathedral, by contrast, "is an outstanding monument of world significance, constructed by the famous architect Rastrelli in 1748–1757 and is under state protection as one of the most outstanding monuments of architecture in Leningrad, in the highest category. It should therefore be protected in all ways possible."[126]

By 1928, Leningrad's leading official responsible for heritage preservation saw his body as being in a profoundly vulnerable position, able to make a stand for Smol'nyi, but not for, say, the Harbor Trinity Church, which had been ranked as a structure of great importance in 1922.[127] But this was still not a once-and-for-all break in attitudes to heritage. The bricks of the Smol'nyi Cathedral were not consigned for reclamation, and although Lev Il'in lost his position as head of the Museum of the City in 1927, he survived as head of the City Bureau. The emphasis on urban renewal that began in 1926 increased pressure on the lessees of historic buildings to carry out improvements, as well as driving a more ruthless attitude to historic buildings among planners. Even the "purging" of buildings was not necessarily seen in a negative light by heritage experts— provided they continued being able to dictate what got "purged." And while the institutional capacities of the preservation bodies might seem fragile, their aesthetic perceptions were reassuringly stable. In 1927, an expanded list of monuments of architecture, also including a greater number of churches than had ever been produced before, was issued by the State Restoration Workshops. The commitment to the "Golden Age" persisted, with only five churches dating from the mid-nineteenth century, and only two from later ("The Savior on the Waters" and "The Savior on the Blood").[128] Leningrad preservationists had learned, they were sure, from the mistakes of their colleagues in Moscow: they were not going to take the risk of trying to save a lesser building and thus putting an outstanding one in jeopardy.

• • •

Between 1924 and 1927, preservationists had been successful in acquiring an overall rationale for their work, based on the sacrosanct concept of the *ansambl'*, preferably one that had survived "untouched" from the late eighteenth or early nineteenth century. They had also been able to ensconce themselves in city planning policy (building on the established association between the state monuments protection bodies and the OSP, an association that also allowed them to exploit the OSP's links with the Museum of the City and the City Bureau). Over the next eight years, the emergence of Il'in, with his enthusiasm for Petersburg neoclassicism, as the genius of city planning, was still further to entrench the importance of the *ansambl'* in the reconstruction of Leningrad as Soviet city.

At the same time, the change of guard in 1926–1928 significantly undermined the cultural hegemony operating in Leningrad in the first years after the Revolution. Museum workers and heritage preservationists lost their institutional base at the center of Soviet power. Those who wished to preserve "cultic buildings" suffered a further defeat when the integrity of the collection of house churches they had put together with such effort and difficulty was lost, leading to a dispersal of these precious *ansambli*. Now, the only category of historic ecclesiastical building that had been left relatively untouched was the parish church. While there might be disputes with parish *dvadtsatki* about priorities, historic buildings were, from the point of view of preservationists, safe in their hands. But a threat was mounting to that assumption also. A secret Party report of April 1928 disapprovingly observed that there were still 152 active Orthodox churches in Leningrad; the vast majority of those that had closed so far were in public buildings. It emphasized the need for an antireligious drive to put right this situation.[129] The protection of historic churches had always been a controversial operation; it was to become still more vexed after the radical hardening of attitudes to religious practices that was to emerge over the next two years.

CHAPTER THREE

Churches in the Socialist City

Crash Industrialization, Rational Atheism, and
City Planning, 1929–1940

AT THE BEGINNING OF 1929, the highest Party body in Leningrad, the Provincial Committee of the Communist Party, held a confidential session to discuss setting up a plan for the mass closure of churches in the city.[1] The timing of the session was no accident. At the start of 1929, the mood at the center toward religious belief and practice had once again shifted. A decree of January 24, 1929, had referred to the importance of the church in encouraging opposition to collectivization and underlined the need for further action against religion in the countryside.[2] But it was not just the rural church that came under assault: "village attitudes" were seen to threaten the culture of the Soviet city also.[3] The First Five-Year Plan had set ambitious targets of industrial production, requiring a population influx to urban areas. Overcrowding and infrastructural strain stood alongside moral panic about the values and behavior of the incomers, particularly *sezonniki* (seasonal workers).[4] The Party leadership began taking measures to tighten social control. One outcome, in 1932, was the reimposition of the passport (state identity card) system, abolished in 1917, accompanied by strict regulation of settlement rights through the *propiska* (registration with the police). Used initially for filtration (those not granted passports were expelled), state registration was later employed, particularly during the Great Terror of 1937–1938, as an instrument of repression: those with the "wrong nationality" (or wrong social profile generally) were summarily arrested.[5] As social paranoia mounted, any kind of association—from Esperanto groups to recreational clubs for the profoundly deaf—fell under suspicion. Religious denominations, as particularly large groups that were heterogeneous in cultural terms, excited sustained hostility. While "Order No. 00447" of July 30, 1937, which unleashed mass persecutions of "former kulaks, criminals, and other anti-Soviet elements," did not mention religious believers specifically, they were rounded up in large numbers under its provisions.[6] Over the course of the 1930s, tens of thousands of priests and faithful were executed, deported, and imprisoned, and there was a concerted drive to close church buildings.[7]

The first move came with the Decree on Religious Organizations of April 8, 1929. Such organizations were now expressly prohibited from any and all activities except worship. They were allowed to raise money only within their own congregations, which added greatly to the difficulty of finding funds to pay for the mandatory repairs. Clauses in the decree also expedited the process of liquidating a "cultic building," stating that this could be initiated by "a well-founded order" passed by the administration of a Soviet republic or region. The decree forbade liquidation in any other circumstances, but the new arrangements made a mockery of contractual law, significantly weakening religious communities' right of tenure in their buildings.[8] Part of the effect of the decree was to synthesize measures that had previously had the status of regulations within different sections of the Soviet bureaucracy (for example, the NKVD and Commissariat of Justice), but this in itself signified a new, integrated, and purposive approach to the "problem of cults." As a leading church historian has put it, "it was no longer mere 'superstition' or 'monarchist clergy,' but the power of the parish and the social status of lay activists that was central."[9]

The winding-up of the relatively cautious Antireligious Commission of the Central Committee in December 1929 took the Soviet government's radical secularization campaign to a new phase.[10] An all-out drive to force church closures began. As well as acting within the specific terms of the law, local administrations did what they could to hasten closures by calling on the network of regulatory mechanisms, such as the requirement to maintain buildings properly and to pay substantial amounts in tax and insurance.[11] Direct protests were rare. Believers could petition to VTsIK, but at most 5 percent of cases were formally reassessed, and the vast majority of these ended in rejection.[12] Some congregations simply gave up the unequal struggle. Closures over the next few years dislocated the spatial association between the Orthodox Church and the city, so that "parish" came to refer merely to the congregation of a working church, whose faithful might live citywide.

Not all the changes that occurred stemmed from the direct intention to repress the church. Many resulted from the transformation of the urban environment through industrial and domestic building, and the creation of the infrastructure to support this as the population grew. Some cities, such as Magnitogorsk, were built from scratch; others, such as Moscow or Nizhnii Novgorod, were transformed by new building.[13] The General Plan for the Reconstruction of Moscow, approved by the Central Committee on July 10, 1935, acted as a model, though emulation in every detail was not expected. Moscow reigned supreme as political and cultural capital; other, secondary, cities were ranked on a technocratic basis, identified by key industries and other grand projects of the era, rather than their historical associations.[14]

The project of political and economic transformation in turn produced a new class of Soviet officials and technocrats—the chief engineers of factories, the staffs of government and municipal agencies, but also many less highly placed beneficiaries of social advancement—who were loyal to Stalin as leader and to "Stalinist values" more generally.[15] The reassertion of the freedom of religious belief in the Constitution of 1936 briefly encouraged hopes that Soviet identity and allegiance to a "cult" might be compatible. This was the background to the embarrassingly high numbers of Soviet citizens (56 percent of those who answered the question) to record themselves as "believers" in the 1937 Census, the results of which were expediently suppressed.[16] But this stark reminder of religious belief's tenacity prompted another drive to force religion out of existence. The radical atheist movement, now also interpreted as a hotbed of voluntarism and a potential threat to central control, was no longer the key ally. The delegation of control over religious affairs to local soviets in 1938 increased the leverage of another traditionally antireligious force, but one easier to manage from within the "power vertical."[17] However, from the point of view of "religious organizations," the issue of who imposed repressive measures was secondary; what they noticed was that closures and liquidations had accelerated once more.

"The Battle for a New Everyday" and the Fight with Backwardness: Cultural Revolution in Leningrad

Leningrad shared to the full this pattern of increased control, increased incentives, and reshaped personal and collective identities. The local papers reported regularly on the glorious achievements of the city's leading plants, such as the Kirov Factory. Leningrad was presented to the public, both inside and outside the city, as an industrial powerhouse, the home of heroic workers, Party officials, and Komsomol activists.[18] Below the surface, defense industries were developed assiduously—shipbuilding at the Admiralty Wharves, for instance. Spy-manias regularly gripped the city.[19] Leningrad was also a city of institutes, producing engineers and other specialists, and was a center for the education of Party officials. These educational institutions were natural homes for the local representatives of "new Soviet man," who took pride in "forward thinking," self-improvement, and the ruthless prosecution of ideological deviance.[20] Sergei Kirov, as a hardliner and a hard worker, a loyal Stalinist, and a spectacularly successful case of upward mobility by a provincial outsider, was a model in every respect for this group.

What was referred to in periodicals of the day as the "battle for a new everyday" (bor'ba za novyi byt), in other words, the campaign to transform domestic practices and private relations, had a significant impact on the city. Architectural projects shaped by the aspirations of rational collectivism were energetically constructed. "House communes" with shared catering, laundering, and childcare facilities went up across the city, along with "factory kitchens" offering ready-prepared meals.[21] Naturally, the new values included radical atheism, with extended programs of lectures at the city's Houses of Culture, energetic publication of brochures, and secular festivals.[22]

With religious practice under a growing cloud, the social and cultural leverage of congregations also went into decline. Most members of dvadtsatki were elderly, often past working age; often, too, they came from a proletarian or peasant background, and had at best limited education.[23] Certainly, the composition of the dvadtsatki did not necessarily reflect the profile of believers more generally (dvadtsatki were likely to be made up of those least susceptible to social pressure, such as threats of dismissal from employment).[24] But religious believers, as well as the "former people," or members of the prerevolutionary social elite, and petty criminals, were particularly vulnerable to exile from Leningrad on political grounds, so that in 1936 a Militant Godless activist could say, "these days, there's more religion to be found 101 kilometers from Leningrad" than in the city itself.[25]

The public face of churchgoing both echoed and reinforced the official understanding of religion as "backward." Large numbers of Leningraders saw conformation to the atheist norms of the day as an essential part of prudent, or "cultured," behavior. To be sure, this did not mean they discarded all vestiges of tradition. Figures mocked by the radical atheist movement included a teacher who took down her icons, but created a Christmas tree out of an umbrella frame and a fir twig because the real things were not on sale, and a doctor who took her children from early Easter mass to the May 1 political parade.[26] But as these cases show, the outward enactment of social expectations was a prerequisite of survival. A British woman who spent two months in Leningrad during the summer of 1937 was told by a friend who had gone to church at Easter that year that "'nobody gave the Easter kiss or spoke the traditional greeting. And,' she added, 'no one now keeps the Lenten fast, not even the pious.'"[27] It was possible to presume, even at the end of the 1930s, that one could be loyal both to Stalin and to God. In the words of an anonymous letter to Stalin dating from February 23, 1939: "Dear c[omrade] I. I. [*sic*] I ask you to open the Orthodox Church bekos I have received the conviction that through this we May become Victors of the World through the construktion of Socialism and Approaching Communism Build with Conviction and Endurance [and] Martyrdom [. . .] Long Live the Great Leeder [*sic: vozhd*, missing the final soft sign] of the October Revolution c[omrade] Stalin."[28] But as the letter's command of style and basic grammar indicated, such a perception was not associated with educational and social advantage.

The spread of at least de facto "godlessness" among Leningraders was not simply attributable to dictate at the highest level. According to Leningrad legend, Kirov himself ordered the demolition of certain churches that he regularly passed on his journey from his apartment on ulitsa Krasnykh zor' (Kamennoostrovskii prospekt) to Party headquarters in Smol'nyi.[29] But there is no evidence of this, or indeed, of any direct intervention by Kirov into antireligious work. His murder in December 1934, and replacement by the equally loyal Stalinist Andrei Zhdanov, did not mark a shift of policy toward religious communities. The militancy of the local soviet in Petrogradskii district, which had already been particularly active in hounding Orthodox parishes in 1926 and 1927, suggests that Kirov's exhortations were not needed.[30] Throughout the 1930s, it was the officials of Lensovet who took the primary role in controlling "religious organizations," and they were assiduous in applying the regulations at their disposal.

Alongside those officially tasked with enacting the new legislation, such as the employees of the Church Offices and Department for the Management of Communal Resources, Leningrad had a zealous branch of the League of the Militant Godless, the atheistic organization founded at the national level in 1925. By 1928, the League had over 11,000 members across Leningrad. Its members cooperated with Party organizations, particularly the Office of Political Enlightenment, to put on programs of lectures, question and answer sessions, exhibitions, and other forms of atheist education.[31] The League lobbied vigorously for the closure of churches, and kept its own tally of "cultic buildings" that were still being used for worship.[32] Once the 1929 decree had been passed, antireligious activists had another weapon in their hands, and they paid close attention to the letter of the law, checking how effectively *dvadtsatki* maintained the buildings they were assigned, and whether the inventories of state property were in order.[33]

Before the 1929 decree was passed, dissatisfaction with the behavior of a *dvadtsatka* had generally been used to motivate offering a "cultic building" to another religious group, rather than closing it altogether.[34] As paranoia rose after the murder of Sergei Kirov on December 1, 1934, the Leningrad branch of the Militant Godless saw its chance, emphasizing the need for vigilance in the "class war," and boasting that "in every works we have not just one person, but two or three who keep watch, then come to our post and give us information."[35] The League's members also monitored the professional background of *dvadtsatka* members, so that representations could be made to employers about the "unreliable" status of a given person; they would then be forced to give up their open attachment to a "cult."[36] In the 1920s, believers had been able to challenge this kind of surveillance by appeal to the Soviet authorities; but such channels of appeal were now ceasing to exist.[37] Believers were also one of the groups that suffered most notably during passportization in 1933–1936, targeted as "social undesirables" and forced into administrative exile.[38]

The population was transformed not just by expulsion of "former" groups, but by the arrival of new ones. Between 1928 and 1935, the city grew from just under 1.7 million to just over 2.7 million, a figure that comfortably surpassed its historical high, 2.4 million in 1916. By 1939, Leningrad had nearly 3.2 million inhabitants. The hand-to-mouth solution of "compression" (*uplotnenie*), the billeting of new tenants in former one-family, "bourgeois" apartments, was patently insufficient. Large-scale building projects were launched, transforming areas such as the territory round the Red Putilov (later renamed Kirov) Factory.

The reconstruction was not simply practical; it had symbolic significance. On December 4, 1931, Leningrad was declared a "model socialist city." As the announcement put it, "being a major proletarian and port center," Leningrad needed to be reshaped to reflect its new role.[39] The General Plan for the Development of Leningrad, completed in 1935, was meant to be an instrument of this reshaping. In thousands of pages of documentation, city officials meticulously analyzed the city's development needs, covering drainage, utilities, transport, roadbuilding and civil engineering as well as domestic and industrial construction. Some elements of the Plan were revised in 1938, after Nikolai Baranov was appointed to the position of Leningrad's first city architect, replacing Lev Il'in as the presiding genius of planning.[40] But the underlying principles and much of the detail were retained. Indeed, the Plan became the basis for all subsequent General Plans of the Soviet period.

Churches in the "Socialist City"

There was a thorny question in the planning of any "model socialist city." What should be done with *pre*-socialist buildings, and particularly with "cult buildings," in an era when the declared aim of planning policy was to transform the urban infrastructure by expanding the tram network and "constructing schools, hospitals, clubs, organizing a network of public catering services, and creating an ever wider network of children's homes, crèches, clubs, libraries, etc.?"[41]

For some, the answer was straightforward. In March 1937, Grigorii Tiurin, a worker in the Leningrad electricity supply system, sent a short article to *Leningradskaia pravda* (Leningrad Truth) under the title "On the Uses of Closed Churches and Houses of Prayer."[42] Tiurin observed that the large numbers of empty ecclesiastical (in the Soviet usage, "cultic") buildings all over the Soviet Union represented a pyrrhic victory for the new order. On the one hand, "these forts of the counterrevolution" were "indications of the enormity of our victories on the antireligious front." But on the other, they presented a constant threat, giving believers cause to press for their reopening. "We are bad crusaders against religion and bad housekeepers [*khoziaistvenniki*]," Tiurin observed. "As a rule, no one in this multi-million city takes any care of them (even when they are in use for some other purposes), the crosses are sawn off in a hurry, any old how (and sometimes not even that is done). Smashed windows, broken window-gratings and railings, and other damage are a common sight. Often, warehouses are fixed up in closed churches, and no one bothers to remove icons and other cultic objects. It goes without saying that this kind of 'antireligious work' is a trump card in the hands of our enemies."

Tiurin went on to give an eloquent, if clumsy, account of his own proposals for rational use of these defunct structures:

> Church buildings are infinitely various and *most* of them [italics original] can be easily adapted for different purposes and sometimes after insignificant rebuilding their architectural appearance can be altered completely [...] some can be used for hospitals or schools, some as stores, but on every occasion reconstruction is needed so that the building can be used to the full, in an economically rational way [*po-khoziaiski*]. I am against the practice of converting them into clubs that was common a few years back, to begin with church buildings aren't too suitable and a lot of reconstruction is needed, and then often there's a negative effect in terms of antireligious propaganda, too. Finally, a proportion of these buildings cannot be used with advantage for other purposes. They should be demolished as quickly as possible.

In November of the same year, another ordinary Leningrader, one F. Sokolov, sent a similar and even more clumsily written text to the press, once again ruminating on the role of "cultic buildings" in the Soviet city:[43]

> In front of the Moscow Station spreads a big square called "Uprising" Square. Until November 1937 that square was "beautified" by a sizeable monstrous bogey on a horse of Tsar Alexander III [...] Now on that same square on the corner of Znamenskaia and 25 October Prospect[44] stands on the central square opposite the central and none other than Moscow station a church an old one[,] religious intoxication [popovskii durman] [,] having outlived its life completely. The church stands out gratingly against the background of our cultured socialist construction[,] schools[,] say[,] and apartment blocks and houses of culture and theaters and such. As a senior worker at a factory I propose removing that erection of old architecture that grates on the eyes of our guests from home and abroad.[45]

Voiced in clogged, semiliterate prose (not for nothing did Sokolov suggest, "If you find some Wrong expression in my letter I ask you to correct it"), Tiurin and Sokolov's texts were examples of a genre, the "note" from a self-appointed "worker correspondent," that was widespread in Soviet culture from its early years.[46] As often with such materials, they never saw the light of print. However, they did get processed in the Soviet administrative machine, ending up in the files of the Commission on the Affairs of Cults of the Leningrad Regional Soviet, where they were used to support the case being mounted by the authorities that the two churches in question should be demolished.[47]

In fact, however, the results were less immediate than Tiurin and Sokolov, or those who cited their letters, might have hoped. The Church of the Sign, to which the second letter referred, was eventually demolished, though not till three years after the letter was sent, and after a good deal of argument. The focus of Tiurin's indignation, the Church of the Resurrection (popularly known as "the Savior on the Blood"), built to mark the spot where Alexander II was killed by terrorists in 1881, survives to this day.

In 1931, a documentary film by Vladislav Mikosha—footage from which was later to become famous—showed, as a moment of dramatic and instant collapse, the demolition of the Church of Christ the Redeemer in Moscow.[48] But in reality, dealing with former churches was not as simple as this, even in Stalin's Russia. Blowing up a large structure in the heart of a major city was expensive in terms of time and resources, technically problematic, and wasteful.[49] But demolition by hand took many months, with the risk of provoking the kind of irritation in believers to which Tiurin referred.[50] Poor information about what was actually happening on the ground augmented the lack of a clear "general line." It is clear from archival documents that Lensovet staff often did not know when, or even whether, buildings had been pulled down, and that officials' response was to visit in person and file reports along the lines of "the church has gone and theres a park on the site," or "building rubble is laying around."[51]

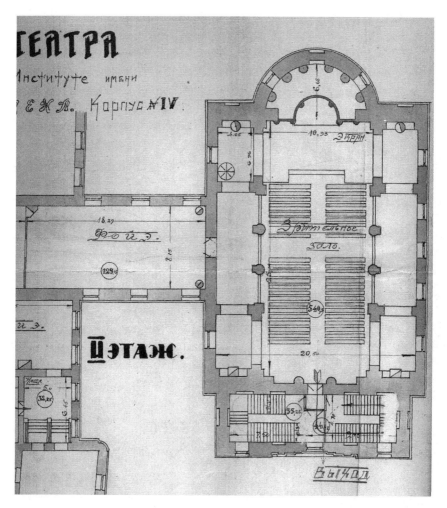

FIGURE 9. Plan of a cinema to be installed in the former Church of St Peter and St Paul (Petr Plavov, 1843–1847), Imperial Institute for the Deaf and Dumb (from 1920, the Herzen Pedagogical Institute). 1927 (TsGANTD-SPb.)

In any case, churches were seen not just as "counterrevolutionary monuments," but as potentially useful buildings that could perform a function in the new society. Like people, buildings that had fallen into the wrong hands were not always "to blame" and did not necessarily have to endure annihilation: they could undergo "rebuilding" (*perestroika*) (a word that evoked both material and spiritual change).[52] A 1932 project to convert the Church of the Elevation of the Cross on Petrograd Side gave a detailed account of the transformative process:

1. The main dome and the top of the bell-tower are removed.
2. The main supporting columns of the dome are removed [...]
3. On the ground floor an 800-seat auditorium is constructed, with a stage and service quarters.
4. On the first floor is the gallery for the auditorium, a buffet, a reading room and service quarters [...][53]

According to the General Plan of 1935, the basic street layout of Leningrad would remain unchanged, save for "partial alterations (demolition of small-scale structures, corner buildings) in some individual cases only in order to facilitate transport flow and to improve the architectural realization of certain streets and squares."[54] Buildings that stood in the way of tramlines and roadways were at particular risk, and naturally there was no mercy for churches in this situation.[55] The planning of the Leningrad underground railway was to be equally costly in terms of "cult buildings" that stood in the way.[56] So far as the Party's Central Executive Committee was concerned, the anticipated reconstruction of an urban area set out in the General Plan constituted adequate grounds for the closure and demolition of a church, even if this was a listed building.[57]

Questions about the appropriate treatment of churches in the "model socialist city" became more complicated when these churches were also classified as "monuments" (*pamiatniki*). This made them part of the national patrimony, to be regulated by the monuments preservation bodies. Yet a church—however resonant the name of its architect, and admirable the artistry of the building—was still most definitely not a shrine of *socialist* memory, of the kind expected to be found at the center of the model city. All the same, the drastic reconstruction of a church (as with the St. Sergius Artillery Cathedral, converted into a stumpy fortress for the OGPU (political police) by I. F. Bespalov in 1934) was rarely the preferred solution.[58] It is the paradox of the "cult building" that was simultaneously a "monument" (listed building), at once admirable and suspect, that was at the heart of difficulties for planners and preservationists alike. In turn, the dilemmas here illustrate not just how regulations were enacted on the ground, but the fault lines that shot through "Soviet subjectivity." As it turned out, there was no easy answer to the question, "Is it 'Soviet' to preserve historic churches, or not?" To trace the detail of the conflict is to expose dilemmas, rather than to discover solutions.

"Socialist Monuments"

One awkward cultural given for socialist planners was that pre-1917 "town construction," *gradostroitel'svo*, placed the Orthodox church at the center of public spaces. According to the Building Regulations (*Ustav Stroitel'nyi*), 1900, it was essential "to select sites for churches on squares, and not among ordinary buildings [*obyvatel'skikh stroenii*]."[59] The result of pre-Soviet planning regulations, then, was to leave cities with buildings that—whatever their other merits—were "in the wrong place."

By the end of the 1920s, a radical tone had entered some statements on city planning. The balance of power in the Old St. Petersburg Society had swung away from local historians. Among members of its governing body now was, for instance, Nikolai Proskurin (1861–1942), an architect whose projects of the day included functional structures such as lifesaving pavilions and cattle pens. Other members included a statistician and a civil engineer.[60] Attitudes became ever more militant where the question of what to do with "former" buildings was concerned. For instance, in 1930, the OSP began lobbying not just for the removal of NEP-era advertisements for private companies, but for the demolition of the chapel next to the Summer Garden, "on the spot where an attempt to assassinate Alexander II took place." Despite an existing decision to get rid of the structure, "this ugly work of Veldten" was still standing, to the indignation of the OSP.[61] Demolition duly followed, despite the fact that the removal of the chapel left a gap in the famous wrought-iron fence around the outside of the Summer Garden, which had to be replaced with a modern reproduction.[62]

The old emphasis on harmonious integration had given way to a sense that intervention was the best way forward. As Professor V. S. Karpovich, addressing the OSP in 1930, put it:

> It is possible that the city will soon witness the construction of gigantic structures built on the block principle. These will allow the through flow of air and traffic, the

erection in countries all over the world of large-scale canteens and laundries, the introduction into life of principles of hygiene, the organization of cultural work.

It remained only for local architects to cease "slavishly copying the West" and to evolve the principles of a new system of treating house exteriors—a problem that in Leningrad, "undoubtedly one of the most beautiful cities in the world," needed particularly close attention.[63]

The sense that the "socialist city" required radically new solutions was widespread. Young architects rapidly began to produce bold projects for revamping historic areas. In *Leningrad—A Model Socialist City* (1932), A. I. Gegello and D. L. Krichevskii presented, among other things, an enormous new structure on the site of the city's main covered bazaar, the central Gostinyi dvor on Nevsky Prospect, a low brick-and-stucco arcade built by Rastrelli and Jean-Baptiste Vallin de la Mothe in 1781–1785:

> On the Perinnaia liniia will be placed a 1000-bed hotel and a 3000-seat cinema. On the corner of October 25 Prospect [Nevsky] and June 3 Street [Sadovaia] will be a six-story department store; along 25 October Prospect, the ground floor will be shops, and in the first, second, and third floors will be a restaurant and a 2000-place canteen. Inside the Gostinyi dvor all the old buildings will be demolished, and a 10-story block erected.[64]

But Gegello and Krichevskii's boast that this project would be realized "in the next few years" turned out to be hollow. The key figure in city planning between the

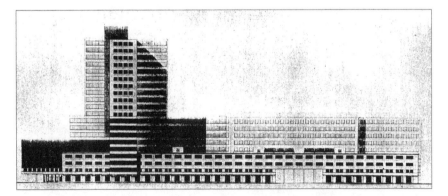

FIGURE 10. A. I. Gegello and D. L. Krichevskii, artists' impression of development on the Gostinyi Dvor site. (From *Leningrad: a Model Socialist City*, 1932.) (Author's collection.)

early 1920s and late 1930s was Lev Il'in, whose very different attitude to "old build-ings" was to be more influential, in the long run, than Gegello and Krichevskii's. Only a year after their Gostinyi dvor project was published, the first issue of the new journal *Arkhitektura v SSSR* resonantly announced, in eye-catching bold type, "The most pernicious manifestation of the backwardness of our architec-ture is that *pseudo-architectural primitivism* of 'box buildings', which have in very many cases forced out the slightest manifestations of a creative attitude to the architect's task."[65]

Lev Il'in immediately took advantage of the new circumstances. In the sec-ond number of *Arkhitektura v SSSR* appeared his article about city planning in Leningrad, which emphasized the importance of the early nineteenth-century architecture of St. Petersburg to the planning of the "model socialist" Leningrad. Following the principles that had been evolved in discussions during the mid-1920s, the article underlined the importance of *ansambli* (as opposed to the "harlequin or faceless mixture" of collections of individual buildings). It also emphasized the importance of preserving what Pushkin had called the city's "severe and harmonious" architecture ("that is what Petersburg was like until the mid-nineteenth century").[66]

In this context, it was not the original function of buildings that was of primary concern, but the era in which they were built. For instance, in the case of Nevsky Prospect, Il'in observed:

> In the mid-nineteenth century, Nevsky was an even chain of uniform three- and four-story houses, quite restrained against the background of the Kazan' Cathe-dral, the Public Library with the entire *ansambl'* in front of Rossi's theater building [i.e., the Pushkin (Aleksandrinskii) Theater], the Anichkov Palace, on the one side, and the three churches on the other, imposing in their richness and scale. All these buildings formed the unified *ansambl'* of the broad street. The later construction of a stylistic medley of banks, with their opulent facing materials, destroyed that unity, and now it is hard to recreate it.[67]

It was the buildings of the capitalist era that were alien to the nature of Leningrad per se, rather than its churches.

Il'in's prominent institutional role anchored in the planning of the "socialist city" the principles espoused by heritage preservationists in the 1920s. Crucial to the General Plan eventually completed in 1935 was the idea of the "museum city." The modern center of Leningrad would be moved southward, on to International

Prospect, which was symbolically extended in the direction of Moscow. Some of the radial routes running southwards, such as ulitsa Dzerzhinskogo (the former Gorokhovaia) would be modernized, as would Sennaia (the Haymarket), whose traditional status as a rather scrubby marketplace was clearly quite unsuitable to the new socialist city.[68] But much of the existing center would remain inviolate. (Indeed, the very idea of remodeling the secondary radial avenues went back to the prerevolutionary era, though it was monuments to the Russian emperors, rather than Party leaders, which were then supposed to act as the cynosures for the new public spaces.)[69] As a participant in a discussion about the integration of monument preservation into planning put it in 1934, "We may not value the gentry era, but all the same, monuments, as the child [sic] of that era, the child produced by slaves, have a colossal value for us."[70] In town planning generally, the work of Carlo Rossi in particular remained exemplary.[71]

An important voice in these discussions belonged to the OSP, whose stated commitment to "the preservation of historical-revolutionary and artistic monuments and the facilitation of new building" concealed enduring commitment to the architecture of the late eighteenth and early nineteenth centuries.[72] In 1930, for example, the OSP was concerning itself not just with memorials to Lenin and other revolutionary heroes, but with Pushkin monuments, Andrei Voronikhin's wrought-iron fence outside the Kazan' Cathedral, and the elegant neoclassical wooden theater on Stone Island.[73] The journal, *Architecture of Leningrad*, set up in 1936, celebrated recent architecture and dwelt on key projects such as the planning of International Prospect. "Soviet architecture will step right over the boundaries that have been set by the best works from the past," the first issue trumpeted. But the journal continued to pay tribute to key figures from the late eighteenth and early nineteenth centuries, as if celebrating the very "boundaries" it boasted would be transgressed.[74]

Preservation in the "Socialist City"

Not surprisingly, the emphasis on the "Golden Age" continued to be entrenched in preservation policy, as well as planning. A circular issued by Glavnauka at the beginning of 1928, "On the Assignment of Monuments of Architecture to Categories and on the Preservation of Monuments," had created four tiers of listed building: three, two, one, and "highest" at the top.[75] The central guidelines saw the watershed date for "stone" (including brick) buildings as 1725. However, if applied in Leningrad, this would have led to the delisting of almost all the city's buildings, and in fact, later buildings were included in large numbers—though, according to the established principle, overwhelmingly those built at periods before 1840. All six churches placed in the "highest" category in a list of protected buildings dating from 1929 were constructed in the eighteenth and early nineteenth centuries, as were all twenty-four churches in category one. Into categories two and three, however, fell churches without neoclassical credentials (such as those built by Konstantin Ton), or those that, though early, had been extensively altered in later periods (such as the Church of St. Panteleimon on ulitsa Pestelia, built in 1735–1739, but with additions and reworkings dating from 1834 to 1896). A list produced in 1930 ranked buildings according to the same principles as the one from 1929, with one early nineteenth-century church (the Maltese Chapel) now demoted to the second rank, and a number of incidental differences in the lower categories, but a similar ordering by period visible in the overall hierarchy.[76]

As well as reducing the numbers of churches in category one and the "highest" category (from twenty-four to twenty-one and six to five), the 1930 list also significantly reduced the overall number of churches listed (from fifty-eight churches to forty-eight), while increasing the numbers of "civic" buildings listed (from 183 to 193). This development partly reflected the demolition, in 1929–1930, of several listed churches.[77] The guidelines of 1928 had in fact anticipated that such demolition might take place, stating, with ominous tautology, "It is superfluous to insist on the complete inviolability of a building if its status as a monument is not especially high." Monuments placed in category three could be modified at the behest of the local authority (district soviet, etc.), though "major alterations or demolitions" were supposed to take place only with the approval of the Museums Department (the responsible section of Glavnauka).[78]

One further effect of the categorization system was to create significant confusion about which precise jurisdiction a monument belonged to and which bodies should be consulted over modifications to it. Until 1930, primary responsibility remained with Glavnauka's Section for Museums and the Preservation of Monuments, but with duties devolved, as in the late 1920s, to the Restoration Workshops. At the end of 1929, however, a new responsible organ was created, the Consultation Bureau on the Preservation of Monuments, attached to Narkompros's Higher Education and Academic Sector, and headed by P. A. Vsevolozhskii, formerly deputy head of the Leningrad State Restoration Workshops.[79] Vsevolozhskii bore the title of plenipotentiary of the Central Committee, but was primarily an employee of Lensovet, being attached to the Department of Education (ONO) as well as to the Department of Political and Cultural Education, also known as the "Section for Work with the Masses" (Massovyi otdel).[80] The Bureau was, however, responsible only for control over monuments in the lower categories; queries relating to monuments in the highest category had to be referred to the central authorities in Glavnauka, a situation that had to be repeatedly explained to the officials of Lensovet as they sought to establish the status of buildings.[81] The Department for the Protection of Monuments of Revolution and Culture attached to the Political Enlightenment Section of Lensovet also retained notional oversight, though this part of the local administration apparently had little to do with the regulation of cultic buildings.[82] This administrative to-ing and fro-ing, punctuated by the table-thumping of officials wanting quick and simple decisions, was the essential rhythm of local planning life in the early Stalin years.

The injection of confusion may well have been deliberate. The Leningrad preservation bodies did not experience a direct purge resembling the "case on the spying and wrecking in the Central Restoration Workshops" that broke out in October 1930, leading to the arrest of members of staff, including Aleksandr Anisimov, and the retirement as director of Igor' Grabar'. But the established experts—Konstantin Romanov as well as Aleksandr Udalenkov—were not reemployed in the new organization, and both spent several years in the political cold. In the bracing world of the "socialist city," preservationists needed to worry not just that they might jeopardize buildings by making the wrong decision, but also that they might jeopardize themselves.[83]

The Past as Raw Material

The tightening up of the heritage preservation statute signified, in essence, that only certain categories of building classified as "protected" on paper were now protected in terms of fact. Buildings in category three were vulnerable to argument on the part of local authorities that conversion or demolition was essential for economic reasons. This was symptomatic of the altered cultural and political priorities operating under the First Five-Year Plan.[84] The program of crash industrialization and urbanization generated ruthless expediency with regard to historic structures. In February 1929, the head of the Landscaping Subsection (Podotdel blagoustroistva) of the Communal Resource Maintenance Section (Otkomkhoz) of Lensovet contacted OSP to inform them that:

Rudmetalltorg has submitted a proposal that the railings of the Winter Palace currently stored at the Volkovo Cemetery should be transferred to them and used as scrap metal. Given that there will be no chance in the near future of using the railings for their original purpose, the Landscaping Subsection of Gorotkomkhoz requests that you urgently inform us of what purpose may be served, in your opinion, by the further preservation of these railings.

By 1932, matters had reached such a pitch that the Presidium of Lensovet was forced to forbid the removal of metal fixtures such as awnings, railings, and bollards without special permission. In a fervent desire to aid the work of "socialist construction" (or a frenzied attempt to comply with planning targets), some housing departments had been systematically removing such structures, "justifying this procedure as a way of mobilizing scrap metal."[85]

In this "hunter-gatherer" atmosphere, churches were especially vulnerable. The Decree on Religious Organizations of April 8, 1929, not only permitted the liquidation of a religious building if this was "essential for the needs of the state and society," but specified that closed churches would be subject to technical inspections that assessed their condition. A church that failed such an assessment could be demolished.[86] An instruction of the executive committees of the Leningrad Regional and City Soviets issued in 1931, On the Regulations for Implementing the Legislation on Cults, promulgated these measures at the local level.[87]

In theory, local authorities had held such powers since 1919, but the legislative instrument granting them had been a circular of the Commissariat of Justice.[88] The new legislative acts had a far higher profile, and were far more effective in normative terms. They unleashed a flood of *zaprosy*, proposals to use church buildings to some practical end—libraries, clubs, warehouses, repositories of building materials. City officials at district and city/regional levels, particularly in the Department of Communal Resource Management and the Section of Administration and Surveillance (Admnadzor), encouraged and coordinated, and in some cases likely initiated, these demands.[89] The work of closing churches did not progress unimpeded. Believers had the right to appeal to VTsIK, which overturned some local decisions, such as the attempt to close the Trinity Cathedral of the Izmailovskii Regiment in 1932. But the majority of decisions went through. In 1929–1930 alone, eighty-eight churches were closed, and between 1931 and 1934, fifty-seven.[90]

Once closed, "cultic buildings" were, on the face of it, eminently dispensable. They stood for backwardness and lack of culture. They were the focus of potential social disaffection. At the same time, they were repositories of valuable commodities: premises that could be converted, or sites that could be built on; metals (for instance, the gilding used on roofs and the bronze for church bells); building materials such as brick, lumber, and tiling. Calls to demolish churches often invoked several of these factors simultaneously. For example, in 1932, Comrade Peshkov, the inspector of cults of Petrograd district, proposed the demolition of one of the churches in his area (a monument in category two, credited to an anonymous architect working in 1800–1802), on the following grounds:

> The St. Matthew Church is very old and not much to look at, it's located in the block between Bol'shaia Pushkarskaia, Kalinina, Kronverkskaia, and Matveevskii pereulok. In that same block (see map) an ATS [automatic telephone exchange] is being constructed, there's wasteland and the fact it's empty is the fault of the church, because you can't build anything on that land without demolishing that church. There are going to be buildings extended upward right by the church and once again that church is a big obstacle because there's nowhere to turn round. Toward ul. Lenina there's a public garden where masses of children play and the fact that right nearby is a church and bells ringing and that stuff is reflected in the children's ideology. That garden could become a nice little garden square, but we have to pull the church down.[91]

Similarly, a call from the City Education Department (GorONO) in 1932 to demolish the eighteenth-century wooden Cathedral of the Trinity on Petrograd Side emphasized both ideological and practical considerations:

> The plot next to the aforementioned church, situated on Petrovskaia ul. and Magazinnyi pereulok, and comprising c. 1.5 ha. has been assigned to LenGorONO for the construction of a Children's Palace of Culture. Yet the plan for the future buildings of the Palace of Culture projects that these will occupy 18000 m., i.e., 1.8 ha., NOT INCLUDING ancillary space [capitals original][92] [. . .]
>
> It is completely clear that it is quite impermissible to allow a collision such as the situation of a church in front of or next to the Children's Palace of Culture. [. . .] And finally, leaving the church and its surrounding land disharmonizes even at the present time in the sense of the architectural *ansambl'* such as Revolution Square with the construction on this of the House of Political Prisoners.[93]

Against this unfortunate "collision" was to be set the entirely appropriate conjunction, should the church be demolished, of "monuments to three generations of

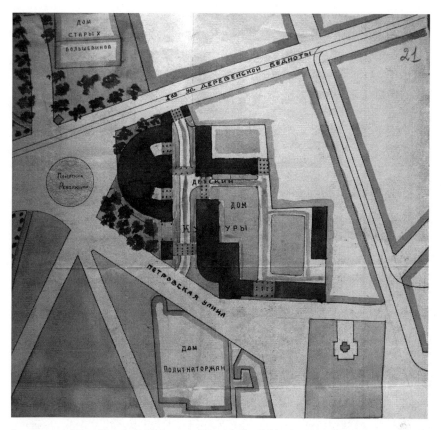

FIGURE 11. Map of Revolution Square, c. 1932, with the Children's House of Culture on the site of the Trinity Cathedral. (TsGA-SPb.)

the Revolution": the Peter and Paul Fortress, about two hundred meters away, the House of Political Prisoners, a flagship "house commune" for surviving radicals imprisoned in the late Imperial era, and the new educational and recreational facility for Leningrad's Young Pioneers, to be built in place of the church.

Historians of the Russian Orthodox Church (ROC) see the practical considerations advanced to justify the demolition of churches as purely hypocritical. The point, they argue, was to efface religious buildings from Soviet life, and the references to the exigencies of city planning—tram junctions, public parks, clubs, expansion of factories and living space, and so on—were mere excuses.[94] In some cases, there is evidence to support exactly this interpretation. On February 8, 1932, the deputy chair of the Organizational Department of Lensovet presented to the Presidium a detailed list of churches that were scheduled for closure and demolition. A year later, the Administrative Department returned to the list and began pushing forward the closures. In September 1933, it put together a "Working Plan for the Removal of Bells from the Churches of Leningrad," so that this important source of scrap metal could be exploited.[95] (The measure was, of course, also intended to ensure that the city's noise environment was embellished by the whine of trams, the clash of steam-hammers, and the striking of clocks, rather than the traditional reminders of sacred time.)[96]

At the Lensovet elections of 1934, the official list of "electors' demands" included several along the lines of, "Adopt measures to assure the immediate closure of all remaining churches," and "reduce the numbers of active churches and religious communities and turn the premises into havens of culture," as well as demands for the closure of individual "cultic buildings."[97] Emboldened by the case of the Kazan' Cathedral, officials pushed to convert remaining churches to "cultural-educational" ends. For example, according to a project of 1933, the Trinity Cathedral in the Alexander Nevskii Monastery was to become a "House of Miracles and Scientific-Technical Achievements."[98] With the Trinity Cathedral of the Izmailovskii Regiment, the sheer grotesqueness of the proposals (including that a circus be built on the church's site) indicates that "demolition for demolition's sake" was the order of the day. Indeed, one of the official grounds given for the destruction was openly ideological: "The church is a monument of monarchism (it used to belong to the Izmailovskii Regiment)."[99]

But reference to considerations other than "the struggle with religion" was not necessarily specious. For example, the Church of the Savior on the Waters was not a regimental church, but a memorial to naval ratings killed in the Russo-Japanese War. Other monuments to the victims of the War (in Kronstadt and on Petrograd Side) were left untouched, suggesting that demolition was not an ideological priority.[100] However, the Church of the Savior stood on the site of Leningrad's most important military shipbuilding wharves. The director's claims that the presence of clergy and believers on the factory site was a threat to security were entirely in accordance with the rising "spy mania" of the day. There is no reason to suppose that the pressure to demolish, in this case, was generated purely by antireligious fervor.[101] When local administrators simply wished to close a church come what may, they had the alternative of citing "cultural and educational purposes" as a failsafe excuse.[102]

Claims that particular churches impeded transport planning, equally, were perhaps not always baseless. The Church of the Trinity (popularly known as "Easter Loaf and Easter Pudding," from the rough pyramid of the bell tower and the

FIGURE 12. Church of the Trinity (Nikolai L'vov, 1785–1790), Schlüsselberg Prospect. 1933. (TsGA-SPb.)

dumpy shape of the church itself), on Schlüsselberg Prospect, in the city's south-eastern industrial heartlands, was scheduled for demolition in 1933 because it was said to obstruct the building of a planned tramline. Archival records indicate that the site was photographed and surveyed in the course of putting forward the proposal, and the area was certainly then under substantial redevelopment.

The Church of the Birth of John the Baptist on Stone Island, an elegant small structure that had been built to serve the area's neoclassical summer villas, was at the opposite end of the social and aesthetic scale, but it too came under threat from road-widening.[103] At this period also, the Church of the Sign was assailed on the grounds of traffic problems: a detailed investigation indicated that the junction where it stood was indeed exceptionally accident-prone, with hundreds of casualties every year.[104] However, the fact that the preservation authorities actually managed to save all three of these churches, at least in the meantime, pointed to the fact that institutional authority was easily as important as the substance of the case put forward by each side.

Sifting the Past

Cases where practical factors may have had substance aside, the political impetus behind the closures and demolitions should not be underplayed, given the

FIGURE 13. Church of the Sign (Fedor Demertsov,1794–1804), photographed in 1934 to indicate that it was a traffic hazard. (TsGA-SPb.)

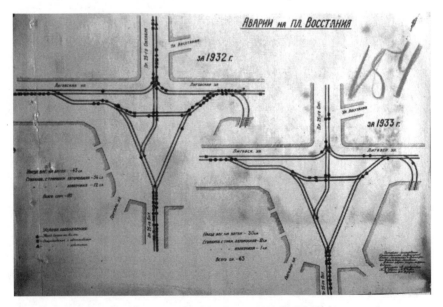

FIGURE 14. Schema of accident rates at Uprising Square, 1934. (TsGA-SPb.)

energetic work by Leningrad's League of the Militant Godless and the Party's own organs of political education to coordinate campaigns for closure.[105] At the same time, petitions from factory workers about closing churches were not necessarily just automatic responses to a campaign organized from above. The files from a campaign to close the Chapel of St. Paraskeva at Porokhovye, launched by *Krasnaia gazeta* in 1929, include a very diverse range of petition materials. At "Bolshevik" factory, workers were asked simply to "sign off" a mimeographed petition form, but in other places, texts were especially composed. Sometimes, signatories even added their own comments. "To hell with her" (i.e., the saint), wrote one; another, signing a petition for the closure of both the Chapel of St. Paraskeva and the Church of the Protection, wrote, "Only the Chapel of St. Paraskeva." And it was common for petitions to include not just clichés of the antireligious struggle (references to this religious building as a "nest of wasps," and the annual pilgrimage organized to it on "St Il'ia's Friday" as a "money-spinner" for the clergy), but comments that the pilgrimage, and particularly the rite of "healing the possessed" that traditionally took place, were out of keeping with the identity of Leningrad.[106] The membership of the League of the Militant Godless was overwhelmingly working-class (84 percent in 1928). Its stance, while not universal, certainly did characterize a particular type of energetically self-improving, politically committed proletarian.[107]

One could describe the demolition of "cult buildings" as "overdetermined"—generated by many different factors at the same time. Yet, despite all the possible reasons for destruction, only a minority of churches in Leningrad came to be demolished. Also (in contrast to some other cities, such as Yaroslavl, Vologda, or indeed Moscow), the city's premier churches survived unscathed.[108] In some cases, the survival can be attributed partly to pragmatic factors: a church was more useful as storage space than as a source of bricks, or was so big that demolition would have been too demanding.[109] But it is also clear that the tastes and perceptions of the officials in the monuments preservation service played a critical role in what survived and what did not.[110]

This did not mean that everything preservationists wanted to save actually survived. On the one hand, they were decidedly lukewarm about the virtues of a masterpiece of the "cockerel style," the Church of the Savior on the Blood, which was conspicuously absent from the OSP list of 1924, and assigned to a low category by Glavnauka. It was described in 1938 as a "typical monument of the Russian style in the time of its degeneration," valuable mainly for some of its mosaics.[111] But this church escaped destruction, perhaps because of the technical difficulties

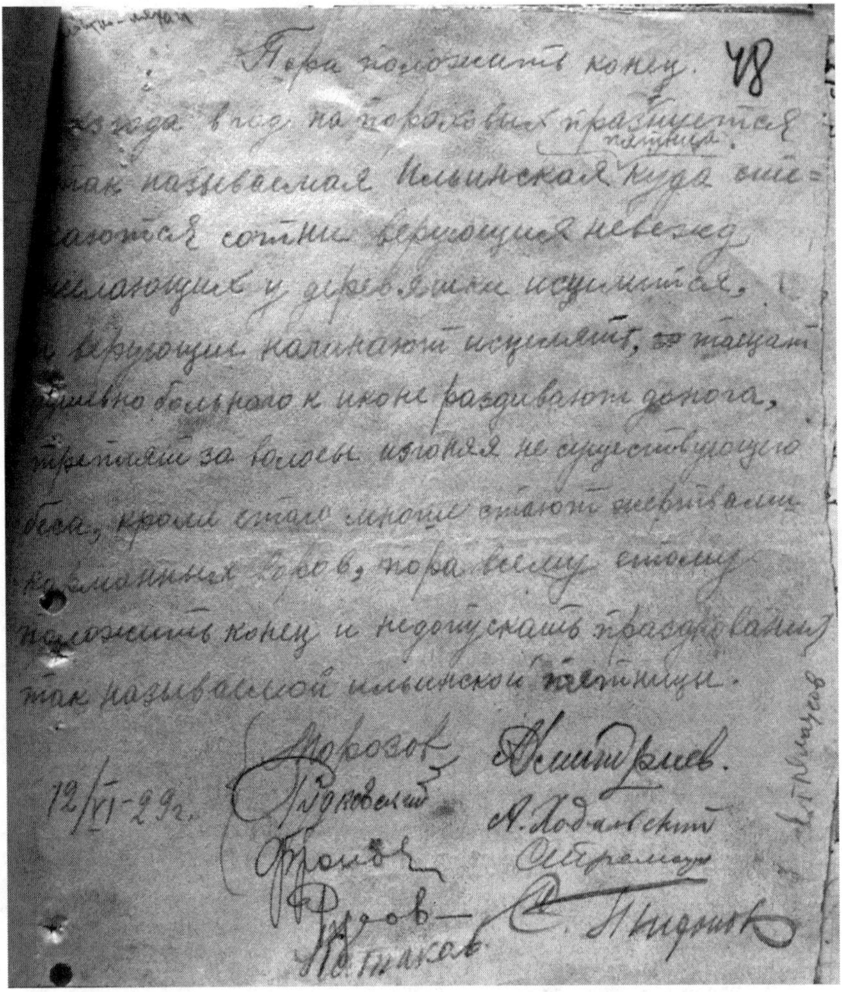
Пора положить конец. 48
Когда в год на церковных празднуется так называемая Ильинская пятница куда стекаются сотни верующих невежд желающих у деревяшки исцелиться.
И верующие начинают исцелять, таскают ужасно больного к иконе раздевают донага, трепят за волосы изгоняя не существующего беса, кроме етого многие стают жертвами карманных воров, пора всему етому положить конец и недопускать празднования так называемой ильинской пятницы.
12/VI-29 г.

FIGURE 15. One of the petitions demanding the closure of the Chapel of St Paraskeva, 1929. (TsGA-SPb.)

presented by demolition, which could have threatened an entire area of historic Leningrad. On the other, preservationists had some notable defeats, for example, the demolition of the Church of the Apostle Paul in 1929. Built by A. D. Zakharov (1761–1811), architect of the Admiralty, who was right at the pinnacle of the preservationists' aesthetic hierarchy, the church was part of a model village at the Obukhovskii Factory, and hence integrated into an "*ansambl'*" of the admired sort. Not surprisingly, its destruction was vehemently opposed by both OSP and Glavnauka.[112] In this case, the "Bolshevik" factory, on whose site the church stood,

FIGURE 16. Church of St Paul the Apostle (Adrian Zakharov, 1804–1826), Bolshevik Factory (formerly the Obukhov Iron Foundry), at the point of being demolished, 1929. Leningrad State Restoration Workshop collection. (FO NA IIMK RAN, neg. II 3370, collection no. 16-969.)

won out; the cultural lobby was not equipped to take on a major player in the "military-industrial complex."

However, there were numerous occasions when protests by the Monuments Office were more successful. For example, officials were able to save the ornamental bronze fence outside the Cathedral of the Transfiguration, sculpted from chains and trophy cannons, despite vehement lobbying from Rudmetallotorg and from the Marti Ship Works to get this "useless" artifact melted down. The efforts to get the Trinity Cathedral of the Izmailovskii Regiment demolished were also averted by a timely reminder of the building's value. As Glavnauka informed Lensovet on March 5, 1932: "The building of Trinity Cathedral, erected by the famous architect Stasov, is of architectural merit, and one of the greatest buildings in the 'empire' style, and therefore the church must be preserved and used for 'cultural needs' [...] without damage to the external architecture (crosses to be removed)."[113] All in all, there was a notable correlation between the buildings in the top categories of the official list of preserved buildings, and those that escaped demolition.[114]

To be sure, this assessment is in a sense artificial, since there is evidence that the lists were adjusted to reflect force majeure. For instance, the Church of the Savior on the Waters, regularly listed until 1927, was dropped at that point, and the Church of the Holy Ghost on Okhta, assigned to the first category in 1929, disappeared from the list in 1930. Both these churches were later demolished. However, both were of relatively late date (the Holy Ghost Church was recorded as "unknown, 1844"). The determination to preserve important church monuments from the "Golden Age" was consistent.

The defense of "outstanding" church buildings seems to have united Leningrad intellectuals, including the administration of the League of the Militant Godless.[115] It emphatically did not go with defense of the interests of believers, whose ideas about "beauty" and "historic interest" were very different. By the 1930s, believers' petitions to keep churches open seldom evoked monuments protection as a ground of protest.[116] For their part, heritage preservationists by now never argued that it was better for churches that happened to be listed buildings to be used for their original purpose. As an official in Glavnauka explained to the local administration in Cherepovets in 1930:

> Placing something on the list absolutely does not mean that these church buildings cannot be used for practical purposes and that they must be preserved for religious worship. The significance of preservation extends only to the conservation of the building's architecture.[117]

The 1931 instruction, On the Regulations for Implementing the Legislation on Cults, instituted a separate form of contract for religious societies leasing a listed "cultic building," which placed considerably more onerous demands on them than on ordinary lessees of listed buildings.[118] Officials responsible for the protection of monuments regularly enforced their own ideas about appropriate priorities and techniques in restoration, independent of the preferences and economic resources of a given "religious society." It was not unknown for a *dvadtsatka* to be pressed into completing restoration works *after* a decision to close the church had been made—but before this was communicated to the faithful.[119]

"The Aforesaid Structure Might Be Used for the Post Office": Repurposing Closed Churches

"Preservation of the fundamental architectural features" of church buildings did not necessarily preclude wide-ranging alterations. A 1932 proposal to convert the Prince Vladimir Cathedral into an "educational complex" inspired the

Monuments Office to insist that the external architecture of the building should be preserved. As a draft letter of agreement dated March 5, 1932, read:

> *The Vladimir Cathedral*, dating from 1789, is the best church building by the famous architect [Antonio] Rinaldi. Therefore, it is possible to use it as an educational complex, provided the external appearance of the building is retained with its cupolas and bell tower (after removal of the crosses). The internal fittings[,] with preliminary photo-documentation before the iconostases are removed[,] must be agreed with the Leningrad Center of Political Enlightenment.[120]

Priorities in preservation appear to have been partly driven by distaste for buildings whose "ecclesiastical appearance" was considered too obvious, and conversely, preference for those that did not look "like churches." For example, in 1931, when the Institute of Automobile Repair Supplies that was leasing the Chesme Memorial Church proposed its demolition (the building had been damaged in a fire, and the bricks were said to be needed for work at the Institute), Glavnauka protested Lensovet's support for this decision, stating that the church

> represents the most striking example of the Russian pseudo-gothic style of the eighteenth century, and is of exceptional interest in terms of the development of the arts and techniques of buildings [. . .]
>
> *Lacking an odiously ecclesiastical appearance* [emphasis added], the building can and certainly should be used for industrial and cultural needs—after removal of the crosses, as religious emblems.[121]

It is notable that the three churches standing on Nevsky Prospect praised by Il'in in 1933 all belonged to non-Orthodox denominations: the Roman Catholic and Armenian Churches of St. Catherine, and the Lutheran Church of St. Peter and St. Paul. The preference for churches that did not look like Orthodox churches may also help explain the survival, right in the center of the city, of St. Isaac's Cathedral and the Kazan' Cathedral, both of which could—in the distance—perfectly well have been secular buildings.[122]

Thus, the essential planning principle of the harmonious architectural landscape could endorse the preservation of churches that looked "secular," as well as prompting the removal of those which seemed "out of place." Drastic clashes, such as the sixteenth-century Moscow church that survived among the steel overhead walkways of a showpiece automobile plant, were not characteristic.[123]

All the same, to see the post-demolition Leningrad landscape as somehow "planned" in any detailed sense would be misplaced. Often, the monuments bodies had little room to maneuver. Most city officials in other departments lacked understanding of or sympathy with the principles of heritage preservation. When demolition of the St. Matthew Church began in 1932, it emerged that the liquidation of the church had taken place without the presence of a representative of the Bureau for the Preservation of Monuments, which was a clear violation of the rules (the church was a monument of the second category). This provoked a panic-struck epistle of self-justification from the local Inspector of Cults to the Commission on the Affairs of Cults:

> On receipt of the decree of the Regional Soviet of June 19, 1932, about the closure of the St. Matthew Cathedral on June 20, 1932, I was called in to the Administration and Supervision Section to see comrade *Negliuevich* to discuss the situation and comrade *Negliuevich* asked me is the St. Matthew Cathedral on the Glavnauka lists and I said I don't know and com. *Negliuevich* told me to ring com. Vsevolozhskii [in the Monuments Office] and say we were going to liquidate Matthew's Church [*sic*] on June 22–23 and if you need anything take it. On June 22 I didn't go over and check the church contents instead I did that on June 24 and on June 23 I rang Glav Nauka [*sic*], on [June] 23–24 I went ahead with the liquidation. On 24-6-26 [*sic*; i.e., 1932] I teliphoned [*sic: pozvanila*] and they kept telling me that Comrade MOROZOV wasn't there he's gone off on business.

After much more exhausting detail about her attempts to reach Comrades Morozov and Vsevolozhskii, the official concluded defensively, "We've always let all the organizations know by telephone."[124]

In the event, the demolition of the St. Matthew Cathedral was retrospectively endorsed by VTsIK, letting Lensovet officials off the hook. However, the episode is revealing not just because it points to "governance by telephone" (*telefonnoe pravo*, the practice of conducting sensitive business so there was no written record), but also because it makes clear the extent of ignorance (real or affected) about which buildings were protected and which were not. City officials, fettered already by the requirement that the different Orthodox subgroups (the "Tikhonites" and later, "Sergeites," Church of Renovation, "Josephites," etc.) should have access to sufficient churches to cater for their separate needs, rarely raised the issue of whether a given church was protected when discussions went on about whether to pull it down. Preservation officials were themselves beleaguered. They were now even more vulnerable to accusations of tacit support for believers and "disruption of antireligious work" than in the 1920s.[125] No doubt as a result, they made little fuss when churches of the second and third rank came under threat, concentrating all their efforts on those from the top categories.[126]

Exhibiting Godlessness

The 1929 decree marked the start of an increasingly aggressive attitude to movable church property as well as to church buildings, since the period of the "cultural revolution" also witnessed a transformation of attitudes to museum work. At the First All-Russian Museum Congress (1930), the slogan "Replace the Museum of Things with the Museum of Ideas" was coined. The educational role was to outweigh the custodial one:

> For us the museum is not a kunstkamera, not a collection of rarities, not a cemetery of monuments, not an aesthetic gallery, and finally, not a closed collection for a minority. For us, a museum is a conglomerate of political enlightenment that creates an exhibition of its collections on the basis of scholarly research, and by this exhibition, by hands-on representation tells the working masses about nature and human society, the historical forms of class war, the fight for socialism, the great project of socialist construction. And in addition, from our point of view the museum should not just tell its visitors about what has been and what is, that is, foster *understanding*, but also demonstrate what ought to be done, that is, to foster action.[127]

In the new ideological climate, a museum of church architecture such as had been proposed by the Old St. Petersburg Society in 1924 was out of the question. *Sovetskii muzei*, which began publishing in 1931, carried regular articles criticizing what it saw as an excessively pious attitude toward "cultic buildings." N. R. Levinson, writing in 1932, conceded that "in the vestries of churches and monasteries, as well as run-of-the-mill cultic theatrical props meant only to have an effect through rich appearance and vulgar glitter, many items of refined craftsmanship were hidden away." But the crudity of his own rhetoric was an indication of the changed attitude, and he was also to remark that the "suspicion toward the entire business" of preservation in Soviet society was down to the "church in-group" (*element tserkovshchiny*) that had dominated preservation so far: after all, around two-thirds of registered monuments were churches.[128] In the following years, the idea that "people often insinuated themselves into the cause who were hostile to Soviet power and who wished to preserve the ideology of their own bourgeois class and keep items of cultural value for themselves" continued provoking wariness toward heritage preservation.[129]

In the museums world, the display of such inflammatory objects as the "theatrical props" of cults was a particularly tricky task. How to achieve the object of undermining, rather than reinforcing, the metaphysical aims of "religious intoxication" (religioznyi durman)? The approved answer, in the world of Sovetskii muzei, was through the agitational exhibitions of the antireligious museum. As an article published in 1931 put it, "A significant advantage of the Perm' Antireligious Museum is that it has been successful in using its displays to annihilate the impact of the church with its heavy altar. The visitors' attention is not absorbed by the church itself."[130]

Similar anxieties about the potential "impact" of church buildings and furnishings haunted the organizers of the major antireligious museums in the country, in Moscow and Leningrad, and similar aggressive techniques of "annihilation" were adopted. Small-scale antireligious displays had been mounted in Leningrad already during the late 1920s. From 1923, the Department of Political Education of the Communist Party's provincial soviet had its own "antireligious museum," which was briefly ensconced in the halls of the Winter Palace.[131] But with the post-1929 wave of church "liquidations" came new opportunities for the development of this work. The opening in November 1929 of the Central Antireligious Museum in Moscow, housed in the former Monastery of the Passion (Strastnoi monastyr'), and run by the League of the Militant Godless, set the tone for the country generally, and the development of work in Leningrad was soon accelerating. On April 12, 1931, the materials from the Department of Political Enlightenment's antireligious exhibition were transferred to St. Isaac's Cathedral, which was now converted from a museum church into a church housing a museum. As well as an enormous Foucault pendulum, intended as a scientific challenge to the traditional cosmogony, the exhibition included modish two-dimensional agitation. Vast display boards in a jaggedly geometrical Constructivist style proclaimed the virtues of the SCIENTIFIC WORLD VIEW, and did much to obscure the sumptuous marbles and gilding of the church's interior.[132] A pamphlet published to mark the museum's opening emphasized its character as a bastion of antireligious activism—one constantly under threat. "Even in recent days, after the Museum was set up, the ill will of the class enemy did all it could to disrupt the Foucault pendulum, engaging in wrecking activities. A malicious wrecker who was familiar with the cathedral's layout climbed to the top of the building and wired up the pendulum cable to one side at its top end so that it did not function correctly."[133]

At the First All-Russian Museums Congress in 1930, S. P. Lebedianskii discussed in detail the objectives of the new museum. "We don't call it an 'antireligious museum,' we call it an 'agglomeration,'" he observed, suggesting the new, "industrial" character of the enterprise. Antireligious work should be the task of all museums; this one should aim, however, "for the maximum thematic clarity in the way the museum is set out and the maximum effectiveness of its expressive principles, so that the visitor should not feel he is visiting a cabinet of curiosities, but gains a clear sense of the [ideological] threads." It was best to avoid the display of concrete objects. "When you exhibit an icon in a specific artistic configuration, then that leads to people coming in and praying. That actually happened in Peter I's Cottage.[134] If the icon is hanging on a plain background, then it can impact on believers that way. If you don't have elements of caricature and lampoon on show, then often the items on display will have a purely religious effect." As for the premises, "the basic task, in our view, when an antireligious museum is organized in a church should be to decanonize it, to subject it to parody [*obygrivat'*]. Often when a museum-church is organized, the material placed in it does not develop the overall *ansambl'* of the church. We, however, are setting up the exhibition in the church so that everyone can sense its antireligious character in a holistic sense. [. . .] An exhibition of this kind must annihilate the church, must display themes of a kind totally alien to it."[135] The antihistorical, agitational character of the exhibitions flowed directly from this set of principles.

A peculiarity of Leningrad was that the city had not one, but two, antireligious museums, both housed in buildings of the first architectural importance.[136] On September 7, 1930, the Presidium of the Academy of Sciences resolved to set up its own museum dedicated to the cause of scientific (rather than militant) atheism, the Museum of the History of Religion. On November 15, 1932, the Museum opened inside the former Kazan' Cathedral. Directed by the well-known ethnographer V. G. Bogoraz-Tan, the Museum placed considerably more emphasis on the historical development of religion than did its counterpart in St. Isaac's Cathedral. Many of the artifacts originally intended for the Museum of Church Daily Life (Museum of Dying Cult) ended up here, but in a markedly more agitational context.

Despite the "scientific" credentials of the Museum of the History of Religion, the cruder and more aggressive displays in St. Isaac's Cathedral in fact signified a

far less radical intervention into the architectural fabric of the church. The Kazan'
Cathedral had been "liquidated" much more thoroughly than St. Isaac's Cathedral. While some of the latter's religious furnishings were removed (communion
vessels and so on), the interiors were left in place, including the magnificent iconostasis.[137] This tension between the surviving architecture of St. Isaac's, and the
antireligious drive of the displays, was to create some serious problems of ideological direction in the following years.

"Recently Monuments of Ancient Architecture Have Begun to Be Demolished": Pushing for Preservation, 1933–1938

St. Isaac's and the Kazan' Cathedral were among the few church buildings in
Leningrad that were firmly considered of "museum" status, even at a period
when it was believed that "the overwhelming majority of architectural monuments can successfully and without notable harm to themselves be used for the
requirements of contemporaneity."[138] However, by the early summer of 1932, the
extent of destruction to monuments had become so overwhelming that even
contributors to Sovetskii muzei were voicing alarm. Once again, it was Moscow
that set the tone:

> In connection with the [re]planning of the city of Moscow that has been necessitated
> by the energetic growth of new accommodation and industry, recently monuments
> of ancient architecture have begun to be demolished, among which are objects that
> are extremely valuable both from the socialist and from the artistic point of view.
>
> This has prompted Glavnauka of Narkompros to intensify protection of these
> monuments.[139]

In the following months, Narkompros succeeded in persuading the architects of
crash industrialization to support such enhanced protection. One reform was
the creation, in 1932, of the Inter-Agency Committee on the Preservation of
Monuments, attached to VTsIK, which appointed plenipotentiaries to serve in
the regions, thus (by design at least) providing a direct link between monument
protection and the executive power. On August 10, 1933, this institutional change
was followed by new legislation. A decree of VTsIK, "On the Protection of Historic Monuments," repeated the strictures in the 1924 decree about the inadmissibility of demolition and alteration to historic buildings without permission. It

introduced the first nationwide integrated list of monuments, to be approved by VTsIK. And it initiated a direct relationship between the heritage preservation bodies and the lessees of historic buildings. The latter would now be required to pay the cost of repairs, and instead of merely regulating building works, heritage preservation bodies would have the monuments themselves under their jurisdiction.[140] The reform was intended both to provide a measure of financial support for monuments preservation, and to facilitate control of historic buildings, since the heritage bodies were empowered to terminate the leases of users who did not carry out the required repairs.[141]

At the same period came a major reorganization of the departments of Lensovet. The practically minded Department of Communal Resources Management, with its focus on roadbuilding and drains, was dismantled in 1933, and a new Department of Architecture and Planning set up.[142] All over the country, city planning was taking on a more urgent tempo, with work going on to create the first integrated General Plan of urban development.[143] Leningrad officials played a major part in creating the new ideal landscapes for other cities; the new arrangements meant that doing the same job on their own city was placed at the center of local government.[144]

The changes at first left heritage preservationists in Leningrad feeling bullish. In March 1934, those attending a liaison meeting between the various agencies concerned with preservation expounded with enthusiasm on the achievements of the Special Inspectorate on the Preservation of Monuments, which had been pressuring the lessees of historic buildings, including churches, to treat the structures in their care with respect.[145]

But no sooner had they resurfaced than preservationists were knocked back again. A mere few months after this meeting, in the summer of 1934, the State Restoration Workshops were closed, sending a clear sign from the top that the cause of preservation had been downgraded. In 1936, the Inter-Agency Committee of VTsIK was disbanded, and its functions assigned to the Directorate of Artistic Affairs, to which the plenipotentiaries were transferred. At this point, P. A. Vsevolozhskii (who was on a 1935 blacklist of Lensovet employees with a dubious class background) disappeared from view, to be replaced by a young and untried appointee, the architect Andrei Pobedonostsev, who appears to have had no background in conservation at all.[146] As for the OSP, in January 1935, it was described by the head of the Department of Political and Cultural Education at Lensovet as "a narrow, closed-off organization with a highly unsatisfactory social composition, acting without any participation from or control by the working-class and Soviet public." Its activities effectively ceased at that point.[147]

At the national level, more and more funding was being poured into strategic and military resources as the geopolitical situation worsened. There was precious little for culture or even education, let alone an ideologically borderline area such as monuments protection.[148] In real terms, the situation of monuments in Leningrad continued to deteriorate, and inspections in 1937 and 1938 established that some of the key sites, for example the Peter and Paul Fortress, were in a desperate condition. Pressure from the Leningrad Department of the Union of Architects led the City Soviet to place its systems for the protection of monuments on a firmer footing. A decree of the Presidium of Lensovet passed on November 26, 1938, transferred responsibility for the regulation of contracts with the users of protected monuments at the "local" level to Lensovet's own Monuments Department (the Department for the Preservation of Monuments attached to the city soviet's Directorate for Artistic Affairs).[149] Despite protests from Narkompros, this act of self-assertion was retrospectively approved by the central ministries at republic level.[150] Yet the reorganization of control over monuments was once again political and ideological, rather than practical, a reflection of Narkompros's precarious status at the time.[151] The changes did not solve the problem of enforcement: lessees were not at all happy with their enhanced responsibilities, and did all they could to contest them.[152] And the essential problem of finance remained. In 1938, the official budget for heritage preservation stood at a mere 9 million rubles.[153] By the end of the decade, the Monuments Department was locked into a defensive position, most of its energies going to arguments about threatened buildings, rather than to the recording or care of listed sites.[154]

"It Is Enemies Who Are Closing the Churches": (Anti)Religious Work, 1935–1939

Where religious affairs were concerned, the picture was also ambiguous. At the national level, "militant godlessness" lost leverage in 1935, when it emerged that the provisions of the new Soviet constitution would include "freedom of worship." At this point, *The Militant Atheist* (*Bezbozhnik*) journal was closed down.[155] In 1936, the Leningrad branch lost its headquarters, in the former Swedish church on ulitsa Zheliabova (Bol'shaia Koniushennaia), off Nevsky Prospect, a clear sign of diminishing institutional power.[156] Like other voluntary societies, the League of the Militant Godless came under suspicion as a haven of likely subversion, and was thoroughly purged, a process that extended to the Leningrad branch as well.[157] Once the 1936 "Stalin Constitution" was promulgated, believers began actively petitioning to retain buildings for worship, or even have these reopened, citing the provisions on freedom of worship as legitimation.[158] Catching the language of the times, a group campaigning against the closure of the Church of St. John Baptist on Mokhovaia referred to closures as the work of political subversives: "For we firmly believe that it is enemies who are closing the churches, in order to excite dissatisfaction with the Government. The elections to the Supreme Soviet are approaching and the enemy is doing his ghastly work[,] he is playing on people's sacred feelings."[159]

But this new confidence turned out to be drastically misplaced. The apparent relaxation of constraints was for show only, a result of the familiar insight that harassment tended to entrench religious practices, rather than eradicate them.[160] Behind closed doors, "cults" were pursued just as vehemently as before. Repression of ordinary clergy reached unprecedented levels, as paranoia about "enemies of the people" raged.[161] By early September 1937, according to an official report, there were a mere ten priests left working in Leningrad, along with two deacons.[162] By 1938, numbers had dropped still further: as a report by League of the Militant Godless noted that year, "many remaining churches are in fact not functioning because they have no priests (they have been arrested)."[163] After management of church affairs was transferred to the local level in 1938, policy toward churches that were still open showed no signs of letting up.[164] An underground system of secret orders now governed the management of religious bodies, embedded in what has been described as the Soviet Union's "second legality."[165] This was to remain the practice throughout the successive decades of the country's existence.[166]

The key factor was now to get churches closed as quickly as possible, using the formidable repertoire of "administrative regulations" that lay at officials' disposal. As Aleksandra Tatarintseva, who as an inspector of the Administrative Section of Lensovet's General Department was one of the key officials with responsibility for the regulation of church affairs, noted in a report of 1938, a colleague had been astonished that Lensovet should be pussyfooting around the closure of the Greek Orthodox Church:

> He was amazed that we weren't loading them with taxes and that generally our Smol'nyi district soviet wasn't squeezing them for all it was worth. I took what he said to heart and in the near future I'm going to do my best to attack those Greeks all

out and in order to get our Soviet laws implemented, and to get the church repaired and the payments for rent coming in.[167]

The files for the era record concerted efforts to close churches come what may, without any pretense that the building was needed for alternative purposes; for example, in the case of the Mother of God Church at the Smolenskoe Cemetery, officials simply referred to the drunkenness on church holidays, and suggested the building could be reused "to antireligious ends." It was duly closed in 1940.[168]

The zeal of Tatarintseva and her colleagues had notable results. According to Lensovet records, as late as September 1, 1937, sixty-seven churches across Leningrad were still in operation. By July 1, 1938, however, the picture looked very different: a mere ten Orthodox churches were still open for worship, along with five Catholic churches, one mosque, one mikvah, and one synagogue. In 1940, there were eight Orthodox churches open across Leningrad, including a mere four in the center, and one Catholic church and one mikvah.[169]

The move back to a mood of resolute atheism was also evident in the history of the Antireligious Museum in St. Isaac's Cathedral. A decree of Lensovet's Presidium on July 7, 1937, had redefined the museum's purpose as "the study and exhibition of the St. Isaac's Cathedral itself as a historical and architectural monument, and the execution of antireligious work." But a secret report to the Provincial Committee of the Communist Party filed on December 20, 1938, then severely criticized the developments that had resulted:

> Instead of subordinating the work done in the museum to the basic political task of antireligious propaganda, the main emphasis in the exhibitions and the excursions alike is the construction and architecture of the St. Isaac's Cathedral and the three churches that preceded the present building. Too much attention is paid to the cathedral's architect, Montferrand, whose work has even been the subject of a special exhibition. At the same time, there are too few materials dealing with the severe conditions of serf labor and the harsh life and daily existence endured by the people of the mid-nineteenth century who were actually responsible for doing the building work. Even such a universally known fact as the death of 60 workers at the Berg factory when the dome was being gilded is not reflected at all.

The report went on to criticize the "poor artistic quality" of the texts discussing the counterrevolutionary role of the church. "Some religious exhibits eclipse the antireligious exhibits and texts in terms of their artistic quality and effect." Above all, not enough use was made of the features to hand:

> The iconostasis with its representations of the "saints" who share the names of Tsar Paul, Tsar Nicholas, and Catherine II is insufficiently exploited to expose the politics of cultic worship of the tsars and the craven attitude of the church to autocracy. The exhibition of mosaics is politically harmful; the small Soviet-era works on show pale into insignificance when set against the background of St. Isaac's Cathedral itself, which gives the viewer altogether the wrong impression of what Soviet artists have achieved in the domain of mosaic art. It is especially unacceptable that portraits of Lenin and Stalin appear alongside the icons that are also on exhibition.[170]

At a blunt discussion in the City Committee of the Communist Party on January 3, 1939, Aleksei Kuznetsov, then second secretary of the Committee, wondered aloud whether there was any purpose in maintaining two museums, and acknowledged the problems of combining, in the St. Isaac's Cathedral, a respect for the "colossal value of the building as a historic work of architecture" with agitational ends:

> Whatever you might say about antireligious propaganda in St. Isaac's Cathedral, the architecture itself and the construction of the building are bound to dominate. Why should we deceive ourselves?

Yet his conclusion was neither that the museum should be shut, nor that a purely architectural display should be mounted. Instead, the antireligious side of the museum's work should be strengthened, and the excursion leaders given a more thorough grounding so that their comments about Foucault's pendulum expressed the due political orthodoxy.[171] A month later, the League of the Militant Godless reported that—perhaps in response to the criticism—"the exhibition, 'The Origins of Religion and Its Harmfulness in Class Terms,' has just been opened."[172] The primary function of antireligious museums definitely remained the struggle with "obscurantism."[173]

In Soviet society more broadly, historic buildings continued to have at best marginal status. Despite the rise of the "National Bolshevik" ethos, with accompanying assiduous promotion of Russian literature and folklore, there was no accompanying surge in the promotion of "national architecture"—perhaps because so many important buildings had actually been constructed by foreigners and "architect unknown." Indeed, in 1938, the journal *Architecture of Leningrad* was severely reprimanded for wasting too much space on historical architecture, and directed to dedicate much more attention to contemporary building technology and other practical subjects.[174]

Allude to "cultural purposes" though they might, the local authorities continued to have pragmatic ends in mind. In 1936, the State Museum of Ethnography was allocated the Church of the Savior on the Blood as a storage facility for its reserve collections, which prompted the museum's administrators to lobby for another church building that was, as they put it, in a "less dilapidated condition."[175] As this suggests, there was an active market in closed churches, with institutions lobbying to get themselves the best deal. Officials disposed of the buildings as best they could, with far less scrupulous attention paid to the pious hopes of "cultural and educational use" than in the early 1930s. If museum storage could perhaps have been understood as "cultural use" of an oblique kind, this was not the case with many of the other purposes to which churches were put—vegetable warehousing, shops, offices, factory workshops, orphanages and kindergartens, and living accommodation. Figures from 1934 indicated that a mere ten of the fifty-seven churches closed in 1931, 1932, and 1933 were then in use for "cultural purposes." In 1936, there were only six out of 122.[176]

Just as in 1923–1924 and 1929–1932, so later in the 1930s, the forced pace of reconstruction was highly problematic in terms of the integrity of monuments. The preservation bodies were jostled into agreeing demolitions of some listed buildings, such as the Church of the Transfiguration at the State Porcelain Factory and the Church of the Nativity in Peski. Even buildings that did survive were often damaged in the hectic process of closure and conversion. At the beginning of 1938, for example, inspectors from the Monuments Department discovered that the Church of St. Simeon and St. Anne, closed a few months earlier, was in appalling condition. "On our visit to the aforesaid building at 16:00 on January 5, 1938, it emerged that the high alter [*sic, predel*] was badly damaged, the iconostasis broken, as well as all the icon stands, pictures had been removed from the walls, the altar-table was destroyed; the entire contents of the church had been rifled without a detailed photographic record having been made."[177] An order signed by Anatolii Kosygin, then chairman of Lensovet, on September 17, 1938, required the removal of crosses from the exteriors of all churches not in use for worship; the Monuments Office responded to this simply by requiring that the removal take place under their supervision and that a finial of some kind should be added to the domes.[178]

The monuments protection agencies also had limited leverage when it came to dealing with the new lessees of churches. Even the thoroughly optimistic report on the Special Inspectorate of Monuments Protection recognized limitations in this area of preservation work:

> In the Chesme charitable institution, there still survives a church built by Feldman [*sic*: Georg Friedrich Veldten], which the Automobile Institute asked permission to use as a museum. We gave our permission for this, subject to the provision that it was kept in good order. But instead of organizing a museum there, the Automobile Institute is using it as a workshop, and when that burned down, so did the church. And now the Institute is refusing to mend it.[179]

If this was the case in 1934, matters were to become still more problematic later. On June 4, 1935, a new, still further reduced, list of protected churches was produced: only thirty-three appeared in the list at all, and under the new binary classification into "local" and "state" monuments, only twelve churches were assigned to the "state" category.[180] In 1936, the number of churches in the "state" category was further reduced, to a mere five.[181] Narkompros—an increasingly beleaguered organization—was not in a position to campaign actively for monument protection, leaving the plenipotentiary of VTsIK's Inter-Agency Committee to struggle with the situation alone.[182]

"The Church Has Lost Any Significance as a Monument of Art"

The increasingly active role, from 1937 onward, of Lensovet's own Monuments Department, which was supposed to concentrate control over listed buildings in one unified body, did not stop the challenges to listed churches.[183] An illustration of this is the case of St. Catherine's Church on S"ezdovskaia liniia, Vasilievskii Island. In 1937, the director of Plant No. 177, Professor N. B. Zavodskoi, approached the chairman of Lensovet with the request that this church (formerly in the first category, now a "local" monument) should be stripped of its status as a monument altogether. The demands of the Monuments Department were a nuisance, and in any case, "the church has lost any significance as a monument of art."[184] In this case, the Monuments Department was able to save the church, after a brisk tutorial in architectural history aimed at the building's lessees and the Presidium of Lensovet:

FIGURE 17. Painted decoration to the conch of the southern exedra, St Catherine's Church, Vasilievskii Island (A. A. Mikhailov Junior, 1811–1823), photographed 1938. (TsGANTD-SPb.)

> The statement made by the Narkomat of Defense Industry about the lack of artistic value in the given building is erroneous and is evidently brought about by total lack of competence in the field of architecture; this is demonstrated by the Narkomat's assignation of this building to the "Graeco-Roman style," a completely nonexistent category. Architect Mikhailov was and remains a master of the empire style.[185]

In the event, both the church and its later bell tower were left standing, despite an order of March 21, 1935, decreeing the demolition of all "freestanding bell towers."[186]

Yet the lessees of the St. Catherine's Church also did nothing to keep the monument in good order. This situation did not change after the transfer of contracts to the Monuments Department, since the typical Leningrad lessee, whether a factory or an institute, could boast a degree of economic and symbolic leverage that was beyond the reach of heritage preservationists. In 1938, the Monuments Office made considerable effort to safeguard the carved wooden iconostasis of the St. Andrew's Cathedral, "a monument of great artistic and historical significance, interesting both in terms of its composition and of the details of the craft techniques used."[187] Yet only months later, it agreed that a window aperture could be bored into the apse at the back of the altar.[188] The November 26, 1938, Lensovet decree on the preservation of monuments specifically prohibited the use of funds raised from liquidating "cultic buildings" under state protection and rental payments on the buildings themselves to finance the upkeep of such "cultic buildings": the monies were instead to be used for the upkeep of all categories of listed monument.[189] The chance that a church would be repaired when a secular building needed restoration was vanishingly small.

Impeded from repairing churches themselves, and unable to enforce repairing leases or even to halt major reconstructions, the staff of the Monuments Department were in an impossible position.[190] The most they could normally do was to attempt to find a lessee who might cause minimum damage. The Monuments Department displayed a strong preference for their buildings to be used to some or other "cultural" and "educational" end. A case in point was the Coreligionists' Church, a building whose severe neo-classical style was much to the taste of preservationists, where officials edged out a theater scenery warehouse in order to give space to the Museum of the Arctic. The conviction that such a purpose was appropriate was so strong that officials were prepared to agree to quite extensive alterations: not just removal of the crosses and domes, according to standard practice, but also the construction of two steel and wood staircases inside the building.[191] The Monuments Protection Office also permitted extensive reconstruction of the Church of St. Simeon and St. Anne to accommodate the stage of a rehearsal theater. The original pillars were removed and a concrete load-bearing beam inserted so that the building's roof would not collapse.[192]

At times, preservationists ran ahead of other city departments in their eagerness to recommend that a given building should undergo conversion. For example, in 1934, commenting on the future of the Church of the Sign on Uprising Square, P. A. Vsevolozhskii observed:

> At the present time, there is a variety of proposals for a building of this kind: from a visual arts cooperative; from the Union of Soviet Architects; from the agitational center [*agitpunkt*] of the Palace Museums Administration; from a poster workshop, and so on. Alternatively, the aforesaid structure might be used for the post office now occupying living space at the October Station. All the above should be borne in mind, especially given that this building could easily, should it be required, be stripped of its specifically ecclesiastical appearance, and that it is in very satisfactory condition.[193]

Yet the background to this was the continuing threat that the Church of the Sign would simply be demolished altogether, because it "impeded replanning of the square."[194] In this context, conversion was understandably considered the lesser of two evils. As it happens, the tactic did not work: the Church of the Sign was once again earmarked for demolition in 1938, "as it stands on the city's main thoroughfare."[195] This time, the Monuments Office appears to have admitted defeat.[196] A projected reconstruction as a station pavilion was simply ignored during new building, and the building was summarily pulled down in 1941.[197] Operating a well-rehearsed and sometimes successful strategy of advocating the retention of churches that did not look like churches—or that could be adapted so as not to look like churches—the Office simply had no other resources should this strategy not work.

• • •

Between 1929 and 1940, a period of crash industrialization, urbanization, and a crescendo in the official campaigns of state atheism, the architectural heritage of Leningrad came under all-out assault, as a massive hunt for raw materials and living and work space was launched. While ordinary churches proved eminently dispensable, the fate of church-monuments was more complicated. On the one hand, they were understood as monuments of architecture, and hence subject to protection. In the city generally (as opposed to Moscow), the survival rate of historic structures was quite high.[198] On the other hand, Leningrad had a robust history of secularism and anticlericalism, and it was a major industrial city, with, in the person of Sergei Kirov, an outspokenly technocratic local leader as well. The result was to make church-monuments the target of contention. Heritage preservationists, caught between rules that encouraged the secular use of such monuments, and the principles of conservation, were—unlike officials in the Commission on the Affairs of Cults—in a far from straightforward position. Where the latter, once the April 8, 1929, Decree on Religious Organizations had come into force, did all they could to hasten the closing of churches, officials in the Monuments Office adopted a variety of different strategies with regard to the churches in their care. They campaigned to have buildings they valued preserved in maximally unchanged form. However, if that failed, they cooperated with plans for alteration, and turned a blind eye to changes and even to demolitions.

The root of policy decisions remained the recognition of the primary aesthetic value of neoclassical architecture from the late eighteenth and early nineteenth centuries, which acted to consolidate the canons established in the second half of the 1920s. Buildings constructed after 1850, or even 1840, were not a priority. By this point, preservationists' deliberations on what was best for a given "church-monument" did not extend to insisting that it was left in the hands of believers, and they behaved toward this group with mildly hostile neutrality (in part in order to protect themselves from accusations of "taking the side" of religious associations). The integrity of church buildings as religious structures was not their concern either. While making efforts to protect the contents of "liquidated cult buildings," they routinely agreed to the separation of these from their original setting, and endorsed the secularization of church exteriors.

To observe all this is not to mount a denunciation post factum. Believers were not legally empowered to protest against the demolition of churches (merely against their closure). The most that they could do, when churches were closed, was to continue paying silent or public tribute to what had once been a religious site. Anatolii Krasnov-Levitin, a member of the Church of Renovation in the 1930s, recalled in his *The Years of Savagery* the shock he felt toward the end of the decade when he visited what had once been his parish church, St. Catherine's on S"ezdovskaia (Kadetskaia) liniia:

> My God! What I saw there: icons toppled face-down, coarse voices echoing below the dome as some crude squabble broke out. The royal gates [of the iconostasis] had been broken off and tossed down on the altar steps, but the sacred image above the altar still remained in place, and through the gap where the royal doors had been, the Savior still looked down, victorious and joyful, with the banner in his right hand.[199]

Occasionally, believers expressed their feelings in a more public way, as Grigorii Tiurin indignantly described in his letter about closed churches:

> There's a so-called "church of the resurrection" here, a counterrevolutionary monument, if you watch it you'll see "holy fool" types come up and walk around it and start praying right in front of everyone to every icon in there. And in February of the current year, I happened to see this quite amazing sight. Walking away from this church was a quite respectably dressed, very well-built old man, but the clothes he had on!—just a thin overcoat and a summer suit, no hat at all on his bare bald head, and bare feet. And that in twenty-three degrees of frost.

"You can't say that's not agitation," Tiurin continued, making this case a key part of his campaign to get the Church of the Resurrection pulled down.[200] With vigilantes anxious to remove churches because they were "counterrevolutionary monuments" (to use Tiurin's words), and factory managers pressing for their demolition on practical grounds, officials in the Monuments Office were the only significant group who were able to oppose destruction, and even then only occasionally. As a relatively disempowered organ of local politics, the Monuments Office often had to compromise: to accept the downgrading of buildings or their exclusion from the lists; to concentrate their efforts on buildings of the higher categories; to agree to projects of extensive reconstruction. Their efforts were remarkably successful, in that almost all the buildings placed in the highest and first categories in 1930 survived undemolished, if not undamaged, the sole exception being the Church of the Sign. The process of whittling down lists of protected monuments was one about which they felt ambivalent at best. But the selection consolidated the architectural canons that preservationists cherished, and—practically speaking— meant that the record of protected monuments had more authority than in its earlier, more inclusive, manifestation.

In any case, the entire context of architectural work militated against nonconformity. Architects (like filmmakers) were directly dependent on commissions for professional survival. As a member of the Leningrad Union of Architects put it in 1936, most members of the Union were "members of state institutions, working in the planning organizations; it's clear that artists, writers, and so on are in a different position."[201] The aesthetic of the "socialist city" was inescapable. By 1934, even Konstantin Romanov was acting as a consultant to Giprogor (the Urban Planning Institute), and sitting in meetings that discussed the construction of new hospital blocks in Petrozavodsk and spa complexes in Gagry.[202]

Obviously, all of this was deeply offensive to believers, creating a sense of resentment that persisted over the next seventy and more years. But the planners' actions had an impact also on the much larger numbers of Leningraders who did not espouse a "cult." By 1940, the prominent churches left standing were mostly those which, to the Russian eye, had never looked like churches at all, or which had been adapted so that their ecclesiastical features had disappeared. It was only the eight remaining working churches in the city, all of which were tucked away from the city's major public space (and in the case of all but three, in outlying suburban areas) that carried crosses.[203] This had transformed the prerevolutionary landscape, since Petersburg's major squares and *ansambli* had focused precisely on cult buildings. But the process of "filtering" the city—in terms both of actual space and of pictorial representations—was not interpreted as a violation of the past. The most influential "Petersburg texts," those by famous writers, had also mainly elided these structures; thus, the "Leningrad landscape" that was created by removing churches could seem to be an authentic continuation of historic "St. Petersburg." By extension, local memory and religious culture were, for most individuals, strictly separate; indeed, there was a strong division between Orthodoxy and local identity.[204]

As for the conversions, these soon came to lead lives of their own. Visitors to the Museum of the Arctic were informed by the notice outside merely that it was constructed in 1820–1827 by Avraam Mel'nikov and had been reconstructed in 1933–1936.[205] A highly innovative reworking of a historic structure, with icons of polar explorers to replace those of saints in the lunettes, and the angularity of the stairs challenging the smoothly expansive barrel vaulting of the original ceiling, it was such a dramatic intervention into the prized architecture of the 1820s that it was criticized by the city Monuments Department only a few years after its completion.[206]

But any criticism of planning was strictly for experts speaking to experts. In the public domain, the discussion was conducted in tones of relentless optimism. A guidebook published in 1933 evoked the transformation of the city in lyrical terms:

> Preserving the *ansambli* that have been created over the course of history in certain parts of the city and restoring a number of old buildings, adapting the heritage of gentry and capitalist Petersburg to the needs of proletarian and socialist Leningrad— turning churches in to museums, luxurious mansions into clubs, resettling works in bourgeois apartments, etc.—the Leningrad city soviet is also executing a grandiose building plan with a rationale that is quite distinct from any in previous eras, a different type of *ansambl'* and architectural realization, and is carrying out a systematic plan to transform Leningrad into a genuinely socialist city.[207]

No matter that only two of the city's actual churches were by then "museums," while others were serving mundane purposes, derelict, or reduced to rubble.[208] The ideal of the rationally transformed city endured through the era, and was to be carried forward into later decades as well.

CHAPTER FOUR

The Great Patriotic Church?

Wartime Destruction, Postwar Reconstruction,
1941–1953

NINETEEN FORTY REPRESENTED A historic low both in the relations of religious denominations and the Soviet state, and in the fortunes of heritage protection. With few churches working across the country, the dynamic of laicization had shifted from activity within the parish to activity beyond. In the context of such illegal religious activity, "the center [...] was no longer the church, but the home of whoever organized the unsanctioned activities: maybe a priest or a monk, but more likely a nun, a former choirmaster, church elder, or simply lay person."[1] Given the background of ambivalence to architectural heritage, at best partially rehabilitated during the late 1930s move to a Soviet nationalism with Russian coloration, historic buildings had a precarious place in the Soviet cultural canon. It was obligatory for any "cultured" Soviet person to read Pushkin, Gogol', and Leo Tolstoy, and to attend the theater at least occasionally. But who had built the Pashkov House in central Moscow, or indeed what it was called to begin with, was, relatively speaking, esoteric knowledge. The invasion of the Soviet Union by the Third Reich on June 22, 1941, and the rise of patriotic fervor that accompanied the defense of what came to be called "the Motherland," dramatically altered both the status of religion and of heritage. Yet, just as in earlier decades, the shift of attitudes worked in contradictory and unpredictable ways.

In the retrospective gaze of late Soviet and post-Soviet heritage experts, the years of the 1940s—the Great Patriotic War and its aftermath—epitomized professional commitment at its heroic best. This was all the more the case with Leningrad, given the dreadful suffering of the city's inhabitants during the "nine hundred days" of the Blockade—over half a million died in the winter of 1941–1942 alone.[2] The story as usually told begins with the evacuation of treasures from conflict-threatened Leningrad, the burying of statues, and the camouflage of the city's landmarks to reduce the threat from the air. It continues with the efforts made by those who remained in the city as the siege began to protect notable collections from looting, the stints as voluntary air-raid wardens, and as members of building and restoration teams doing essential work on the many historic structures damaged by bombs and shell-fires.[3] Undaunted by sickness and starvation, Leningraders flung themselves into the defense of the city's past. After victory, a particularly joyful part of the effort to reconstruct Leningrad was the recuperation of its heritage. The poet Olga Berggol'ts, in her July 15, 1945, broadcast "The Return of the Peace," recalled the moment when the bronze sculptures by Peter Klodt were lifted on to the parapet of the Anichkov Bridge: "We stood and stood, the white night glimmered, the statue rose slowly and then suddenly, all at once, slashed into the pale green night with the entire force of its black, its dun, its tragic silhouette. And we all shuddered, shivered, even, so beautiful was the sight of the sculptures in the sky, so sharply did we once again get a sense of peace and of the world."[4]

As Berggol'ts's essay shows, it was not just restorers who took pride in the survival of the city's major buildings. The salvation of Leningrad's heritage was a matter of reverence among Leningraders generally, not just in the 1940s, but generations later. No matter that contemporary documents and diaries, particularly those produced in the terrible winter of 1941–1942, when over half a million people died, draw a less heartening picture, one that points to the importance of the sheer struggle to survive.[5] Even here, the sense of the city's beauty—the bleak and terrible majesty of its devastation—offset human struggle and squalor. Texts written during the war record the commitment to protecting heritage at all costs, as well as the horror of bread queues, the alternate panic and lassitude of starvation, and the sight of corpses in the streets.[6]

A second set of heroic recollections addresses the role of the Orthodox Church during the Great Patriotic War. Here traditions of a different kind are at issue: the majesty of the services that attracted masses of the faithful; the efforts by priests and congregations to aid the war effort, drawing on the church's long traditions of patriotic service to the Russian nation; the collection of financial aid to support the struggle, and the expression of solidarity with the effort to repel the invader.[7]

Given that both narrative lines have in common the resurgence of Great-Russian patriotism unlike anything previously seen in the Soviet period, they seem on the face of it compatible. The preservation of church buildings should, one might think, have been a crucial part of the work done by those heroic restorers. But where Leningrad was concerned, it was, once again, secular buildings that were at the center of the restoration work, and which have been at the center of memories, professional pride, and mainstream history since. The destruction by the occupying forces of the palaces outside Leningrad, and their meticulous restoration (amounting in some cases to rebuilding) in the years after the war are the best-known episodes in the city's recent architectural history.[8] Far less familiar is the history of the ecclesiastical buildings in and around the city, a history that lays bare tensions in the relationship between the Russian Orthodox Church and state institutions, as well as the considerable extent of their common ground.

"The Façades Will Be Reshaped So They Form a Pendant to Beretti's Guardhouse": The Remodeling of the Haymarket

The war years interrupted the large-scale destruction of ecclesiastical buildings as part of the creation of the Leningrad city landscape, since the manufacture of that landscape itself came to a halt.[9] The proposed new city center along International Prospect was an early victim of the conflict, since its showpiece building, the House of Soviets, was now directly on the front line. Another scheme interrupted by war was the rebuilding of Haymarket Square, a vital link in the chain of new urban spaces that was meant to connect the old center of Leningrad on Nevsky Prospect with its new urban center.

In the words of the General Plan of 1935, "The Haymarket, whose ugly buildings clutter up the whole of the square, is to be liquidated, and International Prospect is to receive its due architectural resolution and consummation."[10] The remodeling of the square fell to Nikolai Baranov (1909–1989), Leningrad's first city architect and planning chief from 1938. Baranov was a very different figure from his predecessor, the urbane neoclassicist and quintessential Petersburg gentleman, Lev Il'in. Born in the Polish small town of Starosielce outside Białystok, and the son of a railway worker, he spent time in an orphanage as a teenager, after his father's death; he then entered the Institute of Civil Engineers (later renamed

LISI). His early professional life was spent at Giprogor (the Urban Planning Institute), the center for the construction of socialist cities across the country.[11] But Baranov had also spent three years training at the former Academy of Arts, giving him an infusion of different values. He felt considerable respect for the traditions that he had inherited from Il'in, and his modifications to the Plan were of modest scale, mainly consisting of minor alterations to the contours of the street planning around Mezhdunarodnyi (International) prospekt itself.[12] At the same time, nothing in his career suggests that Baranov had the slightest direct interest in ecclesiastical architecture, and certainly his plans for the Haymarket strove to play down the Church of the Savior's role.[13]

An article by S. M. Zemtsov published in *Architecture of Leningrad* in 1939 evoked the project of homogenization that was to take place, with the removal of the old trading halls:

> The disorganization of the square's architectural identity, its insanitary character now make extremely pressing the issue of its complete reconstruction in architectural and planning terms. The project that the Architecture and Planning Department

FIGURE 18. The Savior on the Haymarket Church (authorship disputed, 1753–1765), c. 1940. (TsGANTD-SPb.)

of Lensovet has drawn up anticipates that the market halls will be moved to other Leningrad markets.

The building of the Savior on the Haymarket was also to be included in this process of purging and harmonization: it would be rebuilt to echo the design of the guardhouse standing opposite:

> The reconstruction anticipates the preservation of Beretti's guardhouse building on the narrow side of the square and the rebuilding of the church, whose façades will be reshaped so that they form a pendant to Beretti's archway. The opposite side is realized in the form of two five-story blocks with pilasters used to articulate architectural rhythm.[14]

The illustration published with the article presented an integrated plan for the square, with the buildings round it reshaped into uniformity, and the truncated stump of the church visible to one side.

A considerably more detailed plan preserved, in draft form, in the archive of the landscape designer E. A. Poliakova, an associate of Lev Il'in's, and a member of staff at the Museum of the City in Petrograd-Leningrad from 1918 to 1941, fleshed out the proposals in Zemtsov's article. It referred specifically to the intrusive presence of a dilapidated house from the 1750s "in the elaborate and elegant baroque style," not to speak of a far more uncongenial later building, an apartment block from 1912, "a seven-story giant with an amazingly tasteless façade, crudely decorated with colored tiles." Once completed, the new homogeneous five-story blocks would be uniformly rusticated to second-story height, and between the third floors, a frieze would be created "encircling, as it were, the entire square." The plan affirmed the key points in Zemtsov's article: both the central buildings on the square, the church and the guardhouse, would be reconstructed. The bell tower and domes of the church would be removed, while the guardhouse would be broadened and heightened. In the center of the square would be placed "a monument to the heroic defense of Petrograd during the Civil War."[15] An album produced by the Architectural and Planning Department in 1940 added to this a report that "long-living limes" had been planted round the outside of the square, and produced a more meticulous delineation of its remodeling. Tramlines had been replaced by motorcars. But the main elements—the "overbuilding" of the surrounding blocks to five stories high and the reconstruction of the Church of the Savior—were retained.[16]

FIGURE 19. N. V. Baranov et al. Artists' impression of the remodeled Haymarket Square, showing reconstructed Church of the Savior to left. 1940. (TsGANTD-SPb.)

From Internal Enemy to Ally: The Orthodox Church Rehabilitated

In the event, the process of purposive, ideologically and aesthetically inspired destruction of church buildings by the city authorities that took place during the years when "socialist Leningrad" was being constructed, was replaced, once the war started, by large-scale and wholly unpredictable assaults. Right across Leningrad Province, there were serious losses: ecclesiastical buildings might be used to shelter troops or as landmarks to guide missiles, or simply get caught in the crossfire between the two sides. In the city's southern outskirts, six or seven churches had already been so badly damaged by the end of September 1941 that they stopped functioning.[17] Within the city, the Trinity (Alexander Nevsky Monastery), St. Nicholas, and Prince Vladimir Cathedrals were especially badly damaged.[18] Efforts had been made to camouflage the St. Nicholas Cathedral in August 1941, with cloth covers sewn for the crosses, and attempts to cover the dome with concealing paint.[19] But in September 1942, the camouflage needed to be redone, and damage to the windows, roofs, and heating system testified to the limited effects of the concealing work in the meantime.[20] Commandeering churches for the war effort was a matter of routine—whatever their status; so, in 1942, several notable buildings, including the Kazan' and Trinity-Izmailovskii Regiment Cathedrals as well as the Savior on the Blood and the Savior on the Haymarket, were all turned over for use as grain stores on the grounds they would offer "fire resistant" premises.[21] The possible damage to their interiors was, inevitably, a lesser consideration.

But if the war years brought further damage to churches, the fact that this was caused by outside forces made the Soviet authorities treat this very differently. There was, for example, no attempt to shut down bomb-damaged churches on the grounds that they were in "poor condition," though the terms of the April 8, 1929, Decree on Religious Organizations would have permitted this. This inaction was the result of a major shift in the relations between Orthodox religious communities and the state. Certainly, the hounding did not stop when the war started—indeed, believers (like every other class of potential "subversives") were under suspicion (the established assumption that "servants of cults" might be potential spies lived on).[22] However, the third year of the war brought a remarkable reversal of policy, with the famous meeting on September 4, 1943, at which Stalin announced to astonished members of the Orthodox hierarchy, Metropolitans Sergii (Starogorodskii), Aleksii (Simanskii) and Nikolai (Iarushevich), that he proposed a concordat with the Orthodox Church, and agreed to the summoning of a church synod, the reopening of theological academies, and the relaunch of the Patriarchate's journal.[23] The installation of Metropolitan Sergii as patriarch on September 12, 1943, acted as an irreversible public indication of the church's changed status. As "Great Russian" patriotism rose, the denomination now bearing the honorific title "the Russian Orthodox Church" was ensconced as never before in Soviet culture.[24]

Alongside a well-placed awareness that the church was likely to be an effective force in generating loyalty to the Soviet side, Stalin appears to have been swayed by two other considerations.[25] The first related to his relations with his Western allies. For many Western commentators, the oppression of the Orthodox faithful had since the 1920s been a target of regular criticism.[26] The third motivating factor in Stalin's change of policy was the need to nullify the advantage gained by the Nazis when they reopened places of worship that had been closed by the Soviet authorities during the 1930s. This strategy had been adopted right across the occupied territory, and with mosques and churches of all kinds. The largest number of those opened were Orthodox churches, given that this was the majority faith.[27]

The Soviet leadership was acutely aware of this policy and of the leverage that it had given the enemy. As the tide of military action turned, and territory started to be liberated, the issue of what to do with these churches became pressing. Soviet administrators were realistic enough to know that their status as "liberators" would be seriously threatened if they immediately took drastic steps to suppress religious worship on formerly occupied territory. At the same time, appearing to "favor" the population that had lived under the Germans was politically unacceptable.

The rewriting of the relationship with the Orthodox Church represented an effective solution to the dilemma, at least for the time being.[28]

The legislation spelling out the terms of the concordat included a decree passed on November 28, 1943, that introduced procedures for reopening churches when the faithful petitioned for this. At the same time, significant constraints were in operation. One criterion on which decisions to allow reopening were based was that there should be no active church within the locality or easily accessible by public transport. In a city, this was customarily taken to mean "within the same administrative district," whatever the size of the population that district comprised.[29] Easy accessibility by public transport was taken as a given, even though lines were in fact primarily organized to serve home-work trajectories and to take passengers to Nevsky, so that movement across an outlying area was not necessarily easy.[30]

In an effort to maintain control over church openings as well as to harmonize policy nationwide, everyday relations with "cults" were taken out of the hands of local authorities and placed directly under the control of two organs of the Central Committee: the Committee on Religious Affairs, and the Committee on the Affairs of the Russian Orthodox Church. The plenipotentiaries of these committees in a given locality were now responsible for the work that had previously been in the hands of the district- and province-level Church Offices. Primarily responsible to the security services (the first chair of the Committee, Georgii Karpov [1898–1967], was a senior official in the NKVD, as were most of the local appointees), the plenipotentiaries also liaised with the administrations of the various denominations and faiths, which in the case of the Russian Orthodox Church meant those of the local diocese, such as the chancery of the metropolitan, or other senior cleric to whom the authority of the Moscow Patriarchate was locally delegated.[31]

The extent of the religious revival in Leningrad was limited by official policy. Though the city's districts might have populations of at least 100,000, the rule of "one church per district" was still enforced.[32] There was no resurrection of the parish system in a geographical sense that had been destroyed by the closures and demolitions of the 1930s. All the same, the emotional status of religion had changed. During the terrible years of the Blockade, even formerly skeptical members of the intelligentsia had felt wistfully drawn to religious ritual. On September 16, 1942, Nikolai Punin, who two decades earlier had felt so alienated by the ugly and vulgar interior of a local cathedral, imagined what might happen if Leningraders had the sustenance of faith: "If only the churches were open and thousands of people were praying in them, probably weeping as they did so, in the glimmering gloom, how much less one would sense the steely atmosphere in which we now have to live."[33] In fact, some of Leningrad's churches were open during the war years, such as the Prince Vladimir Cathedral, which attracted huge congregations throughout the Blockade. The currency of Orthodoxy could only rise once potential worshippers realized that they were no longer in danger of reprisals.[34]

"They Want It for a Cinema": Campaigns to Open Churches, 1944–1948

As a place that was famous worldwide, Leningrad was of significance in terms of the second objective behind Stalin's concordat—the need to present church-state relations in the best possible light to an international audience. In the postwar decades, emphasis on this element was to become increasingly common. In 1948, for example, TASS, the official news agency, published a photo-reportage about the Catholic Church of Our Lady of France, the only working church belonging to that faith in the city. As the TASS staff put it, "These photographs will be used in the capacity of documents that disprove the slanderous rumors about the Soviet Union that are being put about abroad."[35]

Still more important, though, given that foreign visitors were rare, was the issue of the former occupied territory, where a large number of "cultic buildings" had, according to standard practice, been opened by the Germans. The situation was carefully surveyed by the plenipotentiaries after the war. Exact information was hard to find, since many locals were evasive about whether the church had worked or not during the war, even assuming they knew. But there was reliable information about the bigger places, which indicated that, for instance, in the town of Luga to the south of Leningrad, two of the four churches had worked during the war, in Pavlovsk two, in Krasnoe Selo two, and in Pushkin, two.[36] The St. Petersburg historian of church affairs Mikhail Shkarovskii has recently estimated that the number of working churches in Leningrad Province leapt from 15 to 117 between September 1941 and January 1944.[37]

As territory was recaptured in 1944, Leningrad administrators were faced with the issue of what to do about members of the local population who remarked, for instance, "We want to celebrate Easter like we did under the Germans."[38] The solution was sometimes to avoid cultivating unpopularity, and to accommodate such wishes. This policy was encouraged from the center: a decree of December 1, 1944, required that, if congregations were prevented from using the church building that had been at their disposal during the war years, they should be found a suitable substitute.[39] While over seventy churches were shut in 1944 and 1945, forty-three were working in September 1945, as opposed to twenty-one before the war began, and forty-eight in November 1945.[40] The churches reopened by the Germans and remaining in use included important buildings in sensitive places: the Vladimir Church in Gatchina, a garrison town, which had been reopened in 1943 after closing in 1940, was active until 1962, and St. Paul's Cathedral stayed open throughout the remainder of the Soviet period.

But as these figures also show, it was still a minority of churches opened during the occupation that remained in use once Soviet rule was restored. The local authorities might, in established style, argue that they had a more pressing need for the building. A case in point was the Trinity Church at Krasnoe Selo, a handsome brick building dating from 1733 (though with later alterations) on the southern fringes of Leningrad. The church had, parishioners remembered, been opened by the Germans in 1941.[41] When the parishioners returned at the end of the war from their deportation to Lithuania, they found the building closed. All attempts to get it opened were in vain: the district soviet "sent a written refusal, saying they want it for a cinema." Trying to gain leverage from the fact that the church had been open under occupation was fraught with pitfalls, but the parishioners negotiated them neatly: they stated that they had "with difficulty persuaded" (*uprosili*) the German Kommendant to allow them to use the church.[42] Their petition was not successful, but they did succeed in getting Krasnoe Selo's other church (a smaller, wooden one) reopened, even though this had also been used during the occupation. The general preference for opening smaller churches, where there was a choice, so as not to encourage big crowds, and the greater suitability for "cultural purposes" of a solid brick building than a wooden one, appear to have weighed in the balance.

As for the opening of churches that had been closed since the 1930s, the authorities were soon to be flooded with petitions. Across the Soviet Union as a whole, 6,025 were submitted in 1945. But most of the petitioners were to be disappointed: only 509 of the petitions were successful.[43] In Leningrad Province, though, there seems to have been a more concessive attitude than in some other places. For instance, in 1948, the authorities agreed to the reopening of the Church of St. John the Evangelist in New Ladoga and the Church of the Nativity of the Virgin in Old Ladoga, although this was probably connected with the policy of Russification in Leningrad Province, as a border area and one that was ethnically mixed.[44] The reopening in 1948 of the Cathedral of the Transfiguration in Vyborg was, for instance, a clear signal of this Finno-Swedish city's Russian connections.[45] (By contrast, the city's medieval Western-rite churches remained bombed-out shells into the 2010s.)[46] In Leningrad itself, the countrywide pattern—energetic activity by religious communities met with obstinacy on the part of the authorities—was the rule.[47]

So far as the hierarchy was concerned, the primary task was, in any case, to reconstruct the system of theological education that had been demolished in the early years of Soviet power: there was, obviously, no point in opening churches if there were no priests to run them. One of the first antireligious actions of the Bolshevik government had been to close down the Petrograd Theological Academy, the leading institute of higher education for the clergy in the country. Short-term efforts to organize courses for priests had foundered, with the last such initiative closing in 1928. The newly installed Metropolitan, Grigorii (Chukov), then still Father Nikolai (he became a member of the "black" clergy after being widowed in the war years), had in fact been the organizer of the courses that ran in 1925–1928, so that he was personally as well as institutionally disposed to put education first. On October 14, 1946, came the formal opening of the new Leningrad Theological Academy, now the second phase in an eight-year course that began with four years of basic theological education in the Leningrad Seminary.[48]

Behind the scenes, Metropolitan Grigorii also lobbied to increase the church's presence in the Alexander Nevsky Monastery, and particularly for the opening of the Trinity Cathedral.[49] Otherwise, however, activity mainly came from below. Like Metropolitan Grigorii, rank-and-file petitioners expressed concern about the Alexander Nevsky Monastery. In 1944, one petitioner wrote confidently suggesting that "many followers and zealous allies of those who believe in a true God" would be found to take part in a program of restoration. He suggested an entire package, including not just opening the Trinity Cathedral for worship and clearance of the living accommodation so that it could be used for clergy, but the institution of tax concessions and the organization of animal husbandry (chicken and rabbit farming, beekeeping) to supply the place with food and wax for the church candles.[50]

To sketch out such an elaborate micro-economy was, to put it mildly, unusual. But petitioners did exercise considerable ingenuity in adducing reasons why churches should be open, alongside the official grounds relating to provision of alternative possibilities for worship. These might include the emotional distress of not having access to occasional offices (*treby*) such as christenings, but also the likely benefit to the church if it were taken over.[51] Parishioners would routinely emphasize their readiness to do repairs on the church, while also main-taining a degree of realism about this: "There are many churches on Vasilievskii Island, but the most convenient, the ones needing least repair are the St. Andrew's Cathedral and the former Kiev Monastic Legation," wrote a group of believers in November 1947.[52] The careful argument did not help, however. The St. Andrew's Cathedral, like other major churches that were mentioned in petitions, including the Trinity-Izmailovskii Regiment Cathedral, the Sampson Cathedral, and the Church of the Savior on the Blood, remained firmly closed.[53] Expediency might require an end to persecution, but increasing the visible presence of religion in the city center was still a step too far.

Local officials remained resolutely opposed to concessions in more distant areas too. Already in March 1945, a secret report sent by the Volkhovskii district committee of the Communist Party to the Leningrad provincial committee of the Communist Party observed that the church openings were getting out of hand. It complained that "the Committee on the Affairs of the Orthodox Church *makes no effort to regulate the work of the priests* and these latter are opening churches that were closed a few years ago on their own initiative." It proposed to require the dis-trict soviet itself to prohibit such openings.[54] In fall 1945, a petition to reopen the Marine Cathedral in Kronstadt for worship led to arrests of two of the signatories for anti-Soviet activities, though this was a peculiar case, given the naval garrison located there, the anxiety inspired by reports of religious activity in the armed forces, and the fact that Kronstadt had been the site of a major rebellion in 1921.[55]

On the whole, the authorities in Leningrad and its surroundings seem to have perceived petitioners as a group that might be vocal and persistent, but was not particularly threatening. According to their own estimates, overall numbers of active churchgoers remained small. Reports showed that observance was higher than the authorities might have thought appropriate in this premier "socialist city," but there was no question, objectively speaking, of a surge of piety. By far the most popular rite was the funeral, an indication of the enduring association of faith with the older generation.[56]

"The Inviolable Historic and Artistic Heritage of National Culture": the Protection of Historic Buildings in the Postwar Years

The 1943 concordat had generated an at most insignificant shift in the balance of power between the church and the state bodies of ecclesiastical control; the post-war years also saw a rise in the pull of the bodies responsible for the regulation of architecture. The drive to reconstruct cities was directly in the care of urban planning departments, the monuments offices' parent bureaucracies. Added to this, the new emphasis on heritage also gave these offices considerably greater leverage at the national level.[57]

An important watershed was a new decree of the Council of Ministers of the RSFSR passed on May 22, 1947, which emphasized the significance of monuments not just in terms of "historical and artistic value," but of national heritage and civic pride. Article 1 of the decree stated that "works of Old Russian architecture should be regarded as the inviolable historical and artistic heritage of national culture and the patrimony [*dostoianie*] of the republic, and should be placed under state care." Among those listed were "Kremlins, fortresses, ancient constructions, monasteries, palaces, the architectural *ansambli* of country estates, parks, and landscape gardens, and separate works of civil and cultic significance, and the interior decoration associated with these." The architectural boards of city and provincial soviets were now charged with overseeing the "inviolability, preservation, and proper use" of such works of architecture, which might be reassigned to new users only with the consent of the Council of Ministers of the RSFSR. The Council's Architectural Board was also given oversight of demolition and reconstruction, permitted only "in exceptional cases." Tighter regulation of the ways in which historic buildings were used was also anticipated: those containing "decorative and monumental works of art (frescos, wall paintings) by the greatest masters" could from now on only be used "for the purpose for which they were designed," or turned into museums.[58]

On October 14, 1948, a similar law was passed extending to the whole of the USSR. This made available funding for the restoration of monuments that were not under lease and underlined that lessees were responsible for repairs. It stipulated that "in places where there is a large concentration of monuments of architecture, special scientific-restoration workshops should be organized." An instruction consequent upon the decree, and published in April the following year, instituted a much more elaborate process of registration, requiring that printed archival records, including photographic material and drawings, should be docketed as fully as possible, consultations with local museum staff be held, and detailed site visits take place. The instruction also expressly forbade the storing of dangerous or harmful materials (explosive, inflammable, corrosive, and so on) in monuments of architecture, and their use for the employment and storage of industrial or agricultural machinery. Monuments were also not to be used for living accommodation, except where they had been designed for this (it might, for instance, be permissible for curators to live "on a temporary basis" in a place such as a former country manor house). As well as imposing far stricter guidelines on the use of monuments themselves, the instruction introduced the important new concept of the "preservation zone," directing that the area abutting a monument was also inviolate and should not be altered in any way that would affect the integrity of the monument itself.[59]

Where previous legislation had been proscriptive, the new statutes relating to monuments were prescriptive also. Several points in the instruction related to how buildings should be restored. The two essential methods, it directed, were:

a. the cleansing and laying bare of the entire monument, or a part thereof, of any and all traces of later work that distorts the original forms;
b. the reconstruction and supplementation of elements of the original that have been lost, using new materials, provided that there are reliable data on the character and form of the lost parts or details of the monument that are to be reconstructed.[60]

In the work of restoration, "the monument of architecture must be liberated to the maximum possible extent from later additions that have no independent architectural or historic value."[61]

So far as the arrangements in Leningrad for heritage preservation were concerned, the new legislation in some ways amounted to retrospective sanction of existing practice. In 1943, dedicated courses for the training of restorers had opened, and four years before the 1949 instruction appeared, in 1945, the specialist restoration agency had been reformed as the Restoration Workshops of Lensovet's Architecture and Planning Directorate.[62] The practice of carefully docketing records relating to a specific monument, and paying detailed site visits, was long established, and in some cases, the required information was already in place.[63] The 1949 instruction also retrospectively endorsed the method that had been adopted for restoration work in Leningrad during the immediate postwar years: the use of what was called the "optimal date" (the point when the building had enjoyed greatest aesthetic integrity) as the orientation point of the project. The aim was not necessarily to restore the building's original appearance, because that might mean removing work by the "greatest masters" of architecture, wall painting, and decorative arts. Rather, the structure should be turned into a showcase of canonical practices and of human aesthetic achievements at their height.

This perception had already governed many of the decisions made by the Monuments Office in the prewar years (as shown, for instance, by the disparaging attitude to buildings that had undergone alterations at later periods, such as St. Panteleimon's Church). It was to remain the core assumption of restoration practices in Leningrad over the next decades. In the case of the Winter Palace, for example, Nikolai Belekhov wrote, "The Hermitage is carrying out restoration work and discovering genuine Rastrelli, which has been cluttered by layers of later building."[64] This purism applied, though, only where the showpiece, state-sponsored restorations of exceptionally significant monuments were concerned. So far as the majority of buildings went, the issues were of a different order: how to get the lessees to comply with the new duties imposed on them by legislation, and carry out essential repairs. As experience in Leningrad had shown, the extra jurisdiction accorded to preservation bodies in 1933 had been fiercely resisted. In practice, preventing lessees from using buildings in ways that might damage these and forcing them to organize repairs still remained major challenges.[65] It was difficult finding users to take over church buildings to begin with.[66] Gone were the days when there had actually been competition for vacant "cultic buildings."

There was another, more specific, issue for Leningrad preservationists too: the new legislation's emphasis on "Old Russian" architecture. The term "Old Russian" was customarily used with reference primarily to the medieval period, so that Leningrad architecture was, according to one interpretation, not covered by the specifications of the 1947 and 1948 decrees at all. At the same time, some of the types of building mentioned, particularly "palaces," were abundantly represented in the city and its environs. But when it came to monasteries and churches, things were a little more complicated.

At the national level, churches had been specifically mentioned in an important statement, one could say a proclamation, about the reconstruction of war-damaged historic architecture by Igor' Grabar', the country's most influential champion of the visual arts:

> Now that the Red Army has driven the last fascist invaders from our soil, the time has come to think about recreating the wonderful works of art and heritage upon which the German vandals trampled roughshod in perpetrating their wicked crimes.
>
> Some things cannot be recreated, since some monuments that once astonished the world with their perfection were razed to the very foundations, but anything that has survived in any form can and must be resurrected, no matter what.

> Never before has the world witnessed such a grandiose and enormous work of restoration as faces our country in the approaching decades.[67]

Grabar's article was illustrated with a reproduction of Sergei Gerasimov's painting of the Church of the Savior at Nereditsa, and Grabar' referred explicitly to this church—requiring complete reconstruction—in his article. Writing shortly afterwards, Nikolai Bylinkin celebrated an exhibition of Gerasimov's paintings, and referred particularly to his vision of a church: "It flames in the late evening sky, a church in the Mozhaisk monastery, represented in another of Gerasimov's paintings; it rises on its dark-green mound, like a wondrous vision, a kind of Russian Parthenon."[68]

In keeping with the Great Russian sentiments expressed in these texts, medieval churches were among the buildings on which attention was particularly lavished.[69] While postwar restoration was a central political objective right across Europe, this emphasis on just one nationally significant layer of the past was less characteristic. The rebuilding in modernist style of lost medieval buildings in cities such as Coventry or Groningen was in stark contrast to the elaborate reconstruction for which the authorities in Soviet Russia opted at the same period.[70] The prewar view according to which architecture's primary role was to create utopia, to be the embodiment of optimistic presentism, was never abandoned. Throughout the next decades, architects created showpiece new projects that aimed to break with the planning traditions of the past.[71] However, the treasures of the past now had an equal right to represent Soviet national suprematism—provided they had been filtered by restoration.

But if it had now become much easier to argue for the national importance of historic architecture, including church architecture, this did not mean a wholesale rehabilitation of all its possible meanings. One of the leading younger figures in the campaign to preserve heritage was Nikolai Voronin (1904–1976), a graduate of the Academy of the History of Material Culture in Leningrad (though in the postwar decades mainly resident in Moscow). Forced to mask his devotion to Old Russian buildings in the mid-1930s, Voronin had returned to his subject at the end of the decade, in more clement times. He published two studies of medieval architecture in 1945, and in the spring of the same year, championed heritage at the All-Soviet Architectural Congress. A patriot who in the late 1940s sometimes adopted "anti-cosmopolitan" rhetoric (as when denying Belorussian influence on seventeenth-century Russian culture), Voronin still remained loyal to Communist ideals. He was convinced that religion and rational thought were incompatible: the idea that "an intellectual" might also be a believer made him incredulous.[72] All the same, the *products* of religious thought (if not the thought they had stemmed from) now had an enhanced status—provided their original purpose was tactfully downplayed.

"The Golden Domes of St. Sophia": Preservation in Leningrad's Hinterland

One effect of the new emphasis on Old Russian architecture was to shift the balance between preservation in Leningrad and preservation in the surrounding province. Local policy was affected by the nationwide emphasis on the sacrosanct character of the heritage that had been damaged by the invaders. In the words of a report sent by local party officials in Novgorod to the Leningrad Provincial Committee of the Communist Party:

> The German barbarians have destroyed all the institutions of political education and objects of material value, for instance, in the city of Novgorod, the monument to the Millennium of Russia has been destroyed, and also the eighteenth-century Palace Tower, the twelfth-century Church of St. Theodore the Stratilate, etc., also the library of the city of Novgorod, which had more than 80,000 books in it. The golden domes of the St. Sophia and St. George Cathedrals have been carried off to Germany.[73]

There could hardly be a clearer indication of the evaluative shift toward medieval church architecture, which had lost its association with backwardness and obscurantism, and could now be mentioned in one breath with books, and even "institutions of political education." Precisely such architecture, too, was at the center of a survey of war damage organized by the Board of Architecture of the Leningrad Provincial Soviet in June 1944.[74] This established extensive damage to Novgorod, Pskov, and Gdov, among other places, and an outline budget for repair work. In the following months, a large number of buildings were put forward as "deserving state protection," including six churches and a monastery in New Ladoga and six in Old Ladoga, seven churches in Valdai, and so on. In Pskov and Novgorod alone, over two hundred objects were cited, many of them churches.[75] A list of 157 monuments across the province from December 1944 included 49 wooden churches.[76] The restoration of Novgorod in particular was to be one of the flagship projects of the postwar years.[77]

This represented a major shift from the policies obtaining immediately before the Great Patriotic War broke out. The protection of monuments in the countryside had been even harder hit than the protection of monuments in Leningrad by the retrenchment of staffing and state funds in the mid-1930s. In 1934, there were around 150 official monuments across the whole of Leningrad Province, only 34 of which were located outside Pskov and Novgorod.[78] A revision of the list of protected monuments at local level in 1936–1937 led to the removal of protected status from over 100 structures, all but a dozen of them churches.[79] "Protection" seems in any case often to have existed only on paper. The active archaeological and restoration work of 1919–1921 was at an end.[80] In 1937, A. A. Okoneshnikov, the Central Committee's plenipotentiary on the preservation of monuments, supported by the directors of the Pskov and Novgorod local museums, had written to the head of the Regional Committee of the Communist Party's Department of Cultural and Political Education to complain that the condition of the medieval architecture in Leningrad Province was "catastrophic." Yet the total amount granted for work in Novgorod and Pskov was a mere 100,000 rubles, as against an estimate of need rising to 7.4 million rubles.[81] A draft letter to Commissar of Enlightenment Andrei Bubnov, also written in 1937, painted a similar picture of one of the most important medieval monastic sites in the province, the Kirillovo-Belozersk Monastery. The Church of St. Paraskeva Piatnitsa in Novgorod was said to be on the point of falling down, so grievous was its state.[82] The condition of many parish churches in the province was so dilapidated by the end of the 1930s that even the League of the Militant Godless expressed concern; large numbers of buildings were also being used for practical purposes, such as storage, rather than as clubs, which would have been the approved pattern.[83] If Leningrad's preservation bodies had some traction in the city itself, and in smaller urban centers, their capacity to negotiate was significantly more limited in rural areas, where basic information about buildings might be scanty at best.

From July and August 1944 respectively, Novgorod and Pskov were separate from Leningrad Province in administrative terms, but Leningrad restorers continued to have strong connections with projects there. Conversely, the emphasis on medieval sites anticipated in national legislation was perpetuated in work within the province too. Even in its altered shape, extended westward into the formerly Finnish area of the Karelian isthmus, but retaining the territory stretching eastward toward Vologda, the province included large numbers of important "Old Russian" historic sites that the war had left in a depredated condition. The small city of Tikhvin, for instance, was the site of two late medieval monasteries.

Here, seven sites had been damaged, two very seriously, and the total costs of restoration amounted to nearly 400,000 rubles.[84]

A 1945 report by S. S. Davydenkov, head of the State Inspectorate of Monuments, Leningrad Province, indicated that there were ninety monuments in the new, reduced area of the province. Ecclesiastical buildings—wooden churches as well as the Alexander Svirskii Monastery and the monasteries of Tikhvin—were specifically included among those of "exceptional interest."[85] In 1946, staff in the Architectural Department of the Leningrad provincial soviet began carrying out a survey of all the monuments in the province, dispatching questionnaires to the chairmen of village soviets across the territory and asking for detailed information about the condition and use of listed buildings in the locality, and any recent alterations to these. "Make clear to the surrounding population the value of the building," the chairmen were instructed, and told that they should keep the premises under close supervision and "take measures to impede the entry of unauthorized persons."[86] No precise instructions for how to ensure "supervision," let alone extra funding, were provided, but this was at least a message from the center signifying that the structures were under official care and should not be summarily demolished. Making sure that a notional caretaker was appointed was now an approved act (even if not every local official necessarily took this step).

Two years later, there was a survey of twenty-three sites across the province, including twelve monasteries and churches, and repairs were organized for selected churches, including the Cathedral of the Transfiguration in Vyborg, the Alexander Svirskii Monastery, and the Cathedral of St. Nicholas in Old Ladoga.[87] In 1950 appeared the first integrated list of churches across Leningrad Province, including fifty-seven buildings, twenty-four of which were major monastic sites or churches in small towns, but a further thirty-three of which were individual village churches.[88]

The monuments inspectors at province level were proactive also when it came to challenging would-be or existing lessees. For instance, in 1950, they prevented the Leningrad film distribution agency from leasing part of the Cathedral of the Dormition in Tikhvin in order to store materials (though the section requested was an addition built in 1824).[89] That year, they also saw off attempts to hand over the entire monastery to the local chemical factory in order to house firefighting equipment.[90]

A particularly energetic fight took place over the Monastery of St. Nicholas in the important medieval settlement of Old Ladoga. The monastery's main church, the Cathedral of St. Nicholas, had been used, until the late 1940s, by the local machine-tractor station for storing machinery.[91] In 1948, the head of the Old

Ladoga Museum-Reserve, administered by Leningrad State University, put an end to this arrangement. The local soviet, hoping to get backing further up its own administrative chain of command, protested to the Agriculture Department of the provincial soviet, which duly applied to get the building handed back, suggesting that the Architectural Department should "compel the Volkhovo Machine-Tractor Station to carry out all the rules required by considerations of monument protection."[92] With equal alacrity, the Architectural Department officials got in touch with the head of the Old Ladoga Museum-Reserve, who emphasized that the entire Old Ladoga complex was currently leased by Leningrad State University, and had been undergoing restoration work since 1945. Ignoring this, the director of Volkhovo Machine-Tractor Station had simply "*torn off our padlock and put his newly arrived farming machines*" into the church, after which he had repeatedly refused to move, and was even fixing up a hostel for the station's workers in there. Protests on the part of the Museum Reserve's staff had been useless, since the machine-tractor station director's constant refrain was that he had obtained permission from the executive committee of the provincial soviet.[93]

In terms of the precedents established in the 1930s, the actions of the director of the machine-tractor station were not just understandable, but laudable: the needs of productive work should always come first. However, now the staff of the preservation lobbies had considerably more institutional authority than before. To begin with, there was the site's status as a "museum reserve," a type of institution that had vanished from view when the "museum churches" and "museum monasteries" of the first Soviet years were wound up in 1927, but which had been revived in 1947.[94] Added to this was the engaged attitude of the Architecture Department whose head, V. M. Gal'perin, immediately instructed two inspectors on his staff to research the background to the incident.[95] Gal'perin appears to have sympathized immediately with the view expressed by the Old Ladoga Museum-Reserve's director: the church should either be assigned contractually to the machine-tractor station (meaning that its management would be responsible for upkeep and repairs), or the "impermissibility of his behavior toward a monument under state protection" indicated to its director.[96] Once Gal'perin had grasped that the recent legislation explicitly forbade the use of monuments in order to store machinery, he duly sent a refusal to the local district soviet.[97] Unlike some spokesmen for "productive forces" back in the 1930s, the executive committee of Volkhovo District Soviet meekly accepted this decision, while, in recognition of the "acute shortage of premises for repairing tractors and trailers," allocating the lower floors of the cathedral's side-chapels to the machine-tractor station "on a temporary basis."[98] Gal'perin instructed his staff to pronounce on the acceptability of this attempt to arbitrate the values of production and heritage preservation. But it seems to have passed muster, since at that point the file on the cathedral was closed.[99]

The case of the St. Nicholas Cathedral indicates both the new capacity for enforcement that was granted to monuments protection bodies by the legislation of 1947 and 1948, and its limitations. Here, the institutional backing for preserving the building was unusually strong: the current lessee, Leningrad State University, though based in the regional capital, was directly subordinated to ministries in Moscow. At the same time, the argument about the "needs of production" still had weight, and parts of a building that were considered "later additions" could be commandeered for these needs, even if parts deemed of primary significance were just a wall away.

A further issue was that it was one thing to stop lessees breaking the express provisions of the law, and quite another to press them into manifesting concern of a more active kind for the building that was in their notional care. A draft resolution on monuments protection submitted to the Leningrad Provincial Soviet in 1949 gives a sense of the pervasive dilapidation.

> The lessees of monuments of architecture systematically fail to carry out their contractual duties to repair and reconstruct them (e.g., No. 3 Penal Labor Camp in the former Alexander Svirskii Monastery, Lodeinoe Pole district, Rybkoop [Fish Coop] in the church of St. Clement and Denryba [another fish production or processing plant] in the Church of the Savior Not Made by Human Hands in New Ladoga, the Tikhvin Town Communal Property Administration in the Tikhvin Monastery).[100]

This recalcitrance by bodies in relatively large and accessible places was only the start of the problem. As in the 1930s, some lessees simply refused to sign the contracts with the Architecture Department. But if buildings were left empty, they were in danger of still more severe neglect: the St. Catherine's Cathedral in Kingisepp and the Cathedral of the Annunciation in Petrokrepost' (Schlüsselburg), for instance, were left constantly unlocked and unguarded, "so that unauthorized persons cannot be prevented from entering, and the premises are in a filthy condition."[101]

Local soviets often did nothing to protect monuments either: for instance, the sixteenth-century wall paintings on the Cathedral of the Dormition in Tikhvin were being progressively destroyed. If all these cases related to substantial urban settlements, the situation in rural areas was still less encouraging. "The Gatchina District Soviet has taken no steps of any kind to stop locals dismantling the wooden frames of a church in Malye Kolpany village built in the 1800s," the draft resolution reported. While secular buildings were subject to depredations also— troops stationed in Ropsha had pulled down the service quarters of the palace there in October 1948—it was above all churches that were recorded among the buildings damaged.[102]

Certainly, the very existence of the draft resolution and of an established list of monuments at provincial level represented a significant development, compared with the 1930s. No longer were there demands simply to demolish major monastic complexes and the like.[103] But the Archaeological Department, despite the efforts of its staff to use the new legislation effectively, had an enormous and intractable area to cover from its office in central Leningrad. Even in its reduced state, Leningrad Province extended for many hundreds of kilometers. Traveling to towns in the more distant areas, such as Lodeinoe Pole, the nearest station to the Alexander Svirskii Monastery, took many hours by rail, and beyond them lay huge stretches of forest, bog, and unpaved roads. News of damage and demolition generally arrived after the fact—as in the case of the responses to Gal'perin and his colleagues' survey of listed buildings. The ideological status of Old Russian architecture and traditional culture ensured that efforts were made to stop the attrition, but they could not get at the root of the problem, which lay in the poverty and deprivation of provincial Russia, as a result not only of war damage, but of the miserable years of collectivization and "socialist construction."[104]

Hidden in the City Text: Preservation Policy in Leningrad City

The situation that obtained in Leningrad itself was very different. The dominant figure in the world of monument protection was Nikolai Belekhov (1904–1956). Educated at the Leningrad Building Technicum, Belekhov acquired his architectural expertise from a course in city planning at the Leningrad Society of Architects. From 1936 to 1941, he worked as chief architect in the new Monuments Department of Lensovet. Taking over as its director after Aleksei Pobedonostsev went into the army, Belekhov remained in charge of preservation policy for the next fifteen years, his tour of office ending only with his death.[105]

Even before the postwar statutes were passed, Belekhov had made the Monuments Office (renamed in 1944 the State Inspectorate of Monuments) a force to be reckoned with.[106] He was not only an able and determined administrator, but he was also committed to the city's architecture in an aesthetic and indeed a moral sense. Though the first of the city's preservationists to be a planner first and an architect-conservator second, and very much a "new man" by educational background and generation, his loyalty to historical architecture did not waver. It helped that he lacked the compromising background of his predecessors, having received his higher education entirely under Soviet rule. Belekhov was, in the frame of reference of Soviet officials, "our own man" (*nash chelovek*).[107]

In many respects, Belekhov turned the postwar years into the period when Leningrad heritage policy reached its apogee. But unlike the leading figures in preservation during the 1920s, he had no especial commitment to religious architecture.[108] It was above all the restoration of secular architecture that preoccupied him. As the theater historian Sergei Tsimbal recalled in 1961, "He had an extraordinary knowledge of Leningrad architectural history and was a first-rate organizer; his work combined zealous concern for monuments of the past and passionate dreams of the new Leningrad of the future."[109] Buildings that did not fit this future-driven vision were of less concern.

The concentration on secular buildings was characteristic of conservation policy more widely. In his keynote 1944 article, Igor' Grabar' had named some of Leningrad's buildings among the country's major losses: "The harshest destruction was inflicted by the Germans on the pride of Leningrad, its world-famous palace museums on the outskirts of the city."[110] The palaces were mentioned again in a 1946 statement on planning policy by the chief architect of Leningrad, Nikolai Baranov: "Out of ruins and ashes must rise the wondrous palaces and parks around the city, and also the towns of Pushkin, Pavlovsk, Petrodvorets, Strel'na, Gatchina, and others."[111] As he told a visiting American journalist in 1944, the reconstruction in the city should be "in a style that is heroic and glorious enough to be worthy of Leningrad's heroic and glorious defense." This meant heeding the traditions of national architecture, not "the architecture without principle" of the Bauhaus, say.[112]

The emphasis on war damage concealed from view just how much of a volteface, ideologically speaking, the concentration on old buildings represented. In 1939, a report on the palace-museums had concluded that "income from the palaces and parks is only partially used to finance repairs and almost no major work is done; at the same time, the level at which these incomparable historical and architectural-artistic monuments is displayed is abysmal, and totally unsatisfactory from the point of view of scholarly and scientific standards."[113]

It is no surprise that, before the war, protection of ecclesiastical buildings in Leningrad's environs should also have been exiguous at best. Just one ecclesiastical building across this area—the Church of the Sign at Pushkin—was a monument of "state," as opposed to "local," significance, according to the 1935 list. Just three churches—the Cathedral of the Transfiguration at Strel'na, the St. Sophia Cathedral, and the St. Theodore Settlement (Feodorovskii gorodok) at Pushkin—even had "local" significance. While the demolition of Konstantin Ton's St. Catherine's Cathedral in Pushkin in 1939 was in keeping with planning policies in Leningrad itself, regulation of church buildings was slacker beyond the city; when the Monuments Department decided to add a certain "cultic building" in Kolpino to the list in 1938, they proved unable to specify either its address or its name.[114]

Where the churches of Leningrad and its environs were concerned, there was no postwar shift in attitudes either. Baranov's article mentioned only four ecclesiastical sites in a list of major buildings requiring repair:

> The Hermitage, the Winter Palace, the Russian Museum, the Yusupov Palace, the Admiralty, the Engineers' [Mikhailovskii] Castle, Smol'nyi Convent, the Alexander Nevsky Monastery, the Peter and Paul Fortress, the Public Library, the Pushkin Theater, the St. Isaac's and Kazan' Cathedrals, the Pioneer Palace, the former State Bank building, the Institute of Mines, the Senate and the Synod, the Tauride Palace, and hundreds of other exceptionally valuable monuments of national architecture must be fundamentally reconstructed and carefully restored.[115]

The disproportion between the numbers of named secular and "cultic" buildings gave a sense of the marginal status of churches in the state restoration programs.

Like the *construction* of the socialist city in the 1930s, its *reconstruction* in the late 1940s onward was governed by the ideal of homogeneously planned space. Neoclassical principles continued to dominate, in Leningrad as in other cities undergoing rebuilding.[116] Preparatory materials for the new General Plan of 1949 named the city's main *ansambli* as Palace Square, the Admiralty, St. Isaac's, the Champs de Mars, the Engineer's Castle, ploshchad' Iskusstv, Nevsky Prospect, ploshchad' Ostrovskogo, the Alexander Nevsky Monastery, Smol'nyi, the Strelka of Vasilievskii Island, Petrokrepost' (Schlüsselburg), Elagin Island, the Neva Embankment, the St. Nicholas Cathedral and surrounding square, and the Royal Stables.[117] All of these were from the canonical era of the late eighteenth and early nineteenth centuries.[118] Bomb sites on Suvorovskii prospekt and Nevsky were among those that were raised up again in a style that made the replacement edifices hard to distinguish from surviving buildings of the eighteenth and early nineteenth centuries.[119]

Yet this did not mean that planners' attitudes to the city were fixated on the past. On the contrary, industrialized construction was beginning to be widely supported.[120] Added to that, the central principles of urban planning, as established in the 1935 General Plan for the City of Leningrad, were not revisited in the postwar years. It was still assumed that modernizing infrastructure and creating new urban spaces should be central goals. In this vein, Baranov underlined during 1946 the continuing need for *grands projets*. He anticipated not just the expansion of the city into new suburbs, particularly to the west, but also the reshaping of extant public spaces: "The reconstruction of the Haymarket and of Obukhovo Square, of Kirov Square and the Square of Strikes, must be brought to its culmination."[121]

Indeed, the plans for the city were in some ways more radical than before. The idea of creating a new administrative center had now been quietly dropped: the south of the city had been heavily bombarded during the war, so that further expanding it was simply not practical. This also meant that the idea of a "museum center" with primarily cultural significance had fallen by the wayside. By 1950, Baranov's plans for the city included the construction of new vertical "dominants"—a series of high-rise buildings intended to transform the Neva view. These challenged the traditional predominance of spires and bell towers, no longer needed as vertical relief. The principle of balancing volumes was adduced in Baranov's ruminations on what to do with key areas of the city center. Among places that he nominated for "high-rise accents" were the Tuchkov Embankment, the marine embankments of Vasilievskii Island (where "a rise in the general height to 8–10 storeys can be considered entirely justified,") the area around the Warsaw Station, and Izmailovskii prospekt. In several of these cases (the Tuchkov Embankment, Warsaw Station, and Izmailovskii prospekt), the "high-rise accent" at the time Baranov was writing was provided by a church. His plans, however, envisaged a city skyline where modern, secular buildings would dominate. The only church building that he specifically named as important in the new panoramas was St. Isaac's Cathedral. In a photographic panorama accompanying the text, the dome and bell tower of St. Catherine's Church on Vasilievskii Island were circled in pencil, as if to suggest it was the target the new high rises should meet or exceed—as, in fact, all of them did.[122]

FIGURE 20. Panorama of the Tuchkov Embankment area, 1950, showing new "high-rise accents." (TsGANTD-SPb.)

The only "high-rise accent" in Baranov's plan that actually got constructed was the new building of the Finland Station, and even this with significantly reduced height.[123] But other remodeling ambitions had more impact. A case in point was the Haymarket. As Baranov wrote in 1950, Labor Street had been "cleaned up" (*raschishchena*) in 1928–1930. "Previously, the street was blocked by the architecturally unsuccessful Church of the Annunciation, which also took up much of the space in Labor Square also."[124] This description suggested the likely fate of the Haymarket, particularly since the square was to be provided with a new "vertical accent" in the shape of a large monument with gardens around it.[125]

As the Haymarket was progressively homogenized (with the levels of apartment blocks adjusted so that they formed one long row), the "cultic building" that stood on it started to look more and more incongruous. Despite the abandonment of the plan to move Leningrad's administrative center southward (wartime destruction had been particularly intense in precisely that area), International Prospect remained a key artery of the city, as was underlined by its renaming as Stalin Prospect in 1950. All the prize-winning designs submitted to a competition for the redesign of Stalin Prospect held in 1952–1953 envisaged the removal of the church (and most of them also of the guardhouse).[126] A further indication of the intention to break radically with the past was the renaming of the square in 1952. At this point it became "Peace Square," in a tribute to the cultural diplomacy and "soft power" of the day.[127] Symbolic Sovietization was nearly complete.

All the same, in the meantime, the Savior on the Haymarket survived, and the 1940s did not see a renewal of the all-out demolition that had characterized the "model socialist city" phase of Leningrad's existence. Energies were directed elsewhere: to the repair and replacement of industrial and domestic architecture hit by bombing, and the reconstruction of key areas of the old center. Reworking did not have to mean that "cult buildings" disappeared: the memorial to the "Defenders of Hanko Peninsula" by V. A. Kamenskii and A. A. Leibman (1945), integrated into the wall of a reconstructed building at 11 ulitsa Pestelia, echoed the Dutch gables of St. Panteleimon's Church. However, in 1948, one church of some architectural interest was leveled. This was St. Zachary and St. Elizabeth, which stood on ulitsa Kaliaeva, once named for its sake (Zakhar'evskaia).[128] While not an official monument at this point, the church had been reconstructed, using the neo-baroque style, in 1897–1899 by a noted architect, Leontii Benua (Benois), whose Grand Ducal Mausoleum in the Peter and Paul Fortress was considered one of the most important buildings in the city. In 1922, St. Zachary and St. Elizabeth had been assigned to the second category of protected structure.[129]

More characteristic policy in the late 1940s, though, was to leave churches standing—but do little to stop them from falling down. The amount of funding expended on Leningrad restoration was extremely generous, by prewar standards—over 6 million rubles went toward restoring the Hermitage in 1946–1947 alone.[130] But almost nothing was spent on ecclesiastical buildings, some of which waited decades before undergoing repairs. The Trinity Cathedral in the Alexander Nevsky Monastery (regarded as one of the city's most important churches) was left without a roof till 1956. The Cathedral of the Trinity in Kolpino was a shell from 1943 into the 1950s. Even in the case of major monuments—the Kazan' Cathedral and St. Isaac's Cathedral—work proceeded slowly. On May 15, 1951, participants at a meeting of the Section for the Study, Protection, and Restoration of Monuments of Architecture at the Leningrad Division of the Union of Architects (LOSA) recorded that the façade of St. Isaac's was in a condition that might be dangerous for passersby, and that the roof of the Kazan' Cathedral had a large hole in it, "and the entire building is falling to bits."[131] The former house church of the Winter Palace—one of the few surviving interiors by Rastrelli—underwent superficial restoration only, and was used as a museum hall right up until the twenty-first century.[132]

It was not always easy to get funding for secular construction either: as Nikolai Belekhov pointed out in 1950, it had taken a cartoon by the Kukriniksy, the combination responsible for the country's leading agitational caricatures, to draw the country's attention to the appalling condition of the Bronze Horseman.[133] But the flagship projects—where undertaken at all—involved secular structures.

And the partial rehabilitation of the Orthodox Church had no effect at all on general social perceptions of what empty church buildings should be used for. In March 1947, the executive committee of the Vasilievskii Island District Soviet applied to the plenipotentiary on religious affairs to turn the Armenian Church on the Smolenka Embankment into a footwear factory, and in July that year, the Academician A. N. Krylov Institute requested the use of the St. Catherine's Lutheran Church on Bol'shoi prospekt, Vasilievskii Island, as a laboratory.[134] The Church of St. Simeon and St. Anne, despite partial conversion for use as a theater, was not employed in this capacity after the war. Instead, it was taken over by a "post-box" enterprise (one doing secret defense work), in the course of which a new partition in thick concrete was constructed and the old load-bearing walls and pillars in the building's cellar removed.[135]

Thus, GIOP, despite its new powers, was not always able (and perhaps not always even willing) to prevent damage to historic church buildings. Policy was constrained not just in terms of control over types of use and lessees' behavior, but also in terms of properties listed. There were a mere three new listings of "cultic buildings" in the official inventory of 1947. As well as Giacomo Quarenghi's "English Church" of 1811–1815, on the former English Embankment, these included N. A. L'vov's Church of St. Elijah the Prophet (1782–1786), and the Church of the Trinity (the "house church" of the mansion at 20 Fontanka Embankment, built by Andrei Voronikhin for A. N. Golitsyn in 1812). When compared with earlier lists, the increase in the number of listed churches was even more negligible: there were now thirty-six, as opposed to thirty-four in 1935 and in 1938. The principles of selection were equally conservative. Just as before, all the churches were buildings by renowned architects of the late eighteenth or early nineteenth centuries. Two of them were no longer distinguishable as churches anyway, since the interiors had already been liquidated, and the façades had no details of devotional significance. The inclusion of the Church of St. Elijah the Prophet, the sole Orthodox parish church to appear for the first time, was no doubt intended to make up for the Church of the Sign, demolished after the 1938 list was issued.[136] However, the remote location of the Church of St. Elijah, at Porokhovye, the former Gunpowder Factory, on the city's northern outskirts, made it a replacement for the Church of the Sign exclusively in terms of architectural history, not in terms of spatial significance.

So far as the official Leningrad "city text" was concerned, churches were largely invisible, if not completely so. LOSA's in-house journal, *The Building and Architecture of Leningrad*, which began publishing again in 1946, after a gap of five years, included only a small amount of material about the postwar restoration projects, concentrating on war memorials and the erection of the new monuments to Stalin.[137] Such material as did address restoration focused on Old Russian architecture and on the out-of-town palaces.[138]

At the same time, there was no absolute prohibition on reference to "cultic buildings." Two of the rare publications of material relating to architectural history in the journal included discussion of churches. Alongside a 250th anniversary tribute to Rastrelli, these included an article about Stasov that highlighted his Trinity-Izmailovskii Regiment Cathedral as well as the estate church at Gruzino and the St. Alexander Nevskii Cathedral in Saratov.[139] At a suitably vague distance, "cultic buildings" could also be an acceptable constituent of the city's official panoramas. *Views of Leningrad*, a copiously illustrated album of photographs planned to mark the 250th anniversary of the city, included pictures of the newly planted square in front of the Alexander Nevskii Monastery, the Park of the Laboring People with the mosque in the background, and a smudgy view of the point of Vasilievskii Island with the dome of St. Catherine's Church to one side. But only the Cathedral of St. Peter and St. Paul, and the St. Isaac's and Kazan' Cathedrals, were actually named in the captions. A church still had to be a monument of the "highest" class before its "architectural" function outweighed its significance as a "cultic building."[140]

"The Graves of Our Great Russian Generals": Heritage in Believers' Petitions

For all the limitations of interest in Leningrad's pre-1917 past among professionals, mass-market publications, such as newspapers and journals, gave more space to retrospective materials after the war, compared with the relentlessly technocratic 1930s.[141] Perhaps taking their cue from such sources, as well as the general sense of rising interest in the "history of the Motherland," some petitioners for the reopening of churches decided that it would help to mention the significance of the buildings with respect to the national past.[142] For example, in 1945, the signatory of a letter petitioning for the reopening of the major churches in the Alexander Nevskii Monastery emphasized the positive effects, from a heritage point of view, if believers were to take the church over:

The believing citizens will with pleasure devote their free time, their strength, and their savings to bring about the reconstruction of one of the churches, the cathedral, and the graves of our great Russian generals Alexander Suvorov and Alexander Nevsky.[143]

A petition from residents on Vasilievskii Island requesting the opening of St. Andrew's Cathedral underlined the information that the church "was founded in the time of Peter I (Peter the Great)."[144] A group requesting the Sampson Cathedral be reopened contrasted the magnificent history of the place with its wretched postwar condition, employing great eloquence, if little punctuation:

> This church was founded in memory of Peter I's victory at Poltava and as of the present time it is in a state of destruction during the war three domes were knocked off by shell-fire as a result of which a big gash appeared into which rain and snow are falling and continuing to destroy this historic strukture [*sic, sdanie*] there are many memorial tablets and Peter I's speech to the soldiery and those tables are getting trampled into the ground, the bell tower has not been repaired as it should and the plaster is threatening to fall off and hurt passersby and during the war there was a garage in the cathedral and now there's a sign up saying the Academy of Sciences is looking after it only they're not looking after it[,] well all they care about is using it as a warehouse.[145]

While these letters invoked the churches' status as "monuments of history," rather than specifically architecture, petitioners for the reopening of the St. Catherine's Church in Murino (on the northern borders of Leningrad), referred directly, in their submission of February 27, 1953, to "this remarkable work of Russian architecture." They pointed to an approaching anniversary (always an event of considerable significance in the Soviet ritual calendar) as an appropriate occasion for reopening it:

> This very year, 1953, marks one hundred and fifty years from the date of the death of Architect L'VOV, and the renewal of services in the reconstructed church, as a monument of architecture, would be a just tribute to the memory of this outstanding Russian architect, and underline the preeminence of Russian architecture.
>
> The building is in a state of collapse, and if measures are not taken, it is threatened by total destruction; thus a monument of old, original architecture, as can be seen from the photographs, will be lost for our people and nation [*narod*].[146]

Yet invoking history was far from a universal strategy, even if the church merited this. One petitioner for the opening of the Kazan' Cathedral, for example,

preferred to call on the intercession of Stalin and allude to the religious significance of the Cathedral. This, as she put it "was built by a people just as Orthodox
and pious as we are, to the Tsaritsa of the Heavens, praying to whom for our country and for mankind at large now has such special significance for us."[147] Similarly,
those requesting that the Church of the Sign in Pushkin be reopened did not refer
to its status as an architectural monument, but to their own sufferings in the war
years and the damage, from a religious point of view, to its interior: "The iconostasis is in one piece. All that is missing is the wondrous icons. They look like many
blinded eyes."[148] Such discrepancies suggest that believers were as uncertain about
the relationship of their buildings with the abstract concept of "heritage" as state
administrators were about conferring that status on churches.

To underline a church's historical associations was no guarantee of success in
any case. The petitions for the St. Andrew's and Sampson Cathedrals, and the
Church of St. Catherine at Murino, failed just as conclusively as those citing purely
religious grounds. All the same, it is notable that Metropolitan Grigorii himself
evidently considered that the argument from history was likely to be effective. In
1948, when Father Ioann D'iakonov, the parish priest in Tikhvin, wrote to enquire
about the possibility that the Cathedral of the Dormition might be opened for
worship, the metropolitan's secretary, Father Evgenii Lukin, advised him in considerable detail about how to do this:

> You must make a formal request for permission. The application form on which you
> should do this is enclosed.
>
> In the application, you should particularly emphasize that your Religious Com-
> munity requests the Uspenskii Church should be transferred to it for use simulta-
> neously and sequentially with the Tikhvin Church, and that *this request is prompted
> mainly by the need to support and protect from destruction a monument of history.*[149]

Given the strictly hierarchical understanding of obedience that operated in the
church, Father Lukin could not have made such a suggestion had he not conferred
first with Metropolitan Grigorii and sought his blessing for it. Metropolitan Grigorii
himself was to resort to similar arguments when lobbying for the opening of the
Trinity Cathedral in the Alexander Nevskii Monastery: "The Board of Management
of the Moscow Patriarchate, according to a preliminary agreement of mine there-
with, is prepared to take upon itself the entire costs of repair work to the church, and
in this manner to resurrect this historical monument of eighteenth-century architecture, should the City Executive Committee of Lensovet give permission for this."[150]

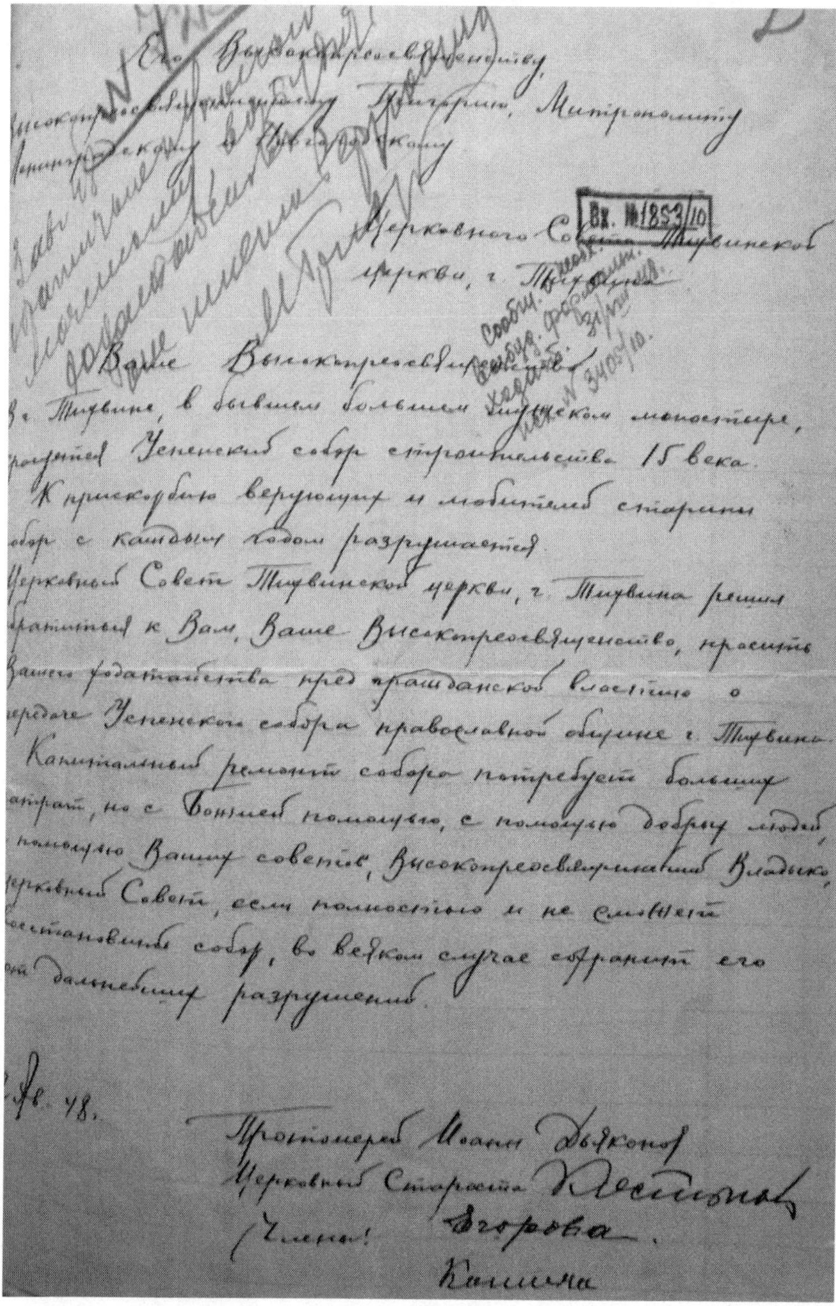
Его Высокопреосвященству
Высокопреосвященнейшему Григорию, Митрополиту
Ленинградскому и Новгородскому

Вх. №1853/10

Церковного Совета Тихвинской
церкви, г. Тихвина

Ваше Высокопреосвященство
В г. Тихвине, в бывшем большом мужском монастыре, …ится Успенский собор строительства 15 века.
К прискорбию верующих и любителей старины собор с каждым годом разрушается.
Церковный Совет Тихвинской церкви, г. Тихвина решил обратиться к Вам, Ваше Высокопреосвященство, просить Вашего ходатайства пред гражданской властью о передаче Успенского собора православной общине г. Тихвина.
Капитальный ремонт собора потребует больших затрат, но с Божией помощью, с помощью добрых людей, с помощью Ваших советов, Высокопреосвященнейший Владыко, Церковный Совет, если полностью и не сможет восстановить собор, во всяком случае сохранит его от дальнейших разрушений.

…48.

Протоиерей Иоанн Дьяконов
Церковный Староста Клесонов
Члены: Егорова
Кошкина

FIGURE 21. Petition for the reopening of the Uspenskii Cathedral, Tikhvin, signed by Father Ioann D'iakonov and parishioners, 1948. (ASPbE.)

For the time being, the historical argument failed to move the authorities so far as these two churches were concerned.[151] However, the only two churches opened in Leningrad after the War (the "Easter Loaf and Easter Pudding" Church, and the Church of the Smolensk Mother of God at the Smolenskoe Cemetery), were, or had been at some point, monuments of architecture.[152] Certainly, the petitions to open them had not played on this fact, and it is more likely that the devotional status of these churches was a factor in the campaigns, or indeed that locals in these outlying areas with poor public transport links hoped to avoid, in future, having to make complicated journeys for Sunday worship.[153] But it is not impossible that the authorities' decision to open these particular churches was at least in part prompted by their status as monuments. Both were in notably poor condition, and the task of finding another lessee would have been difficult. The 250th anniversary of Leningrad's founding fell in 1953, and getting at least the façades of the city's architectural monuments in good condition was a vital and elusive task. A parish would be easier to persuade than a secular lessee that this work was worth doing, since the threat of expulsion was considerably more real. Thus may have run the reasoning. Be that as it may, the Monuments Inspectorate's expectations of religious groups who were already in situ mounted sharply as the anniversary drew near.

"Restoration Must Begin Immediately": Preparing for the 250th Anniversary of Leningrad

On July 20, 1949, with just under four years to go until the anniversary (which was traditionally celebrated on May 27, or May 16 Old Style), Nikolai Belekhov, in his capacity as head of the Monuments Inspectorate, got in touch with the Leningrad Diocesan Works Committee. In order to reinforce the urgency and importance of his communication, he sent it by telegram:

> STATE INSPECTORATE PROTECTION MONUMENTS ARCHITECTURE LENINGRAD REQUIRES YOU WHEN CARRYING OUT RESTORATION WORKS IN PRINCE VLADIMIR CATHEDRAL TO EXECUTE RESTORATION AND GILDING OF ROOFTOP CROSSES[154]

It is easy to imagine the consternation that this announcement caused. In the 1920s and 1930s, the state had stripped ecclesiastical buildings of anything that was deemed valuable, and reduced them to a state where even minor repairs were often a budgetary nightmare. Now, crosses on the *outside* of the church were to be elaborately, and what is more expensively, restored. The metropolitan's response—whatever his respect for the status of listed monuments when it came to exercising leverage so that a church might be opened—was, understandably, to try and evade the order. In this he adopted the classic strategy of playing off one official body against another. Interestingly, in this particular situation, he decided that the weightiest ally would be the plenipotentiary on the affairs of the ROC, Aleksandr Kushnarev. The following month, Kushnarev replied, also by telegram: SUPPORT YOUR DECISION REFERENCE TO NONGILDING CROSSES WIRING BELIKHOV [*sic*] WITH NEGATIVE VIEW KUSHNAREV.[155]

Not to be outdone, a week later, Belekhov, ignoring Kushnarev, once more contacted the Diocesan Works Committee, and insisted that the works should be carried out, including the gilding of the crosses, "according to the agreement with the organizations whose names appear at the foot of this letter."[156] This tactical reminder of the terms of the contract had its due effect, prompting the cathedral's incumbent, two days later, to send a request to the Chancery of the Metropolitan for 195 books of twenty-two-carat gold leaf, "in connection with the demand of the State Inspectorate of Monuments that the cathedral should be gilded."[157] In the unusual circumstances of the late 1940s, heritage preservation could outmaneuver the state agencies in charge of religious affairs—something that had not been the case since the early 1920s.

Still, that was little comfort to Prince Vladimir's parishioners—indeed, rather the reverse. And the *dvadtsatki* of other churches were undergoing comparable travails. On July 18, 1945, for example, Nikolai Belekhov insisted that the Church Council of the Cathedral of the Transfiguration, then carrying out repairs to correct damp and damage caused by aerial bombardment, should take the opportunity also to do corrective work that was, in his view, necessary from an aesthetic perspective. "Given that the wooden internal porches [*tambura*] of the Cathedral of the Transfiguration are recent additions that distort the architectural image of the building as constructed by Stasov, the State Inspectorate for the Preservation of the Monuments of Leningrad informs you that they must be demolished in connection with the restoration works on the building of the Cathedral that are currently in progress."[158] With regard to the wall paintings—already the source of condescension in the 1920s—the preservationists were more accommodating, stating that because these were mostly in poor condition and multiply overpainted, repainting from scratch was permissible, except for the few surviving fragments of the original decoration.[159] The parishioners soon found themselves under added pressure, however, as GIOP, fired up by the approaching 250th anniversary, loaded them with a formidable program of works that had to be completed by the end of 1952, a year from the time the order was issued.

Even the clergy of the Cathedral of the Transfiguration, whose income from candles and the performance of rites such as funerals ran into many thousands of rubles, were forced to apply to the metropolitan for extra funding.[160] Under especial stress was the "Easter Loaf" Church, which, although a small parish church in an industrial region of the city, and far from the routes of ceremonial parades, was faced with a substantial, and costly, program of repairs. As Father Ioann Ptitsyn, the incumbent, reported to the metropolitan on May 9, 1949, the estimate for works inside and outside the church had come in at 162,000 rubles, to cover restoration of the interior and complete repainting of the façades and roofs.[161]

Sometimes *dvadtsatki* could count on gifts—for instance, in 1943, a woman parishioner of the Prince Vladimir Cathedral donated a collection of tsarist-era gold coins to the value of 1190 rubles.[162] But church records suggest that this was very much a one-off event. Church-monuments might be old and beautiful, but maintaining them placed an unusually high level of financial stress on congregations, which likely explains why, in rural areas, communities mostly housed themselves in churches of relatively recent date.[163]

"Getting Work Done [. . .] Is Starting to Be More and More Difficult": Managing Repairs in the Orthodox Parish

Church communities, as non-Soviet organizations, did not have access to the services of the Leningrad Restoration Workshops. They usually carried out works by what was known as "the in-house method" (*khoziaistvennyi sposob*)—that is, they hired workmen, commissioned the repairs and restoration required, and then submitted the results for the approval (or otherwise) of the Inspectorate. But this way of organizing things placed those doing repairs and restoration to "cultic buildings" in the category of "private entrepreneurs" (*chastniki*), who were liable for a special tax on the sums that they earned. Naturally, workmen expected that those commissioning the repairs would make good the difference between the normal rates of pay for building work and those they could earn when they had to pay the extra tax. As Metropolitan Grigorii reported to Patriarch Aleksii on February 5, 1952, this meant that "getting work done, especially in the churches that are under the control of the State Inspectorate for the Protection of Monuments, is starting to be more and more difficult." There were large numbers of requests for help from incumbent priests and parish councils, anxious that they might not be able to complete the work, or would do so much later than the deadlines imposed by GIOP. The regulations relating to taxation made it quite impossible to comply with the tight timing expected by the heritage preservation body. The only sensible solution, Metropolitan Grigorii concluded, was to relax the deadlines on the one hand, and to allow state organizations to work in churches, and tax the work at normal rates on the other.[164] But this type of decision was simply not within the remit of local officials, so Metropolitan Grigorii's arguments got nowhere.

The tax system was not the only cause of headaches for the clergy. Despite the embryonic reemergence of the Orthodox hierarchy, assigned greater powers after the 1943 concordat, the organizer of any building works was generally the church elder (*starosta*). Parish records indicate that this person usually had limited education, and was often without specialist competence in building, let alone elaborate and highly skilled restoration work.[165] Problems quickly cropped up with the repair work to the Easter Loaf Church, for example, as Father Ioann Ptitsyn reported to Metropolitan Grigorii on May 9, 1949. The church elder had a factory job and could not visit the church during working hours to do the essential supervision, and in any case exercised "no initiative at all." The elder was supposed to hire builders for the job and arrange the delivery of building materials, yet he simply had no time to do this. The result was that it had taken him four months even to agree with the hairdressers adjoining the site that water from their supply could be used while the works were going on. "If that is the tempo, one does wonder how on earth a large-scale renovation can possibly be completed in the current building season," Father Ioann concluded.[166].

Caught between the demands of organizing temporary labor, the intransigence of other organizations that did not wish to share "their" water and other resources (let alone with a pariah institution such as a church), and the most inflexible demands of all—those of the seasonal cycle (which made building possible only in the spring, summer, and early autumn), parish councils and incumbent priests carried significant loads of stress.

Matters were not helped by the fact that GIOP officials were extremely fastidious about the standards of finished work. In late October 1951, only eighteen months away from the all-important anniversary of the city's founding, the Executive Council of the St. Nicholas Cathedral ran into serious trouble as they tried to have the repair work they had been ordered to do cleared by the Inspectorate.

A long list of faults was adduced. The restoration of the artworks, certainly, was classed as "wholly satisfactory," but that was hardly a consolation, since almost everything else was severely criticized. For instance, the inspector observed, "The shade of the gloss paint does not match the shade of the soft distemper, and has not been agreed with representatives of the Inspectorate for the Protection of Monuments."[167] "Systematic non-compliance with the demands of the Inspectorate" was identified, and had to be set right without delay:

1. By the end of 1951 at the latest, restoration to the entranceway to the altar must be completed, and gilding with real gold carried out.
2. Work on the restoration of the art works in the iconostasis must begin without delay; the varnish has detached itself in many places.
   The eighteenth-century icons are at the point of disintegrating completely.

An open threat followed: "The Inspectorate for the Protection of Monuments considers that, if the Executive Organ of the Cathedral does not carry out the demands stipulated above, termination of the contract to use the buildings of the monument will be a distinct possibility, given that the user is not carrying out demands whose non-fulfillment will generate damage to a monument of architecture."[168]

The spectacle of the Monuments Inspectors insisting that religious groups regild church exteriors and interiors, or busy themselves scouring Leningrad for the right sort of distemper, has grotesque overtones. The Inspectors did not press for the replacement, let alone gilding, of iconostases and crosses on secularized churches. Yet it is hard to say whether they were necessarily tougher on "religious societies" than on other categories of lessee. Certainly, relations between GIOP and the restorers carrying out work for major state projects, such as the restoration of Leningrad's palaces, seem to have been characterized by warm understanding.[169] But this may be explained less by the always rather tense (and, from 1948, even less cordial) relations of state-church bodies, than by the fact that there was close professional camaraderie between the staff of the Restoration Workshops and the staff of GIOP.[170] The latter were extremely demanding when it came to relations with other non-professionals also, as the management of the Museum of the Arctic were to discover. Certainly, as a state institution, the Museum could count on the support of GIOP in obtaining materials to carry out its programs of restoration.[171] But the fact that the Museum was ensconced in the Soviet establishment did not stop inspectors insisting that repairs were completed as asked.[172]

Sometimes, the director of the Museum tried to answer back. On October 19, 1949, he attributed the continuing delays with restoration work to foot-dragging by the State Restoration Workshop:

> The contractor for the works is the Leningrad Architectural Restoration Workshop. And they are supposed to take responsibility for carrying out the works in time and to a satisfactory standard.
>
> It should be said that the works on this site have right from the beginning and up to the present dragged along very slowly—in an unregulated way [*samotekom*], without respect to the season of the year. In July and August, the painters were busy with the interiors of the former Sheremet'ev Palace, and in October they started on the façades of the Museum of the Arctic. It should all have been the other way round.
>
> The quality of the work being carried out is accordingly no surprise, and when it comes to it, GIOP is not paying sufficient attention to this either.[173]

The official lessee of the Coreligionists' Church was not in fact the Museum—a relatively puny institution—but the much more heavy-weight Institute of the Arctic, subordinated to the Directorate of Northern Sea Routes, a department of the Council of Ministers. Such connections with a Moscow-based institution (and one driving forward the exploitation of the Polar regions, much celebrated in Soviet propaganda), put the Institute way above the reach of any Lensovet department.[174] All the same, GIOP officials continued to chip away, invoking not just their jurisdiction over the building, but their authority over the surrounding "preservation zone." So, for instance, the Inspectorate insisted that a planned dog show could only go ahead if the lawn were left undamaged, and sent letters complaining that the entrance to the site was cluttered with firewood and the local residents were drying their laundry between the columns of the portico: "The drying of laundry on the porch or upon the stylobate of the former church is categorically forbidden."[175]

It is clear that the staff of GIOP did what they could to get repair work done at what they considered an acceptable standard, and generally to exercise influence over how buildings were treated, whoever the lessees happened to be. There was simply greater leverage over religious bodies, because the threat to evict them was real, and supported not just by monument protection legislation, but by the regulations relating to religious societies. In the case of major power brokers, though, GIOP could do no more than wait for a contract to run out and then attempt to lobby Lensovet against its renewal.[176]

There were other factors in play also. In the 1920s and 1930s, the heritage protection bodies had not in any sense favored religious bodies, but had at times exercised flexibility—unavoidably so, not just because of the straitened circumstances in which congregations existed, day to day, but because of the heritage protection bodies' own preoccupation with other problems, such as the threat to churches from demolition. Now that the Monuments Office did not have its energies taxed defending the status of monuments, it could concentrate fully on enforcing the rules relating to usage.[177] Evidently, officials such as Belekhov were inclined to hold the view that the revived Orthodox Church was an institution that could perfectly well afford to carry out repair work to the highest standards.[178] It just needed to be pushed—and, should that not work, coerced.

"That Dust Is So Thick You Can't Hardly Breathe": Parish Life in Postwar Leningrad

So far as their everyday existence went, working church-monuments were churches like all others, and their congregations too experienced the limited revival of parish life that took place after 1943. A ministerial decree of August 22, 1945, had granted to Orthodox communities certain juridical rights, including the manufacture and sale of religious goods to believers, the purchase of dwelling houses and means of transport, and the capacity to call on supplies of building materials from local soviets.[179] As the case in the Cathedral of the Transfiguration showed, overstretched *dvadtsatki* could now apply to the diocese for extra financial help, a possibility that had not existed in the past. The diocese even employed its own architect, who was able to help with organizing works in active churches.[180] It had its own works department, and if necessary, support could also be obtained from the works department of the Moscow Patriarchate.[181] Gone was the era when *dvadtsatki* had to petition unfriendly local soviets for "leftovers," and receive regular refusals. However, dealing with the Monuments Inspectorate had now become quite a lot trickier than in the past.

But the situation was not clear-cut. GIOP's inspectors did not always display relentless aesthetic or historical pedantry (or a sometimes contradictory combination of the two). A case where they did show some understanding was when the parishes of the Smolensk Mother of God Church and the Easter Loaf and Easter Pudding Church got the buildings ready to be used for worship again. Both had been completely "liquidated" in the 1930s, before being used by secular institutions. Their interior furnishings had ended up in a variety of museums and private collections, when they had not simply been destroyed. It might have been possible for the Inspectorate to insist on a full "scientific reconstruction" of the interiors, of the type carried out in the palaces around Leningrad. This would have required months of studying old photographs and architects' plans and drawings—assuming that any such survived. In fact, a quicker, though also demanding, method was agreed—the transfer of objects that were suitable in terms of date and style, irrespective of their origin. Thus, the Easter Pudding Church was furnished with icons and other devotional items in the collections of the St. Isaac's Cathedral Museum. This eminently practical (rather than "scientific") process of recycling was perpetuated in the following years: some of the items originally installed in the Easter Loaf and Easter Pudding Church were transferred to the Church of the Theological Academy when that opened in 1948, and some of those in turn to the Cathedral of the Transfiguration in Vyborg and to the Mother of God of Smolensk Church, and so on.[182]

This did not, of course, mean that church officials could do what they liked with movable property. Every item had to be docketed and its transfer agreed. In particular, the incumbent priest of a given church was personally responsible for the safety of property assigned to the parish, and had to keep strict track of its location and condition (when some icons and church vessels were found to have disappeared from the Easter Loaf and Easter Pudding Church, the result was a prolonged and nasty row).[183]

As well as problems with GIOP, parish councils had other difficulties on their hands. Foremost among these were, as in the past, the relations with the bodies directly charged with regulating church affairs. The Council of Religious Affairs and Council on the Affairs of the Russian Orthodox Church, as effective branches of the security services, required tight surveillance of religious communities in the pursuit of possible deviance. In 1948, for example, the Leningrad plenipotentiaries were instructed to prepare for the issuing of internal passports (identity cards) to "the servants of cults" by supplying the names of individuals whose right to reside in Leningrad should be terminated to the central councils for approval, and then to the local police.[184] But plenipotentiaries were not—unlike the employees of the Church Offices in the 1920s and 1930s—under specific instructions to make life difficult for religious communities and to precipitate their departure from "cultic buildings." Nor did they invariably take this role upon themselves. Indeed, they were sometimes the targets of accusations from the Party and local authorities of being too close to church officials, and not doing enough to enforce the regulations.[185] The small number of churches opened demonstrates Aleksandr Kushnarev's cautious attitude in areas that were of primary interest to the Party hierarchy. But when regulating existing communities, his attitudes were rather different. The case where he stepped in to support the metropolitan by arguing that it really was not reasonable to require gilding of the St. Nicholas Cathedral's crosses is an interesting example of contact with the plenipotentiary that was, from the ROC's point of view, positive. In terms of their duties, the plenipotentiaries trod a wavering line, anxious not to allow religious communities to cause trouble, but also not to cause too much trouble to them.[186]

Indeed, officials were sometimes more temperate than ordinary members of the public when it came to the day-to-day lives of church communities. The latter could at times be as intolerant as any paid-up members of the late lamented League of the Militant Godless.[187] On August 22, 1945, the Council of Ministers of the USSR passed a resolution determining "to place no obstruction before the ringing of church bells by church communities, provided they use bells already in their possession."[188] However, in 1951, the neighbors of the Cathedral of the Transfiguration in Leningrad wrote to complain about the "round-the-clock ringing of church bells," though, as the incumbent priest explained, the bells were rung "only in the morning and the evening at unavoidable times before and during a service, and the bell ringer is also instructed to ring them for the minimum possible time." It turned out to be the Cathedral's clock, recently restored by order of GIOP, which was causing the trouble.[189] If this was in the area of farce, then a case where a man ran into the Cathedral and broke the glass on two icons, including the precious seventeenth-century Savior Not Made by Human Hands, painted by Simon Ushakov, threatened much more serious unpleasantness. What to the parishioners was sacrilege was potentially, to the secular authorities, failure on the part of the "religious association" itself to ensure the due safety of the movable property in its care.[190] In 1949, teenagers who claimed to be "hunting pigeons" in the grounds of the St. Nicholas Cathedral caused serious trouble for the church's watchmen, threatening them with razors and, on one occasion, beating them up.[191]

Relations with the unpredictable collections of sometimes marginal and obsessive individuals who made up the congregations of churches were not easy either.[192] In 1952, a self-described "group of worshippers" at the Prince Vladimir Cathedral wrote to the metropolitan to complain that the repair work was interfering with their devotions.

> Our dear arch-pastor Vladimir [sic] When you see the awful things that are going on in the Prince Vladimir Cathedral, it's enough to wear out your patience

completely. It's been four months now that the repair work to the church has been going on and every day there's more muck, which by the way no one makes any effort to clean up. At ten in the morning the late service starts and . . . at that very moment, at ten in the morning, the workmen arrive and banging and crashing like you can't hardly imagine starts up, and exactly during the "Cherubim" and "We Sing to Thee" that banging and crashing gets even louder . . . And as well as all those, ehem, "delights," just when the singing is going on they have to scrape down the bits of plaster what've been chipped off the walls of the church. And that Dust is so Thick that you can't hardly breathe, not to speak of you can't hear the priest nor the deacons nor the choir neither, and as we see it this is sacrilege and desecration of the church. And what bugs you more than anything else is that round about noon or one in the afternoon, all that banging and crashing and somehow the workman manage to go on without it . . . It's just disgusting. And then in the evening once the service starts again what do you get? More of that banging and crashing. And you don't feel in the least like praying . . . and it pains a believer to see how the administration of the Church loses all sense of the holy in this Holy church. We think you could stop Banging during the Mass and not kick up no dust neither.

The petitioners continued that they had talked about this to the administration of the church, but had been told to mind their own business; the incumbent priest was only in church once a week, "and they say he's afraid to tell the Elder anything." They repeated their urging that the "disgrace" should come to an end.[193] The incumbent disputed the facts of the case, commenting that a section of the parishioners had been out to discredit him since another priest employed in the cathedral had been arrested.[194] Whatever the truth, the incident vividly illustrated not just the fragility of social relations in the micro-world of the working church, but how the demands of architectural conservation could push them to breaking point.

"Much of the Church Was Taken Away Brick by Brick": Parishes in Rural Areas

With very limited information about which churches might be monuments in villages themselves, and conversely (in the province's Architectural Department) about where monuments were actually located, the life of parishes in the countryside was very different from that in towns. Contact with the heritage preservation bodies was extremely rare—indeed, contact with the authorities of any kind was spasmodic. Congregations were largely left to their own devices. Whether monuments or not, working churches had a much better chance of survival than those which were not in use. An example was the wooden Church of the Resurrection at Kurpovo, nearly three hundred kilometers northeast of Leningrad, on the borders of Karelia.

The church, originally built in the seventeenth century as a "tent-roofed" structure with a tall tapering tower, had been remodeled in the early nineteenth century with a rustic neoclassical façade and dome. Had it stood in Leningrad, this kind of drastic reconstruction might have spelled inferiority, but the Architectural Department of Leningrad Province seems not to have hesitated about whether it should be listed, as it uniformly was from the late 1940s. However, not everyone locally (including some of the incumbent priests) was aware of this fact, and its survival was primarily down to action by the district's Orthodox congregation.[195]

The Church of the Resurrection had been closed during the war (when Kurpovo stood near to the front line). However, in 1946, one Mariia Shkurnikova organized a petition for its reopening. Perhaps Shkurnikova herself had looked after the church when it was closed (next to the building was a small dwelling for a custodian).[196] Certainly, Shkurnikova reported it in 1946 to be in good condition:

> No special repairs are necessary the outside is in good condition all the domes have crosses on there's a good tin roof on it too. Inside the church the iconostases in the right side chapel are in place with the heavenly gates [sic] there's lots of different books in the church and its good and clean inside the doors are all in order. The window frames and the metal grilles are in good order. It just needs glass in the windows and no more repairs at all and also all the fittings and vessels for the three altars and vestments. Because the church doesn't have [illegible: presumably, an antimins], though, you can only celebrate the Minor service.[197]

Shkurnikova's representations were successful, and the Church of the Resurrection reopened again for worship on April 10, 1947.

The Church of the Resurrection became the only working church in the whole of Podporozh'e district, which would certainly have cemented the case for its reopening. It probably helped also that it was in a relatively accessible part of the province, only a few kilometers from the railway junction of Vazhiny, on the main line between Petrozavodsk and Leningrad. Certainly, the closeness of the railway meant that church officials were able to visit, and it seems to have been left to them to monitor the condition of the place. There is no evidence from the files of the Architectural Department that anyone from there actually made the six- or seven-hour journey to reach the locality.[198]

The comments of church officials give a good idea of conditions in rural parishes in the postwar years. Father Aleksii Verzin, dean of New Ladoga district, noted during his tour of inspection in late November 1951 that the spiritual side of parish life was not very energetic, as could be gauged from the fact that a dragée box was serving as a container for the consecrated bread. Congregations were small, especially in the winter, and the number of rites very low—not one wedding in the past year, for instance; only a few parishioners joined in the singing during mass. He also noted the condition of the architecture and furnishings:

> This sixteenth-century [*sic*] church represents an architectural monument under the protection of the state. The church has been well preserved and does not require extensive repairs. The roof and walls could do with being painted; the roof in particular should be painted without delay. The façade of the church has been damaged, particularly the cornice and moldings, but these faults are not particularly serious and will be easily fixed.

The "old iconostasis decorated with carving" inside the church had traces of damp "that appeared when restoration of the Church was in progress," and "needs to be skillfully restored by a highly qualified artist-restorer." Kurpovo's summer church (the inner hall of the main building) had become a kind of museum of closed churches, with the icons from the demolished church in Vazhiny removed there, though they, like the icons in the Kurpovo winter church (its outer hall), were of relatively recent date, and therefore of less historical interest.[199]

Desultory as the parish life in Kurpovo might have seemed, the church was in fact unusually well funded, with offerings and takings from candle sales having risen over 130 percent in the last year. The church was a draw for worshippers from all over the district, "despite the difficulties of transport to it."[200] However, so the visiting dean felt, the incumbent priest was more concerned with raising funds than with taking care of the good order (*blagolepie*) of the church, and had done nothing about arranging repair works with the Diocesan Works Department even when he had been visiting the Chancery.[201] He was in due course replaced, but his successor was reported to be still more slovenly. Not till 1954 was the church properly in hand.[202]

But as the case of Kurpovo also shows, parish priests' deficiencies in maintaining churches had some chance of being corrected by the church hierarchy. With the secular authorities, things were more complicated. Site visits by monuments protection officials are not recorded even after the church reopened (evidently, the assiduous on-paper requests for reports were meant to replace them). The secular officials regulating church affairs were only slightly more mobile. In October 1951, Plenipotentiary Kushnarev got as far as Tikhvin (one of the province's most accessible church sites), and visited the Cathedral of the Dormition, the town's most important church from an architectural as well as a spiritual point of view. However, he refused the offer of the senior local priest, Father Ioann D'iakonov, to accompany him to the cathedral: "If people see that, they'll all start chattering about the cathedral, and that's not a good idea." Whether out of discretion, overload, pomposity, or indolence, he otherwise mostly expected business to be conducted by local representatives journeying to Leningrad in order to see him.[203] The fact that Kushnarev was not personally responsible for the condition of churches meant that he concerned himself little about this.

The overall result of geographical and cultural distance was to make country churches extremely vulnerable to fire, theft, and the recycling of their building materials for other construction work. A picture of the likely processes of decay was given by the incumbent priest of the St. John the Baptist Church in Poddub'e when he reported to the Chancery of the Metropolitan in 1949. This "magnificent stone church," built in 1772 "with the financial support and by the efforts of Privy Councillor Nepliuev," had a particularly picturesque situation on the Moglinka River, surrounded by "century-old willows."[204] Its gilded dome "shone for a long distance around." However, the war years had seen its condition precipitately decline: "After the enemy attacked and the locality was taken and retaken by the different sides, strikes by the heavy and siege artillery riddled the dome, the roof, and even parts of the walls." When the conflict ended, other dangers had made themselves felt:

> Exhausted and emaciated [*izmorennye*] people emerge from the forests and the trenches. They collect all kinds of debris from the ruins and all of them start to stock up with what they need there.

The building starts. But materials are terribly short, especially brick. And over there is a half-ruined church, forgotten by everyone. Brick is scattered all around it. Everyone who needs brick rushes to the church to get some.

Thus, much of the church was taken away brick by brick, and some of the "Orthodox faithful" even had the gall to begin breaking up perfectly sound parts of the walls that remained.

The church floor, in line with an order made by the Plenipotentiary on the Affairs of the Orthodox church in Leningrad Province, Al. Iv. KUSHNAREV, has been reused to pave the floors and ceilings of the new presbytery [*tserkovnyi dom*].[205]

Reports about damage to vacant buildings could only consolidate the practice of removing furnishings from closed churches and passing them to churches that were being used. The scavenging of materials from inside was in turn bound to exacerbate the process of predation on the exterior. As this report suggests, accommodation for the clergy was a pressing problem. By the terms of the April 8, 1929, decree, they were forbidden to reside in church buildings, so any working church had to have accommodation provided. An unused church was an obvious, safe place where building materials might be obtained, so "recycling" of bricks and so on was likely a common strategy.

Given the difficulty with protection from hundreds of kilometers away, the only real salvation for village churches lay in the presence of some member of the local population who was prepared to take an interest. As a professional restorer with extensive experience of work in the Soviet period recalled in 2008, it was this kind of informal care that made the difference to whether architectural monuments survived or not, rather than their legal status:

Inf.: There was an enormous—let me repeat that—enormous band of wardens. That is, in essence every monument, especially in a village somewhere, if it is under state protection, was supposed to have a warden. As you understand, a warden, well . . . having someone like that doesn't mean that nothing will happen to the building. But there was a . . . a kind of sense of responsibility. That person would at the very least keep hold of the keys. You'd arrive, and if you've got the right bit of paper, he'll open the church for you and so on.

Int.: So it was usually an elderly man living somewhere locally?

Inf.: Yes. Or . . . yes. Or an old woman. An elderly woman [. . .] And that system of wardens, as I see it, well, it may not be the most important thing about the protection of monuments, but it is [important], particularly if the building's got no owner, I mean isn't being used.[206]

This former restorer went on to cite the most famous example of such an informal warden—Valentin Ivanovich V'iushkin, who expended extraordinary efforts on watching over the Church of the Nativity of the Virgin in Ferapontov Convent, so that one of the most important cycles of late medieval wall paintings survived in relatively complete condition.[207]

But it would be unwise to romanticize this situation. The village population itself was under pressure. The forced collectivization and large-scale repressions of the 1930s might be at an end, but miserable pay, huge taxes, and high levels of migration to the cities all took their toll.[208] The Architectural Department's concern for demolished buildings pointed not just to its officials' own custodial priorities, but to the instability of values in rural parts. The upsurge in religious practice did not always help, since it might bring new building (as in the case of the presbytery in Poddub'e), rather than concern for old churches.

In any case, the Stalin years saw a widespread "privatization" of worship, the emergence of a tenacious popular Orthodoxy that existed as part of, but also alongside, the official church. Church closures fostered the rise of the so-called "catacomb church," existing in private houses, and the widening participation of the laity as carriers of religious faith and ritual. Yet the opening of churches in the late 1940s did nothing to hinder this process, since the numbers opened were way short of demand.[209] In this overall context, church goods might be saved from destruction, but then become the "property" of the person who had rescued them, as a report by Father Konstantin Volkovskii, the incumbent priest of the Church of the Resurrection in Petrovskaya Gorka, recorded:

Close to our church, three kilometers away, in the village of Iustitsy there is a closed and half-collapsed church that has recently been used as a barn for winnowing corn and such. In this Church are preserved many beautiful and precious icons, which at present are covered in a thick layer of dust and cobwebs.

What is more, in the home of collective farm worker Pelageia Petrovna NIKOLAEVA, there in the attic are piled up a large quantity of church vessels and a whole cycle of service books. All this is stored in extremely insanitary conditions: covered in mold, dust, and rot, eaten by moths and mice, and in the not too distant future, it will only be fit for throwing away.

All this property is in the keeping of the former nun Aleksandra Vladimirovna KUZNETSOVA, on the grounds that she allegedly hid it and saved it from being snatched away.

According to Father Konstantin, Iustitsy church was in fact a dependency of his own, and Kuznetsova lived in another village altogether. But Kuznetsova, asked to allow the parishioners in Petrovskaya Gorka to use the icons, vessels, vestments, and books, had remained obdurate, "in the hope that her own Church may be opened, and she even said, 'better may it all rot, than I give it up to some other Church.'"[210]

In the priest's eyes, the project of reopening a "half-destroyed" church was beyond the bounds of practicality; for Kuznetsova, it was only "her own" church that counted as a sacred building. While "the Church" in the spiritual sense was often resilient, its outward tokens—church buildings and their contents—were, for all sorts of reasons, fragile; so, too, might be the sense of universal, as opposed to localized, religious community.

● ● ●

The outbreak of what soon came to be known as the "Patriotic War" had a significant impact on the position both of religious believers and of their churches.[211] Mass destruction of churches in order to create new spaces in the socialist city ceased, and the concordat between Party leadership and ROC hierarchy generated a new attitude to the use of churches for worship. At the same time, there was no commitment—much to believers' disappointment—to mass change of use for what were still known officially as "former churches." Those in which state institutions were ensconced tended to remain with their established lessees, unless they were mistreating the buildings so badly that the new legislation of 1947 was used as the basis for eviction. Whatever the eloquence of church groups' citation of national history and the role of church buildings in this, such arguments did not work on their own, though it appears that, in Leningrad, the consideration that religious communities were likely to be a reliable kind of user for registered monuments did carry some weight, given that the only two churches ceded for worship came into that category.

As for the day-to-day use of historic buildings, whether in city or in countryside, aggressive assaults with the purpose of demolition had become relatively rare (though far from unknown). But active restoration was even less common. Low-key work was done to some major buildings (such as St. Isaac's and the Trinity-Izmailovskii Regiment Cathedrals), but some others (for instance, the Trinity Cathedral in the Alexander Nevsky Lavra) were left untouched.[212] The fact that religious communities were denied access to state funding and the services of the Restoration Workshops did not stop preservation officials taking a tough line in terms of the expected standards, and demanding a commitment to elaborate and expensive repairs.

In short, the relations between those seeking to preserve churches and those seeking to use them for their original purpose had not been reformed so much as adjusted. And while the preservation of "live" spirituality without access to an official church building was widespread, this did not necessarily unify the scattered church communities among themselves, let alone give them a strong sense of identification with the religious hierarchy. The enhanced role of the laity in keeping religious practices going and stopping precious objects from being destroyed was not always compatible with a docile attitude toward ecclesiastical officialdom. Still, in retrospect, the immediate interwar years were to come to seem a period of relative benevolence; just a few years later, the social difficulties of church users were to sharpen markedly once more.

CHAPTER FIVE

The Scientific Assault on God

Church-Monuments in the Khrushchev Era,
1953–1964

ON MAY 4, 1953, Father Ioann D'iakonov, the parish priest in Tikhvin, wrote to Metropolitan Grigorii to report, in his sonorous church Russian, the momentous events of the last two months:

> With deep sorrow has echoed within the hearts of the faithful of Tikhvin the unexpected demise of the great Leader of the Soviet Union, J. V. Stalin. On March 7 during Vespers was read aloud a telegram received from His Eminence the Lord Metropolitan Grigorii. The Lord Metropolitan's telegram made a deep impression upon the faithful. Tears of sorrow and of love for the great Leader stood in everyone's eyes. I announced then that on Sunday, March 8 would be celebrated a universal service of remembrance for J. V. Stalin. Immediately before this service, I once again read out the telegram, and then said a few words of my own. One could feel that the same thoughts were in everyone's hearts: we had lost the dearest, most beloved, the closest of persons. Going by the number of candles that were handed out at the service of remembrance, more than a thousand worshippers took part. They could not all fit into the church.[1]

At the time, the entire population of Tikhvin comprised perhaps 10,000 people; something approaching a quarter of the adult population must have flocked to that church.

Believers' devotion to the former leader seems, retrospectively, misguided, given the appalling harassment they had suffered between 1929 and 1941. However, the declaration of the right to freedom of worship in the 1936 Constitution and the 1943 concordat represented two rare points of remission in the otherwise relentless history of assault on religious worship under Soviet power. Now, with their powerful patron (as they saw him) dead, believers were again in a world of uncertainty.[2]

Their anxieties were well placed. Stalin's successors had their formative experience in the post-revolutionary years, and were wholly shaped by the ideology of the new state. Nikita Khrushchev, who by 1954 had emerged as victor in the tussle for power that succeeded Stalin's death—an event to which the Party elite had long looked forward—soon proved to be both a radical modernizer and an idealist preoccupied with keeping alive the flame of Communism. His championing of early Soviet culture, Leninism, and the ideals of the "Old Communists" was partly strategic: once the Stalin years had been condemned as the era of the "cult of personality," it was essential to recuperate part of the Soviet past and show this in a positive light. But it also stemmed from personal taste. A populist of a demagogic coloration who wanted to create better conditions in this world, and had no time for metaphysics, Khrushchev saw "scientific atheism" as an essential part of rational modernity.[3]

"Their Alcoholic Binge of Religious Ecstasy": Antireligious Campaigning, 1954–1964

As early as July 1954 a shot came across the bows of organized religion, as a decree on propaganda for atheism harshly criticized the current state of antireligious education and the spirit of passivity in which the practice of faith was now regarded.[4] A few months later, a second decree criticized "isolated cases" of offensive behavior to religious people, and stressed the need to perpetuate "militant materialism" with the resources of Soviet socialization.[5] This signaled a switch, for the time being, to an emphasis on scientific propaganda.[6] However, four years later—by which time Khrushchev was securely ensconced as leader—came a further spike in antireligious activity.[7] A report by the Central Committee circulated on September 12, 1958, pointed to a rise in the visibility and social leverage of religious groups—as manifested by rising numbers of priests, increasing levels of income, and growing demands for the opening of churches. It identified attendance at religious services and the regular performance of the occasional offices, such as christenings, in people's homes, as ways of sucking them into cultic practices. Even Communists were known to become involved in such activities, something quite impermissible. The best path to overcoming these undesirable phenomena lay not in "crude administrative bullying" (which would simply encourage the believers), but in "educational work," in greater vigilance by the Soviet media, and in the production of a specialist literature, spearheaded by the new journal, *Science and Religion*.[8] Three weeks later, on October 4, 1958, the Central Committee initiated an all-out antireligious campaign at every level of Soviet society.[9]

Both the report and the October 4, 1958, decree were secret, but the change in the public atmosphere was impossible to overlook. Vulgar rhetoric of a sort unheard since 1941 began being used.[10] For example, an article by Lev Khalif published in *Literature and Life* on February 21, 1960, evoked a dreadful scene of backwardness in a major Soviet city:

> From the wide-open doors of the ancient cathedral resound the bass voices of the protodeacons, drowning out the piping descants of the elderly ladies as they wallow in their alcoholic binge of religious ecstasy. All mixed up with the smoky odor of incense and candles, the gyrating of the cripples and the holy fools crammed onto the steps of the cathedral, and finally, the arrival of the deacon himself, the kissing of the hem of his cloak.
>
> What century is this? Where is all this happening? Slap bang in the center of Perm', in our times, right now.[11]

Scorn was poured on the benighted stupidity of belief; religious education warped minds and distorted perceptions. As in the 1920s, a standard device was to ridicule metaphysics through literalism. After Yuri Gagarin's first space flight in 1961, the fact that he had not seen God in the cosmos was cited as a clinching argument.[12]

The Soviet conquest of the cosmos was not just a metaphysical battle, a drive to assert the values of science and enlightenment in the face of obscurantism.[13] It also had direct social resonance. In contrast with the youth and health of Soviet heroes such as Gagarin, "cultic servants" were represented as self-serving charlatans, embezzling the donations of the faithful. You had to be a pathetic loser, someone irretrievably backward, to be deceived.[14] Atheist propaganda was especially fervent among young people, with the Komsomol taking a leading part in the campaign to stigmatize religion as a negative manifestation of the reactionary

FIGURE 22. The miserable heroine of Oleg Shestinskii's story "Spiders on the Mallows" (E. Astmanov, published in Science and Religion, 1960.)

past.[15] Believers, in *Science and Religion*, were always represented as wretched. Young people were at the mercy of their parents, who forced them into the old ways.

Coercion was added to persuasion. Certainly, the situation had to be handled properly, instructional materials advised. Once more criticizing, in a secret report of 1959, cases of "crude administrative bullying," the chairman of the Council on the Affairs of the ROC insisted, "*The clergy must not only not know about our intentions, but must not have even the faintest suspicion of them*" (emphasis original).[16] The solution was, as in 1926–1927 and 1936–1938, to precipitate church closures by exploitation of "the regulations." For example, a church might be closed down because it was said to be overcrowded or unsafe in terms of fire, or both.[17] Pressure was also placed on the clergy. The mass repressions of the 1930s were not revived, but there was recourse to both legal and administrative harassment. Plenipotentiaries dragged their feet about agreeing new appointments to empty churches, and orchestrated arrests of priests for alleged criminal offenses, such as sexual relationships with minors.[18] An instruction issued by the Council on the Affairs of the ROC in 1960 advised that "carefully thought-out pretexts" be used to disrupt the appointment of clergy; believers should simply be given to understand that no new openings of churches would be allowed.[19] Similar was a "plan of initiatives" for 1962:

> The Council [on the Affairs of the Russian Orthodox Church] will continue to search out and employ, within the boundaries of current legislation, tactical methods of overcoming religious superstitions and curbing the activities of the Church, of weakening its material base and of fostering the exodus of believers from religious faith.

The text went on to add, "so far as may be consonant with laws on the freedom of religious worship," but the general orientation was clear.[20] Among anticipated measures was, for instance, the development of "methods of reducing income from the sale of candles, wafers, and the performance of religious services and rituals." Also envisaged was the "rationalization of the network of religious institutions," and in particular, "the reduction of the network of churches as believers start to abandon religion."[21] The conjunction "as" (rather than "after") accurately suggested that the closures were supposed to be preemptive.

Alongside making use of administrative regulations relating to health and safety and other supposedly non-ideological areas of social control, the officials responsible for church-state relations were expected to apply specialist legislation with severity—and particularly the April 8, 1929, Decree on Religious Organizations, a new redaction of which was produced in 1962. Some of the alterations simply reflected the changed social situation (for example, the names of the bureaucracies responsible for registration had been altered), but others conveyed more significant changes. For example, clause 37 (which had allowed believers the right to petition the Central Executive Committee when a "cultic building" was scheduled for closure) was deleted, and clause 43 rewritten to specify "breaches of the legislation on cults" as grounds for the deregistration of a religious group.[22] The burden of these changes was, obviously, to facilitate the "liquidation" of "cultic buildings," large numbers of which were indeed shut down both before and after the modifications were made. Between 1959 and 1965, more than 6,000 churches, approaching 50 percent of the entire figure of working churches across the Soviet Union, were closed for worship.[23] From petitioning to expand provision for worship, believers had to swap their energies to the defense of churches that were already open.

Swept Away on the Tides of Modernity: The Crisis of Architectural Preservation

The commitment to radical modernization at all costs had its effects on attitudes to historic buildings also. The Decree on Architectural Excesses of 1955 imposed new ideals of strictly functionalist and above all economical architecture; the *tipovoi proekt*, or pattern-built block, was the model for the future. The devotion to "past masters" that had characterized the Stalin years had fallen by the wayside. Certainly, the use of mechanized construction, such as systems building, had been entrenched for a decade in Soviet practice.[24] But mechanization was now adopted on a totally different scale, and there was no longer any attempt to mask reinforced ferroconcrete and plain brick with curlicues on the façade, pillars, balustrades, and other decorative flourishes, or even plain stucco.[25] The shift in taste was partly cost-saving, but it was also allied to a commitment to egalitarianism and rational collectivism that consciously harked back to the 1920s.[26] Nineteen fifty-seven saw the start of an all-out building boom that outstripped even the construction drives of the early 1930s and the postwar years, and with it, of land hunger on citywide scale. Entire areas were redeveloped, and buildings that got in the way were summarily cleared. The most famous example was the new district of Novye Cheremushki, built on territory clawed into Moscow from its rural outskirts, which became a model for intensively developed high-rise "micro-districts" across the entire country.[27] Such districts were, by intention, homogeneous, and if buildings of an earlier date happened to be located on the territory, they were demolished, or at most left as a momentary pause in the flow.[28]

A new decree, "On the Further Improvement of the Protection and Restoration of Monuments," passed on August 30, 1960, worked, despite its title, to weaken the status of monuments as conferred by the laws of 1947 and 1948. It instituted a route for demolitions, which—though they had to be approved by the Council of Ministers of the RSFSR (in the case of monuments of state significance) and the Ministry of Culture of the RSFSR (in the case of monuments of local significance) were now, in theory, permitted.[29] If the May 22, 1947, decree had referred to the "inviolability" of Old Russian monuments, these might now, given the appropriate political will, be duly violated.

That such will was likely to be forthcoming was suggested by Khrushchev's own attitudes. In his push to "catch up and overtake America," the leader had no time for historical pieties. As the Yaroslavl local historian M. G. Meierovich remembered, when Khrushchev was being shown the Castle of Trakai, "where the Lithuanian grand dukes lived in the thirteenth and fourteenth centuries, one of the most important medieval monuments in Eastern Europe," the leader became indignant. So much money essential to the economy being spent on pointless projects:

> Khrushchev's intervention became the signal for an all-out campaign against monument preservation. *Sovetskaia kul'tura* newspaper, for instance, announced that a big project to creatively restore the Astrakhan kremlin, a unique monument of defensive architecture, was "no use to anyone." The bosses in Yaroslavl didn't want to lag behind: they set up a special commission to limit the number of monuments under state care. [...]
>
> I remember the row over the Church of St. Peter and St. Paul in the Krasnoperekopskii district, near the Sixteenth Party Congress Club. The Church had been built in 1736 by I. M. Zatrapezovskii, the founder of the Yaroslavl Greater Manufactory. The only baroque church in the entire city, it closely resembles the Cathedral of Saints Peter and Paul in Petersburg. The 70-meter-high spire of its belfry holds the whole area beyond the Kotorosl' River together. "If that church weren't under government protection," I said, "then the spire could have been condemned as 'beyond repair' when the church was restored recently, and completely pulled down." In fact, the church was one of the few monuments [nominated for delisting] that we actually did manage to save.[30]

It was not just the provinces where this radical attitude held sway. As in the late 1920s and 1930s, Moscow set the tone for the entire country. One flagship project was the Palace of Congresses in the Kremlin, an abrasive exercise in functionalism deliberately intended to sound an alien note amidst the medieval towers and church domes of the historic citadel.[31] Another was the creation of prospekt Kalinina (Novyi Arbat) in Moscow, with its streamlined shop frontages and mid-rise towers, which effaced a corner of the city well loved for its graceful dilapidation and intellectual links.[32]

If all old buildings were threatened by the modernizing tides, churches were particularly likely to be swept away. They were not just useless; they stood for the backward values that were being targeted by radical atheism. Not surprisingly, churches were prominent among the buildings summarily demolished. Among the major ecclesiastical buildings reduced to rubble were the seventeenth-century churches of St. Paraskeva and St. Cyril and St. John the Evangelist in Vologda, the St. Mitrofan Monastery and Trinity and Smolensk Mother of God Cathedral in

Voronezh, the eighteenth-century Coreligionist Church of the Dormition in Tver', and the Church of St. John the Evangelist in Pereslavl'-Zalesskii, also dating from the end of the eighteenth century.[33]

Demolition on this scale had not been seen since 1941. The difference, however, was Khrushchev's commitment to relatively open debate about the social changes that were pushed through. The new, ruthless, attitude to the cultural landscape attracted prominent critics. On August 23, 1956, the flagship newspaper *Literary Gazette* published an open letter from writers, architects, artists, and historians under the title "In Defense of Monuments of Culture."[34] It referred to widespread "indignation" as "wonderful monuments perish." In an effort to employ the leverage granted by Khrushchev's denunciation of the "cult of personality" the same year, the letter described the attitudes to monuments as reminiscent of the Stalinist past. The opening paragraph invoked, in particular, the demolition of a cathedral:

> On the second of June this year, in the town of Ufa, the thunderous noise of an explosion rang out. Before the very eyes of astonished locals, a unique monument of history and architecture—the Cathedral of the Mother of God of Smolensk—collapsed into a heap of rubble. Despite protests from the Academy of Sciences of the USSR and from the Ministry of Culture, and despite the blatant absence of the special government permission that is required, it had been summarily destroyed.

Instances where churches were simply falling down out of neglect were also recounted:

> In spring 1954, in the St. Paphnutius Monastery in Borovsk [...], a wonderful architectural monument dating from the sixteenth century, the vaulting of the cathedral collapsed and buried the discarded remains of farm equipment that a labor reserve college was keeping there. [...] Not far from Moscow is located the Monastery of St. Joseph of Volokolamsk, an amazing monument from the start of the sixteenth century [...] it, too, is visibly disintegrating. [...] The seventeenth-century Church of St. John the Baptist in the Tolchkovskaia Settlement, Yaroslavl, is famous far beyond Russia as one of the exemplary buildings of its time. But its superb frescos are in the process of perishing.

While secular buildings too were mentioned, it was above all ecclesiastical structures on which the letter-writers focused.

The lobbying did not produce concessions in terms of a program of salvation for old churches. But debate was not shut down either. Just under a year later, on July 29, 1957, a decree of the Council of Ministers of the RSFSR sought to draw local museums into the work of "strict control over the protection of monuments of culture." They were tasked with "the popularization of and dissemination of propaganda about" heritage preservation.[35] Emboldened by the encouragement of discussion, in 1959, the secretary of the Union of Architects dispatched a letter to the Central Committee in which he proposed the founding of a nationwide society for the protection of monuments.[36] In early 1960, two articles in *Literature and Life* also lobbied hard for heritage preservation. On February 21, Iurii Chaplygin lamented the neglect and destruction of monuments in Kostroma and other Russian provincial towns, focusing once more on ecclesiastical architecture.[37] Three weeks later, on March 11, appeared an article by Dmitrii Likhachev taking up the theme, and once more pressing for a nationwide society to protect historic architecture.[38] Under the modest rubric "reader's letter," the publication was one of the first public steps in Likhachev's remarkable history as an advocate for heritage preservation.[39]

Behind the scenes, in the editorial office of *Literature and Life*, a major row had taken place about whether the emphasis on ecclesiastical heritage was in line with the commitment to scientific atheism. The cognitive dissonance of the times was underlined by the fact that Chaplygin's article appeared in the very same number, and on the same page, as Khalif's article calling for the closure of the Perm' monastery.[40] For the meantime, the Party leadership considered the proposal to create a monuments preservation society, in the set phrase of Soviet bureaucratese, "not timely."[41] But the August 22, 1960, decree spoke in its article 1 of the need to "involve the public at a broad level in this work, which has great significance in the inculcation of the laboring people, and especially Soviet youth, of feelings of deep respect for the historical past of our people and love of the Motherland."[42]

Dancing to the tune the piper had set, the Soviet media began to publish further articles about the preservation of heritage. A particularly important one appeared in *Novyi Mir*'s issue for November 1962 (the same number as Aleksandr Solzhenitsyn's epoch-making story, *A Day in the Life of Ivan Denisovich*). The writer Viktor Nekrasov, whose participation in the 1959 campaign to erect a memorial to the Holocaust victims of Babyi Iar had made him a central figure in public debates of the day, unfavorably contrasted the deep respect for heritage he had noticed in a recent visit to Italy with the attitude to monuments in the USSR. Like the authors of the 1956 open letter to *Literary Gazette*, Nekrasov condemned neglect of monuments as a throwback to the Stalinist past (though without mentioning the former leader's name): "The lack of respect for the historical and cultural values of the past that made itself felt in the early 1930s caused great (and in some cases irreparable) damage to monuments of culture." He also paid tribute to the "pure" Communist doctrine of an earlier period, recalling "with what rapt and constant attention Vladimir Ilyich Lenin used to keep watch over the preservation of cultural values." This decidedly partial recollection of the Bolshevik figurehead and his era was to become a trope in the preservationist texts of the time.

In Nekrasov's text, ecclesiastical buildings once again exemplified what was going wrong:

> As I left San Giminagno, bade my farewell to its towers, which I will probably never see again, an involuntary thought of my native Kiev entered my mind. As you approach the city these days over the railway bridge and delight in its silhouette, you take involuntary delight in the gleam of the domes of the restored Lavra, the sight of scaffolding on the Vydubichi Monastery. The Cathedral of St. Sophia has also been rejuvenated by the meticulous work of the restorers. But if you stand with your back to the Cathedral, over the other side of the square you see some singularly unimpressive fences and roofs. That is where the St. Michael Monastery of the Golden Domes used to rise. No more: in 1937 it was pulled down. Pulled down so that an office block could be built on the spot, only one never was. The eleventh-century monastery has gone; now there are just fences and roofs. [...]
>
> Just recently, I happened to be present at a meeting in Kiev at which the list of monuments under state care was being reviewed. Quite possibly, not all listed monuments really do deserve to be listed, and not all of them should be under state care, but when a meeting is summoned with the express purpose of "reducing the list by 50 percent," then you feel not just astonishment, but deep alarm.
>
> We love our history and our past, and what has come down to us should not be destroyed; it should be carefully preserved.[43]

Nekrasov's views were not new in Soviet preservation policy. Since the war, the perception of church architecture as part of the national heritage had been an acceptable position. Novel, though, was his demonstrative association of aggressive attitudes to such architecture with radical atheism. Lenin might be a model in terms of the tenderness with which he had regarded the past, but Marx was most certainly not in terms of his attitudes toward religion. Added to this (an inflammatory point in an age when claims that the Soviet Union led the world in everything from space to sport were the rule), Nekrasov was emphasizing that a Western capitalist country, not the Soviet Union, was on the right course when it came to heritage. In its way, the article was every bit as radical as *One Day in the Life of Ivan Denisovich*, and it was perhaps the coincidence of its being published in the same issue that averted the possible consequences for Nekrasov and his editor.[44]

The policy toward heritage, like so many other aspects of policy under Khrushchev, was shot through with irreconcilable contradictions. On the one hand, actual monuments were under a bigger threat than at any time since the Great Patriotic War. On the other, a relatively open discussion of this situation was now taking place, aided not just by the emphasis on lively, if also carefully orchestrated, exchanges that was characteristic of the era, but by the revival of at least limited autonomy for the regions that Khrushchev also favored.[45] "Regional studies"—suppressed in the 1930s—slowly got back off the ground, and local museums once again began to collect material relating to the history of their areas. The Party leadership might stop short of permitting a large-scale state-sponsored movement for the protection of monuments, but it tolerated the promotion of heritage at the level of local grassroots initiatives, in line with the general policy of encouraging activities "on public principles" (the Soviet version of voluntary work).[46]

Hard Lines in Religion and in Architecture: Managing the Church and City Planning in Leningrad

In the Soviet Union's second city, events followed the overall direction of increased antagonism both to religion and heritage, though the situation had certain specific features that emerged directly from the revival of limited regional autonomy. One of Khrushchev's main tasks in the course of his struggle for power had been to get the Party leadership of the Soviet Union's second biggest city on his side. The most significant indication of this was his speech of May 1954 branding the 1949 purge of the Leningrad Communist Party leadership, the so-called "Leningrad Affair," a "falsification." The speech generated not just huge relief on the part of the city's Party elite, but the rise of a powerful local myth—that the Leningrad leaders had been purged because they were more forward-thinking than Stalin was prepared to tolerate. The Leningrad Party leadership, throughout the post-Stalin years, prided itself on this; a local cult of Sergei Kirov as a "progressive" leader was also assiduously promoted. But "progressive" did not mean "liberal": the ideal was an efficient modern technocracy.[47] The city continued to be dominated by the needs of the "military-industrial bloc." Added to this, it was still the center of an extremely active movement for "scientific atheism," boosted by the two-decade history of its pioneering Museum of the History of Religion (renamed in 1954 the "Museum of the History of Religion and Atheism").[48]

Leningrad activists were among the leaders of the new movement for "Soviet traditions," exemplified by the founding of the first Soviet "palace of marriages" in 1959.[49] The antireligious policies of the day were also pushed through assiduously. The plenipotentiary from March 7, 1962, was Grigorii Zharinov, "a man of conviction, far from stupid, and wily," in the words of Father Vladimir Sorokin, who had to deal with him for some three decades in the capacity of theological student, priest, and inspector of the Theological Academy.[50]

In the spirit of the new mood in the central Council on the Affairs of the ROC, Zharinov took a far more interventionist attitude to his position than Kushnarev, beginning with the fact that he tried to ensure the appointment of members of the hierarchy who would be maximally malleable.[51] His testimonial for the then metropolitan of Leningrad, Pimen (Izvekov) when Pimen was in the process of moving to another and more prestigious position in 1963, points to the extent of his ideological micromanagement:

> It is quite easy to decide questions of rational transfers of clergy, and of the senselessness of appointing priests to economically weak parishes, with Pimen. Pimen's correct behavior and reactions have often facilitated the fact that when various churches were closed, e.g., the Chapel of the Blessed Xenia, there were no undesirable manifestations from clergy and believers.[52]

Pimen's successor, Metropolitan Nikodim (Rotov), was a very different character, and far readier to take the side of believers where he was able. But the amount that he could do, given the intransigence of the plenipotentiary and of the law itself, was strictly limited.[53]

Like the tougher line on religion, the drive to produce functionalist architecture also had a strong impact on Leningrad. The Decree on Architectural Excesses had singled out as inappropriate some projects created in the city, such as Boris Zhuravlev's apartment block on Stalin Prospect, "which includes a colonnade two stories high," and Valentin Kamenskii's blocks on prospekt Stachek, "with façades in an archaic style, pilasters with heavy rustication, and complex handling of the cornices." A notably high proportion of the city's buildings had been architect-designed: "Of 353 buildings under construction, only 14 are 'pattern-book built' [*tipovye proekty*]."[54] This was a serious offense, since the Decree was aimed at significantly increasing the number of "pattern-book" projects.[55] The result was a boom in the construction of these, and in neo-functionalist architecture more generally. Leningrad acquired its bus garages and car parks, its covered markets, its *doma byta* (daily life centers, i.e., places offering domestic services, such as launderettes and repair workshops), its steel-and-glass department stores and metro stations. Pivotal in this was the work of Valentin Kamenskii himself, as city architect at the period when most of the work was commissioned and carried out. Though appointed in 1951, Kamenskii espoused the new ethos with enthusiasm, perhaps because he had been singled out for criticism in the 1955 decree.[56]

It was less even the boxy shape of the new buildings than their distinctive proportions (with large areas of glass, and the undercarriage carved out to let in open space), their eschewal of the so-called "line of beauty" (*krasnaia liniia*), or traditional line of the street frontage, and their use of unadorned concrete and steel, that were innovative. The aim was to create new monuments, rather than cosseting old ones. In the late Stalin era, building on city-center streets had usually been safely bland.[57] The early 1960s, by contrast, saw a rush of projects that paraded a brash novelty. S. I. Neimark, V. F. Khrushchev, and A. I. Solodovnikov's Press House (the home of Lenizdat publishers) on the Fontanka, finished in 1964, included several of the key mannerisms of the time: the heavily faceted front, with uniform reticulations continuing across an expanse far wider than the complete façades of the neighboring building; the aggressive retreat from the established street-building boundary; and the presence of a surly awning (*naves*) over the front entrance.

Further down the Fontanka, the eighteen-story Soviet Hotel (not completed until 1967, but designed by E. A. Levinson and his workshop entirely in the spirit of the architectural trends established a decade earlier) made a still louder statement in favor of new dimensions and new materials (the glass panels for the hotel were specially imported from Mexico).[58] Though later interpreted as heralds of a "new barbarism," the buildings had antecedents in Leningrad, including Levinson's own Lensovet House of Culture (1931–1938), and Lensovet Apartment Block No. 1 (1931–1935), the former with blocky tower and vast oblong span of steel-and-glass window, the latter set back from the embankment and supported on slender square stilts. Indeed, the Lensovet building, with its curved frontage and urban garden, was in its own way more adventurous than anything built in the Khrushchev era; the 1955 emphasis on the need for economy gave even

FIGURE 23. The Press House, image from Leningrad: *fotoal'bom*, an album of views of Leningrad published in 1964. The slogan on top reads GLORY TO THE CPSU. (Author's collection.)

one-off projects a conscientiously uniform look. The main form of originality was proportional: with its grille of regular but oversized windows and wide frontage, the Press House bullied the older structures alongside into submission.

While a 1964 draft for the new City Plan of 1964 paid the usual tribute to the importance of "city construction" in Leningrad, and of its architectural *ansambli*, it also underlined the requirement to "construct a city that answers the demands of Communist labor, daily life, and mass leisure." Extensive development was envisaged, including not just work on currently unused land out toward the Gulf of Finland (planned already in the late 1940s), but also building along the city embankments, and in historic quarters such as Lesser Okhta, not to speak of the areas around the Smol'nyi Cathedral and the Alexander Nevsky Monastery.[59] In the press of the time, it was the modernization of the city that took pride of place, with *Vechernii Leningrad* (Evening Leningrad) celebrating in 1961 the expansion of the metro system: "The day is fast approaching when speedy underground trains blazing with light will run beyond the Moscow gates."[60]

But alongside its traditions of radical atheism, and established history of streamlined, modernist architecture, Leningrad also had its decades-long history of commitment to preservation, not to speak of neoclassicism. The imposition of functionalist norms inspired a good deal of soul-searching. Already in 1957, David Gol'dgor, one of the leading architects in the post-1955 crash housing program, confessed to colleagues that he thought the construction of a pattern-book block next to Smol'nyi "was a city planning error of the crudest kind. It's a block on Podgornaia ulitsa and it's just made the whole district look ugly. I feel I'm partly to blame, though in fact I couldn't do anything [to stop it]."[61] Even at the height of the architectural efficiency drive, there were doubts about whether assertively spare buildings would work in every part of Leningrad.

Far from being simply a period of modernist triumphalism, the mid- to late 1950s saw a modest expansion of interest in Leningrad's historic past. The 250th anniversary of the foundation of Leningrad, celebrated in 1957, brought much attention to the city's revolutionary history (the year was chosen partly because it marked forty years from 1917). But the festival was also accompanied by an exhibition in the Museum of the History of Leningrad spanning the three centuries of city history.[62] In 1958 came the publication of *The Monuments of Architecture of Leningrad*, an unusually broad and richly illustrated treatment.[63] Admittedly, some buildings were delisted in 1960 (the precise number is impossible to establish, because the GIOP records for this period have not been declassified, but was certainly far less than the 50 percent that Nekrasov recorded in Kiev).[64] A number of demolitions also took place—notable examples were Luigi Rusca's portico alongside the Gostinyi dvor, dismantled to make way for a pedestrian subway in 1963, and the Pirogov Museum, demolished during the building of the Hotel Leningrad a year or so later.[65] But the wholesale clearing of entire areas that took place in Moscow's Arbat had no parallel here. In this context, the handling of historic churches was—by local if not national standards—abnormal.

"A Shrine of Memory": The Status of Historic Churches, 1954–1958

The renewed vulnerability of "cultic buildings" was not immediately obvious. Once Khrushchev took power, conditions initially got rather better for "religious groups"—to begin with, at the national level. Georgii Karpov, the chairman of the Council on the Affairs of the ROC, was, in the words of the historian Dimitry Pospielovsky, "able to exploit the 'interregnum' of 1954–1956 and the official slogans about restoring 'Leninist legality' to reinforce the Church's legal position."[66] In 1954, churches once again began to be opened, though in small numbers.[67] A case where a local functionary had proposed to the Council of Ministers the demolition of four churches "without due cause" was sharply criticized in 1956 because it had "provoked an activization on the part of believers in terms of petitions to have the churches opened."[68]

A flood of petitions had indeed been unleashed, in the Leningrad diocese as well as in other places.[69] As in the past, petitioners sometimes mentioned a church's historic importance. A petition dispatched in 1957 to request the opening of the Sampson Cathedral referred not just to the fact that there was only one open church in the district, but to the Cathedral's "historic status," and the fact that opening it would "honor the 250th anniversary of Leningrad," an event for which the church "has been restored on the outside."[70] When this appeal was declined, the letter-writers invoked the 250th anniversary of the Battle of Poltava, due to fall in 1959, when "250 years of the church's existence" would also be marked. "We deeply hope that you will enter into the spirit of our sincere request and help us to receive permission to open the Church of St. Sampson, for which the believers will be endlessly grateful and which will enable the preservation of the city of Leningrad's Historic value," the petitioners concluded.[71]

In 1955, a letter to *Leningradskaia pravda* requesting the reopening of the St. Alexander Nevsky Church in Ust'-Izhora, on the outskirts of Leningrad, also invoked history directly: "This church is not only a church, it is [a shrine of] memory, and is linked with the name of the Great General Prince Alexander Nevsky and this church is named with his name and when Alexander Nevsky smashed the Swedes on the Neva on this rock on this spot he rested with his soldiers, after which the church was named with the name of Prince Alexander Nevsky." The group even offered help in funding the restoration of the church.[72]

The letter, forwarded by the newspaper's editorial office to GIOP, provoked an assurance from the deputy head of the Inspectorate, S. V. Korobkov, that the church was being properly looked after by the secular authorities. "An inspection of the building has just been carried out," Korobkov stated, and GIOP had "contacted the executive committee of the Leningrad City Soviet to urge them to request the Kolpino district soviet to carry out works in order to protect the monument from further destruction, for which the Inspectorate is making special funding available."[73] While it did something to goad the authorities into action of a practical kind, as a petition for the opening of the church, the letter was a signal failure.

However, petitions were not always ignored or deflected. The campaign to reopen the Trinity Cathedral in the Alexander Nevsky Monastery took a different course, partly because of the decisive support of the church hierarchy. As Metropolitan Grigorii—now liberated from his efforts to set up the Leningrad

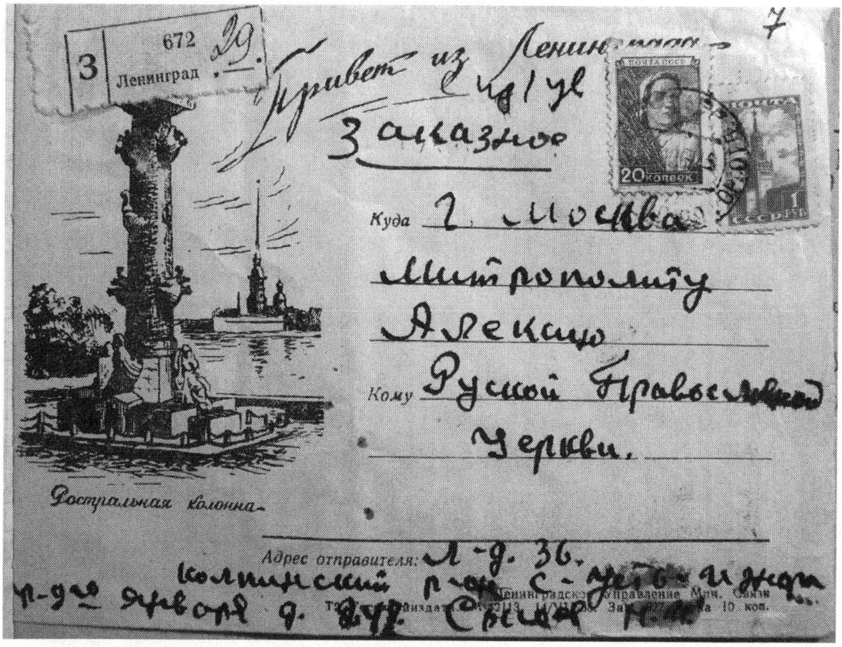

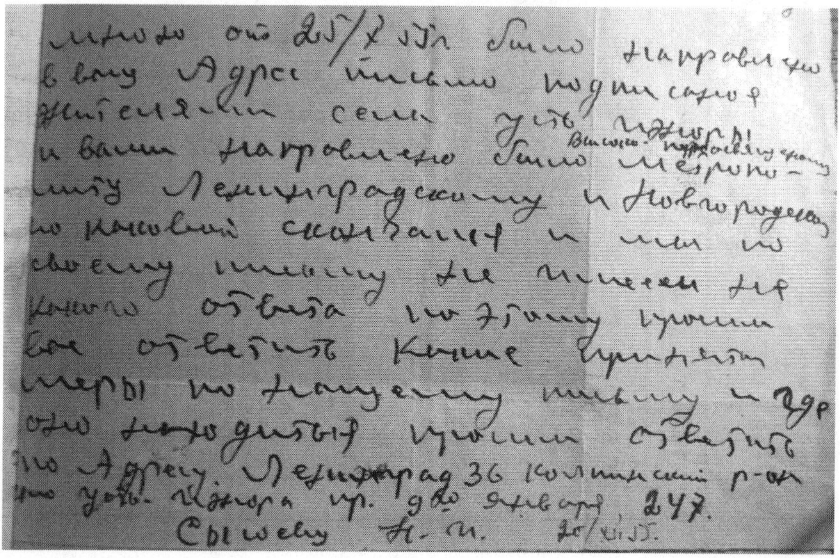
много от 25/X 55г было направлено
в ваш Адрес письмо подписаное
жителями села Усть Ижоры
и вами направлено было Митрополиту Ленинградскому и Новгородскому Высоко-преосвященству
по каковой скандалит и мы по
своему письму не имеем ни
какого ответа по этому прошу
вас ответить какие приняты
меры по нашему письму и где
оно находится прошу ответить
по Адресу Ленинград 36 Колпинский р-он
пос Усть-Ижора пр. 9го января 247.
Сысоеву Н. М. 20/XII 55.

FIGURE 24, 25. Envelope and page from a follow-up letter by N. M. Sysoev enquiring about the response to the petition asking for the opening of the Alexander Nevsky Church in Ust'-Izhora, December 20, 1955. Note the Leningrad architecture (a Rostral Column and the Peter and Paul Fortress) on the envelope. (ASPbE.)

Theological Academy—argued in a report to Patriarch Aleksii on July 15, 1955, there were many reasons why the case to open this building was strong. Not only was there a petition on file from prospective parishioners dating back to 1948 (the minimum required in terms of opening a campaign), but there were other, exceptional grounds. As well as formerly acting as "the center of religious life in Leningrad," the church was "situated at the center of the territory of a State Museum Reservation, amidst the architectural *ansambl'* of the Alexander Nevsky Monastery, and until its closure it was the center of the religious life of the city of Leningrad." Yet it was at present in a dangerously run-down condition:

> At the present time this historical monument, nominally under the protection of the state, is actually in a condition of total decay: the walls have become sodden because of leakage, and it is essential to organize central heating so that the Cathedral can dry out. The cornices have collapsed, and the plaster has fallen off in many places leaving the brick exposed; the reliefs are badly damaged.
>
> Inside the church, the magnificent plaster ceilings are in a state of total dilapidation, as are the sculptural decorations. Major building works are urgently needed. Specialist opinion alone can determine the actual extent of the restoration needed, and the cost will certainly run into millions of rubles. Yet for the Soviet public, the Cathedral evidently holds no interest, and it is currently completely empty—apart from a few piles of boxes, that is.
>
> A whole string of delegations from foreign churches, while visiting the Metropolitan of Leningrad, have taken acerbic note of the wretched condition of the Lavra Cathedral (it is located near the Metropolitan's chambers). They have expressed frank astonishment about this matter, particularly given the information about the inner freedom of the Church and the goodwill felt toward it by the Soviet Government that the Metropolitan of Leningrad has always been careful to pass on to his guests.[74]

The thin excuses that had to be presented to foreigners about why they could not visit the Cathedral (actually closed because of "the totally ugly and neglected state the building is in") Metropolitan Grigorii continued, had created "an impression of insincerity and indeed mendacity." In other words, left as it was, the Cathedral was a supreme example of negative propaganda. This argument displayed astute awareness that the treatment of religious believers remained a key weapon in the ideological battle of the socialist and capitalist worlds, and that this was an area where the Soviet leadership was aware of potential vulnerability.

Metropolitan Grigorii went on to counter, one by one, the list of possible objections to the opening of the Cathedral, as though he were filling in an invisible questionnaire. No, it was not in a prominent place, or one where its activities would impinge on the civic rituals of Soviet life, such as the political parades; no, it would not become so full as to be a danger in terms of public safety, but would instead take the pressure off the Theological Academy church, the only working one in the entire district. Finally, he mentioned two other good reasons for opening the church, both of a specifically religious kind: it would be possible to move the important tombs of Orthodox dignitaries from the closed Nikol'skoe Cemetery alongside, thus removing "temptation" when the cemetery was transformed into a park, and all the graves were cleared; and the opening of this working church would make it possible to honor the memory of St. Alexander Nevsky, to whom the entire monastery and the square outside were dedicated. The possibility of moving the saint's relics back into the Cathedral was not something it would have been prudent to mention, but it is clear that the sense of communing with the sacred place where they had once stood underlay Metropolitan Grigorii's words.[75]

Metropolitan Grigorii's case for opening the Cathedral was a masterpiece of diplomacy. Particularly skillful was his playing on the question of foreign prestige—an issue that was of even greater importance now that far larger numbers of visitors from abroad were visiting Leningrad as part of the closer cultural contact that was a major development of the "Thaw" era.[76] It is unlikely that an argument derived solely from the Cathedral's architectural importance and beauty would have been immediately effective: after all, the place had stood, rapidly deteriorating, for more than a decade. But the information that *foreigners* thought the building attractive and assumed that it was in such dreadful condition because it was a church, and would extrapolate all kinds of conclusions from this about the mistreatment of believers themselves, could be expected to carry immediate weight.

The case for opening the Cathedral was duly accepted, though it was only under Metropolitan Grigorii's successor, Elefterii (Grigorii having died in November 1955) that the actual work of opening it began. However, by November 10, 1956, the administration of the diocese was busy with setting up a committee "in connection with the imminent opening of the Cathedral of the Holy Trinity, as agreed by the Secular Authorities."[77] The Commission's first meeting, beginning and ending with hymn-singing, was held on November 22, 1956.[78] It soon found itself, though, up against the very different bureaucratic style of the "Secular Authorities." To begin with, GIOP insisted on a complicated and detailed renovation to deal with the extensive damage caused to the interiors as the result of war damage, which had left the building not just roofless, but with one its corners destroyed.[79] The estimate for the costs ran into about 10 million rubles, all of which the "Secular Authorities" tried to make the responsibility of the diocese, though, as the Works Department of the Moscow Patriarchate pointed out, it was quite inappropriate to treat the church authorities as though they were to blame for the damage. At the very least, responsibility should be shared with the previous lessee, who had for many years ignored the provisions of the 1948 Decree on the Protection of Monuments.[80] But this case was rejected by GIOP (on the grounds that entering into a contract of lease upon a monument required making good repairs necessary as of that date), and in the end, the diocese had to resort to aid from the Moscow Patriarchate and raising money in whatever ways it could.[81]

As the work itself progressed, the headaches of resolving religious and secular demands proliferated. There was the far from easy question of finding builders with the adequate skills to take on such work.[82] But that was only the start: more complex questions soon arose. It was impossible, the clerics felt, for a significant church of this kind to make do with only one altar, but arranging side altars not in the original building raised difficult questions in terms of architectural preservation. Icons and church furnishings had to be collected across the diocese, and it was essential to ensure that they were stylistically compatible and appropriate in terms of period. An iconostasis of suitable size, period, and style for the high altar proved elusive, and one for a side altar was, at first, easier to locate. But Metropolitan Elefterii did not wish to celebrate the first mass in the Cathedral at anything other than the high altar. Eventually, work on the altar was completed by the Works Department of the Moscow Patriarchate, but not without many obstacles along the way.[83]

As this instance indicates, the clerical authorities remained dependent on their own resources where completing the work was concerned. But the fact that GIOP provided little if any support of a practical kind did not make the inspectors drop their rigorous standards. Their many objections, once work was completed, included a whole series of quibbles about the candelabra (*panikadila*) that dangled from the cathedral ceiling. First the inspectors fussed that these were hard to examine closely, and then when they got them in view, they did not like what they saw. The objects were dirty, but cleaning should leave the patina in place; new ones, just like the old, were to be manufactured in bronze with silver leaf, and missing sections replaced in pierced bronze-work. Finally, after repeated objections, they threatened to take the candelabra away, leading to a full-scale row with the metropolitan, who simply refused to sign the document setting out this threat, and submitted an alternative report of his own.[84] At last, after many vicissitudes, work on the Cathedral reached a stage where the reconsecration could take place (and the building was duly dedicated on September 12, 1957, the Feast of St. Alexander Nevsky). But further restoration was to continue for significantly longer, reaching its conclusion only in 1960.

A year later, the monuments preservation argument surfaced again in the administration of the cathedral, though now in a different context. The staff of officiating priests at the Trinity Cathedral having been reduced by three, parishioners wrote to Khrushchev in indignation:

> We must never forget that rude meddling in the affairs of the church on the part of people who lack all general human qualities, humanism, love, kindness, and a sense of truth and justice not only messes up the work of the church, but damages the entire culture of our country, nurturing disrespect for everything holy and sacred.
>
> And is that not one of the causes of the barbaric attitude of many people to monuments of history, objects of art, to the natural riches of our country, about which so much is written in our press?[85]

At this point, however, the historical argument was probably more of a hindrance than a help. At no stage, in any case, did Khrushchev and his colleagues adopt the position that custodianship of historically valuable buildings entitled Orthodox "religious associations" to a relaxation of pressure in terms of the renewed drive for radical secularization.

Candle Booths That "Impaired the Architectural Appearance of the Buildings": Heritage Legislation and Church-State Relations

The laws on heritage preservation were not only a source of handy rhetoric for clerics and their flocks as they sought for leverage in Soviet society at a time when arguments proceeding from religious rights made little impact. They were also useful ammunition for Soviet officials searching, as the guidelines of the time indicated they should, for ways of using administrative regulations to force religious groups out of existence. Like his colleagues, Zharinov tirelessly cited fire and labor protection legislation and other breaches of rules, such as running an institutional car rather than using one from the pool, in order to harass members of religious groups.[86] He also did all he could to reduce earnings from candle sales, again in obedience to central directives. But the use of monuments protection legislation as a neat way of combining the two strategies (administrative harassment plus reduction of income) seems to have been his invention. As he described on May 11, 1962:

> The reduction of income generation from the sale of candles has also been influenced by the fact that, in almost all the churches in Leningrad, the practice of trading candles in special booths next to the church has now been curtailed. A directive issued to the executive organs of churches by the executive committees of local soviets and the State Inspectorate for the Preservation of Monuments of Architecture enforced the removal of the above booths, which had been constructed without the permission of the appropriate authorities and which impaired the architectural appearance of the buildings.[87]

That said, this instrumental use of monuments legislation in the support of the antireligious drive does not seem to have been adopted as policy in the heritage bodies themselves. GIOP officials were just as ready to pounce on illicit structures outside monuments in secular hands, demanding in June 1964 that booths for selling goods, "etc.," were removed from outside the former Church of the Coreligionists, converted to the Museum of the Arctic in the 1930s. (The "etc." related to an on-street tanker for selling beer, the subject of vehement protests from the museum director at the time.)[88] Conversely, no major row about alleged mistreatment of a "cultic building" by a "religious society" was initiated by the monuments protection office at this point. When the Cathedral of the Transfiguration underwent restoration in 1959, for example, the dealings with GIOP were perfectly businesslike.[89]

For his part, Zharinov never attempted to form a regular alliance with GIOP. When it suited his purpose, he ignored completely the legislation on monuments. For instance, in 1962, he carried out a survey of working churches in Leningrad to establish which lacked valid contracts of use, evidently in the hope that it would be possible to close down some in the process of reregistration. As it transpired, some had out-of-date contracts, and others contracts that Zharinov now considered obsolete, since they had been signed by long-dead or vanished members of the *dvadtsatka*. Also on the list were churches that had no contracts on file at all with the executive committees of local soviets. Five of these (the St. Nicholas Cathedral, the Cathedral of the Transfiguration, the Prince Vladimir Cathedral, the Easter Loaf Church and the Trinity Cathedral in the Alexander Nevsky Monastery) were protected monuments. In these cases, the church communities all had contracts with GIOP (the only type of agreement which, according to accepted legal practice, they actually required). This did not, however, impede Zharinov from noting on his list, "Contracts with local executive committees have never been executed."[90]

Whatever Zharinov's intentions, the churches whose contracts had "never been executed" were not closed down. But the gambit was characteristic of his style—pushing to the extremities of the law, or indeed beyond. He appears also to have employed the classic manipulative strategy of organizing petitions among suitable members of the "Soviet working population" against religious buildings that were open for worship. In 1963, a campaign began (accompanied by letter-writing to local newspapers and so on) to get the Trinity Church on prospekt Obukhovskoi oborony ("Easter Loaf and Easter Pudding") closed. As the incumbent priest, Anatolii Moroz, reported to the metropolitan:

> On Saturday February 2, after evening service, I tried to calm believers down, and in my private capacity answered their questions about whether the church would be closed. I told them that the material in the newspapers was written by a group of workers and I read them out a quotation from the newspaper, but [I added that] the question about the closure of the church would not be decided by an individual group of people, it would be the higher organs of the government and so there was no cause for excitement and all the more since misrule [*beschinstva*] of any kind and loose talk are impermissible in a church.[91]

It is possible that the "group of workers" concerned may well really have been writing on their own initiative—perhaps recalling the central role that had been played by *zaprosy* (change-of-use proposals) during the Cultural Revolution. But the unusualness of the case (there are no records of campaigns of this kind against other churches), suggests that Zharinov likely selected what he thought was a vulnerable parish (in an outlying area of the city, far from interfering members of the local intelligentsia and inconveniently observant foreigners) in order to polish his statistics.

As the case of "Easter Loaf and Easter Pudding" showed, the status as a protected monument was no protection against calls for closure. But it may conceivably have helped parishioners keep the church open. It is notable that two other Leningrad churches without preservation orders actually were closed down in the early 1960s. One of these was the Chapel of the Blessed Xenia in the Smolenskoe Cemetery, Vasilievskii Island; the other was the Church of the Trinity at Lesnovo, the only church open for worship in the whole of Vyborg district (the population of which was expanding rapidly because it was an area scheduled for new building).[92] Certainly, the parishioners of the Holy Trinity Church at Lesnovo seem themselves to have supposed that it would help to be assigned a church with protected status, since one of the strategies they engaged when dealing with the authorities was to state that they were prepared to agree to demolition if they were allowed to move their parish into another empty church in the same district. The two buildings that they mentioned, St. Catherine's Church at Murino and the Sampson Cathedral, were both structures of acknowledged architectural importance.[93]

The Trinity Church at Lesnovo was a modest wooden building without pretensions to architectural significance, and not a protected monument. The parishioners' perception that somewhere more "permanent" would be safer is understandable. They probably also hoped for a secondary line of institutional support, given the church hierarchy's reluctance to make a robust case for church preservation at this period. As Grigorii Zharinov noted in his testimonial for Metropolitan Pimen, the latter had discouraged any protests when the Chapel of St. Xenia was closed. True, the Chapel of the Blessed Xenia had long been the focus of popular cults of a kind that had caused a good deal of discomfort to the Orthodox hierarchy, as well as city officials, over the years.[94] But Pimen displayed no more inclination to take the side of the parishioners from the Trinity Church at Lesnovo, supporting the official line that the place should be demolished. As he wrote to Patriarch Aleksii when the latter forwarded an appeal from the *dvadtsatka*, the destruction of the church was simply inevitable:

> It is correct to suggest that the Executive Committee of the Vyborg District Soviet of the City of Leningrad has approved the demolition of certain buildings and among them the Trinity Church, Lesnovo, in view of the widening of the highway and the planned new construction along the route to the cemetery of victims of the Blockade, where a monument has been erected and an eternal flame lit.
>
> The Executive Committee of the Vyborg District Soviet has informed the community of believers of Lesnovo Church of this decision, giving due notice.

Having made clear that the decision to demolish the church was, in his eyes, legitimate and reasoned, Pimen then went on to dispose of another complaint offered by the parishioners—that their application to use the "large brick church" on the same site had been declined. The church in question, he contended, "is occupied by an organization of the factory type for its industrial equipment, with machines and lathes in place. The claim that the lease on this premises expires in 1964 is not founded on fact. [. . .] Whether the believers themselves have made representations to any official body to the effect that this building should be put at their disposal, I cannot say."[95] Since Pimen could only have had the information about the use of the other church from Zharinov, the metropolitan's inability to say whether the parishioners had made any representations to "any official body" seems more like a piece of coquetry than a likely statement of the facts.[96] The term of his office as metropolitan was also to see the closure of various notable churches across the province, including, for example, the Vladimir Church at Gatchina (shut down in 1962), as well as large numbers of churches in villages.[97] But it is unlikely that Pimen could have achieved much, even with greater goodwill. The more populist and resolute Metropolitan Nikodim was able to do no more than stop the parish of the Trinity Church being wound up at the point when they had to abandon the building. Normally, each parish required its own church; in this case, the parishioners were allowed joint use of the St. Alexander Nevsky Church in Shuvalovo—a significant distance away from the original structure, but still notionally in the same district.[98]

"The List of Churches That Are Architectural Monuments Should Be Thoroughly Revised": Filtering Heritage in Leningrad

The confidence of the Trinity Church parishioners that church-monuments were always invulnerable from assault was certainly unfounded. A report sent by Zharinov to the City Committee of the Communist Party on March 12, 1962, made explicit his desire to see the number of protected churches reduced as part of a plan to arrange demolition of churches that were in a "worn out" (*vetkhii*) condition:

> The commissions of the district executive committees in Leningrad and Leningrad Province have on their inventory 232 non-functioning churches (Orthodox) that retain their ecclesiastical appearance.
>
> 181 of these are made of stone [or brick], 51 are wooden. It has also been established that many church buildings (58 in total) are in a worn-out or semi-ruined condition and subject to demolition.

There is also a fairly small number of churches (15) that are empty and are not used for any purpose, but can be adapted to economic and cultural ends. However, the question about how these churches should be used must be decided quickly, so that believers do not start to make representations about getting them opened.

The buildings of churches and chapels that are on the inventory of architectural monuments should also be put under serious review. There are 76 such churches that are non-functioning, and 11 that are functioning.

As is noted by the commissions, many of the non-functioning churches that are architectural monuments are in a worn-out, or even a half-ruined, condition, and are subject to demolition.

It is clear that the list of church buildings that are architectural monuments should be thoroughly revised with a view to making cuts in the same.[99]

The precise impact of Zharinov's statement is difficult to trace, given that the records of listed churches for this period are, like the records of architectural monuments generally, at best elusive.[100] However, one important church was certainly removed from the lists at this point—the St. Alexander Nevsky Church at Ust'-Izhora, built in 1798–1799. The church had been badly damaged during the war, which may have provoked the decision. In the event, St. Alexander Nevsky's escaped demolition, though the dome was removed in 1962.[101] Another significant site to undergo assault was the Trinity-St. Sergius Monastery in Primorskaia pustyn', Strel'na, which had also suffered heavily during the war. The monastery does not seem ever to have been delisted, but several of the buildings, including the Trinity Cathedral, built by Rastrelli in 1756–1760, were quietly demolished in 1960 (the buildings were in use as a youth detention center at the time).[102]

The most celebrated demolition of the day, however, was of a church in Leningrad itself, the Church of the Savior on the Haymarket ("Peace Square"). Like the Church of the Sign, this incubus was effaced in order to make way for a metro station.[103] The removal of the church was deemed so inevitable that it was not even glossed in any way. The Lensovet minute recording the decision (January 21, 1960) stated simply that "the overground pavilion" was to be placed "on the site of the church."[104]

At this point, however, a member of GIOP's Learned Council, the architectural historian Professor Vladimir Piliavskii (1910–1980), heard of the proposed demolition. Piliavskii, who came originally from a relatively humble background (his parents were teachers in Vilna), was a remarkable Soviet success story. After training as an industrial architect, he had worked in 1942–1946 as chief architect of the Admiralty building, and emerged during the postwar years as one of the leading Leningrad specialists in Russian architecture of the late eighteenth and early nineteenth centuries.[105] His thesis, a meticulous dissection of the career of Vasilii Stasov, abundantly illustrated with archival materials, gave considerable emphasis to church architecture and to the resemblance between the architect's Petersburg churches and their Old Russian prototypes. It resonantly cited Stasov's vision of church architecture as permanent, where lesser buildings might fall by the wayside. "All these relations can charge under the effects of time, but a church, as a sacred monument, will never [change] till faith itself is forgotten, and for this reason everything else should take its tone from the church, and it from nothing, save for the natural landscape." Piliavskii also lamented the desuetude into which some of Stasov's church buildings had fallen, and commented that more rational uses for these were urgently needed. The Trinity-Izmailovskii Regiment Cathedral, for instance, might become "a permanent exhibition of machinery for heavy industry or for the construction industry. The superb lighting of the interior, the smooth white walls, the division of space into five separate sections, all mean that the building is outstandingly well suited to modern purposes." [106] While an exhibition of this kind hardly accorded with the "eternal" function of the cathedral that Stasov had foreseen, there was a striking contrast with the 1930s plans to convert the place for factory or workshop use, if not to pull it down.[107]

While Piliavskii was not a Soviet media figure in the way that Dmitrii Likhachev was to become in the 1980s, or even as well known to the general public as Nikolai Belekhov had been in the 1940s, he was immensely influential among professionals. He was not only a leading figure at the Leningrad Institute of Building and Engineering (LISI), which trained many of the city's architects, but a still more authoritative figure at GIOP than his position as external consultant might have suggested. The head of the Scholarly Section, Lev Mederskii, was writing a candidate's thesis on the architect Aleksandr Mikhailov under his direction; the head of the Section of Architecture and Monument Preservation at the Leningrad Section of the Union of Architects, Aleksandr Rotach, was also a protégé of Piliavskii's.[108]

Aside from Piliavskii's general interest in church architecture, he had begun a project on Matvei Zemtsov in 1959, and is likely to have taken a particular interest in the Church of the Savior because he evidently believed it to be the work of one of the architect's pupils.[109] His intervention must explain why—exceptionally in the case of a building that was no longer a listed monument—the staff at GIOP stirred themselves to contest the demolition. Lev Mederskii, head of the Learned Council of GIOP, along with Iu. M. Denisov, another of Piliavskii's graduate students, compiled a tactically adept memorandum arguing against the demolition on cost grounds. The church had large amounts of usable space and could be entirely reconstructed inside, since the original decoration was lost anyway. There was no need to spend a million rubles tearing it down.[110] But in tune though it might be with the economy drive that the Soviet press tirelessly pressed upon professionals in the construction industry, the memorandum changed nothing.[111] According to Vladimir Smirnov, a former pupil, Piliavskii also organized an emergency meeting in the late autumn of 1960 at LISI—perhaps after efforts to fight the demolition through GIOP had proved unsuccessful.[112] This meeting, assuming it happened, also failed to achieve its ends.

Retrospective commentary was to recall a major public uproar over the planned demolition, inflamed by an article in Leningrad's evening paper referring to the removal of this "disgraceful blot" on the city's landscape. But no such article appears to have been published in any of the city's newspapers; it is doubtful, indeed, whether the local authorities would have run the risk of using such provocative language about a local building.[113] As for the "uproar," there is also no evidence of this, nor is there anything to substantiate a popular local story that Ekaterina Furtseva, then minister of culture of the USSR, sent a telegram to halt the demolition, but some powerful Leningrad official chose "not to have received" it. Such stories are likely the product of classic Soviet myth (the "telegram from Moscow" is proverbial), added to project back onto the Khrushchev era events from the next decade, which actually did see upfront campaigns to save churches.[114] Nor is there foundation in the story that Piliavskii's career suffered as a result of his campaign to save the Church of the Savior. Indeed, everything indicates the opposite. In March 1962 his colleagues at LISI tried to get him appointed chair of the Department of City Planning (*gradostroitel'stvo*) at the Institute. This plan failed when A. A. Liubosh, chair of the Board of LOSA, protested that Piliavskii, whatever his merits as a historian of architecture, was not an expert in modern planning. In 1964, however, he was put forward as candidate for the more suitable post of professor of the history of architecture. He published widely, and even made trips abroad, for example, to France and Hungary, an indication of exceptional reliability in the eyes of the authorities. A Party member who had been a Komsomol activist, and who punctiliously cited Lenin (and Stalin, in the appropriate years), Piliavskii was certainly not a dissident—and nor was he so perceived.[115]

All the same, the campaign to spare the Church of the Savior was, to use a standard Soviet term of denigration, "not timely." January 1960 had seen a call from the Central Committee to step up the antireligious drive, and in the same month, Leonid Brezhnev, Anatolii Kosygin, Anastas Mikoian, and Mikhail Suslov had very publicly attended a conference of the "Knowledge" society, tasked with spearheading rational atheist propaganda.[116] This background was quite possibly what had precipitated Lensovet to opt for building the station right on top of the church's site. Certainly, the time was not ripe for a noisy public campaign: Piliavskii's backstage lobbying was already a risky act. Though this lobbying did not stop the destruction, it did have the result of forcing the Leningrad metro construction authority to permit a survey of the church—not a measure that would usually have been considered necessary when an unlisted building was demolished.[117]

The survey was agreed at speed, and its execution was hasty as well. It took place in severe winter conditions after the initial demolition work had started in early 1961. The team of surveyors was allowed a fortnight, during which they measured and photographed the church as best they could, given the unforgiving temperatures and timetable, using a newly developed system of stereoscopic photography in order to try and accurately record its appearance in three dimensions.[118]

FIGURE 26. One of the images produced by the surveyors of the Church of the Savior on the Haymarket, 1961, showing the entrance portico and bell-tower, with three of the church's domes in the background. (TsGANTD-SPb.)

While the original decision to demolish the church was stated in the survey to be the presence of "later additions that had spoilt the appearance of the building," as well as the absence of evidence as to its authorship, the results of the new work were to indicate that much eighteenth-century detailing had actually survived. For example, once the roofs of the later additions had been removed, it emerged that the walls, the colonnades, "the handling of the upper part of the refectory and of the entire perimeter of the church," the second tier of the bell tower, and the sections of masonry above the porticos and the central apse, all dated from the first phase of construction, which was now firmly attributed to a follower of Matvei Zemtsov.[119] Extensive archival work indicated also that the porticos must be earlier than had been previously supposed, and dated not from after the building of the guardhouse in the 1820s, but from, at latest, the 1790s.[120] Bearing in mind the interventionist nature of Leningrad restoration practice, the reconstruction of something close to the original appearance of the church, with its characteristic domes in the Ukrainian style, would have been entirely feasible. But this was not a line of argument that the authors of the survey were at liberty to pursue.[121]

Once again, the principles of the 1935 General Plan—transport before anything else—had come to the fore. And if Uprising Square station, built on the site of the Church of the Sign, had adopted a neoclassical style, with portico and reliefs, analogous to that used for the park pavilions in the Tauride Gardens, the style of the Haymarket Station was boxy and uncompromising. The office block whose bottom floor it was supposed to occupy never materialized, and instead a low-rise structure with an obtrusive awning, out of scale both with its immediate surroundings and with the broader landscape of the square, was plonked down on the empty space.[122]

The demolition of the Church of the Savior generated a good deal more public indignation in retrospect than at the stage when the decision was made. In the summer of 1961, Dmitrii Likhachev alluded explicitly to this demolition among a list of scandalous past and proposed removals of historic buildings. Despite its "extreme architectural interest" and associations with Dostoevskii, not to speak of its role in forming the "historic gateway to the city," along with the Beretti Guardhouse, the church had been summarily pulled down—and this although there were many other places where a metro station could have been placed. The article in which the comment appeared was a response to a new brochure by N. N. Voronin, *Old Russian Monuments of Architecture Should Be Cherished and Preserved* (1960), and Likhachev warmly endorsed Voronin's exhortation that the *national* significance of churches should not be elided by their *religious* function.

To assume that demolishing a church contributed to the struggle with religion was a "superstition" in itself.[123]

Much of Likhachev's article was concerned, however, with medieval icons and wall painting, and heritage generally, rather than with church architecture. The vanished Church of the Savior was the only ecclesiastical building in Leningrad that he mentioned.[124] A year later, in 1962, came the demolition of another church on a prominent city-center site: the "Greek Church" (the Church of St. Demetrius of Salonica) on Ligovskii prospekt, built in the neo-Byzantine style by R. I. Kuz'min (1861–1865). The vast structure (it could accommodate a congregation of one thousand) had dominated an otherwise architecturally anonymous area. Now, in a re-evocation of the exemplary social and cultural transformations of the 1920s, the church was replaced by the October Concert Hall (completed in 1967), whose lead architect, Aleksandr Zhuk, was responsible for several other key projects of the day, including an enormous housing complex on Krasnoputilovskaia ulitsa (1963), and the Theater of Young Viewers next to the Vitebsk Station (1962). A more substantial building in all respects than Sennaia metro station, the concert hall was all the same tactically out of sorts with its surroundings, skirted by peculiar gaps between it and earlier structures. Its glaring incongruity was enhanced by its shiny white marble facing (the original plan had proposed a more conventional dark brownish red, as already employed for the detailing of A. I. Gegello, A. A. Ol', and N. A. Trotskii's OGPU-NKVD building on ulitsa Voinova [Shpalernaia], 1932). While the concert hall was popular as a venue, as a building in its own right it had few admirers.

Neither in the case of the Savior on the Haymarket nor of the Greek Church did public consultation in a broad sense take place. In itself, this was no surprise, since the non-transparent and categorical nature of planning decisions was a given of established practice. However, in the atmosphere of fervent debate that was characteristic of the era, both demolitions generated fierce indignation. "Why, before reconstruction of historic sites begins, can the proposals not be discussed with artists, writers, historians, and art historians at open meetings and in print?" Likhachev demanded in 1961. The "principle of democratism" was in abeyance here.[125] Thus the Soviet government of the day was judged by its own principles and found wanting. Yet the disappearance of architectural monuments was inflammatory not only because the public had not been consulted. They were valued in themselves—as much as anything *because* they had now disappeared.[126] Indeed, the destruction of these churches was to become a primal wound in Leningrad consciousness over the next few years.[127]

"They Tried to Jimmy Out the Royal Doors": Assaults on the Fabric of "Cultic Buildings" in Leningrad's Hinterland

As for the area beyond Leningrad, it remained largely beyond the reach of the preservation bodies. Crude anticlericalism was widespread. The management of a collective farm might, say, site an intensive livestock unit right next to the church ("and in answer to all my questions about whether it was possible to build it somewhere else, all I hear is 'we've been given the *kolkhoz* lands to use on a permanent basis and so I'm the boss around here'").[128] Or sometimes church property might be destroyed, as with St. George's Church at Lozhgolovo village in the distant west of the province, reported by the Church Council to the patriarch on January 14, 1964. The chair of the local executive committee and the chair of the village soviet had jointly "carried out robbery of this monument of church history and art, [they] have destroyed its sacred treasures of museum rarity, and provoke sorrow and tears in the faithful." The authorities in the diocese, the parishioners complained, had been as little concerned with all this as the secular authorities, referring the villagers to the plenipotentiary, "since they know him to be on the side of closed churches, so he will do all he can to drag the business out and not make decisions."[129] Perhaps hoping for support from other parts of the secular apparatus, the members of the Parish Council also enclosed a detailed account of the church's history and assertion of its value as a work of art:

> This church, according to historical data, was built in 1660 as a wooden one. After a fire, it was rebuilt in stone and consecrated in 1831. The interior of the church, as is obvious from the enclosed photographs, was a real "church museum," decorated with examples of rare art by the finest Russian icon-painters. Worthy of especial remark is an image of the Savior of museum rarity, and also an icon of the Mother of God in a silver case, rare in terms of its manner of painting, evidently also the work of the old Russian masters. The royal gates are crowned by an image of the Holy Trinity of museum rarity. The church was lit by candelabra (chandeliers) from the olden times, well preserved, and of white metal, perhaps even silver. The images and their state of repair is visible in the photographs. The church vessels [include] candlesticks, and banners of metal and of velvet, embroidered with gold thread of a most venerable age. Particularly precious is the epitaphios—of velvet and embroidered in gold thread, handmade with great artistry by old mistresses of the embroiderer's art. It is the pride of Old Russian art. It is all represented in the photograph. Upon the altar stood a sanctuary of silver-gilt, of museum rarity.

The complaint also emphasized that the vessels had been removed despite the fact that the church had never officially closed (though as of 1962, no priest was attached to it), and that the keys had been handed over by the church elder "under threats to her personally and to members of her family." An assault on the church had rapidly followed:

> On December 2, 1963, two motorcars arrived from Kingisepp and in them the chairman of the village soviet, Skvortsov who after arriving in those cars went into the church and before the eyes of everyone in the village flung the church doors open and together with someone from the Kingisepp [district soviet] executive committee[,] a certain citizen Mosin Georgii[,] announced that they were there for the church property, and told the villagers they were to load up the icons, candlesticks, and all the other church property.

The items had been removed without documentation of the incident having taken place, though a list of the icons removed had been made. Worse, a few days later, Skvortsov had turned up again "along with a group of workmen armed with axes and jimmies," and gone into the church without taking any members of the *dvadtsatka* and the church council with him:

> With their axes, the workmen hacked the icons out of their cases, and chopped up the royal gates, hewing out the painted sections. They tried to jimmy out the royal doors themselves, they destroyed the altar and broke up the iconostasis, they tried to hack out the precious grilles over the ambon and kliros, only they did not manage to do this, they broke the glass in the icon stands and the icon frames. They tried to haul down the candelabra, only these were too heavy. Before the very eyes of the villagers, they threw all the icons and paintings, the precious vessels, the candlesticks, the seven-branched candlestick from the altar, the epitaphios, the vestments, the books, and the sanctuary on to their motorcars and made off.
>
> What became of the [church] property, the precious church vessels, no one can say. According to some reports, it was taken down to the bank of the Luga River, had something poured over it, and was set on fire.

After the zealous officials had departed, all that remained of the church property was two icons, a bell, and a cross.[130]

The Lozhgolovo villagers' litany of treasured and destroyed objects reads more like a lament than a request for action, and they probably did not expect to achieve much by it. The church was not actually an official monument; once again, there was a gap between the "treasures of museum rarity" as the faithful saw these, and what the staff of actual "museums" deemed to be valuable. Certainly, the complaint appears to have lain in the files without obvious effect. Soon the exterior of the church too went into a rapid decline: by the 1990s, "it had no dome or crosses, and stood there all stripped bare and unsheltered," as a description on a modern Orthodox website puts it.[131] At least twenty churches across Leningrad Province were completely destroyed during the 1950s and 1960s, a figure that is not far behind the twenty-eight ruined during the 1930s.[132]

Not all the destruction was the result of official action, of however dubious a legitimacy. As in earlier decades, ordinary vandalism was also a serious problem. In 1964, for instance, a group of local youths broke into the Church of the Resurrection in Petrovskaya Gorka and damaged church vessels and icons.[133] The response of the preservation agencies was equally traditional: to remove out of harm's way any artifacts that they considered particularly valuable. A new wave of such removals—above all icons—by museum workers began in 1960. The authorization documents brooked no argument. One issued to a member of staff at the Russian Museum baldly declared that "researcher E. S. SMIRNOVA and artist-restorer S. F. KONENKOV are permitted to survey your church and, in case of necessity, to photograph and remove any icons and objects that may have historic and artistic value."[134] Sometimes church councils hit back. In summer 1963, for instance, a letter arrived in the Chancery of the Metropolitan complaining of a visit from museum works accompanied by removals:

> On June 16, 1963, staff from museums in Leningrad and Petrozavodsk arrived at Olonetsk Church, where they discovered four ancient icons:
> The Sovereign Lord,
> The Nativity of the Most Holy Mother of God,
> The Prophet Elijah,
> The Venerable St. Nicholas the Wonder-Worker.
> The said icons were decreed by the museum workers to be monuments of history, which, in their opinion, ought to be removed or transferred to the Leningrad Russian Museum. For us religious parishioners of the Olonetsk Church of the Dormition from the religious point of view those icons are something inviolable and sacred, which were painted and they were preserved by our ancestors in this holy church, and we are not prepared to give them to a museum, but wish to continue preserving

them in our church, since the Prophet Elijah and the Venerable St. Nicholas are venerated in our parish.[135]

In the case of the Lozhgolovo Church, the "museum" status of the disputed objects had been identified by the parishioners themselves, as a way of adding force to their lament about their church's despoliation. In fact, the church and its contents do not appear to have been highly valued by specialists (certainly, they made no attempt to remove the items the parishioners treasured). But in Petrovskaya Gorka, things stood the other way round: the value attached by parishioners to their icons, when arguing with the secular authorities, was purely spiritual ("from the religious point of view those icons are something inviolable and sacred"). It is possible that groups of parishioners applied the strategy that they felt would be most effective in a given context. However, the difference may equally well have lain in the discrepancy between separate groups of worshippers: the blanket term "believers" covers a wide variety of different possible reactions to, and interpretations of, the changing political, social, and cultural context.[136]

Certainly, for some religious communities, retaining "museum value" church property was the least of their worries. In Vazhiny, for example, the parish priest was perfectly content to hand over a precious icon to the Hermitage for restoration.[137] In marginal areas—and particularly those that were relatively easily accessible from urban areas—parishes themselves had good reason to be worried about the safety of valuable works of art. Whatever the law might decree about the need for *dvadtsatka* members to be "local," their attachment to the given site was likely to be far weaker than in the prerevolutionary parish, with its tight bond between spatial and spiritual community. Given the distances and difficulty of traveling, village priests, too, lived a life less that of traditional village priests before 1917 than like that of district doctors back in Chekhov's lifetime, with an area of around a hundred square kilometers to cover, and often without support. Unlike the village doctors, though, they were hedged about with a mass of petty regulations, and could get into trouble for, say, going on a mercy dash to give the last rites to someone who, technically, was a member of another parish. Retreat into despair and alcoholism was all too possible.[138]

In Leningrad itself, catastrophe and despair were far less serious threats. Churches, with their reduced but devoted circles of active parishioners, were closely cared for, and by far the majority of buildings in use (eleven out of thirteen) were protected monuments in any case.[139] There are no records of an incursion by officials, whether from museums or local soviets, in order to appropriate property, and vandalism, by this period, seems to have become rare.[140] As for harassment of believers, it certainly consolidated the process by which active parishioners were drawn mainly from the older generations, but at the same time, this could be a source of strength, since those who had lived through the persecutions of the 1930s were unlikely to be significantly daunted by the threats of the 1960s (mainly of "unpleasantness at work"). Yet the atmosphere, all the same, was tense. Church property might remain inviolate, but attempts to disrupt services were common. Atheistic education, with its groundswell of contempt for worship as outmoded, could provoke young people to, say, interrupt an Easter service with heckling (as in the "Easter Loaf and Easter Pudding" Church on April 13, 1958), or even incite a teacher to use a visit to a church as the excuse for an attack on religious faith.[141] It was scarcely surprising that religious believers took a hostile view of Khrushchev's liberal credentials; and indeed, only after the leader was deposed did the situation for worshippers, and for church buildings, begin to improve.[142]

• • •

The so-called Khrushchev "Thaw" was in fact the background to a notable chilling of the temperature both for "religious associations," and for representatives of the preservation bodies, particularly after the start of the all-out antireligious drive initiated in 1958. With a revival of the functionalist spirit in architecture and city planning also, historic churches, especially once they had closed, were again vulnerable to demolition. Plenipotentiaries were also making efforts to get churches shut down by using administrative legislation, starting a cycle of "close-condemn on technical grounds-demolish." These patterns were visible in Leningrad also, and several major churches were destroyed in the city itself and its immediate surroundings. In the countryside, local officials representing the district vectors of control, such as the village soviets, could add to the tribulations. Members of religious societies appealed to every level of the administration—in the diocese and Moscow Patriarchate, the Council on the Affairs of the Russian Orthodox Church, the municipal and rural soviets, and the preservation bodies—in order to attempt to press their rights, using the language of historical value that they had sometimes successfully espoused in the late 1940s. But this language was mostly now condemned to failure, both because of the likelihood of mismatch between "museum rarity" as understood by congregations and as understood by professionals, and because of the weakness of the preservation bodies themselves.

GIOP staff do not appear to have participated in church closures and demolitions, but their opportunities to oppose were at best restricted, so that the main method of safeguarding heritage—particularly in the countryside—was often simply to remove objects that seemed to be in danger. At the same time, the general atmosphere of the Khrushchev years meant that a powerful lobby against demolition was starting to gather in the Russian intelligentsia generally, the effects of which would shape social perceptions in the decades after Khrushchev was ousted from power.

FIGURE 27. The Trinity-Izmailovskii Regiment Cathedral (Vasilii Stasov, 1828–1835) in 1961. (GMISPb.)

CHAPTER SIX

Cynosures of the City

Church Buildings as National Heritage, 1965–1988

THE RETROSPECTIVE IMAGE OF the years after Khrushchev's deposition in August 1964 as a period of dreary stasis owes a great deal to the slogan "period of stagnation," coined by Mikhail Gorbachev at the Twenty-Seventh Congress of the Communist Party in 1986. Gorbachev came up with this as a justification for his own campaign of glasnost and perestroika. In due course, that campaign would sweep away the entire system in which church-state relations and the preservation of monuments had previously existed. Symbolic changes may have played as large a role in all this as structural and economic reform: never before had a Soviet leader suggested that stagnation might be a problem *within* the socialist system (as opposed to capitalism).[1]

Whatever the immediate political resonance of Gorbachev's assessment, from a factual point of view it was in many respects misleading.[2] Certainly, the accession of Leonid Brezhnev, consciously selected by the Politburo as a more docile figure than his predecessor, put an end to the startling U-turns and policy shifts that had characterized the Khrushchev years. "Stability of cadres" became the order of the day, and with it, the rising domination of local elites.[3] In Leningrad, the most effective leader of the period, Grigorii Romanov, was first secretary of the Regional Committee for thirteen years between 1970 and 1983. Alongside the move away from radical political intervention went de-radicalization of other kinds. Khrushchev had sought to distance the modern Soviet Union from late Stalinism through a return to the values of the first fifteen years of Soviet rule and by an assiduous promotion of the cult of Lenin. Under Brezhnev, the explicit critique of Stalin's legacy was brought to an end, and a policy of not "smacking one's lips over faults" was the order of the day.[4] Where Khrushchev had courted controversy, Brezhnev and his associates adopted a policy of consensus-building, with commemoration of the 1945 victory (May 9 was reestablished as a public holiday in 1965) becoming a festival of nationwide belonging.[5] However, the emphasis on consensus also opened the way for an inclusive, rather than engaged, assessment of the past more generally. Under Brezhnev, the recuperation of history was often generously accommodating, and included much attention to non-Soviet phenomena and objects, from the salon culture of the 1820s to the boyar palaces of the sixteenth century.[6] This was a phenomenon quite different in kind from the "national Bolshevism" of the Stalin years, with its definition of the national patrimony in terms of a strictly denominated canon of great writers, great artists, and master architects, selected for their "progressive" characteristics.[7]

Yet a highly ideologized view persisted, and some historical objects were still considered more valuable than others. The promptings for preservation were not only, and indeed not mainly, aesthetic. Buildings considered of little architectural importance, but linked with famous figures in the Soviet canon, were, on the whole, better preserved than buildings that were considered to be of high architectural importance, but whose associations were with dubious persons or practices.[8] The whole process of recuperating the national patrimony was fraught with risks. It is at one level reasonable to understand the Brezhnev era as a period when the "Russian party" in government finally gained the ascendancy, to be followed by the all-out resurgence of conservative nationalism in the Gorbachev era and its legitimation as state ideology after the collapse of Soviet power.[9] But there were other forces at work too. Just as in the Khrushchev era, the flight to the past could be inspired by distaste for official nationalism (Iurii Lotman's essay about Petersburg as an "eccentric" capital was a case in point).[10] Added to that, the rise of nationalism was deeply unpopular among some influential Soviet figures, including prominent Party officials. In 1972, B. S. Andreev, a secretary of the Leningrad City Committee, assailed "Slavophile tendencies" during a speech to Leningrad Komsomol propagandists. That too much interest in "the Russian soul" might make one slide away from "interpretation in terms of social classes" (*sotsial'no-klassovyi podkhod*) remained a besetting anxiety.[11] The growing rapprochement with "national traditions" across the USSR vied with belief that a homogeneous "Soviet" culture was just around the corner. This celebration of, versus enduring hostility to, national traditions composed the shifting ground of heritage preservation throughout the last years of Soviet power.

Churches, "Cultural Intimacy," and the Shifting Boundaries of Preservation

The enduring suspicion of "Great Russian" nationalism meant that church preservation remained a ticklish subject. As Steve Smith has pointed out, "the desire to maintain the national patrimony collided with the usually stronger desire to build an industrial, urban, and socialist society emancipated from religious belief."[12] To put it another way, one could say that churches, and religious art more generally, embodied what the anthropologist Michael Herzfeld has termed "cultural intimacy," being seen both as an inalienable expression of the spiritual attainment (*dukhovnost'*) of Russian culture, and as a manifestation of its shameful backwardness.[13]

All the same, the Brezhnev years were characterized by a remarkable change in the attitude to churches, if not necessarily to religious practice. A case that gives an indication of the shifting values was a meeting held at the Union of Architects, an institution whose contribution to the preservation of churches had earlier been vestigial to nonexistent.[14] On July 2, 1975, the Commission for the History, Preservation, and Restoration of Monuments at the Leningrad Section of the Union of Architects (LOSA) and the Union's City Planning Commission met to review yet one more proposed reconstruction of Haymarket Square. Late Soviet culture is often seen as shot through by a division between "public" and "private" (with conversations around the kitchen table replacing frank discussion in the outside world). But the July 2 meeting, described in Russian as "extended" (*rasshirennoe*) was actually typical of the times in that it lay somewhere between the "public" and "private" realms.[15] It was unadvertised, and held in a place that was, technically, open only to members. Yet it was typical, at this period, for events held in the creative unions to be attended by the family members, associates, and assorted hangers-on of actual members.[16] And in this case, those attending by official invitation (more than sixty in all, according to the official minutes) included at least a dozen non-architects, among them members of the Union of Artists, such as the sculptor Valentina Malakhieva (1923–1997), representatives of the All-Russian Society for the Preservation of Monuments of History and Culture (VOOPIiK), and other people from Soviet "public life" (*obshchestvennost'*), such as the historian T. A. Kukushkina from Leningrad State University. Other outsiders may have figured as unlisted members of the audience.[17]

The purpose of the meeting was to discuss a plan that had been drawn up in 1974 by the architect Dmitrii Butyrin (1933–2010).[18] This proposed to offset the erection of a new bus station on Haymarket Square by rebuilding the bell tower of the demolished Savior on the Haymarket.[19] The reconstruction had already been warmly welcomed in Leningrad, but had hit a stumbling block further up the line. In November 1974, a committee at the state construction authority (Gosstroi) had decided that, while a vertical accent in the square would be all to the good, this should not be in a retrospective architectural style.[20] However, the lobbying rumbled on into 1975, and the July 2 meeting was meant to be part of a further drive to get the plan agreed. The discussion rapidly started to range much further, though, with some contributions, such as Malakhieva's, becoming very emotional:

> Not long ago we were here to discuss the preservation of the Cathedral of St. Boris and St. Gleb on the Sinope Embankment. Many vital, important, and valid things were said. And then what? The cathedral got blown up! Never mind all our discussions and motions. And on the thirtieth anniversary of Victory [in World War II] as well.
>
> When our enemies blew up our monuments, it was clear what they were doing—destroying our culture. But what about when we do it ourselves? The last speaker said, "It's dreadful that the church on the Haymarket was blown up, but the people who are guilty aren't around any more, we should make a fresh start." That's a great suggestion—refuse to recognize your mistakes, and make them all over again![21]

Another participant in the discussion, the architect and architectural historian Vladimir Lisovskii, went as far as to argue that "simply reconstructing the bell tower is pointless; we should reconstruct the church too," though he did immediately add, "but that's quite impossible."[22] For T. A. Kukushkina, the demise of the church "damaged our entire culture."[23]

Whatever the extent of their disagreement about what to do with Haymarket Square in the 1975 present, those attending the meeting were firmly agreed about one thing: the demolition of the Church of the Savior had been "a fatal error of city planning" (*rokovaia gradostroitel'naia oshibka*), and an affront to their own relationship with the city as well. As the architect Oleg Bashinskii put it:

In my memories, the only thing that the Haymarket calls to mind is the church.

   The loss is incalculable. If there is any chance of reconstructing it, then that must be done.[24]

It was politically convenient to blame the "incalculable loss" on the former city architect, Valentin Kamenskii, who had retired from his post in 1971 (and who died, at the age of only sixty-eight, in the year this discussion took place). But those who criticized the plans for Sennaia were well aware that the problems amounted to more than the errant taste of one person.[25] In their discreet way, they were seeking to challenge the values of Soviet city planning overall.

Rediscovering History: The Moderation of Late Soviet Modernism

With hindsight, informed by the widespread restitution of churches to religious denominations beginning in the late 1980s, and the reconstruction of demolished ecclesiastical buildings in the following two decades, the events of 1975 perhaps do not appear very surprising.[26] However, at the time, things seemed different. It is difficult to overstate just what a turning point the Brezhnev era represented with regard to the status of churches (and more generally, historic buildings) in the aesthetic hierarchy of the Russian intelligentsia generally, and of the Leningrad intelligentsia particularly. While people did not argue, in the 1970s and early 1980s, that churches should be rebuilt because they were churches (that development came only at the very end of Soviet power), the sense of what a church might stand for shifted from the early Soviet position. Rather than being ideologically suspect unless demonstrated otherwise, more and more churches were recognized as architecturally important.[27] They were important not just in their own right, but in defining the entire urban landscape. The Church of the Sign had been demolished precisely *because* it dominated a major thoroughfare; thirty-five years later, the *absence* of a church was a planning dilemma for those reviewing a central city square.

This radical shift in perception and taste operated on a variety of different levels. As is well known, the Brezhnev era saw official encouragement being given to the celebration of heritage in academic and museum work, city planning, and "propaganda" in the broadest sense (officially published literature and the arts, journalism, and cultural work with "the Soviet masses").[28] On July 23, 1965, came the decree of the Council of Ministers of the RSFSR that established VOOPIiK, a mass-membership association modeled on VOOP (The All-Union

Society for the Protection of Nature, which had a pedigree going back to 1925). The Society's constitution (*ustav*) specified that its purpose was to "actively seek to foster the implementation of the initiatives put forward by the Party and Government for the preservation of monuments of history and culture and the employment of these to the ends of the Communist education of the Soviet people, the improvement of its level of education and culture," and that VOOPIiK was to be run on the principles of "democratic centralism."[29] The Society's annual reports, published in the yearbook of the *Great Soviet Encyclopaedia*, emphasized above all its work in preserving monuments related to the Communist past and its antecedents.[30] But under the surface, the entire drive of VOOPIiK was very different. "Democratic centralist" or no, VOOPIiK was an enormous and quasi-autonomous voluntary organization. Founded in an attempt to mold popular opinion, it was itself molded by this. The effort to involve non-professionals in the discussion of city planning had no precedent in the recent past, and its effects were to be momentous.

Hot on the heels of VOOPIiK's founding was a new decree on the protection of monuments, passed by the Council of Ministers of the RSFSR on May 24, 1966. According to a rhetorical strategy that was to become characteristic of the era, it began with fulsome praise for Soviet achievements so far (particularly "museum reserves" and the admiration they had inspired in foreign tourists). Then it shifted to veiled, but still thoroughgoing, criticism of the status quo and its "serious faults." "In a range of autonomous republics, regions, districts, and provinces, certain monument buildings are in a neglected condition, being used as different types of warehouse and distribution outlet, and for the keeping of materials that harm the condition of these monuments, and especially, the works of art inside them." All of this was a close verbal echo of the laws from 1947–1948. But then came a more pointed observation: "In a range of cases, the building and reconstruction work done in cities takes place with insufficient attention being given to the historical and artistic value of monuments of history and the complexes of building round them, they are not integrated into modern architectural *ansambli*." This represented a challenge to the fundamental premises of architecture over the last few years: previously, non-integration had been precisely the point. Building on this principle of a revision to the current understanding of the place of monuments in the city, the decree required not just, for example, the improvement of training for restorers, a shift in attitude by lessees, more intensive work on maintenance, and the rationalization of ways in which monuments were used, but the further entrenchment of "preservation zones" around monuments, and the creation of "conservation zones" in the wider city landscape.[31]

The May 26, 1966, law referred prominently to the need to protect "revolutionary monuments," but its main focus was on monuments from earlier eras.
One of the effects of the official emphasis on heritage preservation was to further
entrench the preoccupation with relics of medieval Russia, including material
with religious associations, above all icons (as evoked by Vladimir Soloukhin in an
immensely influential essay of 1966, "Black Boards"), the "white stone" churches
of cities such as Vladimir and Rostov Velikii, the early Russian chronicles and
vitae of Russian saints, and so forth.[32] Tourism to the so-called "Golden Ring"
(a range of well-preserved historic sites within easy reach of Moscow, including Pereslavl'-Zalesskii, Yaroslavl, Suzdal', as well as several of the places already
mentioned) was extensively developed, both for foreign and domestic travelers.
During excursions, it was customary to emphasize the "popular" or "folk" (narodnoe) character of the buildings that were visited, including ecclesiastical buildings.[33] As Peter Vail' and Aleksandr Genis entertainingly put it, in their general
study of the Soviet 1960s, this was a time when "every self-respecting intellectual
put a pair of lapti [peasant bast shoes] on his TV set, pinned a postcard of St.
George and the Dragon to his wall, and drank garlic-flavored vodka to the sound
of the bells of Rostov."[34]

Leningrad Preservation in the Brezhnev Era: New Canons for a New Establishment

Given the emphasis on icons and the "bells of Rostov" in late Soviet heritage preservation, Leningrad, a place without medieval Russian remains of any description
(other than artifacts in museums), obviously represented something of a special case. But Leningrad was also seen as a major jewel of the national heritage.
Vladimir Soloukhin's essay "Letters from the Russian Museum" (1966) favorably
contrasted the place with Moscow in terms of what had survived, and in 1965,
a landmark publication in Literaturnaia gazeta (Literary Newspaper) by Dmitrii
Likhachev argued vehemently that it was essential to preserve the city's historic
vertical skyline.[35]

Certainly, these sources were not any more concerned with ecclesiastical
architecture than previous celebrations of Leningrad heritage. Preferences still
continued to be driven by the literary history of Leningrad above all. One concrete case illustrating this was the decision by the Learned Council of GIOP in
1966 to allow a modern painting to be executed directly on the wall of the former

church wing of the Catherine Palace, in order to provide an entrée to the Pushkin Museum in the Lyceum Building.[36] Attitudes to church architecture, among professional architects, were often cautious at best. A letter to the deputy chairman of Lensovet's Executive Committee, drafted by members of LOSA's Department for the Preservation of Monuments in 1965, noted the importance of the Sampson Cathedral on what was then Marx Prospect (now Great Sampson Prospect). "Begun in 1728 as a memorial to the Battle of Poltava," this was a "unique" building that attracted tourists even though it had never undergone "scientific restoration," and was being used as a warehouse. The letter recommended that the building be transferred to the local district soviet and used for "social and cultural purposes," after "a mandatory complete scientific restoration" had taken place. But at this stage, a proposal of this kind was still sufficient to generate panic. The copy in the LOSA archive is endorsed with the comment,

> Aleksandr Lukich!
> Referring to the Sampson Cathedral (and in connection with the objection of K. A. Pavlova [the head of GIOP], who is in charge of the building), Korobkov considers that it would be better not to send this letter.[37]

The writer of this comment continued, "I don't agree myself," but the hesitation reflected the still uncertain status of efforts to ensure that empty churches (as opposed to those used for worship) were properly restored.

Yet by the end of 1965, LOSA was receiving, without apparent consternation, a fiery document from Professor N. A. Kozhin, director of the New Maiden Convent Museum in Moscow, and P. E. Kornilov, an art historian at the Russian Museum, "To Preserve the Beauty of Leningrad."[38] This vehemently attacked the demolition of the Savior on the Haymarket, concluding, "The entire square has been wrecked."[39] Just a few years later, a thoroughgoing rapprochement even with church architecture of the late Imperial era took place. In 1972, the Presidium of VOOPIiK started pressing the Leningrad city authorities to take in hand the restoration of the Church-Mausoleum of the Kazan' Icon of the Mother of God at the former New Maidens Convent (Novodevichii monastyr') on Moskovskii prospekt. From the point of view of traditional Petersburg preservationism, the Mausoleum was triply odious: it was unmistakably a church; it was in an architectural style (the ornate neo-Byzantinism characteristic of its architect, Vasilii Kosiakov) that had long been considered alien to local tradition; and its exuberant, freestanding bulk was out of kilter with the "severe" *ansambli* (such as Rossi's General

Staff Building) that were held to manifest the summit of architectural achievement.[40] After all, in November 1928, when the Mausoleum was placed on a list of churches scheduled for demolition, the then head of Glavnauka (the Narkompros section responsible for the preservation of monuments) had described it as being "of no artistic or historical significance."[41] On February 11, 1972, however, writing to the city architect of Leningrad, Gennadii Buldakov, Boris Piotrovskii, chairman of VOOPIiK, dwelled precisely on the building's exceptional merits:

> The building of the Mausoleum [. . .] is of great architectural and artistic value; it has six domes and is on a square plan; it is richly decorated with art ceramics and carving, and the domes have a magnificent ceramic covering on a lead lining.[42]

FIGURE 28. The Mausoleum (Kazan' Church) at the New Maiden Convent, St Petersburg (Vasilii Kosiakov, 1908–1912). (Author's photo, 2013.)

From "no artistic significance" to "great architectural and artistic value" in just four decades: there could hardly be a better indication of the radical shift in taste that had taken place.

In retrospect, Leningrad preservationism in the Brezhnev era has often been taken as primarily a form of licit opposition to the regime, a way of expressing broadly based hostility in a forum licensed by official policy.[43] It is certainly true that a motif that came up regularly in 1970s protests was the failure of the authorities to consult. An example was Boris Piotrovskii's letter to Gennadii Buldakov, quoted earlier, which went on to observe that the project for reconstructing the New Maiden Convent and Cemetery "was approved in 1967, *without the general public's being given the chance to discuss it*" (emphasis added).[44] (One can compare Valentina Malakhieva's observation at the discussion about the reshaping of the Haymarket that the protests over the demolition of the Church of SS. Boris and Gleb had simply been ignored.)[45] It would be reasonable to suppose that at least some advocates of preservation were motivated by a commitment to transparency and consultation as principles of governance, and irritation at the absence of these from "democratic centralism." This was, after all, the heyday of lobbying for human rights and self-expression, stimulated by Khrushchev's limited encouragement to debate on the one hand, and by growing awareness of Western practices on the other.[46] Emphasis on public participation in planning was to be one of the planks of glasnost, though finally achieved, and then only as a promise, just before the Soviet Union's collapse.[47]

However, the sense that the public ought to be consulted was itself the result of official policy. The Brezhnev-era debates over preservation were a phenomenon *of* the establishment, as well as an antiestablishment phenomenon. As befitted a movement that was not just sanctioned, but positively encouraged, by the authorities, VOOPIiK was permeated by the Soviet "great and good." The chairman of its Leningrad section, Boris Piotrovskii, came from a dynasty of leading archaeologists, and had been, since 1964, the director of the Hermitage, the premier cultural post in the city. Practically everyone on VOOPIiK's board in Leningrad (with the exception of financial administrators, a traditionally menial role) was a Party member.[48]

Yet if VOOPIiK's primary function at its highest levels was to express the views of the cream of the Leningrad "official" intelligentsia, the historical revival also drew in large numbers of Leningraders who would not willingly have cooperated with the authorities on any other issue.[49] For its part, VOOPIiK was not just an on-paper organization that people remember having to belong to whether they chose to do so or not.[50] It was also a serious and effective social force, comparable with the war veterans' associations that became a significant feature of the political landscape at this period.[51] Indeed, the eventual result of the pressure exerted by VOOPIiK campaigners was a marked decline in the authority of the city architect in favor of lobby groups. The new emphasis on zoning put an end to the days of grandiose unitary planning, confining reconstruction to discrete areas of the urban territory. It was no accident that Gennadii Buldakov's replacement in 1986, Sergei Sokolov (b. 1940) is now best remembered as a planner for his work in Hanoi.[52]

A "National" Church?

A further contributing factor to the revival in enthusiasm for church architecture was the shift in attitudes toward the Russian Orthodox Church itself. From late 1965 onward (after assignment of relations with "cults" to the Council on Religious Affairs of the Central Committee), attitudes toward the official groups governed by the Moscow Patriarchate became considerably less aggressive, both across the Soviet Union generally, and in Leningrad. Militancy on the part of officials started to be directed mainly at the so-called "sectarians," particularly illegal (unregistered) groups of Baptists, as well as at Orthodox dissidents.[53] The response from the Orthodox hierarchy, and many members of the clergy, was a careful show of conformity, including extensive participation in civic life, particularly the official peace movement. Indeed, a major anxiety among plenipotentiaries became that the Church was ventriloquizing official discourse so effectively that congregations had got the idea there was no essential contradiction between a Soviet and a religious identity.[54]

Religious life in Leningrad generally reflected the nationwide picture. A typical biography of a younger priest might include the fact that he had taken part in the Sixth International Congress of Youth and had impressed on Spanish guests the Church's patriotism and the complete freedom of worship in the USSR.[55] Just as elsewhere, priests made tribute to issues of the day in their sermons.[56] The point was not lost on the broader public. A popular Leningrad joke told of a unedifying squabble between a priest and a local Party worker when the latter wanted to borrow some chairs: after a series of foul-mouthed threats on both sides ("F— - the Komsomol boys and girls you wanted for your religious procession!" "Then f—- the nuns you wanted for your sauna!"), the Party worker delivered the coup de grace: "Father, language like that could get you kicked right out of the Party."[57]

From the inside, things looked rather different: conformity was usually the result of fear. "There were informers in almost all the churches," a veteran of the era recalled.[58] Some priests collaborated with the authorities; others kept their distance and felt inner distaste, but were extremely careful to avoid controversy. Father Aleksandr Medvedskii, pressured by Grigorii Zharinov to report how the clergy was responding to the Soviet intervention in Czechoslovakia, bravely stated that some priests felt that military action should have been avoided. However, he also emphasized that for the most part, the clergy did not discuss politics and stuck to religious matters. Given that Zharinov privately labeled Medvedskii a "Frondiste" even for these gently voiced objections, caution was only prudent.[59] Church elders often acted as an arm of the security services, using their position to bully congregations, extract personal gain, and as a parishioners' petition of 1966 put it, "treat the church like a fiefdom."[60]

In the wider world, radical atheism had not gone away: one major reason for encouraging the revival of national traditions was precisely to provide an alternative to religious practices.[61] Efforts were made to stop young people from participating in acts of worship even in the semi-tolerated denominations. [62] Police surveillance and tight control under public order legislation and so forth remained a fact of life. Vandalism and petty disruption of church services by Komsomol members were also enduring hazards.[63] But systematic persecution of the kind familiar from the 1930s or even the early 1960s had ended. This partial appeasement with Orthodoxy was one of the reasons why religious art and church architecture could now become more prominent in academic and popular discussions, and why the locution "Church Slavonic" (rather than "Old Slavonic") was now permissible.[64]

Attitudes to users of churches also became more accommodating. A further revision of the 1929 Decree on Religious Organizations passed on June 23, 1975, removed the blanket statement that such organizations were not "juridical sub-jects," and instead (as in the late 1940s) allowed them a range of rights, including the purchase of buildings as well as "cultic objects," means of transport, and the organization of building works. Revisions of clauses 7 and 8 took registration out of the hands of local authorities and made it the responsibility of the Council on Religious Affairs, a stipulation that at least reduced the number of offices that religious organizations had to engage with, and ensured they were dealing with informed personnel.[65] Since it was customary for officials in Leningrad to fall rapidly into line with new directives, the energy of an official such as Zharinov, formerly officious in carrying out to the letter the Khrushchev-era instructions on harassment, notably ebbed. Increasingly, church buildings and artifacts began to be seen as "part of history," something that affected not just the displays at the Museum of the History of Religion and Atheism, but also culture more broadly. It was common, among other things, for directors who were making historical films to request permission to borrow genuine ecclesiastical items to use as props, something that also suggested an association between church culture and authenticity.[66]

The late 1960s and early 1970s was not just a period of institutional and social change. The period also witnessed a shift in aesthetic perceptions. The local historian Aleksandr Margolis recalled in 2007 that attitudes to the Savior on the Blood, for instance, had totally changed during his own lifetime:

> I spent my entire childhood living on the Griboedov Canal Embankment, opposite the Savior on the Blood. I think we moved from there in 1964, yes. And my entire childhood was accompanied by talk about what a hideous church it was and how it would be a great idea to blow it up, simply get rid of it. [...] In the 1960s, you could have counted on the fingers of one hand the people who thought that church was worth keeping. There's been a complete transformation of people's attitudes.[67]

Below the surface, the transformation began before Brezhnev took over as general secretary. The new hard-line attitude to religious belief after 1959 was not of particular concern to the Leningrad intelligentsia in a broad sense, though it certainly impacted the lives of believers themselves. However, the demolitions of churches did now attract attention, as part of a rise in the sensitivity to the loss of historic buildings of all kinds. The architect Iurii Kurbatov was later to remember that the 1961 demolition of the Savior on the Haymarket, and the razing that year of the Greek Orthodox Church, along with the dismantling of the Rusca portico and the destruction of the Pirogov Museum, pushed him and many of his friends into a radical stance.[68]

During the Brezhnev years, the swell of feeling against cultural destruction began to rise. In 1966, Joseph Brodsky's poem "Halt in the Desert," one of the poet's first masterpieces, represented the demolition of the Greek Church as the onset of new barbarism:

> A bulldozer came into the church's garden
> with a ball of iron fixed to its claw,
> and the walls gently began giving way. [...]

Tonight again I'm looking through the window
and wondering to myself: where are we now?
And where are we furthest from right now—
Orthodoxy or Hellenism?[69]

Not for nothing was the destruction of the church glimpsed through the windows
of an apartment owned by the lyric hero's Tatar friends: in Brodsky's Orientalist
world view, "Tatars" stood for the traditional enemies of Christian civilization, as
in the early twentieth-century writings of another Petersburg poet, Aleksandr Blok.

The poet Boris Ivanov later recalled the text's extraordinary impact on
Brodsky's generation.

> He read some sad and bitter verses about the destruction of an *Orthodox* church
> in the center of Leningrad, and not in Stalin's times—but in our own. It was not
> a rebuke to the distant past, but a rebuke to all of us, since we had succumbed to
> cultural anemia and memory loss. This was not the versifying of a politician; it was
> the discourse of a prophet invoking the vacant spaces in our spiritual life.[70]

As the cultural critic Igor' Smirnov remembered, Brodsky and his immediate circle were not preoccupied with spiritual values in the sense of traditional
religious ones. They preferred to live for the moment: "Conversations about
higher things weren't tolerated: Soviet propaganda had usurped them."[71] At this
point, the Greek Church was less important as a "church" than as a token of the
European associations of Leningrad (Petersburg).[72] But the next generation—the
so-called "1970-ers"—had a much closer sympathy with the religious meaning of
church buildings. In their case, a major revival of interest in religio-philosophical
traditions—and in Orthodoxy as part of this—went with a passionate absorption
in the aesthetics of early modernism.[73] Naturally, intellectuals who took a vivid
interest in the activities of the early twentieth-century Religious-Philosophical
Society, and who were deep admirers of Orthodox thinkers such as Father Sergei
Bulgakov and Father Pavel Florensky, were unlikely to take a hostile view of
churches. And it was precisely in the late 1970s that an extraordinarily important work of recuperation aimed at church architecture—the study eventually
published by Vladimir Antonov and Aleksandr Kobak as *The Sacred Places of
Petersburg*—began to take shape.[74] In this publication, the churches of the immediately prerevolutionary period, including *style russe* buildings such as the Church
of the Protection of the Mother of God on Lieutenant Schmidt Embankment

(Vasilii Kosiakov, 1895–1897) were treated just as reverently as those in the previously canonical neoclassical style. It was at this point also that people began to edit the past, looking back to the demolition of the Church of the Savior on the Haymarket as a crucial moment in the development of the civic campaign to save old buildings.[75]

It was not just among cerebral members of the self-styled "unofficial culture" that values were changing. A shift in aesthetic perceptions was making itself felt within "official" culture too. The preliminary materials for the 1966 General Plan placed far more emphasis than before on the importance of historic buildings. Proposed reconstructions, such as those of the Apraksin Market and of the European Hotel on ulitsa Brodskogo, were justified in terms of returning these places to the appearance intended by the original planner (in this case, Rossi). It was underlined that buildings of the "capitalist period" needed to be valued, and that official listed buildings across the city should be used in ways that did not cause damage to their fabric.[76] The completed plan proposed that all the listed buildings in the city should undergo restoration. In 1966, after the passing of the most significant new legislation on monument protection since the late 1940s, GIOP added a number of important early twentieth-century buildings to the list of protected architecture, among them Vitebsk Station and its opulent restaurant hall, apartment blocks such as the Emir of Bukhara's House, banks, and department stores.[77] Over the following years, architectural journals began to give more and more space to buildings in the *style moderne*.[78] Such buildings were also accorded increasing prominence in guidebooks—though not, for the time being, those that had been designed for religious purposes.[79]

Working with Monuments

In the late 1960s, the policy in GIOP also began to shift. There were no dramatic personnel changes—the head from 1965, S. V. Korobkov, had been a staff member before his appointment as acting head in 1964, and his successor, K. A. Pavlova, was also a long-term member of the department—so clearly, the changes were explained by the new institutional situation.[80] On April 4, 1966, the Inspectorate's Learned Council resolved to reconfer the status of monument on the Church of Alexander Nevsky in Ust'-Izhora, delisted in 1960.[81] Certainly, policy remained conservative: not one of the new additions to the list of protected monuments in January 1966 included, say, a church from the late nineteenth or early twentieth century.[82] In 1947, there had been thirty-six churches on the official list of protected monuments; in 1968, there were thirty-five.[83] There was no special focus on churches in the 1968 *Monuments of Leningrad* either, despite the direct participation in the choice of buildings for inclusion by V. I. Piliavskii, and despite his own warm interest in church architecture.[84] However, by the late 1960s, GIOP's inspectors were increasingly ready to intervene when industrial enterprises, scientific institutes, museums, and other bodies mistreated historic buildings that they held under lease, and pressure was also put on the lessees of churches. For example, the "post-box institute" (carrying out secret military research) that occupied the Church of St. Simeon and St. Anne on Mokhovaia built by the Russian baroque architect M. G. Zemtsov in 1731–1734 was repeatedly cajoled to carry out the repainting of the façade that was required by the Inspectorate. The director of the Museum of the Arctic and Antarctic on ulitsa Marata was nagged about the hooks for Soviet flags that had been drilled into the façade of the building it occupied, the former Church of the Coreligionists.[85] Pressure increased after I. P. Sautov took over in 1975; despite the new head's relative youth (he was then only in his late twenties), he was a considerably more effective boss than Korobkov or Pavlova. In 1975, Sautov managed to force the director of the Museum to pay up 2,000 rubles (a considerable sum) after part of the ornamental railings around the church were removed, even though the latter protested that it was the local house maintenance office that had caused the damage.[86]

True, there was a limit to what even the most determined GIOP boss could do. Though a thorn in the side of church congregations and indeed local architects, particularly those of innovative ambitions, the Inspectorate was institutionally weak compared with the "military-industrial base" and the scientific organizations embedded into it.[87] The Institute of the Arctic and Antarctic, as it was now named, retained the strategic importance and prestige it had enjoyed in the prewar years.[88] Threats to eject it would have to remain threats. But the effort to regulate lessees was in itself significant, compared with the wide-ranging alterations that had been allowed to lessees in previous decades.[89] It was at this period, too, when restorers began at least a partial reconstruction of the "house churches" in the showpiece palaces at Tsarskoe Selo and elsewhere.[90]

Yet care for ecclesiastical buildings went only so far. A 1975 plan to save the Alexander Nevsky Lavra from its current state of dilapidation proposed turning the entire complex into a museum reserve. But it was the fate of the historic cemeteries on the monastery site (including the 1920s "Communist Square" right beside the Trinity Cathedral) that was used as the clinching argument. The monastery buildings mostly remained in a variety of secular uses till the end of the post-Soviet period.[91] Poets might mourn the demolition of churches, but those concerned with the history of preservation had a different focus. In 1972, for example, VOOPIiK received a letter from the widow of the engineer who in 1930 had been delegated to reproduce the missing section of the fence round the Summer Garden, filling the gap created when the Chapel of St. Alexander Nevsky was demolished. Her husband, she proudly recollected, had worked day and night to make sure that a piece of fencing was produced that would be worthy of the original. His workplace—an electrical welding workshop then located at a technical college housed in the Grenadier Barracks—had no specialists in restoration, and they had not been forwarded any instructions about how to carry out the manufacture, let alone any plans. All the same, he and the welders in the workshop had duly produced a piece of wrought-iron that was indistinguishable from the original.[92] Hesitation about the level of craftsmanship—could electro-welding really reproduce hand-made wrought iron; is a copy, constrained by the requirements of imitation, ever *exactly* like the original?—did not cross anyone's mind. The main point was to replace the loss—indeed to *better* what had previously existed, if possible. As for the loss of the chapel, that was simply off the radar.

One significant manifestation of historicism as applied to architectural monuments generally was the effort on the part of preservation bodies to ensure that such buildings should be used for their original purposes (at any rate, where these were "cultural" in nature).[93] A book published in 1981 claimed that "the most [architecturally] valuable" buildings in the city "are used in the ways envisaged by their architect creators." Among those listed were "theaters, educational institutions, covered markets, and dwelling houses."[94] Churches were conspicuously absent from the list. Occasional suggestions from members of the public that historic church buildings might be restored to worship died in the private files of the local authorities. This was the case, for example, when the parishioners of the Trinity Church at Lesnovo petitioned on March 16, 1966, using the "monuments card," for the opening of the Sampson Cathedral as a replacement for their soon-to-be-demolished church, despite their citation of authority in the Soviet media:

> After all, in the article "The Living Past," published in *Izvestiia* on 25 January this year, famous figures from the world of science, scholarship, and culture called for the salvation of that past from complete destruction! Yet all the while, in actual living reality, it somehow turns out that the most ancient monument of church architecture in one of the most beautiful cities in the world, our city, is collapsing and

disintegrating, and being used for purposes that do not in the least accord with its original function.[95]

In 1969, a group of would-be parishioners living in and around Murino, just north of the Leningrad city boundaries, mounted a concerted and well-organized campaign for the reopening of the St. Catherine's Church (built by the leading architect Nikolai L'vov in 1786).[96] The group's spokesman, one Georgii Ivanovich Slukhov, sent pages of documentation in which he detailed the rude response that he had received from local officials ("we don't need the church, we'll pull it down, and we'll have you in one by one and then see how many of you want to go through with this"). He laid out at length his own war record, and the war record of the Orthodox Church, the millions of rubles that it had raised for tanks. The eloquence failed to hit home, however. Even the claims by believers that they would look after the church (which contemporary photographs indicate was in a badly distressed condition) better than its current lessees did not produce a change of heart.[97] The suggestion that churches should reopen was treated no more favorably when it did not come from religious organizations. A letter passed by GIOP in 1970 to the plenipotentiary on religious affairs put forward a suggestion that it would be historically appropriate to return the Church of the Sign in Pushkin (Tsarskoe Selo) to believers. The response came back that this was out of the question, since no believers had actually expressed an interest in the building. GIOP's own preferred use for it was to house a historical exhibition.[98]

Just as had been the case in the 1920s and 1930s, the appropriate use for an ecclesiastical building was deemed to be "cultural education." As early as 1964, preparatory documents for the 1966 General Plan had drawn attention to the specific case of buildings that had once had a "cultured character" (the authors had intended to write "cultic," but the slip of the pen was significant). It had expressed disquiet that a number of buildings by "architects of the greatest significance," including Smol'nyi Cathedral, Trinity-Izmailovskii Regiment Cathedral, St. Catherine's Roman Catholic Church on Nevsky Prospect, St. Catherine's Orthodox Church on Vasilievskii Island, the Savior on the Blood, and the Chesme Church, were being used in ways that might damage them. The document proposed banning the construction of internal partitions; Smol'nyi Cathedral should be transferred to another use by 1970 at latest.[99]

The immediate effect of the transfer of use instruction was at best limited. As a former Leningrad Communist of reformist tendencies who held various responsible positions in the 1960s and 1970s remembered in 2009, "I grew up with deep

FIGURE 29. Smol'nyi Cathedral, 1966, photographed by the British architect Eric Lyons (The Robert Elwall Photographs Collection, RIBA British Architectural Library, SCUR 108).

atheist principles, when I was a schoolboy and student and so on, and the function and meaning of religion was totally alien to me. [. . .] When I was working for the Komsomol, none of us had the slightest doubt that Smol'nyi should be used as a hall for weight lifting and so on."[100] These attitudes still colored practices through the post-Stalin era: the Trinity-Izmailovskii Regiment Cathedral remained a warehouse right to the end of the Soviet period.

All the same, there was now pressure at the national level. In 1972, the vice-president of the Presidium of the Leningrad Section of VOOPIiK, evidently in response to a request from the Central Council of the organization, forwarded the latter a list of monuments in Leningrad and details of what purposes they were currently serving. Four of the thirteen buildings that were described as being used in "impermissible" ways were churches: the Church of the Annunciation on Primorskoe shosse, which was then a rubber factory; the Church of the Annunciation on Eighth Line, Vasilievskii Island, which was in use as a metalworks; the Alexander Nevsky Monastery (a scientific institute and an "experimental factory"); and the former Catholic Church of St. Stanislav, serving as a warehouse.[101] But what VOOPIiK considered preferable was not ecclesiastical use, but making a structure over as an exhibit hall, as now happened with Rastrelli's Smol'nyi Cathedral, taken over by the Museum of the History of Leningrad for its display, "The Development of Modern Leningrad," and with VOOPIiK's own premises, the former Church of the Mother of God Joy of Those Who Grieve. The plans for conversion of the latter were entirely secular: a cloakroom was to be created as well as "radiator cases like the ones in the House of Friendship"; the windows were to have special drapes fixed up, and the parquet was to get a coat of lacquer.[102]

At the same time, unlike the "redundant" churches of which the Church of England disencumbered itself at the same period, the disused "cultic buildings" of Leningrad were not turned into living accommodation. In this respect at least, a certain sense of the sacral persisted. It was one thing to turn a former church into a temple of art, and quite another to sully it with "daily life" (*byt*) of the kind that intellectuals disdained.[103] And general local legislation relating to the preservation of interiors, introduced in 1972, was at least notionally applicable to church buildings too.[104]

However, the legislation on interiors prescribed, in time-honored style, that features thought to be at risk should be removed to museums, not that they should be retained where they had originally been placed. Preserving the integrity of *ansambli* at this level proved next to impossible.[105] This was one symptom of the fact that the prominence of monuments in ideological terms was not necessarily underwritten by real administrative force, let alone economic support. Indeed, in 1966, members of the Section of Monuments Preservation at the Union of Architects pointed to the fact that the founding of VOOPIiK had been offset by a steep decline in restoration standards: "The work it does now is no better than the work the city rebuilding and redecoration department does. Many of the master craftsmen are no longer with us. Attitudes were different after the war, when there was a lot of restoration being done. Now the workshops spend about 30 percent of their time not on monuments and those are often the ones that count—the other work gets fitted in round them."[106] In these circumstances, churches in use, where parish councils had long built up relationships with their own teams of workmen, tended to remain the best-kept ecclesiastical buildings. As V. I. Piliavskii noted in 1970, the only major ecclesiastical building by Vasilii Stasov that was in "good condition" was the Cathedral of the Transfiguration; the others were mainly in need of work, being used for unsuitable purposes, and in some cases badly damaged as well.[107]

This insight did not stop the monuments authorities from continuing to pressure religious congregations. The GIOP file on the very same Cathedral of the Transfiguration records a familiar series of interactions: the removal of a painting by Grigorii Ugriumov, *Hagar and Her Young Son Ishmael in Their Desert Exile* (1785) to the Russian Museum, on the grounds that it "has no cultic character either in terms of plan or purpose"; queries about the status of works (whether restoration or repairs) from the tax authorities; close regulation of conservation, such as the regilding of icon kiots. As late as 1985, the official contract with GIOP stated that this could be terminated "if the monument of architecture is declared to be a museum reserve by the government," along with the usual provisions about upkeep. As before, the tone set by central government was all-important: one of the instruments for regulating church congregations in the locality was a 1980 Instruction on the Registration and Preservation of Cultural Objects in the Use of Religious Societies, issued not by the Ministry of Culture but by the Council on Religious Affairs, which reminded religious groups that "the careful treatment of these objects of value is the obligation of religious societies, and the patriotic and moral duty of all citizens of the USSR."[108] But the atmosphere was now a great deal more businesslike, and threats to expel the parish had come to an end. The officials of GIOP were only too well aware that finding another tenant who would maintain the building as carefully was out of the question.[109]

Planning the New City

The growing historicism, and new aesthetic permissiveness, did not simply have an impact on individual buildings. It fundamentally altered the principles according to which important *ansambli* were shaped. A case in point was the treatment, at this juncture, of the Haymarket area. In 1965, M. Z. Vil'ner, presenting yet another plan for redevelopment, spoke of the widespread dissatisfaction with the square's current state:

> The Haymarket—or Peace Square as it is now called—is one of the few open spaces in the city of Leningrad whose architecture and general disorganization excite dissatisfaction among most of those living in the city, and not just among professionals. Despite all the efforts to make the square architecturally elegant, it remains a conglomerate of diverse buildings. In short, it is a mishmash. And no architect can avoid confronting the issue.[110]

Interestingly, even at this stage one of the participants in the discussion, B. A. Razodeev, the head of the department of city planning at the State Inspectorate for the Protection of Monuments, was prepared to argue that the removal of churches from city squares had been an architectural disaster, resulting in desolation.

> Things like those buildings [i.e., two houses that Vil'ner proposed replacing by a modern building] should be preserved. It's not the point that they aren't official monuments. Demolishing is dead easy, but preservation isn't. In Hungary, in Italy, you can see lots of examples of a new building done really well, with marble and aluminum, next to an old one, and they rub along together, and the problem is solved with reference to the entire square. And with us? We had Uprising Square, and we pulled the church down, and built a metro station that looks like the church, only worse. So, now we've pulled down the church on Haymarket, so are we to put up a hotel? No, that won't do. So let's put up an office block, the kind you'd get anywhere ... It's not good: demolish first, think up the solution later.[111]

"We've made too big a success of the demolition," concluded Razodeev, to laughter and applause.[112]

Once an obstacle to the square's integration and elegance, the Church of the Savior was seen, by 1965, as an important constituent of its character and beauty. A decade later, preservationist attitudes had become still more assertive, with architects openly arguing that the *dominanta*, or cynosure, of many areas in central Leningrad was and should be an ecclesiastical building. In the spring of 1975, this principle was invoked to argue for the retention of the Church of SS. Boris and Gleb:

> The building of the former Church of Saints Boris and Gleb is not an official monument of architecture. However, its picturesque silhouette enlivens the humble panorama of the ordinary buildings on the embankment. After the construction of the hotel and the automated telephone exchange, the significance of the building as a kind of "buffer" between old and new buildings will grow still further. [. . .] The unjustified demolition of the Church of St. Boris and St. Gleb would be yet one more mistake of city planning comparable with the demolition of the Church of the Savior on Peace Square [the Haymarket] or the demolition of no. 16 Rimsky-Korsakov Prospect and other sites that will be extremely difficult to replace.

The case is particularly interesting because St. Boris and St. Gleb had been condemned under the General Plan of 1935. When it was allocated to a factory in 1940, the director was warned that "the building is scheduled for demolition as part of the reconstruction of the city."[113] By 1975, the aesthetic had changed. Rather than being presented as a "foreign body" in the landscape of the Neva embankments, adorned toward the center of the city by structures from the "Golden Age," it was now interpreted as an important complement to these long-valued buildings. It was itself one of a triangle of buildings (all, as it happened, ecclesiastical) that made up the core *ansambl'* of this particular area:

> The Church of St. Boris and St. Gleb plays the role of the third basic *dominanta* of the embankment. Its city planning role is quite different from that of Smol'nyi Cathedral or the Alexander Nevsky Monastery. To begin with, the building of the former church, with its picturesque silhouette, works to harmonize and organize the domestic buildings around it; in addition, its well-chosen location, on a bend of the Neva, means that, without jarring against the main architectural dominant of the site, the church nonetheless contributes to the rhythmic articulation of the three-kilometer-long embankment [on which it stands].[114]

Thus, the "city planning significance" (*gradostroitel'noe znachenie*) of church buildings was now a generally accepted principle of Leningrad architecture—in professional discussions, if not the mainstream press. The discussion of Haymarket

Square that took place a few months later was entirely in accordance with the shifting views, as was the concern on the part of VOOPIiK's board to provide money for church restoration. In 1972, for example, the Society spent 5,000 rubles (about double the annual salary of a middle-ranking academic) in order to draw up plans for a restoration of the crumbling exterior of St. Catherine's Church at Murino, and four times that on work at the Chesme Church, in very poor condition after a fire back in the 1930s.[115]

Yet there were still only two church-museums with a display that at least partly focused on architecture: the Cathedral of St. Peter and Paul in the eponymous fortress, and St. Isaac's Cathedral. Even here, religion was not the main point. The Cathedral of St. Peter and Paul was mainly presented to tourists as the shrine of Peter the Great's sarcophagus, and the Foucault's pendulum hanging from the dome of St. Isaac's as an aid to "atheist education" continued to hark back to an era when defusing the "counterrevolutionary" character of these structures had been a prime objective.[116] And most churches, including architectural monuments, which were not used for worship, remained in dire condition, particularly in areas where tourists were unlikely to see them.[117] At the eighteenth-century Church of Prophet Elijah in the Gunpowder Factory district, repairs after a fire in 1974 dragged on inconsequentially for years; the fine neo-Gothic Church of Saints Peter and Paul at Shuvalovo was in a ruinous state.[118] All the same, ideals of city preservation now accommodated and indeed focused on these structures, despite the continuing severe control of the religious belief that had been the original force behind their construction. The shift from "counterrevolutionary monument" to valued achievement of national and popular tradition was differently nuanced, and more gradual, in Leningrad than in some other Russian cities. But by the mid-1970s, it was well entrenched.

As for Leningrad's hinterland, the effects of the new interest in history were rather muted. Despite their antiquity, none of the towns in the province were restored and repackaged in "Golden Ring" style (instead, tourists were bussed to Novgorod). Important monastic sites such as the Alexander Svirskii Monastery and the Great Monastery of Tikhvin continued falling down, as did many of the wooden churches out in the villages, unless some local warden, perhaps self-appointed, stopped this happening. And the rise of interest in church culture was not a uniformly positive development, since the emergence of a semi-legal market for icons and other artifacts meant that theft became increasingly attractive.[119] The files of GIOP, VOOPIiK, and the Union of Architects give a clear sense of the pervasive neglect. As reported to the Monuments Preservation Section of LOSA in 1966:

It's essential to work on the cathedral in Kingisepp, or else they [presumably, the local city soviet] will blow it up. It's completely filthy. The estimate specifies 200,000 [rubles]. We've asked the [State Restoration] Workshops to do the planning and no more. Local volunteers will do all the actual work. That'll cost only a third as much.[120]

At the same time, as the description also indicates, there was now more likelihood that closed churches would attract the attention of the rank-and-file members of the intelligentsia who were the core audience for the publications and broadcasts about Russian history. This was particularly true in the vicinity of Leningrad. A striking case in point is a letter written by a VOOPIiK member in Sestroretsk, expressing concern about "a badly damaged church" in the nearby resort of Zelenogorsk, on the Primorskoe shosse:

We know it was built in 1912. The architect is unknown.[121] At the moment, the Zelenogorsk Food Trade Depot is in it. You can see war damage inside and outside, it looks quite pitiful. The bell towers are damaged, the plaster's coming off, so you can see red brick in places. But once it was a grandiose and impressive building. Now it would cost lots to restore it. It stands on a prominent place, right by the coastal highway, where tourists going out for trips are always passing by, and foreigners among them. The Sestroretsk Executive Committee [of the local soviet] often gets letters from members of the working people and intelligentsia expressing the desire that the building should be restored. But it is hardly unique and possessing of such architectural and artistic virtues as to deserve preservation. The Sestroretsk District Committee of the CPSU and the Executive Committee of the District Soviet are unanimous—pull the building down and put something new up there instead.

The letter-writer's obvious confusion about the situation did not dissipate as he continued to ponder what should be done. Perhaps an organization should be found to build a tourist center and repair the church? Locals of long standing were unanimous that it should be preserved, and that would be a "far-sighted step in a political sense," bearing in mind, once again, those foreign tourists. At the same time, it seemed that the Architecture and Planning Committee had already made a formal or informal decision in favor of demolition.[122] While the response in the highest levels of VOOPIiK to this artless missive has not survived, the church did; restoration commenced in 1980 (to have it looking respectable in time for the Moscow Olympics), and plans were laid to convert it from a warehouse into a local museum.[123]

From "Buildings" to "Zones": The Historicization of *ansambli*

By the start of the 1980s, the last barriers to the preservation of churches on equal terms were beginning to shift. One factor behind this was the spread of "preservation zones" (*zapovednye zony*, introduced by the heritage preservation law of 1966, but implemented considerably later in most places, including Leningrad, where local legislation came through only in 1969).[124] These represented a radical break with the old principles of preservation according to historical and aesthetic value, since the idea was to conserve an entire city quarter, complete with its different historical layers. In 1980, once again in response to legislation at republic level, Lensovet widened the concept of the "preservation zone" (or, as the term now was, "reservation zone," as with "nature reservation" in ecology, and the "museum reservations" set up in the 1940s).[125] Over the following years, planning began on a large "reservation zone" in central Leningrad, running from the Winter Palace around to ulitsa Zheliabova (whose historical and modern name is Bol'shaia Koniushennaia). The intention was to turn the entire area into an outdoor museum, complete with woodpiles and carts in external courtyards. Rather than focus on the Golden Age, the zone was meant to cut a transverse slice through the historical evolution of Petersburg.[126] Certainly, the plan for the Royal Stables quarter did not spell out what was to happen to the church that was part of the complex in Koniushennaia ploshchad' itself, but the commitment to integration pointed away from the previous method of preserving historic buildings on an "atomized" (*tochechnaia*) basis while new structures were raised all round them, as had happened to the Chesme Church in the three previous decades.

Another sign of shifting attitudes was that concern about the "eyesore" effect of disused churches and the likely impact of these ruins on tourists had become still more acute than in the past. This now applied to sites well beyond the city center also. In 1982, for instance, Grigorii Zharinov was instructed to check the condition of all church buildings that were visible along major tourist routes leading out of Leningrad, and inform the Council on Religious Affairs whether they were receiving any visitors.[127]

Alongside the rise in stock of churches came a further softening of the line toward religious communities. The rapid leadership changes of the next years— with four leaders in less than three years, after Brezhnev died on November 10, 1982, to be replaced by Yuri Andropov until February 9, 1984, and then Konstantin Chernenko until March 10, 1985, before finally a haler and longer-lasting general

FIGURE 30. The Chesme Church (Georg Felten, 1777–1780), photographed in 1974 by the British architect Bernard H. Cox. (The Robert Elwall Photographs Collection, RIBA British Architectural Library, SU 322.)

secretary emerged in the person of Mikhail Gorbachev—did not affect the drift toward greater and greater accommodation with Orthodoxy.

The approaching millennium of the Christianization of Russia, due in 1988, acted as an important incentive to this process. In Poland, the Catholic Church had used the putative millennium of Poland's Christianization (which fell in 1966) to extract concessions from the Communist government, going as far even as the building of new churches.[128] No doubt the Orthodox leadership had watched these events closely and thirsted for parity of esteem, while from another point of view, the events in Poland may have persuaded the Soviet leadership that concessions to religion would likely strengthen church-state relations and act as a force for consolidation, rather than disruption. Whichever way, a softening of control at the central level began to be evident several years in advance of the festival.

Already by 1982, the Council on Religious Affairs was preparing a new codex of legislation whose drafts manifested subtle shifts in terminology: the term "canon law" had managed to find its way into the document. The code now linked together the release of a particular church and the registration of a given religious community and failed to mention that meetings of the *dvadtsatka* should only take place with prior notice to the authorities. Not all these changes went down well with local plenipotentiaries. Grigorii Zharinov, for instance, sharply criticized the term "canon law" and the coupling of registration and release of churches, and argued vehemently that allowing meetings without consultation "deprives us of an important lever of control over the religious association, and the possibility of influencing them in a timely way."[129] His assessment that leverage had been curtailed was entirely accurate. But by now, his understanding of the plenipotentiary's role was out of step with the general direction of policy. As Zharinov would discover, a simple "no" was now a more problematic reply to religious groups than it had been in the past. In the latter half of 1982, an Old Believers' group refused to accept that it could not expect to claim for its own use the Sampson Cathedral, since this was scheduled to become the home of a branch of the Suvorov Museum dedicated to the Battle of Poltava. The community leader, Zharinov complained, had insisted on the group's right to the cathedral, speaking in "a rude and provocative manner."[130] Less than fifteen years previously, that was the tone that believers could expect from officials; now the balance of power was beginning to shift.

The approach of the millennium did not bring with it a complete abandonment of antireligious work. In 1985, the Council on Religious Affairs commended to plenipotentiaries across the country the Ukrainian regional "campaign against bourgeois clerical propaganda in connection with the millennium of the Christianization of Russia."[131] Zharinov took care to bring the document to the attention of his staff.[132] In Leningrad, the drive to promote rational atheism lasted until the very end of Soviet power. As late as 1986, the Komsomol, in collaboration with the State Museum of Ethnography in Leningrad, mounted an expedition to Pskov province in order to carry out an investigation of religious beliefs among young people, and to inculcate new, secular traditions.[133] Zharinov did his best to prevent the canonization of Blessed Xenia as part of the celebrations for the millennium, first attempting to undermine the historical validity of the cult (there were no objective facts about Xenia's life), before turning to the likely negative impact of the canonization on rational secularism: "We are convinced that the canonization of Blessed Xenia absolutely must not be allowed, because it will strengthen religious fanaticism and increase the number of adherents of her cult, who are resident by no means only in Leningrad."[134]

But arguments that had formerly been accepted without further ado were starting to lose traction. The Chapel of the Blessed Xenia, restored to the Orthodox faithful in 1984, was only the first of four churches in Leningrad and its outskirts to be handed over in preparation for the millennium.[135] Metropolitan Aleksii of Leningrad now dealt directly with the chairman of the Council on Religious Affairs, bypassing Zharinov in order to argue with the central authorities for more church openings and expanded space to house his own quarters.[136] The millennium, with thousands of leading churchmen expected from all over the world, was the quintessential example of an occasion when Soviet international prestige depended on underlining that "religious associations" were being treated by the strict letter of constitutional rights. Metropolitan Aleksii exploited the situation with consummate skill.[137] In similar vein, the official "Information Bulletin" produced for in the run-up to the celebrations delicately reminded the reader of the oppressions visited on the faithful in the past, before concluding, "But the main thing is that in Leningrad now, as in the entire country, perestroika reigns, with the renewal of all sides of life and social activity."[138]

By the middle of the 1980s, churches were firmly ensconced in the "heritage landscape" for secular Leningraders as well.[139] For example, in December 1984, a woman by the name of Valentina Toporovskaia wrote to VOOPIiK to express her distress over the condition of Smol'nyi Cathedral, which she had seen on a recent nostalgic visit to her former district:

> I spent my girlhood years on Tverskaia Street, which is next to Smol'nyi—the headquarters of the Russian Revolution. I often used to go walking across the gardens

outside it to Smol'nyi Cathedral, admiring the beauty of the architecture and the shining domes. The Cathedral is linked for me with deeply personal memories that have stayed with me all my life. It was painful to see, I felt as though a bit of my heart had been ripped out, when they took one of the side golden domes down. I can see that maybe it was necessary to do this, and the hope that it'll soon be restored won't leave me alone.

Now I live at the address given on the envelope [in a different part of Leningrad], but I often visit the spots that hold so many memories for me, and I look with sadness at the beheaded tower—and for how long already! I went into the Institute of Party History to ask, since it's in the wing under that tower, but they couldn't tell me anything much.

Dear editors! Please answer: why did they take the dome down? Who was responsible? And, most important of all, when will that yawning gap be filled?[140]

Certainly, it was not the religious significance of Smol'nyi that mattered for Toporovskaia, but "deeply personal memories." But the fact that a church building could have such associations was an indication of how the cultural landscape had shifted.

For the most part, Leningraders still perceived churches in a "secular" way, but they were increasingly convinced also that they were not buildings like any others. As Galina Burkazova, a resident of Moskovskii district, put it in 1984 when writing to complain about the condition of the Trinity-Izmailovskii Regiment Cathedral,

It's just standing there like a big dirty blotch on the center of the city and also by the way it's on a main street and after all it could make a big impression on people if it was turned into a picture exhibition or children's crafts or something, but all there is there now is some warehouse or whatnot. For instance in Yaroslavl all the churches have been freed from warehouses and even the frescoes on the walls are being restored. Why can't they restore such a big cathedral[?] It would be so good to see the cathedral in proper condition.[141]

To restore a church to "proper condition" might not require the revival of its original function, but it did now mean extensive repairs and use for "cultural purposes." In cases such as these, staff at the monuments preservation bodies hastened to reassure the letter-writers that the situation was in hand. Valentina Toporovskaia was informed that the dreadful state of Smol'nyi was down to the fact that restoration was currently in progress, while G. L. Burkazova received a letter from the district soviet to the effect that pressure was being put on the lessees to complete the necessary repair work.[142] Again, the shift in attitude from just a few years previously was marked.

Equally insistent was A. V. Bukvalov, a Leningrad scientist and amateur local historian who wrote in 1986 to Dmitrii Likhachev to complain about the fate of another piece of church architecture. In this case, it was plans to return the exterior of the St. Panteleimon Church to its appearance in the early eighteenth century that had provoked the sense of affronted memory. The Church, used for storage in the postwar years, had recently been handed over to the Museum of the History of Leningrad as the premises for a museum dedicated to the naval battle of Gangut, the occasion for its original construction. Work on the reconstruction had been assigned to Irina Benua (Benois), a relation by marriage of the city's most famous architectural dynasty; in the 1940s, she had been responsible for the reconstruction of the Kikin Chambers, another of the city's important early eighteenth-century buildings. This decision was an indication of the rising significance of churches in city planning; in 1934, there had been pressure to demolish the church because of its awkward location on a street corner.[143]

Despite the pedigree of the architect and the approbatory press coverage, Bukvalov was not impressed. He failed to get anywhere with a reader's letter to *Leningrad Panorama*, which got published in the journal along with a patronizing response from a member of the editorial staff suggesting he did not know what he was talking about. But Bukvalov was not to be deterred, insisting to Likhachev that the restoration of just this one building would be a historical aberration. The entire environment had altered since the early eighteenth century, with the Particular Wharf long gone. However, just down the street was the monument to the Battle of Hanko, a remarkable artifact of the recent past, and one designed with the current architecture of the church in mind. The "optimal date" that mattered was not that of the building, but of the *ansambl'* as a whole.[144]

Part of the background to such complaints, as the letters themselves indicated, was the surging interest in heritage preservation right across Leningrad. Bukvalov's letter in particular displayed a detailed familiarity with the arguments appearing in the architectural press about conservation zones (he clearly read every issue of *Leningrad Panorama* with the greatest care). By the mid-1980s, this preoccupation was beginning to acquire increasing political salience. As Bukvalov wrote, architecture was too important to be left to mere experts.[145] In other Soviet cities, the freedom of association allowed under Gorbachev's politics of glasnost—according to which citizens might legally hold demonstrations and register so-called "informal groups"—acted as the engine for environmental protests. In Leningrad, however, it was the demolition of buildings that brought people on to the streets. The crucial cases were secular buildings—the Del'vig House on Vladimirskaia ploshchad' and the Hotel Angleterre. In both these instances, the literary associations of the buildings concerned were crucial, true to the common Leningrad pattern whereby architecture that was not sanctified by text tended not to break the surface of memory politics.[146] However, there was no longer any hostility to the preservation of churches, which—admittedly mainly to a public beyond the heritage movements themselves—had come to seem a priority.

After the millennium in 1988, the tide turned once and for all. Metropolitan Aleksii himself described this as "the beneficial process of normalization of relations between the Church and the state."[147] In the altered circumstances, heritage preservation bodies had also changed their attitude to "religious associations." A harbinger of the new trend was Metropolitan Aleksii's capacity to secure backing from the committee steering Leningrad's bid to be accorded the status of a UNESCO World Heritage Site when he put forward a request to return the Cathedral of St. Peter and Paul at Petrodvorets (Peterhof) to the Orthodox Church.[148] Alongside buildings, Metropolitan Aleksii busied himself with applications for the return of key devotional objects from state collections, such as a "sculptural icon" from Il'esha village church that in the past had been transferred to the Russian Museum.[149] By the spring of 1990, Metropolitan Aleksii had agreed with the Council on Religious Affairs a "stage-by-stage" return of important architectural monuments, such as the churches in the Varlaam Monastery on Lake Ladoga.[150] Aleksii's election as Patriarch on June 7, 1990 brought the drive for restitution into the center of the ROC and ensured that the possession of churches would henceforth be a fundamental issue of church-state relations.

The fact that state institutions were, once perestroika started, working in an ideological frame that was at best only notionally Communist obviously made the rapprochement with Orthodoxy easier. Once the Church was no longer seen as an intrinsically anti-Soviet institution, it made sense to level the field of negotiation. Added to that, with greater emphasis on individual budget control (*khozraschet*), the return of churches to Orthodox worship made good financial sense—because that way the costs of restoration and the administration of repairs were also diverted to the Church. Fully aware of this, Metropolitan Aleksii did his best, in early 1990, to press for state funding, but his hopes were, in the meantime, foiled.[151] For decades, heritage preservation specialists had simply accepted that the vast majority of historic churches would be in secular hands, and less than optimally kept; now, they accepted that working together with the Church was the way forward.

Once the process of accommodating religious values began, events rapidly progressed—as with glasnost generally—from exclamations that certain developments were "unthinkable" to the proposal, within months or even weeks, of exactly such reforms. In 1986, Professor N. S. Gordienko wrote that the cult of Blessed Xenia was "a rotting haven of religious obscurantism," and that the canonization of this imaginary saint would precipitate Soviet culture down a slippery slope. "Now it's Blessed Xenia; before long there'll be talk of canonizing John of Kronstadt—a blatant reactionary and obscurantist. And what then? Are we to follow these Karlovci canonizations by canonizing Nicholas II and other 'new martyrs'?"[152] But it was the language of "forward-thinking" godless agitation that now sounded obsolete. Within four years, John of Kronstadt had indeed been canonized, and a decade later, he was joined—as if in Gordienko's worst nightmare—by Nicholas II and his family. In between these two dates—the canonization of John of Kronstadt in 1990 and of Nicholas in 2000—also lay a total transformation of the legislative landscape. The Decree on Freedom of Conscience of 1990 restored conditions of religious toleration not experienced in Russia since the period between February and October 1917. This was followed by a new post-Soviet statute "On the Freedom of Conscience and Religious Associations," passed on September 26, 1997, which began to shape the religious landscape explicitly in favor of "traditional faiths." From now onward Orthodoxy, nominated in the legislation as Russia's primary faith, in historical and cultural terms, would begin to develop an ever closer relationship with the state, with its premier buildings understood as the appropriate places for the Russian Federation's rituals of power.

• • •

The Brezhnev era saw a fundamental reassessment of the existing principles of city planning in Leningrad, and of the place of ecclesiastical architecture within this. The heritage preservation movement started to gain real momentum after the founding of VOOPIiK in 1965. The society's files, like those of the heritage preservation section of the Union of Architects, point to a remarkably dynamic debate on the role of churches in city planning, and make clear the underlying links of the argument with broader shifts in attitude to aesthetics and national identity. While in terms of everyday practices such as maintenance, churches often

FIGURE 31. The St Peter and St Paul Cathedral (Domenico Trezzini, 1712–1733), photographed by Ian Thompson, 1988.

continued to be neglected, symbolically they were starting to play a far larger role in the "Petersburg text" than at any period since 1917.

At the same time, there was persisting uncertainty about the role of churches in the landscape and a tenacious commitment to the secular use of buildings that were considered to be of historical and aesthetic value. It was not until the end of the 1980s that churches listed as architectural monuments began being returned to believers for worship in significant numbers, and not till the post-Soviet period when the return of some of Leningrad's premier buildings was agreed. Attitudes to the role of the church in city planning also changed slowly, with new building mostly confined to small commemorative structures, or to the city's suburbs.[153]

As well as reflection on the tangled paths of church-state relations in the late Soviet period, the history of attitudes to "cultic buildings" from 1964 onward also provokes reflection on the history of "socialist cities" in a broader sense. Classic studies of late socialist urban geography, such as R. A. French and F. E. Hamilton's *The Socialist City* (1979), have tended to emphasize the peculiarities of spatial structure, such as the absence of suburbs, the different configuration of industrial/residential zoning, and the lack of correlation between social status and place of residence (i.e., the nonexistence of "working-class" and "middle-class" areas, districts denominated by particular ethnic groups, and so on).[154] Commentators from post-socialist Russia have tended to make arguments along similar lines.[155] The discussions over the fate of churches, by contrast, show increasing preoccupation with a feature that was *not* specific to the socialist city. Certainly, these discussions were ideologically localized (it was not until the mid-1980s that Soviet newspapers and journals began to give space to the issue of church conservation), but at the same time, they happened in institutionally significant places, such as the Union of Architects, an indication that ecclesiastical architecture was increasingly becoming part of "official" Soviet culture.

The handling of religious buildings in Soviet Russia was, by the 1970s, no longer "Soviet" in the way this would have been understood in the early 1920s (when the non-Soviet character of these structures had regularly been underlined).[156] Added to that, contemporary Western Europe was seeing a drop in church attendance, not infrequently accompanied by the demolition or radical conversion of "redundant churches."[157] But the popular alternative paradigm of "normalization" (often applied to developments such as the increasing importance of private life in late socialist culture) does not fit the situation either, since the social and economic constriction of religious communities' activities (for instance, the ban on fundraising and on access to state grants) still expressed a radical secularism that owed something to the socialist past. And if the decline in church attendance in Western Europe was accompanied by (or symptomatic of) a decline in association-ism more broadly, the rise of interest in religious practice in Brezhnev-era Russia was paralleled or generated by a rise of interest in alternative forms of social prac-tice, including rock music and yoga as well as Orthodox Christianity.[158] Whichever way, individualism was becoming increasingly apparent, expressed in city plan-ning projects as well as beliefs. As Blair Ruble observed in 1990, "A socialist state system explicitly concerned with promoting collective values clings to an urban design philosophy that elevates *res privata* over *res publica*"[159]—though it was less a case of "clinging" to such a philosophy and more one of *asserting* it by the con-struction of urban spaces that expressed a commitment to one-family housing and conceded, behind the scenes at least, a good deal of leeway to at least some citizens in the expression of their own concepts of how cities should develop.

From the late 1960s to the early 1980s, Soviet culture became less socialist, in terms of commitment to rational collectivism, egalitarianism, and radical athe-ism. But the urban landscapes that resulted did not necessarily resemble those in Western Europe or the United States. The very conservatism with which the fab-ric of historic cities was handled was something exceptional.[160] It is unclear that what happened in Leningrad was "typical" of processes in other Soviet urban centers, given that the rise of local identity was a key development of the period. But the arguments in the city certainly expressed the paradoxicality and diver-sity of an era when the boundaries between "official" and "unofficial," like those between "public and "private," became increasingly permeable. Architecture and city planning were, of all the art forms, most closely integrated with the Soviet state-making project, with the planning institutes subordinated to the munici-pal and national "power vertical."[161] Yet "cognitive dissonance" was visible even there, with views of appropriate strategy varying from explicitly *passéiste* to avant-garde. For those involved in these arguments, even the Brezhnev years seemed a period less of enduring stability and predictability, when "everything was forever until it was no more" than one of "frozen conflict"—of a kind that would come radically to the surface when Mikhail Gorbachev's policy of glas-nost allowed broad public discussion of debates previously circulating in narrow circles of the professional intelligentsia.[162]

Conclusion

THE "SOCIALIST CHURCH" REPRESENTED a bundle of contradictions that the proponents of heritage policy in Leningrad and Petrograd could never entirely unravel. On the one hand, commitment to preservation in the city was, compared to other major Soviet cities, unusually high; on the other, its church buildings belonged to what, in the context of preservation policy generally, was considered a late, and therefore inferior, epoch. This background stripped professionals and the general public of the clarity that accompanied discussions of, say, the Winter Palace or the Stock Exchange. It meant that the overall contours of discussion followed those at national level, with policy toward churches becoming more or less accommodating at different eras depending on changes in the legal regulation of religious affairs on the one hand, and historic buildings on the other. Alongside questions about the Soviet "usable past" and how state control over the cultural patrimony should be asserted and defended, the debates over the fate of churches invoked crucial questions about the role of public organizations and about how immovable property should be administered. Discussion was never disinterested; the constantly changing cargo of "heritage objects" became the target of different groups (museum workers, planning officials, religious associations, interested members of the public) both in and outside the state administration. "Cultic buildings" and objects might be treated instrumentally (monetized, regarded as usable space, or a source of raw materials), but they might equally well be cherished for their symbolic value, and their role in boosting the political, social, and cultural capital of people and groups, both within the state administration and outside. Rather than answering simplistic questions about the efficacy of "state power" in the abstract, or presenting a totalized world of "Soviet values," this narrative shows us a thickly peopled and often confused territory of fallible individuals reactively making haphazard and contradictory decisions. Though it was rhetorically convenient for Brezhnev-era preservationists such as Dmitrii Likhachev to refer to the 1920s as the pinnacle of Soviet achievement (thus suggesting preservation's "Leninist" credentials), the creators of Soviet heritage policy struggled then and at all times to combine cohesiveness and inclusivity at the conceptual level, let alone to settle the pressing issues of legal enforcement and financial viability. In this they were no different from their counterparts in other countries, but in a country torn apart by political and natural disasters, the demands placed on them were higher, and the ingrained suspicion of the voluntary sector between the mid-1930s and the mid-1960s robbed conservation work of a vital source of ancillary support at precisely the point when it was most needed.

The collapse of the old order in 1917 left both Orthodox churchmen and heritage preservationists with hopes of change for the better, but in precisely opposite directions. Orthodox clergy anticipated, when the Church Council began work in August 1917, "the opportunity for and right to self-determination," free of interference from the state. Heritage specialists, however, eagerly awaited "the recognition of all buildings and movable property belonging to churches, monasteries, chapels, dioceses, and the vestries and treasuries attached to these as the property of the state in general."[1] Both groups regarded state aid as their inalienable prerequisite, but accompanied by freedom from control on the one hand, and freedom to control on the other. This led to a painful process of adjustment, as it emerged that state paymasters expected them to contribute directly to the process of creating a new Soviet ideology and identity if they were to receive anything at all. "Self-determination" was more or less ruled out, and "recognition" strictly limited.

While it would go too far to describe the separation of church and state initiated by the January 20, 1918, decree as "a legal fiction" (since the expulsion of religious interests from the school system, for example, was a decisive and overt process), the Orthodox Church was faced with exactly the opposite of the political and social autonomy plus financial aid that had been the ideal set out at the Church Council in 1917.[2] Unlike *associations cultuelles* under the French secularizing law of 1905, Soviet "religious associations," after surrendering jurisdiction over "cultic buildings," did not receive subsidies, but increased financial burdens. It was this key point—the assignment of responsibility for church buildings to "religious associations" without the allowance to these of means to support conservation measures, or even of ways to generate funding on their own initiative— that, right to the end of Soviet power, bedeviled efforts by parish associations to maintain buildings in the condition that the representatives of state associations required. Officials in the organs controlling church-state relations might spy on congregations and comb sermon texts for subversive content, but they did not interfere with the substance of the liturgy or with theological debates. Inspectors of the monuments protection offices did, however, directly dictate to congregations which icons might be repainted, how to repair the iconostasis, and whether a worn-out carpet could be replaced. They could, and did, disrupt church life with their surveillance and control.[3] These were interventions like no others into the daily life and material world of religion.

Yet heritage preservation was itself a marginal area of the state administration. Certainly, the preservation bodies were (unlike religious bodies) fully "Soviet" organizations, ensconced into the "power verticals" of the time, both at the national (ministerial) and at the municipal level. But their activities often took an "on-paper" form and were fraught with retreat and compromise. Only with reservations can their activities over the decades be fitted into the customary "rise in state capacity" model that sees the 1930s as representing a transformation in effective control from the center.[4] Even in the postwar era, when more powerful legislation and a greater ideological commitment to cherishing the past gave them a support they had lacked before 1941, officials often found it hard to enact the legislation whose exemplary status was trumpeted at the national and international level. At this period too, the Orthodox Church (renamed the "Russian Orthodox Church" as a token of its new national-patriotic status) had more political and cultural leverage than before. The plenipotentiaries on religious affairs took a less punitive position than the officials of the local "church offices" who had pressed for closures and demolitions. But their shift of position when top-level policy changed in 1959 indicated that their capacity to accommodate was fragile. The preservationists' ideal—the rationally organized museum in the former cultic building—was mostly impossible to realize. Unlike some cities and towns, where church buildings stood empty, in Leningrad there was intense pressure on space. Often unused religious buildings had to be used for purposes that were damaging to their fabric. This became increasingly embarrassing as concern for heritage preservation rose. Once Orthodoxy was rehabilitated as an essential part of the national past, the stand-off with religious users became a battle that architect-restorers could no longer win.

The trajectory to reach this point was long and indirect. In France, it took only a few years for the rupture between church and state engineered in 1905 to be at least partially repaired—though the underlying principle of division survived into the twenty-first century. The secularization process in Soviet Russia was pushed through far more brutally. Certainly, the original January 20, 1918, decree was at first enforced erratically. But by the start of 1924, the spatial separation of churches and other types of public building was nearly complete. After several years of mainly administrative attrition, the April 8, 1929, Decree on Religious Organizations brought the resumption of all-out hostilities, with war declared on the parish churches. By this point the political leverage of the Orthodox Church, divided as it was into competing factions, was more or less nonexistent. Congregations and clerics backed away from open protest, and used any legislative loophole they could, including the laws relating to heritage preservation. In correspondence among themselves, clergy and laity adhered to prerevolutionary linguistic norms: a request to the authorities was always a *proshenie* (petition), and not (in the Soviet term) *zaiavlenie* (announcement). But when dealing with state officials, they invoked Soviet legal instruments, and underlined their loyalty to Soviet power. Yet alongside this accommodation to the demands of the time (widely recognized in church history over recent decades), they stubbornly retained a view of church property that saw churches as more than piles of bricks, and icons as more than painted boards.

In the first two decades of Bolshevik rule, significant sections of the population, particularly grassroots activists and officials of local soviets, regarded church buildings themselves as "havens of obscurantism," best torn down lest they encourage insidious feelings of piety in the benighted masses. Such feelings were widespread in Leningrad, which had an active and vocal antireligious movement, with (by 1931) two museums to its name, and where local officials were relatively well-educated, and heeded (indeed, anticipated) the demands of higher political authority. When churches survived, it was for secular reasons: they had been created by great architects, and lacked an "odiously ecclesiastical appearance."

The "Great Patriotic War" only partially changed this attitude to the "city text" in Leningrad. The churches that were at the center of the nationwide upsurge in patriotic feeling for architecture came from a period long before the city was built. Added to this, the drive to implement the General Plan of 1935 continued into the

1960s. The idea of transferring the administrative center to the southern extreme of the city was abandoned, but work began on turning the Haymarket (renamed "Peace Square") into a public space fit for a prestige district in a "model socialist city." The demolition of the Church of the Savior on Peace Square both crystallized and precipitated anxieties about the radical transformation of Leningrad. At the same time, it was, even now, not primarily as "churches" that the Church of the Savior, and later the Church of St. Boris and Gleb, and Vasilii Kosiakov's Funerary Church in the New Maiden Convent, stirred up feelings in many members of the Russian intelligentsia.[5] Rather, these were seen as architectural features, "dominants" in the city panorama—a status that reflected a vacuum at the heart of Soviet planning as much as it did regret for the past. Soviet planners and architects were uneasily aware that they had not arrived at a consensus about what a suitably distinctive modern feature in a historic public space might be. The attachment to churches as buildings was still possible only if the religious aspects of the building were screened out.

This was one reason why relations with heritage preservationists and the Orthodox faithful did not become significantly warmer in the postwar era. Another was that the greater institutional leverage of the preservation bodies and their enhanced capacities to enforce the letter of the law—at any rate, where relatively weak institutions were concerned—generated higher numbers of conflicts than in the prewar decades. Petitioners might invoke protection legislation when trying to get churches opened, but congregations also did their best to stave off the expensive "counsels of perfection" that architect-conservators forced upon them (as in when Metropolitan Grigorii sought backing from the plenipotentiary on the affairs of the ROC in an effort to reject demands to have the domes of the Prince Vladimir Cathedral regilded). The heritage bodies continued to attach value to churches exclusively as works of architecture (as the statutory instruments, indeed, required them to do). The basic standpoint of mildly hostile neutrality did not alter before the late 1980s, by which time the "general line" across the country had shifted to one of tolerance and accommodation. Churches functioned as the "transient objects" of Michael Thompson's theory of cultural recycling, according to which objects are "rescued" from the category of waste by recognition of their artistic status.[6] There was a rise in the value precisely of those buildings (Russian revivalist, early twentieth century) that ranked lowest in the canons of the 1920s and 1930s. But the ideological freighting of all church buildings delayed this process; to "rescue" a church was significantly more difficult than to "rescue," say, a 1910 apartment block.

With this background, it was inevitable that the Orthodox faithful mainly saw heritage preservation as yet one more form of interference. Alongside local tax offices, the secret police, and the authorities directly responsible for religious affairs, the monuments preservation bodies were empowered to implement central and local policy and to force closures of church buildings if these were violated. Compliance was reluctant at best. Where they could, congregations tried to renew decoration and fittings in ways that they considered aesthetically pleasing, which did not necessarily harmonize with the preferences of heritage specialists.

A further cause of friction was the removal of treasured artifacts to museums "for safe-keeping." The attachment to objects and buildings rather than to those who used them was characteristic of Soviet heritage preservation throughout its existence.[7] In the circumstances, it is unsurprising that much religious life existed without reference to ecclesiastical buildings, not just in the self-declared "catacomb church" movements, but among villagers honoring holy wells and other sacred sites. Those who bypassed working churches might end up by having little sense of connection with churches at all. While not undergoing "de-Christianization," they had moved a considerable distance from the practices of early twentieth-century official Orthodoxy.[8] Just as importantly, those who did have access to churches developed a different attitude to religious property—at once more reverential and more curatorial—than had characterized parishes in the nineteenth century. Where the latter had often resented being made by experts to care for old and (as they saw it) ritually valueless items, Soviet Orthodox Christians resented the implication that they were somehow less historically sensitive and less competent in conservation than the employees of museums and monuments offices.[9]

For all the many instances of miscommunication, however, the management of the ecclesiastical heritage was not only a history of how human rights and freedoms were put at risk. During the most problematic period for heritage preservation (1928–1940), the officials in the Leningrad preservation bodies, despite the winding-up of the voluntary organization whose support had been so important, and despite considerable encroachment on their powers, achieved something that was close to miraculous. They managed to preserve the city's main churches, while in other Soviet urban centers of any size, such structures were usually demolished. They did not defend "religious associations" whose churches were scheduled for closure, but they did not themselves precipitate such closures. If preservations and demolitions reflected the artistic tastes of the time, the same can be said of the fate of "redundant" churches even in countries that had not shut their face against Christian tradition.[10]

Still, much was lost, particularly from the preservationists' least favorite period (1840–1900). Their sense that neo-Byzantine and *style russe* buildings were inimical to the city's character meant that, right up to the 1970s, there was little done to protect these. A purist attitude to structures of mixed date was another continuum, leading to extensive rebuilding as well as to demolitions. Yet the way in which the preservers of heritage themselves preferred to understand the past was to emphasize what had been improved, not what had been lost. The sense that the missing buildings, architectural details, and objects represented no real deprivation—the city was now superior to what it had been before the Soviet period began—was widespread in the general public also. In 1965, Dmitrii Likhachev went so far as to claim that, if Leningrad was beautiful now, it was "the achievement of Soviet town planners" to have made it so.[11] While a particularly large proportion of important churches survived in Leningrad, compared with Moscow and many Old Russian cities (for instance, Yaroslavl and Vologda), their presence in the landscape was not something of which most locals were aware.

This perception persisted into the post-Soviet era—and not just among people professionally involved in the defense of heritage.[12] The belief that the city's historic destiny was to be Russia's "cultural capital," bare of advertisements and commercial enterprises, but thronged with galleries, museums, and concert halls, continued to be widespread.[13] Nationwide, the headline story was the vastly increased political, social, and cultural authority of the Russian Orthodox Church, which by the late 1990s had the status of a de facto state religion, participating in all major government ceremonies, and buttressed by reforms that substituted tax advantages for the old discriminatory tax burdens. Like other faiths, the church also benefited from restoration en masse of religious buildings to the denominations that had used them. The popularity of religion among new elites was expressed not just in the restoration of buildings with the support of the burgeoning plutocracy, but in the complete reconstruction of some buildings (the most famous or infamous case was the Cathedral of Christ the Redeemer in Moscow), and in the building of many completely new churches, not to speak of chapels on the sites of churches that could not, in the meantime, be rebuilt.[14]

Against this background, St. Petersburg looked in many ways unusual. As of the mid-2010s, only one new church had been built at the heart of the city.[15] The church was dedicated to St. Xenia of Petersburg, the local saint, and was in a fairly nondescript back street on Petrograd Side. Its building had been proposed by a local organization for the disabled, and it was to be the first wheelchair-accessible church in the city.[16] Nevertheless, local residents and others bitterly opposed its appearance, on the grounds that precious green space would be lost and that the site was architecturally inappropriate.[17] Not one major religious building was reconstructed in the first twenty-five years after the Soviet Union collapsed. The rebuilding of the Church of the Savior on the Haymarket was the regular subject of debate from the early 1990s into the 2010s, but the site stood empty year after year, while discussions on how to reshape the square, still interpreted as scrubby and unsatisfactory in appearance, went on gripping not just professional planners and architects, but the city's population more generally.[18] By 2015, a preservation order on the site of the Savior Church because of the "archaeological significance" of the foundations had stymied further development. In the contest between two types of retrospective gaze—archaeology and reconstruction—the former had, at least in the meantime, won out.[19] A carefully evolved architectural project to restore the church in its late eighteenth-century form had been shelved, despite the enduring commitment of the parish council to the rebuilding.[20]

In the wake of what Metropolitan (later Patriarch) Aleksii had expectantly seen as the "normalization of church-state relations," the revival of religious use was, on the whole, low-key. The extremely elaborate and costly restoration of the Church of the Protecting Veil on the Lieutenant Schmidt Embankment—financed by a local businessman—was the exception rather than the rule. Here, a team of over fifty highly qualified restorers toiled to reconstruct the wall paintings, which had been catastrophically damaged when the building was in use as an ice rink in the Soviet period.[21] A project executed at a comparable level was Vasilii Kosiakov's Kazan' Church in the New Maiden Convent, returned to resplendent condition after nearly fifteen years of effort.[22] But some other work was carried out to a much lower standard, as church insiders readily admitted.[23] Even in the Kazan' Cathedral (returned to the church in 1989), man-made substances were used to replace the original gilding and marble. As a feature in the parish newspaper argued, "In our country, reconstructions are the only way of acquiring a cultural heritage and sacred places and objects. The forced approximation that characterizes restoration works and the loss of authenticity are the price that one has to pay for bringing a monument to life."[24] In some of the city's nineteenth-century churches, even "forced approximation" was impossible. The vast spaces of the Gutuevskaia Church, built to encourage sailors in ways of temperance, and the Church of the Protecting Veil next to the Warsaw Station, dwarfed their modern congregations, and here a coat of emulsion and some newly painted icons were at the outer limit of what could be managed in terms of *blagolepie*.[25]

FIGURE 32. Aleksandr Strugach and Andrei Trifonov, Simmetria practice, St Petersburg. Artist's impression of the reconstructed Church of the Savior on the Haymarket, 2011. (Courtesy of the architects.)

In the churches that were regarded as highly significant works of architecture, the emphasis was generally on careful restoration rather than radical intervention of the former "Leningrad School" kind. Once the Orthodox Church had taken over St. Panteleimon, the plan to return the building to its early eighteenth-century appearance was abandoned, and instead the emphasis switched to the reconstruction of the religious paintings and iconostasis, which were required for ritual purposes.[26] At most, an Orthodox parish might aim to landscape the territory around a church in the historic style, fusing the traditional commitment to *blagolepie* with the delight in parks and gardens that was a central part of Soviet-era planning.

The monuments preservation bodies rapidly descended from the high they had attained in 1990, with the denomination of St. Petersburg as a UNESCO World Heritage Site. The post-Soviet period saw an assault on the fabric of the

FIGURE 33. Design by O. A. Gordan' and I. A. Iusfin, 1991, for the landscaping of the church of the Vladimir Icon of the Mother of God (authorship disputed, 1761–1769). (TsGANTD-SPb.)

city not witnessed since the 1930s, as a new generation of leaders tried to leave
their own mark on the landscape, and as property development became one of
the most lucrative local occupations.[27] But monument preservation was still a
central concern of many educated locals, acquiring additional political salience
as buildings came under threat. The city also remained the capital of museum
culture across the Russian Federation, with its extraordinary concentration of
historical repositories of all kinds, headed by the world-famous Hermitage. The
secularized understanding of church architecture and artifacts as "art" proved
tenacious. Even in the 2010s, four major ecclesiastical buildings still made up
the "Museum of Four Cathedrals," with a focus on architecture, rather than on
religious practice, in the displays.[28] By no means all Petersburgers with an interest
in architecture were concerned about church preservation—there was, indeed,
a widespread view that this could now be left to the Orthodox Church itself.[29]
And where architectural historians and historians of the city did preoccupy
themselves with such themes, this was often in a perspective that emphasized the
history of architecture generally. Smol'nyi Cathedral was, from this point of view,
still of primary importance as a building illustrating the genius of Rastrelli. An
admiration for church architecture by no means always translated into sympathy
towards religion as such.[30]

Religious leaders themselves tended to be cautious, when it came to claims
on historic church buildings, with none of the mass agitation for the return of
buildings that was evident in, say, Moscow.[31] The process of restitution was slow
even after legislation of 2010 (incorporated locally in 2013) stipulated that all
buildings once in possession of religious denominations that were legal prior to
1917 must be restored to those denominations upon demand.[32] The process of
returning former house churches was particularly gradual; efforts to evict the
Mayakovsky Library, housed in one of these, came to nothing after a vigorous
campaign by staff and users to keep the library where it was.[33] Ecclesiastical artifacts of acknowledged artistic and historic value mostly remained in museums,
which justified their curatorial preeminence by giving far more space to these than
in the past, organizing special displays and publishing lavish albums.[34] Museum
facilities attached to churches (as in the treasuries of Italian or English cathedrals)
remained no more than a dream.

All in all, St. Petersburg of the late twentieth and early twenty-first century
illustrated some of the failures of the Soviet campaign of secularization, but also
the extent of its success. Anti-religious activists had not managed, whether in the
early Soviet period or the late, to force religion out of existence altogether, or even

to force all religious practice underground. Once opportunities presented themselves to worship openly, large numbers of people seized them—including many new converts.[35] The number of working churches was much larger than in Soviet days—150 by 2009, rather than just 14, as in 1991.[36] All had devoted congregations, some of significant size. There were priests engaged in civic projects with resonance far beyond the immediate neighborhood, such as the commemoration of war dead organized by Father Viacheslav Kharinov, or the Book of Memory founded by Father Vladimir Sorokin.[37] In a society where bureaucratic regulation remained intrusive and where greed of a commercial kind now sat alongside pettifogging interference, every restoration project demanded huge determination. But parishes and clergy were able to command it. One priest, fighting off the monuments authority's attempts to foist upon him the services of firms run by contacts of their own, arranged training for several parishioners in craft building; another did much of the initial manual work himself.[38] The energy of parish life was obvious even to a casual visitor dropping into, say, the Church of the Prophet Elijah, with its bicycle racks and crowds of families with children, or St. Catherine's Church at Murino, with its beautifully redecorated vaults, or the Church of St. Peter and St. Paul at Shuvalovo, with its meticulously re-carved iconostasis. At the end of the Soviet period, all three had been near-wrecks.

But, with a city population of over 5 million, 150 churches was rather a modest number, and on most Sundays, the numbers of those attending Mass were modest also. As in other cities across Russia, "believers" in the sense of those who were vaguely sympathetic to the church considerably outstripped "believers" in the sense of those who attended services regularly, and otherwise observed the tenets of the faith (the so-called *votserkovlennye*, or "enchurched").[39] There were far more local businessmen who asked the local priest to bless a new car and secretaries who bought an Easter loaf to eat with tea in the office than there were Petersburgers who regularly attended communion or confession, or made donations to religious charities.[40] Orthodox belief accorded more with the late Soviet revival of "traditions" than with the thickly interwoven texture of religious observance and everyday life before 1917. Individual members of staff might place icons about the workplace (including even on the microwave), but offices did not have an official "red corner." Easter, the most important Orthodox festival, was not a public holiday (Orthodox Christmas was, but for the majority of Petersburgers, this simply extended the New Year break for an extra few days).

This was typical of other post-Soviet cities also. Yet in Petersburg, the hold of religious life was perhaps more tenuous—as a function of the very lack of

"ecclesiastical appearance" that had allowed the city's major churches to survive.[41] There were quite a few in the city's intelligentsia who were resistant to
the rise of church culture ("the Orthodox Church is a disgusting organization").
And many others were little concerned whether churches were opened or not,
but certainly did not like the idea of forfeiting green space or cultural ameni-
ties if a building was reconstructed on a church site that had been a park for
eighty years. Sometimes they even resented no longer being able to visit the
cinemas and swimming pools once housed in now functioning churches. "The
Foucault pendulum is part of *my* city memory," commented a woman born in
the 1960s, irked that her stake on St. Isaac's had been swept away.[42] The Museum
of the Arctic and Antarctic remained one of the city's best-loved places to take
children, its icons of polar explorers still untouched after seven decades; in a
city that proudly recognized layered memory, the church was now considered a
monument to the *Soviet* past.[43]

As this book came to completion, the conflict over the sacred versus secular
associations of city memory blew up in a major fight. At the end of August 2015,
a bas-relief on the side of an art nouveau apartment block constructed in 1910,
showing the head of Mephistopheles, was summarily destroyed. A self-nominated
group of "Russian Cossacks" (not necessarily with any historical links to that eth-
nicity) immediately claimed responsibility. The incident instantly became a cause
célèbre, covered on every city news and discussion site. The fact that the building was a short distance away from building work on the new St. Xenia Church
increased suspicions: mere geographical proximity suggested parishioners *must*
be involved (and this despite the fact that the organizing group at the church was
made up of people not physically capable of the destruction). The flames were
further fanned when a local priest accused Sergei Burov, director of the Museum
of Four Cathedrals, of having organized the attack so as to distract attention from
the Orthodox Church's request, lodged the previous month, to have St. Isaac's
Cathedral returned to its sole care. Swirls of rumor and conspiracy theory suggested that the governor of St. Petersburg, Georgii Poltavchenko, was against
the return of St. Isaac's, and that the new metropolitan, Varsonofii, installed
in January 2015, was behind the slur on Burov. "Well might St. Petersburg be
described as 'the Northern Palmyra,'" Internet commentators fumed, referring
to the campaigns by the Islamic State against supposedly idolatrous works of art
in Syria.[44]

All this suggests that to attempt grasping post-Soviet Russia purely in terms of
the religious revival (important as this was in political and cultural terms) may

lead to false conclusions. As has been argued for other places in "post-Soviet space," the social role of religion was strongly shaped by community-building endeavors analogous to those of the Soviet period (something that both explained and derived from the prominence of former Soviet-era activists among the faithful).[45] Religious processions resembled Communist demonstrations, with banner-carrying columns and at best vaguely interested spectators—except that the numbers participating were far lower, there being no attempt to force workers across the city to turn up.[46] A sturdy tradition of skepticism about religious ideas persisted, not just among those of current or former socialist convictions but in many sections of the intelligentsia.[47] Priests might be asked to address school congregations, but the reopened chapels of universities and other institutions of higher education led an existence both discreet and discrete, and it was impossible to imagine research institutes marking rites of passage with prayer meetings, or getting in a cleric to sanctify a new library.[48] With liberal views completely marginalized in the post-Soviet Orthodox hierarchy, those who originally joined the church as a gesture of nonconformism had been left deeply uncomfortable by its recent history.[49]

Indeed, even grassroots Orthodox faithful were far from always enamored of the new church-state configuration, often perceiving recent history in terms of opportunities for activity *without* the supervision of the state, rather than in terms of the chance to inscribe their "religious association" into the heart of political relations.[50] "Under Lenin they took [the churches] away, and under Stalin they took them away, during the War they gave them back, under Khrushchev they closed them again, and then under Brezhnev things stayed as they were, then under Gorbachev they started giving them back, and under Yeltsin. Well, today they're returning them— tomorrow they'll take them away," one senior St. Petersburg priest summed up.[51] From the outside, the Orthodox Church looked safely ensconced in Russia's political fabric, but insiders were keenly aware that the institution's status would endure exactly as long as people in government considered association with it politically expedient. In sum, the Soviet story was not just about unsuccessful secularization masking tenacious faith. In certain quite significant ways, the anti-religious campaign achieved what its proponents had hoped for—if one speaks of the creation of a new society, a new attitude to property rights (structured round the opposition "state-private"), and a new kind of urban landscape, rather than total eradication of metaphysical belief.

Until detailed work on preservation in other Soviet cities over the whole of the Soviet period may become available, it is difficult to tell how far the intricacies of the decisions made by Leningrad planners are reflected in other places, and the extent to which those campaigning to preserve the prerevolutionary heritage were led by "bourgeois specialists" whose aesthetic perceptions had been shaped by architectural and preservation work before 1917, but who at the same time adapted the prerevolutionary legacies in significant respects. A provisional conclusion would suggest that the confidence and consistency of Leningrad practices and their fidelity to a certain vision of the "city text" were indeed exceptional.[52] Yet the overall process of construction of the "socialist city" certainly had parallels elsewhere. The title accorded to Leningrad in 1931, "model Socialist city," suggested that it represented the best of the typical. It was, of course, Moscow rather than Leningrad that was the pattern for Soviet cities (particularly, its vast squares for parades commemorating the Revolution, its major avenues, its "culture parks" and pantheons of revolutionary and Communist heroes).[53]

Admittedly, the "Moscow style" itself was shaped by architects trained in the former capital (notably Ivan Fomin, 1872–1936). The imperial architecture of late tsarist St. Petersburg, above all the grandiose Kamennoostrovskii prospekt, became the model for Moscow high-style apartment blocks and "administrative buildings." But the influence of Petersburg heritage was not advertised and thus, in a real sense, did "not exist" so far as Soviet culture was concerned.[54] The desired effect of integrated city planning was—in typically Soviet style—to efface regionalism.[55] The template socialist buildings, whether newly built, or restored and recreated from old ones, were to be integrated into a spatially and temporally homogeneous world, in which the restructured past looked forward to a uniform and harmonious future, rather than giving testimony to the chaotic and disorderly world of years gone by.[56]

The "socialist city" functioned not merely on this elite level. Not only officials in local government, but ordinary citizens were committed to the creation of new landscapes. Just as Soviet citizens learned to "speak Bolshevik," so they learned to "build socialist." They espoused "socialist construction" not simply in the abstract sense, but in the sense of "socialist building" and "socialist architecture."[57] Both with building and language, the dramatic and highly ideologized moments of rupture with the past that were orchestrated in the political and cultural elite of Soviet society went with a complicated and gradual process of negotiating with inherited cultural forms. In turn, this process generated forms of speaking and living that were, in international context, recognizably "Western," while at the same time striving to be distinct from those characterizing the so-called "capitalist countries" of the further world. The tragedy of all those involved in the struggle over religion during the Soviet period was that when the Soviet system they had often criticized and creatively modified collapsed, so did many of the ideals that they had not even realized they shared. Once again, ecclesiastical architecture had been marginalized, but now by the drive to create a city fit for business and commerce.[58]

FIGURE 34. Smol'nyi Cathedral competing for attention with high-rise office and apartment blocks, April 2015. (Author's photo.)

A Note on Sources

The marginal status of historic churches in terms of heritage preservation, and of heritage preservation in terms of church-state relations, means that research on the subject requires access to a large number of different repositories and materials. For the most part, I have concentrated on sources at the local level, since regulation of these areas at the central level is well recorded in published document collections and in secondary discussions. But research in the city is more complicated than it might seem, since documentation is scattered across a range of different repositories, both inside and outside the state archive system.

The main holdings for church-state affairs up to 1943 are in TsGA-SPb (with a limited amount of material, mainly on the antireligious campaigns, in TsGAIPD-SPb). The diocesan archive (ASPbE) is invaluable for the postwar decades, particularly the mid-1940s to the late 1960s. The best places to access the spotty evidence on preservation before 1941 are RA IIMK (where the personal archive of Konstantin Romanov includes copies of reports that I have not come across anywhere else) and TsGALI-SPb, which has patchy but useful holdings for the Old St. Petersburg Society. The extremely sparse photographic evidence is dispersed among IIMK (for the 1920s), TsGANTD-SPb, TsGAKFFD-SPb, and TsGA-SPb (the last mainly for the 1930s). Correspondence from members of the public (what in Russian are known as "letters of the toiling people," *pis'ma trudiashchikhsia*) is held in the fonds of the church offices and other bureaucracies dealing with church-state affairs (mainly in TsGA-SPb), and, for the postwar era, in ASPbE and in TsGALI-SPb. TsGANTD-SPb has significant amounts of material about city planning (mainly the technical side), and some procedural documents from GIOP. NA UGIOP is valuable as a cross section of correspondence relating to individual buildings, but the religious use of these was outside the remit of the city preservation bodies.

Even with the best will in the world, research cannot be exhaustive. Some repositories, such as the archives of the political police or the Leningrad metro system, are open to few, if any, external visitors. Others (for instance TsGA-SPb, the main city archive) have gaps in the documentation, partly because some materials were destroyed in the Blockade, but also because others have not yet been declassified, or indeed catalogued. The materials relating to local governance at the Party level (in TsGAIPD-SPb) are also accessible only partially, with material from the City Committee of the CPSU from the 1960s onward, in particular, still largely treated as confidential. In the archive of UGIOP (the Board of the State Inspectorate of Monuments) in St. Petersburg, the procedural documentation is generally available to in-house researchers only; I draw in chapters 4, 5, and 6 on a small number of records that are available to the general public in TsGANTD-SPb. By and large, available material related to the political and social control of religious practice is confined to scattered materials from the administrative section of the city and provincial soviets (for the 1920s and 1930s) and the reports to Party and local authorities of the plenipotentiaries on religious affairs and on the affairs of the Russian Orthodox Church (for the period 1943–1991); these are held in TsGA-SPb, TsGAIPD-SPb, and (for the post-1943 period only) the ASPbE.

From the mid-1960s, material in all the main city repositories thins out radically; the likely explanation is that documents were archived by individual city and Party offices on a rolling twenty-five-year deadline; once Soviet governance collapsed, in 1991, the old regulations were ignored, or thought irrelevant, and archiving mainly stopped. (An exception is the recent transfer to TsGA, presumably from the secret police archives, of documents relating to the activities of the plenipotentiary for religious affairs at the end of the Soviet period, though this consists exclusively of circulars, draft reports, and other "public" materials.)

The flaws and gaps are, of course, themselves revealing. The compartmentalization and territorial strife of the different bodies that the archives reflect, and the way in which public concerns and urgent case resolutions fell through the cracks, are part of the history of church-monuments themselves. And documents are not just (and often not primarily) repositories of information about action; rather, they expose world views, aspirations, professional self-awareness, and ideological and aesthetic attitudes. Since no source exists where such issues of subjectivity and sensitivity to genre requirements are not significant, I have not glossed these specially. The naïve enthusiasm, as archives opened in the

1990s, about the possibility of acquiring from documents a factually reliable and demonstrably authentic command of the Soviet past has been dissipated by a mature awareness that documents for internal circulation were also shaped by power games, and created in the hall of mirrors of career advancement and self-protection. Business done by telephone was seldom recorded, and vital "conversations in the corridor" (*kuluarnye besedy*) remained unfixed. Yet we can acquire from these deficiencies a grasp of process. The chaos and obfuscation that they reveal lend a sense of the stresses and contradictions of bureaucratic life both for those who governed, and for those subjected to control (two groups that, in the end, cannot be fully separated).

Those who wish to gain a further sense of the on-paper world in which officials moved are directed to the appendices, published online at https://oxford. academia.edu/CatrionaKelly. These include official lists of protected churches, 1922–1968 (appendix 1); materials relating to the fate of churches in Leningrad and region after 1918 (e.g., lists of those scheduled for demolition, the uses of those to be retained) (appendix 2); materials on civic buildings under state protection (appendix 3); and materials on the legal regulation of churches (appendix 4). In appendix 2, the reader will also find tables relating to the proportion of churches destroyed in a range of years—these figures are, of necessity, tentative, since the documentation makes it clear that even officials themselves often had no idea exactly when buildings were finally closed or destroyed (see chapter 3). It is traditional to see statistics as representing a kind of evidential gold standard, but in the Soviet context, the scant figures that exist, or can be adduced, were as much as anything else a contribution to the smoke and mirrors game, having a discursive or performative function ("we are supposed to produce tables, and so we will, but what goes in them is up to us").

Alongside collecting written materials, I have myself visited most of St. Petersburg's surviving churches of architectural note, as well as some outside the city (Gatchina, Kronstadt, Tsarskoe Selo, Pavlovsk, Vyborg, Old and New Ladoga, Tikhvin, Kurpovo, Sogintsy, Zelenograd, Oranienbaum). Like most visitors (and indeed locals), prior to the late 1980s, I had been inside only a very few religious buildings (in my case, these were mainly working churches: the St. Nicholas Cathedral, the Smolenskoe Cemetery Church, the Trinity Cathedral of the Alexander Nevsky Monastery). The many closed churches had a dismal look, though none was as strikingly disfigured as the pink sixteenth-century church in Vladimir emblazoned, in 1980, with the words BOOT FACTORY (attempts to photograph this were foiled by workers emerging from the building at the end of their shift). From the early 1990s, once more churches opened, I would often drop in while passing, and from 2009, having started work on this project, visited more systematically. Conversations with priests and members of congregations, and with Petersburgers generally, have formed part of the background to this book, and I have drawn on interviews conducted by others also. While this testimony may not be reliable in terms of exact dates, it is uniquely revealing about the status of the churches in people's perceptions of their city, and about the different understandings of the structures used for worship, from refuges of the sacred to "temples of art."

Notes

Introduction

1. From 1921, Berestechko, an ethnically mixed town whose population included Ukrainians and Jews as well as Poles, was in the territory of the newly independent Poland; in 1939, as part of "Western Ukraine," it was annexed by the Soviet Union. It is currently part of Ukraine.

2. Here and below, all quotations are from the first publication of the story: Babel', "U sviatogo Valenta," *Krasnaia nov'* 3 (1924): 13–16 (here, 14).

3. Ibid., 16.

4. Ibid., 15.

5. Ibid., 14.

6. There was a clear parallel here with the situation in France after 1789 (see Suzanne Desan, *Reclaiming the Sacred: Lay Religion and Popular Politics in Revolutionary France* [Ithaca, NY: Cornell University Press, 1990], 5–7), though events took a different trajectory in the two countries: if "most churches in France were closed or transformed into revolutionary temples by about March 1794" (ibid., 9), it took over twenty years for mass closures to take place in Soviet Russia, which subjected Christian communities to attrition, so that the surge of "religious initiative and zeal" evident in France (ibid., 13–14) was less significant there.

7. The distinction between anticlerical feeling (and more broadly, hostility to organized religion as counterrevolutionary, which was pervasive in the worker movement), and spiritual beliefs and traditions (which were equally widespread) is underlined in Jean Bruhat, "Anticléricalisme et mouvement ouvrier en France avant 1914," *Mouvement social* 57 (1966): 61–100. As historians of religion in Russia have also emphasized, the late nineteenth and early twentieth centuries were as much a period of religious reform and renewal as of secularization. See, for example, Robert Greene, *Bodies Like Bright Stars: Saints and Relics in Orthodox Russia* (DeKalb: Northern Illinois University Press, 2010); Simon Dixon, "The Orthodox Church and the Workers of St. Petersburg, 1880–1890," in *European Religion in the Age of Great Cities, 1830–1930*, ed. Hugh McLeod (London: Routledge, 2005), 117–39. For the correspondence between hostility to the ancien régime and hostility to religion as a general pattern in revolutionary societies, see W. Bruce Lincoln, "Notes toward a Theory of Religion and Revolution," in *Religion, Rebellion, Revolution: An Interdisciplinary and Cross-Cultural Collection of Essays* (London: Macmillan, 1985), 266–92. The Bolshevik campaigns against "superstition" have been addressed in detail in work by Stephen A. Smith, for example, "The First Soviet Generation: Children and Religious Belief in Soviet Russia, 1917–41," in *Generations in Twentieth-Century Europe*, ed. Stephen Lovell (Basingstoke: Palgrave, 2007), 79–100; "Bones of Contention: Bolsheviks and the Exposure of Saints' Relics, 1918–30," *Past and Present* 204 (2009): 155–94.

8. "Kratkii otchet o deiatel'nosti Petrogradskogo Otdela Muzeev i okhrany pamiatnikov iskusstva i stariny, narodnogo byta i prirody Aktsentra i podvedomstvennykh emu uchrezhdenii za vremia ot 25 Oktiabria 1917 g. po 1922-i god" (undated, probably early 1923), Gosudarstvennyi arkhiv

Rossiiskoi Federatsii (hereafter GARF), f. 2307, op. 3, d. 272, l. 127. There is a large literature on revolutionary iconoclasm: an influential study is Orlando Figes and Boris Kolonitskii, *Interpreting the Russian Revolution: The Language and Symbols of 1917* (New Haven, CT: Yale University Press, 1999).

9. See the list of staff at GARF, f. 2307, op. 3, d. 272, ll. 36–37. My account simplifies the early history of the Museums Department, which was originally founded as the All-Russian College on the Affairs of Museums on May 28, 1918, under the chairmanship of I. E. Grabar', before being reformed on July 6, 1918, as the Committee on the Affairs of Museums. The Restoration Commission was set up by Grabar' on June 10, 1918. See L. N. Krylova, "I. E. Grabar' i okhrana pamiatnikov: Chetyre etapa ego zhizni," *Grabarevskie chteniia* 5 (2004), online at http://art-con.ru/node/1765.

10. "Dekret o registratsii, prieme na uchet i okhrane pamiatnikov iskusstva i stariny, nakhodiashchikhsia vo vladenii chastnykh lits, obshchestv i uchrezhdenii," *Dekrety Sovetskoi vlasti* (hereafter *DSV*) 3:399–400.

11. *Sobranie uzakonenii i rasporiazhenii raboche-krest'ianskogo pravitel'stva* (hereafter *SU*) 15 (1922): item 102.

12. "Proekt postanovleniia VTsIK RSFSR ot . . . 1923 g." (exact date left blank), GARF, f. 2306, op. 1, d. 2319, l. 9. However, in the Criminal Code of 1926, the sole article relating to monuments was the same one criminalizing failure to declare collections (now numbered as article 188). See M. N. Gernet and A. N. Trainin, eds., *Ugolovnyi kodeks: Nauchno-populiarnyi prakticheskii kommentarii s dopolneniiami i izmeneniiami po 15 avgusta 1927 g.* (Moscow: Pravo i zhizn', 1927), and compare *Ugolovnyi kodeks RSFSR: Ofitsial'nyi tekst s izmeneniiami na 1 oktiabria 1953 g.* (Moscow: Gosudarstvennoe izdatel'stvo Iuridicheskoi literatury, 1953). The criminalization of willful damage to monuments was introduced only to the revised Criminal Code of 1960 (article 230, with a penalty of up to two years' custodial sentence, or up to one year's forced labor or a fine of one hundred rubles): *Ugolovnyi kodeks RSFSR: Priniat tret'ei sessiei Verkhovnogo soveta RSFSR piatogo sozyva* (Moscow: Iuridicheskaia literatura, 1960), 382–84. These penalties were raised to up to two years' forced labor or a fine of 300 rubles in 1982, and remained unchanged till the end of the Soviet legal system. *Ugolovnyi kodeks RSFSR s izmeneniiami i dopolneniiami na 5 maia 1990 g.* (Moscow: Iuridicheskaia literatura, 1990), 146.

13. These statutes, as well as the history of VOOPIiK, are discussed in detail below (see chapters 3–5).

14. See, for example, I. E. Grabar', *Moia zhizn'* (Moscow: Iskusstvo, 1937), 73–78; B. M. Kirikov, *Okhrana arkhitekturnykh pamiatnikov Leningrada v gody sovetskoi vlasti* (Leningrad: Znanie, 1988); V. A. Demen'teva, O. V. Taratynova, and B. M. Kirikov, eds., *Okhrana pamiatnikov Sankt-Peterburga: K 90-letiiu Komiteta po gosudarstvennomu kontroliu, ispol'zovaniiu i okhrane pamiatnikov istorii i kul'tury Sankt-Peterburga* (St. Petersburg: Propilei, 2008). Some of the ambiguities of monument preservation are briefly acknowledged in B. Kirikov, "Kakie pamiatniki okhraniaem?," *Leningradskaia panorama* 11 (1991): 15–17. Exceptional in its range and relative detachment is the collection edited by A. S. Shchenkov, *Pamiatniki arkhitektury v Sovetskom Soiuze: Ocherki istorii arkhitekturnoi restavratsii* (Moscow: Pamiatniki istoricheskoi mysli, 2004). This emphasis on achievement began in the Brezhnev era: the Berezhkovskaia naberezhnaia reading room of GARF contains a special handlist of documents relating to monuments preservation dating from the early 1970s, a period that also saw the publication of such collections of legislation as G. G. Anisimov, ed., *Okhrana pamiatnikov istorii i kul'tury; Sbornik dokumentov* (Moscow: Sovetskaia Rossiia, 1973) (henceforth *OPIK* 1973). It continues into the present. The only time I have been grilled by the director of an archive about my intentions ("you do know that historians are supposed to treat evidence carefully?") was when applying for permission there to work on monuments preservation.

15. Grabar's *Moia zhizn'*, for example, referred to the 1922–1923 confiscations of church property as a period when "museums were enriched by a far larger collection of objects than had ever been placed there before 1917" (278), an account so partial as to be positively mendacious (for the chaos and pointless destruction that actually accompanied the confiscations, see chapter 1). Kirikov's *Okhrana arkhitekturnykh pamiatnikov* is misleading in its strategic omissions, rather than through obvious misrepresentations of this kind.

16. See the introduction to the first issue of the specialist publication *Voprosy restavratsii* [Questions of restoration] 1 (1907): 1, and "Vremennyi ustav Akademii Khudozhestv ot 15 oktiabria 1893," article 5 (*Polnoe sobranie zakonov Rossiiskoi Imperii* [hereafter *PSZ*], 3rd series, vol. 3, p. 570, no. 9982, clause 11). The arrangements for regulating work on buildings deemed to be of historic and aesthetic importance were later incorporated into the 1900 version of the Buildings Statute (*Ustav stroitel'nyi*), which remained in force till 1917. See, for example, I. D. Mordukhai-Boltovskii, ed., *Svod zakonov Rossiiskoi Imperii* (St. Petersburg: Knizhnoe tovarishchestvo Deiatel', 1912), vol. 12, pt. 1, p. 120.

17. For a list of the Committee's membership, see the note by V. V. in "Khronika," *Starye gody* 3 (1909): 146–47. Three of the Committee's eighteen members, clearly the "first among equals," were from the State Council, the Russian Empire's highest bureaucratic body.

18. The point about the absence of lists is made in Kirikov, *Okhrana arkhitekturnykh pamiatnikov*, though efforts to register monuments had gone forward on a piecemeal basis in the last decades of the nineteenth century (on this, see Ekaterina Pravilova, *A Public Empire: Property and the Quest for the Common Good in Imperial Russia* [Princeton, NJ: Princeton University Press, 2014], 136–38), and in fact Soviet Russia had no integrated lists either till the late 1930s (see chapter 3). For material at architects' congresses, see, for example, *Trudy III-go S"ezda Russkikh Zodchikh v S-Peterburge* (St. Petersburg: Ekonomicheskaia Tipo-Litografiia, 1905), 58–59; *Dnevnik V Vserossiiskogo S"ezda Zodchikh, 15–22 Dekabria 1913 g.* (St Petersburg: Tipografiia Sankt-Peterburgskogo Gradonachal'stva, 1913), pt. 1, p. 33 (G. G. Pirang, "Ob okhrane pamiatnikov, kak o predmete izucheniia v vysshikh uchebnykh zavedeniiakh"); ibid., pt. 3, p. 7 (A. P. Aplaksin, "Registratsiia pamiatnikov iskusstva i stariny").

19. E. E. Baumgarten and L. A. Il'in, "Vandalizm reklamy," in *Dnevnik IV S"ezda Russkikh Zodchikh, sostoiashchego pod pochetnym Predsedatel'stvom Avgusteishego Prezidenta Imperatorskoi Akademii Khudozhestv Velikoi Kniagini Marii Pavlovny* (St. Petersburg: Tipografiia Sankt-Peterburgskogo Gradonachal'stva, 1911), pt. 2, p. 8. In the event, the Congress decided to support a limit only on commercial advertising. On debates over ownership of the arts generally, see Pravilova, *A Public Empire*, parts 2 and 3.

20. GARF, f. 2307, op. 3, d. 76, l. 1 (from an undated document placed in a file in which other material is dated to 1921).

21. This interpretation is made clear by the outraged response of the Civil War hero and Red Cavalry commander Semen Budennyi, whose public denunciation under the offensive title "Babizm Babelia" (the womanishness of Babel', a puerile pun on the author's name) contended that the writer "invents taradiddles, pours filth over the best Communist commanders, fantasizes and simply tells lies" (*Oktiabr'* no. 3 [1924], 197). In later versions of his Red Cavalry cycle, Babel' toned down the description of the shenanigans in "At St. Walenty's" to make this less shocking: Sashka is not stripped naked by the Cossacks, but her skirt billows up to show her legs, she is seized by the "arm" not the "breast," and the "sacred books" and "vestments" become simply "books" and "silks": see Babel', *Konarmiia* (Moscow: Gosudarstvennoe izdatel'stvo, 1926), 110–11.

22. For an authoritative discussion of the "spontaneity/consciousness" dichotomy, see Katerina Clark, *The Soviet Novel: History as Ritual* (Chicago, IL: University of Chicago Press, 1981). Indeed, political officials in responsible positions might even feel suspicious of new rituals, on the grounds that they were potentially uncontrollable. In 1924, participants in a discussion at Lensovet expressed disquiet over the antireligious ritual of the "red baptism," commenting that it should be "brought into organized channels"; a resolution was passed forbidding the conferral of names "of a kind contradictory to the new way of life," among which was mentioned "Anarchist" ("Protokol soveshchaniia predsedatelei raionnykh ispolkomov," March 13, 1924, Tsentral'nyi gosudarstvennyi arkhiv Sankt-Peterburga [hereafter TsGA-SPb], f. 1001, op. 9, d. 10, l. 19).

23. The Soviet cinema was seen as a particularly valuable resource for popular education. See, for example, Denise Youngblood, *Movies for the Masses: Popular Cinema and Soviet Society* (Cambridge: Cambridge University Press, 1992); Peter Kenez, *Cinema in Soviet Society from the Revolution to the Death of Stalin* (London: I. B. Tauris, 2001). A rich range of primary sources is accessible in Ian Christie and Richard Taylor, eds., *The Film Factory: Russian and Soviet Cinema in Documents, 1896–1939* (London: Routledge, 1988).

24. Potentially, of course, literary and musical works had value on the international market, but state institutions never displayed the same sensitivity to this as they did to the market value of artworks. There was, for example, no attempt to ship the manuscripts of Alexander Pushkin or Petr Tchaikovsky to London or New York for auction; indeed, over the decades, state institutions did their best to purchase manuscripts that came up for sale so that they could end up in Soviet archives.

25. See chapter 2 below.

26. "Postanovlenie SNK o poriadke rekvizitsii i konfiskatsii blagorodnykh metallov, deneg i tsennostei, [...]," *DSV* 9:213–21.

27. See the document from 1923 held in GARF, f. 2307, op. 3, d. 163, ll. 58–59, which lists, for example, the removal from the Hermitage of a platinum ingot weighing three and a half poods (just over a hundred pounds).

28. Tsentraln'yi gosudarstvennyi arkhiv literatury i iskusstva Sankt-Peterburga (hereafter Ts-GALI-SPb), f. 36, op. 1, d. 40, l. 21. For instance, antique sheets might simply be destroyed when embroidery and lace was torn off, and rare, valuable chairs might be dumped because they lacked obvious ornamentation.

29. There is an extensive literature on censorship. Archive-based studies of literary censorship include Arlen Blium, *Za kulisami "Ministerstva pravdy": Tainaia istoriia sovetskoi tsenzury, 1917–1929* (St. Petersburg: Akademicheskii proekt, 1994); Blium, *Zapreshchennye knigi russkikh pisatelei i literaturovedov 1917–1991: Indeks sovetskoi tsenzury s kommentariiami* (St. Petersburg: Gosudarstvennyi universitet kul'tury i iskusstv, 2003); Samantha Sherry, *Discourses of Regulation and Resistance: Censoring Translation in the Stalin and Khrushchev Era Soviet Union* (Edinburgh: Edinburgh University Press, 2015). In Petrograd, the first drive to institute film censorship came in 1919, with the institution of the Regional Cinematographic Committee, which aimed to "purge the sphere of cinematography from the flood of films" that ran contrary to the Committee's own didactic ends, and that displayed "revolutionary" tendencies, were politically subversive, or fostered "criminal and base passions of human nature" (TsGA-SPb, f. 1000, op. 3, d. 146, l. 205). Later materials are available in, for example, K. M. Anderson et al., eds., *Kremlevskii kinoteatr 1928–1953: Dokumenty* (Moscow: ROSSPEN, 2005); V. P. Mikhailov, ed., *Zapreshchenye fil'my: Dokumenty, Svidetel'stva, Kommentarii* (Moscow: Nauchno-issledovatel'skii institut kinoiskusstva, 1993).

30. The flagship project here was the transformation, from 1918 onward, of what had been Tsarskoe Selo into "Detskoe Selo" (Children's Village), where orphanages and houses of rest were concentrated. Later projects included the conversion of the Anichkov Palace into the Pioneer Palace, opened in 1936.

31. The most famous example was the conversion of the Winter Palace into a public museum, the "Palace of Arts" (later to be part of the "State Hermitage"), but the Russian Museum's Ethnographical Section also operated such "museums of daily life," as did the Museum of the City.

32. The Philharmonia retains the hall to this day, while the Free Theater was replaced by the Working Youth Theater (which organized a complete reconstruction of the building), and then, in 1945, the Lensovet Theater, which is still ensconced there.

33. See, for example, Anatole Kopp, *Town and Revolution: Soviet Architecture and City Planning, 1917–1935* (London: Thames and Hudson, 1970); O. A. Shvidkovskii, *Building in the USSR, 1917–1932* (London: Studio Vista, 1971); Hugh Hudson, *Blueprints and Blood: The Stalinization of Soviet Architecture, 1917–1927* (Princeton, NJ: Princeton University Press, 1994); S. O. Khan-Magomedov, *INCHUK i rannii konstruktivizm* (Moscow: Arkhitektura, 1994); Catherine Cooke, *Russian Avant-Garde: Theories of Art, Architecture, and the City* (London: Academy Editions, 1995); Alexei Tarkhanov and Sergei Kavtaradze, *Stalinist Architecture* (London: Laurence King, 1992); Richard Pare, *The Lost Vanguard: Russian Modernist Architecture, 1922–1932* (New York: The Monacelli Press, 2007).

34. One could still get a sense of the "making do" ethos in the 2010s by visiting such academic establishments as the Institute of the History of Material Culture or the Institute of Russian Literature (both part of the Academy of Sciences), and (until it was closed) the Institute of the History of Arts on St. Isaac's Square.

35. This is evident even today if one visits the offices of the city administration on ulitsa Rossi, which are housed in what was once the Ministry of Popular Enlightenment (i.e., Education), and acted as the offices of departments of the city soviet in the 1918–1991 period.

36. A useful anthology of the relevant statutes is V. S. Dediukhina et al., eds., *Sokhranenie pamiatnikov tserkovnoi stariny v Rossii v XVIII–nachala XX vv.: Sbornik dokumentov* (Moscow: Otechestvo, 1997). Among general studies of preservation before 1917 are A. S. Shchenkov, ed., *Pamiatniki arkhitektury v dorevoliutsionnoi Rossii: Ocherki istorii arkhitekturnoi restavratsii* (Moscow: Terra-Knizhnyi klub, 2002), and Mariia V. Medvedeva, "Izuchenie i okhrana pamiatnikov arkheologii i arkhitektury epokhi srednevekov'ia Severo-Zapada Rossii v deiatel'nosti Imperatorskoi Arkheologicheskoi Komissii" (Avtoreferat diss., Institut istorii material'noi kul'tury RAN, 2007).

37. See Richard Wortman, *Scenarios of Power: Myth and Ceremony in Russian Monarchy*, 2 vols. (Princeton, NJ: Princeton University Press, 1995–2000).

38. "O predostavlenii eparkhial'nym Arkhiereiam prava samim razreshat' postroiku, perestroiku i rasprostranenie sobornykh, prikhodskikh, kladbishchenskikh tserkvei v gorodakh, krome stolits," synodal ukase of July 29, 1865, no. 42349, *PSZ*, 2nd series, vol. 40, cols. 830–31. While directed at places outside the capitals, the ukase enshrined the principles traditionally in use there, too.

39. According to a synodal instruction of 1857, "if churches are so dilapidated that they have started to list because of rotten timbers, have leaks, and threaten collapse, or at the very least, are in such a dilapidated condition that they make a most holy place unfit to be seen," parishioners were to be directed to exert themselves to construct a new church (Dediukhina, *Sokhranenie pamiatnikov tserkovnoi stariny*, doc. 73, p. 94).

40. See the reference to the "renewal of ancient paintings in a certain Cathedral without the solicitation of permission" in the synodal ukase of December 31, 1842, no. 16401, *PSZ*, 2nd series, vol. 17, col. 288.

41. For the requirement to consult with the Archaeological Commission, see *Voprosy restavratsii* 1 (1907): 1. Alongside building works, consultation with regard to works of monumental art (wall paintings, etc.) was compulsory, this time with the Imperial Academy of Arts: see "Vremennyi ustav Imperatorskoi Akademii Khudozhestv ot 15 oktiabria 1893," article 5, *PSZ*, 3rd series, vol. 3, p. 570 (no. 9982), clause 11. On the publications of Snegirev and others, and the growing tourist interest, see M. E. Kaulen, *Muzei-khramy i muzei-monastyri v pervoe desiatiletie Sovetskoi vlasti* (Moscow: Luch, 2001), 15–16. An example of a guidebook that placed churches in the position of prime architectural monuments is Grigorii Moskvin, *Peterburg i ego okrestnosti: Illiustrirovannyi prakticheskii putevoditel'* (1888), which had reached its eleventh edition by 1915. See also P. Preobrazhenskii, *Isaakievskii sobor: Istoriia postroiki khrama, ego sviatilishcha i khudozhestvennye dostoprimechatel'nosti (po povodu 75-letiia ego vozobnovleniia)* (St. Petersburg: Izdanie tovarishchestva M. O. Vol'f, 1894). Of course, even before this, churches had been the source of civic pride, widely represented in panoramas: see the splendid examples in P. Iu. Klimov, comp., *Religioznyi Peterburg* (St. Petersburg: Palace Editions, 2006). I am grateful to Rosamund Bartlett for drawing my attention to this edition. The serial publication, *Lavry, monastyri i khramy na Sviatoi Rusi*, a gazetteer of church buildings published in St. Petersburg in installments starting 1909, was another sign of rising interest in ecclesiastical architecture.

42. See N. V. Pivovarova, "Khristianskie drevnosti v Sankt-Peterburge: Iz istorii sobraniia i muzeefikatsii pamiatnikov tserkovnoi stariny," *Voprosy muzeologii* 1, no. 3 (2011): 57–66. The Treasury of Antiquities was the subject of a fascinating exhibition from December 2014 to March 2015.

43. As indicated in the importance of synodal ukases noted above.

44. There is an excellent account of this in Pravilova, *A Public Empire*, 139–77.

45. NA IIMK, f. 68, op. 1, d. 1, l. 71.

46. Ibid., l. 74–74 ob.

47. Famous examples included, besides, of course, Lenin, the "Decembrists," the leaders of the abortive 1825 coup against Nicholas I; Stepan Khalturin, who in 1880 attempted to blow up the Winter Palace; and the woman radical Sof'ia Perovskaia, hanged in 1881 for her part in the assassination of Alexander II. All were the subjects of street renamings in Petrograd in 1918.

48. "O svobode sovesti, tserkovnykh i religioznykh ob"edineniiakh," January 20 (February 2), 1918, *DSV* 1:371–4.

49. For instance, in the first edition of the *Great Soviet Encyclopedia* (*Bol'shaia sovetskaia entsiklopediia* or *BSE*) (Moscow: OPIZ, 1937), 35:462–64, "cult" was described as "a manifestation of governing religious beliefs" that had originated in the battle of "primitive peoples" with natural phenomena, and an instrument of imperial authority in slave-owning societies; the Orthodox cult, "like other religious cults," had a "vividly expressed reactionary character" before 1917. The second edition of the *BSE* (Moscow: Bol'shaia sovetskaia entsiklopediia, 1953, 24:25) repeated much of this material, adding that "in C[ults] the status of religion as 'opium of the people' is especially clear." This also, of course, explains the contextual force of Khrushchev's condemnation of Stalin's "cult of personality" in 1956.

50. For a detailed treatment of this side of Soviet cultural transformation, see Kelly, "Competing Orthodoxies: Identity and Religious Belief in Soviet and Post-Soviet Russia," in *Soviet and Post-Soviet Identities*, ed. Mark Bassin and Catriona Kelly (Cambridge: Cambridge University Press, 2012), 299–320. Soviet policy toward other Christian and non-Christian denominations was also harsh, and increasingly so from the mid-1930s, as international tensions grew and anxiety about the diplomatic resonance of action against groups with powerful supporters abroad began to wane. See, for example, Artur G. Dalgatov, *"Oppozitsionnaia religioznost'" v sovetskoi Rossii (oktiabr' 1917 g.–konets 1930 gg.* (St. Petersburg: Petropolis, 2002); Anna Shternshis, *Soviet and Kosher: Jewish Popular Culture in the Soviet Union, 1923–1939* (Bloomington: Indiana University Press, 2006); and the articles collected in Marjorie Mandelstam Balzer, ed., *Religion and Politics in Russia: A Reader* (Armonk, NY: M. E. Sharpe, 2010). But the conflict between the religious and the historical and aesthetic significance of non-Orthodox buildings was, in Russia itself, less sharp, because to the uniformed eye they were much less likely to look like "religious buildings" to begin with (on the significance of an "odiously ecclesiastical appearance," see chapter 3 below).

51. *SU* 62 (1918), item 685. For a detailed description of the responsibilities of religious associations, see chapter 1.

52. A case in point was the St. Isaac's Cathedral (see chapter 3). For the phrase, "havens of obscurantism," see, for example, L. Finn,et al., *Iz ochaga mrakobesiia v ochag kul'tury* (Leningrad: OGIZ-Priboi, 1931).

53. For instance, the author of a recent university course-book on monuments preservation sententiously observes that between 1917 and 1991, country houses, churches, and monasteries "were condemned to oblivion and destruction" (M. A. Poliakova, *Okhrana kul'turnogo naslediia Rossii: Uchebnoe posobie dlia vuzov* [Moscow: Drofa, 2005], 7, 9). This is a significant overstatement of the facts, if one is speaking in strictly legal terms (neglect in practical terms is a different matter, as I shall illustrate).

54. For a more detailed discussion of this issue, see Catriona Kelly, "Religion and *nauka*: Churches as Architectural Heritage in Soviet Leningrad," in *Science, Religion, and Communism during the Cold War*, ed. Paul Betts and Stephen A. Smith (Basingstoke: Palgrave, 2016), 227–51.

55. For the legend about the skyscrapers ("the attribution of the design to Stalin [. . .] is indisputable"), see Owen Hatherley, *Landscapes of Communism: A History through Buildings* (London: Allen Lane, 2015), 213–15. On the Stalin prizes, see Marina Frolova-Walker, *Stalin's Music Prize* (New Haven, CT: Yale University Press, 2016).

56. These processes are discussed in further detail in chapter 3.

57. I discuss these points further in chapters 4, 5, and 6.

58. See Talal Asad, *Formations of the Secular: Christianity, Islam, Modernity* (Stanford, CA: Stanford University Press, 2003), 9: "An atheist will not read [the Bible] in the way a Christian would." Similarly, a tourist taking a selfie in St. Peter's, Rome, is using the building in a totally different way from a pilgrim or someone attending Mass, though in practice all three categories may sometimes overlap. On the specific case of religious objects transferred to museums, see Crispin Paine, "Religion in London's Museums," in *Godly Things: Museums, Objects, and Religion* (Leicester: Leicester University Press, 2000), 151–70, and his *Religious Objects in Museums: Private Lives and Public Duties* (London: Bloomsbury, 2013).

59. Architecture, from the Soviet point of view, was less easy to assign to the category of the national patrimony than literature, because of the preponderance of architects of foreign origin in the historical canon (for example, Francesco Rastrelli, Carlo Rossi, Auguste de Montferrand, and Georg Friedrich Veldten). However, this made the great buildings of the past congenial in terms of another objective of Soviet culture: its pretension to the role of custodian of world culture (on which, see Katerina Clark, *Moscow, the Fourth Rome: Stalinism, Cosmopolitanism, and the Evolution of Soviet Culture, 1931–1941* [Cambridge, MA: Harvard University Press, 2011]).

60. Earlier work on the subject includes Michael Bourdeaux, *Opium of the People: the Christian Religion in the USSR* (London: Faber and Faber, 1965); Dimitry Pospielovsky, *The Russian Church under the Soviet Regime 1917-1982* (2 vols; New York: St Vladimir's Seminary Press, 1984); idem, *Russkaia Pravoslavnaia Tserkov' v XX veke* (Moscow: Respublika, 1995); Jane Ellis, *The Russian Orthodox Church: A Contemporary History* (London: Croom Helm, 1986). Among more recent studies are John Anderson, *Religion, State, and Politics in the Soviet Union and its Successor States* (Cambridge: Cambridge University Press, 1994); Arto Luukkanen, *The Party of Unbelief: The Religious Policy of the Bolshevik Party, 1917–1929* (Helsinki: Suomen Historiallinen Seura, 1994) and his *The Religious Policy of the Stalinist State, a Case Study: The Central Committee on Religious Questions* (Helsinki: SHF, 1997); Nathaniel Davis, *A Long Walk to Church: A Contemporary History of Russian Orthodoxy* (Boulder, CO: Westview Press, 1995); Glennys Young, *Power and the Sacred in Revolutionary Russia: Religious Activists in the Village* (University Park: Pennsylvania State University Press, 1997); Tatiana Chumachenko, *Church and State in Soviet Russia: Russian Orthodoxy from World War II to the Khrushchev Years*, ed. Edward E. Roslof (Armonk, NY: M. E. Sharpe, 2002); and Gregory L. Freeze, "Counter-Reformation in Russian Orthodoxy: Popular Response to Religious Innovation, 1922-1925," *Slavic Review* 2 [1995]: 305-39; Freeze, "The Stalinist Assault on the Parish, 1929-1941," *Stalinismus vor dem Zweiten Weltkrieg: Neue Wege der Forschung*, edited by Manfred Hildermeier, 209-32 (Munich: Oldenburg Verlag, 1998); Freeze, "From Dechristianization to Laicization: State, Church, and Believers in Russia," *Canadian Slavonic Papers* 1 [2015]: 6-34; as well as the treatments of specific subjects: Roslof, *Red Priests* (Renovationism); Scott M. Kenworthy, *The Heart of Russia: Trinity-Sergius, Monasticism, and Society after 1825* (New York: Oxford University Press, 2010) (monasticism); Greene, *Bodies Like Bright Stars* (relics), and Alexander Panchenko, Jeanne Kormina, and Sergei Shtyrkov, *Izobretenie religii: Desekuliarizatsiia v postsovetskom kontekste* (St. Petersburg: Evropeiskii universitet v Sankt-Peterburg, 2015) (popular Orthodoxy). On Leningrad, see particularly the work of M. V. Shkarovskii, e.g., *Peterburgskaia eparkhiia v gody gonenii i utrat, 1917-1945* (St Petersburg: Liki Rossii, 1995); Shkarovskii, *Sankt-Peterburgskaia eparkhiia v dvadtsatom veke v svete arkhivnykh materialov* (St. Petersburg: Liki Rossii, 2000); Shkarovskii, *Tserkov' zovet k zashchite Rodiny: Religioznaia zhizn' Leningrada i Severo-Zapada v gody Velikoi Otechestvennoi voiny* (St. Petersburg: Satis-Derzhava, 2005) (alongside monographs, Shkarovskii, working with N. Iu. Cherepnina, has made available to researchers an enormous amount of primary material, particularly from TsGA-SPb).

61. See, for example, Willem van den Bercken, *Ideology and Atheism in the Soviet Union* (Berlin: Walter de Gruyter, 1988); Daniel Peris, *Storming the Heavens: The Soviet League of the Militant Godless* (Ithaca, NY: Cornell University Press, 1998); William B. Husband, *"Godless Communists": Atheism and Society in Soviet Russia, 1917–1932* (DeKalb: Northern Illinois University Press, 2000); Victoria Smolkin-Rothrock, "The Ticket to the Soviet Soul: Science, Religion, and the Spiritual Crisis of Late Soviet Atheism," *Russian Review* 73, no. 2 (2014): 171–97; Michael Froggatt, "Science in Propaganda and Popular Culture in the USSR under Khrushchëv (1953–1964)" (DPhil thesis, University of Oxford, 2006); and others. Pospielovsky's *A History of Soviet Ideology and Atheism in the Soviet Union* (2 vols. Berlin: Walter de Gruyter, 1988), is also useful, particularly on the impact of atheism upon the religious population.

62. Generally on the past, see, for example, David Brandenberger, *National Bolshevism: Stalinist Mass Culture and the Formation of Modern Russian National Identity, 1931–1956* (Cambridge, MA: Harvard University Press, 2002); David Brandenberger and Kevin Platt, *Epic Revisionism: Russian History and Literature as Stalinist Propaganda* (Madison: University of Wisconsin Press, 2006); Denis Kozlov, *The Readers of Novyi Mir: Coming to Terms with the Stalinist Past* (Cambridge, MA: Harvard

University Press, 2013). On Leningrad particularly, see Emily Johnson, *How St. Petersburg Learned to Study Itself: The Russian Idea of Kraevedenie* (University Park: Pennsylvania State University Press, 2006); on museums, Anne Odom and Wendy R. Salmond, eds., *Treasures into Tractors: The Selling of Russia's Cultural Heritage, 1918–1938* (Washington, DC: Hillwood Estate, 2009); Susan N. Smith, "The Accidental Museum: Expropriating and Appropriating the Past," *Russian Review* 67, no. 3 (2008): 438–53; Adam Jolles, "Stalin's Talking Museums," *Oxford Art Journal* 28, no. 3 (2005): 49–55; on the built environment, see Alexei Elfimov, *Russian Intellectual Culture in Transition: The Future in the Past* (Münster: Lit, 2004); Steven Maddox, *Saving Stalin's Imperial City: Historic Preservation in Leningrad, 1930–1950* (Bloomington: Indiana University Press, 2015).

63. The definitive study is V. V. Antonov and A. V. Kobak's *Sviatyni Sankt-Peterburga: Entsiklopediia khristianskikh khramov*, 3rd ed. (St. Petersburg: Fond Spas, 2010), hereafter *SSPb*. See also A. P. Popov, *Khramy Sankt-Peterburga: Khudozhestvenno-istoricheskii ocherk* (St Petersburg: Lenizdat, 1995); S. Kuriashov, I. Rumiantseva, *Monastyri Sankt-Peterburgskoi eparkhii. Spravochnik palomnika* (St Petersburg, 2000), and G. V. Dluzhnevskaia, *Utrachennye khramy Peterburga* (St. Petersburg: Litera, 2003) and L. Protsai, "Utrachennye sviatyni," in Klimov, *Religioznyi Peterburg.*

64. Dluzhnevskaia, *Utrachennye khramy Peterburga*, 5–6. Despite its melodramatic tone here, this is a well-researched scholarly publication illustrated with photographs from the IIMK collection, whose archive Dluzhnevskaia headed until her untimely death in July 2014. A more uncompromising viewpoint is evident in Sergei Bychkov, *Bol'sheviki protiv russkoi tserkvi* (Moscow: Tetis Pablishn, 2006), whose proclaimed purpose is history to devotional ends, and which describes most other historians in the field, for example, M. V. Shkarovskii, as "mythographers" (2:25).

65. Interview with Father N., a priest in one of St. Petersburg's cathedrals, 2009 (author's field diary, April 2009).

66. According to the general belief, the largest number of *namolennye* churches are to be found in Moscow, but such churches exist in Petersburg too, and the concept was ubiquitous among our informants. See, for example, Oxf/AHRC SPb-11 PF21 MS (interview with a nun, b. c. 1975); Oxf/AHRC SPb-09 PF2 VM ("yes, a new church can also be *namolennaia*, but if it's an old one, if services were given without interruption [throughout the Soviet period], that's also very important"). The informants in Oxf/AHRC SPb-09 PF10 VM, Oxf/AHRC SPb-09 PF4 VM, Oxf/AHRC SPb-09 PF6 VM, Oxf/AHRC SPb-09 PF5 CK, Oxf/AHRC SPb-09 PF6 CK, Oxf/AHRC SPb-09 PF7 CK, and Oxf/AHRC SPb-09 PF9 CK express similar sentiments.

67. A priest at one of St. Petersburg's cathedrals whom I interviewed in April 2009 expanded at length on these issues. He requested that the interview should not be taped, but there is a detailed synopsis in my field notes (FN, April 2009).

68. Studies focus above all on the titanic efforts to save monuments during the Great Patriotic War and reconstruct them in the years following. See, for example, the two collections edited by Kedrinskii et al.: *Letopis' vozrozhdeniia: Vosstanovlenie pamiatnikov arkhitektury Leningrada i prigorodov, razrushennykh v gody Velikoi Otechestvennoi Voiny nemetski-fashistskimi zakhvatchikami* (Leningrad: Lenizdat, 1971), and *Vosstanovlenie pamiatnikov arkhitektury Leningrada* (Leningrad: Lenizdat, 1983). See also Iu. Bakhareva and N. S. Tret'iakova, comp., "Iz dnevnikov khranitelei prigorodnykh dvortsov-muzeev Leningrada, 1941–1945," *Otechestvennye arkhivy* 1 (2007), http://www.rusarchives.ru/publication/mobil.shtml.

69. For interviews with conservators taking a nostalgic view, see, for example, Oxf/AHRC SPb-08 PF 2 AP; Oxf/AHRC SPb-08 PF5 AP; Oxf/AHRC SPb-08 PF6 AP.

70. See the conclusion below.

71. A rare source to point out that church buildings were sometimes demolished with the knowledge and consent of the Monuments Office is L. Protsai, "Utrachennye sviatyni," 447–59.

72. Traditional Roman Catholic attitudes to sacred space are comparable, though in post-Vatican II practice there has been a strong ecumenical drive, and the presence of a non-Catholic or non-Christian would no longer create problems, nor would the use of a church for a concert be seen as peculiar. But even so, it is notable that recent plans in Berlin to create a space for multi-faith worship (the "House of One") have been led by a Lutheran pastor, rather than members of other Christian

denominations, and some Catholics have expressed disquiet, with novelist Martin Mosebach brand-ing the development bulky and featureless, a "pharaoh's grave" (Philip Ottermann, "Berlin's House of One: A Church, a Mosque and a Synagogue under One Roof," *Guardian*, June 25, 2014, http://www.theguardian.com/world/shortcuts/2014/jun/25/berlin-house-of-one-unity-christian-muslim-jew).

73. Petr Nechaev, *Prakticheskoe rukovodstvo dlia sviashchennosluzhitelei*, 5th ed. St. Petersburg: Tip. I. N. Skorokhodova, 1893. For a detailed discussion of the highly specific resonance of ecclesias-tical space in Russia, see Victoria Arnold, "The Experience of Sacred Place in Post-Soviet Russia: A Geography of Orthodoxy and Islam in Perm' Krai" (DPhil thesis, University of Oxford, 2012), ch. 1.

74. As recounted, for instance, by the German traveler Adam Olearius in his famous account of his 1636 voyage to Muscovy (Olearius, *Vermehrte newe Beschreibung der muscowitischen und per-sischen Reyse . . . welche zum andern mahl heraus gibt Adam Olearius* [Schlesswig: J. Holwein, 1656]).

75. The example of a bible in a lavatory comes from my interview with a liberal Orthodox priest (Oxf/AHRC SPb-09 PF7 CK); of the self-portrait icon, from a conversation with a professional restorer in 2007 (FN March 2007).

76. From my interview with a priest at one of Petersburg's cathedrals (FN April 2009).

77. See articles 3–12 of the *Ustav o preduprezhdenii i presechenii prestuplenii* (1890 edition), in Mordukhai-Boltovskii, *Svod zakonov*, 14:98–99.

78. "There have been reports that Father V. Ivanov sometimes celebrates the Liturgy in peo-ple's homes. This is not permitted, except in cases of emergency, and then with episcopal permission, since a home where the Liturgy is performed becomes a religious building [*khram*]." 1958 letter from Metropolitan Elefterii of Leningrad; Arkhiv Sankt-Peterburgskoi eparkhii (hereafter ASPbE), f. 1, op. 11, d. 78, l. 2. The background was a country priest who had, out of the kindness of his heart, been covering for colleagues in other parishes who were too lazy to travel out to distant villages. Only the occasional offices (*treby*, for example, funerals, christenings, blessings) may normally be performed in secular premises. As I mention in chapter 1, the Church Council (Pomestnyi Sobor) of 1917–1918 gave dispensation for masses to be performed outside churches, but this was an emergency measure precipitated by the impending confiscation of church premises.

79. For the suggestion about multi-denominational use, see TsGA-SPb, f. 1001, op. 7, d. 18, l. 2. In the early Soviet period, shared use of "cultic" premises was sometimes unavoidable, but Or-thodox believers from the conservative mainstream did their best to minimize contact: an article in the *Zhurnal Moskovskoi Patriarkhii* (1 [1931]: 17) counseled strongly against using the same order as "those of other churches" (*inotserkovniki*); each group should have its own portable altar.

80. P. A. Florenskii, "Khramovoe deistvo kak sintez iskusstv," in *Iz istorii sovetskoi nauki o teatre, 20-e gody: Sbornik trudov*, ed. S. V. Stakhorskii (Moscow: GITIS, 1988), 31.

81. I discuss this situation in more detail in chapter 3. The fact that icons and church property were, in practice, sometimes simply dumped (or sold for cash) (see further below) has not affected these debates, which are based on canonical tradition and on transcendent ideals.

82. As I was in the middle stages of work on this book, the Russian Federation was dominated by the Pussy Riot case, an especially ugly clash between aggressive piety and vehement anticlericalism. On the one side stood those for whom the group had an absolute right to free speech, and for whom references to "offense to the feelings of believers" was mere hogwash, and on the other, those who thought that those guilty of the offense should have received an even stiffer prison sentence, or, in-deed, been executed. Moderate commentary, for instance from the liberal Orthodox writer Aleksandr Arkhangel'skii (who argued that the young women had committed a "sin" that was outside the juris-diction of secular law) was almost non-existent. For a useful discussion, see Olga G. Voronina, "Pussy Riot Steal the Stage in the Moscow Cathedral of Christ the Saviour: Punk Prayer on Trial Online and in Court," *Digital Icons: Studies in Russian, Eurasian and Central European New Media* 9 (2013): 69–85.

83. I return to this topic in the conclusion.

84. In *The Hermitage: The Biography of a Great Museum* (London: Jonathan Cape, 1997), Geraldine Norman records that the Hermitage staff whom she spoke to were far more distressed by recollecting the forced de-accessions of the late 1920s and early 1930s than the political purges of 1937–1938.

85. The *Oxford English Dictionary* records this meaning from 1704.

86. A study that attempts to place such interpretations in perspective, while continuing to subscribe to them, is Bryan Wilson, *Religion in Sociological Perspective* (1982; repr., Oxford: Oxford University Press, 2002), which contends, for example, that religious authority was able to persist only where development was particularly rapid (39), and that "the social system of advanced societies functions on rational premises" (47).

87. Wilson's *Religion in Sociological Perspective*, originally given as a course of lectures in Japan, includes an attempt to deal with the relationship between the state and Buddhism, for instance.

88. For an uncompromising assertion of the old secularization models, see Steve Bruce, *God Is Dead: Secularization in the West* (Oxford: Blackwell, 2002). Pippa Norris and Ronald Inglehart, *Sacred and Secular: Religion and Politics Worldwide* (Cambridge: Cambridge University Press, 2004) also emphasize the continuing importance of secularization, relating the strength of traditional religion to socioeconomic deprivation. On the market-driven model of US religious sociology, where the multiplicity of creeds is seen as a sign of strength, rather than of fragmentation and decline, see R. Stephen Walker, "Work in Progress: Towards a New Paradigm for the Sociological Study of Religion in the United States," *American Journal of Sociology* 98, no. 5 (1993): 1044–55. Peter Berger has also employed a market-based model in order to explain the persisting strength of religion (see, for example, "The Desecularization of the World: A Global Overview," in *The Desecularization of the World: Resurgent Religion and World Politics* [Washington DC: Ethics and Public Policy Center, 1999], 1–18).

89. See particularly Paul Froese, *The Plot to Kill God: Findings from the Soviet Experiment in Secularization* (Berkeley: University of California Press, 2008). A more complicated picture is suggested by the detailed work on religious life in the Soviet and post-Soviet period; for a good selection, see Mark D. Steinberg and Catherine Wanner, eds., *Religion, Morality, and Community in Post-Soviet Societies* (Bloomington: Indiana University Press, 2008); Sonja Luehrmann, *Secularism Soviet Style: Teaching Atheism and Religion in a Volga Republic* (Bloomington: Indiana University Press, 2011); Catherine Wanner, ed., *State Secularism and Lived Religion in Soviet Russia and Ukraine* (New York: Oxford University Press, 2012).

90. Bruce, *God Is Dead*, 33.

91. On the League of the Militant Godless, see especially Peris, *Storming the Heavens*.

92. Here I have been influenced by the sophisticated discussion of "religion" and "the sacred" in a generalized (as well as institutionalized) sense by Danièle Hervieu-Léger, *Religion as a Chain of Memory*, trans. Simon Lee (Cambridge: Polity Press, 2000); originally published as *La Religion pour mémoire* (Paris: Editions du Cerf, 1993). The central argument is that a self-conscious and ceremonial link with the past is a defining feature of religious or quasi-religious activity: thus, a football match is not "religious," but the rite at which Liverpool fans spontaneously massed at Anfield to honor the fans who had died in the Hillsborough disaster was a manifestation of "metaphorical religion."

93. David Powell, "The Effectiveness of Soviet Anti-Religious Propaganda," *The Public Opinion Quarterly* 31, no. 3 (1967): 379–80. See also the same author's *Anti-Religious Propaganda in the Soviet Union: A Study of Mass Persuasion* (Cambridge, MA: MIT Press, 1975).

94. I have discussed this more fully in "Religion and *nauka*."

95. Here I draw on a body of recent work that has dealt precisely with the mutually defining relations of the sacred and the secular. See particularly Asad, *Formations of the Secular*.

96. For the distinction between "project" and "process," see Jonathan C. D. Clark, "Secularization and Modernization: The Failure of a 'Grand Narrative,'" *The Historical Journal* 55 (2012): 189.

97. The quotation comes from David Nash, "Reconnecting Religion with Social and Cultural History: Secularization's Failure as a Master Narrative," *Cultural and Social History* 3 (2004): 308. On the anthropology of secularism, see, for example, Philip S. Gorski and Ateş Atinordu, "After Secularization?," *Annual Review of Sociology* 34 (2008): 73–74.

98. Callum G. Brown, "The Secularisation Debate: What the 1960s Have Done to the Study of Religious History," in *The Decline of Christendom in Western Europe*, ed. Hugh McLeod and Werner Ustorf (Cambridge: Cambridge University Press, 2003), 42. See also Hugh McLeod, Introduction to

The Decline of Christendom, 3; S. Filatov and R. Lunken, "Statistics on Religion in Russian Reality," *Religion, State and Society* 34 (2006): 33–49.

99. The "tokens of exchange" view of monuments can be seen, for example, in Katherine Verdery, *The Political Lives of Dead Bodies: Reburial and Post-Socialist Change* (New York: Columbia University Press, 1999), and Mark Bassin, Christopher Ely, and Melissa T. Stockdale, eds., *Space, Place, and Power in Modern Russia: Essays in the New Spatial History* (DeKalb: Northern Illinois University Press, 2010). For a useful discussion of the different possible responses to buildings, see William Whyte, "How Do Buildings Mean? Some Issues of Interpretation in the History of Architecture," *History and Theory* 45, no. 2 (May 2006): 153–77.

100. For example, the church reform movement was particularly strong in Petrograd, with Metropolitan Veniamin playing a crucial role as mediator between the Moscow Patriarchate and the new directions of thought; later figures such as Metropolitan Grigorii were to exercise a rare spiritual authority. On the importance of regional variations in church life generally, see Gregory L. Freeze, "Subversive Atheism: Soviet Antireligious Campaigns and the Religious Revival in Ukraine in the 1920s," in Wanner, *State Secularism*, 27–62.

101. A. A. "Pro doma sua," *Starye gody* 2 (1909): 94. On the prerevolutionary history of preservation in Petersburg, see, for example, Katerina Clark, *Petersburg, Crucible of Cultural Revolution* (Cambridge, MA: Harvard University Press), ch. 1.

102. The picture, based on holdings in GARF, was extremely mixed. In Yeneseisk province, a list of churches deserving protection was forwarded to the central Museums Department as early as 1920 (GARF, f. A-353, op. 4, d. 377, passim). But this was a rich and cultivated part of the provinces. Contrast the need to nag Vladimir, for example, in 1923 (GARF, f. 2307, op. 3, d. 163, ll. 140, 143). The bulk of documentation in the Glavnauka (Scientific Directorate) files relates to Moscow and the surrounding areas, but there was a mixed picture here too: cf. the materials on the dire condition of Zagorsk (GARF, f. 259, op. 37, d. 287, passim).

103. "The Monuments Office" is used as a shorthand here for the department charged with recording and protecting *pamiatniki*, the name of which altered at different times: in the late 1920s and early 1930s (from c. 1924), it was the "Bureau for the Protection of Monuments of Revolution and Culture" attached to the Mass Section (Massovyi otdel) of Lensovet; from 1937 it was the "Section for the Protection of Monuments of History and Culture" attached to the Directorate of the Arts (Upravlenie iskusstv). During the Second World War, the title changed to the "State Inspectorate of Monuments" (GIOP), a title used right to the end of Soviet power. The Office was answerable both to local government (Lensovet—in tandem with Lenoblispolkom between 1931 and 1953), and to central government. The term "Museums Department," however, refers to the department of the Scientific Directorate (Glavnauka) of Narkompros, the name of which, confusingly, became between 1930 and 1934 the "Bureau for the Protection of Monuments of Art and History." The link with the city authorities was unusual in terms of overall Soviet policy, and in 1938–1939, this led to a major standoff with Narkompros, won by the Leningrad city authorities (see chapter 3).

104. See the claim made in 1934 by the then head of the Monuments Office (Otdel okhrany pamiatnikov) at Lensovet, P. A. Vsevolozhskii, TsGALI-SPb, f. 32, op. 1, d. 71, l. 6.

105. Work is now being done on the biographies of local officials (see, for example, Tracy McDonald, *Face to the Village: The Riazan Countryside under Soviet Rule, 1921–1930* [Toronto: University of Toronto Press, 2011]), but this area of research is tricky because facts about educational profile, parental background, service record, and so on, are difficult to locate in archives and subject to confidentiality regulations, and because the information given may not be accurate in any case, given the widespread practice, in the 1920s and 1930s, of adjusting biographical data to avoid discrimination.

106. See my note on sources below.

107. A few documents relating to the City Planning Council's work in the late 1940s are held in TsGANTD-SPb, which also holds limited materials for the APU and its predecessors and successors. The City Planning Council was comprised of city officials working in planning and construction and notable figures from the field of architecture, for example, architects and historians. See also my note on sources below.

294 NOTES TO INTRODUCTION

108. Typical of this is Antonov and Kobak's compendious *SSPb*, which simply provides the dates of alterations, demolitions, etc.

109. For the importance of intersubjectivity as well as, or rather than, meaning in religious history, see Robert A. Orsi, *Between Heaven and Earth: The Religious Worlds People Make and the Scholars Who Study Them* (Princeton, NJ: Princeton University Press, 2005), 5–9.

110. See, for example, Clark, *Petersburg*, ch. 1; Blair Ruble, *Leningrad: Shaping a Soviet City* (Berkeley: University of California Press, 1990); Lev Lur'e and Aleksandr Kobak, "Rozhdenie i gibel' peterburgskoi idei," *Muzei i gorod*, a special issue of the journal *Petersburg ars* (1993): 25–31; Johnson, *How St. Petersburg Learned*.

111. See, for example, Solomon Volkov, *St. Petersburg: A Cultural History* (New York: Free Press, 1995); Svetlana Boym, *The Future of Nostalgia* (New York: Basic Books, 2001); Lisa Kirschenbaum, *The Legacy of the Siege of Leningrad, 1941–1995: Myth, Memories, and Monuments* (Cambridge: Cambridge University Press, 2006); and the introduction and different contributions in Helena Goscilo and Steven Norris, eds., *Preserving Petersburg: History, Memory, Nostalgia* (Bloomington: Indiana University Press, 2008). A rare source to point to *discontinuities* is Elena Hellberg-Hirn, *Imperial Imprints: Post-Soviet St. Petersburg* (Helsinki: SKS, Finnish Literature Society, 2003), which emphasizes that there was almost no discussion of the prerevolutionary history of Leningrad in official Soviet sources (a point that, while overstated, acts as an important corrective to the customary arguments about the city).

112. See, for example, the architectural studies of William Brumfield (*A History of Russian Architecture* [Cambridge: Cambridge University Press, 1993], and "St. Petersburg and the Art of Survival," in Goscilo and Norris, *Preserving Petersburg*, 1–38, both of which are illustrated with Brumfield's own handsome photographs, or the various publications of Boris Kirikov (*Arkhitektura peterburgskogo moderna: Osobniaki i dokhodnye doma* [St. Petersburg: Neva, 2003]; *Pamiatniki arkhitektury i istorii Sankt-Peterburga: Vasileostrovskii raion* [St. Petersburg: Kolo, 2006]; *Pamiatniki arkhitektury i istorii Sankt-Peterburga: Petrogradskii raion* [St. Petersburg: Kolo, 2004], which are mainly based on Soviet-era materials from the archive of the Monuments Office. For this book, I have tried where possible to use photographs contemporary with my historical discussion, though the amount of material available is often limited. The ideologically marginal character of churches meant that much photography was associated with campaigns for closure and demolition (for this reason, the worst represented period is the 1970s and 1980s, when government officials had stopped pushing for the removal or reconstruction of churches, but were still not much concerned with their condition). The otherwise extraordinarily rich holdings in the Tsentral'nyi gosudarstvennyi arkhiv kino- foto- fonodokumentov Sankt-Peterburga (hereafter TsGAKFFD-SPb) and the Gosudarstvennyi muzei istorii Sankt-Peterburga (hereafter GMISPb) have no more than twenty to thirty images available between them.

113. See, for example, the reference to this practice in the material on the demolition of the St. Matthew Church quoted in chapter 3—its bricks were to be used for the *nadstroika* of the buildings standing round it.

114. To date, discussion of Stalinist culture has focused mainly on canon formation in written texts (see, for example, Brandenberger, *National Bolshevism*; Brandenberger and Platt, *Epic Revisionism*; Evgeny Dobrenko, *The Making of the State Reader: Social and Aesthetic Origins of Soviet Literary Culture*, trans. Jesse Savage [Stanford, CA: Stanford University Press]). Art history has also received some attention (see, for example, Jan Plamper, *The Stalin Cult: A Study in the Alchemy of Power* (New Haven: Yale University Press, 2012); Johnson, *How Petersburg Learned*), as has the ballet (for example, Christina Ezrahi, *Swans of the Kremlin: Ballet and Power in Soviet Russia* [Pittsburgh, PA: University of Pittsburgh Press, 2012]). But the process could be matched in architectural history. For an account focusing mainly on political purges in the architectural world, see Hugh Hudson, *Blueprints and Blood: The Stalinization of Soviet Architecture, 1917–1927* (Princeton, NJ: Princeton University Press, 1994); for a brilliant symbological schematization, Vladimir Papernyi, *Kultura "dva"* (Ann Arbor: Ardis, 1985). A thorough history of Soviet architecture based on archival documentation remains to be written.

115. Alexander Rabinowitch, *The Bolsheviks in Power: The First Years of Soviet Rule in Petrograd* (Bloomington: Indiana University Press, 2007), 56.

116. It is worth emphasizing this point because so much of the literature on officialdom deals with Party loyalties: see, for example, Boris Firsov, *Raznomyslie v SSSR: 1940-e–1960-e gody; Istoriia, teoriia i praktika* (St. Petersburg: Evropeiskii dom, 2008); Caroline Humphrey, "The 'Creative Bureaucrat': Conflicts in the Production of Communist Party Discourse," *Inner Asia* 10, no. 1 (2008): 5–35. Much of a heritage protection (more broadly, city planning) official's life had little to do with producing "discourse" in the ideological sense, but rather with implementing directives and contributing to policy discussions. Ideology had to be invoked, but its production could be left to others. As I shall show, professional training at LISI or the Academy of Arts was more important than a stint at the Higher Party School.

117. Again, I am departing here from a line of argument—entirely valid in some contexts—that sees Soviet language as essentially self-reinforcingly ritualistic and performative in nature, with no referential function at all: see particularly the work of Alexei Yurchak, *Everything Was Forever, Until It Was No More: The Last Soviet Generation* (Princeton, NJ: Princeton University Press, 2006). For a broader study of Soviet public language, see Nikolai Vakhtin and Boris Firsov, eds., *Public Debate in Russia: Matters of (Dis)order* (Edinburgh: Edinburgh University Press, 2016).

118. There is a large literature on the history of these issues in Western Europe and the United States. Along with the classic citation, Pierre Nora, ed., *Les Lieux de mémoire*, 3 vols. (Paris: Gallimard, 1984–1992), see, for example, Daniel Bluestone, "Academics in Tennis Shoes: Historic Preservation and the Academy," *Journal of the Society of Architectural Historians* 58, no. 3 (1999): 300–307; Felix Urban, "Recovering Essence through Demolition: The 'Organic' City in Post-War Berlin," *Journal of the Society of Architectural Historians* 3 (2004): 354–69; Neil Sharp, "The Wrong Twigs for an Eagle's Nest? Architecture, Nationalism, and Sir Hugh Lane's Scheme for a Gallery of Modern Art, Dublin, 1904–13," in *The Architecture of the Museum: Symbolic Structures, Urban Contexts*, ed. Michaela Giebelhausen (Manchester: Manchester University Press, 2003), 32-53; Astrid Swenson, *The Rise of Heritage: Preserving the Past in France, Germany, and England, 1789–1914* (Cambridge: Cambridge University Press, 2013); the special issue of *Nations and Nationalism* on heritage preservation, edited by Mark Thatcher (forthcoming); and also the material on the associations' websites about the history of the Georgian Group (http://www.georgiangroup.org.uk); and English Heritage (http://www.english-heritage.org.uk).

119. On the reshaping of the material world of the Catholic Church during the English Reformation, see Eamon Duffy, *The Stripping of the Altars: Traditional Religion in England, c. 1400–c. 1580* (New Haven, CT: Yale University Press, 1992). The rational detachment from church art may have been a specifically Petrograd/Leningrad feature. In 1922, Nikolai Kharlamov, director of the Viazniki Museum of History and Art in Vladimir province wrote to protest the removal of the jeweled covering of a sixteenth-century icon held in the local Kazan' Cathedral. "With all the force of my reasoning and feeling, I can only urgently desire the restoration of this monument whose genuine beauty makes it unique in this place." (N. N. Pokrovskii, S. G. Petrov, *Arkhivy Kremlia: Politbiuro i tserkov'* (Moscow: ROSSPEN, 1998), vol. 2, doc. 66, p. 108).

120. During the Revolution and Civil War, reality was often significantly worse than the events depicted by Babel, with churches damaged and desecrated, and members of the clergy murdered (see the extensive documentation in A. A. Valentinov, ed., *Chernaia kniga: "Shturm nebes"; Sbornik dokumental'nykh dannykh, kharakterizuiushchikh bor'bu sovetskoi kommunisticheskoi vlasti protiv vsiakoi religii, protiv vsekh ispovedanii i tserkvei* [Paris: Izd. Russkogo natsional'nogo studencheskogo ob"edineniia, 1925]). One can compare the events of the Spanish Civil War, as well as those of revolutionary France; see, for example, Franz Borkenau, *The Spanish Cockpit: An Eye-Witness Account of the Political and Social Conflicts of the Spanish Civil War* (London: Faber and Faber, 1937), 71, 75. But there was a difference between these events and the purposive, government-sponsored assault on the material culture and practices of religion in Soviet Russia, which began with the assault on monasteries and saints' shrines in 1918 and continued with the confiscation of church goods in 1922, as I discuss in chapter 1 below.

121. On the demolitions, and the removal of architectural fragments to the Guildhall Museum, see Francis Sheppard, *The Treasury of London's Past: An Historical Account of the Museum of London*

and Its Predecessors, the Guildhall Museum and the London Museum (London: HMSO Publications, 1991), 8–9.

122. The work of Astrid Swenson places the history of preservation policy in England, France, and Germany since the late eighteenth century in broad comparative perspective, emphasizing the convergence of ideals and practical norms: See her *The Rise of Heritage.*

123. As set out, for example, in Peter Holquist, *Making War, Forging Revolution: Russia's Continuum of Crisis* (Cambridge, MA: Harvard University Press, 2002); the contributors to Amir Weiner, ed., *Landscaping the Human Garden: Twentieth-Century Population Management in a Comparative Perspective* (Stanford, CA: Stanford University Press, 2003); and more recently by David Shearer, *Policing Stalin's Socialism: Repression and Social Order in the Soviet Union, 1924–1953* (New Haven, CT: Yale University Press, 2009), and Paul Hagenloh, *Stalin's Police: Public Order and Mass Repression in the USSR, 1926–1941* (Washington, DC: Woodrow Wilson Center, 2009).

124. For the presentation and implementation of a schematic topology of different forms of Marxism in early Soviet culture, see David Priestland, *Stalinism and the Politics of Mobilization: Ideas, Power, and Terror in Inter-War Russia* (Oxford: Oxford University Press, 2007). This schema is deployed on a transnational level in Priestland's *The Red Flag: Communism and the Making of the Modern World* (London: Allen Lane, 2009).

125. This point has tended to be obscured by the abundant use of sources generated by the most highly ideologized branches of the state bureaucracy—what the Russian historian Nikolai Mitrokhin has termed "the morbid condition called 'The Archive of the State Plenipotentiary'" (see his comment in "Bolezn' pod nazvaniem 'fond upolnomochennogo' ili neskol'ko stranits ob aktual'nykh problemakh izucheniia religioznosti v SSSR," *Gosudarstvo, religiia, tserkov'* 30, nos. 3–4 [2012]: 505–11)—or the files of the antireligious organizations. Once the files of other bureaucracies are consulted, the picture becomes significantly more complicated. For an instructive discussion of the difficulties of local soviet and Party officials in grasping exactly what the division between church and state was supposed to signify in the changed world of the late 1940s, see Jeanne [Zhanna] Kormina, "Ispolkomy i prikhody: Religioznaia zhizn' Pskovskoi oblasti v pervuiu poslevoennuiu piatiletku," *Neprikosnovennyi zapas* 59, no. 3 (2008), http://magazines.russ.ru/nz/2008/3/ko11.html. Sonja Luehrmann has pointed out that reports written to provide higher authorities with what they "needed to know" often omitted the local knowledge of activists, so that these might suppress even traditional beliefs they in fact shared, such as *porcha* (ritual pollution), etc.: "Chto my mozhem znat' o religioznoi zhizni sovetskogo perioda? Sopostavlenie arkhivnykh i ustnykh istochnikov," *Gosudarstvo, religiia, tserkov'*, nos. 3–4 (2012): 485–504.

126. Work on the specific case of the "Renewal" or "Renovationist" movement, which explicitly sought accommodation with Soviet power (see, for example, Roslof, *Red Priests*), naturally espouses a "partial convergence" model. A good primary source on this for Leningrad is the remarkably accurate memoir (to judge by archival evidence) by Anatolii Krasnov-Levitin, *Likhie gody, 1925–1941* (Paris: YMCA, 1977). Douglas Rogers, *The Old Faith and the Russian Land: A Historical Ethnography of Ethics in the Urals* (Ithaca, NY: Cornell University Press, 2009), seeks to obviate a simplistic "resistance" paradigm in the case of an Old Believer community. Indeed, the Old Believers were not subject to the same level of persecution as the Orthodox (since, as a persecuted minority under the Old Regime, they had the luster of oppositional status). Up to the "Stalinist Concordat" of 1943, there is quite a lot of evidence for systematic self-differentiation on the part of Orthodox communities other than those who espoused "renewal" (see Glennys Young, *Power and the Sacred in Revolutionary Russia: Religious Activists in the Village* [University Park: Pennsylvania State University Press, 1997]; Panchenko, "Popular Orthodoxy in Twentieth-Century Russia: Ideology, Consumption, and Competition," in *Soviet and Post-Soviet Identities*, ed. Mark Bassin and Catriona Kelly [Cambridge: Cambridge University Press, 2010], 321–40; Kelly, "Competing Orthodoxies"). At the same time, by the late 1930s, believers, at least in Leningrad, sometimes employed strategies they thought would appeal to representatives of Soviet power—for instance, references to the Stalinist Constitution of 1936: see chapter 3 below.

127. Quotation from Caroline Humphrey, *The Unmaking of Soviet Life: Everyday Economies after Socialism* (Ithaca, NY: Cornell University Press, 2002), xix. For further work in the field of

cultural anthropology emphasizing the dialogic relationship between the material world and human actors, see, for example, Arjun Appadurai, ed., *The Social Life of Things: Commodities in Cultural Perspective* (New York: Cambridge University Press, 1986); Daniel Miller, ed., *Anthropology and the Individual: A Material Culture Perspective* (Oxford: Berg, 2009). On the materiality of architecture, see, for example, Michael Thompson, *Rubbish Theory: The Creation and Destruction of Value* (Oxford: Oxford University Press, 1979); Victor Buchli, *An Anthropology of Architecture* (London: Bloomsbury Academic, 2013).

128. An instructive study of the role of material objects in religious practice is Colleen McDannell, *Material Christianity: Religion and Popular Culture in America* (New Haven, CT: Yale University Press, 1995).

Chapter One

1. Lev D. Trotskii [Leon Trotsky], note to the Politburo, March 30, 1922, cited here from N. N. Pokrovskii and S. G. Petrov, eds., *Arkhivy Kremlia: Politbiuro i tserkov', 1922–1925* (Moscow: ROSSPEN, 1998), vol. 1, doc. no. 23.29, p. 161. A more literal translation of the original would read, "The October Revolution has only now rolled up to the church."

2. For the original title, see *DSV* 1:371. In portraying the slide toward more repressive policies, this work follows Alexander Rabinowitch's archive-based *The Bolsheviks in Power: The First Years of Soviet Rule in Petrograd* (Bloomington: Indiana University Press, 2007), rather than Richard Pipes's *Russia under the Bolshevik Regime, 1919–1924* (New York: Vintage, 1995), which draws on printed sources to make a case for purposive control from the very beginning (exactly the narrative that was propounded by official Soviet studies of the October Revolution).

3. On the moves against the periodical press, which were particularly effective in Petrograd, under the notoriously severe Commissar of Print and Propaganda Moisei Ionovich Lisovskii (1887–1938), see G. V. Zhirkov, "Istoriia sovetskoi tsenzury perioda komissaroderzhaviia (1917–1919 gg.)," *Vestnik Sankt-Peterburgskogo universiteta, 2nd ser.* 1 (1994), 82–92, http://www.pseudology.org/Tsenzura/TsetzuraHistory/library_view_book4df3.html.

4. V. I. Lenin, "Sotsializm i religiia" (first published in *Novaia zhizn'*, December 3, 1905), in *Polnoe sobranie sochinenii* (hereafter *PSS*), 5th ed. (Moscow: Izdatel'stvo politicheskoi literatury, 1960), 12:143. The radical secularization program of the Bolsheviks, and the place of the antireligious campaign in their ideology, has been the subject of an enormous literature. For recent discussions, see Arto Luukkanen, *The Party of Unbelief: The Religious Policy of the Bolshevik Party, 1917–1929* (Helsinki: SHS, 1994), esp. 21–163; Dimitry Pospielovsky, *The Russian Church under the Soviet Regime, 1917–1982*, vol. 1 (Crestwood, NY: St. Vladimir's Seminary Press, 1984); Pospielovsky, *Russkaia pravoslavnaia tserkov' v XX veke* (Moscow: Respublika, 1995); Robert Greene, *Bodies Like Bright Stars: Saints and Relics in Orthodox Russia* (DeKalb: Northern Illinois University Press, 2010); A. N. Kashevarov, *Pravoslavnaia rossiiskaia tserkov' i sovetskoe gosudarstvo 1917–1922* (Moscow: Izdatel'stvo Krutitskogo podvor'ia, 2005).

5. The main measures passed by the Provisional Government were the March 20, 1917, law "On the Abolition of Confessional and National Restrictions" [Ob otmene veroispovednykh i natsional'nykh ogranicheniiakh], which ended discrimination against non-Orthodox citizens of Russia, and the July 14, 1917, law "On the Freedom of Conscience" [O svobode sovesti]. At the same time, a statute of July 5, 1917, affirmed the status of Orthodoxy as "the first among religious faiths" (Dimitry Pospielovsky, "Na puti k sobornosti," *Kontinent* 121 [2004], http://magazines.russ.ru/continent/2004/121/po10.html).

6. Article 2, "Dekret o zemle S"ezda sovetov rabochikh i soldatskikh deputatov," *DSV* 1:17–18.

7. "Deklaratsiia prav narodov Rossii," *DSV* 1:40 (article 3, referring to the "abolition of all and any national and national-religious privileges and restrictions").

8. "O rasstorzhenii braka," December 16 (29), 1917, *DSV* 1:237–39; "O grazhdanskom brake," December 18 (31), 1917, *DSV* 1:260–63.

9. "Konstitutsiia (Osnovnoi Zakon) Rossiiskoi Sotsialisticheskoi Federativnoi Sovetskoi Respubliki," July 10, 1918, *DSV* 2:545–66.

10. Monasteries could continue to exist only if they reformed themselves as "labor workshops" (*trudovye arteli*), and even then were subject to repression: the Lavra of the Trinity and St. Sergius, for example, was closed down in November 1919 (the premises were formally nationalized by government decree on November 1 of that year), and the remaining monks were transferred to sketes formerly in the monastery's dependency. See Scott Kenworthy, *The Heart of Russia: Trinity-Sergius, Monasticism, and Society after 1825* (New York: Oxford University Press, 2010), 296–328, 332–38; on monasticism more broadly, see Jennifer Wynot, *Keeping the Faith: Russian Orthodox Monasticism in the Soviet Union, 1917-1939* (College Station, TX: Texas A & M University Press, 2004), ch. 2; on underground monasticism, Aleksei Beglov, *V poiskakh "bezgreshnykh katakomb": Tserkovnoe podpol'e v SSSR* (Moscow: Izdatel'skii sovet Russkoi pravoslavnoi tserkvi, 2008), 40–52.

11. *SU* 18 (1918): item 263. In the original draft was the statement "religion is a private matter" (as in Lenin's "Sotsializm i religiia," see below), but Lenin himself deleted this (ibid.).

12. Lenin's "Sotsializm i religiia" also rhetorically hesitates between a "religious freedom for all" position and a clear hostility to "religion" and "superstition" as socially harmful practices: "We demand that religion should become a private matter with regard to the state, but we cannot demand that it becomes a private matter with regard to the Party" (*PSS* 12:143).

13. An alternative and perhaps preferable translation of *obnovlenie* would be "renewal" rather than "renovation," since the latter, with its connotations of strictly material improvement (redecoration of buildings, etc.) is awkward when applied to the spiritual process that the promoters of *obnovlenie* had in mind. However, the rendering "renovation" is adopted here for familiarity's sake.

14. For an important source from the 1900s, see *K tserkovnomu soboru: Sbornik*, authored by a self-styled "group of Petersburg clergy" (*gruppa peterburgskikh sviashchennikov*) (St. Petersburg: Tip. M. Merkusheva, 1906). Historical discussions of this era include the study by an ecclesiastical historian associated with "Renovation," Boris V. Titlinov (e.g., *Novaia tserkov'* [Petrograd: Tipografiia L. Ia. Ganzburg, 1923]); and the lively narrative history coauthored by a former Church of Renovation worshipper, Anatolii Krasnov-Levitin (with Vadim Shavrov), *Ocherki po istorii russkoi tserkovnoi smuty*, 2 vols. (Moscow: Krutitskoe patriarshee podvor'e, 1994). More recent academic histories include Gregory Freeze, "Subversive Piety: Religion and the Political Crisis in Late Imperial Russia," *Journal of Modern History* 68, no. 2 (1996): 308–50; M. V. Shkarovskii, *Obnovlencheskoe dvizhenii v Russkoi Pravoslavnoi Tserkvi XX veka* (St. Petersburg: Nestor, 1999); and Edward E. Roslof, *Red Priests: Renovationism, Russian Orthodoxy, and Revolution, 1905-1946* (Bloomington: Indiana University Press, 2002). John S. Curtiss, *The Russian Church and the Soviet State, 1917-1950* (Boston: Little, Brown and Company, 1953), written without access to unpublished sources, is a valuable guide to the contents of contemporary publications. A general study of conservative Orthodoxy in the last years of the Russian Empire is John Strickland, *The Making of Holy Russia: The Orthodox Church and Russian Nationalism before the Revolution* (Jordanville, NY: Holy Trinity Publications, 2013). A notorious conservative (who later ended up on the side of "renovation," see below) is portrayed in Simon Dixon, "The 'Mad Monk' Iliodor in Tsaritsyn," *The Slavonic and East European Review* 88, nos. 1–2 (2010): 377–415. On the period of upheaval immediately leading up to the Bolshevik Revolution, see Pavel Rogoznyi, *Tserkovnaia revoliutsiia 1917 goda: Vysshee dukhovenstvo Rossiiskoi Tserkvi v bor'be za vlast' v eparkhiiakh posle Fevral'skoi revoliutsii* (St. Petersburg: Liki Rossii, 2008). For more general studies, see, for example, George L. Kline, *Religious and Anti-Religious Thought in Russia* (Chicago, IL: University of Chicago Press, 1968); Nadieszda Kizenko, *A Prodigal Saint: Father John of Kronstadt and the Russian People* (University Park: Pennsylvania State University Press, 2000); Laura Engelstein, "Holy Russia in Modern Times: An Essay on Orthodoxy and Cultural Change," *Past and Present* 173 (2001): 129–56; Scott M. Kenworthy, "To Save the World or to Renounce It: Modes of Moral Action in Russian Orthodoxy," in *Religion, Morality, and Community in Post-Soviet Societies*, ed. Mark D. Steinberg and Catherine Wanner (Bloomington: Indiana University Press, 2008), 21–53.

15. On parish reform, see Gregory Freeze, "All Power to the Parish? The Problem and Politics of Church Reform in Late Imperial Russia," in *Social Identities in Revolutionary Russia*, ed. Madhavan

K. Palat (London: Macmillan, 2001), 174–208; L. S. Bokareva, "Reforma pravoslavnogo prikhoda 1914–1917 gg.: Sinodal'noe vedomstvo," *Vestnik Leningradskogo gosudarstvennogo universiteta im. A. S. Pushkina* 4 (2012), 133–42.

16. The copious materials from the Church Council were published as *Deianiia Sviashchennogo Sobora Pravoslavnoi Rossiiskoi Tserkvi 1917–1918 gg.* 3 vols. (1918; repr., Moscow: Izdatel'stvo Novospasskogo monastyria, 1994). For discussion of the Church Council, see G. Kravetskii et al., eds., *Sviashchennyi Sobor Pravoslavnoi Rossiiskoi Tserkvi, 1917–1918 gg.: Obzor deianii,* 3 vols. (Moscow: Krutitskoe Patriarshee Podvor'e, 2000–2002); James W. Cunningham, *The Gates of Hell: The Great Sobor of the Russian Orthodox Church, 1917–1918* (Minneapolis: University of Minnesota Press, 2002); Gunther Schulz et al., eds., *Bolschewisitische Herrschaft und Orthodoxe Kirche in Russland: Das Landeskonzil 1917/1918; Quellen und Analysen* (Münster: Lit, 2005); and Irina Papkova, "The Freezing of Historical Memory? The Post-Soviet Russian Orthodox Church and the Church Council of 1917," in Steinberg and Wanner, *Religion, Morality, and Community,* 57–65.

17. *Deianiia Sviashchennogo Sobora,* 1:3.

18. "Opredelenie Sviashchennogo Sobora Pravoslavnoi Rossiiskoi Tserkvi o pravovom polozhenii Pravoslavnoi Rossiiskoi Tserkvi," in *Sobranie opredelenii i postanovlenii Sviashchennogo Sobora Pravoslavnoi Russkoi Tserkvi* (1918; repr., Moscow: Izdatel'stvo Novospasskogo monastyria, 1994), issue 2, pp. 6–8.

19. See, for example, "Programma tserkovnykh reform, namechennykh gruppoi dukhovenstva i mirian," *Zhivaia tserkov'* 10 (1922): 17, which refers to "the struggle with superstitions, religious prejudices and omens, which grew in the soil of popular ignorance and the monastic exploitation of the religious feelings of the credulous masses." B. V. Titlinov's *Pravoslavie na sluzhbe samoderzhaviia v russkom gosudarstve* (Leningrad: Gosizdat, 1924), 206, argued that the relationship between the Orthodox Church and power before 1917 had been the result not just of cultural inertia, but of self-interest: "Only in autocracy did they perceive a reliable foundation for Orthodoxy, suspecting, quite rightly, that no other type of government would play the role of the policeman of conscience, and defend them by all means at the state's disposal."

20. Lenin, "Sotsializm i religiia," 143.

21. "Sovetskaia politika v religioznom voprose," *Revoliutsiia i tserkov'* 1 (1918): 1. (The style has been slightly edited here to make the meaning easier to follow.)

22. Ibid.

23. As Roslof points out (*Red Priests,* 27), Lenin also adopted a conciliatory position at this point, with a speech on November 19, 1918, warning against offense to religious believers.

24. The wording of the "certificate of protection" (*okhrannoe svidetel'stvo*) issued by Glavnauka did not give grounds for the listing either, citing merely the date of the building and an attribution of its architect. For the example from the Admiralty "house church," see TsGA-SPb, f. 1001, op. 7, d. 1, l. 9 (printed in M. V. Shkarovskii and N. Iu. Cherepnina, eds., *Spravochnik po istorii pravoslavnykh monastyrei i soborov g. Sankt-Peterburga, 1917–1945 gg.: Po dokumentam TsGA-SPb* [St. Peterburg: Memorial, 1996], doc. no. 40, pp. 116–17).

25. On the 1850 watershed, see "Instruktsiia Gubmuzeia po osushchestvleniiu nadzora za remonto-restavratsionnymi rabotami po tserkovnym zdaniiam [i] nakhodiashchimsia v nikh predmetam istoriko-khudozhestvennogo znacheniia" (1923), GARF, f. A2307, op. 3, d. 19, l. 12; for the general principles of restoration, ibid., l. 42.

26. See also the useful discussion in S. A. Gorelova, "Pervaia Vserossiiskaia restavratsionnaia konferentsiia 1921 goda," *Khudozhestvennoe nasledie* 21, no. 51 (2004), http://art-con.ru/node/1193. However, there were important differences between groups of restorers as well (see chapter 2 below on the conflict between the Moscow-based Aleksandr Anisimov and Petr Pokryshkin in Petrograd).

27. *Instruktsiia po uchetu, khraneniiu i peredache religioznogo imushchestva, imeiushchego istoricheskoe, khudozhestvennoe ili arkheologicheskoe znachenie* (Moscow: Narkompros, 1920). (GARF, f. 2307, op. 3, d. 19, ll. 28–33.)

28. See a list of "monuments of all-Soviet significance" dating from c. 1923 (GARF, f. 2307, op. 10, d. 147, ll. 455–56), which includes large numbers of "cultic buildings," for instance the St. Sophia

Cathedral and Cave Monastery in Kiev, the Churches of St. Cyril and of St. Andrew in Chernigov, the churches at Kizhi, the Peter and Paul Church in Kazan', and numerous churches in Georgia and Armenia.

29. See the report from the Petrograd Department for the Preservation of Monuments sent to Narkompros's Collegium on the Affairs of Museums and the Preservation of Monuments, December 16, 1918, requesting the return to Petrograd of communion vessels and vestments, etc., removed from the former Ministry of Foreign Affairs house church to the Kirillovo-Belozersk Monastery, and thence to the Moscow Kremlin. GARF, f. 2307, op. 3, d. 266, l. 46.

30. "Otchet o rabotakh tserkovnoi sektsii, 1918–1923 gg.," GARF, f. 2307, op. 8, d. 252, l. 13–13 ob. For an excellent study of the church-museums, see M. E. Kaulen, *Muzei-khramy i muzei-monastyri v pervoe desiatiletie Sovetskoi vlasti* (Moscow: Luch, 2001). This issue is discussed further in chapter 2 below.

31. See, for example, "Dokladnaia zapiska (Mozaichnoi sektsii Restavratsionnogo otdela)" (1922), Rukopisnyi arkhiv Instituta material'noi kul'tury Rosiiskoi Akademii Nauk (hereafter RA IIMK), f. 67, op. 7, ed. khr. 73; "Muzei i pamiatniki stariny" (1925), GARF, f. 2307, op. 10, d. 147, l. 418. For a good historical discussion of restoration work in the early to mid-1920s, see A. S. Shchenkov, ed., *Pamiatniki arkhitektury v Sovetskom Soiuze: Ocherki istorii arkhitekturnoi restavratsii* (Moscow: Pamiatniki istoricheskoi mysli, 2004).

32. "Il est interdit, à l'avenir, d'élever ou d'apposer aucun signe ou emblème religieux sur les monuments publics ou en quelque emplacement public que ce soit, à l'exception des édifices servant au culte, des terrains de sépulture dans les cimetières, des monuments funéraires, ainsi que des musées ou expositions." [Henceforth it is prohibited to raise or fix any sign or emblem of a religious kind to public buildings or in any public place whatever, except for buildings serving cultic purposes, sepulchures in cemeteries, funerary monuments, and museums or exhibitions.] "Loi concernant la séparation des Églises et de l'État [Law on the Separation of Churches and the State]," December 9, 1905, article 28, http://www.legifrance.gouv.fr/. There is a large literature on the background and effects of the French secularizing decree. See, for example, Louis Capéran's monumental *Histoire contemporaine de la laïcité française*: vol. 1, *La Crise du 16 mai et la revanche républicaine* (Paris, Marcel Rivière, 1957); vol. 2, *La Révolution scolaire* (Paris, Marcel Rivière, 1959); vol. 3, *La Laïcité en Marche* (Paris: Nouvelles éditions latines, 1961); Maurice Larkin, *Church and State after the Dreyfus Affair: The Separation Issue in France* (London: Macmillan, 1974); John McManners, *Church and State in France, 1870–1914* (New York: Harper and Row, 1972). My thanks to Ruth Harris for her advice here.

33. "Il sera procédé à un classement complémentaire des édifices servant à l'exercice public du culte (cathédrales, églises, chapelles, temples, synagogues, archevêchés, évêchés, presbytères, séminaires), dans lequel devront être compris tous ceux de ces édifices représentant, dans leur ensemble ou dans leurs parties, une valeur artistique ou historique." [This is to be preceded by a complementary classification of all buildings serving for the public exercise of cult (cathedrals, churches, chapels, Protestant churches, synagogues, archbishops' and bishops' palaces, presbyteries and seminaries) in which are to be included all such buildings as may wholly or partly represent an artistic or historical value.] "Loi concernant la separation," art. 16.

34. M. S. Trubacheva, "Neizvestnoe pis'mo P. A. Florenskogo k I. E. Grabariu," *Grabarevskie chteniia* 5 (2003), http://art-con.ru/node/1766 (quoting from a document held in the archive of the State Tretyakov Gallery).

35. Grabar''s career is the subject of an abundant specialist literature: for an outline biography, see L. N. Krylova, "I. E. Grabar' i okhrana pamiatnikov: Chetyre etapa ego zhizni," *Grabarevskie chteniia* 5 (2004), http://art-con.ru/node/1765.

36. It was not until 1923, after Patriarch Tikhon had been under house arrest for months, that he formally acknowledged the authority of the new government at all.

37. Materials from 1919 indicate that the standard form ran thus: "The Department requests the District Soviet to extend all possible aid in the protection of objects upon the inventories of the Department and under its protection, and in cases where some institution or person wishes to occupy premises where works of art are kept, to inform the Department" (TsGALI-SPb, f. 36, op. 1, d. 40, l. 19

ob.). This old-fashioned courtliness can have cut little ice with rank-and-file Petrograd Bolsheviks. For complaints about malpractice, see ibid., l. 4, l. 21.

38. This stipulation in terms of numbers was also modeled on the French statute of December 9, 1905, though the latter had a sliding scale depending on the local population. In communes with a population of under 1,000, a membership of just seven was sufficient to facilitate registration of a religious group, though this rose to fifteen for communes with a population of 1,000–20,000, and to twenty-five for those that were larger.

39. For the generic contract, see the August 24, 1918, instruction of the People's Commissariat of Justice, *SU* 62 (1918): item 685. While the first stipulations were to do with an undertaking not to use the "cultic building" for non-religious purposes (e.g., political meetings), clauses 4–7 of the contract made members of the religious group responsible for the upkeep of the building and its contents.

40. "Akt o peredache imushchestva," included in *Instruktsiia po uchetu*, GARF, f. 2307, op. 3, d. 19, ll. 22–23. The August 24, 1918, instruction referred to special contracts drawn up by the Museums Department for churches of architectural importance (*SU* 62 [1918]: item 685), but did not include an example of these.

41. "Postanovlenie SNK o poriadke rekvizitsii i konfiskatsii blagorodnykh metallov, deneg i tsennostei, meditsinskie i farmatsevskie imushchestva," *DSV* 9:216. It would appear that the legislation did not apply only to items held in churches, but did include such items (no details are given).

42. *SU* 62 (1918): item 685. See also the introduction.

43. See the note to clause 29, "O poriadke provedeniia," *SU* 62 (1918): item 685: "The removal of religious images that have an artistic or historical significance, and the determination of what should be done with these, is to be carried out in consultation with the People's Commissariat of Enlightenment."

44. Here and below the emphasis follows the original text.

45. *Instruktsiia po uchetu*, GARF, f. 2307, op. 3, d. 19, l. 29.

46. A draft of this statement is held in the personal archive of the leading archaeologist and restorer K. K. Romanov. RA IIMK, f. 29, ed. khr. 12, ll. 7–9. It was likely written by Romanov himself, who was also the author of various draft statutes on monument preservation. Typewritten in the old orthography, the text likely dates from the autumn of 1917. The Union of Art Activists (Soiuz deiatelei iskusstv), which held its inaugural conference in March 1917, and ceased its existence in September of the following year, is best-known as a force for the defense of artistic autonomy, but as the present case shows, state-public relations were more complicated than this interpretation might suggest.

47. For the painter Aleksandr Benua (Alexandre Benois), addressing the Academy of Arts in 1912, the state-sponsored building of Petersburg in the late eighteenth and early nineteenth centuries was vastly superior to the commercialized voluntarism of his own age ("Chem mogla by byt' Akademiia Khudozhestv v nastoiashchee vremia," in *Trudy Vserossiiskogo s"ezda khudozhnikov, sostoiashchegosia pod Vysochaishim Pokrovitel'stvom Ego Imperatorskogo Velichestva Gosudaria NIKOLAIA ALEKSANDROVICHA i pochetnym predsedatel'stvom Ee Imperatorskogo Vysochestva Avgusteishego Prezidenta Imperatorskoi Akademii Khudozhestv Velikoi Kniagini Marii Pavlovny, Dekabr' 1911–Ianvar' 1912*, 3 vols. (St. Petersburg-Petrograd: Tipografiia P. Golike i A. Vil'borg, 1912–1914), 3:92–98. There is an interesting parallel here to the arguments about natural resources that are traced by Ekaterina Pravilova in her "Les res publicae russes: Discours sur la propriété publique à la fin de l'empire," *Annales: Histoire, Sciences Sociales* 3 (2009): 579–609, which also makes the point about the preference of state to individual ownership in the late Imperial era.

48. As discussed by Susan N. Smith, "The Accidental Museum: Expropriating and Appropriating the Past," *Russian Review* 67, no. 3 (2008): 438–53.

49. G. A. Kuzina, "Gosudarstvennaia politika v oblasti muzeinogo dela v 1917–1924 gg.," in *Muzei i vlast': Sbornik nauchnykh trudov NII kul'tury*, ed. S. A. Kasparinskaia (Moscow: NIIK, 1991), 1:155. Cited from E. V. Minkina, "P. P. Veiner: Muzeinyi rabotnik," in *Ot Muzeia Starogo Peterburga k Gosudarstvennomu muzeiu istorii Sankt-Peterburga: Issledovaniia i materialy*, ed. V. A. Frolov (St. Petersburg: GMI-SPb, 1997), 28–29.

50. "Monastyri," *Revoliutsiia i tserkov'* 9–12 (1920): 83.

51. "Monastyri," *Revoliutsiia i tserkov'* 1 (1919): 39.

52. "Tsirkuliar po voprosu otdeleniia tserkvi ot gosudarstva," *Revoliutsiia i tserkov'* 1 (1919): 31.

53. As in the case of Father Pavel Florensky (see the introduction above). It is notable that an early, well-supported denunciation of the attack on the church, A. A. Valentinov, ed., *Chernaia kniga: "Shturm nebes"; Sbornik dokumental'nykh dannykh, kharakterizuiushchikh bor'bu sovetskoi kommunisticheskoi vlasti protiv vsiakoi religii, protiv vsekh ispovedanii i tserkvei* (Paris: Izdatel'stvo Russkogo natsional'nogo studencheskogo ob"edineniia, 1925), 28–30, reported the secularization of house churches as sacrilege, alongside defecation in church sanctuaries, etc. See the comment at the Pomestnyi Sobor, classifying the closure of chapels in schools as "persecution": Kravetskii, *Sviashchennyi Sobor*, 204, 224.

54. For example, an article by Mikhail Gorev about the exposure of the relics of St. Mitrofan of Voronezh and St. Tikhon Zadonskii ("Vskrytie moshchei Tikhona Zadonskogo i Mitrofana Voronezhskogo," *Revoliutsiia i tserkov'* 2 [1919]: 9–23) emphasized the dramatic effects of the ritual and its impact on the spectators, which had been "like an exploding bomb." A standard destination for relics was the antireligious displays of local museums (as in the arrangements for the relics of St. Varnava (Barnabas), Abbot of Vetluga, in Kostroma, which were "to be transferred to the Gubmuzei [provincial museum department] or Moscow," according to the order given in April/May 1922 by the deputy commissar of justice, P. A. Krasikov: Pokrovskii and Petrov, *Arkhivy Kremlia*, vol. 1, doc. 23.39, p. 172). For an excellent study of this period in the context of shifting attitudes to sainthood in the late nineteenth and early twentieth centuries, see Greene, *Bodies Like Bright Stars*. Good discussions of the relic exposure itself include Stephen A. Smith, "Bones of Contention: Bolsheviks and the Exposure of Saints' Relics, 1918–1930," *Past and Present* 204, no. 1 (2009): 155–94. A. B. Rogozianskii, *Strasti po moshcham* (St. Petersburg: Obshchestvo sviatitelia Vasiliia Velikogo, 1998), is a short account of a popularizing kind.

55. The "artistic and historical" value of mummified relics themselves do not seem to have been addressed in materials produced by the Museums Department, or indeed anywhere else; the governing discourse presenting these simply as "fakes" that had been made in order to dupe the benighted masses seems to have been too powerful to challenge. On the preservation of the casket, see the material below on the stripping of St. Alexander Nevsky's relics.

56. This was comparable with the overall history of museum collection in the Soviet Union, which was also shaped by perceptions of the didactic value of the objects housed. For example, an early Narkompros circular ("Kak ustroit' muzei i vesti ego. Programmnoe rukovodstvo. V muzeinyi otdel," c. 1920) listed the museum's functions as "science and scholarship," "education" (particularly as a "visual aid"), and "as a social and political center." A later section of the text underlined the museum's significance as "one of the main methods outside the schoolroom of combating popular ignorance," and "a center of popular enlightenment" (GARF, f. 2307, op. 10, d. 147, l. 6–6 ob.). Precisely this meant that shifting attitudes to the objectives and methods of education had a direct impact also upon museum work. (See further chapters 2 and 3 of this book.) For a useful discussion of museum work in the early Soviet years and its ideological context, see Smith, "The Accidental Museum."

57. "Instruktsiia Kollegii po delam muzeev i okhrane pamiatnikov iskusstva stariny Narodnogo Komissariata Prosveshcheniia," *Revoliutsiia i tserkov'* 1 (1919): 30.

58. As Ekaterina Pravilova has discussed, the situation relating to church property was extremely complicated: non-parish churches ("house churches," etc.) could belong to private individuals, while hospital and regimental churches were owned by "the state" (more exactly, the ministries that ran the institutions housing them), and there was even a ruling by the Synod in 1884 making parish churches themselves autonomous property owners (rather than handing them over to the fallible humans who made up the "parish" in a community sense): Ekaterina Pravilova, *A Public Empire: Property and the Quest for the Common Good in Imperial Russia* (Princeton, NJ: Princeton University Press, 2014), 142–44.

59. A. I. Mramornov, ed., *Dokumenty Sviashchennogo Sobora Pravoslavnoi Russkoi Tserkvi, 1917–1918 godov* (Moscow: Izdanie Novospasskogo monastyria, 2012), 1.1:528–29, 542–50; 1.2:713–19. This outline summary considerably simplifies the complicated discussions, which also ranged over whether property ownership should be vested in "the Church" generally, whether bishops and others

could act as agents on the Church's behalf when Imperial law forbade them from owning property, and so on.

60. V. Vorob'ev and N. A. Krivova, eds., *Sledstvennoe delo Patriarkha Tikhona: Sbornik dokumentov po materialam Tsentral'nogo arkhiva FSB RF* (Moscow: Pamiatniki istoricheskoi mysli, 2000), 149.

61. John F. Pollard, *Money and the Rise of the Modern Papacy: Financing the Vatican, 1850–1950* (Cambridge: Cambridge University Press, 2005), 94–98.

62. For the benefits of the laicization initiated by the separation of church and state, see Gregory Freeze, "The Stalinist Assault on the Parish, 1929–1941," in *Stalinismus vor dem Zweiten Weltkrieg: Neue Wege der Forschung*, ed. Manfred Hildermeier (Munich: Oldenburg Verlag, 1998), 209–10.

63. In England and Wales, for example, "churches in use" were exempted altogether from preservation legislation until the late 1940s (Astrid Swenson, "Preservation Policies and Nationalism in Britain," forthcoming in *Heritage Preservation in Europe, 1800–2015*, special issue of *Nations and Nationalism*, ed. Mark Thatcher). Thereafter, work on Scheduled Ancient Monuments required permission from the relevant body (then the Office of Public Works, later English Heritage/Cadw). Churches that were listed buildings, however, were from 1994 under the jurisdiction of an "ecclesiastical exemption order" that made alterations subject to assessment by the Diocesan Advisory Committee rather than local planning offices.

64. A comparable contradiction lay between a Sovnarkom decree of December 26, 1919, "O likvidatsii bezgramotnosti sredi naseleniia RSFSR" (*DSV* 7:50–51), which specified that churches might be used for anti-illiteracy events, and another decree from the Presidium of VTsIK (Vserossiiskii tsentral'nyi ispolnitel'nyi komitet, or All-Russian Central Executive Committee) (June 13, 1921) that gave religious associations the right to decide what non-religious events they wanted to hold in their buildings.

65. The documentation around the founding of the Petrogubsovet Board of Building and Architecture in 1920 indicates that the city's housing stock was in a very bad condition: "Over the three years of revolution, living accommodation, sometimes of very high quality and significance, has been destroyed and damaged on a systematic basis, with all the symptoms of open and unsupervised vandalism [. . .] the number of senselessly destroyed brick buildings that were perfectly habitable is so great that the current living accommodation crisis is directly attributable to this, and also to the chaotic demolition of all types of building for firewood." "Zakliuchenie Komissii po voprosam obshchikh prichin, vyzvavshikh takoe ukhudshenie v sostoianii zdanii," Tsentral'nyi gosudarstvennyi arkhiv nauchno-tekhnicheskoi dokumentatsii Sankt-Peterburga (hereafter TsGANTD-SPb), f. 386, op. 1–2, d. 29, l. 20.

66. For a brief discussion of these figures, see M. V. Shkarovskii, *Russkaia Pravoslavnaia Tserkov' v XX veke* (Moscow: Veche, 2010). The general history of conservatism is handled in Gregory Freeze, "Counter-Reformation in Russian Orthodoxy: Popular Response to Religious Innovation, 1922–1925," *Slavic Review* 54, no. 2 (1995): 305–39.

67. The Church Council (Pomestnyi Sobor) of August 15, 1917, to September 7, 1918, the first since pre-Petrine times, marked the beginning of the transition, since it was held in the Church of the Dormition in the Kremlin. At this point, the use of Moscow as a location (and the decision by the assembly that the patriarch and the managing council of the Orthodox Church, the Synod, should also be based in that city) underlined the separation of spiritual and temporal power, since the capital was still in Petrograd. Once the Soviet capital had moved to Moscow, the relocation had the effect of subordinating spiritual affairs to the direction of the new government—not something anticipated in 1917.

68. "Prikhodskoi ustav: Opredelenie Sviashchennogo Sobora Pravoslavnoi Rossiiskoi Tserkvi o Pravoslavnom Prikhode, 7 (20) aprelia 1918 goda," in *Sobranie opredelenii i postanovlenii*, issue 3, pp. 14, 27, 34, 56, 59–60.

69. *Sobranie opredelenii*, issue 4, pp. 28–30.

70. "O poriadke provedeniia v zhizn' dekreta 'Ob otdelenii tserkvi ot gosudarstva i shkoly ot tserkvi' (Instruktsiia)," August 24, 1918, *SU* 62 (1918): item 685.

71. To avoid confusion, the term "house churches" is used to apply to a chapel within an institution or public building, and "chapel" is reserved for translations of *chasovnia*. See glossary.

72. An informative catalogue of the *domovye tserkvi*, supported by extensive research in the archives relating to prerevolutionary St. Petersburg, is included in the various editions of Antonov and Kobak, *SSPb*—see particularly the expanded and revised edition of 2010, though even this is not exhaustive, as it fails to include some of the churches ensconced in private residences (for example, Vladimir Nabokov's *Speak, Memory* [London: Penguin, 1967], 19, implies—with the reference to his parents correcting the priest's misunderstanding of the preferred name "through the half-closed door"—that there was one in the family mansion on Bol'shaia Morskaia).

73. I. D. Mordukhai-Boltovskii, *Svod zakonov Rossiiskoi Imperii* (St. Petersburg: Knizhnoe toverishchestvo Deiatel', 1912), 6:50, 13:141–42. On hospitals run by the Ministry of the Interior, see ibid., 13:318.

74. Mramornov, *Dokumenty Sviashchnennogo Sobora*, 1:546. On palace churches, see ibid., 1:545.

75. "Tsirkuliar po voprosu," 31.

76. See, for example, "Domovye tserkvi," *Revoliutsiia i tserkov'* 2 (1919): 44–47.

77. "'Prikhod' ili kollektiv?", *Sobornyi razum* 3–4 [1918]: 1.

78. On the eventual assault on the relics of St. Alexander Nevsky, see below.

79. Kollontai ordered the requisitioning of the monastery on January 13, 1918, but the effects were not immediate, though the living accommodation was handed over to the city authorities later that year, and land in the monastery's courtyard began being used as a burial ground for Soviet notables (the so-called "Communist Square"). See the account of the Lavra's history on its official website, http://lavra.spb.ru/about/history/18–1917–1989-.html.

80. Nauchnyi arhiv Upravleniia Gosudarstvennoi inspektsii okhrany pamiatnikov (hereafter NA UGIOP), f. 150, pap. 481, t. 1, b. Edinovercheskaia Nikol'skaia tserkov', l. 141.

81. Over the first two decades of Soviet power, there was a gradual move toward the investment of expanded powers in the local authorities. In 1921, the Church Offices took over from the Commissariat of Justice as the main regulatory body for church-state relations, though with the Committee on Religious Affairs of the Central Executive Committee (VTsIK) left as final arbiter. At the same time, both the General Section (Obshchii otdel) of the NKVD and the Administrative Sub-Section (Administrativnyi pododtel) of the local soviet continued to be charged with "enacting the decree on the separation of church and state" (see the VTsIK and Sovnarkom decree, "O Narodnom komissariate vnutrennikh del," June 10, 1921, *DSV* 16:42, 52).

82. The different attitudes to religious communities in the different political and bureaucratic interest groups are dealt with in detail by N. A. Krivova, *Vlast' i tserkov' v 1922–1925 gg.*, *Makhaon* 1 (1999), http://krotov.info/history/20/krivova/kriv01.html. The deputy commissar of justice, P. A. Krasikov, was one of the most formidable proponents of radical secularization in the country (on his role in the exposure of relics, see Smith, "Bones of Contention").

83. Throughout the Soviet period, priests were assigned to parishes only with the permission of the bodies regulating church affairs, such as the Church Offices (until 1943), and the Committee on the Affairs of the Russian Orthodox Church (1943–1965), and from 1966, the Committee on Religious Affairs. The interpretation of *dvadtsatka* as "parish" was enshrined, for example, in a statement by the Holy Synod on August 30, 1918, that churches should be used "not by casual associations of people who happen to term themselves Orthodox, but exclusively by Orthodox parishes, brotherhoods, and other church organizations, on the basis of general principles of ecclesiastical and canon law" (V. S. Dediukhina et al., eds. *Sokhranenie pamiatnikov tserkovnoi stariny v Rossii v XVIII–nachala XX vv.: Sbornik dokumentov* [Moscow: Otechestvo, 1997], 314–15, no. 218). Administrative responsibility was divided between the parish council (*prikhodskoi sovet*) and the church elder (*tserkovnyi starosta*), with the latter acquiring a progressively more important role as time went on: see the letter of protest from the parish council of the Church of the Smolensk Mother of God, Smolenskoe Cemetery, July 31, 1922, objecting to the decision by the Petrograd Diocese on July 7, 1922, to assign primary responsibility for property management to elder and clergy, TsGA-SPb, f. 7384, op. 33, d. 85, l. 175.

84. The New Maiden Convent in Petrograd, for example, continued to operate in this capacity through the 1920s. By 1928, the authorities were becoming much more wary of such work communes: a report to the Obkom, April 28, 1928, contended: "All these 'artels' and 'communes' are leading a parasitic mode of life." It went on: "Processions with icons round villages, and the letting of summer dacha accommodation to incomers, are providing the support for priests and exiles who in turn support the anti-Soviet agitation of the churchmen. Pictures of the former royal family are on show" (TsGAIPD-SPb, f. 24, op. 8, d. 53, l. 29 ob.). The combination of antireligious legislation, arrests, and (in rural areas) collectivization was, in the course of the next few years, to wipe them out.

85. As discussed further in chapter 2, the word *ansambl'*—a transliteration of the French *ensemble*—was an enormously important value term in St. Petersburg preservation. Since it does not have an exact equivalent in English (and "ensemble" would risk confusion with the usual musical meaning of that term), the transliteration is used here and throughout the book. See also glossary.

86. "Obrazets opisnoi kartochki na zdanie khudozhestvenno-istoricheskogo znacheniia," GARF, f. 2306, op. 28, d. 157, l. 32. See also appendix 2.

87. "Kratkii otchet o deiatel'nosti Petrogradskogo Otdela Muzeev i okhrany pamiatnikov iskusstva i stariny, narodnogo byta i prirody Aktsentra i podvedomstvennykh emu uchrezhdenii za vremia ot 25 Oktiabria 1917 g. po 1922-i god," GARF, f. 2307, op. 3, d. 272, l. 130.

88. See the 1922 figures for spending, GARF, f. 2307, op. 3, d. 272, ll. 176–77. The sum expended on the Cathedral of the Transfiguration (at 100,000 rubles to replace the roof after a fire) could not compare with the amounts spent on the Elagin Palace (200,000), the Rostral Columns (400,000), let alone the Marble Palace (1,000,000). (In Moscow, by contrast, churches soaked up most of the funds for restoration: see ibid.)

89. For the prohibition on using integral parts of a building, see, for example, "Domovye tserkvi," 44–45: "If the given premises that was formerly used for religious services is part of a building connected with the rest, then it must without doubt share the fate of the entire building and may not be in the possession of private individuals and used for needs of private individuals that do not correspond to the general aims of the given institution."

90. *Instruktsiia po uchetu* (1920), GARF, f. 2307, op. 3, d. 19, ll. 29–30.

91. As late as July 9, 1922, after a complaint to Rabkrin (the Worker and Peasant Inspectorate, a kind of early Soviet ombudsman), it was pronounced that the "house church" at no. 59, Fontanka embankment "does not belong to the category of house churches and chapels referred to in the compulsory decree of the Council of the Party Committee of the Northern Labor Commune, 'On the Liquidation of House Churches and Chapels'" (*Severnaia Kommuna*, August 8, 1918, p. 1). (See also TsGA-SPb, f. 1001, op. 7, d. 1, l. 301.) The August 8, 1918, decree did not specify criteria for adjudicating what was a "house church," so such decisions were evidently made on an ad hoc basis. In this particular case, the "house church" concerned was the Resurrection Church at the Apraksin Market, which was directly next to the market, but had a separate entrance, the presence of which was certainly an important factor in the decision ("the experts have come to the conclusion that neither the external nor the internal features of the building give it the character of a house church").

92. A case in point was the Royal Stables Church, the use of which by believers was endorsed by the Department of Justice on December 28, 1919, according to a petition against its closure dating from April 22, 1922 (TsGA-SPb, f. 1001, op. 7, d. 1, l. 163).

93. In 1918–1919, for instance, the Museums Department inspected nearly 3,000 different sites and registered several thousand works of art, removing the most important to the Museums Fund. Over 1,500 collections comprising more than 18,700 objects were transferred to the Museums Fund. Eighteen collections were immediately handed over the Hermitage, and twenty-five to the Russian Museum. There were thirty-nine museums in Petrograd as of 1922, of which fifteen had been founded since the October Revolution. See "Kratkii otchet o deiatel'nosti Petrogradskogo Otdela Muzeev i okhrany pamiatnikov iskusstva i stariny," GARF, f. 2307, op. 3, d. 272, ll. 126–46 ob. For the material on the collections, see l. 130, on the museums, ll. 127–29 ob.

94. "Kratkii otchet o deiatel'nosti Petrogradskogo Otdela Muzeev i okhrany pamiatnikov iskusstva i stariny," GARF, f. 2307, op. 3, d. 272, l. 132. Twenty monasteries in all were the subjects

of detailed surveys between 1917 and 1922 (ibid.). The documentation in the fond of the Museums Department of Petrograd Glavnauka held in the Institute of the History of Material Culture indicates that much organizational initiative went into making sure that supervision would be adequate "at district level" (*na mestakh*) (see "Zhurnal zasedaniia po sostavleniiu Soveta po Otdelu Muzeev i Okhrany Pamiatnikov," December 31, 1918, RA IIMK, f. 67, d. 1, l. 3, where Georgy Iatmanov, the commissar of the Museums Department, put forward the idea of "emissaries" who would regulate protection work out in the provinces).

95. The Monuments Department is referred to regularly in documents from early 1922, though the date of its foundation is not mentioned. "Kratkii otchet o deiatel'nosti Otdela po delam muzeev i okhrany pamiatnikov iskusstva i stariny Komissariata Narodnogo prosveshcheniia," TsGA-SPb, f. 1000, op. 3, d. 146, ll. 8–9 ob. (1923), gives the date when this was founded as November 1, 1918. O. M. Kormil'tseva and A. G. Leont'ev, in "V nasledstvo budushchim pokoleniiam: Nekotorye stranitsy istorii restavratsii Peterburga," http://www.d-c.spb.ru/archiv/29/34–37/34–37.htm, give the date of the founding of the Museums Department as November 15, 1918. It is possible that the latter date refers to the founding of the *city* department, since official histories of the State Inspectorate of Monuments regularly confuse the Narkompros agency and the city one.

96. M. V. Galkin, "V kakoi mere osushchestvlena Petrogradskim sovdepom i vsemi raionnymi sovdepami vyrabotanaia komissariatom iustitsii instruktsiia po provedeniiu v zhizn' dekreta ob otdelenii tserkvi ot gosudarstva: Doklad," undated (late 1918 or early 1919), GARF, f. 353, op. 2, d. 691, l. 254. Galkin also complained that the nationalization of the cemeteries (also ordered by the August 24, 1918, instruction) had not taken place either.

97. GARF, f. 353, op. 3, d. 398, l. 29–29 ob., March 31, 1919. There was a comparable attempt to chivvy Red Cross institutions in 1919: see the documentation in TsGA-SPb, f. 5325, op. 7, d. 102.

98. These were encoded in two circulars: of the Commissariat of Justice (January 3, 1919) and of the Commissariat of Internal Affairs (December 28, 1919): see "Instruktsiia po voprosam, sviazannym s provedeniem v zhizn' dekreta ob otdelenii tserkvi ot gosudarstva," *SU* 72 (1923): item 699.

99. Figures calculated from Antonov and Kobak, *SSPb*. The fact that there were any school churches in operation is perhaps the biggest anomaly, since these were the subject of a special local decree ordering their liquidation by August 10, 1918 (*Severnaia kommuna*, August 8, 1918, p. 1).

100. Antonov and Kobak, *SSPb*, no. 389, no. 368.

101. For the closure date, see Antonov and Kobak, *SSPb*, no. 140. For the Monument Department's tenure of the building, see "Spisok domov GLAVMUZEIA imeiushchikh pereiti v arendnoe pol'zovanie nazvannogo uchrezhdeniia," RA IIMK, f. 67, ed. khr. 73, l. 3.

102. For the closure dates (1920, 1923, 1923, 1923, and 1922), see Antonov and Kobak, *SSPb*, nos. 121, 119, 135, 141, 124. The sole exception to the general rule was the chapel of the Presbyter to the Army and Navy, constructed in 1893, which stayed open till 1923 (see ibid., no. 114).

103. The association of Clemenceau and Hermant with the 1905 law is a little curious, as its main architects were Aristide Briand and Emile Combes, though Clemenceau, during his government of 1906–1909, was directly involved in putting into practice the 1905 law. However, the main measures of his period of office were in fact to soften its effects (e.g., the decree of April 11, 1908, classifying religious buildings as "communal property"), a point that undermines the case being made here.

104. TsGA-SPb, f. 1001, op. 7, d. 18, l. 45.

105. Ibid. The Gostinyi dvor to which the official referred was not the central one on Nevsky, but the 1720 building on Birzhevaia liniia, Vasilievskii Island, razed to allow construction of Marian Peretiatkovich's 1914–1915 building for the Ministry of Trade and Industry.

106. The specialization in church architecture of these leading preservation officials is interesting, given that Narkompros was one of a number of People's Commissariats—the others being the Commissariat of Justice and the Commissariat of Internal Affairs, as well as the Commissariats of Food Supply and of Agriculture—where there was a *Berufsverbot* [occupational prohibition] on the employment of "servants of cults," though these had the right to take other state employment. (January 13, 1921, cited in "Instruktsiia po voprosam, sviazannym s provedeniem v zhizn' dekreta ob otdelenii tserkvi ot gosudarstva," *SU* 72 [1923]: item 699).

107. Udalenkov was present at the first recorded meeting of the Museums Department, when he is listed as the head of the Archaeological Section ("Zhurnal zasedaniia 27 noiabria 1918 g. po sostavleniiu smety na 1919 g.," RA IIMK, f. 67, ed. khr. 1, l. 1). Romanov was also active from an early stage: he is listed, for example, among the participants of the Museums Department meeting on December 31, 1918 (ibid., l. 8), and in early 1919, he and Udalenkov were among the participants in a highly critical discussion of the methods of restoration work used by Aleksandr Anisimov, then leader of work on medieval icons in Novgorod (see "Protokol zasedaniia Osoboi Komissii, organizovannoi Arkheologicheskim Otdelom dlia osmotra rabot po restavratsii ikon v g. Novgorode i okrestnostiakh," February 11, 1919, RA IIMK, f. 67, ed. khr. 3, ll. 18–19). Kotov is listed as a member of the Restoration Section in the minutes of the discussion on how to respond to the Decree on the Confiscation of Church Valuables (see below). Another Museums Department member (also present at this meeting) with significant interests in church architecture was the art historian Leonid Matsulevich, author of a celebrated monograph on Byzantine architecture, but he did not have the same impact as the others on discussions in Petrograd-Leningrad. The biographical account here is based on materials in RA IIMK: see f. 2, op. 3, d. 675 (personal file of A. P. Udalenkov, 1931–1937, including numerous copies of his autobiography); f. 2, op. 5, d. 319 (work record card [*trudovoi spisok*] of A. P. Udalenkov); f. 2, op. 5, d. 273 (work record card of K. K. Romanov); f. 2, op. 3, d. 809 (work record card of G. I. Kotov). For material on Udalenkov's study visit to Samarkand in 1922, see GARF, f. 2307, op. 3, d. 272, l. 42. Romanov's activities are also abundantly documented in his personal fond, RA IIMK, f. 29. An example of a specialist in church art who was a religious believer was Petr Pokryshkin, who before his early death in 1922 had undergone ordination and retreated to the Lukoianovskii-Tikhnovskii Convent as chaplain. See Pravilova, *A Public Empire*, 353n176.

108. TsGA-SPb, f. 1001, op. 7, d. 1, l. 7. In the event, the petition was unsuccessful, possibly because the mutiny by the naval garrison at Kronstadt had made the Petrograd authorities wary of any possible focus of anti-Communist feeling among the armed forces, or possibly because the petition was forwarded to the City Soviet by the naval high command on December 7, 1921, so that review of it would have coincided with the discussions of church property sequestration.

109. "Ob iz"iatii tserkovnykh tsennostei," *Krasnaia gazeta* (hereafter *KG*), February 23, 1922, 3.

110. Vorob'ev and Krivova, *Sledstvennoe delo Patriarkha Tikhona*, 15.

111. For an overview of the statistics of repression in 1918–1919, see Stéphane Courtois et al., eds., *Chernaia kniga kommunizma: Prestupleniia, terror, repressii* (Moscow: Tri veka istorii, 1999), ch. 3.

112. This is suggested, at any rate, by the list in Valentinov, *Chernaia kniga*, 28–30.

113. Smith, "Bones of Contention."

114. On the festivals in 1920, see Tsentraln'yi gosudarstvennyi arkhiv istoriko-politicheskikh dokumentov Sankt-Peterburga (hereafter TsGAIPD-SPb), f. K-601, op. 1, d. 86, l. 1; on May 1 (ibid., l. 3); subbotniki (ibid., l. 9); Union Days (ibid., d. 224, l. 2); July Days (ibid., l. 3). A festival that combined celebration with the harnessing of iconoclastic drives was the removal, on May 1, 1920, of the ornamental fencing around the Winter Palace (Roman Mel'tser, 1900). As a recent addition to the palace, the fence was considered an eyesore in aesthetic terms, and its removal also reshaped the relationship between the building and the public areas outside, symbolically indicating that this was now the Palace of Arts, a museum for everyone in the city to visit.

115. For this argument, see particularly James Ryan, "Cleansing NEP Russia: State Violence against the Russian Orthodox Church in 1922," *Europe-Asia Studies* 65, no. 9 (2013): 1807–26.

116. As explained at greater length in Kelly, "The Bolshevik Reformation: February 1922," in *Historically Inevitable?*, ed. Tony Brenton (London: Profile Books, 2016, 244-62), the evidence suggests a reactive process, rather than one masterminded by, say, Trotsky from the beginning. For example, the records of Politburo agendas from 1919–1925 indicate that the removal of church goods was first discussed formally on March 11, 1922, which was followed by discussions on March 16, 20, 22, 23, and April 12. From then onward, the subject surfaced only occasionally, for example, during the Moscow clergy trials (May 11 and 18) and the Petersburg trials (July 13). G. M. Adibekov, K. M. Anderson, and L. A. Rogovaia, eds., *Politbiuro TsK RKG(b)-VKP(b): Povestki dnia zasedanii, 1919–1952; Katalog*, 3

vols. (Moscow: ROSSPEN, 2000–2001), 1:166–83. S. G. Petrov, *Russkaia pravoslavnaia tserkov' vremeni patriarkha Tikhona* (Novosibirsk: Izdatel'stvo Sibirskogo otdeleniia Russkoi Akademii Nauk, 2013), 47–48, suggests that Trotsky probably purged his archive of materials relating to church-state affairs, since his private papers contain little relating to these. But there seems no reason why Trotsky would have felt that his antireligious line was retrospectively shameful; it is far more likely that the struggle with religion was, so far as he was concerned, a relatively minor and short-term concern.

117. The Party leadership eventually conceded the Church's right to fundraise in support of famine victims, but very late in the day (the legislation went through only on December 8, 1921, and was not ratified until February 1, 1922 (Pokrovskii and Petrov, *Arkhivy Kremlia*, vol. 2, doc. 4, pp. 8-10), by which time the imminent imposition of sequestration had essentially made the concession redundant). The Central Executive Committee of the official Soviet agency charged with famine relief, Pomgol (Aid to the Starving), however, had agreed as early as August 19, 1921, not to obstruct the Orthodox Church's fundraising efforts: A. Mazyrin, V. A. Goncharov, and I. V. Uspenskii, eds., *Iz"iatie tserkovnykh tsennostei v Moskve v 1922 g.: Sbornik dokumentov iz fornda Revvoensoveta Respubliki* (Moscow: Izdatel'stvo Pravoslavnogo Sviato-Tikhonovskogo gumanitarnogo universiteta, 2006), 140.

118. Commentators on church history, understandably, tend to view the confiscations as purely an effort to crack down on religion (see, for example, Jonathan Daly, "'Storming the Last Citadel': The Bolshevik Assault on the Church, 1922," in *The Bolsheviks in Russian Society: The Revolution and Civil Wars*, ed. Vladimir N. Brovkin [New Haven, CT: Yale University Press, 1997], 236–59). However, at the stage when the escalation began, the Bolshevik government was under pressure to tap into its gold reserves, since this was a factor in US government negotiations over aid in the autumn of 1921. On September 2, 1921, President Hoover wrote to Colonel Haskell of the ARA: "As you are aware, it is reported here that Soviet Government has still some resources in gold and metals, and it does seem to me fundamental that they should expend these sums at once in the purchase of breadstuffs from abroad. While even this will be insufficient to cover their necessities, they can scarcely expect the rest of the world to make sacrifices until they have exhausted their own resources." Harold H. Fisher, *The Famine in Soviet Russia, 1919–1923: The Operations of the American Relief Administration* (New York: The Macmillan Company, 1927), 155.

119. "O tsennostiakh, nakhodiashchikhsia v tserkvakh i monastyriakh," *SU* 19 (1922): item 215.

120. On the January 2, 1922, decree (which did not appear in *SU*, maybe because it was considered to have been superseded by the February 16 decree), see Krivova, *Vlast' i tserkov'*, ch. 2; Anatoly Eldashev, "Utrachennye monastyrskie nekropoli Kazani," http://archive.is/Kyto. In sources such as the March 4, 1922, Glavnauka instruction (see below), it is usually stated that the January 2, 1922, decree was published in *Izvestiia* on January 6; but that was actually the text of the December 27, 1922, decree. The January 2, 1922, decree appears to have remained unpublished, perhaps because of its sensitive nature. A third decree of February 9, 1922, ordained that sums raised from deaccessioning objects in museums were to go into the funds of the museums themselves: "O peredache otdelu po delam muzeev i okhrane pamiatnikov iskusstva i stariny chasti summy, vyruchennykh ot prodazhi muzeinykh tsennostei," *SU* 19 (1922): item 216.

121. *Sic.* Elsewhere the date is more accurately given as "more than 125 years."

122. Letter from Galunov (no first name given), chairman of the Post Office Church *dvadtsatka*, to "The Artistic Commission for the Preservation of Monuments of Art and Culture," January 11, 1922, RA IIMK, f. 67, ed. khr. 67, l. 5–5 ob.

123. The church was listed as still functioning in a list compiled no earlier than late February 1922 by the Special Commission on the Removal of Church Valuables ("Spisok tserkvei funktsionirui-ushchikh," RA IIMK, f. 67, ed. khr. 847, ll. 17–18).

124. TsGAIPD-SPb, f. 16, op. 9, d. 9256, ll. 1–2.

125. "O poriadke iz"iatii tserkovnykh tsennostei, nakhodiashchikhsia v pol'zovanii grupp ver-uiushchikh," *SU* 19 (1922): item 217. See also the instruction, ibid., item 218. There are two alternative dates for this decree—February 16, 1922, when it was passed by VTsIK, and February 23 (the date when it appeared in *SU*, *KG*, etc.). To complicate matters further, the decree was first published in

Petrograd between those two dates (see *Petrogradskaia pravda* [hereafter *PP*], February 19, 1922, 2). Since there is not the slightest doubt that the text was communicated to local Party leaderships as soon as it was first agreed (as is indicated, inter alia, by the appearance of Fr. Aleksandr Vvedenskii's sermon exhorting the Orthodox faithful to cooperate with the requisitions as early as February 18, 1922), I have preferred the February 16, 1922, date here.

126. N. N. Pokrovskii, "Predislovie", in Pokrovskii and Petrov, *Arkhivy Kremlia*, vol. 1, 113–15.

127. Krivova, *Vlast' i tserkov'*, ch. 2.

128. "Instruktsiia" (March 4, 1922), GARF f. 2307, op. 1, d. 166, l. 27–27 ob.

129. "Zapis' obsuzhdeniia Osoboi Komissii, sozdannoi po porucheniu Zav. Petrogradskim Otdeleleniem Aktsentra" (March 4–5, 1922), RA IIMK, f. 67, ed. khr. 73, l. 79–79 ob. This meeting also evolved its own three-tier classification, of a similar chronological kind, but lacking the bewildering references to "Louis XV," and so on. In a note on the progress of the sequestrations that he wrote while these were going on (probably in the summer of 1922), Konstantin Romanov claimed that the March 4, 1922, decree was written on the basis of a draft from the Petrograd Special Commission (see RA IIMK, f. 67, ed. khr. 847, l. 75); but in that case, there must presumably have been an earlier text than the one included with the record of this discussion, a text that could have acted as the foundation for both the Petrograd text and the Moscow one.

130. The same was true of the instruction of January 23, 1922, setting up the sequestration boards, which comprised the head of the local Financial Section (the district fiscal authority), as well as representatives of the Cheka and the armed forces (see Krivova, *Vlast' i tserkov'*, ch. 2). Representatives of the Petrograd "Special Commission" were forced to recognize this omission directly, though the Commission tried to cover its embarrassment by emphasizing that the provisions of the January 2, 1922, law on church valuables still retained their force: RA IIMK, f. 67, ed. khr. 73, l. 79.

131. "Tserkov' i golod," *PP*, February 18, 1922, 2.

132. "Tserkov [*sic*] i golod," *PP*, March 14, 1922, 2.

133. For claims of support by the clergy, see, for example, "Tserkov' i golod," *PP*, March 18, 1922, 18; for the "Declaration" (*Vozzvanie gruppy petrogradskikh sviashchennikov*), *PP*, March 25, 1922, 1; see also "Vozzvanie gruppy sviashchennikov", *Izvestiia*, March 29, 1922, 2.

134. For detailed accounts of this complicated episode in religious history, see Roslof, *Red Priests*; Krasnov-Levitin, *Ocherki po istorii*; Krasnov-Levitin, *Likhie gody, 1925–1941* (Paris: YMCA Press, 1977). The collaboration with the Bolshevik government represented a significant volte-face, since the "renovation" movement had traditionally taken an anti-statist position, and the result was equally paradoxical—the expression of support for the position of "renovation" by some major figures from the reactionary clerical wing, such as the so-called "mad monk" Iliodor, whose assimilation seems to have come about on the grounds of their statist convictions. This particular type of ducking and weaving does not seem to have characterized Petrograd, however, where most of the leading figures in the "renovation" movement were ones (such as Vvedenskii) whose involvement went back well before 1917.

135. "Khleb nasushchnyi dlia golodaiushchikh," *PP*, March 21, 1922, 1.

136. All this refers exclusively to the *public* face of the campaign. There was a complicated back story that included secret negotiations between Petrosovet, Pomgol, and Metropolitan Veniamin during the first days of March 1922, which appear to have broken down after directions from the central government to escalate the confiscations. For Metropolitan Veniamin's letter to the Petrograd Committee of Pomgol on March 5, 1922, stipulating that he should himself oversee the melting-down of the vessels, as it would be "sacrilege" if unordained hands touched them, see Pokrovskii and Petrov, *Arkhivy Kremlia*, vol. 2, doc. 21, pp. 28-30.   See also Pospielovsky, *Russkaia pravoslavnaia tserkov'*, 104–7, and Kelly, "The Bolshevik Reformation." Compare Patriarch Tikhon's reference to inconsistent behavior on the part of the Soviet officials he dealt with in fall 1921 through spring 1922, in Vorob'ev and Krivova, *Sledstvennoe delo Patriarkha Tikhona*, 130–35.

137. "Soglashenie ob iz"iatii tsennostei" (the measure allowing "buying off" of items valued by believers, and Metropolitan Veniamin's call to the faithful), *PP*, April 14, 1922, 2; ibid., April 15, 2 (the mocking reader's letter); "Perelom v tserkvi," ibid., May 31, 1922, 2 (on the split between "progressives"

and "reactionaries"); "Sud nad tserkovnikami," ibid., June 2, 1922, 3 (the start of the trial). Again, behind the scenes, as made clear by documents in *Arkhivy Kremlia*, vol. 2 (see e.g. Sedova-Trotskaia's May 3, 1922 letter protesting the removal of church vessels even from museum displays, doc. 119, pp. 228-30), the central and local Commissions on the Removal of Church Valuables gave no quarter at all, whether to believers or to Museum Department initiatives.

138 .The confiscation of church property was part of an entire "politics of requisition" embracing the personal property of the prerevolutionary social elite in general. A major consideration when it came to the former property of the royal households was the potential value of this when sold abroad. The Soviet government seems to have made less effort to market chalices and icons in the West than, say, Fabergé eggs (on July 1, 1922, Sedova-Trotskaia wrote to Pomgol pointing out that items had been melted down that could have been sold abroad [*Arkhivy Kremlia*, vol. 2, doc. 147, p. 272]). However, such items could be disposed of on the internal market. Western travelers of the early Soviet period recall that they were, for example, easily available in hard currency shops: Una Pope-Hennessey, *The Closed City: Impressions of a Visit to Leningrad* (London: Hutchinson, 1938), 12, recalled the "vast curiosity shop" at Leningrad port, with "vast quantities of altar furnishings, chalice covers, and other ecclesiastical embroideries." On the marketing of confiscated goods through Western auction houses, etc., see particularly the chapters by Yuri Pyatnitsky in N. Iu. Semenova and N. V. Iljine, eds., *Selling Russia's Treasures: The Soviet Trade in Nationalized Art, 1917–1938* (Paris: The M. T. Abraham Center for the Arts Foundation, 2013).

139. Stenograficheskii otchet zasedaniia Petrogradskogo soveta, 20 marta 1922 g.," TsGA-SPb, f. 1000, op. 6, d. 266, ll. 52. My thanks to Alexandra Piir for transcribing this document. The ungrammatical style reflects the stylistic register of the original.

140. TsGA-SPb., f. 1000, op. 6, d. 266, ll. 47-50.

141. TsGA-SPb, f. 1000, op. 6, d. 266, l. 60.

142. TsGA-SPb, f. 1000, op. 6, d. 266, ll. 61–72. One assumes that the speaker who criticized going "against God" was either cowed by the general mood of the meeting, or (more likely) simply did not have his vote against or abstention recorded.

143. Telegram from Molotov to the North-Western Bureau of the Communist Party, Ts-GAIPD-SPb, f. 16, op. 9, d. 9256, l. 8. As Pokrovskii points out in his introduction to *Arkhivy Kremlia*, vol. 1, pp. 25-26, the Party leadership was initially divided as to the best strategy for handling the expropriations. In December 1921, Felix Dzerzhinsky, the chief of the Cheka, urged a head-on confrontation with the Orthodox Church, spearheaded and managed by the secret police, contrary to Anatoly Lunacharsky's suggestion of attempting cooperation with amenable clergy. Trotsky, who as chair and special plenipotentiary of the Commission on the Registration and Concentration of Valuables had a direct interest in maximizing requisitions, also pressed for a tough line; Molotov, though, held out for gradualism. Serious riots in Shuia on March 14–15, 1922, acted to convince many, including Lenin, of the need to "smash the enemy's head in and secure our fighting positions for several decades" (see his letter to the Politburo of March 19, 1922, *Arkhivy Kremlia*, vol. 1, doc. 23.16, p. 141). A consistent element in policy-making, though, was that action against the Church must be carried out behind closed doors—as manifested in the "top secret" character of the documents in which it was discussed, in the concealing of the activities of the Commissions on the Confiscations of Church Goods, and in the negative reaction to openly satirical coverage of the clergy in the mainstream press (see, for example, Trotsky, in Pokrovskii and Petrov, *Arkhivy Kremlia*, vol. 1, doc. 23.29, pp. 162-3). The strategy of cultivating amenable clergy was still pursued, though now with the aim of splitting the Orthodox community and exploiting the "forward-thinking" clergy in the meantime as an instrument of hastening requisition (see Trotsky, ibid., and the extensive discussion in Roslof, *Red Priests*, 39–71).

144. Even in the secret discussions at the Politburo, Grigory Zinoviev, Party leader in Petrograd, was one of those who held out for gradualism; as Pokrovskii points out in *Arkhivy Kremlia*, vol. 1, p. 25, the likely explanation for this is his sense that the situation might easily spiral out of control in his home city.

145. TsGAIPD-SPb, f. 16, op. 9, d. 9256, l. 3.

146. Ibid., op. 1, d. 482, l. 147.

147. The opening of the casket, revealing "some brown decayed bones, and not many of those, a mere handful," was triumphantly recorded in *PP* ("Vskrytie moshchei Aleksandra Nevskogo," May 13, 1922, 2). This article also mentioned that the casket itself, pronounced by the preservation bodies to be "of enormous artistic value," was to be transferred to the Hermitage. On the dating of the transfers, see http://lavra.spb.ru/about/history/18–1917–1989–.html.

148. See (on the living accommodation) the decision of the Presidium of the Moskovsko-Narvskii district soviet, June 6, 1923, and (on the Kazan' Church) the petition against the conversion by the religious community using the church and cemetery, TsGA-SPb, f. 1001, op. 8, d. 13, l. 124. The case of the latter was to resurface in the late 1920s and in the Brezhnev era: see chapter 2, chapter 6.

149. TsGA-SPb, f. 1001, op. 7, d. 6, l. 46. After complaints from fourteen different religious communities, Rabkrin declared this intrusive questioning unlawful (but not the collection of data required by the March 5, 1922, ruling). However, in 1923, Vasilieostrovskii district was still exceeding its legal brief, insisting that *dvadtsatka* members produce identity documents and extracts from the *domovye knigi* (house registry books): see the file for the Mother of God of Smolensk Church, TsGA-SPb, f. 7384, op. 33, d. 60, ll. 208–308.

150. "O vvedenii Ugolovnogo kodeksa RSFSR," *SU* 15 (1922): item 153, section 3, articles 119–25.

151. For a reference to this decree, see "Instruktsiia o poriadke registratsii religioznykh obshchestv," *SU* 37 (1923): item 384.

152. See the exchange of documents in TsGA-SPb, f. 1001, op. 7, d. 18, ll. 28–29.

153. As explicitly mentioned in an article about the confiscations in Smol'nyi district, "Iz"iatie tserkovnykh tsennostei v pomoshch' golodaiushchim," *PP*, April 8, 1922, 2: "The removal of valuables from closed churches proceeded without significant difficulties."

154. TsGA-SPb, f. 151, op. 2, d. 79, l. 258; see Shkarovskii and Cherepnina, *Spravochnik po istorii*, doc. 17, p. 64. The word *nastoiatel'* refers to the senior priest in a church or cathedral (see glossary).

155. N. Iu. Cherepnina and M. V. Shkarovskii, *Pravoslavnye khramy Sankt-Peterburga 1917–1945 gg.: Spravochnik* (St. Petersburg: BLITs, 1999), doc 8, p. 315.

156. TsGA-SPb, f. 1001, op. 7, d. 18, l. 13. (This was, evidently, the house church of St. Nicholas in the former Officers' Cavalry School, 49 Shpalernaia, which lies opposite the city waterworks.) The authorities at the level of the provincial committee were less than impressed with this argument: the document has a pencil note at the end, "The church must be closed, all the more since it's a school." All the same, the church remained open until 1923, when it was turned into a club (Antonov and Kobak, *SSPb*, 196).

157. TsGA-SPb, f. 1001, op. 7, d. 18, l. 37.

158. "Dokladnaia zapiska sviashchennika khrama-pamiatnika moriakam (Vladimira Rybakova)," February 20, 1924. TsGA-SPb, f. 7384, op. 33, d. 13, l. 5. For a reference to the protected status of the church, see the inspection record of March 1924, ibid., l. 7.

159. See, for example, TsGA-SPb, f. 1001, op. 7, d. 18, ll. 29, 32, 37.

160. RA IIMK, f. 29, ed. khr. 847, ll. 79–80.

161. RA IIMK, f. 29, ed. khr. 104, l. 11 (entry of June 19, 1922).

162. RA IIMK, f. 29, ed. khr. 847, ll. 79–80.

163. See the letter to Romanov from V. Molas written on March 14, 1922, RA IIMK, f. 29, ed. khr. 847, l. 82. One of the most notorious episodes of the confiscation campaign was the destruction in early summer 1922 of the Kazan' Cathedral's silver iconostasis, designed by Konstantin Ton in 1836. See the telegrams of protest from A. A. Vasil'ev, then director of the Academy of the History of Material Culture, and the Rector of the Academy of Arts, A. E. Belogrud, May 16, 1922, *Arkhivy Kremlia*, vol. 2, doc. 133, p. 242, doc. 134, p. 243.

164. For the categories, see RA IIMK, f. 29, ed. khr. 847, l. 1 (document of February 8, 1922).

165. The statistics are given in RA IIMK, f. 29, ed. khr. 847, l. 14.

166. For instance, there is little overlap between the list of closed churches under protection dating from 1923 (TsGALI-SPb, f. 32, op. 1, d. 30, ll. 1–2) and a separate list of protected house churches also dating from this point (TsGALI-SPb, f. 32, op. 1, d. 30, l. 60). The lists in RA IIMK,

f. 29, ed. khr. 847, ll. 1–20, etc., are still more confusing: see the examples on l. 19, l. 25; in the latter, five churches have been added to category 1, but one demoted to category 2, and five churches in the palaces outside St. Petersburg are listed that appear nowhere else, and so on. For a sampling of this material, see appendix 1.

167. For the confusion, see TsGA-SPb, f. 1001, op. 7, d. 18. For conflicting instructions about liquidation compare (a) a circular on the liquidation of house churches from the Administrative Department of Petrogubispolkom [the Executive Committee of the Petrograd Provincial Soviet] dated September 15, 1922, which told officials that they could sell vestments to the religious society that had formerly used the church, and give to them icons and books once "recorded in special lists," but should remove valuables to the local financial department, while non-ritual objects such as chairs and carpets of no special value might be removed by the local soviet for its own purposes (RA IIMK, f. 29, ed. khr. 847, l. 62), and (b) the note of August 22, 1922, from the Administrative Department to the Presidium of Petrogubispolkom stating that the only item of church property that believers were allowed to take when the church was stripped was the antimins (the ritual cloth containing a saint's relics and blessed and signed by a bishop, which was required for the full liturgy to be performed—see introduction): TsGA-SPb, f. 1001, op. 7, d. 18, l. 26.

168. TsGA-SPb, f. 1001, op. 9, d. 10, l. 15. The "no consultation without representation" rule also applied to other churches—for example, the Kazan' Cathedral (RA IIMK, f. 29, ed. khr. 847, l. 82).

169. M. V. Shkarovskii, *Sankt-Peterburgskaia eparkhiia v dvadtsatom veke v svete arkhivnykh materialov* (St. Petersburg: Liki Rossii, 2000), 86.

170. TsGA-SPb, f. 1001, op. 7, d. 18, l. 11 (report of the Moskovskii district soviet to the Administrative Section of Petrogubispolkom).

171. In February 1922, the Administrative Section of the Church Office (Tserkovnyi Stol) of Petrogubispolkom informed the Health Department that all house churches in hospitals and other medical institutions should now be closed, including that in the Second Psychiatric Hospital; if a place were required for worship, the former chapel could be used, once "cleansed from items of religious cult," by the members of any religious group. TsGA-SPb, f. 1001, op. 7, d. 18, l. 2. In fact, this church (which was freestanding) remained open for the meantime, but most other hospital churches had closed by the end of 1923 (see chapter 2).

172. "Akt komissii," June 15, 1922, TsGA-SPb, f. 1001, op. 7, d. 1, l. 340.

173. TsGA-SPb, f. 1001, op. 7, d. 18, l. 12.

174. Newspaper reports also gave primary attention to the weight of the objects that had been removed: see, for example, "V pomoshch' golodaiushchim," *PP*, April 8, 1922, 3, which reported that four poods of silver had been removed from churches in Smol'nyi district.

175. This was true in Moscow also: on criticism of Sedova-Trotskaia in this vein, see Krivova, *Vlast' i tserkov'*, ch. 3.

176. TsGA-SPb, f. 1001, op. 7, d. 18, l. 49.

177. Ibid., l. 52.

178. These figures (157 Orthodox churches, "2 or 3 Catholic and Jewish" ones) were given in a letter from the Board of Management (Upravlenie) of the Petrograd Provincial Soviet, responding to representations from Jewish communities against the closure of their "house churches." TsGA-SPb, f. 1001, op. 7, d. 1, l. 310.

179. TsGA-SPb, f. 1001, op. 7, d. 19, l. 24.

180. For the 1921 figure, see RA IIMK, f. 67, ed. khr. 55, l. 103; for the 1922 figure, RA IIMK, f. 67, ed. khr. 73, l. 19. These are typed staff lists of the time. Konstantin Romanov claimed an even bigger drop in his note of summer 1922: from 140 to 13 (RA IIMK, f. 29, ed. khr. 111, l. 6). It is possible that the discrepancy in the figures is explained by whether part-time employees and consultants were counted. As Romanov pointed out (ibid.), until the end of 1921, there was also a technical department to call on.

181. The church in question is the house church of the Raising of the Cross in the Community of Sisters of Charity, 154 Fontanka Embankment, built by the architect Iu. Iu. Benua [Benois] in 1903–1904 as part of his conversion of the early nineteenth-century mansion housing the Community. See Antonov and Kobak, *SSPb*, no. 280, pp. 257–58. (Here the information,

however, is a little different from the archival record, stating that under the last incumbent priest to serve before the closure, Father Ioann Blagodatov, the house church was, in 1919, "removed to the lower floor and closed on September 21, 1922; the priest took the altar and communion vessels home, and transferred the icons to the Catherine Church" [which of the several Catherine Churches in the city is not indicated].)

182. That is, the well-known painter Viktor Vasnetsov (1848–1926), one of the leading artists of the Russian revival movement.

183. See the report of December 15, 1922, TsGA-SPb, f. 1001, op. 7, d. 19, l. 18. This kind of friction was typical of the Museum Department's relations with other Soviet bodies at central level too. The Department's push for final say in deciding which objects had "historic and artistic value" was opposed by Trotsky on March 22, 1922 (*Arkhivy Kremlia*, vol. 2, doc. 54, p. 90), and on April 5, 1922 officials from the Central Commission on Confiscations and the Deputy Plenipotentiary on Inventorization and Concentration of Valuables wrote to Sedova-Trotskaia to complain of "the endless red tape that slows our work down" (ibid. vol. 2, doc. 83, pp. 138-9).

184. "Instruktsiia po voprosam, sviazannym s provedeniem v zhizn' dekreta ob otdelenii tserkvi ot gosudarstva," *SU* 72 (1923): item 699. The instruction amounted to a reiteration of earlier measures (e.g., decrees on the removal of churches needed for cultural and other purposes dating from January 3 and December 28, 1919), but the consolidation and codification of the rules clearly acted as a stimulus to their enactment. For the material on registrations, see *SU* 37 (1923): item 384 (though the original deadline of three months given here had to be extended later in 1923: see *SU* 71 [1923]: item 692). Another trajectory was the winding-up of contracts with religious groups on grounds of breach of contract, as facilitated by a decree of VTsIK on April 19, 1923: see the September 20, 1923, Narkomiust circular in *Ezhenedel'nik sovetskoi iustitsii* 37 (1923): 860. As of May 13, 1924, church buildings were subject to compulsory insurance (at the expense of the religious society): *Biulleten' NKVD* 15–16 (1924): 66.

185. See the list of closed churches at TsGALI-SPb, f. 32, op. 1, d. 30., ll. 1–2 (and appendix 2).

186. TsGA-SPb, f. 1001, op. 8, d. 13, l. 163. For other demands of this kind dating from summer 1923 (July 4, 1923, for the Trinity house church in 44 Fontanka—which was in the process of conversion to the Old and New Guard Club, see above—and July 28, 1923), see RA IIMK, f. 29, ed. khr. 848, l. 4, l. 8.

187. This is recorded in the minutes of the Old St. Petersburg Society (OSP) (see chapter 2) for December 14, 1923: TsGALI-SPb, f. 32, op. 1, d. 7, l. 136. The report by S. N. Nasedkin that set out this information also recorded that the Preservation Committee had stipulated that the iconostasis (*sic*; i.e., the altar painting, in the case of the Maltese Chapel) should not be removed, but simply covered with a cloth, so that it could be inspected by art historians. According to Antonov and Kobak, *SSPb*, no. 514, the church furnishings were removed from the Maltese Chapel only in 1928–1930; the iconostasis of the Orthodox chapel remained in place till 1927 (ibid., no. 238).

188. TsGA-SPb, f. 1001, op. 7, d. 1, ll. 333–35.

189. *KG*, December 23, 1923, 2. For the listing of the building, see RA IIMK, f. 29, ed. khr. 847, l. 19 ob. See also E. Shubina, "Klub 'Staraia i Molodaia Gvardiia,'" *Fontanka: Kul'turno-istoricheskii al'manakh* 2 (2007): 8.

190. See, for example, O. Barabashev, comp., "Za krasnyi byt, ili operativnaia svodka s fronta, o kotorom nel'zia zabyt'," *Iunyi proletarii* 1 (1924): 4–7, which describes the various types of "red rituals," with examples from different parts of the Soviet Union.

191. The adumbration of Ilya Il'f and Evgenii Petrov's famous comic novel, *The Twelve Chairs*, is fortuitous, but entertaining.

192. "Dokladnaia zapiska arkhitektorov N. I. Postnikova i G. Z. Levi v Restavratsionnyi P-Otdel," April 24, 1922, RA IIMK, f. 67, ed. khr. 73, l. 72–72 ob.

193. Letter from the commandant of Smol'nyi to Il'in, deputy head of the Section for the Management of State Property (OUPGI), June 28, 1923, TsGA-SPb, f. 1001, op. 8, d. 13, l. 113. The cathedral at Smol'nyi was partly stripped in September 1923, with some items sent to the Museum

Fund, others (carpets, chrism, etc.) to the Domestic (Khoziaistvennyi) Fund, and a third category denominated for use in "antireligious demonstrations" (TsGALI-SPb, f. 32, op. 1, d. 7, l. 117).

194. "Tsirkuliar no. 21: Sekretno," March 21, 1923, TsGAIPD-SPb, f. 16, op. 9, d. 9547, l. 4 ob.

195. This is based on information from Aleksandr Kobak when he was interviewed in 2009. Oxf/AHRC SPb-09 PF10 CK.

196. In the case of the Senate Church, the Special Commission drew up an elaborate contract for the State Archives Directorate, the lessee of the entire complex in which it was housed, requiring them to "foster in every way the restoration of the historic and everyday *ansambl'* of the church," to report regularly on its condition, to eschew alterations without permission from the Monuments Department, and so on ("Akt o peredachi na okhranu Domovoi tserkvi Senata Glavarkhivu," RA IIMK, f. 29, ed. khr. 847, l. 72). However, the document was not enforced, and the church was liquidated in 1923 (Antonov and Kobak, *SSPb*, no. 112).

197. There seem to have been serious disagreements over preservation policy between Konstantin Romanov and other members of the Monuments Department in the late summer and autumn of 1923. In August 1923, Udalenkov wrote to Romanov politely thanking him for his contribution, and suggesting that, as he no longer approved of preservation policy, he might wish to stand down as inspector for the Department. In the meantime, the tiff was patched up, and Romanov continued working, but in October 1923, he was recorded as having left the staff of the Department (though he continued to belong to its advisory board). RA IIMK, f. 29, ed. khr. 848, ll. 10–11, 23.

198. There are plenty of examples of draconian behavior in Valentinov, *Chernaia kniga*. As for "literacy levels," the comment is based less on the (extremely limited) information about actual education than on the character of the documents themselves, which is very different from those of provincial places in the early Soviet period (to judge by materials held by the Party and local archives in Ekaterinburg, for instance).

Chapter Two

1. Dates here are taken from Antonov and Kobak, *SSPb*.

2. A. Men'shoi, "Gorod pyshnyi, gorod bednyi," *Petrograd* 14 (1923): 16. The oblivion of the earlier names among some Petrograders was likely aided by population turnover (between 1916 and 1920 the city's population dropped by over two-thirds, but by 1923 it had risen by over 250,000 compared with 1920). Renamings in 1918 included Znamenskaia (ploshchad' Vosstaniia), Bol'shoi Sampsonievskii (prospekt Marksa), Blagoveshchenskaia ulitsa (ploshchad' Truda). Among those renamed in 1923 were Troitskaia ploshchad', Voznesenskii prospekt, Tserkovnaia ulitsa, Aleksandro-Nevskaia ploshchad', as ploshchad' Revoliutsii, prospekt Maiorova, ulitsa Blinova, and Krasnaia ploshchad' respectively.

3. On the *obnovlentsy* (Renovationists) at this period, see Anatolii Krasnov-Levitin (with Vadim Shavrov), *Ocherki po istorii tserkovnoi smuty*, 2 vols. (Moscow: Krutitskoe patriarshee podvor'e, 1996); Edward E. Roslof, *Red Priests: Renovationism, Russian Orthodoxy, and Revolution, 1905–1946* (Bloomington: Indiana University Press, 2002); M. V. Shkarovskii, *Obnovlencheskoe dvizheniie v Russkoi Pravoslavnoi Tserkvi XX veka* (St. Petersburg: Nestor, 1999).

4. These groups were specifically mentioned in the 1923 "Instruktsiia po voprosam, sviazannym s provedeniem v zhizn' dekreta ob otdelenii tserkvi ot gosudarstva," *SU* 72 (1923): item 699.

5. In Leningrad, it would appear, the League was mainly active against Orthodox believers in the countryside at this point, and action against Evangelical Christians was more of a preoccupation than relations with Orthodoxy: see, for example, the materials for March–November 1925 in TsGAIPD-SPb, f. 16, op. 9, d. 9994.

6. V. V. Lobanov, ed., *Protokoly komissii po provedeniiu otdeleniia tserkvi ot gosudarstva pri TsK-RKP(b)-VKP(b) (Antireligioznoi komissii), 1922–1929* (Moscow: Izdatel'stvo Pravoslavnogo Sviato-Tikhonovskogo gumanitarnogo universiteta, 2014), 47.

7. Ibid., 73. In his "The Stalinist Assault on the Parish, 1929–1941," in *Stalinismus vor dem Zweiten Weltkrieg: Neue Wege der Forschung,* ed. Manfred Hildermeier (Munich: Oldenburg Verlag, 1998), 209, Gregory Freeze sees the change as motivated by the need to placate Russia's rural population (citing a speech to this effect made by Grigory Zinoviev at the Twelfth Congress of the Russian Communist Party in April 1923), but this may simply have been an excuse: another possible explanation is the leadership vacuum in the face of Lenin's worsening condition, after his third stroke in March 1923 left him paralyzed and unable to speak.

8. "O prodlenii sroka registratsii religioznykh obshchestv," *SU* 59 (1924): item 577.

9. *SU* 73 (1923): item 711, section 4.

10. *OPIK* 1973, 43.

11. See N. Trotskaia, "Muzeinoe stroitel'stvo i revoliutsiia," *Nauka i iskusstvo* 1 (1926): 30–32, 40–42. The comments are notably defensive, underlining that care for churches before 1917 was poor, and brushing off suggestions that churches had suffered significant damage in the Soviet period, but conceding that "the preservation of churches and monasteries was often, in the heat of early revolutionary creation, regarded as a masked way of indulging religious prejudices" (41).

12. GARF, f. 2307, op. 3, d. 163, l. 141.

13. GARF, f. 2307, op. 3, d. 264, ll. 3–4.

14. The dwindling of the Monuments Department is reflected in the dramatic shrinkage of archival materials. RA IIMK, f. 67, holds seventy-seven files covering its activities between 1918 and 1922, and eleven covering its activities between 1923 and 1927.

15. TsGA-SPb, f. 7384, op. 33, d. 13, l. 9.

16. "Paskhal'nye chastushi: Stikhi Nikolaia Semenova," *Iunyi proletarii,* no. 7 (1925): 16.

17. The church was closed in 1925 in the aftermath of the campaign against factory churches (though freestanding and officially registered as a parish church, it stood next to the entrance to the Red Putilov Works).

18. See G. A. Ol', *Aleksandr Nikol'skii* (Leningrad: Lenizdat, 1980), 20–24 (on the diploma project), 68–69 (on the Putilov Church conversion, including a rare illustration of the building's façade).

19. "Spisok osmotrennykh tserkvei Moskovsko-Narvskogo raiona," TsGALI-SPb, f. 32, op. 1, d. 4, l. 38 ob. This report was carried out by the Old St. Petersburg Society (OSP), on which see below. In 1926, the OSP made efforts to save the interior ("in an idiosyncratic Eastern Romanesque style and planned down to the last detail") for the Museum of Dying Cult (see TsGALI-SPb, f. 32, op. 1, d. 30, l. 45)—with what success is unclear.

20. For the suggestion that the construction of the stadium (followed in 1971 by the Jubilee Palace of Sport) had antireligious promptings, see the comments of Father Vladimir Sorokin, "'Teper' oni bol'she ne smeiutsia,'" http://krotov.info/spravki/history_bio/21_bio/1939_sorokin.html.

21. A photograph of the original building, badly damaged during the war and replaced by stands for spectators in a more traditional diluted neoclassical style, is available on the official stadium site, http://en.petrovsky.spb.ru/docs/id51.html.

22. On the work of voluntary institutions, such as the "Children's Friend Society" in the NEP period, see Catriona Kelly, *Children's World: Growing Up in Russia, 1890–1991* (New Haven, CT: Yale University Press, 2008), ch. 6.

23. On the OSP's relation to prerevolutionary antecedents such as the Commission for the Study and Description of the Monuments of Old St. Petersburg, founded in 1907, see Katerina Clark, *Petersburg, Crucible of Cultural Revolution* (Cambridge, MA: Harvard University Press, 1995), ch. 1. The Society of Architects was another obvious force in its emergence, since this had been a major forum for discussions of preservation policy before 1917 (see introduction above).

24. "Godovoi otchet za 1921–1922 gg.," TsGALI-SPb, f. 32, op. 1, d. 3, l. 2.

25. See, for example, Emily Johnson, *How St. Petersburg Learned to Study Itself: The Russian Idea of Kraevedenie* (University Park: University of Pennsylvania Press, 2006).

26. On the biography of Il'in, see G. A. Popova, "L. A. Il'in: Pervyi director Muzeia Goroda," in *Ot Muzeia Starogo Peterburga k Gosudarstvennomu muzeiu istorii Sankt-Peterburga: Issledovaniia i*

materialy, ed. V. A. Frolov (St. Petersburg: GMI-SPb., 1997), 48–56, and her *Muzei Goroda v Anichkovom dvortse: Sobytiia, sud'by, kollektsii* (St. Petersburg: Almaz, 1998). See also E. P. Busyreva, *Lev Il'in* (St. Petersburg: Muzei istorii Sankt-Peterburga, 2008). Il'in's mansion burned down in the late 1910s, leaving only two park buildings, but was completely reconstructed in 1997. For recent photographs, see http://babs71.livejournal.com/765856.html?nojs=1.

27. These initiatives are abundantly documented in the files of the OSP, held in TsGALI-SPb, f. 32.

28. As is evident from the files of VOOPIiK (TsGALI-SPb, f. 229). See also chapter 6.

29. "Zhurnal Soveshchaniia, sostoiavshegosia 12 sentiabria 1922 g. v Otdele Muzeev," Ts-GA-SPb, f. 1000, op. 6, d. 234, l. 45.

30. See, for example, "Otchet Sektsii Okhrany pamiatnikov stariny i iskusstva, 1 okt. 1924 g.–1 okt. 1925 g.," TsGA-SPb, f. 1001, op. 6, d. 277, ll. 172–76.

31. Records of a meeting on July 16, 1923, indicate that Aleksandr Udalenkov was then acting as chair of the Presidium of the Council of OSP: see TsGALI-SPb, f. 32, op. 1, d. 1, l. 6. In January 1924, Konstantin Romanov (along with the well-known local historian Nikolai Antsiferov) stated their intention of resigning from OSP, because of a disagreement at the general meeting; the response of the Council was to call another meeting, apparently to everyone's satisfaction; in March 1924, Antsiferov was still a member of the society (see l. 21), at which point he put forward the argument on cooperation with state organizations.

32. See chapter 1 for the example of P. P. Veiner. This expediency, or simple recognition of the absence of an alternative, was characteristic of many other professionals as well, among them educators, scientists, physicians, and engineers; see Sergei Iarov, *Konformizm v sovetskoi Rossii: Petrograd 1917–1920-kh godov* (St. Petersburg: Evropeiskii Dom, 2006).

33. TsGALI-SPb, f. 32, op. 1, d. 27, l. 13, l. 11.

34. TsGALI-SPb, f. 32, op. 1, d. 3, l. 77. For another version of the report, also containing this passage, and said to relate to activities in "July 1925," see TsGA-SPb, f. 1001, op. 6, d. 277, l. 173.

35. TsGALI-SPb, f. 32, op. 1, d. 3, l. 16.

36. TsGALI-SPb, f. 32, op. 1, d. 41, l. 4a. The document is undated, but must be later than the debates about placing a statue of Lenin (or alternatively, Red Army soldier) on the Alexander Column (to replace the angel originally there), which took place in the months after Lenin died (on this episode, see N. B. Lebina and V. S. Izmozik, *Peterburg sovetskii: "Novyi chelovek" v starom prostranstve; Sotsial'no-arkhitekturnoe mikroistoricheskoe issledovanie* [St. Petersburg: Kriga, 2010]); but since it does not refer to flood damage, it likely predates the deluge of September 23, 1924. (The latter event, which caused serious damp problems in, for example, the Russian Museum, does not seem to have adversely affected the major ecclesiastical buildings of the city, perhaps because of the traditional choice of higher land for building.) Also in early 1924 (TsGALI-SPb, f. 32, op. 1, d. 61, l. 102), the OSP produced a list of buildings that merited reconstruction work, including the bell tower of the St. Nicholas Cathedral, the Smol'nyi Cathedral (needing underpinning), and the St. Isaac's and St. Peter and St. Paul Cathedrals, as well as numerous "civic" structures, e.g., the embankments.

37. TsGALI-SPb, f. 32, op. 1, d. 3, l. 77.

38. Ibid., d. 1, l. 29 (April 1, 1924). For the results, see "Spisok osmotrennykh tserkvei Moskovsko-Narvskogo raiona," ibid., d. 4, l. 38–38 ob.

39. An early record of an OSP meeting (January 15, 1921) includes Asaf'ev, Benua, Zharnovskii, Il'in, and M. D. Filosofov (TsGALI-SPb, f. 32, op. 1. d. 1, l. 2). For later records, see, for example, the lists of members held in TsGA-SPb, f. 1001, op. 6, d. 277, l. 4 (not dated, probably 1923), l. 23 (1924), ll. 85–86, l. 96, l. 163 (biuro from 1924, including A. N. Benua). On the biography of Petr Stolpianskii (1872–1938), see http://www.nlr.ru/ar/staff/stolp.htm; on Sergei Zharnovskii, http://convolut.ru/?paged=5. Il'in is the only one of these figures to be the subject of a detailed modern biography: see Busyreva, *Lev Il'in*.

40. For a detailed discussion of these issues, see Catriona Kelly, "'A Dissonant Note on the Neva': Historical Memory and Local Identity in Russia's Second City during the Post-Stalin Era," *Journal of Eurasian Studies* 1, no. 1 (2010): 72–83.

41. TsGALI-SPb, f. 32, op. 1, d. 41, l. 6 ob.

42. Ibid., d. 4, l. 140.

43. *Style russe* or Russian revivalism applies to the movement in Russian architecture that aimed to echo the style of medieval Russian buildings, though in the 1840s the effect tended to more closely resemble neo-Byzantinism. In the Soviet architectural establishment generally, Ton was decried because of his official role as court architect to a reactionary emperor (hence the spectacular demolition of the Cathedral of Christ the Redeemer, see chapter 3). But in Petersburg, it was mainly the "ugliness" of his churches that was considered offensive. As a result of city remodeling in the 1930s, only one survived, and that in rebuilt form—the Church of the Transfiguration on Apothecary Island, which was still only at the start of the process of being converted back in the mid-2010s (visit, FN January 2015).

44. Vladimir Kurbatov, *Peterburg: Khudozhestvenno-istoricheskii ocherk* (St. Petersburg: Izd. Obshchiny sv. Evgenii, 1913). The "cockerel style" (*petushinyi stil'*) refers to the decorative red brick that was used for many late nineteenth-century public buildings, including churches. Indeed, even the diocesan architect, Aleksandr Aplaksin, had commented unfavorably on the low quality of modern church architecture—"There has never been such shocking lack of taste in any era; even in the epoch of Ton you could find the odd good building." *Russkoe tserkovnoe iskusstvo i ego sovremennye zadachi* (St. Petersburg: Tipografiia Aleksandro-Nevskogo Obshchestva Trezvosti, 1911), 43. Aplaksin's own, rather interesting, modernist churches have mainly not survived, a distinguished exception being the Church of St. Anna of Kashin on Bol'shoi Sampsonievskii prospekt.

45. G. I. Kotov, "O razvitii russkoi arkhitektury XVIII veka," in Mashkov, N. P., and A. A. Netyksa, eds. *Dnevnik Vysochaishe utverzhdennogo II S"ezda russkikh Zodchikh v Moskve, 1895 goda* (Moscow: Biuro S"ezda/Politekhnicheskii Muzei, 1895), pt. 4, p. 4. For a typical attack on "architectural vulgarity," see A. P. Krasnosel'skii, "Arkhitekturnaia poshlost'," *Dnevnik V Vserossiiskogo S"ezda Zodchikh, 15–22 Dekabria 1913 g.* (St. Petersburg: Tipografiia Sankt-Peterburgskogo Gradonachal'stva, 1913), pt. 8, p. 3.

46. Nikolai Punin, *Mir svetel liubov'iu: Dnevniki, pis'ma*, ed. L. A. Zykova (Moscow: Slovo, 1998), 242. The "cathedral" in question was probably either the Cathedral of the Transfiguration or the late eighteenth-century Cathedral of St. Sergius, both of which were located not far away from Punin's apartment behind the Sheremet'ev Palace.

47. On the "Petersburg text," see particularly V. N. Toporov, "Peterburg i 'Peterburgskii tekst' russkoi literatury" (1971, 1993), in *Peterburgskii tekst russkoi literatury: Izbrannye trudy* (St. Petersburg : Iskusstvo-Sankt-Peterburga, 2003), 7–118. Examples of scenes in churches to satirical ends include Pushkin's "From Pindemonte" (where an armed guard watches over the image of the Crucifixion), Gogol's *The Nose* (where the escaped Nose is glimpsed by Kovalev saying his prayers "very piously"), and Tolstoy's *Father Sergius* (where the worldly monastery in which Kasatskii is ordained is clearly intended as a portrait of the Alexander Nevsky Lavra).

48. Boris Eikhenbaum, "Dusha Moskvy," *Sovremennoe slovo* 1 (1917), http://philologos.narod.ru/eichenbaum/eichen_moscow.htm.

49. Ariadna Tyrkova-Williams, *Vospominaniia* (1954; repr., Moscow: Slovo, 1998), 242.

50. Saki [H. H. Munro], "The Old Town of Pskoff," in *The Complete Short Stories* (London: Penguin Books, 2000), 559. The piece was first published in 1924 (eight years after Saki's death), but was evidently written considerably earlier, in late 1914 or 1915.

51. A striking illustration of early twentieth-century distaste for the Victorian is the poet and writer John Betjeman, who in the 1960s began crusading for the retention of Victorian buildings, but in the 1930s felt that the surroundings of St. Paul's would be much improved by modern buildings: "We must give up the building rule which restricts the height of buildings, and we must not only do that, but we must build office blocks twice as high as St. Paul's, and have green spaces and wide roads in between the blocks.... Two dozen skyscrapers, though they would obviously dwarf St. Paul's, would not take away from its beauty if they were beautiful themselves." Quoted (no source given) in David Kynaston, *A World to Build: Austerity Britain, 1945–48* (London: Bloomsbury Publishing, 2007), 29.

52. TsGALI-SPb, f. 32, op. 1, d. 7, 53 (minutes of meeting of November 17, 1922: proposal to inspect); ibid., l. 60 (results of inspection, December 15, 1922).

53. That is, artists who were professors at the Academy of Arts.

54. TsGALI-SPb, f. 32, op. 1, d. 30, l. 34.

55. Ibid., l. 36.

56. See the information on chapels in Antonov and Kobak, *SSPb*.

57. See, for example, "Godovoi otchet o deiatel'nosti Obshchestva Starogo Peterburga i ego okrestnostei, 1921–1922 gg.," TsGALI-SPb, f. 32, op. 1, d. 3, l. 15, and the list of protected objects for early 1925 at TsGA-SPb, f. 1001, op. 6, d. 277, l. 65. This oratory is regularly referred to in the OSP documentation as "the oratory of the Fedoseevo Concord" (the Fedoseevo Concord being one of the "priestless" groups of Old Believers, whose members in this case repudiated marriage and led lives of quasi-monastic communality). Confusingly, there was also another prayer-house at 3 Volkovskaia ulitsa (now renamed River Volkova Embankment) that sometimes appears on preservation lists (such as the OSP's "Spisok arkhitekturnykh (tserkovnykh) sooruzhenii," c. 1924, TsGALI-SPb, f. 32, op. 1, d. 30, l. 60). Alongside their official association with this Old Believer oratory, individual members of the OSP sometimes acted as custodians for other churches on an informal basis: for example, P. V. Lutsenko was in charge of the house church of the Trinity in 20 Fontanka embankment (the so-called "Golitsyn church"), built by Andrei Voronikhin and Karl Magnus (Aleksandr) Vitberg in 1812, and with icons by Vladimir Borovikovskii and others (TsGALI-SPb, f. 32, op. 1, d. 1, l. 22).

58. TsGALI-SPb, f. 32, op. 1, d. 3, l. 15. This oratory was one of the flagship projects of the OSP. It was closely supervised, and the religious community used the premises under the terms of a special contract with the Society that (like the official contracts issued by Narkompros) required them to obtain permission for any alterations, as well as allowing inspections and excursions (TsGA-LI-SPb, f. 32, op. 1, d. 30, l. 49). In 1930, a Lensovet decision to close it down was reversed by VTsIK (a submission reiterating the aesthetic and historical importance of the ensemble was made at this point by Glavnauka), but a second effort in 1935–1936 was successful, after which it was liquidated and the premises converted into living accommodation for a nearby factory (TsGA-SPb, f. 7384, op. 33, d. 5, ll. 1–18). It was generally the case that Old Believer religious groups, because of the history of persecution before 1917, were treated more considerately than Orthodox groups, which may be another reason why the OSP occupied itself so enthusiastically with the oratory. In 1924, the NKVD even evolved a special way of coming to contractual arrangements with groups of Old Believers who refused to countenance drawing up written contracts (a formal spoken statement): see "O poriadke peredachi khramov staroobriadtsam," September 13, 1924, *Biulleten' NKVD* 34 (1924): 164. The special arrangements continued until the April 8, 1929, Decree on Religious Organizations was passed (see chapter 3).

59. RA IIMK, f. 67, ed. khr. 3, ll. 16–49. This conflict is discussed using different, but comparable, evidence from 1919–1920 in V. M. Roslavskii, *Stanovlenie uchrezhdenii okhrany i restavratsii pamiatnikov iskusstva i stariny v RSFSR 1917–1921 gg.: Igor' Grabar' i restavratsiia* (Moscow: Polimag, 2004): see esp. 308–16, 354–71. The emphasis on punctilious conservation went back well before 1917: in 1892, a session at the Congress of Architects had drafted a set of rules for restoration that included detailed sketching and photography, and decreed that later additions to buildings that were of "artistic and historic interest" should be allowed to remain: "O nekotorykh pravilakh pri vozobnovlenii drevnikh zdanii," *Dnevnik Vysochaishe utverzhdennogo S"ezda russkikh Zodchikh v S-Peterburge, 1892 g.* (St. Petersburg: Biuro S"ezda/Akademiia Khudozhestv, 1892), pt. 3, p. 5.

60. RA IIMK, f. 67, ed. khr. 73, l. 79–79 ob.

61. RA IIMK, f. 67, ed. khr. 32, l. 6.

62. For the architectural details, see Antonov and Kobak, *SSPb*, no. 213.

63. For the instruction, RA IIMK, f. 67, ed. khr. 73, l. 80; for Romanov's comments, RA IIMK, f. 29, ed. khr. 847, l. 76. Among those advocating 1825 as a cutoff was likely Lev Il'in (for his presence at the meeting, see RA IIMK, f. 67, ed. khr. 73, l. 79).

64. See the penciled note by Romanov in the paperwork of the Special Commission, RA IIMK, f. 29, ed. khr. 847, l. 52. This file also contains a draft outline by Romanov for a history of Petersburg architecture that is organized by era, and takes the era of Nicholas I as its culminating point (ll. 21–22).

65. *SU* 73 (1923): item 711, part 4.

66. "Spisok otdel'no stoiashchikh tserkvei priniatykh pod okhranu Osoboi Komissii Restavratsionnogo P[od]otdela (v Petrograde)," TsGA-SPb, f. 1001, op. 8, d. 13, l. 84. See also appendix 1. This is the earliest list that has come to light in local or central archives, and it would appear that it may be the earliest in existence. Prior to that, "certificates of protection" had been issued to individual buildings, as noted in chapter 1. The lists obviously represented a step forward in terms of organization, but there were occasional mistakes and omissions, just as there were in all lists up to the late Soviet period (see chapter 4 for some comments on the 1950 list of churches in Leningrad Province).

67. "Spisok arkhitekturnykh (tserkovnykh) sooruzhenii," TsGALI-SPb, f. 32, op. 1, d. 30, l. 60. See also appendix 1.

68. As stated above (n. 43), the Church of the Transfiguration was the only major ecclesiastical building built by Ton to survive the Soviet period; after being taken over for use as a laboratory in 1930, it was repeatedly restructured, most recently in the 1980s. (See Antonov and Kobak, *SSPb*.) Here and below, dates and attributions follow those in contemporary lists, which in some cases differ from modern ones. For example, the Church of the Mother of God Joy of Those Who Grieve on Voinova (Shpalernaia) is now usually attributed to Ruska and dated 1817–1818.

69. *Sobor* is often translated "cathedral," but strictly, this would be *kafedral'nyi sobor*. In the 1920s, the title of *sobor* was given to a number of buildings (e.g., the St. Matthew Church on Petrograd Side) that had not formerly held the title, partly as a result of the division of the Orthodox faithful into a variety of competing groups (see chapter 1). For the sake of familiarity, "cathedral" is routinely used here to translate "sobor."

70. "Spisok arkhitekturnykh (tserkovnykh) sooruzhenii," TsGALI-SPb, f. 32, op. 1, d. 30, l. 60. See also appendix 1.

71. The exception being the Old Believer Oratory.

72. "Muzei i pamiatniki stariny" (1925), GARF, f. 2307, op. 10, d. 147, l. 417. Underlining follows original.

73. This narrowing of the canons was a general process across the art forms. On literature, for example, see Evgeny Dobrenko, *The Making of the State Reader: Social and Aesthetic Origins of Soviet Literary Culture*, trans. Jesse Savage (Stanford, CA: Stanford University Press, 2001).

74. "Otchet o rabotakh tserkovnoi sektsii, 1918–1923 gg.," GARF, f. 2307, op. 8, d. 252, l. 13–13 ob.

75. See M. E. Kaulen, *Muzei-khramy i muzei-monastyri v pervoe desiatiletie Sovetskoi vlasti* (Moscow: Luch, 2001).

76. A 1919 list of buildings in the care of the Museum Department does not include the St. Peter and St. Paul Cathedral and the Church of the Savior on the Blood (TsGALI-SPb, f. 36, op. 1, d. 40, l. 17), but salary records from 1921 (TsGALI-SPb, f. 36, op. 2, l. 4, l. 6) include a doorman and four watchmen and a cleaner (*podenshchitsa*) in the latter; l. 6, ibid., is a semi-literate chit for pay to a "dor-Man" and one other member of staff from the official in charge of the St. Peter and St. Paul Cathedral. On the peculiarity of Petrograd and Leningrad practices in the national context, see Kaulen, *Muzei-khramy*, 58. As Kaulen's appendix indicates (157), the Gothic Church in Alexandria and the house church of the Great Palace at Peterhof were also church-museums, which was likewise a result of their former royal status.

77. "Sektsiia Okhrany: Otchet za 1923–1924 gg." (undated, probably early summer 1924), TsGA-SPb, f. 1001, op. 6, d. 277, ll. 63–67.

78. In the case of Smol'nyi, the iconostasis was not removed until the 1960s; the St. Andrew's Cathedral remained in use for storage purposes until after the collapse of Soviet power (it was transferred to the Orthodox Church by the Kunstkamera in 1993), but the iconostasis survived (as in the case of the Sampson Cathedral, also used for storage in the Soviet period).

79. Antonov and Kobak, *SSPb*. In 2014, the Cathedral was reopened after restoration, to mark the 250th anniversary of the Hermitage's founding.

80. The Karlova Mansion and the Anichkov Palace were in the care of the Museum of the City, while the Sheremet'ev Palace was run by the Russian Museum. See Catriona Kelly, *Remembering St.*

Petersburg (Oxford: Triton Press, 2014), https://www.academia.edu/6847211/REMEMBERING_ST_PETERSBURG, ch. 4.

81. See, for example, "Otchet Restavratsionnogo Otdela," undated (c. 1923), GARF, f. 2307, op. 8, d. 252, ll. 14 ob.–15 ob., which reports work on various ecclesiastical buildings in Moscow (e.g., the Cathedral of the Twelve Apostles in the Kremlin), but work exclusively on secular buildings in Petrograd: for instance, the Hermitage and Winter Palace, the Russian Museum, and the palaces at Peterhof, Detskoe (Tsarskoe) Selo, Pavlovsk, and Oranienbaum. This point is also made by Kaulen, *Muzei-khramy*, 58, who—reasonably enough—also describes the museum world in the city as characterized by "a certain snobbery."

82. See, for example, "Kak ustroit' muzei i vesti ego. Programmnoe rukovodstvo. V muzeinuiu sektsiiu," GARF, f. 2037, op. 10, d. 147, l. 6–6 ob. The document is undated, but has been classified by the archivist as dating from 1918.

83. Trotskaia, "Muzeinoe stroitel'stvo," 42 (removal of *lishnee, zagromozhdaiushchee*), 41 (occasional excesses and list of Kremlin cathedrals, Trinity-St. Sergius and Don Monasteries, New Maiden Convent, St. Basil's Cathedral, Kolomenskoe and D'iakovo, New Jerusalem, "and others" as the sites worthy of preservation).

84. See the material from Vasilieostrovskii district cited in the previous chapter, p. 58.

85. Ibid, p. 59.

86. For the date of 1923, see the oral report by A. K. Nevolin, November 16, 1923, in which he describes the transfer of the Royal Stables Church to the OSP (TsGALI-SPb, f. 32, op. 1, d. 7, l. 126–126 ob.). Cf. the record of a meeting held on October 25, 1927, between representatives of the OSP and the Scientific Office in Moscow (TsGALI-SPb, f. 32, op. 1, d. 4, l. 88); on the contents of the meeting, see also below. The idea of a "church museum" went back further than this: at the Museum Conference in 1919, Konstantin Romanov had presented a paper arguing for the importance of this type of institution (RA IIMK, f. 29, ed. khr. 84, ll. 1–12).

87. TsGALI-SPb, f. 32, op. 1, d. 1, l. 15.

88. "Plan organizatsii Istoriko-Bytovogo Tserkovnogo Muzeia" (May 1924), TsGA-SPb, f. 1001, op. 6, d. 277, l. 31–31 ob.

89. See, for example, TsGA-SPb, f. 1001, op. 6, d. 277, l. 44 (report for July 1924); on the transfer of the category 1 churches, see the documentation in TsGALI-SPb, f. 32, op. 1, d. 37, ll. 8–13. In 1925, items from the Admiralty Church and the earliest (eighteenth-century) St. Isaac's Cathedral were also transferred (ibid., ll. 17–18).

90. See the references dating from January 1925, TsGALI-SPb, f. 32, op. 1, d. 27, l. 26. Note also the use of a new, "ideologically sound" (*ideologicheski vyverennyi*) rhetoric in order to justify the inclusive collection policy: another document of 1925 reiterated the established case that church furnishings should be preserved as *ansambli* with a reference to the decadence of church furnishings in the recent past: "This perfunctory attitude to the requirements of a dying religion was what gave rise to the purely decorative content of church art, which was calculated to make a big impact on the masses with its dramatic character [*obstanovochnost'*], its overwhelming majesty, its abundant use of gilding" (TsGA-SPb, f. 6, op. 277, l. 183–183 ob.).

91. TsGA-SPb, f. 1001, op. 6, d. 277, l. 199 ob. Note that another record from TsGALI, f. 32, op. 1, d. 13, l. 22, records the transfer from the "Miatlev church" of a number of other items, including a carved wooden iconostasis, eight bronze candelabra, various religious artworks, some mahogany pilasters, etc.

92. TsGA-SPb, f. 1001, op. 6, d. 277, ll. 183–88.

93. TsGALI-SPb, f. 32, op. 1, d. 13, l. 26 (June 25, 1926).

94. TsGA-SPb, f. 1001, op. 6, d. 277, l. 185 ob.

95. On the small grant, see TsGALI-SPb, f. 32, op. 1, d. 37, l. 21; on the backing of the Scientific Office, ibid., l. 24. A report on the OSP's activities from October 6, 1923, until October 1, 1926 (TsGA-SPb, f. 1001, op. 6, d. 277, l. 147) mentions the plans to request Glavnauka's support, suggesting that the funding probably came through in late autumn 1926.

96. See TsGA-SPb, f. 1000, op. 11, d. 290, l. 90; and on the Stroganov Palace, TsGA-SPb, f. 1000, op. 11, d. 290, l. 32 (document from March 9, 1927).

97. For the accusations, see "Akt Obsledovaniia 'MUZEIA GORODA' pri otkomkhoze [sic] chlenami sekstii Kommunal'nogo Khoziaistva Leningradskogo Soveta XI sozyva" (c. June 2, 1928), TsGALI-SPb, f. 72, op. 1, d. 3, ll. 72–75; for the results, see the undated report to members of the Provincial Department of Communal Property Management (Oblotkomkhoz) (evidently from 1929), TsGALI-SPb, f. 72, op. 1, d. 3, ll. 65–66. A similar process of deaccessioning also affected, for example, the "museum of daily life" in the Sheremet'ev Palace on the Fontanka (Iu. N. Zhukov, Stalin: Operatsiia Ermitazh [Moscow: Vagrius, 2005], 103), where a decision was made to replace saleable objects with less valuable ones, supposedly equally suitable for display.

98. TsGALI-SPb, f. 32, op. 1, d. 4, l. 88.

99. Museum "rationalization" is one of the best-known episodes of the early Stalin era, but it has most often been discussed from the point of view of the mega-museums themselves, in particular the Hermitage. See, for example, the collection of documents Ermitazh, kotoryi my poteriali, ed. N. M. Serapina (St. Petersburg: Zhurnal Neva, 2001); Zhukov, Stalin; Anne Odom and Wendy Salmond, eds., Treasures into Tractors: The Selling of Russia's Cultural Heritage, 1918–1938 (Washington, DC: Hillwood Estate, 2009). On the Museum of the City, see also chapter 4 of Kelly, Remembering St. Petersburg. For informative discussions that include material about what happened to the displaced objects, see the articles collected in N. Iu. Semenova and N. V. Iljine, eds., Selling Russia's Treasures: The Soviet Trade in Nationalized Art, 1917–1938 (Paris: The M. T. Abraham Center for the Arts Foundation, 2013).

100. L. N. Finn et al., Iz ochaga mrakobesiia v ochag kul'tury (Leningrad: OGIZ-Priboi, 1931), 6. In more detail, this meant a display of "the material from which it is constructed in the light of theoretical problems of the natural sciences," and "drawing a contrast between the principles of construction in the aristocratic empire and those of our modern socialist construction" (ibid.). For further details of the exhibition strategy, see chapter 3.

101. See Kaulen, Muzei-khramy, 132–35. For the quotation, see 133 (citing a statement by the Moscow Trade Unions' Culture Department, 1928). It should be said that even in 1919, Romanov's plan for a church museum met a divided response. The Museums Conference voted by fifteen to twelve to reject it, and the session chair, Nikolai Punin, and leading avant-garde pundit, Osip Brik, were among those who spoke against, though Nikolai Marr, the famous linguist and influential director of the Academy of the History of Material Culture (AIMK), spoke in favor. See K. K. Romanov, "Tserkovnyi muzei: Doklad na Gumanitarno-Khudozhestvennoi Sektsii Muzeinoi Konferentsii; Preniia po dokladu," RA IIMK, f. 29, op. 1, d. 84, ll. 6–11.

102. GARF, f. 2307, op. 3, d. 19, ll. 11–12.

103. NA UGIOP, pap. 173, t. 1 (former Church of Saints Simeon and Anne, 1922–1940), ll. 164–65. Soft distemper (kleevaia kraska) is a paint medium made of limewash, with glue used as a fixative; it was used for wall paintings as well as rendering surfaces.

104. NA UGIOP, pap. 171, t. 1, Spaso-Preobrazhenskii sobor: Perepiska, 1919–1940, l. 119, l. 112 (leaves in reverse chronological order).

105. TsGA-SPb, f. 1000, op. 6, d. 266, l. 33, August 27, 1927. This was a case where the executive committee of the local soviet behaved with more understanding: "Given that the dvadtsatka of the St. Andrew's Cathedral has already purchased the building materials and that painting with oil-based paint has already started, and the very late announcement by Glavnauka to the dvadtsatka about how they were supposed to use lime-based paint and not oil-based paint, it is proposed to require the dvadtsatka to use the materials already prepared (the paint) in according to the anticipated purpose." Quoted from A. G. Lipman, "Materialy istoriko-arkhitekturnoi pasportizatsii b. Andreevskogo sobora," 1941, NA UGIOP, pap. 8/2, file 151, l. 37.

106. TsGA-SPb, f. 7384, op. 33, d. 13, l. 17–17 ob.

107. See the letter from Otkomkhoz to the Management Department of the Petrograd District Soviet, December 12, 1922, TsGA-SPb, f. 1001, op. 7, d. 19, l. 9.

108. See the report signed by the guberniia architect, S. Korchagin, presented to the presidium of the Leningrad Gubispolkom, October 28, 1926, Tsentral'nyi gosudarstvennyi arkhiv nauchno-tekhnicheskoi dokumentatsiia Sankt-Peterburga (hereafter TsGANTD-SPb), f. 192, op. 3–1, d. 9277, l. 6.

109. Only a couple of important cases relating to listed monuments are mentioned here, but the materials in the fond of the Leningrad Regional Directorate of Buildings Control (Leningradskoe oblastnoe upravlenie stroitel'nogo kontrolia), TsGANTD-SPb, f. 192, op. 3–1, d. 9277, include over twenty other cases where the religious associations using buildings were subjected to inspections at this time (in some cases, such as the Trinity-Izmailovskii Regiment Cathedral and the Church of the Transfiguration at the Porcelain Factory, both also listed monuments, the results for the users were less threatening, since only minor repairs were required).

110. See, for example, the plan of the Museums Department's Architectural Section for 1921, RA IIMK, f. 67, ed. khr. 58, l. 6.

111. "Obrashchenie ot Dvadtsatki Troitsko-Petrovskogo sobora" (with stamp of receipt, August 22, 1927), TsGANTD-SPb, f. 192, op. 3–1, d. 9277, l. 293.

112. For the complete text of Sergii's Declaration, see http://www.sedmitza.ru/lib/text/440043/. For a discussion of its consequences in the long-term "accommodation" of the Church to state directives, see Natalia Shlikhta, "'Orthodox' and 'Soviet': On the Issue of the Identity of Christian Soviet Citizens (1940s–early 1970s)," *Forum for Anthropology and Culture* 11 (2015), pp. 140–64.

113. See the NKVD circular, "O poriadke zakrytiia molitvennykh zdanii i likvidatsii tserkovnogo imushchestva" (September 19, 1927), *Biulleten' NKVD* 26 (1927): 456–59. It is possible that the public safety objections raised up mid-1927 were not wholly the product of an antireligious drive (it is notable that the documents on necessary repairs are filed with other materials from the Leningrad Regional Directorate of Buildings Control [f. 192 of TsGANTD-SPb], rather than in the district or citywide Church Offices). But the September 19, 1927, circular marked a shift to a campaign specifically directed against church users.

114. "Vypiska iz protokola No. 31 Prezidiuma Leningradskogo soveta ot 30/X-1926," TsGANTD-SPb, f. 192, op. 3–1, d. 9277, l. 5.

115. There is evidence for the systematic reassignment of churches to the Renovationists in 1924 (as well as the Prince Vladimir Cathedral; another case was the Mother of God of Smolensk Church: see TsGA-SPb, f. 7384, op. 33, d. 60, l. 317). On June 5, 1925, OGPU (Unified State Political Directorate) officials recommended leaving the Cathedral of the Transfiguration in the hands of Renovationists, "as the most loyal group toward Soviet power" (TsGA-SPb, f. 7384, op. 33, d. 18, l. 1 ob.). But in 1926–1927, Church of Renovation groups were harassed just as readily on administrative grounds. One effect of Metropolitan Sergii's July 29, 1927, declaration was to fissure Orthodoxy's conservatives (the "Tikhonites," "Josephites," and "Philippites" all had representation in Leningrad). (See M. V. Shkarovskii, *Iosiflianstvo: Techenie v Russkoi Pravoslavnoi Tserkvi* [St. Petersburg: Memorial, 1999].) But another was to strip away the Renovationists' former advantage. After 1929, churches belonging to all the different groups were harassed in equal measure. A planning document from 1932 recognized the need to "preserve the current proportions between the different directions [of Orthodoxy]," but in the all-out campaign for closures, such niceties were forgotten, and the policy was to have no more than one Orthodox church working in any city district, irrespective of denomination (see the list of 1940, TsGA-SPb, f. 7384, op. 33, d. 74, l. 1). Post-Soviet historians of the Orthodox Church writing in Russia itself have generally presented the Church of Renovation in a uniformly negative light, alleging that the Church not only pullulated with pro-government spies, but was responsible for other types of unsavory behavior, such as neglect of the churches that it was assigned. See, for example, the comments in A. K. Galkin, A. V. Bertash, and M. V. Shkarovskii, *Kniaz'-Vladimirskii sobor: Kratkii istoricheskii ocherk* (St. Petersburg: Kniaz'-Vladimirskii sobor, 2005), 13: "The 'care' exercised by the 'Protopresbyter of All Rus'" V. Krasnitskii extended merely to the construction of an angled awning above the western parvis. This construction was supposed to protect the members of the Living Church from falling plaster, proper repairs to the church being beyond their capacities." It would be risky, however, to take evidence from the 1926–1927 crackdown on health and safety as an

indication of the objective conditions in the buildings inspected (one could equally conclude that the strictures of the heritage protection bodies against members of the Tikhonite and Sergievite tendencies demonstrated that they did not "care" about repairing their churches). A more cogent argument would be that, since the Church of Renovation had little popular support in Leningrad (on which, see Anatolii Krasnov-Levitin, *Likhie gody, 1925–1941* [Paris: YMCA, 1977]), raising funds for repairs was particularly difficult.

116. On Bishop Antonin's experiments, see Krasnov-Levitin and Shavrov, *Ocherkii po istorii*, vol. 1, chapter "1922."

117. "O poriadke zakrytiia molitvennykh zdanii," September 19, 1927, *Biulleten' NKVD* 26 (1927): 459.

118. For an incisive discussion of this period, see Sheila Fitzpatrick, "The 'Soft Line' on Culture and Its Enemies," in her *The Cultural Front: Power and Culture in Revolutionary Russia* (Ithaca, NY: Cornell University Press, 1992), ch. 5.

119. RA IIMK, f. 67, ed. khr. 86, l. 3. Mikhail Rogov (1880–1942), at the time chairman of Mossovet, the organ of city governance in Moscow, was promoted in 1930 to chairman of Gosplan (the state planning organization), a clear sign of high favor with the Party leadership.

120. RA IIMK, f. 67, ed. khr. 86, ll. 4–5.

121. A background to this was, of course, the general replanning of what a 1926 article had termed Moscow's "narrow crooked streets with their irregular façade lines" and sidewalks of varying widths, and the provision of avenues to rival Nevsky Prospect, or Kiev's Kreshchatik and Odessa's Deribassovskaia: G. Bebutov, "K voprosu o regulirovanii ulichnogo dvizheniia," *Kommunal'noe khoziaistvo* 1 (1926): 13–14. See also V. A. Lozhkin, "Chto takoe urbanizm?," *Kommunal'noe khoziaistvo* 17 (1925): 15–26; G. Krasin, "K voprosu o budushchei 'Bol'shoi Moskve,'" *Kommunal'noe khoziaistvo* 2 (1926): 17–20.

122. These furnishings are preserved in Kirov's museum apartment (visit, 2005).

123. RA IIMK, f. 67, ed. khr. 86, l. 3.

124. RA IIMK, f. 67, ed. khr. 86, l. 13.

125. "Spisok pustuiushchikh tserkvei, sostavlennyi na osnovanii dannykh Administrativnogo otdela Leningradskogo oblastnogo ispolkoma," TsGA-SPb, f. 3199, op. 2, d. 428, l. 6.

126. TsGA-SPb, f. 3199, op. 2, d. 428, l. 7.

127. It was then in the first category, as recognized by the Special Commission on the Sequestration of Church Valuables: see RA IIMK, f. 29, ed. khr. 847, ll. 3–4.

128. "Spisok zdanii kul'ta v g. Leningrade nakhodiashchikhsia pod gosudarstvennoi okranoi" (1927), TsGANTD-SPb, f. 192, op. 3–1, d. 9277, ll. 459–62. See also appendix 1.

129. "Material k Agitpropkollegii Oblastkoma VKP/b/ 24 Aprelia 1928 g.," TsGAIPD-SPb, f. 24, op. 8, d. 53, l. 26. The file also contains a draft decree of the Party provincial committee on antireligious propaganda dating from May 1928 (ibid., ll. 35–36).

Chapter Three

1. TsGAIPD-SPb, f. 24, op. 2v, d. 12, l. 15.

2. Gregory Freeze, "The Stalinist Assault on the Parish, 1929–1941," in *Stalinismus vor dem Zweiten Weltkrieg: Neue Wege der Forschung*, ed. Manfred Hildermeier (Munich: R. Oldenburg Verlag, 1998), 213.

3. Ibid.

4. See, for example, David L. Hoffmann, *Peasant Metropolis: Social Identities in Moscow, 1929–1941* (Ithaca, NY: Cornell University Press, 1994).

5. Albert Baiburin, "The Wrong Nationality: Ascribed Identity in the 1930s Soviet Union," in *Russian Cultural Anthropology since the Collapse of Communism*, ed. Albert Baiburin, Catriona Kelly, and Nikolai Vakhtin (London: Routledge, 2012), 59–76; Paul Hagenloh, *Stalin's Police: Public Order and Mass Repression in the USSR, 1926–1941* (Washington, DC: Woodrow Wilson Center, 2009);

David Shearer, *Policing Stalin's Socialism: Repression and Social Order in the Soviet Union, 1924–1953* (New Haven, CT: Yale University Press, 2009).

6. See, for example, Tat'jana Leont'eva, "Kirchen und Religionsgemeinschaften in den Jahren der "bolschewistischen Perestrojka" im Gebiet Kalinin," in *Stalinismus in der sowjetischen Provinz 1937–1938: Die Massenaktion aufgrund des operativen Befehls no. 00447*, ed. Rolf Binner, Bernd Bonwetsch, and Marc Junge (Berlin: Akademie Verlag, 2010), 235–66; Andrej Kolesnikov, "Die Verfolgung der Russischen Orthodoxen Kirche im Altaj," ibid., 267–86.

7. There is an abundant literature on the repression of the Church in the prewar years. Recent studies include M. I. Odintsov, ed., *Russkaia Pravoslavnaia Tserkov' nakanune i v epokhu stalinskogo sotsializma 1917–1953 gg.* (Moscow: ROSSPEN, 2014); M. V. Shkarovskii, *Russkaia Pravoslavnaia Tserkov' v XX veke* (Moscow: Veche/Lepta, 2010). Shkarovskii's publications on Leningrad, particularly *Sankt-Peterburgskaia eparkhiia v dvadtsatom veke v svete arkhivnykh materialov* (St. Petersburg: Liki Rossii, 2000), and *Peterburgskaia eparkhiia v gody gonenii i utrat, 1917–1945* (St. Petersburg: Liki Rossii, 1995) are invaluable sources of information about the process in Leningrad. A. A. Pogrebskaia, "Ob ispol'zovanii tserkvei Leningrada, zakrytykh v 1930-e gody", *Trudy Istoricheskogo fakul'teta Sankt-Peterburgskogo universiteta* 2 (2010), 317-326, is a useful outline of the fate of some notable churches, particularly the Cathedral of the Savior on the Blood, based on official orders and letters from members of the public, though its representation of the situation in terms of a straightforward divide between "the authorities" and "society" over-simplifies the situation.

8. "O religioznykh ob"edineniiakh," *SU* 35 (1929): item 36. See also appendix 3.

9. Freeze, "The Stalinist Assault," 213.

10. On the political position of the Antireligious Committee, see the useful commentaries in Ludwig Steindorff and Günther Schulz, *Partei und Kirchen im frühen Sowjetstaat: Die Protokolle der antireligiösen Kommission beim Zentralkomitee der Russischen Kommunistischen Partei (Bol'ševiki) 1922–1929* (Münster: LIT, 2007).

11. Freeze, "The Stalinist Assault," 224, cites a figure of thirty-three churches in Leningrad closed officially in 1930–1932, but 322 that had ceased to function over the same period.

12. According to figures given by Roslof (*Red Priests*, 181, table 6.2), on February 6, 1931, the Central Standing Commission on Religious Questions returned thirty-seven out of forty-two closed churches to believers; on April 6, 1931, fourteen out of seventeen; but on May 6, 1931, only fifteen out of forty-five; on June 16, 1931, twenty-one out of sixty-one; on July 26, 1931, one out of nineteen, and on August 6, 1931, zero out of ten. Odintsov, *Russkaia Pravoslavnaia Tserkov'*, 202, points to a steep rise in petitions from 1929 to 1934 (5,242 to 8,229); in 1934, only fourteen out of 105 reassessed cases declined the proposal to close a religious building. The numbers of reassessments went up in 1935–1937 (323, 420, 359), but the proportions of agreed closures remained high (323, 308, 253) (ibid., 212).

13. On Magnitogorsk, see Stephen Kotkin, *Magnetic Mountain: Stalinism as a Civilization* (Berkeley: University of California Press, 1995); on Moscow, see, for example, Timothy Colton, *Moscow: Governing the Socialist Metropolis* (Cambridge, MA: Belknap Press, 1995).

14. See, for example, Evgeny Dobrenko and Eric Naiman, eds., *The Landscape of Stalinism: The Art and Ideology of Soviet Space* (Seattle: University of Washington Press, 2003).

15. There is a large literature on the new subjectivity. See, for example, Sheila Fitzpatrick, *The Cultural Front: Power and Culture in Revolutionary Russia* (Ithaca, NY: Cornell University Press, 1992); Jochen Hellbeck, *Revolution on My Mind: Writing a Diary under Stalin* (Cambridge, MA: Harvard University Press, 2006); David L. Hoffmann, *Stalinist Values: The Cultural Norms of Soviet Modernity, 1917–1941* (Ithaca, NY: Cornell University Press, 2003).

16. For a useful discussion of the complexities of the results at a detailed level (typical responses ran, "I work in the construction industry, so I suppose I must be a non-believer," and "Only God knows whether I am a believer"), see V. B. Zhiromskaia, "Religioznost' naroda v 1937 godu," *Istoricheskii vestnik* 1 (2000), http://krotov.info/history/20/1930/1937_zher.htm.

17. On the transfer to the localities, see, for example, A. L. Beglov, *V poiskakh "bezgreshnykh katakomb": Tserkovnoe podpol'e v SSSR* (Moscow: Izdatel'skii sovet Russkoi Pravoslavnoi Tserkvi, 2008), 114.

18. This can be seen in the press of the day—*Leningradskaia pravda* (*LP*), *Vechernii Leningrad* (*VL*), and *Smena*, and in literary sources, such as the poetry of Ol'ga Berggol'ts, photography, and memoirs. This image of the city persisted into the late 1950s and 1960s onward—see Catriona Kelly, *St. Petersburg: Shadows of the Past* (New Haven, CT: Yale University Press, 2014), ch. 4.

19. On the rising importance of the defense industry at this period, see A. N. Shcherba, *Voennaia promyshlennost' Leningrada v 20-30-e gody* (St. Petersburg: Nestor, 1999).

20. See particularly Igal Halfin, *Stalinist Confessions: Messianism and Terror at the Leningrad Communist University* (Pittsburgh, PA: University of Pittsburgh Press, 2009); Andy Willimott, *Living the Revolution: Urban Communes and Soviet Socialism, 1917–1932* (Oxford: Oxford University Press, 2016).

21. Julia Obertreis, *Tränen des Sozialismus: Wohnen in Leningrad zwischen Alltag und Utopie, 1917–1937* (Cologne: Böhlau, 2004); Anatole Kopp, *Town and Revolution: Soviet Architecture and City Planning, 1917–1935* (London: Thames and Hudson, 1970).

22. See, for example, *Bezbozhniki sotsialisticheskoi derevni navstrechu 4-mu godu piatiletki: Antirozhdestvenskii Sbornik* (Leningrad: Lenizdat, 1931); *Bezbozhniki za rabotoi: Iz opyta raboty iacheek Soiuza voinstvuiushchikh bezbozhnikov Leningrada i Leningradskoi oblasti* (Leningrad: Lenizdat, 1938).

23. See, for example, "Spisok chlenov 20-ki tserkvi Sv. Simeoniia i Anny, chto na ulitse Belinskogo d. No. 6 na 1933 god," TsGA-SPb, f. 7384, op. 33, d. 28, l. 170 ob.–171 ob.; "Spisok chlenov 20-ki na 1-e fevralia 1937 g." (Troitsko-Izmailovskii sobor), TsGA-SPb, f. 7384, op. 33, d. 168, l. 70; for the Znamenskaia Church in 1937, see TsGA-SPb, f. 7384, op. 33, d. 68, ll. 9–11. It should be said that the increasing ages (accompanied by feminization, see below) of church populations had advantages in terms of their survival, since it kept them "below the radar" of surveillance. However, it did represent a transformation of the previous situation, in contrast to, say, the communities of "priestless" Old Believers, among whom it had always been customary for piety to be expected of older generations, allowing younger people to live "in the world." See Douglas Rogers, "Old Belief between 'Society' and 'Culture': Remaking Moral Communities and Inequalities on a Former State Farm," in *Religion, Morality, and Community in Post-Soviet Societies*, ed. Mark D. Steinberg and Catherine Wanner (Bloomington: Indiana University Press, 2008), 118–24.

24. See Anatolii Krasnov-Levitin's recollections: "The working classes didn't go to church much. It was mostly the small fry of Petersburg: janitors and watchmen, clerks. Members of the intelligentsia too." There was also a marked gender imbalance: "Mostly women in kerchiefs, old and young" (*Likhie gody, 1925–1941* [Paris: YMCA, 1977], 75–76). The prevalence of requests to resign from *dvadtsatki* in church files at dates when pressure was being applied to close the churches (ubiquitous in f. 7384 of TsGA-SPb) is an indication of manipulation behind the scenes. The 1937 Census, by contrast, suggested that there was a high proportion of believers among educated people in their twenties: see Zhiromskaia, "Religioznost' naroda," but without a detailed regional breakdown, it is impossible to tell whether this also applied in Leningrad.

25. "Doklad tov. Dulova," TsGAIPD-SPb, f. 24, op. 8, d. 293, l. 101 (he attributed this to "the presence of class-alien elements"). A standard form of exile allowed those penalized to settle only 101 kilometers or more from the city limits.

26. As recounted in a June 2, 1940, letter to the Party authorities from one Iulii Blom, who claimed that acquaintances of his had behaved like this: TsGAIPD-SPb, f. 24, op. 2v, d. 4410, ll. 41–43. As related by I. N. Donina, "Obyknovennyi ateizm," *Klio* 82, no. 8 (2008) (my thanks to Aleksandr Burov for providing me with a copy of this text), "believing atheists" were often just as confused about the boundaries of acceptable and unacceptable practices.

27. Una Pope-Hennessey, *The Closed City: Impressions of a Visit to Leningrad* (London: Hutchinson, 1938), 217.

28. TsGA-SPb, f. 7834, op. 33, d. 76, l. 12.

29. See Ioann (Snychev), *Ocherki istorii Sankt-Peterburgskoi eparkhii* (St. Petersburg: Andreev i synov'ia, 1994), 262. The problem with this argument is that Kirov's regular route into the city center would have taken him past just one church, the Trinity Cathedral on Revolution Square.

30. This militancy continued in later years also. See, for example, the materials for 1932 in TsGA-SPb, f. 1000, op. 49, d. 40.

31. See the material in the Politprosvet files of the Obkom from 1928 in TsGAIPD-SPb, f. 24, op. 8, d. 53, ll. 31–33. There is a brief account of the League's work in N. B. Lebina, "Deiatel'nost' 'voin-stvuiushchikh bezbozhnikov' i ikh sud'ba," *Voprosy istorii* 5–6 (1996): 154–57. Daniel Peris, *Storming the Heavens: The Soviet League of the Militant Godless* (Ithaca, NY: Cornell University Press, 1998), emphasizes the unusually active work of the Leningrad League.

32. For the lobbying, see *KG*, June 11, 1929, which refers to the participation of the League in the campaign to close St. Paraskeva's Church, and the petition mounted in the same cause by the "Proletarian List of the Foundry of the proletarian [*sic*] factory [and] the Militant League [*sic*] of the godless," TsGA-SPb, f. 1000, op. 13, l. 92, l. 222. For the tallies of churches, see, for example, the report from 1936 at TsGAIPD-SPb, f. 24, op. 8, d. 293, ll. 60–63.

33. For example, the report of 1936 complained that officials right across Leningrad and its province were slack in their surveillance: "The conduct of affairs relating to the preservation and maintenance of cultic buildings is poor. Inventories are present by no means everywhere, and as a rule there are no regular checks on the condition of preservation of church goods" (TsGAIPD-SPb, f. 24, op. 8, d. 293, l. 59).

34. See, for example, the item in the minutes of a March 27, 1924, meeting of the presidium of the Executive Committee of the Leningrad provincial soviet relating to the Mother of God of Smolensk Church, which proposed that the contract should be terminated and the church given to another group of worshippers, "bearing in mind the fact that the *dvadtsatka* of the Smolensk cemetery churches has, instead of its primary duties, carried out agitation hostile to Soviet power and by acting in this way, has brought about a series of intolerable excesses" (TsGA-SPb, f. 7384, op. 33, d. 60, l. 317). This was, of course, a strategy to place churches in the hands of amenable groups, such as the Church of Renovation (as in this case), and was therefore particularly common when the rapprochement with the Church of Renovation was at its height, in the mid-1920s. See also chapter 2.

35. "Doklad tov. Dulova o sostoianii i deiatel'nosti religioznykh organizatsii i religioznosti naseleniia Leningradskoi oblasti," March 29, 1936, TSGAIPD-SPb, f. 24, op. 8, d. 293, l. 123.

36. "Doklad tov. Dulova," l. 105, reported that the *dvadtsatka* of the Church of the Sign in Leningrad included a train driver, and that there were nurses in the *dvadtsatka* of the Prince Vladimir and Trinity Cathedrals. This information had been passed to "directors of the enterprises in question."

37. For a case of an appeal in the 1920s, see chapter 2.

38. See, for example, the provisions on priests in TsGA-SPb, f. 7384, op. 2, d. 20, ll. 5–6.

39. "O nachal'nykh meropriiatiiakh po preobrazovaniiu i razvitiiu Leningrada v obraztsovyi sovetskii i podlinno sotsialisticheskii gorod" (signed V. Molotov), *Izvestiia*, December 4, 1931; reprinted in *Vestnik Leningradskogo Oblispolkoma i Leningradskogo Soveta* 161 (1931): 1.

40. On Baranov's biography, see chapter 4.

41. "O nachal'nykh meropriiatiiakh", 1.

42. Here and below, quotations are from G. A. Tiurin, "Ob ispol'zovanii zdanii zakrytykh tserkvei i molitvennykh domov," TsGA-SPb, f. 7384, op. 33, d. 50, ll. 10–13. My English translation here and below attempts to capture the ungainly nature of the original.

43. Again, my translation attempts to capture the style.

44. The official name of Nevsky Prospect between 1918 and 1944.

45. TsGA-SPb, f. 7384, op. 33, d. 163, l. 89.

46. See, for example, Michael Gorham, "Tongue-Tied Writers: The *Rabsel'kor* Movement and the Voice of the New Intelligentsia," *Russian Review* 55, no. 3 (1996): 412–29; Matthew Lenoe, *Closer to the Masses: Stalinist Culture, Social Revolution, and Soviet Newspapers* (Cambridge, MA: Harvard University Press, 2004).

47. See further in TsGA-SPb, f. 7384, op. 33, d. 50, l. 170; TsGA-SPb, f. 7384, op. 33, d. 76, ll. 26–44.

48. Mikosha's film, viewed from beginning to end, emphasizes the hard work of prizing off sculptures and marble cladding, removing icons from their cases and dismantling them, stacking

the dynamite against the walls, and so on. However, it was a clip of the demolition itself that was to become famous, making its way into, for instance, the film show about the reconstruction of Moscow in Aleksandr Medvedkin's 1938 film *New Moscow* (shelved before release after hostile reviews in the Soviet press, but an iconic film in the post-Soviet period). To this day, clips from Mikosha's film are much easier to find than the complete movie, for which, see www.net-film.ru.

49. See an estimate from 1931 that to blow up the Chesme Church would have raised 34,000 rubles' worth of building materials, but the demolition, plus the cost of the detailed survey required by the Monuments Office, would have added up to 21,500 rubles, "not including the cost of the church" (in the sense, presumably, of what would now be termed "opportunity costs," or the expense of finding other space to replace that lost, etc.). See TsGA-SPb, f. 1000, op. 49, d. 37, l. 34. On the risks, see, for example, the top secret report to Iakov Kapustin, a secretary of the Leningrad City Committee, in 1941, which noted that work on blowing up the Church of the Sign, because of the carelessness of the builders doing the demolition, needed to be delayed for several days because "if an explosion takes place, the buildings nearby may be damaged" (TsGAIPD-SPb, f. 27, op. 2b, d. 983, ll. 86–87).

50. See the June 20, 1933 report by K. M. Negliuevich, the head of Admnadzor (the Administration and Surveillance Section of Lenoblispolkom), and head of the Commission on Religious Issues, established in early summer 1930: "Sixteen objects [i.e., buildings] are being demolished with long delays and a check has established that the work has ground to a halt and almost nothing is happening" (Shkarovskii, *Sankt-Peterburgskaia eparkhiia*, 183). Negliuevich's initials and role as head of the Commission on Religious Issues, see Pogrebskaia, "Ob ispol'zovanii tserkvei Leningrada", 318.

51. See the reports in appendix 2, for example, TsGA-SPb, op. 51, d. 35, l. 13. My thanks to Alexandra Piir for copying this material.

52. A remarkable case of transformation at the national level was Aleksandr Aleksandrov (1883–1946), co-founder in 1928 of the Red Army Chorus and Stalin Prize winner, who until 1922 had been the choir-master at the Cathedral of Christ the Redeemer. See Marina Frolova-Walker, *Stalin's Music Prize* (New Haven, CT: Yale University Press, 2016).

53. TsGA-SPb, f. 1000, op. 49, d. 40, l. 13. One could perhaps compare the "rehabilitation" of "bourgeois" dwellings as "communal apartments" in the 1920s, a strategy that was both practical (because of housing shortages) and ideological—the apartments were supposed to propound "communal values." The fullest study of the history of this process is Obertreis, *Tränen des Sozialismus*.

54. "General'nyi plan razvitiia Leningrada," TsGA-SPb, f. 7384, op. 20, d. 1, l. 17. The tram would, the plan stated, remain the "basic form of transport" during the period in question. On the importance of the embankments and the plan to extend the granite casing to Rybatskoe southward and up the Malaia and Bol'shaia Nevka, see ibid., l. 66, l. 129.

55. An early example of a "cultic building" demolished on these grounds (or ostensibly so) was the Church of the Annunciation on Labor Square (ploshchad' Truda), pulled down in 1929 (Antonov and Kobak, *SSPb*).

56. On the Church of the Sign, see below. A later example of a metro station built on the site of a church was Sennaia (see chs. 4, 5). It is tempting to regard stations as alternative "temples," as argued for Moscow by Andrew Jenks, "A Metro on the Mount: The Underground as a Church of Soviet Civilization," *Technology and Culture* 41, no. 4 (2000): 697–724, but a comment by Lazar' Kaganovich, "These aren't cathedrals, after all, but stations for an underground railroad," quoted by Jenks himself on p. 718, suggests that the authorities specifically sought to play down this analogy. And the eventual design for the station pavilion on ploshchad' Vosstaniia was more closely analogous to the Soviet-era park architecture of the Tauride Gardens than to Orthodox churches.

57. See, for example, the documentation relating to the Church of the Savior Not Made by Human Hands in the Volkovo Cemetery: on August 2, 1935, the APU of Lensovet stated that it had no objection to the building's demolition, but on October 28, 1935, VTsIK replied, "This memorandum [*spravka*] is not sufficient for our purposes. We require accurate information about whether the church is included in the plan for the reconstruction of the city and the cemetery" (TsGA-SPb, f. 7384, op. 33, d. 177, ll. 11, 14).

58. This project, realized in 1934, was the last important conversion of an ecclesiastical building, and took place at the last possible moment, since Constructivist architecture was at the point of falling out of favor. Despite its remodeling by a rated architect, Fedor Demertsov, in 1796–1800, the St. Sergius Artillery Cathedral was a building of mixed date (never a point of favor with conservationists), and as a military church, it was also ideologically objectionable (cf. the case of the Trinity-Izmailovskii Regiment Cathedral below). P. M. Grinberg and G. S. Raits's reconstruction of the German Reformed Church on the Moika as the Palace of Culture of the Communication Workers' Union (1932–1939) is the only other comparable rebuild, this time with a building that was not a listed monument.

59. "Ustav Stroitel'nyi," article 90, point 3. I. D. Mordukhai-Boltovskii, ed., *Svod zakonov Rossiiskoi Imperii* (St. Petersburg: Knizhnoe tovarishchestvo Deiatel', 1912), 12:1:220.

60. "Spisok chlenov soveta Obshchestva" (1930), TsGA-SPb, f. 1000, op. 48, d. 99, l. 11. For Proskurin's career, see http://www.snor.ru/?an=pers_402.

61. "Otchet Obshchestva 'Staryi Peterburg-Novyi Leningrad' za 1930 g.," TsGA-SPb, f. 1000, op. 48, d. 99, l. 5. The actual architect of the chapel, finished in 1866, was R. I. Kuz'min; Georg Friedrich Veldten, court architect to Catherine II, had died in 1801. This is a striking indication of the loss of expertise (or interest) among the members of the OSP. It should be said that these public calls for demolition were certainly accompanied by less public attempts to save churches that the OSP did value: for instance, the minutes of a meeting held on February 7, 1930, record that A. G. Iatsevich had reported on his visit to Glavnauka on January 18, 1930, to discuss "issues relating to the church of the Widows' Refuge at Smol'nyi and to the destruction of the Golitsyn church" (TsGALI-SPb, f. 32, op. 1, d. 62, l. 15).

62. See letter from Zoia Novikova, widow of the engineer at the electrical welding works that had been charged with making the section of fencing, December 5, 1972, TsGALI-SPb, f. 229, op. 1, d. 72, ll. 131–32. There is further on this letter in chapter 6 below.

63. Quotation from a lecture given by Professor V. S. Karpovich, "Problema Leningrada, kak sotsialisticheskogo goroda," in "Otchet Ob-va 'Staryi Peterburg-Novyi Leningrad' za period vremeni s 1 Maia po 1 Oktiabria 1930 g.," TsGALI-SPb, f. 32, op. 1, d. 3, ll. 149–50.

64. *Leningrad—obraztsovyi sotsialisticheskii gorod: Novostroiki 1932 g.* (Leningrad: OGIZ-IZOGIZ, 1932), 11.

65. "Nashi zadachi," *Arkhitektura SSSR* 1 (1933): 1. Emphasis original.

66. L. Il'in, "Ansambl' v arkhitekturnom oblike Leningrada," *Arkhitektura SSSR* 2 (1933): 9–11.

67. Ibid., 9.

68. The principle of a new southern center was retained after Nikolai Baranov took over directing work on the Plan: see the decision of the Executive Committee of Lensovet, February 28, 1941, TsGALI-SPb, f. 341, op. 1, d. 78, ll. 8–10. The planned transformation of the Haymarket, and Baranov's role, is discussed in chapter 4.

69. F. E. Enakiev, *Zadachi preobrazovaniia Sankt-Peterburga* (St. Petersburg: Tovarishchestvo R. Golike i A. Vil'borg, 1912). See also Vadim Bass, *Peterburgskaia neoklassika 1900–1910-kh gg.: Arkhitekturnye konkursy; Zodchii, tsekh, gorod* (St. Petersburg: NP-Print, 2005); Bass, *Peterburgskaia neoklassicheskaia arkhitektura 1900–1910-kh gg. v zerkale konkursov: Slovo i forma* (St. Petersburg: Evropeiskii universitet, 2010).

70. Comrade Kryzhanovskii, "Stenograficheskii otchet sovmestnogo zasedaniia shefov po okhrane pamiatnikov i spetsinspektsii Lensoveta o blagoustroistve i uluchshenii okhrany pamiatnikov stariny v Leningrade," February 15, 1934, TsGALI-SPb, f. 32, op. 1, d. 71, l. 9.

71. Rossi was the subject of five monographs published between 1937 and 1956, as well as a candidate of sciences dissertation (see the catalogue of the Russian National Library). Among them were V. A. Panov, *Karlo Rossi 1775–1849* (Moscow, 1937); G. G. Grimm, *Ploshchad' Iskusstv i Ploshchad' Ostrovskogo* (Moscow: Iskusstvo, 1946); V. I. Piliavskii, *Zodchii Rossi* (Moscow: Gos. izd-vo arkhitektury i gradostroitel'stva, 1951). Most other leading architects were the subject of just one monograph at best. As Owen Hatherley points out (*Landscapes of Communism: A History through Buildings* [London: Allen Lane, 2015]), knock-offs of Rossi's General Staff Building archway were used along Gorky Street

(and, one could add, in many other prestigious developments of the 1930s, for instance the model flats along ulitsa Polyarnikov in Leningrad).

72. "Otchet OSP-NL za 1930 god," TsGA-SPb, f. 1000, op. 48, d. 99, l. 3.

73. Ibid., ll. 4–9.

74. "Nashi zadachi," *Arkhitektura Leningrada* 1 (1936): 6–9. For material on the past, see, for example, the articles by OSP members N. E. Lansere, "Adrian Dmitrievich Zakharov," *Arkhitektura Leningrada* 1 (1937): 40–46, and A. Iatsevich, "Peterburg v tvorchestve Pushkina," ibid., 60–62.

75. "Tsirkuliar NKP po Glavnauke vsem krai-, obl- i gubono i muzeinym p/otdelam pri nikh, No. 500/002/66 ot 17/1 1928 g.," *Biulleten' Narkomprosa*, January 17, 1928, 2.

76. "Spisok arkhitekturnykh pamiatnikov g. Leningrad, sostoiashchikh pod Gosudarstvennoi Okhranoi," TsGALI-SPb, f. 32, op. 1, d. 61, ll. 78–87 ob. See also appendix 1. The Old St. Petersburg Society's report on activities in 1930 refers to "the assignment from the Department of Communal Property Management [Otkomkhoz] to compile an exhaustive list of all the monuments in Leningrad," to be carried out by the OSP's plenipotentiaries (TsGA-SPb, f. 1000, op. 48, d. 99, l. 3), of which the earlier and later lists are presumably different versions.

77. "Spisok arkhitekturnykh pamiatnikov g. Leningrada, sostoiashchikh pod Gosudarstvennoi Okhranoi," TsGALI-SPb, f. 32, op. 1, d. 61, ll. 4–15.

78. "Tsirkuliar NKP po Glavnauke vsem krai-, obl- i gubono i muzeinym p/otdelam pri nikh," 2.

79. For Vsevolozhskii's former position, see NA UGIOP, pap. 171 (Cathedral of the Transfiguration), t. 2 (1918–1940), l. 106 (letter of June 15, 1928); l. 90 (letter of November 24, 1929); for the record of his headship of the Monuments Office, see TsGA-SPb, f. 1000, op. 51, d. 39, l. 17 (letter of September 21, 1930). His name regularly appears in this capacity in documents up to and including November 27, 1934 (see TsGA-SPb, f. 7384, op. 33, d. 163, l. 15). His personal file does not appear to have survived, but the 1935 list of politically suspect individuals working for Lensovet (see also below) gives him as b. 1873 and of gentry origins, resident at 7 Griboedov Canal (TsGA-LI-SPb, f. 9, op. 2, d. 11, l. 155). Nikolai Petrovich Vsevolozhskii (1904–1971), whose personal file also gives him as of gentry origins, and who worked as an architect (early projects included the "factory kitchen" on Vyborg Side), was possibly P. A. Vsevolozhskii's son (see TsGALI-SPb, f. 341, op. 3, d. 89, ll. 1–6). The Vsevolozhskii family had emerged to prominence in the eighteenth century and was particularly distinguished by military service in the nineteenth, including generals and admirals in the line.

80. For the ONO link, see TsGA-SPb, f. 1000, op. 51, d. 39, l. 17 (document of September 21, 1930). On his connection with the Massovyi otdel, see the staff list from 1935, where he is described as a "consultant," TsGALI-SPb, f. 9, op. 2, d. 11, l. 155. The plenipotentiary for Leningrad Province, A. A. Okoneshnikov, worked in collaboration with a learned council that included a number of consultants, among them Konstantin Romanov and Aleksandr Udalenkov (see RA IIMK, f. 29, ed. khr. 872, l. 8, l. 34, etc.), but it is not clear how big a staff Vsevolozhskii had. Given that all the limited paperwork is signed by him, there is the strong impression he worked more or less alone, with perhaps a typist and clerical assistant.

81. See, for example, the exchange relating to the Chesme Church in November 1931 at TsGA-SPb, f. 1000, op. 49, d. 37, l. 35.

82. Available archival materials contain two references to this department, the first dating from 1924 (see the NA UGIOP, pap. 171 [Cathedral of the Transfiguration], t. 2, l. 146, where the context is the fence of trophy cannons around the Cathedral, considered a memorial of military significance, rather than the building itself; and the second relating to the plan to convert the Prince Vladimir Cathedral into a house of culture (see below).

83. In September 1930, Konstantin Romanov was given a formal reprimand for allegedly anti-Soviet articles that had appeared in a collection published by Russian émigrés in Prague, and to which he was a contributor: see his work record card (*trudovoi spisok*), RA IIMK, f. 2, op. 3, d. 273, l. 5 ob. He seems to have reappeared in the preservation world only in 1935, and then mainly as a consultant to surveys in Leningrad Province, rather than in the city itself (the same was true of Udalenkov). (See RA IIMK, f. 2, op. 3, ed. khr. 675—personal file of A. P. Udalenkov; RA IIMK, f. 29,

[op. 1], ed. khr. 872—papers from the Monuments Preservation Section of the Leningrad Provincial Soviet, 1936–1940.)

84. On the economic background, see Oscar Sanchez-Sibony, "Depression Stalinism: The Great Break Reconsidered," *Kritika* 15, no. 1 (2014): 23–50.

85. "O poriadke sniatiia zontov nad vkhodnymi dver'mi," Postanovlenie Prezidium Lenoblispolkoma i Leningradskogo soveta, *Vestnik Leningradskogo Oblispolkoma i Leningradskogo Soveta* 20 (1932): 1.

86. *SU* 35 (1929): item 353.

87. "O poriadke provedeniia v zhizn' zakonodatel'stva o kul'takh," *Vestnik Leningradskogo Oblispolkoma i Leningradskogo Soveta* 64 (1931): 3.

88. As noted in chapter 1, a recodification of these measures in 1923 had some impact—but at that date mainly on "house churches."

89. See, for example, "Spisok namechennykh k zakrytiiu tserkovnykh zdanii" (1932), TsGA-SPb, f. 7384, op. 2, d. 50, ll. 11–16 (appendix 2).

90. TsGA-SPb, f. 7384, op. 33, d. 38, ll. 1–5; TsGA-SPb, f. 7384, op. 33, d. 38, ll. 1–3.

91. "Doklad Inspektora kul'tov Petroraisoveta po voprosu snosa Matveevskoi tserkvi," TsGA-SPb, f. 1000, op. 49, d. 40, l. 92. Peshkov's first name and initials are not given.

92. Russian: "TOL'KO poleznoi ploshchadi": literally "useful space alone"—i.e., not including sanitary facilities, kitchens, etc.

93. "Zaiavlenie Zam. Zav. LenGorONO i Zav. Stroisektorom LenGorONO," May 10, 1933, TsGA-SPb, f. 1000, op. 50, d. 33, l. 15. The rendering here attempts to capture the awkward style of the original.

94. See, for example, Antonov and Kobak, *SSPb*. For a similar line in the context of Moscow's redevelopment, see Catherine Merridale, *Red Fortress: The Secret Heart of Russia's History* (London: Allen Lane, 2013), ch. 10.

95. For the list of churches, see TsGA-SPb, f. 1000, op. 11, d. 92, ll. 7–16, ll. 33–34; for the material on bells, ibid., ll. 64–70 ob. A campaign to try and ban the ringing of church bells took place in 1928–1929 (see *KG*), and the issue was discussed by the Provincial Committee of the Communist Party in that year (TsGAIPD-SPb, f. 24, op. 2v, d. 12, l. 46), but judging by the references in antireligious materials (e.g., the petition to close the wooden Trinity Cathedral in 1932), no order was in fact made.

96. For an imaginative study of church bells and their function, see Richard J. Hernandez, "Sacred Sound and Sacred Substance: Bells and the Auditory Culture of Russian Villages during the Bolshevik *Velikii perelom*," *The American Historical Review* 109, no. 5 (2004): 1475–1504.

97. "Dopolnenie k Nakazu izbiratelei Leningradskomu sovetu XIV sozyva" (1934), TsGA-SPb, f. 7384, d. 33, l. 163, l. 20.

98. M. V. Shkarovskii and N. Iu. Cherepnina, *Spravochnik po istorii pravoslavnykh monastyrei i soborov g. Sankt-Peterburga, 1917–1945 gg.: Po dokumentam TsGA-SPb* (St. Petersburg: Memorial, 1996), 18, no. 1. In 1934, P. A. Vsevolozhskii advanced a plan for the conversion of Smol'nyi Cathedral into a planetarium (see Potrebskaia, "Ob ispol'zovanii tserkvei Leningrada", p. 320). This desperate search for "cultural" uses by monuments preservation officials continued into the 1980s, but it is important to remember that the realistic alternatives at the time – use for industrial purposes or storage, or indeed demolition – were even less compatible with the integrity of historic buildings than conversion to planetariums and the like.

99. TsGA-SPb, f. 1000, op. 49, d. 39, l. 41. When the church was finally closed in 1937, the reasons given were equally hypocritical: at a preliminary discussion, none of the officials in the Commission on the Affairs of Cults could find a suitable "cultural-educational" use for the place (someone half-heartedly suggested a planetarium), but the grounds given to VTsIK were that it was essential for the city archive. Eventually, the church was actually assigned to an electrical workshop (TsGA-SPb, f. 7384, op. 33, d. 168, ll. 82, 155, 164, 188). On the history of the military churches of St. Petersburg and their dismal fate after 1917, see especially A. Iu. Gusarov, *Pamiatniki voinskoi slavy Peterburga* (St. Petersburg: Paritet, 2010).

100. It is notable also that the arguments about the democratic nature of the memorials had spared the church from destruction just a few years earlier, though they had not led to the release of funding for repairs. See chapter 2.

101. TsGA-SPb, f. 1000, op. 49, d. 39, l. 21; cf. ll. 10–24. There is similar material on the Church of St. Michael Archangel in Kolomna, whose liquidation was said to have been "insisted upon in a whole list of instructions to Lensovet by all the nearby industrial concerns" (ibid, l. 7, ll. 9–10).

102. In a 1933 list of church closures (TsGA-SPb, f. 1000, op. 51, d. 35, ll. 1–52), such purposes are listed on numerous occasions, alongside redesignation as factory premises, schools, kindergartens, etc.

103. See the Administrative Department's list of 1933, TsGA-SPb, f. 7384, op. 2, d. 20, ll. 11–16.

104. On the 1934 investigation relating to road safety issues as part of the remodeling of the ploschad' Vosstania area, see TsGA-SPb., f. 7384, op. 33, d. 163, ll. 2-6 etc., and illustrations, p. 116 below.

105. On the central coordination of the campaigns, see, for example, the minutes of the Central Committee's Antireligious Committee, July 21, 1928, suggesting that such campaigns should be headed by a non-Party member: V. V. Lobanov, ed., *Protokoly Komissii po provedeniiu otdeleniia tserkvi ot gosudarstva pri TsK RKP(b)-VKP(b) (Antireligioznoi komissii), 1922–1929* (Izdatel'stvo Pravslavnogo Sviato-Tikhonovskogo gumanitarnogo universiteta), 247. By contrast, information about the mechanisms of control in Leningrad is at best circumstantial, because the files for that period in the Party archive are still secret (and in 2011, even the inventories [*opisi*] of these were reclassified as confidential). But the pattern of educational work and lobbying suggests general instructions from above and liberal interpretation of these below.

106. TsGA-SPb, f. 7384, op. 12, d. 92, l. 222, l. 82. For an example of a "Leningrad" objector, see, for example, the text by P. Marov ("worker at the okhta [*sic*] chemical factory"), l. 49: "it's interesting that the believers and admirers of this holiday are old women and provincials [crossed out] and incomers from nearby villages there are very few workers." "St. Il'ia's Friday" is mentioned in prerevolutionary sources (for example, Il'ia Goncharov's essay "Slugi" [Servants]), but it is not clear at which point the "healing of the possessed" ritual began. In Russian folk religion, St. Il'ia's Day is traditionally a day for casting out demons. However, "St. Il'ia's Friday" is not a usual term. It appears to have been generated by a confusion between the usual sobriquet of St. Paraskeva, "Piatnitsa," or "Friday," and the actual day of the week—encouraged by the fact that the Chapel of St. Paraskeva was a dependency of the Church of St. Il'ia in Porokhovye. (My thanks to Albert Baiburin for help with the folk background here.)

107. See the figures from 1928 in TsGAIPD-SPb, f. 24, op. 8, d. 53, ll. 31–33. The membership was predominantly male as well as working-class: only 32 percent of those who belonged were women.

108. This point is unlikely to derive simply from the nature of Leningrad preservationism, since Moscow and the old Russian cities had vigorous movements before 1917, and also in the 1920s. See M. E. Kaulen, *Muzei-khramy i muzei-monastyri v pervoe desiatiletie Sovetskoi vlasti* (Moscow: Luch, 2001); A. S. Shchenkov, ed., *Pamiatniki arkhitektury v Sovetskom Soiuze: Ocherki istorii arkhitekturnoi restavratsii* (Moscow: Pamiatniki istoricheskoi mysli, 2004). However, it seems that local pride was a key factor. It is interesting that Vladislav Mikosha, whose film documentary about the Cathedral of Christ the Redeemer contains the canonical footage of the building's demolition (see above) was himself a Leningrader. In an interview from the 1980s (www.net-film.ru), he remarked that he found the spectacle of the demolition barbaric—"I asked them, will you be pulling down St. Isaac's next?"—but was simply told a commission was a commission, and he should do what he was told.

109. The enormous Gutuevskaia Church on Obvodnyi Canal was scheduled for demolition in 1932, but then saved and returned to believers by VTsIK (see TsGA-SPb, f. 1000, op. 49, d. 38, l. 19).

110. Believers did not have the right to petition against the demolition of a church, only against its liquidation, so this lobby group could exercise no leverage where the retention of former cultic buildings was concerned.

111. TsGA-SPb, f. 7384, op. 33, d. 76, l. 36.

112. See the impassioned defense of the church's architectural value in TsGALI-SPb, f. 32, op. 1, d. 4, l. 95–95 ob., l. 98.

113. TsGA-SPb, f. 1000, op. 49, d. 39, l. 39.

114. This remained true in later years as well. See below.

115. See Lebina, "Deiatel'nost'," 55 (no sources are given for this assertion, but it is circumstantially likely, given the housing of antireligious museums in the city's two leading cathedrals).

116. A rare exception was the *dvadtsatka* of the Church of the Presentation, Petrograd Side, who noted in an appeal to VTsIK in 1932 that their church was "one of the oldest buildings in Leningrad built in 1793, is honored by the whole believing population of the district and is under the supervision of Glavnauka" (TsGA-SPb, f. 1000, op. 49, d. 40, l. 2). However, the monuments authority does not seem to have tried to save the building.

117. TsGA-SPb, f. 7179, op. 4, d. 25, l. 75.

118. "Prilozhenie No. 9 k Instruktsii," *Vestnik Leningradskogo Oblispolkoma i Leningradskogo Soveta* 73 (1931): 3. This had been true in 1920, of course (see chapter 1), but at that point, the contract had been issued by the Museums Department and had advisory force.

119. This happened with the Church of St. Simeon and St. Anne: the Presidium of Lensovet passed a resolution to hand over the place "for cultural ends" on July 13, 1937, but throughout the spring and summer of 1938, the Monuments Department was still insisting on repairs. See NA UGIOP, pap. 173, t. 1, ll. 130–36. There were other signs of pressure on parishes too: for instance, on March 20, 1934, the *dvadtsatka* of St. Andrew's Cathedral was billed 9,250 rubles by the Museums Department for valuable objects stolen from the church (NA UGIOP, pap. 8/2, l. 37).

120. TsGA-SPb, f. 1000, op. 49, d. 40, l. 48. Emphasis original.

121. TsGA-SPb, f. 1000, op. 49, d. 37, l. 42.

122. The widespread demolition of bell towers can also be seen in this light: they were often described as "late" structures, but their role as landmarks was certainly equally important.

123. This made an extraordinary impact on a first visit to the building in 1990, by which time the church was functioning again.

124. TsGA-SPb, f. 1000, op. 49, d. 40, l. 81. The final words, "*my vsegda vsem organizatsiiam soobshchali po telefonu*," as well as the surnames of the officials Levitskaia talked to, have been added by hand to the typescript, ibid. At the national level, Narkomfin (the People's Commisariat of Finance) had to issue a reminder on February 20, 1931, that it was improper to close and seal up a church before the executive committee of the local soviet had issued an order to do this, and that officials superintending confiscations must not confiscate property belonging to individual members of the religious community. *Zhurnal Moskovskoi Patriarkhii* 3 (1931): 47.

125. In 1930, Glavnauka was forced to explain that an expert carrying out an investigation of church contents in Ustiuzhnia was not colluding with believers: TsGA-SPb, f. 7179, op. 4, d. 25, l. 75.

126. See the letter on file from February 4, 1933: "For the second time, the Bureau for the Preservation of Monuments informs you that inasmuch as the Scientific Section of Narkompros has permitted the demolition of the Trinity Cathedral on Revolution Square, the Bureau does not object, provided preliminary photo-documentation and a complete survey of the building is carried out to the specifications of the Bureau." TsGA-SPb, f. 1000, op. 50, d. 33, l. 24.

127. "Zadachi sovetskogo muzeia," *Sovetskii muzei* 1 (1931): 1. Emphasis original.

128. N. R. Levinson, "Okhrana vnemuzeinykh pamiatnikov," *Sovetskii muzei* 6 (1932): 54, 57.

129. See, for example, Ia. Lidak, "Zabota o pamiatnikakh proshlogo," *Sovetskii muzei* 5 (1938): 20.

130. "Chem boleiut muzei v provedenii antireligioznoi propagandy" (unsigned article), *Sovetskii muzei* 4 (1931): 111.

131. For a mention of the Museum, see "Svodka o sostoianii religoznykh organizatsii," TsGAIPD-SPb, f. 24, op. 8, d. 53, l. 33. The founding date of 1923 is given in the 1941 report on the first ten years' activities of the Antireligious Museum: see TsGALI-SPb, f. 276, op. 1, d. 55, l. 3.

132. The Museum's character is vividly expressed in the collection of polemical articles by L. N. Finn et al., *Iz ochaga mrakobesiia v ochag kul'tury* (Leningrad: OGIZ-Priboi, 1931). See Adam Jolles, "Stalin's Talking Museums," *Oxford Art Journal* 28, no. 3 (2005): 429–55, for a good discussion of the Antireligious Museum in its museological context.

133. Finn, *Iz ochaga mrakobesiia*, 9.

134. Until 1929, Peter the Great's Cottage was still arranged as a chapel, according to the reconstruction ordained by Empress Elizabeth in the mid-eighteenth century. At that point, the cottage was closed to visitors, and the interior once more rearranged, using "in-period" historical objects to recreate the "authentic" interior as in Peter's time (most of Peter's actual possessions, other than his clothes, had not survived). The icon of the Savior Not Made by Human Hands, particularly venerated by Peter, was transferred to the Cathedral of the Transfiguration, where it is still kept. Peter's bedroom now contains a replica of the icon (Museum visit, July 2014).

135. S. P. Lebedianskii, "Voprosy ekspozitsii antireligioznykh muzeev," in *Trudy Pervogo Vserossiiskogo muzeinogo s"ezda*, vol. 2, ed. I. K. Luppol (Moscow: Gosudarstvennyi uchebno-pedagogicheskoe izdanie, 1931), 123–28. Quotations, 125–26.

136. This has caused understandable confusion in retrospective accounts: for example, Jolles, "Stalin's Talking Museums," refers to Vladimir Bogoraz-Tan as the director of the Antireligious Museum in St. Isaac's (he was actually director of the Museum of the History of Religion in the Kazan' Cathedral).

137. This did not mean that the staff of the Museum were much concerned with exercising a curatorial role. In 1935, an inspection indicated that many exhibits were displayed in an unsecured condition, where they could be easily reached, handled, and indeed removed, by the public (TsGALI-SPb, f. 9, op. 1, d. 2, l. 152). Another inspection in 1938 established that the reserve collections, including items of significant value, were housed in damp and chaotic basement areas, and that no proper inventories had been carried out. The many and confusing lists had totally unprofessional descriptions of the items: "Oil painting 158 x 120 cm," etc. Among the jumble of files were folders titled "Sum ole trash" (*vsiakaia irunda*) and "Look inside for contents" (TsGALI-SPb, f. 276, op. 1, d. 14, l. 2).

138. "Sektsiia po okhrane pamiatnikov revoliutsionnogo dvizheniia, iskusstva i stariny," in Luppol, *Trudy Pervogo Vserossiiskogo muzeinogo s"ezda*, 2:161.

139. Ia. Lidak, "Bol'she vnimaniia pamiatnikam stariny," *Sovetskii muzei* 5 (1932): 116–17.

140. "Ob okhrane istoricheskikh pamiatnikov," in *OPIK* 1973, 60. It is not clear whether a more detailed "instruction" was published along with this document; certainly, none appears to have been made public.

141. Ibid.

142. This organ, later known as the Board of Architectural Affairs (1943–1957), the Architecture and Planning Directorate (1957–1966), and the Chief Directorate of Architecture and Planning (1966–1988) (and Lenglavarkhitektura, or "Lenboardarch," from 1988), retained authority over planning throughout the Soviet period. For the details of names and dates, see http://www.kgainfo.spb.ru/about/history.html.

143. For a good discussion of how planning visions and techniques were disseminated, see Heather DeHaan, *Stalinist City Planning: Professionals, Performance, and Power* (Toronto: University of Toronto Press, 2013).

144. *Arkhitektura Leningrada* carried occasional information on the planning of provincial towns: see, for example, N. V. Baranov, "Bol'shoi Iaroslavl'," *Arkhitektura Leningrada* 1–3 (1937): 30–37; and the articles on Yerevan, Gorky, and Ordzhonokidze, *Arkhitektura Leningrada*, 2 (1938). DeHaan, *Stalinist City Planning*, includes some interesting material on the pitfalls of long-distance planning in Nizhnii Novgorod, where Leningraders proceeded without adequate knowledge of local conditions.

145. "Stenograficheskii otchet sovmestnogo zasedaniia," TsGALI-SPb, f. 32, op. 1, d. 71. Among the cases mentioned was the Marble Palace (where the Inspectorate had forced the removal of a shack made of parquet from the roof), the Dutch Church (where the Inspectorate hoped to compel the lessees to reconstruct the fire-damaged hall, now a theatre, according to historical principles, rather than rebuilding it in reinforced concrete), a church in the provincial town of Slutsk now in use by a factory, with whose "pig-headed" director the Inspectorate had run into conflict, and the Armenian Church on Nevsky.

146. For the staff list of 1935, where Vsevolozhskii is given as having gentry origins (*dvorianin*), see TsGALI-SPb, f. 9, op. 2, d. 11, l. 155; see also n. 79 above. No information is traceable on

Pobedonostsev, though since he was called up in 1941 (on which see the memoirs of Natal'ia Ust-vol'skaia, http://old.iremember.ru/grazhdanskie/ustvolskaya-natalya-mikhaylovna/stranitsa-17.html), he must have been significantly younger. The crackdown on members of "former classes" in the early to mid-1930s was accompanied by the promotion of young people with appropriate credentials (the so-called *vydvizhentsy*), which had its impact on preservation work also. See, for example, the anonymous letter of complaint written by employees at the Detskoe (Tsarskoe) Selo Museums complex on October 31, 1934, asserting that the new director had no background in museum work at all, and that his predecessor had been a former bathhouse manager who was now running a hairdresser's shop: TsGALI-SPb, f. 9, op. 2, d. 11, l. 27.

147. For the description, see TsGALI-SPb, f. 9, op. 2, d. 11, l. 39. The text accompanies a draft decree of Lensovet closing the OSP down, though it is not clear whether this was enacted at this point. However, the archival materials in TsGALI-SPb and TsGA-SPb peter out at much the same time.

148. The diversion of resources to rearmament is discussed, for example, in Larry E. Holmes, *Stalin's School: Moscow's Model School no. 25, 1931–1937* (Pittsburgh, PA: University of Pittsburgh Press, 1999).

149. "Ob okhrane pamiatnikov," GARF, f. 259, op. 37, d. 304, ll. 25–26.

150. See the documentation in GARF, f. 259, op. 37, d. 304, l. 1.

151. The decree, On Pedological Perversions, of July 4, 1936, marked a direct assault on the educational policy of Narkompros and on the standing of education and culture in central government generally. See Holmes, *Stalin's School*. In October 1937, Lunacharsky's replacement as commissar, Andrei Bubnov, was arrested, and in August 1938, executed.

152. A case in point was the directorate of the Museum of the Arctic, which sent to the Monuments Office a report from a lawyer arguing that the imposition of the requirement to carry out repairs was unlawful. NA UGIOP, pap. 481, t. 1, ll. 76–77.

153. See a 1949 report by Nikolai Belekhov, then chief of the State Inspectorate of Monuments, quoted by Steven Maddox, "Healing the Wounds: Commemorations, Myths, and the Restoration of Leningrad's Imperial Heritage, 1941-1950." Ph.D Thesis, University of Toronto, 2008, 92. As a comparison, note the costs of repairs to Novgorod in 1936 had been estimated at 7.4 million rubles. See chapter 4 below.

154. As discussed below. See also, O. M. Kormil'tseva, "Nachalo deiatel'nosti po sokhraneniiu kul'turnogo naslediia v Petrograde-Leningrade," in *Okhrana pamiatnikov Sankt-Peterburga: K 90-letiiu Komiteta po gosudarstvennomu kontroliu, ispol'zovaniiu i okhrane pamiatnikov istorii i kul'tury Sankt-Peterburga*, ed. V. A. Demen'teva, O. V. Taratynova, and B. M. Kirikov (St. Petersburg: Propilei, 2008), 39–40.

155. Peris, *Storming the Heavens*, 197.

156. See the letter of protest to *LP* written in 1939 by a supporter of the League, TsGAIPD-SPb, f. 24, op. 8, d. 421, l. 9. The newspaper replied that the League had been assigned "fully satisfactory" premises in 59 Moika Embankment, "the former school for propagandists," but this represented a downsizing in spatial and symbolic terms: as one of the League's officers pointed out in a letter of January 14, 1938, the only entrance to the offices was through a back courtyard (ibid., l. 6).

157. See Lebina, "Deiatel'nost."

158. As testified in a speech by Comrade Gurchenko to the League of the Militant Godless, "Stalinskaia Konstitutsiia i vopros o religii," October 20, 1937, in which he complained, "the popes [clergy] treat the constitution to suit their own ends" (TsGAIPD-SPb, f. 24, op. 8, d. 471, l. 12).

159. TsGA-SPb, f. 7384, op. 33, d. 50, l. 98. For other examples of petitions invoking the Constitution, see ibid., l. 21, l. 87; for a comment on this as a general tendency, ibid., l. 67.

160. This point was addressed, for instance, in a document proposing that the Leningrad Obkom should pass a decree on antireligious work (Comrade Nikanorov, "Ob antireligioznoi rabote: Proekt postanovleniia biuro Obkoma VKP(b)," August 8, 1936, TsGAIPD-SPb, f. 24, op. 2v, d. 1610, ll. 53–57), which advocated changing the name of the League to something less confrontational (such as the "Society for Scientific and Antireligious Propaganda"), and warned: "When carrying out such scientific-educational and antireligious [work], it is essential to carefully avoid offending the feelings

of religious believers, which leads only to the intensification of religious fanaticism." This passage has been underlined in red by a member of the Party hierarchy. (In the postwar era, the League's activities were replaced by the more decorous work of the "Knowledge" [Znanie] Society, exactly along the lines suggested here.)

161. For a good account of this, see Father Dionisii Burmistrov, "Leningradskaia eparkhiia v usloviiakh antitserkovnykh gonenii v 1929–1939 gg. (po materialam arkhivov Sankt-Peterburga i Leningradskoi oblasti)," http://www.religare.ru/2_65553.html; see also Shkarovskii, *Peterburgskaia eparkhiia*. Note that this strategy of concealment too turned out to have drawbacks: as an activist of the League of the Militant Godless complained in 1938, "In the course of this year, many priests [*popy*] have been caught red-handed in the midst of spying and wrecking activities, but there is little explanatory work going on in the localities. The result is that rumors are crawling round the villages on the lines, 'they've arrested the father so as they can shut the church,' and our local organizations are powerless to combat those rumors, since they don't have any concrete material relating to those cases" (TsGAIPD-SPb, f. 24, op. 8, d. 420, l. 25).

162. TsGA-SPb, f. 7384, op. 33, d. 50, l. 79; for similar data, see ibid., l. 66.

163. TsGAIPD-SPb, f. 24, op. 8, d. 420, l. 25. The report recorded that thirteen churches remained notionally open at this point (the city soviet figures were slightly different—see below—a discrepancy perhaps explained by whether priestless churches were counted as "closed" or "open").

164. The General Section of Lensovet managed church affairs as of October 7, 1938: see the reference to chasing up materials from certain districts that had still not transferred them: TsGA-SPb, f. 7384, op. 33, d. 76, l. 85.

165. Documents relating to the management of "cults" were invariably placed at one or other level of hidden circulation: "confidential" (*ne podlezhit oglasheniiu*), "for official use only" (*dlia sluzhebnogo pol'zovaniia*), "secret" (*sekretno*), "top secret" (*sovershenno sekretno*), etc. For the phrase, "second legality" (*pravo-2*), see Baiburin, "The 'Wrong' Nationality," 59–80.

166. An example is the revision of the April 8, 1929, decree in 1962, in order to further tighten its provisions: see chapter 5.

167. "Dokladnaia zapiska A. V. Tatarintsevoi tov. Andreevu (NKVD)," TsGA-SPb, f. 7384, op. 33, d. 50, l. 111. The career history of Tatarintseva—one of the few Lensovet officials whose biographical details can be located in accessible local archives—indicates the extent to which suppressing religious practices was "just another job" for employees of local government at this period. She worked as the inspector of cults in Vasilievskii Island district from December 19, 1931, to August 8, 1935, but her earlier career had nothing to do with religious affairs. Born in 1904, after parish primary school, "incomplete secondary education," and two years of higher education at a workers' faculty, she worked as a teacher and *vospitatel'* (educator) before joining local government as a clerk in the registry office (ZAGS). (See her personal file, TsGA-SPb, f. 7384, op. 34, d. 2103, ll. 143–45.) After the Second World War, she acted as legal advisor to the Protocol and Rights Section of Lensovet (from 1945 onward), and as secretary to the Chancery of the General Department of Lensovet (see TsGA-SPb, f. 9620, op. 2, d. 5, l. 33). M. V. Shkarovskii provides supplementary information. Tatarintseva was born in Samara, and the workers' faculty was at the Herzen Pedagogical Institute; her educator position was at the Demiansk Penal Colony for young people; and she also worked from August 8, 1935, as political instructor of the Commission on the Restoration of Electoral Rights. (See Shkarovskii, *Iosiflianstvo: Techenie v Russkoi Pravoslavnoi Tserkvi* [St. Petersburg: Memorial, 1999], 270n11. The source—not cited—is no doubt another official autobiography by Tatarintseva.)

168. TsGA-SPb, f. 7384, op. 33, d. 66, ll. 50–52, l. 184, l. 187. The closure of the church was accompanied by the usual chaos and willful damage: see ibid., ll. 192–94.

169. TsGA-SPb, f. 7384, op. 33, d. 74, l. 1. The synagogue, not mentioned on this list, was in fact still functioning, and continued to do so without interruption throughout the Soviet period. The mosque had been closed by order of Lensovet on June 8, 1940 (TsGA-SPb, f. 7384, op. 33, d. 37, l. 111), with the official reason given that the *dvadtsatka* "had systematically failed to carry out the major renovations identified as essential by inter-departmental commissions in 1935, 1936, 1937, and 1938." The document went on to state that the mosque was now in a terrible condition; the requisite inventory

had also not been compiled. The reason why the Catholic church remained open was almost certainly geopolitical: in 1933, local officials setting out the program of planned church closures mentioned "the links of Catholic, Lutheran, and Greek [religious] communities with countries with which we have normal diplomatic relations—France, Germany, Sweden, Poland, and Finland" (TsGA-SPb, f. 7834, op. 2, d. 20, l. 7 ob.). Relations with most of those countries (and also with Greece) worsened sharply at the end of the 1930s, but France was an exception.

170. "O sostoianii raboty v Gosudarstvennom anti-religioznom muzee (b. Isaakievskom so-bore)," TsGAIPD-SPb, f. 25, op. 2, d. 2000, ll. 64–65. Note the populist use of "tsar" rather than the formally correct, in pre-1917 usage, "emperor."

171. TsGAIPD-SPb, f. 25, op. 2, d. 2000, ll. 10–11.

172. TsGAIPD-SPb, f. 24, op. 10, d. 421, l. 20.

173. The antireligious mission was set out, for instance, in the planning materials for the Museum (see TsGALI-SPb, f. 276, op. 1, d. 37; ibid., d. 45). It continued to produce pamphlets such as *Bor'ba tserkovnikov Isaakievskogo sobora protiv naroda* (Leningrad: Gosudarstvennyi antireligioznyi muzei, 1941), and even a self-declaredly "scholarly" publication concentrated on the socially oppressive effects of religion, ignoring the cathedral's architectural history (*Soobshcheniia nauchnoi chasti Gosudarstvennogo antireligioznogo muzei—byvshego Isaakievskogo sobora* [Leningrad: Gosudarstvennyi antireligioznyi muzei, 1940]). An aggressively antireligious policy was also supported by rank-and-file "militant atheists": see, for example, the letter from Iulii Blom, June 2, 1940, which contrasts the light and crowds in the Leningrad working churches for Easter 1940 and the power-cut state of St. Isaac's: TsGAIPD-SPb, f. 24, op. 2v, d. 4410, ll. 43–44.

174. On "national Bolshevism," see David Brandenberger, *National Bolshevism: Stalinist Mass Culture and the Formation of Modern Russian National Identity, 1931–1956* (Cambridge, MA: Harvard University Press, 2002); Brandenberger and Kevin Platt, *Epic Revisionism: Russian History and Literature as Stalinist Propaganda* (Madison: University of Wisconsin Press, 2006). For the rebuke to *Arkhitektura Leningrada*, see the July 5, 1938, decision of the Presidium of Lensovet, TsGALI-SPb, f. 341, op. 1, d. 19, l. 108.

175. TsGAIPD-SPb, f. 24, op. 10, d. 148, l. 20.

176. "Spisok zakrytykh tserkvei po g. Leningradu za vremia 1931, 1932 i 1933 g.," TsGA-SPb, f. 7384, op. 33, d. 38, ll. 6–11; "Spiski tserkvei, zakrytykh v period s 1917–1936 gg.," TsGA-SPb, f. 7384, op. 33, d. 60, ll. 1–19. See also appendix 2.

177. "Akt 5 ianvaria 1937 g." [*sic*] (this is clearly a scribal error of the kind often made at the beginning of the year, since in October 1937 the church was still being used by the parish), NA UGIOP, pap. 173, t. 1, l. 152.

178. See the Monuments Department (OOP) order of September 26, 1938, signed by Pobedon-ostsev, TsGA-SPb, f. 7384, op. 33, d. 177, l. 37.

179. "Stenograficheskii otchet sovmestnogo zasedaniia" (1934), TsGALI-SPb, f. 32, op. 1, d. 71, l. 15.

180. TsGA-SPb, f. 7384, op. 33, d. 74, ll. 11–15.

181. NA IIMK, f. 29, op. 1, d. 872, ll. 101–4. At this point, there were only thirty-two buildings and structures (including bridges and embankments) under state protection in Leningrad, and only five hundred across the Russian Federation (ibid.; see also appendix 1.7). It seems almost incredible that, for instance, St. Isaac's and the Kazan' Cathedrals were not on the "state monument" lists, but the fact that these were museums (and thus in the care of Narkompros's Museums Department) no doubt meant that they were considered to be in relatively safe hands.

182. On Narkompros's beleaguered situation, see above. In Leningrad, the lack of activity on Narkompros's part, and the fact that the Central Executive Committee plenipotentiary "had in essence no rights and powers at all, and could only send out signals when things were going badly with the protection of monuments," was used to motivate the concentration of regulatory powers in the local Monuments Department; see GARF, f. 259, op. 37, d. 304, l. 19. Records of the plenipotentiary's activities in 1935 and 1936 are indeed thin on the ground: in August 1935, the signature of Lebedianskii (possibly S. P. Lebedianskii, one of the activists involved in the Antireligious Museum) appears in the

capacity of plenipotentiary on a document referring to the transfer of the St. Panteleimon Church in ulitsa Pestelia for use as storage by Zagotovzerno (the state corn processing plant), TsGA-SPb, f. 7179, op. 10, d. 849, ll. 86–87.

183. For the plan to concentrate resources in one body, see GARF, f. 259, op. 37, d. 304, l. 19.

184. TsGA-SPb, f. 7384, op. 33, d. 50, ll. 50–51.

185. Ibid., l. 51.

186. On the order, see Shkarovskii, *Peterburgskaia eparkhiia*, 162.

187. A. G. Lipman, "Materialy istoriko-arkhitekturnoi pasportizatsii b. Andreevskogo sobora" (1941), NA UGIOP, pap. 8/2, No. H-151/II, l. 40.

188. Ibid., l. 41. The Monuments Office staff noted that plywood partitions had been put up without permission, but did not suggest these should be removed, though they did suggest a brazier for heating glue should be in the church's annex, not the main church (ibid.).

189. GARF, f. 259, op. 37, d. 304, l. 7.

190. If one compares the 1938 list of monuments to be transferred to the direct control of the Monuments Department (GARF, f. 259, op. 304, ll. 31–33; see also appendix) with the 1935 list, it is clear that a further three buildings had been downgraded to "local" status (the Cathedral of the Vladimir Mother of God, the Trinity-Izmailovskii Regiment Cathedral, and the Chesme Church), while the Church of the Finland Regimental Hospital, a handsome early nineteenth-century former "house church," had disappeared from the list altogether, presumably after removal of most of its fittings upon conversion to the Baltic Factory's House of Culture (Antonov and Kobak, *SSPb*).

191. N. N. Belekhov and A. N. Petrov, "Istoriko-arkhitekturnyi Pasport na zdanie Muzeia Arktiki" (1937–1938), NA UGIOP, f. 150, N-202/1, ll. 112–15.

192. NA UGIOP, pap. 173, t. 1, ll. 129, 107.

193. Ibid., l. 7.

194. Ibid., l. 2.

195. Ibid., l. 131.

196. Certainly, the main file on the church (TsGA-SPb, f. 7384, op. 33, d. 163) does not contain any representations from the Monuments Department at this point.

197. The design was on display at an exhibition in TsGAIPD-SPb in 2009. The final document relating to the church in TsGA-SPb, f. 7384, op. 33, d. 163, l. 138 is a July 3, 1938, request for the keys from a demolition specialist on the basis of an order from Lensovet. On its demolition, see TsGAIPD-SPb, f. 27, op. 2b, d. 983, ll. 86–87.

198. Two well-known secular structures demolished in the 1920s were the Ekateringof Palace and the Litovskii Castle. Both were in a decayed condition, and the latter, as the "Russian Bastille," was ideologically inflammatory into the bargain. See *Sankt-Peterburg: Entsiklopedicheskii slovar*', www.encspb.ru.

199. Krasnov-Levitin, *Likhie gody*, 73.

200. Tiurin, "Ob ispol'zovanii zdanii," TsGA-SPb, f. 7384, op. 33, d. 50, l. 12.

201. TsGALI-SPb, f. 333, op. 1, d. 119, l. 3 ob.

202. RA IIMK, f. 29, ed. khr. 866.

203. The working churches as of 1940 were, besides the St. Nicholas, Transfiguration, and Prince Vladimir Cathedrals (all in the center, but none located on a major square or street), the wooden church of St. Demetrius of Salonica in distant Kolomiagi, the church of St. Seraphim at the Serafimovskoe Cemetery, and the Trinity Church at Lesnaia (both of which were also wooden), the Church of Suffering Job at the Volkovo Cemetery, and the St. Nicholas Church at the Georgievskoe Cemetery. TsGA-SPb, op. 33, d. 74, l. 1. The removal of crosses had been haphazard in the first two decades of Soviet power, but an order of the Presidium of the Supreme Soviet passed on September 7, 1938, and implemented in Leningrad ten days later, demanded that all further ones be taken down (ibid., l. 16). A simultaneous order that churches should be used only for the purposes approved by VTsIK when they were liquidated appears to have been honored only in the breach, though Lensovet went through the motions of compiling a survey questionnaire (ibid., l. 17). A rare exception, as a non-working church that preserved its crosses, was the Trinity-Izmailovskii Regiment Cathedral (see the illustration of the building in 1960, chapter 5). The cause of this was perhaps the lateness of its closure and the importance of its architect.

204. This might be supposed to be the case everywhere. But in some small towns, a much more traditional attitude to church culture survived for considerably longer, as an informant born in 1918 in Tula province recalled when interviewed in 2004 (CKQ-M04 PF5).

205. See the 1939 chit agreeing the text of the inscription, NA UGIOP, f. 150, p. 481, t. 1, l. 91. The document emphasizes that the "secular" (*grazhdanskii*) character of the monument should be made clear.

206. For the embarrassment, see Belekhov and Petrov, "Istoriko-arkhitekturnyi Pasport na zdanie Muzeia Arktiki" (1937–1938), NA UGIOP, f. 150, N-202/1, l. 150, which refers to the building as "marred" (*iskazheno*).

207. M. A. Orlov, *Leningrad: Putevoditel'*, 2nd ed., 2 vols. (Moscow: OGIZ, 1933), 1:258.

208. Of the Lavra, Una Pope-Hennessey recalled in 1937, "With stone scaling, plaster peeling, bricks disintegrating, it is rapidly becoming a depressing relic of an unheeded past" (*The Closed City*, 144).

Chapter Four

1. Aleksei Beglov, *V poiskakh "bezgreshnykh katakomb": Tserkovnoe podpol'e v SSSR* (Moscow: Izdatel'skii sovet Russkoi pravoslavnoi tserkvi, 2008), 70.

2. For a recent documentary history of the Blockade, see Richard Bidlack and Nikita Lomagin, eds., *The Leningrad Blockade, 1941–1944: A New Documentary History from the Soviet Archives* (New Haven, CT: Yale University Press, 2012). On the history of Blockade commemoration, see Lisa Kirschenbaum, *The Legacy of the Siege of Leningrad, 1941–1945: Myth, Memories, and Monuments* (Cambridge: Cambridge University Press, 2006); Catriona Kelly, "The Leningrad Affair: Remembering the 'Communist Alternative' in the Second Capital," *Slavonica* 17, no. 2 (2011): 103–22.

3. See, for example, Dement'eva et al., *Okhrana pamiatnikov Sankt-Peterburga: K 90-letiiu Komiteta po gosudarstvennomu kontroliu, ispol'zovaniiu i okhrane pamiatnikov istorii i kul'tury Sankt-Peterburga* (St. Petersburg: Propilei, 2008).

4. Ol'ga Berggol'ts, "Vozvrashchenie mira," in *Dnevnye zvezdy: Govorit Leningrad*, ed. Mariia F. Berggol'ts (Leningrad: Khudozhestvennaia literatura, 1985), 200.

5. On the danger and hardship endured by restoration workers, see Steven Maddox, *Saving Stalin's Imperial City: Historic Preservation in Leningrad, 1930–1950* (Bloomington: Indiana University Press, 2015), 57–61. For instance, restoration workers could be refused permission to evacuate, or denied rations if they did not complete their targets. This was, one might add, in line with the general "military command" attitude to workers of all kinds during the Blockade—so that latecomers might be sacked for a single offense and so on. On the daily life of the Blockade, see particularly Nikita Lomagin, *Neizvestnaia Blokada*, 2 vols. (St. Petersburg: Neva, 2001–2002).

6. For excellent accounts of the aesthetic sense of Leningrad in the Blockade, see Polina Barskova, "The Spectacle of the Besieged City: Repurposing Cultural Memory in Leningrad," *Slavic Review* 69, no. 2 (2010): 327–54, and her *Zhivye kartiny: Leningradskaia blokada v litsakh* (St. Petersburg: Limbus, 2014). Examples of wartime diaries with material on heritage preservation include Iu. Bakhareva and N. S. Tret'iakova, comp., "Iz dnevnikov khranitelei prigorodnykh dvortsov-muzeev Leningrada, 1941–1945," *Otechestvennye arkhivy* 1 (2007), http://www.rusarchives.ru/publication/mobil.shtml. See also the writings of Vera Inber, in whose *Pochti tri goda: Leningradskii dnevnik* (Moscow: Sovetskii pisatel', 1946), the evacuation of the palace museums in the Leningrad area was given much attention; and the diary for 1941–1942 of A. A. Chernovskii, who worked at the Museum of the History and Development of Leningrad (City Museum): L. P. Baklan, "Dnevnik goroda," in *Ot Muzeia Starogo Peterburga k Gosudarstvennomu muzeiu istorii Sankt-Peterburga: Issledovaniia i materialy* (St. Petersburg: GMI-SPb, 1997), 57–62.

7. On the Church in the war years, see M. V. Shkarovskii, *Tserkov' zovet k zashchite Rodiny: Religioznaia zhizn' Leningrada i Severo-Zapada v gody Velikoi Otechestvennoi voiny* (St. Petersburg:

Satis-Derzhava, 2005); O. I. Khodakovskaia, ed., "Blokadnyi khram: Religioznaia zhizn' blokadnogo Leningrada," http://blokada.mrezha.ru/duhov.htm.

8. See, for example, A. A. Kedrinskii et al., *Letopis' vozrozhdeniia: Vosstanovlenie pamiatnikov arkhitektury Leningrada i prigorodov, razrushennykh v gody Velikoi Otechestvennoi Voiny nemetsko-fashistskimi zakhvatchikami* (Leningrad: Lenizdat, 1971); A. A. Kedrinskii et al., *Vosstanovlenie pamiatnikov arkhitektury Leningrada* (Leningrad: Lenizdat, 1983); B. M. Kirikov, *Okhrana arkhitekturnykh pamiatnikov Leningrada v gody sovetskoi vlasti* (Leningrad: Znanie, 1988); Dement'eva et al., *Okhrana pamiatnikov Sankt-Peterburga*; Bakhareva and Tret'iakova, "Iz dnevnikov khranitelei."

9. Some plans, for example, to demolish the Chapel of St. Xenia at the Smolenskoe Cemetery, agreed in 1940, simply fell by the wayside; there was no longer the energy to destroy buildings deliberately when so much was being wrecked in any case. For the plans, see TsGA-SPb, f. 7384, op. 33, d. 66, l. 184.

10. "General'nyi plan po razvitiiu Leningrada," TsGA-SPb, f. 7384, op. 20, d. 1, l. 90.

11. On Baranov's biography, see Father Aleksandr Fedorov, "Glavnyi arkhitektor goroda perioda Velikoi Otechestvennoi voiny i vosstanovleniia goroda Nikolai Baranov," in *Tserkov' sviatoi velikomuchenitsy Ekateriny v Akademii Khudozhestv*, n.d., http://www.art-acad-church.ru/arh/spb/br.html. Though written by Baranov's grandson and not without family piety, this provides interesting background information.

12. For the later modifications to the 1935 General Plan, see, for example, "O vnesenii korrektiv v general'nyi proekt planirovki goroda Leningrada," decision of Lensovet on February 28, 1941, TsGALI-SPb, f. 341, op. 1, d. 78, l. 8. In 1951, Baranov moved to the Academy of Architecture in Moscow, a significant promotion (he was the only Leningrad city planner ever to be so honored), and in 1963, he took up a still more important post as the vice-chair of the Committee on Civil Engineering and Architecture at Gosstroi (the central state construction planning agency). But he continued to see his work in Leningrad as a model, as in his guide for planners, *Glavnyi arkhitektor goroda (Tvorcheskaia i organizatsionnaia deiatel'nost')* (Moscow: Izdatel'stvo arkhitektury po stroitel'stvu, 1973).

13. It is notable that the most even his grandson could find to suggest sympathy for church architecture was to say that Baranov's penchant for verticals was derived from the traditional massing of Old Russian bell towers (Fedorov, "Glavnyi arkhitektor goroda").

14. S. M. Zemtsov, "Rekonstruktsiia Sennoi i Obukhovskoi ploshchadei," *Arkhitektura Leningrada* 3 (1939): 47–48.

15. Untitled note on the reconstruction of the Haymarket (no author given), c. 1940, Otdel rukopisei Rossiiskoi natsional'noi biblioteki (hereafter OR RNB), f. 606, ed. khr. 127, ll. 1–5. For a sketch of Poliakova's biography and her work on green space in Leningrad, see T. V. Barabko, "'Zelenoe stroitel'stvo' Leningrada v 1920-kh–1940-kh godakh (po materialam arkhiva E. A. Poliakovoi)," *Universitetskii istorik* 10 (2012): 135–41.

16. "Proekt rekonstruktsii tsentral'nykh i severnykh raionov g. Leningrada (Fotoal'bom)," 1940, TsGANTD-SPb, f. 386, op. 3–4, d. 2, l. 27. See also illustration 4.2.

17. Shkarovskii, *Tserkov' zovet*, 277.

18. On the Trinity Cathedral, see below. On the St. Nicholas and St. Vladimir Cathedrals, see Khodakovskaia, "Blokadnyi khram."

19. TsGA-SPb, f. 7834, op. 33, d. 62, l. 73.

20. See the estimate for these works, TsGA-SPb, f. 7834, op. 33, d. 62, ll. 97–98 ob.

21. TsGAIPD-SPb, f. 25, op. 2a, d. 204, l. 83.

22. Shkarovskii, *Tserkov' zovet*.

23. See the record of the meeting by G. G. Karpov in M. I. Odintsov, *Russkie patriarkhi XX veka: Sud'by Otechestva i Tserkvi na stranitsakh arkhivnykh dokumentov* (Moscow: Izd. RAGS, 1999), 283–90.

24. In the pre-1917 period, the usual style was "the Orthodox Russian Church." In the early Soviet period, the common usage was to refer to the various subdivisions—"Renovationists," "Tikhonites," etc. The rehabilitation of the Patriarchate was accompanied by a drive against alternative

forms of Russian Orthodoxy, which had been forced from the scene by the late 1940s. See Shkarovskii, *Tserkov' zovet*; Edward E. Roslof, *Red Priests: Renovationism, Russian Orthodoxy, and Revolution, 1905–1946* (Bloomington: Indiana University Press, 2002).

25. According to the record of the meeting made by G. G. Karpov, Stalin told the church leaders that the government was aware of the "patriotic work" being done by the Church, and was receiving "many letters from the Front" with positive evaluations of this. See the note written by Karpov in September 1943, Odintsov, *Russkie patriarkhi*, 284. Odintsov's own explanation ("Veroispovednaia politika sovetskogo gosudarstva v 1939–1958 gg.," in *Vlast' i tserkov' v SSSR i stranakh Vostochnoi Evropy, 1939–1958: Diskussionnye aspekty*, ed. M. I. Odintsov [Moscow: Institut slavianovedeniia RAN, 2003], 17–18), concentrates more on the need to outflank the Germans.

26. Early examples include F. A. Mackenzie, *The Russian Crucifixion: The Full Story of the Persecution of Religion under Bolshevism* (London: Jarrolds, 1927), and B. L. Cederholm, *In the Clutches of the Tcheka*, trans. F. H. Lyon (London: George Allen and Unwin, 1929). Persecution of religious minorities was among the factors delaying diplomatic recognition of the USSR by the USA, and caused regular friction also with the Vatican.

27. Beglov, *V poiskakh "bezgreshnykh katakomb,"* 215, points out that a compromise with practical ends had already been made in 1940, when the Baltic states and Western Ukraine were absorbed into the Soviet Union: the strategy was to assign church hierarchs at the center, rather than to institute an immediate crackdown on religion.

28. For example, on March 10, 1942, Lavrenty Beria wrote to Stalin that the Germans were making efforts to exploit the Orthodox Church as an instrument of legitimation in the occupied zones (the letter is quoted in Shkarovskii, *Tserkov' zovet*, 106). Felix Corley, ed., *Religion in the Soviet Union: An Archival Reader* (Basingstoke: Macmillan, 1996), no. 84, pp. 132–33, cites a secret report from the High Command of the Red Army, dated September 16, 1942: according to this, the Germans were restoring churches in the Dno district of Novgorod, and sermons given by priests in the Novgorod area were expressing favorable views of Germans (Rossiiskii gosudarstvennyi arkhiv noveishei istorii [hereafter RGANI], f. 17, op. 125, d. 92, l. 129). The assignment to the Patriarchate of the former German embassy in Moscow (see the 1943 note by Karpov in Odintsov, *Russkie patriarkhi*, 289) surely also had symbolic, as well as practical, significance.

29. On the legislation, see, for example, T. A. Chumachenko, "Pravovaia baza gosudarstvenno-tserkovnykh otnoshenii v 1940-e–pervoi polovine 1960-kh godov: Soderzhanie, praktika, primeneniia, evoliutsiia," *Vestnik Cheliabinskogo gosudarstvennogo universiteta* 15 (2008): 138–56; M. I. Odintsov, *Vlast' i religiia v gody voiny: Gosudarstvo i religioznye organizatsii v SSSR v gody Velikoi Otechestvennoi voiny, 1941–1945* (Moscow: Rossiiskoe ob"edinenie issledovatelei religii, 2005), 331–32. Petitions in ASPbE suggest that in the countryside, public transport connections were also taken as a discriminator.

30. Memoirs of the period also make clear that in the postwar era, public transport was often erratic and overcrowded; see, for example, Mikhail German, *Slozhnoe proshedshee* (St. Petersburg: Iskusstvo, 2000).

31. A thorough and detailed account of church-state relations at this period in Leningrad is given in Elena Shun'gina, "Politika Sovetskogo gosudarstva v otnoshenii Russkoi pravoslavnoi tserkvi v 1940–1950-kh gg.: Vozvrashchenie kul'tovykh zdanii tserkvi (po materialam Leningrada)" (Candidate diss., St. Petersburg Institute of History of the Russian Academy of Sciences, 2009). There is a large literature on the period generally. See, for example, Dimitry Pospielovsky, *The Russian Church under the Soviet Regime, 1917–1982* (Crestwood, NY: St. Vladimir's Seminary Press, 1984), 2:301–46; and Tatiana A. Chumachenko, *Church and State in Soviet Russia: Russian Orthodoxy from World War II to the Khrushchev Years*, ed. Edward E. Roslof (Armonk, NY: M. E. Sharpe, 2002), chs. 1–2, which focus on the Council on the Affairs of the Russian Orthodox Church.

32. There were fifteen city districts at this period and an overall city population of around 1.5 million in 1946 and 2.2 million in 1950.

33. Nikolai Punin, *Mir svetel liubov'iu: Dnevniki, pis'ma*, ed. L. A. Zykova (Moscow: Slovo, 1998), 347.

34. Shkarovskii, *Tserkov' zovet.*

35. TsGA-SPb, f. 9620, op. 1, d. 9, l. 25. For an indication of the possible prompting of this—a story in the French press about the arrest on charges of spying of Madame Bovard, a parishioner of the Church of Our Lady of France, and a resident of the city since 1911, as well as a holder of two medals for wartime bravery and "noble labor" (*doblestnyi trud*), see ibid., ll. 1–2.

36. On the Luga churches, see TsGA-SPb, f. 9260, op. 1, d. 9, l. 11. This file also contains numerous examples of churches whose war history is specified as unknown (see, for example, ll. 28–29), or where the church is specified as having been closed "for a very long time" (e.g., l. 14). On Pavlovsk, see ASPbE, f. 1, op. 24, d. 10, l. 11.

37. Shkarovskii, *Tserkov' zovet*, 227, 279.

38. The remark is recorded in a top secret report of March 22, 1945, "Informatsionnaia svodka o faktakh aktivizatsii deiatel'nosti tserkovnikov v raionakh [Leningradskoi] oblasti," TsGA-SPb, f. 9324, op. 32, d. 5, l. 3 ob.

39. I. Iu. Fedotova, "Deiatel'nost' upolnomochennogo Soveta po delam Russkoi Pravoslavnoi Tserkvi po otkrytiiu tserkvei v Molotovskoi oblasti (1940-e–achalo 1950-kh gg.)," page of Perm' State Archive of Modern History (PGANI), permgani.ru.

40. Shkarovskii, *Tserkov' zovet*, 495–96.

41. According to the Trinity Church's official site, http://sobory.ru/article/?object=01569, it was open for another two years.

42. "Zaiavlenie-pros'ba," with twenty-four signatories, TsGA-SPb, f. 9324, op. 1, d. 24, l. 39–39 ob.

43. See the report from G. G. Karpov, the chairman of the Committee on the Affairs of the Russian Orthodox Church, January 1, 1945, GARF, f. 6991, op. 1, d. 29, ll. 2–3 ob., and the annotations to this: http://www.rusoir.ru

44. See TsGANTD-SPb, f. 388, op. 1–1, d. 115, l. 7. The Church of the Nativity of the Virgin in Old Ladoga is not mentioned in the official lists; possibly there was a confusion with the Church of the Nativity of St. John the Baptist, or the Cathedral of the Dormition in the Convent of the Dormition.

45. Ibid. The promotion of the architectural merits of Vyborg began shortly after the annexation at the end of the Finno-Soviet "Winter War" of 1939–1940; see, for example, N. A. Solofnenko, "Arkhitektura i zastroika Vyborga," *Arkhitektura Leningrada* 1–2 (1941): 57–60. Yet at this period there were genuine efforts to save Finnish architecture as well: for example, in 1941, Aleksandr Gegello, a leading architect and chair of the Board of LOSA, wrote to the Presidium of the Supreme Soviet of the Karelian ASSR in order to intercede for the main Lutheran church in Vypuri (the Russian transcription of the Finnish name, Viipuri, another sign of cultural tact), which he described as "a building of great skill" that could easily be converted into a cinema, concert hall, or exhibition center, citing as model the German Reformed Church in Leningrad, rebuilt in the Constructivist style as a club for the Union of Communications Workers (TsGALI-SPb, f. 341, op. 1, d. 78, ll. 18–19; it turned out, however, that the church had already been demolished: ibid., l. 20).

46. Visit to Vyborg, FN, July 2014.

47. Compare the confused reactions of officials in Pskov to the new situation: Jeanne [Zhanna] Kormina, "Ispolkomy i prikhody: Religioznaia zhizn' Pskovskoi oblasti v pervuiu poslevoennuiu piatiletku," *Neprikosnovennyi zapas* 59, no. 3 (2008), http://magazines.russ.ru/nz/2008/3/ko11.html.

48. See the useful short history on the official site of the St. Petersburg Theological Academy, http://spbda.ru/academy/history-of-academy/brief-history/; M. V. Shkarovskii, "Sankt-Peterburgskie dukhovnye shkoly vo 2-i polovine XX–nachale XXI veka," *Vestnik dukhovnoi istorii* 12, no. 4 (2008): 171–210, http://www.sedmitza.ru/data/015/999/1234/171_211.pdf; ibid., 13, no. 1 (2009): 259–66, http://www.sedmitza.ru/data/2009/11/27/1234916973/258_265.pdf; O. I. Khodakovskaia and A. A. Bovkalo, *Leningradskaia (Sankt-Peterburgskaia) dukhovnaia akademiia: Professora i prepodavateli* (St. Petersburg: Divnyi ostrov, 2011).

49. See further below.

50. TsGA-SPb, f. 9324, op. 1, d. 24, l. 6.

51. This was no doubt a response to clause 3b in the November 28, 1943, decree, which made the "condition" of a given church, and "the use to which it is being put" criteria of importance in judgment about whether to open it.

52. ASPbE, f. 1, op. 11a, d. 52, l. 4.

53. On the Trinity-Izmailovskii Regiment Cathedral and the Sampson Cathedral, see Shkarovskii, *Tserkov' zovet*, 496, citing TsGA-SPb, f. 9274, op. 1, d. 21, ll. 112–13, l. 121, ll. 126–27 and ibid., d. 14, l. 63, l. 72. See also Lomagin, *Neizvestnaia blokada*, 1:409–10.

54. Top secret police report, "Informatsionnaia svodka o faktakh aktivizatsii deiatel'nosti tserkovnikov v raionakh oblasti," March 22, 1945, TsGA-SPb, f. 9324, op. 32, d. 5, l. 3. The underlining was made by the plenipotentiary on the affairs of religious cults, N. M. Vasil'ev.

55. See the report from the chairman of the executive committee of the Kronstadt district soviet, November 10, 1945, TsGA-SPb, f. 9324, op. 32, d. 5, l. 20. For another fuss over religious activity with a link to the armed forces, see "Informatsionnaia svodka," ibid., l. 4 (on the circulation of letters suggesting prayer among soldiers at the front).

56. The information from 1945 held in TsGA-SPb, f. 9324, op. 1, d. 29, l.13, indicated that, for instance, around 5,000 funerals were carried out in the Prince Vladimir Cathedral, as opposed to around 500 christenings and twelve weddings; figures for the city's other churches were comparable. However, the popularity of confessions (which spiked steeply in the second third of the year, around Easter) points to a broader public that was at least occasionally observant.

57. For an informative discussion of the leverage of planners and heritage specialists, see Karl D. Qualls, *From Ruins to Reconstruction: Urban Identity in Soviet Sevastopol after World War II* (Ithaca, NY: Cornell University Press, 2009).

58. "Postanovlenie Soveta Ministrov RSFSR," May 22, 1947, in *OPIK* 1973, 62–64.

59. "Instruktsiia o poriadke ucheta, registratsii, soderzhaniia i restavratsii pamiatnikov arkhitektury, sostoiashchikh pod gosudarstvennoi okhranoi," October 14, 1948, in *OPIK* 1973, 92–128.

60. Ibid., section 85, 118.

61. Ibid., section 87, 118.

62. The Central Restoration Workshops were reopened on September 1, 1944.

63. In the archives of the State Monuments Inspectorate, the bulk of the records accessible at the time of visiting (e.g., those related to the St. Nicholas Cathedral and Cathedral of the Transfiguration, and to the Church of SS. Anne and Simeon and the former Coreligionists' Church) are comprised of material dating from before 1941. Where a "passport" (i.e., a detailed historical and technical account specifying which alterations were made to the fabric and when) is on file, this also dates from the prewar era—as in the case of the former Coreligionists' Church, for example (the document was compiled in 1938).

64. TsGALI-SPb, f. 341, op. 1, d. 245, l. 11. The Russian for "cluttered," *zakhlamlennyi*, suggests the building was of low quality (*khlam* = junk). For the principles of "restoration" (*vosstanovlenie*) and "recreation" (*vossozdanie*), see ibid., l. 27. On the trope of "liberation" in writing about Leningrad restoration, see Catriona Kelly, "'Ispravliat' li istoriiu?' Spory ob okhrane pamiatnikov v Leningrade 1960-kh–1980-kh godov," *Neprikosnovennyi zapas* 2 (2009), https://www.academia.edu/2001169/. For a good general history of Leningrad restoration at this point, see Maddox, *Saving Stalin's Imperial City*.

65. See chapter 3 above.

66. As a meeting of LOSA on May 8, 1950, was told by Nikolai Belekhov: "It's hard to find a lessee for the Izmailovskii cathedral, the Lutheran Church, and the Catholic Church on Nevsky, but we're doing our best." TsGALI-SPb, f. 341, op. 1, d. 245, l. 13. The speaker also made clear that the special funding promised by the 1947 law had not yet materialized from Lensovet.

67. Academician Igor' Grabar', "Vosstanovlenie pamiatnikov stariny," *Sovetskoe iskusstvo*, November 28, 1944, 2.

68. N. Bylinkin, "Obrazy russkogo iskusstva," *Sovetskoe iskusstvo*, December 5, 1944, 3. Nikolai Bylinkin (1900–1989) was an architect and the coauthor of a textbook on Soviet architecture (1957).

69. The objects did not include the Mozhaisk Luzhki Monastery, which was restored only in the 1960s (see the brief history on the site http://www.pravoslavie.ru/put/080110173653.htm), but they did include the churches of Novgorod (see below).

70. A more obvious model for Soviet architects was the postwar restoration of Warsaw, which was sometimes mentioned approvingly in commentaries on Leningrad practices (though I have come across such mentions only in 1970s sources, for example, D. A. Butyrin at the meeting of LOSA to discuss the reconstruction of the Haymarket [Peace Square] on July 2, 1975, TsGALI-SPb, f. 229, op. 1, d. 117, l. 26).

71. On architecture and utopia in the prewar period, see, for example, Katerina Clark, "Socialist Realism and the Sacralizing of Space," in *The Landscape of Stalinism: The Art and Ideology of Soviet Space*, ed. Evgeny Dobrenko and Eric Naiman (Seattle: University of Washington Press, 2003), 3–8. The persistence of utopian ideals can be sensed in the projects described by Owen Hatherley, *Landscapes of Communism: A History through Buildings* (London: Allen Lane, 2015), and Kate Brown, *Plutopia: Nuclear Families, Atomic Cities, and the Great Soviet and American Plutonium Disasters* (New York: Oxford University Press, 2013).

72. See the critical, but balanced account of his life in A. A. Formozov, "Rol' N. N. Voronina v zashchite pamiatnikov kul'tury Rossii," *Rossiiskaia arkheologiia* 2 (2004): 173–80.

73. "Spravka o sostoianii narodnogo obrazovaniia v raionakh oblasti, osvobozhdennykh ot nemetsko-fashistskikh zakhvatchikov," January 1944 (exact date not given), TsGAIPD-SPb, f. 24, op. 11, d. 198, ll. 1–2.

74. "Tablitsa stoimosti ushcherbov, prichinennykh otdel'nym pamiatnikam arkhitektury, nakhodiashchikhsia v gorodakh Novgorode, Gdove, Staroi Russe, Tikhvine, Gatchine, Ropshe, Usad'be, Gruzino i sostoiashchim pod gosudarstvennoi okhranoi." TsGANTD-SPb, f. 388, op. 1–1, d. 2, l. 1–3.

75. See "Spisok pamiatnikov arkhitektury, podlezhashchikh vziatiiu pod gosudarstvennuiu okhranu po Leningradskoi oblasti," ibid., ll. 5–10; "Spisok arkhitekturnykh pamiatnikov Leningradskoi oblasti, podlezhashchikh vziatiiu pod mestnuiu okhranu," ibid., ll. 11–13.

76. "Predvaritel'nyi spisok pamiatnikov arkhitektury Leningradskoi oblasti, priniatykh k peredache," December 4, 1944, ibid., ll. 14–20.

77. The restoration of Novgorod is discussed in detail in M. P. Pavlova and A. S. Shchenkov, "Restavratsionnaia praktika Novgoroda," in *Pamiatniki arkhitektury v Sovetskom Soiuze: Ocherki istorii arkhitekturnoi restavratsi*, ed. A. S. Shchenkov (Moscow: Pamiatniki istoricheskii mysli, 2004), 358–72. See also Victoria Donovan, "*Nestolichnaya kul'tura*: Regional and National Identity in Post-1961 Russian Culture" (DPhil thesis, University of Oxford, 2011).

78. RA IIMK, f. 29, ed. khr. 872, ll. 43–50. See also appendix.

79. RA IIMK, f. 29, ed. khr. 872, ll. 1–29. This material also provides useful information about the process of the filtering, which was done on the basis of information from local museums, as well as the inspectors reporting to the plenipotentiary, and then reviewed by the Scholarly Council of the Lenoblsovet Monuments Office. Buildings that were considered run-of-the-mill or clumsily constructed were prime candidates for removal from the lists, though in most cases no information is provided, suggesting that date or location were the primary factors (in one case, l. 3, "difficulty of ensuring preservation" is explicitly given as a reason for dropping a church). Konstantin Romanov was more concerned to get larger numbers of secular wooden buildings added to the list than to defend the churches. See the materials in RA IIMK, f. 29, ed. khr. 877.

80. The records of RA IIMK (both the manuscript and photographic sections) indicate that trips to monuments in the province were mainly limited to Pskov and Novgorod, and that these were mainly fact-finding visits: see, for example, the papers of Konstantin Romanov (f. 29).

81. TsGAIPD-SPb, f. 24, op. 8, d. 463, l. 8. The report also claimed that no restoration work had been done since before the First World War, but this was surely an exaggeration for rhetorical effect; the holdings of IIMK make clear that there was activity in the 1920s (see chapter 1). For Okoneshnikov's initials, see NA IIMK, f. 29, op. 1, d. 872, l. 8.

82. TsGAIPD-SPb, f. 24, op. 8, d. 463, l. 22, l. 25.

83. Ibid., d. 420, l. 25, l. 97. Usually, the League was zealously concerned about putting an end to all forms of "superstition" in rural areas, and regarded preservation issues as mere irritants: Glavnauka, stated a report of 1936, was "an institution with which we are carrying out a very active struggle, since it just insists on protecting everything." TsGAIPD-SPb, f. 24, op. 8, d. 293, l. 120 (the particular objects under contention were some sacred stones in Liadskii district).

84. TsGANTD-SPb, f. 388, op. 1–1, d. 2, l. 3 ob. See also appendix 2.

85. TsGANTD-SPb, f. 388, op. 1–1, d. 23, ll. 1–2. By 1950, this had been reduced to fifty-seven (see appendix 1.9).

86. TsGANTD-SPb, f. 388, op. 1–1, d. 46, e.g., l. 8 (the Church of the Dormition in Vinnitskii district).

87. TsGANTD-SPb, f. 388, op. 1, d. 115, l. 3, l. 8.

88. "Spisok pamiatnikov arkhitektury religioznogo kul'ta po Leningradskoi oblasti, sostoiashchikh na uchete," TsGA-SPb, f. 9620, op. 2, d. 7, ll. 77–79.

89. See the exchange of letters dating from October to December 1951, TsGANTD-SPb, f. 388, op. 1, d. 177, ll. 21–22.

90. Ibid., ll. 18–19.

91. A machine-tractor station was not only a functional installation, but also a key symbolic space of agricultural development, featuring in propaganda materials about "heroes of labor," and so on. So this was not just a conflict with local bumpkins.

92. Letter from the deputy head of the Leningrad Provincial Agricultural Department (Zuev, initials not given) to the head of the Agricultural Department (V. M. Gal'perin), December 7, 1948 , TsGANTD-SPb, f. 388, op. 1–1, d. 115, l. 13.

93. Ibid., l. 14–14 ob. Emphasis follows original.

94. See chapter 3. In the 1935 list of state monuments in Leningrad Province (RA IIMK, f. 29, ed. khr. 872, l. 43), only the medieval fortress at Old Ladoga and some burial mounds just outside the settlement formed part of the "reserve"; the Monastery of St. Nicholas was not listed at all, though it may have had "local" status.

95. See the handwritten note by Gal'perin, TsGANTD-SPb, f. 388, op. 1–1, d. 115, l. 14–14 ob., instructing B. P. Andreev and N. A. Gukov to investigate.

96. Ibid., l. 14. The phrase "the inadmissibility of his behavior" has been underlined by Gal'perin.

97. The refusal cites "section 14 of the 'Directive on the Protection of Monuments of Culture,' approved by the Council of Ministers of the USSR on October 14, 1948," and the accompanying instruction. Ibid., l. 16 (copy of letter from V. M. Gal'perin, December 17, 1948). The letter was also copied to the rector of Leningrad State University.

98. "Vypiska iz protokola No. 52 zasedaniia Ispolnitel'nogo Komiteta Volkhovskogo Raisoveta deputatov trudiashchikhsia," January 13, 1949, TsGANTD-SPb, f. 388, op. 1–1, d. 149, l. 1.

99. For the instruction—"B. P. Andreev. Your comments needed by 17.02.1949"—see the handwritten note, ibid.

100. "Reshenie Ispolkoma Leningradskogo Oblastnogo Soveta ot . . . 1949 g. Po voprosu: Ob uluchshenii dela okhrany pamiatnikov arkhitektury Leningradskoi oblasti," TsGANTD-SPb, f. 388, op. 1–1, d. 149, l. 16.

101. Ibid.

102. Ibid., ll. 16–17.

103. For example, in 1932, there was a proposal to blow up the Ferapontovo Convent and the Kirillovo-Belozersk Monastery, recognized since well before 1917 as architectural and artistic monuments of the first importance (the former is now a UNESCO World Heritage site). See M. V. Shkarovskii, *Peterburgskaia eparkhiia v gody goneniia i utrat, 1917–1945* (St. Petersburg: Liki Rossii, 1995), 150.

104. See, for example, Elena Zubkova, *Russia after the War: Hopes, Illusions, and Disappointments, 1945–1957* (Armonk, NY: M. E. Sharpe, 1998).

105. See the brief biography prepared by the staff at KGIOP (the Committee of the State Inspectorate of Monuments), "Belekhov Nikolai Nikolaevich," on the page "70 let Pobedy—70 let Leningradskoi shkole restavratsii," https://gov.spb.ru/gov/otrasl/c_govcontrol/70-let-pobedy-70-let-leningradskoj-shkole-restavracii/. However, note the slightly different details given in n. 107 below.

106. It helped that the office was now considerably larger than in the 1930s—documents from 1947 list around a dozen GIOP employees (TsGANTD-SPb, f. 386, op. 1–4, d. 29, l. 16).

107. According to a biographical sketch in a brochure published for the sixtieth anniversary of May 9, 1945 (*60 slavnykh let, 1945–2005: Leningrad–Sankt-Peterburg; Spasennoe i sokhranennoe* [St. Petersburg: GASU/Peterburgskii gosudarstvennyi universitet putei soobshcheniia, 2005], 8), Belekhov was born in Beloostrov, a dacha and resort area outside St. Petersburg. He attended the *gimnaziia* (classical high school) attached to the Institute of History and Philology (which in the 1920s was amalgamated with the corresponding faculty of Petrograd University, but at this point was independent). He spent a short time at the Electro-Technical Institute in Petrograd before moving to "the Architectural Institute" (a title occasionally applied to the architecture section of the Leningrad Higher Institute of Art and Technology [LVKhTI], the former Academy of Arts). After military service in Kronstadt (1930–1932), he joined the Lensovet Planning Department. All of this indicates a solidly middle-class background, but not an aristocratic or exceptionally privileged one (at the Electro-Technical Institute, he was a member of the "worker faculty"). For his association with the Monuments Department, see, for example, his co-signature on an OOP order of September 26, 1938, signed by Pobedonostsev, Ts-GA-SPb, f. 7384, op. 33, d. 177, l. 37.

108. Certainly, an obituary of Belekhov published in *Praktika restavratsionnykh rabot: Sbornik vtoroi* (Moscow: Akademiia stroitelst'va i arkhitektury, 1958), available on http://art-con.ru/node/4954, suggested that prior to his work in the Monuments Office, he worked as the plenipotentiary of the Central Executive Committee responsible for Leningrad Province, and had taken part in the restoration of medieval sites in Pskov, Novgorod, Kirillovo-Belozersk, and Gdov, but no corroboration of this has proved traceable in contemporary documentation (where he appears only as chief architect of the Lensovet monuments preservation office), and, as indicated above, it may be doubted how much practical work actually got done at this point in any case.

109. S[ergei] Tsimbal, ". . . Kotoryi est' i kotoryi budet!," in *U nas v Leningrade: O primetakh vremeni; Rasskazyvaiut zhurnalisty, khudozhniki, fotografy*, ed. I. K. Avramenko et al. (Leningrad: Sovetskii pisatel', 1961), 74.

110. Grabar', "Vosstanovlenie pamiatnikov stariny," 2.

111. N. V. Baranov, "Zadachi leningradskoi arkhitektury v realizatsii piatiletnego plana vosstanovleniia i razvitiia g. Leningrada i oblasti," *Stroitel'stvo i arkhitektura Leningrada* (November 1946): 1–7.

112. John Hersey, "The Reconstruction of Leningrad," *Architectural Forum* 12 (1944): 121–22.

113. GARF, f. 259, op. 37, d. 296, l. 8. This was a particularly dismal period for the palace museums, as a number of leading experts (for instance, Nikolai Arkhipov, working at Petergof) had been arrested during the Great Terror; see the unannotated, but informative, article by A. G. Raskin and T. V. Uvarova, "Vozvrashchenie imeni: Nikolai Il'ich Arkhipov," *Pskov: Nauchno-prakticheskii, istoriko-kraevedcheskii zhurnal* 33 (2010), http://cyberleninka.ru/article/n/vozvraschenie-imeni-nikolay-ilich-arhipov.

114. GARF, f. 259, op. 37, d. 304, l. 31. The church was presumably the Cathedral of the Trinity (1758–1773), which had been closed for worship in 1938.

115. Baranov, "Zadachi," 3.

116. On Sevastopol, see Qualls, *From Ruins to Reconstruction*.

117. TsGANTD-SPb, f. 386, op. 3–6, d. 43, l. 3.

118. See TsGANTD-SPb, f. 386, op. 3–6, d. 42, l. 10, describing the era up to "the mid-nineteenth century" as "the most valuable in a city planning sense."

119. Take, for example, the reconstruction of nos. 112–113 (now no. 68) Nevsky Prospect, on the corner of the Fontanka (the so-called "Lopatin Mansion" or "House of Literature") after bomb damage in 1942. The former modest, flat-fronted façade dating from the 1870s was not restored after the war, and instead, after a competition, the house was turned into a uniform four-story structure in the neoclassical

style, its central section with pediment. The scale and statues of factory and collective farm worker were new, but the neoclassical detailing came from the most favored period of Petersburg architecture.

120. For a discussion of mechanization in postwar construction generally, see Mark B. Smith, *Property of Communists: The Urban Housing Program from Stalin to Khrushchev* (DeKalb: Northern Illinois University Press, 2010). The journal *Stroitel'stvo i arkhitektura Leningrada* frequently carried materials on new building in the postwar era: see, for example, S. E. Brovtsev, "Proekt rekonstruktsii ulitsy Lenina," in no. 17 (1951): 19–24.

121. Baranov, "Zadachi," 3.

122. Nikolai Baranov, *Obobshchenie opyta planirovki i zastroiki gorodov*, Akademiia arkhitek-tury SSSR, Leningradskii filial, Sektor planirovki i zastroiki gorodov (typescript, Leningrad, 1950). TsGANTD-SPb, f. 17, op. 2–1, d. 2, l. 202–5. On l. 225, Baranov refers to the importance of St. Isaac's as a vertical accent and calls for a general plan for the placement of tall buildings, as with Moscow. Interestingly, in 1944 Baranov had insisted to John Hersey ("The Reconstruction of Leningrad," 121) that there would be no "skyscrapers" in Leningrad, but this was before the construction of the "high rises" (*vysotki*) in Moscow had set the tone elsewhere.

123. On the Finland Station, see Baranov, *Glavnyi arkhitektor goroda*, 171–72. Baranov stated here that the height reduction was because the construction site would not carry a building of the dimensions originally planned, but the shift from a horizontal to a vertical aesthetic in the post-Stalin era (see chapter 5) was clearly of importance also.

124. Baranov, *Obobshchenie opyta*, l. 137.

125. Ibid., ll. 164–65.

126. See Zoia Iurkova, *Sennaia ploshchad': Vchera, segodnia, zavtra* (Moscow: Tsentropoligraf, 2011), http://lib.rus.ec/b/375320/read.

127. The founding of the Soviet Committee for the Defense of Peace in 1949 marked a new chapter in Soviet cultural diplomacy, as the "world revolution" models of the first two decades of Soviet power were replaced by the "ideological hegemony" models of the country's last four decades.

128. On October 4, 1991, the street's name reverted to Zakhar'evskaia once more.

129. See RA IIMK, f. 29, ed. khr. 847, l. 11.

130. Maddox, *Saving Stalin's Imperial City*, 86.

131. TsGALI-SPb, f. 341, op. 1, d. 283, l. 17. A rare case where restoration did go on was the Church of the Annunciation in the Alexander Nevsky Lavra, and even this, as Nikolai Belekhov re-ported on May 8, 1950, was "being carried out by an odd organization—Teakhozkombinat [The De-partment of Works for Theaters], and they're getting things wrong—it's a real struggle, but the work isn't being done too badly" (TsGALI-SPb, f. 341, op. 1, d. 245, l. 15 ob.).

132. The Winter Palace house church was reopened in December 2014, as part of the celebra-tions for the Hermitage's 250th anniversary that took place that year.

133. TsGALI-SPb, f. 341, op. 1, d. 245, l. 10.

134. TsGA-SPb, f. 9620, op. 2, d. 1, l. 53, l. 64. My thanks to Alexandra Piir for transcribing this document.

135. The records of work in the Church of St. Simeon and St. Anne for 1941–1956 inclusive have disappeared from the NA UGIOP repository (perhaps because of the secret nature of the work done in the enterprise occupying it at the time), but the construction of the partition "in the early 1950s" is recorded in a written exchange of June–July 1980 between the director of the institute then occupying the building and the head of GIOP, Ivan Sautov (NA UGIOP, pap. 173, t. 3 [Tserkov' svv. Simeona i Anny: Perepiska 1971–1989 gg.], sheets not numbered).

136. Putatively, as the 1938 list only gives churches of local significance. Following the number-ing in the lists themselves, there were thirty-three in 1935 and thirty-four in 1938—but that is because the St. Andrew's Cathedral and Three Priests Church were counted separately in 1938 (and in 1935, as a single site).

137. On war memorials, see, for example, E. I. Katonin, "Parki-pobedy," *Stroitel'stvo i arkhitek-tura Leningrada* (June 1946): 9–13; A. I. Gegello, "Pamiatniki na mestakh boev pod Leningradom," ibid., 5–8; on Stalin monuments, "Arkhitektura Stalinskoi epokhi" (editorial), *Stroitel'stvo i arkhitek-tury Leningrada* 1, no. 12 (1950): 2–6; A. Markov, "Rekonstruktsiia Obvodnogo kanala," ibid., 1–12.

138. F. F. Oleinits, "Vosstanovlenie Pavlovskogo dvortsa," *Stroitel'stvo i arkhitektury Leningrada* (November 1946): 36–39; A. I. Naumov, "General'nyi plan vosstanovleniia Pskova," *Stroitel'stvo i arkhitektury Leningrada* (November 1946): 42–48.

139. "K 250-letiiu so dnia rozhdeniia V. V. Rastrelli: Master russkoi arkhitektury," *Stroitel'stvo i arkhitektury Leningrada* 14 (1951): 35–39; V. I. Piliavskii, "Zodchii V. P. Stasov i ego tvorchestvo," *Stroitel'stvo i arkhitektury Leningrada* 10 (1949): 33–42.

140. M. E. Kunin, ed., *Leningrad: Vidy goroda*, designed by G. D. Elifanov, photographs by M. A. Velichko, S. P. Ivanov, and M. A. Mitskevich (Moscow: Gosudarstvennoe izdatel'stvo izobrazitel'nogo iskusstva, 1954). The book, according to its colophon, was cleared for publication in February 1954. Clearly, it would have been typeset significantly earlier (censors only agreed to pass the text of a book once they had seen examples of the finished publication, and signing off often took several months), and must have been planned well in advance of that. The obvious conclusion, especially given its celebratory tone, is that it was intended for the cancelled city jubilee in May 1953.

141. For example, an attractive set of black-and-white postcards widely circulated in the late 1940s portrayed Klodt's equestrian bronzes on the Anichkov Bridge. My thanks to Alim Sabitov for the kind donation of some of the cards in question.

142. This was part of a widely attested strategy of playing up to state expectations and language in petitions (like "letters to the authorities" generally). See, for example, the discussion in Natalia Shlikhta, "'Orthodox' and 'Soviet': On the Issue of the Identity of Christian Soviet Citizens (1940s–early 1970s)," *Forum for Anthropology and Culture* 11 (2015), forthcoming.

143. TsGA-SPb, f. 9324, op. 1, d. 24, l. 5.

144. ASPbE, f. 1, op. 11, d. 52, l. 1.

145. Petition of April 16, 1948, ASPbE, f. 1, op. 11, d. 13, ll. 5–6.

146. ASPbE, f. 1, op. 24, d. 20, l. 144–144 ob. In 1953 also fell the 250th anniversary of the founding of Leningrad (see below), which no doubt meant that anniversaries were in the air.

147. ASPbE, f. 1, op. 11a, d. 18, l. 5. The same petitioner, one Liudmila Kruglova, also wrote to the Metropolitan complaining that "the St. Isaac's and Kazan' Cathedrals, which are meant for Praise to the Lord, serve the cause of impudence [*kramol*] masquerading as science"—a reference to the antireligious displays housed therein. Ibid., l. 1–1 ob.

148. See the petitions in TsGA-SPb, f. 9324, op. 1, d. 24, l. 7 (suffering during the war), l. 8 (the icons).

149. ASPbE, f. 1, op. 11a, d. 10, l. 3. Emphasis added.

150. ASPbE, f. 1, op. 24, d. 6, l. 11.

151. It was only in the mid-1950s, after Metropolitan Grigorii's death, that the Trinity Cathedral was restored to worship. See chapter 5.

152. On the campaign to save the "Easter Loaf and Easter Pudding" Church in 1933, see chapter 3.

153. Certainly, the *dvadtsatka* of Kulich and Paskha petitioned in that vein (TsGA-SPb, f. 9324, op. 1, d. 24, l. 10): "The believers of Volodarskii district request you to open the Church of the Trinity on prospekt Obukhovskoi Oborony. In our district, there is not one single church and we hope that you will let us open the church."

154. ASPbE, f. 1, op. 7, d. 18, l. 27.

155. Telegram of June 21, 1949, ibid., l. 29.

156. Letter from N. N. Belekhov, June 28, 1949, ibid., l. 30.

157. ASPbE, f. 1, op. 7, d. 18, l. 34. On this request is a handwritten note: "Gold leaf issued. July 30, 1949."

158. NA UGIOP, pap. 171, t. 3, l. 101. The chairman of the *dvadtsatka* objected that the porches had a practical function and that removing them would increase condensation "and may lead to children becoming ill"; in any case, the alteration had not been specified at the stage when the estimate for building works was agreed by GIOP; however, as a compromise, he proposed building a substitute porch inside the building (ibid., l. 101a).

159. ASPbE, f. 1 op. 24, d. 10, l. 310 ("Kulich and Paskha"); ASPbE, f. 1, op. 7, d. 11, l. 100 (Cathedral of the Transfiguration).

160. In 1945, for example, the Cathedral of the Transfiguration's income was nearly 250,000 rubles in the highest quarter, and just under 60,000 rubles in the lowest quarter; the income range of the Easter Loaf Church at the same time was around 6,000 rubles up to just over 125,000 rubles. TsGA-SPb, f. 9324, op. 1, d. 29, l. 11.

161. ASPbE, f. 1, op. 24, d. 10, l. 310.

162. Report by the incumbent to Metropolitan Grigorii, April 10, 1948, ASPbE, f. 1, op. 7, d. 18, l. 2.

163. Only six of the churches in a list of monuments of architecture from 1950 ("Spisok pamiatnikov arkhitektury religioznogo kul'ta Leningradskoi oblasti," TsGA-SPb, f. 9620, op. 2, d. 7, ll. 77–79, see also appendix 1) were in use for worship. Two further churches, the Church of the Resurrection at Vazhiny (or Vazheny), on which see below, and the "Little Porch" Church at the Great Monastery of Tikhvin, not included in this list, were also official monuments, as is indicated by documents in ASPbE and elsewhere. Incomplete lists of working churches dating from 1962 (by which time several churches on the monuments list had been closed) are available in ASPbE, f. 1, op. 26 (2), d. 21, ll. 19, 26, 33, 39. See also A. V. Bertash, V. V. Antonov et al., *Zemlia Nevskaia pravoslavnaia: Pravoslavnye khramy prigorodnykh raionov Sankt-Peterburga i Leningradskoi oblasti* (St Petersburg: Pravoslavnaia Rus', 2000), a detailed gazetteer of the region's churches.

164. ASPbE, f. 1, op. 7, d. 18, l. 199.

165. As with the priest, the elder was appointed by the bodies with oversight of religious affairs—the Church Offices or, after 1944, the office of the plenipotentiary on the affairs of the Russian Orthodox Church. These bodies were, predictably, more concerned with the political reliability of the church elder than his or her competence in other respects. Church histories uniformly underline elders' role as part of the state surveillance network. Added to this, there is evidence that at times elders exploited their position for financial gain: in 1950, for example, it turned out that the elder in the Cathedral of the Transfiguration had siphoned off over 23,000 rubles from the receipts of around 35,000 rubles for votive candles (ASPbE, f. 1, op. 7, d. 11, l. 142).

166. ASPbE, f. 1, op. 24, d. 10, l. 310.

167. ASPbE, f. 1, op. 7, d. 1, l. 237.

168. Ibid., l. 237 ob.

169. Elena Shun'gina, "Politika," has contrasted the attitudes of GIOP with the Stroganov Palace (p. 180), but without making allowances for this important point of corporate solidarity.

170. On worsening church relations at the start of the Cold War, see Pospielovsky, *The Russian Church*, 1:311–12. For the professional camaraderie, see the description by Nikolai Belekhov to an audience at the Union of Architects on May 8, 1950 (TsGALI-SPb, f. 341, op. 1, d. 245, l. 18): "The crowning glory of our work, work under our guidance, what people in the theater call 'the highlight of the season' for 1949 is the Shuvalov Palace—the reconstruction of ceiling-painting that was totally ruined in the fire. The work was done by our own restoration workshops, making use of the few scraps that could be collected the day after the fire, when something was still left." The phrase "our own restoration workshops" makes the relationship clear.

171. See NA UGIOP, pap. 150, t. 3, Edinovercheskaia tserkov'/Muzei Arktiki, 1939–1951, l. 89.

172. See, for example, NA UGIOP, pap. 150, t. 3, l. 88—delays with planning, May 15, 1948, l. 32—faults in the repairs of the façade, November 6, 1949.

173. NA UGIOP, pap. 150, t. 3, l. 36. The Sheremet'ev Palace was, at the time, the headquarters of the Institute of the Arctic, the parent institution of the Museum of the Arctic. According to the letter of the 1949 Instruction on the Protection of Monuments, the State Restoration Workshops were supposed to work on monuments in the "museum" category (i.e., those that were preserved in their original state), but they evidently worked on some lease-held sites as well, as in this case.

174. The "conquest" of the Arctic regions, celebrated in the Museum of the Arctic, was a pan-Soviet cult, but Leningrad was the place from which many of the expeditions had departed, giving the city a special sense of ownership. However, it was the currency of the Arctic expeditions in Moscow that was crucial to the Institute's political leverage. On the polar heroes, see Karen Petrone, *Life Has Become More Joyous, Comrades: Celebrations in the Time of Stalin* (Bloomington: Indiana University

Press, 2000). For an early history of the Institute, see Ia. Ia. Gakkel', *Za chetvert' veka: Obzor deiatel'nosti Arkticheskogo Instituta Glavsevmorputei za 25 let* (Moscow: Izdatel'stvo Glavsevmorputi, 1945) (the Museum, with its "polar relics," is mentioned on pp. 104–5). A measure of the Institute's leverage was that it occupied one of the premier architectural monuments in Leningrad, the Sheremet'ev Palace, from 1929 until 1988.

175. NA UGIOP, pap. 150, t. 3, l. 100, l. 97. Both incidents relate to 1947.

176. As happened in July 1949, when Nikolai Belekhov instructed a junior official in GIOP to draw up a draft resolution by the Executive Committee of Lensovet relating to a recently received request from the head of GlavSevmorput' (the Directorate of Northern Sea Routes) to use St. Catherine's Church on Vasilievskii Island for laboratory facilities. "You should attach to it the increasingly indignant letters that have had to be sent regarding non-completion of required repair works." NA UGIOP, pap. 150, t. 1, l. 42.

177. In this context, it is interesting to note inspectors' persnickety behavior over the restoration work done to the Rostral Columns in 1946, though here their reservations seem to have been more substantive than in the case of the paint colors of the St. Nicholas Cathedral: they remarked that the metalwork on the Columns was done to such a low standard that it was already corroding. TsGA-LI-SPb, f. 333, op. 1, d. 341, l. 9.

178. As mentioned above, the income from candles and *treby* in one or two Leningrad churches genuinely was substantial, but this was by no means true of all of them. However, the "rich pope" stereotype of early Soviet propaganda was an abiding feature of the Soviet psychological landscape and even well-educated officials seem to have given it credit.

179. The decree called on local soviets to "incorporate into planning the supply of building materials to religious communities doing repair work on churches" (see the Instruction of the Executive Committee of the Leningrad Provincial Soviet publicizing this decision, TsGA-SPb, f. 9324, op. 32, d. 5, l. 16). The other terms of the decree are mentioned in "Informatsionnoe pis'mo no. 2" (1956), TsGA-SPb, f. 9324, op. 3, d. 40, l. 29.

180. For example, when GIOP insisted in 1951 that the Cathedral of the Transfiguration should employ, on a permanent basis, the services of an architect, the *dvadtsatka* was able to arrange that this duty was assigned to the diocesan architect (ASPbE, f. 1, op. 7, d. 11, ll. 190, 194).

181. This is evident from, for example, the order for gold leaf in the case of the St. Nicholas Cathedral (see above).

182. ASPbE, f. 1, op. 7, d. 66, l. 105. See also the petition from the parishioners of Liugovich village about the transfer of property from St. George's Church in Iugostitsy village (February 4, 1949)—at this point, the property was being kept in the home of a parishioner of the latter. ASPbE, f. 1, op. 24, d. 10, l. 85.

183. See, for example, ASPbE, f. 1, op. 7, d. 65, ll. 34–36; ASPbE, f. 1, op. 7, d. 66, ll. 113–19.

184. TsGA-SPb, f. 9620, op. 1, d. 9, l. 32.

185. See, for example, the top secret "Informatsionnaia svodka" of March 22, 1945, which repeats an allegation from the Volkhovskii district committee of the Communist Party that "the plenipotentiary on the affairs of the Orthodox church is not imposing any control on the priests at all" (TsGA-SPb, f. 9324, op. 32, d. 5, l. 3 [underlining original]).

186. As Elena Shun'gina has argued, plenipotentiaries were dependent on the tenor of the times, even if some were temperamentally inclined to take a harder line than others ("Politika," pp. 50–56).

187. The League was shut down during the Second World War and never revived.

188. The resolution is cited in the Instruction of the Leningrad Provincial Soviet implementing the decision at the local level, TsGA-SPb, f. 9324, op. 32, d. 5, l. 16.

189. ASPbE, f. 1, op. 7, d. 11, l. 124.

190. Ibid., l. 207.

191. ASPbE, f. 1, op. 7, d. 1, l. 15. As this file also reveals, other issues worrying the Cathedral clergy at this period included cars mysteriously cruising around the place at night, and efforts by the city police to crack down on begging outside the church, which the incumbent bravely argued was

not appropriate in terms of church traditions. If the last case refers to explicit police harassment, it is possible that the car drivers and pigeon-hunters were undercover agents of the security services, as the intonation in the reports tends to suggest.

192. Even during the war, petty squabbling and score-settling (what in Russian is known as *skloka*, or "barnyard squawking") did not cease. For instance, on May 25, 1942, an anonymous letter signed "From the Parishioners," sent to the Department of Cults in Lensovet, complained that "money collected by parishioners for the upkeep of the Cathedral is being squandered on who knows what and must be getting used by the presidium of the *dvadtsatka* to look after their own needs" (TsGA-SPb, f. 7384, op. 33, d. 62, ll. 82–82 ob.).

193. ASPbE, f. 1, op. 7, d. 18, l. 231–231 ob.

194. Ibid., l. 233.

195. As noted above, whether the church appeared on official lists was also haphazard.

196. Shkurnikova is registered in the petition as coming from "Melotovo," which may be a version of "Melyotovo" in Pskov province. This may, however, have been her official place of residence according to her passport. None of the other parishioners is given as resident at Kurpovo, though all came from villages in the northeast districts of Leningrad Province.

197. ASPbE, f. 1, op. 7, d. 151, l. 5–5 ob.

198. Modern fast trains reach Vazhiny in about five hours from St. Petersburg (visit, September 2012), but stopping services still take considerably longer, and in the late 1940s, train times generally were slower than in the late twentieth and early twenty-first centuries. Kurpovo is then around an hour's walk beyond Vazhiny.

199. ASPbE, f. 1, op. 7, d. 151, ll. 81–91.

200. In the late Soviet period, two bunkhouses were built to house parishioners wishing to attend mass long-distance (the local bus timetables were arranged so that a return visit was not possible on a Sunday). (Visit, FN, September 2012.)

201. ASPbE, f. 1, op. 7, d. 151, ll. 81–91.

202. Ibid., l. 111, 164–204.

203. ASPbE, f. 1, op. 11, d. 10, l. 8 ob. See also this report on visits by D'iakonov to see Kushnarev in Leningrad; D'iakonov stated that repeated petitions for the opening of the church in 1949 had not been acknowledged, let alone answered, by Kushnarev.

204. The church was, evidently, built of brick (hence the attrition by local visitors), but the use of the word *kamennyi* for brick structures is common in Russian.

205. ASPbE, f. 1, op. 24, d. 11, ll. 330–31.

206. Oxf/AHRC-SPb-08 AP PF4. C. 2.

207. "Valentin Ivanovich V'iushkin," *Ferapontovskii sbornik* 2 (1988): 22–81.

208. For the general picture of rural life at this period, see Zubkova, *Russia after the War*.

209. Beglov, *V poiskakh "bezgreshnykh katakomb,"* 59–121; Alexander Panchenko, "Popular Orthodoxy in Twentieth-Century Russia: Ideology, Consumption, and Competition," in *Soviet and Post-Soviet Identities*, ed. Mark Bassin and Catriona Kelly (Cambridge: Cambridge University Press, 2012), 321–40; Ulrike Huhn, *Glaube und Eigensinn: Volksfrömmigkeit zwischen orthodoxer Kirche und Sowjetischem Staat, 1941 bis 1960* (Wiesbaden: Harrassowitz, 2014).

210. ASPbE, f. 1, op. 24, d. 10, l. 85.

211. During the war itself, the term "Patriotic War" was in wide circulation; after the war concluded, the term "Great Patriotic War" (to suggest its superiority even to the 1812 victory) became the characteristic style.

212. In 1949, Nikolai Belekhov claimed that it was planned to repair the Trinity Cathedral in the Lavra "out of the 8 million rubles received in leasehold payments," with the 250th jubilee of the city as the main motivating force (TsGALI-SPb, f. 341, op. 1, d. 245, l. 24). However, nothing was in fact done about this. The architect A. A. Ol' vigorously argued that the Cathedral was far more important than the removal of firewood in the gardens of the Academy of Arts (ibid., l. 30). But this was evidently not a popular line, since everyone else concentrated exclusively on secular monuments.

Chapter Five

1. ASPbE, f. 1, op. 26, d. 7, l. 318.

2. Another important prompt for mourning over Stalin (as with the Soviet population generally) was his role as a war leader, but, as the readiness of some churchmen to make common cause with the invaders illustrates (see chapter 4), the leader's rapprochement with religion was fundamental.

3. As Michael Froggatt has pointed out ("Science in Propaganda and Popular Culture in the USSR under Khrushchëv [1953–1964]" [DPhil thesis, University of Oxford, 2006], 108), there was also an immediate strategic goal behind the antireligious campaign—it was precipitated by a report of early 1954 that saw religion as a factor in continuing rural backwardness. However, the fact that the report hit home is also an indication of predisposition to the arguments advanced in it. Equally, the assiduous lobbying of veteran Bolshevik Vladimir Bonch-Bruevich (on which see M. V. Shkarovskii, comp., *Russkaia pravoslavnaia tserkov' i Sovetskoe gosudarstvo v 1943–1964 godakh: Ot "peremiriia" k novoi voine* [St. Petersburg: Izdatel'skoe ob"edinenie DEAN + ADIA-M, 1995], 50; Froggatt, "Science in Propaganda," 112) was successful not just because of its nuisance value, but because of existing sympathy to the arguments in favor of a new atheist campaign. William Taubman, *Khrushchev: The Man and His Era* (New York: W. W. Norton, 2003), emphasizes the strategic resonance of the antireligious campaign in the context of de-Stalinization (512–13), underlying Khrushchev's own residual religious feelings (the evidence for which is that Khrushchev crossed himself when visiting his mother's grave). But it is hard to tell from such remembered cases whether, for instance, Khrushchev was primarily expressing a sense of piety toward his mother's memory and doing "as she would have liked." Alternatively, Khrushchev's religiosity may simply have been an act, as suggested by Aleksei Fedotov, "Pervyi etap antireligioznykh reform N. S. Khrushcheva (1958–1961 gg.)," *Bogoslov.ru*, December 26, 2013, http://www.bogoslov.ru/text/3698574.html.

4. "O krupnykh nedostatkakh v nauchno-ateisticheskoi propaganda i o merakh ee uluchsheniia," Postanovlenie TsK KPSS, July 7, 1954, in *O religii i tserkvi: sbornik dokumentov*, ed. F. I. Garkavenko (Moscow: Izdanie Politicheskaia literatura, 1965), 71–77.

5. "Ob oshibkakh v provedenii nauchno-ateisticheskoi propagandy sredi naseleniia," November 10, 1954, *Pravda*, November 11, 1954, 1–2.

6. See the discussion in Froggatt, "Science in Propaganda," 114–18.

7. Dimitry Pospielovsky is certainly right to attribute the U-turn in 1954 to "lack of unity in the Soviet leadership after Stalin's death" (*The Russian Church under the Soviet Regime, 1917–1982* [Crestwood, NY: St. Vladimir's Seminary Press, 1984], 2:330), since Khrushchev's ascendancy was just beginning (in May that year, for instance, he made a notable speech to the Leningrad party *aktiv* (assembly of senior officials) describing the purge of 1949–1951 in the city (the so-called "Leningrad affair") as based on fabricated evidence). See below, p. 199.

8. "Zapiska Otdela propagandy i agitatsii TsK KPSS po soiuznym respublikam 'O nedostatkakh naucho-ateisticheskoi propagandy,'" September 12, 1958, RGANI, f. 4, op. 16, d. 554, ll. 5–13; see online version, http://www.rusoir.ru. *Nauka i religiia* had been planned as early as 1955 (see Froggatt, "Science in Propaganda"), but the first number came out only in 1959.

9. For a discussion of the foundation of the Institute of Scientific Atheism as a key step in the campaign, and its struggles to align a rather primitive conceptual apparatus with the complex status of belief in Soviet society, see Victoria Smolkin-Rothrock, "'Sviato mesto pusto ne byvaet': Ateisticheskoe vospitanie v Sovetskom Soiuze, 1964–1968," *Neprikosnovennyi zapas* 65. no. 3 (2009), http://magazines.russ.ru/nz/2009/3/sm5.html. On the history of *Nauka i religiia*, see her "The Ticket to the Soviet Soul: Science, Religion, and the Spiritual Crisis of Late Soviet Atheism," *Russian Review* 73, no. 2 (2014): 171–97. On the period generally, see Herbert Bodewig, *Die russische Patriarchatskirche: Beiträge zur äusseren Bedrückung und inneren Lage 1958–1979* (Munich: E. Wewel, 1988). For an excellent overview of antireligious campaigns in the last "Soviet decades," see Jeanne Kormina and Sergei Shtyrkov, "'Eto nashe iskonno russkoe, i nikuda nam ot etogo ne det'sia': Predystoriia postsovetskoi desekuliarizatsii," in *Izobretenie religii: Desekuliarizatsiia v postsovetskoi kontekste* (St. Petersburg: Evropeiskii universitet v Sankt-Peterburge, 2015), 7–45.

10. There had been some antireligious publications in 1953–1954, but generally of a more moderate kind, directed against "superstition" in a broad sense; see, for example, "Durnoi glaz" (*Komsomol'skaia pravda*, December 18, 1953), and "Tam, gde bezdeistvuet klub: Pis'mo v redaktsiiu" (*Komsomol'skaia pravda*, September 8, 1954), available online at http://www.krotov.info/acts/20/1950/shtric_12.htm.

11. Lev Khalif, "Permskaia obitel'," *Literatura i zhizn'*, February 21, 1960, 2.

12. Yuri Gagarin's own *Doroga v kosmos* (Moscow: Pravda, 1961) seems to have been the original source of what became a propaganda slogan: "V kosmos letal—boga ne vidal" (I flew into space—of God I saw no trace). See 170–71: "Up to our house [in Smolensk province, which Gagarin visited during his triumphal progress round the country after landing his spacecraft safely] came whole crowds of people: schoolchildren and their teachers, farm workers, even a group of withered old women. They wanted to know whether I'd see the lord god up there in the heavens? I had to disappoint them, and my answer did a lot to shake their faith." A year later, German Titov was to repeat this insight when he made the second Soviet manned flight into space: see *New York Times*, May 7, 1962 (quoted in Asif Siddiqi, "The Cause of the Cosmos: Science and the Occult at the Root of the Soviet Space Program," paper presented at "Science, Religion, and Communism in Cold War Europe," St. Antony's College, Oxford, May 16–17, 2014).

13. On Soviet cosmism of this period generally, see, for example, the essays collected in James T. Andrews and Asif A. Siddiqi, eds., *Into the Cosmos: Space Exploration and Soviet Culture* (Pittsburgh, PA: University of Pittsburgh Press, 2011), and in Eva Maurer, Julia Richers, Monica Rüthers, and Carmen Scheide, eds., *Soviet Space Culture: Cosmic Enthusiasm in Socialist Societies* (Basingstoke: Palgrave, 2011).

14. On the propaganda of the time, see Alexander Panchenko, "Popular Orthodoxy in Twentieth-Century Russia: Ideology, Consumption, and Competition," in *Soviet and Post-Soviet Identities*, ed. Mark Bassin and Catriona Kelly (Cambridge: Cambridge University Press, 2012), 321–40.

15. Both *Komsomol'skaia pravda* and *Pionerskaia pravda* regularly carried antireligious materials, and there was an entire genre of antireligious horror stories aimed at the young (for a key example, the story of Zoia, see Panchenko, "Popular Orthodoxy", 333).

16. RGANI, f. 5, op. 34, d. 57, l. 37; emphasis original. Cf. "Spravka o narushenii sovetskogo zakonodatel'stva o kul'takh v gorode Murmanske," RGANI, f. 5, op. 34, d. 96, l. 101. This "tactful" approach was highly characteristic of later periods too: see Irina Maslova, "Deiatel'nost' Soveta po delam religii pri Sovete Ministrov SSSR v 1965–1985 gg.: 'Politika sderzhivaniia,'" *Religiia i pravo: Informatsionno-analiticheskii zhurnal* 1 (2005): 17–23.

17. See, for example, the instances cited in Georgii Karpov's letter to plenipotentiaries, 1959, RGANI, f. 5, op. 34, d. 57, ll. 37–38 (in one case in Primorskii territory, the local health and hygiene inspection had even closed a church because it was "too close to a cemetery"). While this was cited as "crude administrative bullying," the central authorities sometimes exploited similar cases against the clergy: for instance, in May 1959, a crush in a Vologda church during a fire led to criminal action against the local bishop and sexton (their failure to update wiring had allegedly caused the fire to begin with) (ibid., l. 62; later that year, a charge of poor crowd control was added, ibid., l. 71).

18. For example, in 1959, a priest in Yaroslavl was arrested on charges of seducing a minor: see the collection of documents from RGASPI published by Nikolai Mitrokhin, "Religioznost' v SSSR v 1954–1965 godakh glazami apparata TsK KPSS," *Neprikosnovennyi zapas* 73, no. 5 (2010), http://magazines.russ.ru/nz/2010/5/re8.html.

19. Tatiana A. Chumachenko, *Church and State in Soviet Russia: Russian Orthodoxy from World War II to the Khrushchev Years*, ed. Edward E. Roslof (Armonk, NY: M. E. Sharpe, 2002), 157. Chapter 3 of Chumachenko's book gives a thorough account of changed policy based on materials generated by the Council on the Affairs of the ROC.

20. Shkarovskii, *Russkaia pravoslavnaia tserkov'*, 182.

21. Ibid., 184, 185. See also the detailed discussion in Fedotov, "Pervyi etap."

22. Compare "O religioznykh ob"edineniiakh: Postanovlenie VTsIK," April 8, 1929, *SU* 35 (1929), art. 353, and "O religioznykh ob"edineniiakh: Postanovlenie VTsIK i SNK RSFSR ot 8 aprelia 1929 g. s izmeneniiami, vnesennymi postanovleniem VTsIK i SNK RSFSR ot 1 ianvaria 1932 g. i Ukazom Prezidiuma Verkhovnogo Soveta RSFSR ot 19 dekabria 1962 goda," TsGA-SPb, f. 9620, op. 2, d. 25, ll. 1–10. My thanks to Alexandra Piir for transcribing the latter document. See also appendix 4.

23. Nathaniel Davis, "The Number of Orthodox Churches before and after the Khrushchev Antireligious Drive," *Slavic Review* 50, no. 3 (1991): 614; Kira V. Tsekhanskaia, "Russia: Trends in Orthodox Religiosity (Statistics and Reality)," in *Religion and Politics in Russia: A Reader*, ed. Marjorie Mandelstam Balzer (Armonk, NY: M. E. Sharpe, 2010), 8–10; Andrew B. Stone, "'Overcoming Peasant Backwardness': The Khrushchev Antireligious Campaign and the Rural Soviet Union," *Russian Review* 67, no. 2 (2008): 296–300; Irina Paert, "Demystifying the Heavens: Women, Religion, and Khrushchev's Anti-Religious Campaign, 1954–64," in *Women in the Khrushchev Era*, ed. Melanie Ilic, Susan E. Reid, and Lynne Attwood (Basingstoke: Palgrave, 2004), 203–21.

24. As mentioned in chapter 4 above, it was widely used from the late 1940s.

25. There is a good discussion of this decorative shift and its effects in Owen Hatherley, *Landscapes of Communism: A History through Buildings* (London: Allen Lane, 2015).

26. See, for example, Feliks Novikov and Vladimir Belogolovskii, *Sovetskii modernizm, 1955–1985: Antologiia* (Ekaterinburg: Tatlin, 2010); David Crowley and Susan E. Reid, eds., *Socialist Spaces: Sites of Everyday Life in the Eastern Bloc* (Oxford: Berg, 2002).

27. For example, in Leningrad, the Lenproekt planning agency discussed insights from this project (in a not uncritical spirit) in October 1957: see TsGANTD-SPb, f. 36, op. 1, d. 234. On the new building nationwide, see Mark B. Smith, *Property of Communists: The Urban Housing Program from Stalin to Khrushchev* (DeKalb: Northern Illinois University Press, 2010).

28. For instance, both the Troitsko-Cheremushki Church and the manor house disappeared when the estate was built.

29. *OPIK* 1973, 139.

30. M. G. Meierovich, *U menia poiavilas' mechta* (Iaroslavl': Aleksandr Rutman, 2004), 177.

31. For a short excursus on this project, see Catherine Merridale, *Red Fortress: The Secret Heart of Russia's History* (London: Allen Lane, 2013), ch. 10.

32. An excellent case-study of urban transformation under Khrushchev is Stephen Bittner, *The Many Lives of Khrushchev's Thaw: Experience and Memory in Moscow's Arbat* (Ithaca, NY: Cornell University Press, 2008).

33. On St. Paraskeva and St. Cyril and St. John in Vologda, see http://cultinfo.ru/infoproject/temples/; this site also includes several other Vologda churches dating from the seventeenth century and demolished in the 1960s); on Voronezh, see Elena Fediasheva, "Khramy Voronezha," *Komsomol'skaia pravda*, September 17, 2011, http://www.vrn.kp.ru/daily/25755/2740963/; on Tver', Sergei Pogorelov, "Sud'by Tverskoi Volyni," http://hram-tver.ru/tver/uspeniebogrutv.html; on Pereslavl'-Zalesskii, "Utrachennye khramy Pereslavlia-Zalesskogo," http://www.tourismpereslavl.ru/content.html?page=sightseeing_losttemples.

34. "V zashchitu pamiatnikov proshlogo," *Literaturnaia gazeta*, August 23, 1956, 1. The signatories included Igor' Grabar', Konstantin Fedin, and Il'ia Erenburg, among others, but A. A. Formozov ("Rol' N. N. Voronina v zashchite pamiatnikov kul'tury Rossii," *Rossiiskaia arkheologiia* 2 [2004]: 173–80) has convincingly argued that the text was actually authored by Nikolai Voronin, who had raised the issue of monuments protection in an earlier article, "Ob okhrane pamiatnikov kul'tury," *Pravda*, March 30, 1956, 2, though here he had talked generally about returning to the achievements of the Lenin era in preservation terms, and had not mentioned churches.

35. "Ob uluchshenii dela okhrany i restavratsii pamiatnikov kul'tury v RSFSR," Postanovlenie SM RSFSR ot 29 iiunia 1957, No. 781, in *OPIK* 1973, 133–34. The strengthening of the role assigned to local museums was also linked with the revival of "regional studies" (see below).

36. Letter of Pavel Abrosimov, secretary of the governing body of the Union of Architects of the USSR to A. B. Aristov in the Central Committee of the Communist Party of the Soviet Union (1959),

RGANI, f. 5, op. 34, d. 60, l. 1 Noted on the corner is: "The authors of the letter have been informed that the question of the creation of a voluntary society for the protection of monuments is currently under discussion."

37. Iurii Chaplygin, "Ne pomniashchie rodstva," *Literatura i zhizn*, February 21, 1960, 2.

38. D. S. Likhachev, "Vo imia budushchego," *Literatura i zhizn*, March 11, 1960, 2.

39. The very earliest contribution by Likhachev seems to have been a reader's letter, with cosignatories Nikolai Voronin and the writers Aleksei Iugov (1902–1979, an avid nationalist who believed that Achilles was of Slavonic origin) and Aleksandr Morozov (1906–1992, a specialist on the Russian and European baroque) to *Literaturnaia gazeta* on January 15, 1955, p. 2. Morozov was a colleague of Likhachev's at the Pushkin House Institute of Russian Literature, but Iugov and Likhachev's connection was entirely fortuitous, as the latter was the author of a rival translation of *The Lay of Igor's Campaign* and had no time for the theories about Achilles. Likhachev also coauthored a piece with Nikolai Voronin and Vladimir Kostochkin, an architect-restorer who in the 1970s was to be deputy chairman of the scientific and methodological council on monuments preservation at the USSR Ministry of Culture, which appeared in *Sovetskaia Rossiia* (June 27, 1957, 2). On Likhachev's later career, see chapter 6.

40. There is an interesting discussion of *Literature and Life*'s internal politics and the dipping and weaving of its editor, Aleksandr Dymshits, in Viacheslav Ogryzko, "Na razdache indul'gentsii," *Literaturnaia Rossiia*, July 6, 2012, http://litrossia.ru/archive/item/5861-oldarchive.html.

41. Ogryzko, "Na razdache," notes that Dymshits's equivocal attitude to heritage preservation turned out to be a more accurate assessment of the mood at the top than Chaplygin or Likhachev's advocacy for it.

42. "O dal'neishem uluchshenii dela okhrany i restavratsii pamiatnikov kul'tury v RSFSR," Decree of the Council of Ministers of the RSFSR, August 30, 1960, No. 1327. *OPIK* 1973, 139–42. See also docs.cntd.ru/document/9012089

43. Viktor Nekrasov, "Po obe storony okeana," *Novyi Mir* 11 (1962): 122.

44. On the exceptional impact of *Ivan Denisovich*, see Denis Kozlov, *The Readers of Novyi Mir: Coming to Terms with the Stalinist Past* (Cambridge, MA: Harvard University Press, 2013).

45. For an in-depth examination of the key case of discussions about the "cult of personality," see Polly Jones, *Myth, Memory, Trauma: Rethinking the Stalinist Past in the Soviet Union, 1953–70* (New Haven, CT: Yale University Press, 2013). On regional politics in the Khrushchev era generally, see Oleg Khlevniuk et al., eds., *Regional'naia politika N.S. Khrushcheva: TsK KPSS i mestnye partiinye komitety 1953–1964 gg.* (Moscow: Rosspen, 2009).

46. On the revival of "local studies," see, for example, Emily Johnson, *How St. Petersburg Learned to Study Itself: The Russian Idea of Kraevedenie* (University Park: Pennsylvania State University Press, 2006). On voluntary work generally, see, for example, "O nekotorykh novykh formakh organizatsii vospitatel'noi raboty sredi trudiashchikhsia po mestu zhitel'stva v Moskve i Leningrade" (1961), RGANI, f. 6, op. 34, d. 95, ll. 36–51. Komsomol work in this area is covered in Katharina Barbara Uhl, "Building Communism: The Young Communist League during the Soviet Thaw Period, 1953–1964" (DPhil thesis, University of Oxford, 2014).

47. For a further discussion of these contradictions, see chapter 1 of Catriona Kelly, *Remembering St. Petersburg* (Oxford: Triton Press, 2014).

48. Igor Polianski, in "The Antireligious Museum: Soviet Heterotopia between Transcending and Remembering Religious Heritage," in *Science, Religion and Communism during the Cold War*, ed. Paul Betts and Stephen A. Smith (Basingstoke: Palgrave, 2016), 253–73, has argued for a move toward religious history in the post-Stalin era, but in the Khrushchev era, the idea of "science" and more broadly "knowledge" as an antidote to religious misinformation was still the primary drive of the Leningrad museums, particularly the Museum of the History of Religion and Atheism. Out of fifty publications by the Antireligious Museum from 1956–1991 listed in the catalogue of the Russian National Library, the single one not to mention the word "atheism" in the title is *Pravoslavie v drevnei Rusi*, ed. L. N. Emeliakh, published in 1989. The museum in St. Isaac's dropped the adjective "antireligious" from its title when it reopened in 1957, and the brochures issued in the 1960s were classified

in library catalogues under the categories "architectural monuments" and "ecclesiastical architecture," and included considerably more material about the building's history than those published in the 1940s. See, for example, M. G. Kolotov, *Muzei-pamiatnik "Isaakievskii sobor": Al'bom* (Leningrad: Khudozhnik RSFSR, 1961); A. L. Rotach, *Isaakievskii sobor, vydaiushchiisia pamiatnik russkoi arkhitektury*, ed. V. I. Piliavskii (Leningrad; Znanie, 1962); G. P. Butikov, *Gosudarstvennyi muzei-pamiatnik Isaakievskii sobor* (Leningrad: Khudozhnik RSFSR, 1973). However, Foucault's pendulum remained in place until 1986 (N. Iu. Tolmacheva, *Isaakievskii sobor* [St. Petersburg: Paritet, 2003], 16), and it was not until the 1990s that the cathedral's pre-1917 history started to receive extensive treatment (cf. the much-expanded edition of Butikov's guide as *Muzei "Isaakievskii sobor"* [Leningrad: Lenizdat, 1991]).

49. On the Palace of Marriages, see K. L. Emel'ianova, *Pervyi v strane* (Leningrad: Lenizdat, 1964). The promotion of "new Soviet traditions" was a nationwide movement, whose first harbinger seems to have been a proposal from a woman in Saratov province forwarded in 1956 to the Central Committee by Aleksei Surkov, general secretary of the Soviet Writers' Union (RGANI, f. 5, op. 34, d. 14, l. 3). While this was rejected as "serving no purpose" (a standard Soviet form of refusal intended to deflect argument), in 1959, *Izvestiia* began running a series of articles on "new traditions," and this was followed by a surge of brochures. See Catriona Kelly, "'The Traditions of Our History': 'Tradition' as Framework for National Identity in Late Soviet and Post-Soviet Russia," in *Loyalties, Solidarities and Identities in Russian Society, History and Culture*, ed. Philip Ross Bullock et al. (London: School of Slavonic and East European Studies, 2013), 141–60. On the "palaces of marriage" specifically, see Sergei Shtyrkov, "'V gorode otkryt Dvorets schast'ia': Bor'ba za novuiu sovetskuiu obriadnost' vremen Khrushcheva," in *Topografiia schast'ia: Etnograficheskie karty moderna; Sbornik statei*, ed. Nikolai Ssorin-Chaikov (Moscow: Novoe literaturnoe obozrenie, 2013), 261–75.

50. Father Vladimir Sorokin, "Interv'iu zhurnalu 'Gorod,'" December 2, 2002, http://www.vladimirskysobor.ru/klir/nastojatel/intervju-zhurnalu-gorod/. The article is illustrated with a striking photograph, taken c. 1966, and showing the suavely suited Zharinov, clean-shaven and sprucely coiffed, alongside the luxuriantly bearded Nikodim in his well-worn cassock.

51. The late 1950s and early 1960s saw an exceptionally rapid turnover of metropolitans: after Elevferii (Vorontsov) died in office in 1959, he was succeeded by Pitirim (Sviridov) and Gurii (Egorov), each of whom spent only just over a year in Leningrad.

52. Quoted from Shkarovskii, *Russkaia pravoslavnaia tserkov'*, 188. Like his immediate predecessors, Metropolitan Pimen spent less than two years in Leningrad before promotion. On October 9, 1963, he became metropolitan of Krutitsy and Kolomna, an ancient and prestigious seat previously occupied by Metropolitan Pitirim (Sviridov) that Pimen held until 1971, when he was elevated to patriarch. Pace Pimen, the closure of the Chapel of the Blessed Xenia was deeply unpopular, as the patriarch's postbag indicates: see, for example, the petitions of December 1962 included in Aleksii, *Pis'ma Patriarkha Aleksiia I v Sovet po delam Russkoi Pravoslavnoi Tserkvi pri Sovete narodnykh komissarov—Sovete ministrov SSSR, 1945–1970 gg.* (Moscow: ROSSPEN, 2009–2010), 1:386–88. On the increasing cooperation between the Church and the security services in the late Soviet period, see Irina Maslova, "Russkaia pravoslavnaia tserkov' i KGB," *Voprosy istorii*, no. 12 (2005), 86–96.

53. There is an excellent biography of this remarkable and contradictory figure by Archimandrite Avgustin (Nikitin), *Tserkov' plenennaia: Mitropolit Nikodim (1929–1978) i ego epokha* (St. Petersburg: Izdatel'stvo Sankt-Peterburgskogo universiteta, 2008).

54. More exactly, a *tipovoi proekt* was one constructed to ministerially approved plans published for use all over the Soviet Union, irrespective of landscape or local building traditions. In low-prestige Soviet cities, most construction was in this form. See Elsa-Bair Guchinova, "From the USSR to the Orient: National and Ethnic Symbols in the City Text of Elista," in *Soviet and Post-Soviet Identities*, ed. Mark Bassin and Catriona Kelly (Cambridge: Cambridge University Press, 2012), 191–211.

55. The text is available online at http://www.sovarch.ru/postanovlenie55/.

56. Valentin Kamenskii (1907–1975) had a very different background from his predecessors. Like Baranov, he was a provincial outsider (from Tula—biographical materials about him are more easily available on a website there than in St. Petersburg, http://tulamen.ru/publ/2-1-0-29). But unlike Baranov, Kamenskii found it hard to shake off the taint of provincialism. He studied at the

Institute of Industrial Architecture (a far less prestigious place than LISI or the former Academy), and joined LISI only when he became a member of its teaching staff, in 1941. According to widespread report in St. Petersburg, there was no love lost between Kamenskii and Baranov, and certainly the former must have found his position as chief architect difficult, with a significantly promoted predecessor in a position to exercise control over his own efforts. In his *Glavnyi arkhitektor goroda (Tvorcheskaia i organizatsionnaia deiatel'nost')* (Moscow: Izdatel'stvo arkhitektury po stroitel'stvu, 1973), 170–71, Baranov went out of his way to criticize the unduly high first version of the Hotel Leningrad, describing this as the result of "a wrong decision by the city's chief architect."

57. A typical late-Stalinist public building was M. Ia. Klimentov's School No. 171 on ulitsa Maiakovskogo, completed in 1950.

58. One striking example was the pavilion of the metro station at Vasilieostrovskaia, whose architect specifically referred to the need to provide visual interest in an area of (by implication bland and boring) nineteenth-century buildings. See the discussion in Kelly, *St. Petersburg: Shadows of the Past* (New Haven, CT: Yale University Press, 2014), ch. 3.

59. "Proekt General'nogo plana Leningrada," vol. 1, "Svodnaia poiasnitel'naia zapiska" (Leningrad, Arkhtekturno-planirovochnoe upravlenie, 1964), TsGANTD-SPb, f. 386, op. 3–3, d. 36, l. 4, l. 74. Some of these projects, for example, building around the Lavra and on Okhta, had been anticipated in the 1949 General Plan, but the 1966 Plan abandoned many of the central ideas in that, particularly the elaborate projects of highway reconstruction, including a relief avenue to take pressure off Nevsky, the extension of Ligovskii prospekt to cross the Neva, etc. (TsGANTD-SPb, f. 386, op. 3–6, d. 42).

60. K. Belov, "Otvechaem na voprosy chitatelei: Takimi budut novye stantsii Leningradskogo metro," *VL*, September 9, 1960, 1. Cf. Belov, "Pod Moskovskim prospektom," *VL*, November 1, 1960, 1.

61. See the minutes of a meeting of the Technical Council of Lenproekt, March 5, 1957. TsGANTD-SPb, f. 36, op. 1–1, d. 216, ll. 19–20.

62. For a discussion, see introduction to Kelly, *Remembering St. Petersburg*.

63. A. N. Petrov et al., eds., *Pamiatniki arkhitektury Leningrada* (Leningrad: Stroiizdat, 1958). It is notable that the first edition of this album, and indeed later editions of the same book, were issued in very small print runs: 10,000 for the first, 25,000 for the second (1969), and 20,000 for the third and fourth (1972 and 1975 respectively). By comparison, collected works by leading authors of the day such as Anna Akhmatova and Ol'ga Berggol'ts were issued in significantly larger editions—50,000–80,000 copies.

64. The minutes of the GIOP Learned Council for 1966–1970 are available in TsGANTD-SPb (see chapter 6), and refer in general terms to the delisting policy: the minutes of a meeting on February 14, 1966, for example, refer to the need to compile an official list of monuments "that were mistakenly removed from [state] protection and that should be restored to it" (TsGANTD-SPb, f. 386, op. 1, d. 13, l. 12). However, materials from the Khrushchev era have not been deposited in TsGANTD-SPb, and procedural documents of this kind are closed to researchers in NA UGIOP. The list of state monuments in Leningrad and province for 1960 appears to have remained much the same as it was, if the published record is anything to go by (see Council of Ministers of the RSFSR, "O dal'neishem uluchshenii dela okhrany pamiatnikov kul'tury v RSFSR," August 30, 1960, "Prilozhenie," docs.cntd.ru/document/9012089; See also appendix 1). This list includes over thirty Orthodox sites in Leningrad, and thirty in the province. The latter represents a significant decline compared with 1950, but this may have been partly related to higher quality of information about what exactly still survived.

65. The Portico was reerected in its current position on Feather Row (Perinnaia liniia) in 1971.

66. Dimitry Pospielovsky, "Kak Stalin tserkov' vozrozhdal," *Vesna* 2 (2005), http://ricolor.org/journal/s2005/13/.

67. Pospielovsky, *The Russian Church*, 2:327; Nathaniel Davis, *A Long Walk to Church: A Contemporary History of Russian Orthodoxy* (Boulder, CO: Westview Press, 1995), 27, 31. Between 1947 and 1954, the numbers of working churches in the USSR dropped slightly, from 14,039 to 13,422; between 1954 and 1958, they rose slightly, from 13,376 to 13,415.

68. "Informatsionnoe pis'mo No. 2 Soveta po delam RPTs," January 31, 1956, TsGA-SPb, f. 9324, op. 3, d. 40, l. 1. Cf. "Informatsionnoe pis'mo No. 4 Soveta po delam RPTs," August 27, 1956,

ibid., l. 37, which blames officials' refusing permission to perform occasional offices such as funerals in people's homes for the rise in the numbers of petitions about opening churches.

69. "Svedeniia o khodataistvakh po otkrytiiu tserkvei," ASPbE, f. 1, op. 24, d. 41, ll. 9–10. The petitions in question referred to three separate churches: the Church of St. Nicholas at Zaozer'e (with six petitions from July 3, 1956; May 18, 1957; July 24, 1957; August 27, 1957; December 26, 1957; May 14, 1958); the Church of St. Ol'ga at Luga (with two petitions from April 16, 1957 and May 22, 1957); and the Trinity Cathedral, Kolpino (with five petitions from March 11, 1948; July 27, 1948; November 26, 1953; June 6, 1956; June 9, 1958). Interestingly, according to this file, the only church to have been the subject of petitions in the 1940s was the Church of St. Nicholas at Zaozer'e, related to which three petitions from 1949 are also listed.

70. ASPbE, f. 1, op. 11, d. 13, l. 8.

71. Ibid., l. 10 (November 28, 1958).

72. Letter by N. M. Sysoev and forty-eight other signatories, ASPbE, f. 1, op. 11a, d. 11, l. 2.

73. ASPbE, f. 1, op. 11a, d. 11, l. 4.

74. ASPbE, f. 1, op. 7, d. 40, ll. 12–13. The reference to the "State Museum-Reservation" was inaccurate; the Museum of City Sculpture was certainly situated in the Alexander Nevsky Lavra, and two cemeteries had museum status, but most of the territory was in use for workshops, etc. It is possible that the slip was intentional on Metropolitan Grigorii's part—a way of suggesting delicately that the entire monastery *should* be under state protection.

75. ASPbE, f. 1, op. 7, d. 40, ll. 12–13.

76. Indeed, one could plausibly argue that the popularity of the term "Thaw" among Western commentators came precisely from the success, in propaganda terms, of this (apparent) openness: the commitment to firm and indeed harsh social control that also characterized the Khrushchev years was less obvious to journalists and other visitors than was the considerably freer contact with foreigners that was now allowed. See, for example, Ronald Hingley, *Under Soviet Skins: An Untourist's Report* (London: Hamish Hamilton, 1961).

77. ASPbE, f. 1, op. 7, d. 40, l. 14.

78. Ibid., ll. 30–34.

79. Ibid., ll. 37–42.

80. Ibid., ll. 64–67; ll. 87–88.

81. Ibid., l. 90, l. 101.

82. Ibid., l. 125–26.

83. Ibid., ll. 146–47, l. 155.

84. For the material on the *panikadila*, see ibid., ll. 130–32, ll. 169–72, ll. 303–4.

85. Letter to N. S. Khrushchev from the parishioners of the Trinity Cathedral, June 26, 1961. Quoted from Shkarovskii, *Russkaia pravoslavnaia tserkov'*, 178–79.

86. On church cars, see Zharinov's memo to the City Committee of the Communist Party, March 12, 1962, TsGAIPD-SPb, f. 25, op. 89, d. 122, ll. 3–4. "The fact that churches have access to car transport of their own is justified by nothing, and all the more since at the moment, even many state organizations and enterprises do not have capacities of this kind." This was part of the crackdown on the maintenance of individual service cars under Khrushchev (see Lewis Siegelbaum, *Cars for Comrades: The Life of the Soviet Automobile* [Ithaca, NY: Cornell University Press, 2008], 225–27), though as non-state organizations providing their own transport purchased from their own funds, religious groups were not in the same position as the "state organizations and enterprises" that Zharinov mentions, since the vehicles for these were of course provided by the government, which might therefore quite reasonably decide to withdraw them.

87. TsGAIPD-SPb, f. 25, op. 89, d. 80, ll. 37–38. Zharinov was forced to admit (ibid.) that this strategy had actually failed—"the church people simply moved their trade into various woodsheds, etc.," an example of how practiced in brinkmanship both sides had become.

88. NA UGIOP, pap. 150, volume unnumbered: 4?, Edinovecherskaia tserkov', 1959–1986 gg., l. 157.

89. ASPbE, f. 1, op. 1, d. 35, ll. 32–33.

90. TsGAIPD-SPb, f. 25, op. 89, d. 122, l. 1.

91. ASPbE, f. 1, op. 24, d. 43, l. 30.

92. As a church that had functioned continuously in the Soviet era, this had an established and close-knit parish with its own highly specific and traditionalist ethos. Between 1927 and 1943, it was a Josephite parish. The special character was preserved well into the 1960s, according to a priest's wife who grew up there (FN, September 2012).

93. ASPbE, f. 1, op. 7, d. 122, ll. 57–58.

94. See, for example, the strictures of Metropolitan Grigorii about informal saints' cults in the Smolenskoe Cemetery, "O 'sviatykh' mestakh na Smolenskom kladbishche i trebakh na mogile I. Kronshtadtskogo," Resolutsiia Mitropolita Grigoriia, August 16, 1951, ASPbE, f. 1. op. 26 (3), d. 20, l. 40.

95. "Rapport Mitropolita Pimena Patriarkhu Aleksiiu," April 24, 1963, ASPbE, f. 1, op. 7, d. 122, l. 61.

96. Any "official body" that the parishioners had contacted would immediately have gotten in touch with the plenipotentiary; Pimen could only have gotten the information about the date of the lease from the latter. Therefore, he must certainly have known about any representations they had made, but either chose to ignore these, or wished to cover up the extent of his collaboration with an official from the secular authorities, or both. One may contrast the attitude of Metropolitan Grigorii, who, for example, had the courage to eschew open approbation of the November 13, 1954, decree, even after the patriarch had warmly commended it—a point that did not escape Georgii Karpov. Aleksii, *Pis'ma Patriarkha Aleksiia I*, 1:97.

97. As indicated in chapter 4, forty-five churches were working in Leningrad Province even in 1945, before the postwar reopenings. By 1962, this had declined to thirty-nine (ASPbE, f. 1, op. 26, d. 21, ll. 1–39).

98. See ASPbE, f. 1, op. 7, d. 122, ll. 123–31. The move to the new church was completed, however, only in December 1966.

99. TsGAIPD-SPb, f. 25, op. 89, d. 122, l. 2.

100. No list of church-monuments from 1960 survives in the archival materials consulted for this study; it seems likely that both the heritage bodies and the Orthodox Church simply disposed of such lists once they had been superseded.

101. Antonov and Kobak, *SSPb*.

102. Antonov and Kobak, *SSPb*. See also the information on http://sobory.ru/article/?object=00734.

103. The placing of a station on the square had, as noted in chapter 4, been planned since the 1930s. It had also been public knowledge for some time. See, for example, a late 1950s map showing the development of the metro "up to 1980": http://podzemka.spb.ru/history/. In the autumn of 1960, the Leningrad press published numerous reports on the development of the "Moskovskaia-Petrogradskaia Line" that included reference to ploshchad' Mira; see esp. "Pod ploshchad'iu Mira," *Smena*, September 28, 1960, 2, and also E. Arenin, "Podzemnye marshruty," *LP*, November 13, 1960, 2.

104. "O stroitel'stve vtorogo uchastka Moskovsko-Petrogradskoi linii metropolitena imeni Lenina v Leningrade," TsGANTD-SPb, f. 36, op. 1, d. 353, l. 7. Similarly, when the Architecture and Planning Directorate (APU) reviewed the building of the October Concert Hall on Ligovskii prospekt (meeting of June 1, 1960), A. I. Kniazev, presenting the proposal, stated simply, "The Greek Church will be demolished." This decision was not questioned or even mentioned in the subsequent discussion of the plans (TsGANTD-SPb, f. 386, op. 1–5, d. 112, l. 22).

105. For Piliavskii's position as architect of the Admiralty building, see his personal file (autobiographical form of 1951, Arkhiv Sankt-Peterburgskogo arkhitekturno-stroitel'nogo universiteta [hereafter ASPbGASU], d. 106, t. 1, l. 107). As the file also indicates, Piliavskii's original training was as a modern architect, but even at this stage, his 1933 graduation project included "elements of the architectural heritage of the past" (ibid., l. 10).

106. V. I. Piliavskii, "Tvorchestvo V. P. Stasova: Dissertatsiia na soiskanie stepeni doktora arkhitekturnykh nauk," TsGANTD-SPb, f. 205, op. 2–2, d. 487, 488, 489 (quotations d. 488, l. 66, l. 108).

The dissertation, 1,500 pages in length, and with a supplement of photographic plates, was based on enormous archival research (Piliavskii claimed to have worked in thirty-five repositories), and was a monument of positivistic historical scholarship.

107. See chapter 3.

108. For Mederskii's dissertation, see TsGANTD-SPb, f. 205, op. 2–2, d. 454; for Rotach's connection, see Rotach, *Isaakievskii sobor*, which was edited by Piliavskii and had an introduction by him. Piliavskii had played a major role in the restoration works on St. Isaac's Cathedral.

109. For the project on Zemtsov, see "Novye materialy o tvorchestve vydaiushchikhsia zodchikh (Plan raboty sektsii okhrany pamiatnikov LOSA na 1959 g.)," TsGALI-SPb, f. 341, op. 1, d. 550, l. 2. For the attribution, see the survey report on the Church of the Savior below.

110. L. A. Mederskii and Iu. M. Denisov, "Istoricheskaia spravka po zdaniiu b. tserkvi Spasa na Sennoi pl. (pl. Mira)," KGIOP, NMIIS Inventory no. H-2889. Cited from Zoia Iurkova, *Sennaia ploshchad': Vchera, segodnia, zavtra* (Moscow: Tsentropoligraf, 2011), http://lib.rus.ec/b/375320/read.

111. For an example of hortatory talk about economy, see M. Oporkov, "Proektirovanie i zhizn'—pokonchit' s raspyleniem sil i sredstv pri novoi zastroike," *LP*, September 1, 1960, 2.

112. For a description of this episode, which is not documented in any of the archival material in publicly accessible collections,, including that in SPbGASU, see V. V. Smirnov, "Skvernaia istoriia," *Neva* 3 (2004), http://magazines.russ.ru/neva/2004/3/smir19.html. There are other details in Smirnov's account that seem questionable (such as his unsubstantiated recollection of an article in *VL*, discussed below), but he was a graduate student of Piliavskii's at LISI, and may have been aware of an informal meeting.

113. Smirnov claims that the article appeared in *VL* in September 1960, but a detailed search of this newspaper, *LP*, and *Smena* turned up nothing analogous. In Smirnov's recollection, antireligious material such as Khalif's "Permskii obitel'" may have gotten fused with the reporting on the metro construction in the three Leningrad newspapers.

114. This is worth emphasizing since, in contrast to the baldness of the decision to demolish Spas na Sennoi, the folklore relating to the demolition is rich. It is recorded not just in local legends (such as the tale of how Valentin Kamenskii would daily spend time sighing on a street bench overlooking the site of the demolished church, as expiation for his role in demolishing it), but in written sources. For references to a "telegram from Moscow" see, for example, Ioann (Snychev), ed., *Ocherki istorii Sankt-Peterburgskoi eparkhii* (St. Petersburg: Andreev i synov'ia, 1994), 272; Evgenii Popov, "Dmitrii Likhachev," *LitMir Eketronnaia Biblioteka*, http://www.litmir.net/br/?b=179777&p=49; Smirnov, "Skvernaia istoriia," etc. While Smirnov's recollection that the Savior was visited by a commission from Moscow headed by Nikolai Baranov (the former Leningrad city architect) may be more reliable, and quite possibly also his recollection that Baranov and his colleagues expressed indignation at the proposed demolition, this does not of course prove that Baranov reported back to Furtseva in this vein, let alone that he chose to act on the report. The evidence is that Baranov (for example his ambiguous behavior with regard to the 1974 proposal to reconstruct the bell tower of the Savior Church, on which see chapter 6) was not incapable of playing two contrary roles at the same time. In a similar vein, informants sometimes claim to remember the meeting when the demolition was discussed in the Union of Architects and even having voted against the proposal to demolish —though there was no such meeting, or not at least till 1965, several years after the church disappeared (on the later meetings, see chapter 6). The sole recorded meeting in 1961 was one to discuss projects for the metro station (see the invitation from the chairman of the Moscow District Soviet to attend a discussion in LOSA, July 4, 1961, TsGALI-SPb, f. 341, op. 1–2, d. 592, l. 5). As the frequent confusion over dates in retrospective recollections indicates (people recall the demolition as happening in 1962 or even 1964), command of detail is often unreliable.

115. For the claim about damage to Piliavskii's career, see Smirnov, "Skvernaia istoriia." I base my rebuttal on Piliavskii's personal file, ASPbGASU, d. 106, t. 1, ll. 2–8 (autobiographical forms and letter of recommendation from 1933); l. 106 (information about Party membership from autobiographical form of 1951); t. 2, l. 31 (Piliavskii's application for the chair of City Planning); ll. 33–34 (Liubosh's letter). As for visits abroad, ibid., t. 1, l. 271, indicates that in October 1960, supposedly the

height of the fuss over the Church of the Savior, Piliavskii was given permission by the director of LISI to visit France, and t. 2, l. 19 is an invitation from the Hungarian Academy of Sciences dating from January 19, 1962.

116. Pospielovsky, *The Russian Church*, 2:332.

117. This conclusion is circumstantial—detailed documentation relating to the construction of the metro is not held in publicly accessible collections, so one important class of materials relating to city planning is simply not available for discussion.

118. P. I. Poliakov, "Otchet po dogovoru No. 2 s Lenmetroproektom po teme 'Stereofotogram-metricheskii obmer b. tserkvi na pl. Mira'" (July 1961), TsGANTD-SPb, f. 205, op. 2–4, d. 574, ll. 4–7. Here the details corroborate the gripping first-hand account of the survey that is given by Smirnov, "Skvernaia istoriia." As presented, the photographs are not in fact stereoscopic, but possibly materials of that kind survive elsewhere.

119. TsGANTD-SPb, f. 205, op. 2–4, d. 574, l. 5.

120. Ibid., l. 6. The reason given was that the structures were shown not just on engravings from the 1800s, but also on a map dating from 1798.

121. An interesting side-effect of Soviet demolition policy was the research expertise acquired in areas such as photo-fixation and the archaeology of construction, as here; in the 2010s, the archaeological approach to this church was to triumph again (see my conclusion).

122. For a view of ploshchad' Mira from the steps of the new metro station dating from not long after its opening, see a collection of souvenir postcards, "Leningrad-1966" (November 19, 2011), on the page "Peterburgskie starosti," http://spbstarosti.ru/vidy-na-peterburg/leningrad-1966.html.

123. D. S. Likhachev, "Pamiatniki kul'tury—vsenarodnoe dostoianie," *Istoriia SSSR* 3 (1961): 5–6.

124. See also the response by Likhachev to another publication by a prominent Moscow author, Vladimir Soloukhin: Likhachev, "Berech' pamiatniki proshlogo (Po povodu stat'i V. Soloukhina 'Berech' proshloe—dumat' o budushchem,' *Neva* 11 [1962])," *Neva* 3 (1963): 195–96, which repeats the reference to the Savior on the Haymarket more or less word-for word, and again addresses mainly cases outside Leningrad.

125. Likhachev, "Pamiatniki kul'tury," 8.

126. For an interesting study of how demolition and new building transformed attitudes to the district of Zariad'e in Moscow, see Pavel Kupriyanov and Larisa Sadovnikova, "Historical Zaryadye as Remembered by Locals: Cultural Meanings of City Spaces," in *Russian Cultural Anthropology since the Collapse of Communism*, ed. Albert Baiburin, Catriona Kelly, and Nikolai Vakhtin (Abingdon: Routledge, 2012), 220–53.

127. See chapter 6.

128. Report from Father P. Lebedev, the incumbent priest of the St. Michael the Archangel Church at Zazhupan'e village, Os'minskii district, Leningrad, July 27, 1954, ASPbE, f. 1, op. 24, d. 27, l. 144.

129. ASPbE, f. 1, op. 24, d. 43, l. 206.

130. ASPbE, f. 1, op. 24, d. 43, ll. 208–9. On ll. 326–28 of this file is another petition from the Lozhgolovo Church Council to the patriarch. All the petitions were forwarded to Metropolitan Pimen, and by him to the plenipotentiary (see l. 326), but without results. The photograph referred to has disappeared from the file.

131. http://open-terra.ru/miniexp/4kraev/lozhgolovo.html

132. My calculations from the information in the detailed gazetteer of churches in Leningrad Province, *Zemlia Nevskaia pravoslavnaia: Pravoslavnye khramy prigorodnykh raionov Sankt-Peterburga i Leningradskoi oblasti*, comp. A. V. Berman, E. V. Isakova, N. S. Krylov, M. V. Sharovskii, and N. A. Iakovlev (St. Petersburg: Pravoslavnaia Rus', 2000); see also appendix 2.

133. ASPbE, f. 1, op. 24, d. 43, l. 281.

134. ASPbE, f. 1, op. 26 (2), d. 19, l. 229.

135. Letter of July 1, 1963, ASPbE, f. 1, op. 24, d. 43, l. 96.

136. This point is underlined, for example, in Alexander Panchenko, *Ivan i Iakov—neobychnye svyatye iz bolotistoi mestnosti* (Moscow: Novoe literaturnoe obozrenie, 2012), see, for example, pp. 7–8.

137. Exchange of letters, 1958, ASPbE, f. 1, op. 7, d. 152, ll. 17–18. It is not clear whether the icon was ever returned to the Vazhiny church.

138. On the trouble caused by informal "mutual aid," see, for example, the 1958 case of Father Vasilii Ivanov who helped out parishioners who were not his own, because their own parish priests would not travel. He got a mild rebuke from Metropolitan Elevferii (ASPbE, f. 1, op. 11, d. 78, ll. 1–2). Reading between the lines, descent into alcoholism is what seems to have happened to one of the priests in Vazhiny in 1953–1954, who was said to have acknowledged the "disorder" in his running of the parish (ASPbE, f. 1, op. 7, d. 151, l. 165).

139. According to documentation in the records of the Leningrad Diocesan Chancery, whose officials were presumably in a position to know (ASPbE, f. 1, op. 26 (2), d. 21, ll. 1, 19, 26, 33, 39), there were fifty-two working churches in 1962, of which thirteen were in Leningrad and its surroundings, and the rest in smaller towns and villages. For the figure of eleven church-monuments, see the quotation from Zharinov above. In the province, the list of working churches and the list of monuments still overlapped very little.

140. Documentation of vandalism in city churches from the Khrushchev period has proved elusive, though it should be said that parish records generally thin out significantly, perhaps because more business was done by telephone.

141. ASPbE, f. 24, op. 1, d. 41, l. 23, l. 104. The second incident took place in 1959.

142. For a case of a hostile view from a religious believer, see, for example, the March 29, 1981, letter from the writer L. Panteleev to Lidiia Chukovskaia: *L. Panteleev—L. Chukovskaia: Perepiska, 1929–1987* (Moscow: Novoe literaturnoe obozrenie, 2011), 475: "I was distressed by the fact that [the poet] Akhmatova would, even in a half-joking way, describe herself as 'a Khrushchevian.' The XX Congress? He let Leva [Akhmatova's son, Lev Gumilev] out of the camps? But he closed 10,000 churches. And the blood of the murdered innocents in Novocherkassk?" One important prompting of irony was that believers easily saw through the use of administrative regulations in order to justify church closures: for example, in April 1964, the Trinity Church at Lesnovo parishioners tartly observed that the traffic problems the local soviet was invoking were not caused by the church, but by poor traffic management, notably the absence of lights at the junction outside or even a *regulirovshchik* (traffic policeman detailed to direct traffic with a baton) (ASPbE, f. 1, op. 7, d. 122, l. 79).

Chapter Six

1. "Natsional'nyi korpus russkogo iazyka" (www.ruscorpora.ru) lists many usages of the word *zastoi* prior to Gorbachev's epoch-making employment of the term at the Twenty-Seventh Congress of the Communist Party in 1986, but invariably in contexts such as "the moral *zastoi* of the capitalist system." For a study arguing that Gorbachev also revalued his positive terminology, such as perestroika and glasnost, see Kristian Petrov, "Construction, Reconstruction, Deconstruction: The Fall of the Soviet Union from the Point of View of Conceptual History," *Studies in East European Thought* 60, no. 3 (2008): 179–205.

2. Edwin Bacon and Mark Sandle, eds., *Brezhnev Reconsidered* (Basingstoke: Palgrave, 2002), was a pioneering example of the attempt to look beyond the label of "stagnation." As increasing historical attention is devoted to the Brezhnev era, this interpretation is gaining ground. See, for example, "The Apogee of the Soviet Experience: Culture and Society in the Brezhnev Years," the special two-volume issue of *Cahiers du monde russe* devoted to the period (54, nos. 1–4 [2013]); Christina Ezrahi, *Swans of the Kremlin: Ballet and Power in Soviet Russia* (Pittsburgh, PA: University of Pittsburgh Press, 2012).

3. The entrenchment of provincial elites at this period has been thoroughly studied by Yoram Gorlizki. See, for example, "Too Much Trust: Regional Party Leaders and Local Political Networks under Brezhnev," *Slavic Review* 69, no. 3 (2010): 676–700.

4. The Russian phrase is *ne smakovat' nedostatki*. For a discussion of this side of the Brezhnev era, see Nikolai Koposov, *Pamiat' strogogo rezhima: Istoriia i politika v Rossii* (Moscow: Novoe literaturnoe obozrenie, 2011).

5. On the cult of the war, see Amir Weiner, *Making Sense of War: The Second World War and the Fate of the Bolshevik Revolution* (Princeton, NJ: Princeton University Press, 2001).

6. Two major figures here, both Leningraders, were Dmitrii Sergeevich Likhachev and Iurii Mikhailovich Lotman; crucial publications by them include Likhachev's *Poetika drevnerusskoi literatury* (Leningrad: Nauka, 1967), and Lotman's *Aleksandr Sergeevich Pushkin: Biografiia pisatelia* (Leningrad: Prosveshchenie, 1981). On the recuperation of medieval buildings, see Aleksei Elfimov, *Russian Intellectual Culture in Transition: The Future in the Past* (Münster: Lit, 2004). For the so-called "historical turn" at this period generally, see Denis Kozlov, "The Historical Turn in Late Soviet Culture: Retrospectivism, Factography, Doubt, 1953–91," *Kritika* 2, no. 3 (2000): 577–600.

7. See introduction and chapter 3 above.

8. In Leningrad, the "monuments of history" (as opposed to "monuments of architecture") on the official lists included, alongside the buildings linked with the October Revolution and its historical actors, headed by Lenin, the various apartments and other places associated with famous writers and artists, headed by Pushkin. Great efforts were made to preserve these sites in a manner appropriate to their perceived historical importance: for example, when a rank-and-file Communist wrote in 1978 to the Lenin Museum in Moscow that the setting of the Lenin memorial in Razliv (where the leader had camped out between revolutions in 1917) was being "ruined" by the construction of hotels and "amusement venues" nearby, the result was an exhaustive enquiry by the Leningrad Party authorities (TsGAIPD-SPb, f. 24, op. 210, d. 2, ll. 29–35). The Brezhnev era was also the heyday of the so-called "museum-apartment": for a discussion of these in Leningrad, see Kelly, *Remembering St. Petersburg* (Oxford: Triton Press, 2014), ch. 4.

9. For influential discussions of the revival of nationalism under Brezhnev, see John Dunlop, *The Faces of Contemporary Russian Nationalism* (Princeton, NJ: Princeton University Press, 1983); Dunlop, *The New Russian Nationalism* (New York: Praeger, 1985); Geoffrey Hosking, *The Awakening of the Soviet Union* (Cambridge, MA: Harvard University Press, 1990); Yitzhak M. Brudny, *Reinventing Russia: Russian Nationalism and the Soviet State, 1953–1991* (Cambridge, MA: Harvard University Press, 1998); Nikolai Mitrokhin, *Russkaia partiia: Dvizhenie russkikh natsionalistov v SSSR, 1953–1985 gody* (Moscow: Novoe literaturnoe obozrenie, 2003).

10. Iu. M. Lotman, "Simvolika Peterburga i problemy semiotiki goroda" (1984), in *Izbrannye stat'i* (Tallinn: Aleksandra, 1992–1993), 1:9–22. There is, of course, also an international debate on whether heritage preservation is invariably a symptom of romantic, right-wing nationalism: in the case of the UK, for instance, Raphael Samuel's *Theatres of Memory*, 2 vols. (London: Verso, 1994–1998) offers a robust defense from the left of the role of heritage as popular history, while much greater cynicism is expressed by, say, Patrick Wright (see, for example, *A Journey through Ruins: The Last Days of London* [Oxford: Oxford University Press, 2009], 51–77).

11. Speech by B. S. Andreev, secretary of the Leningrad City Committee of the Komsomol: "Stenograficheskii otchet seminara propagandistov komsomol'skogo politprosveshcheniia i komsomol'skogo aktiva," September 25, 1972. TsGAIPD-SPb, f. K-598, op. 27, d. 457, l. 98.

12. Stephen A. Smith, "Contentious Heritage: The Preservation of Churches and Temples in Communist and Post-Communist Russia and China," in *Heritage in the Modern World: Historical Preservation in Global Perspective*, ed. Paul Betts and Corey Ross, Past and Present Supplement 10 (Oxford: Oxford University Press, 2015), 178.

13. Michael Herzfeld, *Cultural Intimacy: Social Poetics in the Nation State* (New York: Routledge, 1997). Herzfeld's study addresses modern Greek culture and the place in it of customs considered at once authentic and embarrassing, such as plate-smashing at weddings.

14. For instance, the file for LOSA's Section for the Preservation and Restoration of Monuments for 1959 (one of the rare years where any materials are preserved) runs to a mere five pages of handwritten notes recording the desultory discussion over just three meetings (TsGALI-SPb, f. 341, op. 1, d. 549, ll. 1–5). The institutional appointment books (*zhurnaly ezhednevnogo ucheta*) for 1959–1960 and

1961–1965 (TsGALI-SPb, f. 341, op. 1–2, d. 543, and TsGALI-SPb, f. 341, op. 1–2, d. 588) record about two events per year.

15. For studies that emphasize the public/private division, see, for example, Vladimir Shlapentokh, *Public and Private Life of the Soviet People: Changing Values in Post-Stalin Russia* (New York: Oxford University Press, 1989); Elena Zubkova, *Russia after the War: Hopes, Illusions, and Disappointments, 1945-1957* (Armonk, NY: M. E. Sharpe, 1998). For work that takes a more complex view of this divide, see, for example, Alexei Yurchak, *Everything Was Forever, Until It Was No More: The Last Soviet Generation* (Princeton, NJ: Princeton University Press, 2006); Lewis Siegelbaum, ed., *Borders of Socialism: Private Spheres of Soviet Russia* (Basingstoke: Macmillan, 2006).

16. For example, in the Dom kinematografista (the filmmakers' central club in Leningrad), as direct observation in 1981 suggested.

17. There is no overall list of those attending: those mentioned are those who actually spoke.

18. Butyrin, who had graduated from LISI in 1957, worked thereafter in the studio of Igor' Solodovnikov (also born in 1933). Neither specialized in restoration work; it was not until the 1990s that Butyrin began regularly working in this area (see the obituary note, "Umer peterburgskii arkhitektor Dmitrii Butyrin," *Fontanka.ru*, March 26, 2010, http://www.fontanka.ru/2010/03/26/048/). Solodovnikov worked in a variety of fields, including resort planning, defense institute planning, and housing (http://www.spb-business.ru/show.php?directory=60123). Butyrin's own recollections provide no indication of why he decided to design the project or how it progressed to the level of serious consideration, except that "the city architect" approved it (presumably Buldakov: see "Mnenie," undated, http://www.portal-credo.ru/site/?act=authority&id=69). But Butyrin had been a member of the Union of Architects since 1969, so would have been aware of the widespread discussion of the Haymarket.

19. On the demolition, see chapter 5 above.

20. For the minutes of the meeting, see TsGALI-SPb, f. 229, op. 1, d. 117, ll. 4–6. The chair of the meeting was Nikolai Baranov, Leningrad's former chief architect, evidently approached as a *zemliak*, or "local contact," in Moscow. He responded by agreeing to organize a discussion with the Leningrad Zonal Scientific Research Institute of Experimental Planning, responsible for work on the bus station (see ibid., l. 3). The meeting, however, which was clearly driven by Baranov's own agenda, went the opposite way from what the Leningraders surely expected when they got in touch. This double act, which one could describe as diplomatic or duplicitous depending on one's point of view, may throw light on Baranov's behavior when efforts were made to save the church from demolition in 1960 (see chapter 5).

21. "Protokol rasshirennogo zasedaniia komissii okhrany pamiatnikov istorii i kul'tury gradostroitel'noi LOSA, sovmestno s Leningradskim otdeleniem VOOPIiK," July 2, 1972, TsGALI-SPb, f. 229, op. 1, d. 117, l. 21. The reference to "cathedral" here is a slip of the tongue—the Church of St. Boris and St. Gleb was never accorded that status.

22. Ibid., l. 24.

23. Ibid., l. 21.

24. Ibid., l. 28.

25. Indeed, the official who replaced Kamenskii as city architect, Gennadii Buldakov (1924–1990), who held the position from 1971 until 1986, had still fewer credentials in terms of the city's planning traditions. Also a provincial outsider, he had worked in a factory from 1941 and reached higher education (in LISI) only in 1951. In the 1960s he worked on war memorials, and while city architect, he engineered the controversial remodeling of the areas around Smol'nyi Convent and on the Sinope Embankment (the latter involving the demolition of the Church of St. Boris and St. Gleb, see below). An appreciative memoir by a former work colleague (see V. F. Nazarov, "Gennadii Buldakov," in *Arkhitektory ob arkhitektorakh: Leningrad-Peterburg XX vek*, ed. Iu. Kurbatov [St. Petersburg: Ivan Fedorov, 1999]) emphasizes his emollient style and "true Petersburg" spirit, but the latter at any rate would have surprised his critics in the 1970s.

26. For a usefully broad discussion of the changes, see Smith, "Contentious Heritage." See also Sanami Takahashi, "Church or Museum? The Role of State Museums in Conserving Church Buildings,

1965–85," *Journal of Church and State* 51, no. 3 (2009): 502–17; and Victoria Arnold, "The Experience of Sacred Place in Post-Soviet Russia: A Geography of Orthodoxy and Islam in Perm' Krai" (DPhil thesis, Oxford, 2012), which includes a discussion of Soviet attitudes to "sacred space." A general study of property restitution is Csongor Kuti, *Post-Communist Restitution and the Rule of Law* (Budapest: Central European University Press, 2009); on the Orthodox Church, see 199–201.

27. Takahashi, "Church or Museum?," describes this process with regard to two important sites, the complex of wooden churches at Kizhi and the Solovki Monastery. Both were turned into museums, the former in 1965, and the latter in 1967. As Takahashi points out, it became possible to classify religious culture as "progressive" at this period (508); one could add that once churches had become the proper subject of "scientific investigation" (*nauka*), their status vis-à-vis "scientific atheism" also shifted. One could add that, though the Kizhi museum reserve was set up in the 1940s, it was formalized only at this period (see the report of May 16, 1968, TsGALI-SPb, f. 341, op. 1–3, d. 743, l. 7, reporting that it as yet had no legal status as a reserve).

28. This development was noted at the time by scholars such as John Dunlop and Geoffrey Hosking, and has since been extensively discussed in studies such as Elfimov, *Russian Intellectual Culture*. On heritage, see also the later chapters of the enormous and informative volume edited by A. S. Shchenkov, *Pamiatniki arkhitektury v Sovetskom Soiuze: Ocherki istorii arkhitekturnoi restavratsii* (Moscow: Pamiatniki istoricheskoi mysli, 2004).

29. *OPIK* 1973, 157.

30. See, for example, *Ezhegodnik Bol'shoi sovetskoi entsiklopedii*, 1969 (p. 147), 1970 (p. 142), 1971 (p. 159), 1972 (p. 145), etc. These records also claimed a steady rise in the membership, which had reached 4 million by 1970 and 7.5 million by 1972, over 10 million by 1975 (p. 155) and over 16 million by 1987 (p. 140).

31. "O sostoianii i merakh uluchsheniia okhrany pamiatnikov istorii i kul'tury v RSFSR," decree of the Council of Ministers of the USSR, May 24, 1966, quoted from http://www.bestpravo.ru/sssr/eh-zakony/c2v.htm. An extract from the statute is available in *OPIK* 1973, 150–54.

32. Vladimir Soloukhin, "Chernye doski: Zapiski nachinaiushchego kollektsionera" (1969), reprinted in his *Slavianskaia tetrad'* (Moscow: Sovetskaia Rossiia, 1972).

33. The same was true of a trip to Vladimir in 1980, when particular attention was drawn to the little animal sculptures outside the Cathedral of St. Demetrios, as works of "folk art"/"the art of the people" (*narodnoe iskusstvo*).

34. Petr Vail' and Aleksandr Genis, *60-e: Mir sovetskogo chekoveka* (Ann Arbor: Ardis, 1988), 218.

35. Soloukhin's article was later collected in his *Slavianskaia tetrad'*. D. S. Likhachev, "Chetvertoe izmerenie," *Literaturnaia gazeta*, June 10, 1965, 2.

36. Meeting of March 28, 1966, TsGANTD-SPb, f. 386, op. 1–1, d. 13, l. 31. It is notable that six out of sixteen present in fact voted against the proposal, a sign of changing tastes. See Catriona Kelly, "'A Dissonant Note on the Neva': Historical Memory and Local Identity in Russia's Second City during the Post-Stalin Era," *Journal of Eurasian Studies* 1, no. 1 (2010): 72–83, for a discussion of the importance of literary and historical associations in Leningrad preservationism generally.

37. TsGALI-SPb, f. 341, op. 1, d. 691, l. 3. S. V. Korobkov was the official in GIOP who was to be sent a copy of the letter; by 1966, he himself was the head of GIOP (TsGANTD-SPb, f. 386, op. 1, d. 31, l. 86).

38. For their biographies, see A. A. Kharshak, "Petr Evgen'evich Kornilov (1896–1981): Tvorcheskii put', sluzhenie," *Noveishaia istoriia Rossii* 1 (2013): 208–41.

39. TsGALI-SPb, f. 341, op. 1, d. 691, l. 38.

40. On the emergence of the canonical status of the *ansambl'*, see chapters 2 and 3 above. The status endured into the late Soviet period as well; see, for example, V. I. Piliavskii's list of *ansambli* to be included in *Monuments of Leningrad* (1968) (TsGANTD-SPb, f. 386, op. 1–1, d. 31, l. 5), as well as the insistence on the *ansambl'* as an identifying feature of Russian architectural tradition specifically (as opposed to any other) in his *Natsional'nye osobennosti russkoi arkhitektury: Metodicheskoe posobie v pomoshch' lektoru* (Leningrad: Znanie, 1970), 15–16.

41. TsGA-SPb, f. 3199, op. 2, d. 428, ll. 6–7. See also chapter 3.

42. TsGALI-SPb, f. 229, op. 1, d. 72, l. 22.

43. See, for example, the comments by Aleksandr Kobak on the entire preservationist movement as "anti-Communist" in the 2006 TV film *The Twilight of a Big City* (later removed from circulation after adverse comments from then-governor Valentina Matvienko that it was "not timely").

44. Letter from B. B. Piotrovskii to the chief architect of Leningrad, G. N. Buldakov, February 11, 1972, TsGALI-SPb, f. 229, op. 1, d. 72, l. 22.

45. See above.

46. A particular spur to the anti-dirigiste opposition was the role of the Soviet Union as a joint signatory of the Helsinki Accords in 1975, which generated pressure for the Soviet government to live up to the international standards to which it had subscribed. See Geoffrey Hosking, *A History of the Soviet Union* (London: Fontana, 1985, and subsequent editions), esp. ch. 14.

47. On the centrality of pressure for consultation on planning to the glasnost era in Leningrad, see E. K. Zelinskaia, O. N. Ansberg, and A. D. Margolis, eds., *Obshchestvennaia zhizn' v Leningrade v gody perestroiki, 1985–1991* (St. Petersburg: Serebrianyi vek, 2009). For a promise of widened participation, see "Obsuzhdaiut gradostroitel'nye sovety," *Leningradskaia panorama* 1 (1991): 14. This article proposed widening membership of the City Planning Council, which had traditionally comprised city officials and senior architects (see N. V. Baranov, *Glavnyi arkhitektor goroda [Tvorcheskaia i organizatsionnaia deiatel'nost']* [Moscow: Izdatel'stvo arkhitektury po stroitel'stvu, 1973]). Its deliberations were not and never would be subject to public scrutiny (even now, this material is not available in archives for the period from the early 1960s on).

48. See, for example, "Spisok razovyi rukovodiashchego sostava LGO VOOPIiK" (1985), which indicates that twelve out of fourteen people holding official positions in the organization's administration were Party members; the non-party members included the society's accountant and the head of its "social inspectorate." TsGALI-SPb, f. 229, op. 1, d. 563, l. 97.

49. On this, see Oxf/AHRC SPb-07 PF2 CK.

50. It was, admittedly, also this; see, for example, Oxf/AHRC-SPb-08 PF46 ANK (woman b. 1969, interviewed by Anna Kushkova): "Suppose there's a collection, some membership dues or whatever for the monuments protection society. So, say, someone from work turns up and says, 'Give me 50 kopecks.' I've no idea what society she's talking about, and [. . .] I'm not bothered about protecting monuments either, given the state does that very well by itself. Why should I hand over 50 kopecks? But there was all this stuff about collectivism, common rules, and so on, and not coughing up was just not done. So you did cough up."

51. Mark Edele, *Soviet Veterans of the Second World War: A Popular Movement in an Authoritarian Society, 1941–1991* (Oxford: Oxford University Press, 2008).

52. Sokolov and most of his successors also held the position for only short periods of time (five to six years), another factor meaning that their contribution was at the level of *tochechnaia zastroika*, or building on individual sites. Even Oleg Kharchenko (b. 1948), city architect from 1992–2004, mainly managed to build hospitals and clinics. Of course, an additional factor here was that, after 1991, state commissions all but dried up, which meant that the position of city architect became considerably less appealing—the holders were unable to take on financially and professionally rewarding projects themselves, or (equally important) hand these out to their friends.

53. Material from the archive of the plenipotentiary for religious affairs in Leningrad (see TsGA-SPb, f. 2017, op. 1, d. 3 [1966]; d. 18 [1969], etc.) confirms this picture of passivity with reference to Orthodoxy. For discussion of the action against "sectarians" contemporary with the events, see particularly the work of Michael Bourdeaux, for instance *Aida of Leningrad: The Story of Aida Skripnikova* (London: Mowbrays, 1976).

54. See the interesting discussion in Natalia Shlikhta, "'Orthodox' and 'Soviet': On the Issue of the Identity of Christian Soviet Citizens (1940s–early 1970s)," *Forum for Anthropology and Culture* 11 (2015), 140–64.

55. Biography of a priest b. 1929, ASPbE, f. 1, op. 24, d. 41, l. 146.

56. See, for example, ASPbE, f. 1, op. 24, d. 41, l. 149.

57. Arie Zand, *Political Jokes of Leningrad* (Austin, TX: Silvergirl Paperbacks, 1982).

58. Oxf/AHRC SPb-03 PF10 VM.

59. Letter from Father A. Medvedskii, August 30, 1968, and comments by Zharinov, TsGA-SPb, f. 2017, op. 1, d. 18, ll. 53–55.

60. ASPbE, f. 1, op. 7, d. 73, petition of February 9, 1966.

61. See, for example, "O roli zhenshchiny po vnedreniiu v byt novykh sovetskikh obriadov," February 17, 1969, TsGAIPD-SPb, f. 25, op. 102, d. 58, l. 2.

62. For instance, in 1970 a report from Grigorii Zharinov to the Council on Religious Affairs in Moscow reported that the numbers of young people lighting candles in the churches of Leningrad over Easter were worrying (even if some young people could be found using the candles to light their cigarettes): "Dokladnaia zapiska o prazdnovanii v tserkvakh Leningrada paskhi v 1970 godu," May 19, 1970, TsGA-SPb, f. 2017, op. 1, d. 24, ll. 56–58.

63. On vandalism, see, for example, NA UGIOP, pap. 171, Spaso-Preobrazhenskii Sobor: Perepiska 1968–1995 gg., l. 78 (report of 1983). An informant of mine born in the early 1950s recalls that when transistors first became fashionable in the Soviet Union, it was a popular practice among Komsomol members in Leningrad to take these into churches and switch them on, loudly, during the service. (Pers. inf.)

64. As in D. S. Likhachev's discussions of Old Russian literature, for example.

65. "O vnesenii izmenenii i dopolnenii v postanovlenie VTsIK i SNK RSFSR ot 8 aprelia 1929 goda 'O religioznykh ob"edineniiakh,'" Decree of the Presidium of the Supreme Soviet of the RSFSR, June 23, 1975, *Vedomosti Verkhovnogo Soveta RSFSR* 27 (1975): 487–91.

66. See, for example, the letter sent by Lenfil'm studio to Zharinov in 1969, TsGA-SPb, f. 2017, op. 1, d. 18, l. 44. Lenfil'm also built up its own collection of ecclesiastical props, still visible in the stores today (FN, April 2015). That said, religious materials in films were still closely monitored: in discussion of Valerii Frid and Iulii Dunskii's *Victory Day* (later filmed as *The Widows* by Sergei Mikaelian), the scriptwriters were exhorted to remove a scene in which the two old women talked about asking a priest to remember their husbands and two unknown soldiers at prayers in the church. TsGALI-SPb., f. 257, op. 24, d. 1048, l. 6, l. 9.

67. AHRC-SPb.-07 PF2 CK (interview by Catriona Kelly with Aleksandr Margolis). A symptom of changing attitudes was that in an architecture guide aimed at specialists, *Arkhitekturnyi putevoditel' po Leningradu*, ed. V. I. Piliavskii et al. (Leningrad: Izdanie literatury po stroitel'stvu, 1971), the Church of the Savior on the Blood was listed as an architectural attraction and even assigned a star (though the three-star attractions were still all from the "Golden Age").

68. Iu. I. Kurbatov, "Istoricheskaia sreda i kontseptual'nost' novykh form: Opyt Leningrada 1970-kh–1980-kh godov," in *Pamiatniki istorii i kul'tura Sankt-Peterburga*, ed. B. M. Kirikov and L. V. Kornilova (St. Petersburg: Beloe i chernoe, 2005), 398–401.

69. Iosif Brodskii [Joseph Brodsky], "Ostanovka v pustyne," in *Stikhotvoreniia i poemy*, ed. Lev Losev (Moscow: Vita Nova, 2011), 1:210.

70. Boris Ivanov, "Po tu storonu ofitsial'nosti," in *Sochineniia* (Moscow: NLO, 2009), 2:412. Emphasis original.

71. Igor' Smirnov, *Deistvuiushchie litsa* (St. Petersburg: Petropolis, 2008), 22. My thanks to the author for providing a copy of this material.

72. Compare the very limited interest shown by Brodsky in the two important churches, the Cathedral of the Transfiguration and the St. Panteleimon Church, visible from the building in which he grew up, the Muruzi House, in his memoir *Less Than One: Selected Essays* (Harmondsworth: Penguin, 1987).

73. See Josephine von Zitzewitz, "The 'Religious Renaissance' of the 1970s and Its Repercussions on the Soviet Literary Process," DPhil thesis, University of Oxford, 2009. Several of the figures dealt with here, including Elena Shvarts and Viktor Krivulin, were Leningraders.

74. The first edition of Antonov and Kobak's *SSPb*, in three volumes, came out in 1994. In an interview conducted by Catriona Kelly in 2009 (Oxf/AHRC SPb-09 PF10 CK), Aleksandr Kobak described the process of researching the book, whose topic was not conveyed to the staffs of the

archives where he and Antonov worked (instead, their declared topic was "the public buildings of Leningrad"). However, as Kobak observes, the pair "only ever ordered material on churches," so that the archivists "must have understood pretty well what we were up to"—a further indication of a general shift in values. The manuscript was then smuggled out to Paris in 1983, but the hoped-for appearance of the book was delayed by the inability of Nikita Struve, the director of the YMCA Press, to obtain funding (perhaps, one assumes, because of the size and complexity of the manuscript).

75. For instance, a contributor to the 1975 discussion of planning for the Haymarket claimed that "the public protested against it being blown up. A telegram signed by the chairman of the society for the protection of monuments, B. B. Piotrovskii, was sent to the Council of Ministers saying it was essential to save the church. But it was still blown up" (Architect Smetannikov (Giproteatr), TsGA-LI-SPb, f. 229, op. 1, d. 117, l. 30). This accurately describes what would have happened in 1975, or indeed 1967, but not before VOOPIiK had time to establish its lobbying credentials—the organization itself did not, of course, even exist in 1961.

76. "Proekt General'nogo plana Leningrada, t. 1. Svodnaia poiasnitel'naia zapiska" (1964), TsGANTD-SPb, f. 386, op. 3–3, d. 36, l. 93, ll. 105–11. The completed plan proposed that all monuments in the city should undergo restoration: General'nyi plan razvitiia Leningrada (Leningrad: Lengorispolkom, 1966), 17.

77. "Protokol zasedaniia Uchenogo Soveta GIOP," January 10, 1966, TsGANTD-SPb, f. 386, op. 1, d. 13, l. 1–3.

78. Style moderne is the Russian term for the early twentieth-century architectural styles known in France and the English-speaking world as art nouveau and art-and-crafts. For Brezhnev-era discussion of the moderne, see, for example, G. Lisovskii, "Master shkoly natsional'nogo romantizma," Leningradskaia panorama 4 (1975), 42–44 (on N. V. Vasil'ev, architect of the mosque, whose work is also considered in A. Shchukin, "Golubye kupola mecheti," Leningradskaia panorama 8 [1987]: 38–39); B. M. Kirikov and S. G. Fedorov, "Zodchii-entsiklopedist: O tvorcheskom puti arkh. G. V. Baranovskogo," Leningradskaia panorama 2 (1985): 29–32 (includes material on the Eliseev Store); V. G. Isachenko, "V shirokom diapazone: Tvorcheskoe nasledie P. Iu. Siuzora," Leningradskaia panorama 10 (1985): 28–31. By the year 2000, there were 347 buildings from the period 1890–1917 under state protection, more than from all other periods after 1850 put together (V. I. Andreeva et al., eds, Pamiatniki istorii i kul'tury Sankt-Peterburga, sostoiashchie pod gosudarstvennoi okhranoi: Spravochnik [St. Petersburg: Al'tsoft, 2000]).

79. On guidebooks, see Kelly, Remembering St. Petersburg, ch. 2.

80. Judging by their signatures on documents, Pavlova replaced Korobkov in c. 1971 and remained in office until 1975, when she was replaced by I. P. Sautov (see below).

81. "Protokol zasedaniia Uchenogo soveta GIOP," April 4, 1966, TsGANTD-SPb, f. 386, op. 1, d. 13, l. 54.

82. "Protokol zasedaniia Uchenogo soveta GIOP," January 10, 1966, TsGANTD-SPb, f. 386, op. 1, d. 13, ll. 1–3.

83. Compare TsGA-SPb, f. 9620, op. 2, d. 1, l. 55–55 ob., and TsGALI-SPb, f. 229, op. 2, d. 2, ll. 1–30. See also appendix.

84. This interest was less evident in Piliavskii's publications, though Natsional'nye osobennosti russkoi arkhitektury included many examples of churches (St. Isaac's among them), but all the same, fewer than in his unpublished work, particularly his thesis on Stasov (see chapter 5).

85. See the material in files no. 173 (Saints Simeon and Anne) and 481 (Coreligionists), NA UGIOP.

86. NA UGIOP, d. 150, Nikol'skaia Edinovercheskaia tserkov', Perepiska 1959–1986 gg. (no file or vol. no.), ll. 69–83 (folios in reverse chronological order). Ivan Petrovich Sautov (1947–2008) graduated from LISI in 1974 and headed GIOP until 1987, when he was appointed director of the Tsarkoe Selo Palace Museums.

87. The architects interviewed for this book uniformly rolled their eyes when the Inspectorate was mentioned and it was common to hear restorers described as "architects who couldn't make it on their own," etc.

368 NOTES TO CHAPTER SIX

88. A measure of the Institute's standing was the scale of the new building constructed for it on Vasilievskii Island, and the fact that the street on which it stood was renamed after Bering as a tribute to its research subject.

89. See, for example, chapter 3 above, on the Church of the Coreligionists and the Church of St. Simeon and St. Anne.

90. An example was the Catherine Palace at Tsarskoe Selo. On November 30, 1964, Kedrinskii reported to the Section for the Protection of Monuments at the Union of Architects that he was not planning on restoring the chapel as remodeled by Stasov, but had done substantial work to the decorative elements, and was transferring two angels from a church at the Monastery of St. Trinity and St. Sergius (presumably the cathedral, demolished in 1960—see chapter 5). (TsGALI-SPb, f. 341, op. 1–2, d. 655, l. 10.)

91. For the proposal, from the plenipotentiary of the Presidium of the Academy of Sciences in Leningrad, V. M. Tuchkevich, and the president of the Academy of Arts, N. Tomskii, see TsGAIPD-SPb, f. 24, op. 159, d. 39, ll. 30–37. As for the later fate of the monastery complex, even at the start of the 2010s, not all of it was in use by the Lavra itself (the Museum of City Sculpture, for example, was still housed in the St. Lazarus Church and the Church of the Annunciation).

92. Letter from Zoia Novikova to VOOPIiK, December 5, 1972, TsGALI-SPb, f. 229, op. 1, d. 72, ll. 131–32.

93. Obviously, it was also not proposed to turn banks back into banks, palaces into elite accommodation, and so on. That would be a development of the post-Soviet era.

94. A. S. Raskin and N. N. Vesnina, *Okhrana i restavratsiia pamiatnikov arkhitektury Leningrada* (Leningrad: Stroiizdat, 1981).

95. ASPbE, f. 1, op. 7, d. 122, l. 111. The article referred to did not appear in *Izvestiia* on January 25, 1966, so the parishioners may have had in mind one of the articles that appeared around the first convention of VOOPIiK on February 17, 1966; see, for example, February 18, 1966, 2.

96. The St. Catherine Church appeared in Leningrad Province lists from the moment when these were compiled in 1935 (see NA IIMK, f. 29, op. 1, ed. khr. 872, ll. 43–50), and was transferred to the city lists after Murino itself was integrated into the city boundaries. It did not appear in the lists of 1968, but in a letter of April 15, 1971, sent by K. A. Pavlova, then head of GIOP, to B. B. Piotrovskii, is stated as having been transferred to the care of VOOPIiK (TsGALI-SPb, f. 229, op. 1, d. 50, l. 97b).

97. The extensive correspondence to do with the case is held in the files of VOOPIiK at TsGALI-SPb, f. 229, op. 1, d. 224, ll. 1–12. Murino was a bone of contention at other stages too: there are documents on file with submissions about the church's importance and its poor condition from the late 1950s and the 1980s as well. See, for example, ASPbE, f. 1, op. 24, d. 20, ll. 144–45 (petition from 1953); ibid., d. 36, ll. 188–90 (petition from 1958); TsGALI-SPb, f. 229, op. 1, d. 564, ll. 39–40 (representations to VOOPIiK from 1985). Not surprisingly, it was taken over by parishioners at an early stage (a 1990 report by the local dean [*blagochinnyi*] refers to "resurrection of the parish going on actively," ASPbE, f. 1, op. 26 [1], d. 23, l. 123). As of the 2010s, it was a particularly active and welcoming parish (FN January 2010), partly explained by the area's status as a prestigious place for dachas.

98. TsGA-SPb, f. 2017, op. 1, d. 18, l. 89.

99. "Proekt General'nogo plana Leningrada," vol. 1, "Svodnaia poiasnitel'naia zapiska" (Leningrad, Arkhtekturno-planirovochnoe upravlenie, 1964), TsGANTD-SPb, f. 386, op. 3–3, d. 36, l. 109-10.

100. Oxf/AHRC SPb-09 PF5 CK.

101. TsGALI-SPb, f. 229, op. 1, d. 72, ll. 127–28.

102. "Spisok rabot v khrame Vsekh Skorbiashchikh," TsGALI-SPb, f. 229, op. 1, d. 39, l. 70, June 23, 1970. At this period, the Church of St. Simeon and St. Anne was removed from its "post-box institute," and transferred to the Meteorological Museum: see *Biulleten' Ispolkoma Lengorsoveta* 15 (1972): 21. On Smol'nyi, see "Delo po kontrol'iu za Muzeem istorii Leningrada za 1975 g.," TsGALI-SPb, f. 105, op. 2, d. 1120, ll. 13–14, l. 48.

103. Some monastic legations (*podvor'ia*) were turned into domestic accommodation in the early Soviet period, as were parts of the Alexander Nevsky Lavra, but this does not seem to have

happened in the 1960s and 1970s (in contradistinction to Moscow, where some actual church buildings were in service as accommodation right up to the 2010s). Indeed, the general Leningrad preservation policy was to try and prevent mundane activities from taking place in architectural monuments:
the files of VOOPIiK include some entertaining examples of this, such as fuss about refreshments in
the Coffee Pavilion in the Summer Gardens (definitely not to include alcohol or anything more than
soft drinks and biscuits), and about sunbathing outside the Peter and Paul Fortress (supposedly an
offense to the building's solemn history as a prison for sainted revolutionaries). See Kelly, *Remembering
St. Petersburg*, p. 160.

104. "O merakh po sokhraneniiu khudozhestvennogo ubranstva v zdaniiakh," *Biulleten' Ispolkoma Lengorsoveta* 22 (1972): 9.

105. T. Iu. Degtiareva, *Istoricheskii tsentr Leningrada—problemy okhrany i restavratsii inter'erov:
V pomoshch' lektoru* (Leningrad: Znanie, 1988), provided much gloomy discussion of losses to the
fabric.

106. "O sostoianii pamiatnikov arkhitektury Petrovskogo vremeni, nakhodiashchikhsia v Leningrade," February 4, 1966, TsGALI-SPb, f. 341, op. 1–2, d. 701, l. 18.

107. V. I. Piliavskii, *Zodchii Vasilii Petrovich Stasov (1769–1848)* (Leningrad: Izdanie literatury
po stroitel'stvu, 1970), 26–36. In his dissertation of 1959, Piliavskii had been much franker about the
dilapidated condition of some of Stasov's churches, particularly the estate church at Baran'ia gora,
Tver' province, calling for its urgent restoration (TsGANTD-SPb, f. 205, op. 2–2, d. 487, l. 78). As of
February 2015, however, the church was still in appalling condition (see, for example, the photographs
on http://hram-tver.ru/kuvshinovorn/baranovagorakuvshinovo.html), as was another important estate church by Stasov at Bronnitskaia gora in Novgorod province (http://urban3p.ru/object2650/).

108. *Instruktsiia o poriadke ucheta i khraneniia kul'turnykh tsennostei, nakhodiashchikhshsia v
pol'zovanii religioznykh ob"edinenii* (Moscow: Sovet po delam religii, May 29, 1980), 1 (imeographed
typescript, uthor's collection).

109. NA UGIOP, pap. 171 Spaso-Preobrazhenskii Sobor: Perepiska 1968–1995 gg., ll. 3–213
(folios in reverse chronological order).

110. "Stenograficheskii otchet obsuzhdeniia proekta zastroiki ploshchadi Mira v Leningrade,"
November 18, 1965, TsGALI-SPb, f. 341, op. 1, d. 682, l. 18.

111. Ibid., l. 38. For Razodeev's role at the State Inspectorate of Monuments, see the article on
the website of the St. Petersburg Union of Restorers, "Tat'iana Ivanovna Nikolaeva" (author not credited), http://www.srspb.ru, rubric "Alleia slavy".

112. "Stenograficheskii otchet obsuzhdeniia," l. 38.

113. TsGA-SPb, f. 7384, op. 33, d. 76, l. 101.

114. "Chernovik obrashcheniia Prezidiuma Soveta LGO VOOPIiK," April 1975, TsGALI-SPb,
f. 229, op. 1, d. 168, l. 1, l. 7.

115. TsGALI-SPb, f. 229, op. 1, d. 72, l. 53.

116. On a visit in summer 1985, Foucault's pendulum could be seen displayed: otherwise, the
compulsory guided tour of St. Isaac's mainly consisted of viewing the city from the upper galleries.
Equally, on visits to the Cathedral of SS. Peter and Paul, guides did not comment on the building's
iconostasis, or other specifically liturgical features; attention was always concentrated on the tombs of
the Romanovs, above all, of course, the honorary Bolshevik, Peter the Great, whose grave was always
decorated with flowers.

117. The sense that tourists were offended by churches in poor repair was routinely used as an
argument in favor of restoration; see, for instance, the comments on the church at Zelenogorsk cited
above.

118. On the Shuvalovo church, see S. Karishnev, "Vozrodim khram!," *Vyborgskaia storona* 4
(1992): 2; on the Church of St. Elijah the Prophet, see Father Aleksandr Budnikov, *Tserkov' Sviatogo
Proroka Ilii* (St. Petersburg: Izdanie khrama Svatogo Proroka Ilii, 1998).

119. See the circular from the Council on Religious Affairs, 1977, "O roste chisla krazh ikon iz
tserkvei," TsGA-SPb, f. 2017, op. 1, d. 56, l. 36.

120. TsGALI-SPb, f. 341, op. 1–2, d. 701, l. 37.

121. The building the writer had in mind was the Church of the Kazan' Icon of the Mother of God, at no. 547, Primorskoe shosse, constructed by N. N. Nikonov (beginning in 1910) in the "Moscow-Sudzal'" style. It was closed after the war (when the Soviet forces invaded Zelenogorsk, then called Teriokki), and used as a warehouse. In the 1960s, the Orthodox Church petitioned for its return, but received a refusal. It was returned to Orthodox use in 1989. See http://al-spbphoto.narod.ru/Hram/zelenogorsk.html.

122. TsGALI-SPb, f. 229, op. 2, d. 45, l. 12.

123. http://al-spbphoto.narod.ru/Hram/zelenogorsk.html.

124. Zones of "restricted building" were proposed as early as 1964, in the preparatory work for the General Plan (see "Proekt General'nogo plana Leningrada: Svodnaia poiasnitel'naia zapiska" (Leningrad, Arkhtekturno-planirovochnoe upravlenie, 1964), TsGANTD-SPb, f. 386, op. 3–3, d. 36, l. 108–9), and the General Plan of 1966 implemented the specific zones suggested in reduced form (e.g., Vasilievskii Island up to the 8-ia not 13-ia liniia). A. V. Makhrovskaia, *Rekonstruktsiia zhilykh raionov Leningrada (Obzor)* (Moscow: Gosudarstvennyi komitet po grazhdanskomu stroitel'stvu i arkhitekture pri Gosstroe SSSR, 1974), 5–7.

125. "O merakh po uluchsheniiu okhrany, restavratsii i ispol'zovaniia pamiatnikov istorii i kul'tury", 16 June 1980, *Biulleten' Ispolkoma Lengorsoveta* 16 (1980): 7–10. The RSFSR legislation had been passed on January 14, 1980 (ibid., p. 7).

126. B. M. Kirikov and A. D. Margolis, "Ugolok starogo goroda," *Leningradskaia panorama* 8 (1984): 30–31; Kirikov and Margolis, "O sozdanii zapovednoi zony Leningrada," in *Gradostroitel'naia okhrana pamiatnikov istorii i kul'tury*, ed. A. Iu. Bekker (Moscow: Nauchno-metodicheskii sovet po okhrane pamiatnikov kul'tury Ministerstva kul'tury RSFSR, 1987), 151–57.

127. TsGA-SPb, f. 2017, op. 1, d. 77, ll. 54–55.

128. For an interesting discussion of the new churches in Poland from an architectural point of view, see Owen Hatherley, *Landscapes of Communism: A History through Buildings* (London: Allen Lane, 2015), 191–200.

129. See Zharinov's strictures in "Zamechaniia po proektu 'Osnov zakonodatel'stva Soiuza SSR i soiuznykh respublik o religioznykh kul'takh,'" TsGA-SPb, f. 2017, op. 1, d. 77, ll. 13–15.

130. TsGA-SPb, f. 2017, op. 1, d. 77, ll. 62–63.

131. Ibid., op. 1, d. 100, l. 20.

132. The copy of the document in TsGA-SPb (ibid.) is inscribed by Zharinov, "Make yourselves familiar with this."

133. "O rabote komitetov Komsomola Pskovskoi oblasti po ateisticheskomu vospitaniiu iunoshei i devushek, vnedreniiu novykh obriadov v zhizn' molodezhi" (1986). Rossiiskii gosudarstvennyi arkhiv sotsial'no-politichestkoi istorii, Dokumenty Komsomola i molodezhnykh organizatsii (RGASPI-M), f. 1, op. 95, d. 371, ll. 12–25.

134. TsGA-SPb, f. 2017, op. 1, d. 100, ll. 36–40. Zharinov endeavored to support his case with learned opinion—a paper by Professor N. S. Gordienko, a leading antireligious writer at the Herzen Pedagogical Institute (ibid., ll. 33–35), which referred to Xenia as "a legendary and half-witted figure" (something of a contradiction!). Even the prerevolutionary government, Gordienko went on, had thought canonizing her a step too far.

135. ASPbE, f. 1, op. 11, d. 99, ll. 1–6.

136. See, for example, his letter of December 11, 1986, pressing for more church openings, ASPbE, f. 1, op. 11, d. 99, ll. 1–3.

137. As, for instance, in his December 11, 1986, letter, ibid. The official diocesan newsletter produced in the run-up to the millennium gives a good idea of the scale of the enterprise; see TsGA-SPb, f. 2017, op. 3, d. 18, ll. 11–12.

138. TsGA-SPb, f. 2017, op. 3, d. 18, l. 21; the following bulletins treated Soviet history in the same "many trials, but much good" mode, writing with enthusiasm about the church's role in the war effort and the Soviet peace movement, etc. (ibid., ll. 32–45).

139. There are occasional examples of heritage-oriented letters from members of the public written earlier: for instance, in 1978 a man whose careful handwriting, slightly stilted style, and

address suggest he was a village teacher wrote to the Leningrad Directorate of Culture to suggest that the dome of the Cathedral of the Transfiguration, "built under Peter I," should be gilded. I. P. Sautov replied with icy politeness to point out the absurdity of this suggestion. It cannot have helped the letter-writer's case that the cathedral was actually built a century after Peter died. NA UGIOP, pap. 171, Spaso-Preobrazhenskii Sobor: Perepiska 1968–1995 gg., ll. 110–111a (folios in reverse chronological order).

140. Letter from Valentina Toporovskaia, December 8, 1984. TsGALI-SPb, f. 229, op. 1, d. 564, l. 6.

141. Letter of G. L. Burkazova, sent to the Leningrad TV Studios, and from there to VOOPIiK. No later than November 13, 1984, TsGALI-SPb., f. 229, op. 1, d. 540, l. 154–154 ob. (Burkazova, it should be said, was something of a professional letter-writer—for her letter on the Moscow Triumphal Arch, see ibid., ll. 179–80).

142. TsGALI-SPb, f. 229, op. 1, d. 564, l. 4; ibid., d. 540, l. 152.

143. On the history of the church, see N. I. Batorevich and T. D. Kozhitseva, *Khramy-pamiatniki Sankt-Peterburga: Vo slavu i pamiat' rossiiskogo voinstva* (St. Petersburg: Dmitrii Bulanin, 2008), 218. On the life of Irina Benua in particular relation to this project, see *Katalog vystavki nerealizovannykh proektov* (St. Petersburg: Arkhitektura-Arkheologiia, 2004), 4–5.

144. Letter from A. V. Bukvalov to D. S. Likhachev, October 7, 1986. Personal archive of D. S. Likhachev, Rukopisnyi otdel Instituta russkoi literatury Rossiiskoi Akademii Nauk (hereafter RO IRLI RAN), f. 769, pap. 1, no. 30, ll. 1–7. For a discussion of the debate over the restoration of St. Panteleimon's as a case study in the history of attitudes to restoration in Leningrad, see Catriona Kelly, "'Ispravliat' li istoriiu?' Spory ob okhrane pamiatnikov v Leningrade 1960-kh–1980-kh godov," *Neprikosnovennyi zapas* 2 (2009), https://www.academia.edu/2001169/. The Monument to the Battle of Hanko (literally, "to the defenders of Hanko," though the place is on Finnish territory and was in use for a Soviet naval base subsequent to the Finno-Soviet "Winter War") was erected in 1945, and designed by Valentin Kamenskii and Anna Leiman. It is indeed a striking example of the neo-baroque style.

145. Letter from Bukvalov to Likhachev, October 7, 1986, RO IRLI RAN, f. 769, pap. 1, no. 30, ll. 1–7.

146. There is a detailed discussion of the heritage preservation of this period in Kelly, *Remembering St. Petersburg*, ch. 3. On the political resonance of the heritage protests in the late Soviet period, see the excellent article by Boris Gladarev, "Rozhdenie obshchestvennosti iz dukha goroda," in *Ot obshchestvennogo k publichnomu*, ed. Oleg Kharkhordin, Res Publica 5 (St. Petersburg: Izdatel'stvo Evropeiskogo universiteta, 2011), 70–304, particularly 109–51.

147. Letter from Metropolitan Aleksii to Iu. F. Sokolov, first secretary of the Leningrad City Community of the Communist Party, January 16, 1989, ASPbE, f. 1, op. 11, d. 99, l. 7. Church sources generally agree on seeing this as a watershed (e.g., Oxf/AHRC SPb-09 PF2 VM, interview with a senior cleric in one of the city's cathedrals).

148. ASPbE, f. 1, op. 11, d. 99, ll. 11–12, l. 31.

149. Ibid., ll. 20–22.

150. Ibid., l. 34.

151. For the refusal of state funding, see TsGA-SPb, f. 2017, op. 1, d. 100, ll. 34–35.

152. TsGA-SPb, f. 2017, op. 1, d. 100, l. 34. In 1921, the board of the Russian Orthodox Church in Exile moved to Sremski Karlovci in Serbia, where it remained till 1944. Right through the Soviet period, "Karlovci schismatics" was current in Soviet official usage as a denigratory term for the émigré church.

153. Examples in the first category include the memorial church to the Blockade victims incinerated in a brick factory that once stood on the site (Victory Park, Moskovskii prospekt), and the memorial to the demolished Cathedral of the Trinity on Trinity (formerly Revolution) Square.

154. R. A. French and F. E. Ian Hamilton, eds., *The Socialist City: Spatial Structure and Urban Policy* (New York: Wiley, 1979).

155. See, for example, the contributions to "City Culture, Urban Culture" in the journal *Forum for Anthropology and Culture* 7 (2011): 8–187.

156. See chapter 2 above.

157. On the history of the Redundant Churches Fund (now the Churches Conservation Trust), which was set up in 1968, see Matthew Saunders, "The Redundant Churches Fund Comes of Age" (1990), http://www.ihbc.org.uk/context_archive/28/redundant.htm. For the consensus on the 1960s as a turning point in church attendance ("The '1960s' were an international phenomenon"), see, for example, Hugh McLeod, *The Religious Crisis of the 1960s* (Oxford: Oxford University Press, 2007), 3.

158. For the point about the decline of associationism, see J. C. D. Clark, "Secularization and Modernization: The Failure of a 'Grand Narrative,'" *The Historical Journal* 55 (2012): S 164.

159. Blair A. Ruble *Leningrad: Shaping a Soviet City* (Berkeley: University of California Press, 1990), 93.

160. As emphasized, for example, by Hatherley, *Landscapes of Communism*, ch. 6.

161. This is clearly spelled out in Baranov, *Glavnyi arkhitektor goroda.*

162. Alexei Yurchak, in *Everything Was Forever*, argues strongly that the group at which he looks in detail—his own contemporaries, or those born around 1960—did not have a sense of "cognitive dissonance," instead taking a "performative" stance to the Soviet language of power. But it is clear that for older historical subjects, the reexamination of the past launched in the Khrushchev era was a cataclysmic event. Those who had lived through it (such as the people involved in the debates discussed here) were often left with a sense of deep internal confusion, which extended to no longer knowing what the canons of historical memory should be. On this see Vladislav Zubok, *Zhivago's Children: The Last Russian Intelligentsia* (Cambridge, MA: Harvard University Press, 2009), and Polly Jones, *Myth, Memory, Trauma: Rethinking the Stalinist Past in the Soviet Union, 1953–70* (New Haven, CT: Yale University Press, 2013).

Conclusion

1. See chapter 1.

2. For the term "legal fiction," see Edward E. Roslof, *Red Priests: Renovationism, Russian Orthodoxy, and Revolution, 1905–1946* (Bloomington: Indiana University Press, 2002), x. The removal of religious practices and emblems from schools was, in a sense, the core of the legislation. Already on December 11 (24), 1917, a rider had been added to the decree removing all church schools from the ecclesiastical administration: "The question relating to the churches in these institutions will be decided in connection with the decree on the separation of the church from the state" ("O peredache dlia vospitaniia i obrazovaniia iz dukhovnogo vedomstva v vedenie Narodnogo komissariata po prosveshcheniiu," *DSV* 1:211).

3. Note for instance the permit issued by the General Department of Lensovet to a certain V. G. Kulikov in 1933 permitting him to take photographs "during church services of both the exterior and the interior" of Leningrad's churches and cathedrals (TsGA-SPb, f. 7384, op. 33, d. 76, l. 144).

4. For an influential discussion of Soviet history in terms of the rise of state capacity, see Stephen Kotkin, *Magnetic Mountain: Stalinism as a Civilization* (Berkeley: University of California Press, 1995).

5. Obviously, there were exceptions, as pointed out in chapter 6, particularly the groups who were attracted to Orthodoxy and other forms of religious-philosophical enquiry.

6. Michael Thompson, *Rubbish Theory: The Creation and Destruction of Value* (Oxford: Oxford University Press, 1979).

7. For a discussion of comparable attitudes in scholars working with Old Believer groups, see Douglas Rogers, *The Old Faith and the Russian Land: A Historical Ethnography of Ethics in the Urals* (Ithaca, NY: Cornell University Press, 2009).

8. Gregory Freeze, "From Dechristianization to Laicization: State, Church, and Believers in Russia," *Canadian Slavonic Papers* 57, nos. 1–2 (2015): 6–34, rightly argues for discrimination in understanding believers' relations with their faith, but one should not underestimate the extent to which popular cults of streams, unofficial saints' gravestones, etc., excited disfavor with the Orthodox

hierarchy as well as with government and municipal officials. Popular cults in Leningrad graveyards are discussed briefly in chapter 9 of Catriona Kelly, *St. Petersburg: Shadows of the Past* (New Haven, CT: Yale University Press, 2014). The case of icons—universally recognized as sacred objects both inside the official Orthodox Church and beyond, yet with a more secure niche in national heritage than church buildings—deserves detailed historical study, sensitive to the many shifts and contradictions, in its own right. An interesting preliminary survey is Irina Sandomirskaja, "Catastrophe, Restoration, and Kunstwollen: Igor Grabar, Cultural Heritage, and Soviet Reuses of the Past," *Ab Imperio* 20, no. 2 (2015), 339–62.

9. For the nineteenth-century patterns, see Ekaterina Pravilova, *A Public Empire: Property and the Quest for the Common Good in Imperial Russia* (Princeton, NJ: Princeton University Press, 2014), 139–77.

10. Take the striking case of St. John Horsleydown in Southwark, left roofless after the Blitz and demolished for its masonry in the early 1970s. A modern brick box now stands on the original foundations, to frankly hideous effect. It houses the London City Mission, an institution of the Church of England itself. As Patrick Wright points out (*A Journey through Ruins: The Last Days of London* [Oxford: Oxford University Press, 2009], 27), "redundant" churches were also vulnerable in the late twentieth century (he gives the example of St. Bartholomew's, Dalston, summarily torn down under an "ecclesiastical exemption order").

11. D. S. Likhachev, "Ansambli Leningrada," *Leningradskaia pravda*, August 1, 1965, 1.

12. Our interviews with professional heritage experts almost uniformly pointed to a conviction that things were done better back in the Soviet past. It is only specialists in church history who have reservations.

13. This is discussed in more detail—for instance, the drive to ban ordinary shops from Nevsky and the river embankments—in Kelly, *St. Petersburg: Shadows of the Past.*

14. It is not just piety, but money-laundering and prestige reasons that drive the building boom generally (see Nikolai Mitrokhin, *Russkaia pravoslavnaia tserkov': Sovremennoe sostoianie i aktual'nye problemy* [Moscow: Novoe literaturnoe obozrenie, 2004], 168–71); on the religious significance, see Victoria Arnold, "The Experience of Sacred Place in Post-Soviet Russia: A Geography of Orthodoxy and Islam in Perm' Krai" (DPhil thesis, University of Oxford, 2012).

15. Two chapels had been raised near the sites of destroyed churches, on the Haymarket and Trinity (formerly Revolution) Square, but otherwise memorials (e.g., in ploshchad' Kulibina, on the site of the former Church of the Resurrection) were generally simple Orthodox crosses. On building in the city outskirts (usually to serve new residential areas or as part of Blockade commemoration), see Aleksandr Bertash, "O sovremennom tserkovnom stroitel'stve," *Kapitel'* 2, no. 6 (2009): 58–65.

16. Ol'ga Nikishina, "Dom Ksenii Blazhennoi," on the portal of Russian charities, miloserdie.ru, https://www.miloserdie.ru/article/dom-ksenii-blazhennoj/.

17. See, for example, the report on a petition to President Putin, "Protivniki khrama Ksenii Peterburgskoi prosiat pomoshchi u V. V. Putina," August 8, 2013, http://top.rbc.ru/spb_sz/08/08/2013/5592a87a9a794719538d0119.

18. On Sennaia ploshchad' in the post-Soviet period, see, for example, the material on the site of the preservation organization Zhivoi Gorod (Living City), http://www.save-spb.ru. On February 11, 2013, it was reported that the Church of the Savior might be rebuilt as part of yet another reconstruction of the square: see Galina Artemenko, "V Sankt-Peterburg pristupili k 'samomu statusnomu tserkovnomu proektu," IA Regnum, http://archi.ru/events/news/news_present_press.html?nid=46135. After a discussion on TV about vanished buildings in St. Petersburg on April 13, 2013, the other participants (including a representative of the lobby group Living City, a curator at the Museum of the History of St. Petersburg, an architectural historian, and a specialist in the history of St. Petersburg's theaters) unanimously agreed off-air that while rebuilding the Savior on the Haymarket might be acceptable, that church was a special case; the proposal to rebuild the Church of the Archangel Michael on Kulibin Square (in Little Kolomna) was, for instance, quite ridiculous; the square looked better without it.

19. A major development of the 1990s and first decade of the twenty-first century was the placing of some major church sites whose foundations survived on the lists of the Monuments Office, with the advice of Aleksandr Kobak and Vladimir Antonov (Oxf/AHRC SPb-09 PF10 CK). This was another case of conservation trumping reconstruction.

20. Interview with Aleksandr Strugach, January 2015 (AHRC SPb-15 PF13 CK) and Aleksei Kuznetsov (AHRC SPb-15 PF14 CK); FN January 2015.

21. In an interview with me in 2009, one of the restorers at the church described this process (which could also be seen on a visit to the church, including ascent up the scaffolding), but he also made highly critical remarks about restorations taking place in some other ecclesiastical buildings, including an eighteenth-century parish church where the local priest had arranged for overpainting of damaged wall paintings without consulting GIOP. Oxf/AHRC SPb-09 PF6 CK.

22. In this case, the restoration began in 1992 and the church was rededicated in 2006. See the material on the site of SPbGASU, http://www.spbgasu.ru/Universitet/Istoriya/Rukovoditeli_vuza/Kosyakov_Vasiliy_Antonovich/Hram_Kazanskoy_ikony_Bojiey_Materi/.

23. Oxf/AHRC SPb-09 PF6 CK.

24. E. A. Sevast'ianova, "Restavratsiia ubranstva inter'era Kazanskogo sobora," Kazanskii sobor: Ofitsial'noe izdanoe Kazanskogo kafedral'nogo sobora 41, no. 5 (2009): 9. The famous silver iconostasis was likewise replaced with electroplated nickel silver: see "Vozvrashchenie Kazanskogo sobora: beseda s istorikom Mikhailom Shkarovskim", Pravoslavie.ru, September 19, 2011, http://www.pravoslavie.ru/48725.html.

25. Site visits (FN November 2010, January 2010). The same is true, for example, of the former Church of the Putilov Factory, now no longer in use as a factory premises, but still barely restored, despite the efforts of an enthusiastic and friendly, but small, parish (FN, September 2010).

26. On the abandonment of the plan—here convincingly attributed both to the collapse of state funding in the perestroika period and to the new use of St. Panteleimon's as an actual church—see Vladimir Frolov, "Arkhitektor I. N. Benua," in Katalog vystavki nerealizovannykh proektov (St. Petersburg: Arkhitektura-Arkheologiia, 2004), 5.

27. For a detailed discussion of post-Soviet restoration, see Kelly, "'Scientific Reconstruction' or 'New Oldbuild'? The Dilemmas of Restoration in Post-Soviet St. Petersburg," Revue des études slaves 1 (2015): 17–39. For a good analysis of the transformation of the city landscape in another historic city, Baku, see Bruce Grant, "The Edifice Complex: Architecture and the Political Life of Surplus in the New Baku," Public Culture 26, no. 3 (2014): 501–28.

28. In March 1990, Metropolitan Aleksii declined to accept a further twenty churches on behalf of the diocese of Leningrad and Ladoga, including the Royal Stables Church and St. Isaac's Cathedral, on the grounds that this was simply not practical (ASPbE, f. 1, op. 11, d. 99, l. 50). In the same year, he emphasized the church's preparedness, in the meantime, "to make use of the St. Isaac's Cathedral for religious purposes without making changes to its museum status, that is, to use it alongside state organizations" (ASPbE, f. 1, op. 1, d. 99, l. 43). By the early twenty-first century, pressure to return the Cathedral was growing, and a formal application was submitted in July 2015. In April of the same year, it was announced that Smol'nyi Cathedral was to be returned to the Orthodox Church: "Smol'nyi sobor peredadut RPTs," http://www.colta.ru/news/7003. It is possible that the background to this was the replacement of Metropolitan Vladimir (Kotliarov), an academic theologian with long ties to the St Petersburg Theological Academy, by Metropolitan Varsonofii (Sudakov), the holder of a highly placed post in the Moscow Patriarchate, and without direct Petersburg connections. The Russian Orthodox Church in Moscow has been characterized by a far more proactive attitude to the return of buildings. For commentary from Deacon Mikhail Kuraev to the effect that it was mainly the visitor revenue that was behind the push, see Anton Mukhin, "Vriad li kto-to khochet krestit' svoego rebenka posred' tolpy kitaiskikh turistov," 812ru, August 31, 2015, http://www.online812.ru/2015/08/31/001/.

29. At a meeting of the Living City lobby group in 2008, someone who was not part of the organization, a young man who described himself as a professional restorer ("I've worked on more than one church myself") took up the case of the mosaic icon on the façade of the building that once housed the Schools Council of the Holy Synod (ulitsa Pravdy, formerly Kabinetskaia), which was plastered and painted over in the Soviet period. "Our group wants to liberate these sacred faces from the sacrilegious paint, even if it's more than fifty years now since it [the desecration] happened," he explained. This intervention was very coolly received, and he was told that church restoration was not a concern of Living City (FN, June 2008).

30. One of the informants in the project interviews, an employee of the Museum of Four Cathedrals, emphasized that while she and some others working there long-term had ended up as religious converts, others had not and were still fervent atheists: Oxf/AHRC SPb-09 PF 8 VM.

31. See the interview with a priest at a church used for occasional services only, who repeatedly insisted, "That's up to the people who run the diocese." (Oxf/AHRC SPb-09 PF3 VM). Another priest regretfully suggested that civil disobedience was simply not part of church tradition: Oxf/AHRC SPb-09 PF2 VM. At the same time, everyone from the church sees the restoration of church buildings as the ultimate objective (see our interviews with members of the clergy: FN April 2009, Oxf/AHRC SPb-09 PF2 VM, Oxf/AHRC SPb-09 PF3 VM, Oxf/AHRC SPb-09 PF7 CK, etc.). The Petersburg manner of agitation is polite contributions to media debate—see, for example, an internet discussion on Rosbalt-Peterburg, August 4, 2008: "Ekspert: Muzei pukhnut ot bogatsv, prinadlezhashchikh tserkvi," http://www.rosbalt.ru/2008/08/04/510128.html.

32. The issues of restitution are discussed at greater length in Catriona Kelly, "Competing Orthodoxies: Identity and Religious Belief in Soviet and Post-Soviet Russia," in *Soviet and Post-Soviet Identities*, ed. Mark Bassin and Catriona Kelly (Cambridge: Cambridge University Press, 2012), 299–320. As Konstantin Erofeev, a lawyer specializing in church property, emphasized, the law has significant ambiguities—for instance, are the Baptists to be classified as a "legal" group prior to 1917 or not? And it is also discrepant in terms of the overall legislation of the Russian Federation, since post-Soviet governments have not seen fit to restore property to other categories of pre-1917 legal owners en masse. Nevertheless, the political clout of the Orthodox Church particularly is such that challenges to the basic principle of restitution have not so far ensued.

33. David Genkin, "Tserkov' khochet zabrat' zdanie administratsii Tsentral'nogo raiona," *Komsomol'skaia pravda* (St. Petersburg), October 17, 2013, http://www.spb.kp.ru/daily/26147.4/3036063/.

34. An example is the Russian Museum's superb compendium of materials from its collection, *Religioznyi Peterburg*, comp. Pavel Klimov (St. Petersburg: Palace Editions, 2006).

35. For a good discussion of the resilience of religious groups, see the articles collected in Mark D. Steinberg and Catherine Wanner, eds., *Religion, Morality, and Community in Post-Soviet Societies* (Bloomington: Indiana University Press, 2008).

36. According to Father Vladimir Sorokin, dean (*blagochinnyi*) of the Central district, interviewed by Veronika Makarova on May 10, 2009.

37. For more about these projects, see Catriona Kelly *St. Petersburg: Shadows of the Past*, ch. 9.

38. For the first case, see Oxf/AHRC SPb-09 PF10 VM; for the second, Oxf/AHRC SPb-09 PF4 VM.

39. This applies not just to Orthodoxy, but to other faiths also. For instance, only around 5 percent of Jews in St. Petersburg regularly attend synagogue, though the numbers claiming interest in Judaism are much higher, while many Moscow Muslims mainly engage with imams when getting family rituals performed. See the contributions by Elena Nosenko-Shtein and Marat Safarov to "Religion in the Contemporary City," forthcoming in *Forum for Anthropology and Culture* 11 (2015).

40. These remarks are based on intensive first-hand observation of Leningrad and Petersburg since the early years of the century, but they accord with statistical evidence also; see, for example, Boris Dubin, "'Legkoe bremia': Massovoe pravoslavie v Rossii 1999–2000kh godov," in *Religioznye praktiki v sovremennoi Rossii*, ed. Kathy Rousselet and Aleksandr Agadzhanian (Moscow: Novoe izdatel'stvo, 2006), 68–86. It is customary to distinguish between the "church-going" (*votserkovlennoe*) and the "believing" (*veruiushchee*) populations.

41. By the early twenty-first century, tour groups were running excursions under the title "Churches of St. Petersburg," but the main draw for visitors was still the church-museums, in particular St. Isaac's.

42. This is all based on comments from informants in the years of researching this project (2009–2015). At the stage of completing work on this book in autumn 2015, the return of St. Isaac's was becoming a major controversy, with a court case in the offing—see below.

43. An Orthodox priest recalled in 2009 that he had taken his son along to visit, and had been struck (but apparently not offended) by the airplane over the entrance, etc. (FN). The small numbers and limited clout of the Coreligionists partly explain the persisting secular character of the building, but in principle the mainstream Russian Orthodox Church could coordinate a restoration if this were thought appropriate, since the Coreligionists are in communion with them.

44. The story about the Mephistopheles bas-relief broke on August 26, 2015; and the story about the Cossack group on August 27—the group was said to have claimed they were disgusted by tourists who took pictures of "the devil": "'Kazaki Peterburga' vziali otvetstvennost' za razrushenie Mefistofelia na istoricheskom zdanii Peterburgskoi storony," http://echo.msk.ru/news/1611340-echo.html. On the accusations made by the priest (Father Aleksandr Pelin of the Sampson Cathedral), see Aleksandr Ermakov, "Kogo Mefistofel' zakusil chernym PR," http://www.fontanka.ru/2015/08/31/177. The comments and rumors come from social websites such as Facebook and VKontakte. In recent years, so-called Cossack groups have often acted as self-appointed defenders of ecclesiastical safety and honor.

45. See Douglas Rogers, "Old Belief between 'Society' and 'Culture': Remaking Moral Communities and Inequalities on a Former State Farm," in Steinberg and Wanner, *Religion, Morality, and Community*, 115–47. In St. Petersburg, one can sometimes encounter prominent religious activists who, under Soviet power, were in ideologically significant positions, such as teaching philosophy (from a Marxist-Leninist point of view), work in the Komsomol or Party apparatus, etc. The elder of one city-center parish is a former judge, and so on.

46. Based on observation of St. Alexander Nevsky Day (FN September 2012). This is a kind of counterpart to the symbological dependence of British neo-pagan processions on Christian ones; see Amy Whitehead, *Religious Statues and Personhood: Testing the Role of Materiality* (London: Bloomsbury, 2013), 83.

47. At the national level, the site scepsis.net acted as a platform for anticlerical and humanist views. Social media also gave widespread expressions of these, with attitudes to churches sometimes of the "blow them all up" kind.

48. It was relatively rare even for book exhibits at major libraries to focus on religious topics—"history of academic life" predominated.

49. For the feelings among the liberal clergy, see Oxf/AHRC SPb-09 PF7. On the domination of the Orthodox Church by conservative tendencies, see Mitrokhin, *Russkaia pravoslavnaia tserkov'*; Irina Papkova, "The Freezing of Historical Memory? The Post-Soviet Russian Orthodox Church and the Church Council of 1917," in Steinberg and Wanner, *Religion, Morality, and Community*, 55–83.

50. This is discussed in more detail in Kelly, "Competing Orthodoxies."

51. Oxf/AHRC SPb-09 PF2 VM. The informant continued: "The entire twentieth century we had triumphantly stupid people [*samodury*] sitting up top," and gave pungent characterizations of these, including not just Soviet leaders too, but also Nicholas II.

52. The material in A. S. Shchenkov, ed., *Pamiatniki arkhitektury v Sovetskom Soiuze: Ocherki istorii arkhitekturnoi restavratsii* (Moscow: Pamiatniki istoricheskoi mysli, 2004), suggests that the record in Leningrad could be matched in few other places, certainly of any size. Even in Kiev and Moscow, demolition was more extensive, partly because of the demand for high-profile buildings to celebrate Soviet rule.

53. There is a large and growing literature on such "socialist spaces"; see, for example, Katharina Kucher, *Der Gorki-Park: Freizeitkultur im Stalinismus 1928–1941* (Cologne: Böhlau, 2007); M. Rüthers, *Moskau bauen von Lenin bis Chruščev: Öffentliche Räume zwischen Utopie, Terror und Alltag* (Cologne: Böhlau, 2007); Stephen V. Bittner, *The Many Lives of Khrushchev's Thaw: Experience and Memory in Moscow's Arbat* (Ithaca, NY: Cornell University Press, 2008); Mark Bassin, Christopher Ely, and Melissa T. Stockdale, eds., *Space, Place, and Power in Modern Russia: Essays in the New Spatial History* (DeKalb: Northern Illinois University Press, 2010).

54. In his influential study of Soviet architecture, *Kul'tura "dva"* (Ann Arbor: Ardis, 1985), Vladimir Papernyi argued that the role of neoclassical influences on Stalin-era architecture had been much exaggerated, and it is notable that *Arkhitektura SSSR* cited many other prototypes as well,

particularly Gothic architecture (as well as the modern buildings and *grands projets* of the capitalist West). However, in city planning terms, the neoclassical ethos of squares and straight avenues reigned supreme.

55. On the emergence of a supra-regional and supra-national Soviet sense of space, see, for example, Emma Widdis, *Visions of a New Land: Soviet Film from the Revolution to the Second World War* (New Haven, CT: Yale University Press, 2003); Evgeny Dobrenko and Eric Naiman, eds., *The Landscape of Stalinism: The Art and Ideology of Soviet Space* (Seattle: University of Washington Press, 2003), and the various publications of Galina Orlova, for example, "Istoriia s geografiei: Osobaia rol' kart i fizicheskoi geografii v stalinskoi sisteme," http://urokiistorii.ru/history/soc/2010/15/istoriya-s-geografiei.

56. In this context, it is interesting to note the emphasis in Soviet newspaper coverage of the late 1920s of the rubbish heap as a metaphor of the old-style city; see, for example, "Sanitarnoe litso Leningrada," *KG*, June 5, 1929, 3. The rubbish heap precisely suggests a layered and anarchic past that is only manageable by burning or burial.

57. For the coinage "speaking Bolshevik," see Kotkin, *Magnetic Mountain*. It is interesting that while the term *bol'shevistskii iazyk* ("Bolshevik language") was widely used in Soviet culture, the term *bol'shevistskaia arkhitektura* ("Bolshevik architecture") sounds completely unconvincing (a search of Runet produces only three examples, all of them modern, as opposed to 211 for *bol'shevistskii iazyk* and 1520 for *sotsialisticheskaia arkhitektura*). The National Corpus of the Russian Language, http://www.ruscorpora.ru, produces four hits for *sotsialisticheskaia stroika*, but none for *bol'shevistskaia stroika*.

58. The fight over the new Church of St. Xenia on Petrograd Side was precipitated when the church's chosen site was handed over for use as a business center. Commercial interests of this kind have replaced the city's factory and institute leaderships as the city's most effective negotiators with the political administration.

Select Bibliography

Archival Sources

ASPbE f. 1 (Perepiska i deloproizvodstvo Leningradskoi Mitropolii)
ASPbGASU d. 106 (Lichnoe delo Piliavskogo V. I.)
GARF f. 2306 (Narodnyi komissariat prosveshcheniia RSFSR)
    f. 2307 (Glavnoe upravlenie nauchnykh i muzeinykh uchrezhdenii)
NA UGIOP, papka 8/2, delo 150 (Andreevskii sobor)
    papka 171 (Spaso-Preobrazhenskii sobor)
    papka 173 (Tserkov' Simeoniia i Anny)
    papka 481 (Muzei Arktiki/b. Nikol'skaia Edinovercheskaia tserkov')
OR RNB f. 606 (lichnyi fond Poliakovoi E. A.)
    f. 1015 (lichnyi fond Ostroumovoi-Lebedevoi A. P.)
    f. 1062 (lichnyi fond Olia A. A.)
RA IIMK f. 29 (lichnyi fond Romanova K. K.)
    f. 67 (Otdel muzeev)
RGANI f. 4 (Sekretariat TsK KPSS)
    f. 5 (Apparat TsK KPSS)
    f. 6 (Komitet partiinogo kontrolia TsK KPSS)
TsGAIPD-SPb f. 16 (Petrogradskii gubernskii komitet VKP[b])
    f. 24 (Oblastnoi komitet KPSS)
    f. 25 (Gorodskoi komitet KPSS)
    f. 116 (Leningradskii shtab partizanskogo dvizheniia)
    f. K598 (Leningradskii obkom VLKSM)
    f. K601 (Petrogradskii/Leningradskii gubkom VLKSM)
TsGALI-SPb f. 32 (OSP)
    f. 229 (VOOPIiK)
    f. 401 (LOSA)
TSGANTD-SPb f. 17 (Leningradskii zonal'nyi nauchno-issledovatel'skii institut eksperimental'noi planirovki, LZNIIEP)
    f. 36 (Lenproekt)
    f. 192 (Leningradskoe oblastnoe upravlenie stroitel'nogo kontrolia)
    f. 205 (LISI)
    f. 386 (GlavAPU Lenispolkoma)
    f. 388 (APU Lenoblispolkoma)
TsGA-SPb f. 1000 (Leningradskii gubernskii ispolkom)
    f. 1001 (Otdel upravleniia Soveta rabochikh deputatov)
    f. 2017 (Upolnomochennyi po delam religii)

f. 3199 (Otkomkhoz Lensoveta)
f. 7384 (Petrogradskii/Leningradskii sovet narodnykh deputatov)
f. 9324 (Upolnomochennyi po delam kul'tov)
f. 9360 (Upolnomochennyi po delam Russkoi Pravoslavnoi Tserkvi)

Oral History: Transcripts of Interviews

Oxf/AHRC SPb-07 PF1 CK–Oxf/AHRC SPb-15 PF14 CK: Fourteen interviews with architects, conservators, local historians, and parish representatives in St. Petersburg, conducted from 2007 to 2015 by Catriona Kelly.

Oxf/AHRC SPb-08 PF1 AP–Oxf/AHRC SPb-09 PF17 AP: Seventeen interviews with architect-restorers, local historians, and parish representatives in St. Petersburg, conducted in 2008 and 2009 by Alexandra Piir.

Oxf/AHRC SPb-09 PF1 VM–Oxf/AHRC SPb-15 PF10 VM: Ten interviews with parish representatives in St. Petersburg, conducted in 2010 by Veronika Makarova.

Oxf/AHRC SPb-10 PF1 MS–Oxf/AHRC SPb-12 PF44 MS: Forty-four interviews with St. Petersburg residents about their attitudes to the city, conducted from 2010 to 2012 by Marina Samsonova.

Periodicals and Serials

Arkhitektura Leningrada
Arkhitektura SSSR
Biulleten' Ispolnitel'nogo komiteta Leningradskogo gorodskogo soveta deputatov trudiashchikhsia
Dekrety sovetskoi vlasti
Ezhegodnik Bol'shoi sovetskoi entsiklopedii
Izvestiia
Krasnaia gazeta
Leningradskaia panorama
Leningradskaia pravda
Literatura i zhizn'
Nauka i zhizn'
Novyi Mir
Petrogradskaia pravda
Polnoe sobranie zakonov Rossiiskoi Imperii
Pravda
Severnaia Kommuna
Sobranie uzakonenii i rasporiazhenii Raboche-Krest'ianskogo Pravitel'stva
Sovetskoe iskusstvo
Stroitel'stvo i arkhitektura Leningrada
Vechernii Leningrad
Vestnik Leningradskogo Oblispolkoma i Leningradskogo Soveta

Primary Sources

A. A. "Pro doma sua." *Starye gody* 2 (1909): 94.

Adibekov, G. M., K. M. Anderson, and L. A. Rogovaia, eds., *Politbiuro TsK RKG(b)-VKP(b): Povestki dnia zasedanii, 1919–1952; Katalog*, 3 vols. Moscow: ROSSPEN, 2000–2001.

Aleksii. *Pis'ma Patriarkha Aleksiia I v Sovet po delam Russkoi Pravoslavnoi Tserkvi pri Sovete narodnykh komissarov—Sovete ministrov SSSR, 1945–1970 gg.* 2 vols. Moscow: ROSSPEN, 2009–2010.

Aleshina, L. S. *Leningrad i okrestnosti: Spravochnik-putevoditel'*. Moscow: Iskusstvo, 1980.

Anderson, K. M., et al., eds. *Kremlevskii kinoteatr 1928–1953: Dokumenty*. Moscow: ROSSPEN, 2005.

Andreeva, V. I., et al., eds. *Pamiatniki istorii i kul'tury Sankt-Peterburga, sostoiashchie pod gosudarst-vennoi okhranoi: Spravochnik*. St. Petersburg: Al'tsoft, 2000.

Anisimov, G. G., ed. *Okhrana pamiatnikov istorii i kul'tury; Sbornik dokumentov*. (Hereafter *OPIK* 1973).Moscow: Sovetskaia Rossiia, 1973.

Antonov, V. V., and A. V. Kobak. *Sviatyni Sankt-Peterburga: Entsiklopediia khristianskikh khramov*. 3rd ed. St. Petersburg: Fond Spas, 2010. First ed. published as *Sviatyni Peterburga: Istoriko-tserkovnaia entsiklopediia*. 3 vols. (St. Petersburg: Izdatel'stvo Chernysheva, 1994).

Aplaksin, A. P. *Russkoe tserkovnoe iskusstvo i ego sovremennye zadachi: Doklad Sankt-Peterburgskogo Eparkhial'nogo Arkhitektora A. P. Aplaksina, prochitannyi 8-go Ianvaria 1911 goda na IV S"ezde Russkikh Zodchikh v prisutstvii Ego Imperatorskogo Vysochestva Velikogo Kniazia PETRA NIKOLAEVICHA*. St. Petersburg: Tipografiia Aleksandro-Nevskogo Obshchestva Trezvosti, 1911.

Arenin, E. "Podzemnye marshruty." *Leningradskaia Pravda*, November 13, 1960, 2.

Arkheologiia arkhitektury: Katalog vystavki nerealizovannykh proektov. St. Petersburg: Arkhitektu-ra-Arkheologiia, 2004.

Avramenko, I. K., et al., eds. *U nas v Leningrade: O primetakh vremeni; Rasskazyvaiut zhurnalisty, khudozhniki, fotografy*. Leningrad: Sovetskii pisatel', 1961.

Babel', Isaak. "U sviatogo Valenta." *Krasnaia nov'* 3 (1924): 13–16.

———. *Konarmiia*. Moscow: Gosudarstvennoe izdatel'stvo, 1926.

Bakhareva, Iu., and N. S. Tret'iakova, comp. "Iz dnevnikov khranitelei prigorodnykh dvortsov-muzeev Leningrada, 1941–1945." *Otechestvennye arkhivy* 1 (2007), https://archive.is/9cEtO.

Barabko, T. V. "'Zelenoe stroitel'stvo' Leningrada v 1920-kh–1940-kh godakh (po materialam arkhiva E. A. Poliakovoi)." *Universitetskii istorik* 10 (2012): 135–41.

Baranov, N. V. "Bol'shoi Iaroslavl'." *Arkhitektura Leningrada* 1–3 (1937): 30–37.

———. *Glavnyi arkhitektor goroda (Tvorcheskaia i organizatsionnaia deiatel'nost')*. Moscow: Izdatel'stvo arkhitektury po stroitel'stvu, 1973.

———. *Obobshchenie opyta planirovki i zastroiki gorodov*, Akademiia arkhitektury SSSR, Leningradskii filial, Sektor planirovki i zastroiki gorodov (typescript, Leningrad, 1950). TsGANTD-SPb, f. 17, op. 2–1, d. 2.

———. "Zadachi leningradskoi arkhitektury v realizatsii piatiletnego plana vosstanovleniia i razvitiia g. Leningrada i oblasti." *Stroitel'stvo i arkhitektura Leningrada* (November 1946): 1–7.

Bebutov, G. "K voprosu o regulirovanii ulichnogo dvizheniia," *Kommunal'noe khoziaistvo* 1 (1926): 13–14.

Belov, K. "Otvechaem na voprosy chitatelei: Takimi budut novye stantsii Leningradskogo metro." *Vechernii Leningrad*, September 9, 1960, 1.

———. "Pod Moskovskim prospektom." *Vechernii Leningrad*, November 1, 1960, 1.

Berggol'ts, Ol'ga. *Dnevnye zvezdy: Govorit Leningrad*. Edited by Mariia F. Berggol'ts. Leningrad: Khudozhestvennaia literatura, 1985.

Bertash, A. V., V. V. Antonov et al. *Zemlia Nevskaia pravoslavnaia: Pravoslavnye khramy prigorodnykh rainov Sankt-Peterburga i Leningradskoi oblasti*. St. Petersburg: Pravoslavnaia Rus', 2000.

Bertash, Aleksandr. "O sovremennom tserkovnom stroitel'stve." *Kapitel'* 2, no. 6 (2009): 58–65.

Bezbozhniki sotsialisticheskoi derevni navstrechu 4-mu godu piatiletki: Antirozhdestvenskii Sbornik. Leningrad: Lenizdat, 1931.

Bezbozhniki za rabotoi: Iz opyta raboty iacheek Soiuza voinstvuiushchikh bezbozhnikov Leningrada i Leningradskoi oblasti. Leningrad: Lenizdat, 1938.

Bidlack, Richard, and Nikita Lomagin, eds. *The Leningrad Blockade, 1941–1944: A New Documentary History from the Soviet Archives*. New Haven, CT: Yale University Press, 2012.

Bor'ba tserkovnikov Isaakievskogo sobora protiv naroda. Leningrad: Gosudarstvennyi anti-religioznyi muzei, 1941.

Brodsky, Joseph. *Less Than One: Selected Essays*. Harmondsworth: Penguin, 1987.

————. [Iosif Brodskii]. *Stikhotvoreniia i poemy*. Edited by Lev Losev. 2 vols. Moscow: Vita Nova, 2011.

Budennyi, Semen. "Babizm Babelia."*Oktiabr'* 3 (1924): 196–98.

Budnikov, Aleksandr. *Tserkov' Sviatogo Proroka Ilii*. St. Petersburg: Izdanie khrama Sviatogo Proroka Ilii, 1998.

Butikov, G. P. *Gosudarstvennyi muzei-pamiatnik Isaakievskii sobor*. Leningrad: Khudozhnik RSFSR, 1973.

————. *Muzei "Isaakievskii sobor."* Leningrad: Lenizdat, 1991.

Bylinkin, N. "Obrazy russkogo iskusstva." *Sovetskoe iskusstvo*, December 5, 1944, 3.

Cederholm, B. L. *In the Clutches of the Tcheka*. Translated by F. H. Lyon. London: George Allen and Unwin, 1929.

Central Committee of the CPSU. "Ob oshibkakh v provedenii nauchno-ateisticheskoi propagandy sredi naseleniia, November 10, 1954." *Pravda*, November 11, 1954, 1-2.

Chaplygin, Iurii. "Ne pomniashchie rodstva." *Literatura i zhizn'*, February 21, 1960, 2.

Corley, Felix, ed. *Religion in the Soviet Union: An Archival Reader*. Basingstoke: Macmillan, 1996.

Council of Ministers of the RSFSR. "O dal'neishem uluchshenii dela okhrany pamiatnikov kul'tury v RSFSR." August 30, 1960, docs.cntd.ru/document/9012089

Courtois, Stéphane et al., eds., *Chernaia kniga kommunizma: Prestupleniia, terror, repressii*. Moscow: Tri veka istorii, 1999.

Dediukhina, V. S., et al., eds. *Sokhranenie pamiatnikov tserkovnoi stariny v Rossii v XVIII–nachala XX vv.: Sbornik dokumentov*. Moscow: Otechestvo, 1997.

Degtiareva, T. Iu. *Istoricheskii tsentr Leningrada—problemy okhrany i restavratsii inter'erov: V pomoshch' lektoru*. Leningrad: Znanie, 1988.

Deianiia Sviashchennogo Sobora Pravoslavnoi Rossiiskoi Tserkvi 1917-1918 gg. 3 vols. 1918. Facsimile reprint, Moscow: Izdatel'stvo Novospasskogo monastyria, 1994.

"Dekret o registratsii, prieme na uchet i okhrane pamiatnikov iskusstva i stariny." *Kommersant*, September 29, 2003, http://www.kommersant.ru/doc/414844.

Dnevnik IV S"ezda Russkikh Zodchikh, sostoiashchego pod pochetnym Predsedatel'stvom Avgusteishego Prezidenta Imperatorskoi Akademii Khudozhestv Velikoi Kniagini Marii Pavlovny. St. Petersburg: Tipografiia Sankt-Peterburgskogo Gradonachal'stva, 1911.

Dnevnik V Vserossiiskogo S"ezda Zodchikh, 15–22 Dekabria 1913 g. Moscow: Organizatsionnyi komitet S"ezda, 1913.

Dnevnik Vysochaishe utverzhdennogo S"ezda russkikh Zodchikh v S-Peterburge, 1892 g. (Sankt-Peterburgskoe Obshchestvo Arkhitektorov). St. Petersburg: Biuro S"ezda/Akademiia Khudozhestv, 1892.

"Domovye tserkvi." *Revoliutsiia i tserkov'* 2 (1919): 44–47.

Eikhenbaum, Boris. "Dusha Moskvy." *Sovremennoe slovo* 1 (1917), http://philologos.narod.ru/eichenbaum/eichen_moscow.htm.

Emel'ianova, K. L. *Pervyi v strane*. Leningrad: Lenizdat, 1964.

Enakiev, F. E. *Zadachi preobrazovaniia Sankt-Peterburga*. St. Petersburg: Tovarishchestvo R. Golike i A. Vil'borg, 1912.

Fedorov, Aleksandr. "Glavnyi arkhitektor goroda perioda Velikoi Otechestvennoi voiny i vosstanovleniia goroda Nikolai Baranov." *Tserkov' sviatoi velikomuchenitsy Ekateriny v Akademii Khudozhestv*, n.d., http://www.art-acad-church.ru/arh/spb/br.html.

Finn, L. N., et al. *Iz ochaga mrakobesiia v ochag kul'tury*. Leningrad: OGIZ-Priboi, 1931.

Fisher, Harold H. *The Famine in Soviet Russia, 1919–1923: The Operations of the American Relief Administration*. New York: The Macmillan Company, 1927.

Gagarin, Iurii. *Doroga v kosmos*. Moscow: Pravda, 1961.

Gakkel', Ia. Ia. *Za chetvert' veka: Obzor deiatel'nosti Arkticheskogo Instituta Glavsevmorputi za 25 let*. Moscow: Izdatel'stvo Glavsevmorputi, 1945.

Galkin, A. K., A. V. Bertash, and M. V. Shkarovskii. *Kniaz'-Vladimirskii sobor: Kratkii istoricheskii ocherk*. St. Petersburg: Kniaz'-Vladimirskii sobor, 2005.

German, Mikhail. *Slozhnoe proshedshee*. St. Petersburg: Iskusstvo, 2000.

Gernet, M. N., and A. N. Trainin, eds. *Ugolovnyi kodeks: Nauchno-populiarnyi prakticheskii kommentarii s dopolneniiami i izmeneniiami po 15 avgusta 1927 g.* Moscow: Pravo i zhizn', 1927.

Goland, I. B. *Leningrad—fotoal'bom.* Leningrad: Lenizdat, 1964.

Grabar', I. E. *Moia zhizn'.* Moscow: Iskusstvo, 1937.

———. *Pis'ma, 1917–1941.* Moscow: Nauka, 1977.

———. "Vosstanovlenie pamiatnikov stariny." *Sovetskoe iskusstvo,* November 28, 1944, 2.

Grimm, G. G. *Ploshchad' Iskusstv i Ploshchad' Ostrovskogo.* Moscow: Iskusstvo, 1946.

Gruppa peterburgskikh sviashchennikov. *K tserkovnomu soboru: Sbornik.* St. Petersburg: Tip. M. Merkusheva, 1906.

Hersey, John. "The Reconstruction of Leningrad." *Architectural Forum* 12 (1944): 117–22.

Hingley, Ronald. *Under Soviet Skins: An Untourist's Report.* London: Hamish Hamilton, 1961.

Iatsevich, A. "Peterburg v tvorchestve Pushkina." *Arkhitektura Leningrada* 1 (1937): 60–62.

Il'in, L. A. "Ansambl' v arkhitekturnom oblike Leningrada." *Arkhitektura SSSR* 2 (1933): 9–11.

Inber, Vera. *Pochti tri goda: Leningradskii dnevnik.* Moscow: Sovetskii pisatel', 1946.

"Instruktsiia Kollegii po delam muzeev i okhrane pamiatnikov iskusstva stariny Narodnogo Komissariata Prosveshcheniia," *Revoliutsiia i tserkov'* 1 (1919): 30.

Instruktsiia o poriadke ucheta i khraneniia kul'turnykh tsennostei, nakhodiashchikhsia v pol'zovanii religioznykh ob"edinenii. Mimeographed typescript. Moscow: Sovet po delam religii, 1980. (Author's personal archive.)

Instruktsiia po uchetu, khraneniiu i peredache religioznogo imushchestva, imeiushchego istoricheskoe, khudozhestvennoe ili arkheologicheskoe znachenie. Moscow: Narkompros, 1920. (GARF, f. 2307, op. 3, d. 19, ll. 28–33.)

Isachenko, V. G. "V shirokom diapazone: Tvorcheskoe nasledie P. Iu. Siuzora." *Leningradskaia panorama* 10 (1985): 28–31.

Ivanov, Boris. *Sochineniia.* 2 vols. Moscow: NLO, 2009.

"K 250-letiiu so dnia rozhdeniia V. V. Rastrelli: Master russkoi arkhitektury." *Stroitel'stvo i arkhitektury Leningrada* 14 (1951): 35–39.

Karishnev, L. "Vozrodim khram!" *Vyborgskaia storona* 4 (1992): 2.

Khalif, Lev. "Permskaia obitel'." *Literatura i zhizn',* February 21, 1960, 2.

Kirikov, B. M. *Arkhitektura peterburgskogo moderna: Osobniaki i dokhodnye doma.* St. Petersburg: Neva, 2003.

———. "Kakie pamiatniki okhraniaem?" *Leningradskaia panorama* 11 (1991): 15–17.

———. *Okhrana arkhitekturnykh pamiatnikov Leningrada v gody sovetskoi vlasti.* Leningrad: Znanie, 1988.

———, ed. *Pamiatniki arkhitektury i istorii Sankt-Peterburga: Petrogradskii raion.* St. Petersburg: Kolo, 2004.

———, ed. *Pamiatniki arkhitektury i istorii Sankt-Peterburga: Vasileostrovskii raion.* St. Petersburg: Kolo, 2006.

Kirikov, B. M., and S. G. Fedorov. "Zodchii-entsiklopedist: O tvorcheskom puti arkh. G. V. Baranovskogo." *Leningradskaia panorama* 2 (1985): 29–32.

Kirikov, B. M., and L. V. Kornilova, eds. *Pamiatniki istorii i kul'tura Sankt-Peterburga.* Vol. 8. St. Petersburg: Beloe i chernoe, 2005.

Kirikov, B. M., and A. D. Margolis. "O sozdanii zapovednoi zony Leningrada." In *Gradostroitel'naia okhrana pamiatnikov istorii i kul'tury,* ed. A. Iu. Bekker, 151–75. Moscow: Nauchno-metodicheskii sovet po okhrane pamiatnikov kul'tury Ministerstva kul'tury RSFSR, 1987.

———. "Ugolok starogo goroda." *Leningradskaia panorama* 8 (1984): 30–31.

Klimov, P. Iu., comp. *Religioznyi Peterburg.* St. Petersburg: Palace Editions, 2006.

Kolotov, M. G. *Muzei-pamiatnik "Isaakievskii sobor": Al'bom.* Leningrad: Khudozhnik RSFSR, 1961.

Krasin, G. "K voprosu o budushchei 'Bol'shoi Moskve,'" *Kommunal'noe khoziaistvo* 2 (1926): 17–20.

Kravetskii, G., et al., eds. *Sviashchennyi Sobor Pravoslavnoi Rossiiskoi Tserkvi, 1917–1918 gg.: Obzor deianii.* 3 vols. Moscow: Krutitskoe Patriarshee Podvor'e, 2000–2002.

Kurbatov, Vladimir. *Peterburg: Khudozhestvenno-istoricheskii ocherk*. St. Petersburg: Izd. Obshchiny sv. Evgenii, 1913. http://www.nasledie-rus.ru/redport/00302.php.

Kuriashov, S, and I. Rumiantseva, *Monastyri Sankt-Peterburgskoi eparkhii. Spravochnik palomnika*. St Petersburg, 2000.

Lansere, N. E. "Adrian Dmitrievich Zakharov." *Arkhitektura Leningrada* 1 (1937): 40–46.

Lebedianskii, S. P. "Voprosy ekspozitsii antireligioznykh muzeev." In *Trudy Pervogo Vserossiiskogo muzeinogo s'ezda*. Vol. 2, *Materialy sektsionnykh zasedanii*, ed. I. K. Luppol, 123–28. Moscow: Gosudarstvennyi uchebno-pedagogicheskoe izdanie, 1931.

Lenin, V. I. *Polnoe sobranie sochinenii*. 5th ed. 55 vols. Moscow: Izdatel'stvo politicheskoi literatury, 1958–1965.

Leningrad—obraztsovyi sotsialisticheskii gorod: Novostroiki 1932 g. Leningrad: OGIZ-IZOGIZ, 1932.

Likhachev, D. S. "Ansambli Leningrada." *Leningradskaia pravda*, August 1, 1965, 1.

———. "Berech' pamiatniki proshlogo: (Po povodu stat'i V. Soloukhina 'Berech' proshloe—dumat' o budushchem,' *Neva* 11 [1962])." *Neva* 3 (1963): 195–96.

———. "Chetvertoe izmerenie." *Literaturnaia gazeta*, June 10, 1965, 2.

———. "Pamiatniki kul'tury—vsenarodnoe dostoianie." *Istoriia SSSR* 3 (1961): 3–12.

———. "Pamiatniki velikogo proshlogo." *Literatura i zhizn'*, December 16, 1959, 2.

———. *Poetika drevnerusskoi literatury*. Leningrad: Nauka, 1967

———. "Vo imia budushchego." *Literatura i zhizn'*, March 11, 1960, 2.

Lisovskii, G. "Master shkoly natsional'nogo romantizma." *Leningradskaia panorama* 4 (1975): 42–44.

Lobanov, V. V., ed. *Protokoly komissii po provedeniiu otdeleniia tserkvi ot gosudarstva pri TsK RKP(b)-VKP(b) (Antireligioznoi komissii), 1922–1929*. Moscow: Izdatel'stvo Pravoslavnogo Sviato-Tikhonovskogo gumanitarnogo universiteta, 2014.

Lotman, Iu. M. *Aleksandr Sergeevich Pushkin: Biografiia pisatelia*. Leningrad: Prosveshchenie, 1981.

———. "Simvolika Peterburga i problemy semiotiki goroda" (1984), in *Izbrannye stat'i* (Tallinn: Aleksandra, 1992–1993), 1:9–22.

Lozhkin, V. A. "Chto takoe urbanizm?," *Kommunal'noe khoziaistvo* 17 (1925): 15–26.

Luppol, I. K., ed. *Trudy Pervogo Vserossiiskogo muzeinogo s'ezda*. Moscow: Gosudarstvennoe Uchebno-pedagogicheskoe izdanie, 1931.

Mackenzie, F. A. *The Russian Crucifixion: The Full Story of the Persecution of Religion under Bolshevism*. London: Jarrolds, 1927.

Mashkov, N. P., and A. A. Netyksa, eds. *Dnevnik Vysochaishe utverzhdennogo II S'ezda russkikh Zodchikh v Moskve, 1895 goda*. Moscow: Biuro S'ezda/Politekhnicheskii Muzei, 1895.

Mazyrin, A., V. A. Goncharov, and I. V. Uspenskii, eds. *Iz"iatie tserkovnykh tsennostei v Moskve v 1922 g.: Sbornik dokumentov iz fonda Revvoensoveta Respubliki*. Moscow: Izdatel'stvo Pravoslavnogo Sviato-Tikhonovskogo gumanitarnogo universiteta, 2006.

Meierovich, M. G. *U menia poiavilas' mechta*. Iaroslavl': Aleksandr Rutman, 2004.

Mikhailov, V. P., ed. *Zapreshchennye fil'my: Dokumenty, Svidetel'stva, Kommentarii*. Moscow: Nauchno-issledovatel'skii institut kinoiskusstva, 1993.

"Monastyri," *Revoliutsiia i tserkov'* 1 (1919): 39.

"Monastyri," *Revoliutsiia i tserkov'* 9–12 (1920): 83.

Mordukhai-Boltovskii, I. D., ed. *Svod zakonov Rossiiskoi Imperii*. 16 vols. St. Petersburg: Knizhnoe tovarishchestvo Deiatel', 1912.

Morozov, A., D. Likhachev, N. Voronin, and A. Iugov. "Nel'zia tak otnosit'sia k pamiatnikam dereviannogo zodchestva." *Literaturnaia gazeta*, January 15, 1955.

Moskvin, Grigorii. *Peterburg i ego okrestnosti: Illiustrirovannyi prakticheskii putevoditel'*. 1888. Reprint, St. Petersburg, 1915.

Mramornov, A. I., ed. *Dokumenty Sviashchennogo Sobora Pravoslavnoi Russkoi Tserkvi, 1917–1918 godov*. 3 vols. Moscow: Izdatel'stvo Novospasskogo Monastyr'ia, 2012–2013.

Narodnyi komissariat iustitsii (Narkomiust). "O poriadke provedeniia v zhizn' dekreta 'Ob otdelenii tserkvi ot gosudarstva i shkoly ot tserkvi' (Instruktsiia), August 24, 1918." *Sbornik uzakonenii i rasporiazhenii RK RSFSR* 62 (1918): 764.

Narodnyi komissariat vnutrennikh del (NKVD). "O poriadke peredachi khramov staroobriadtsam," September 13, 1924. *Biulleten' NKVD* 34 (1924): 164.

"Nashi zadachi." *Arkhitektura Leningrada* 1 (1936): 6–9.

"Nashi zadachi." *Arkhitektura SSSR* 1 (1933): 1.

Naumov, A. I. "General'nyi plan vosstanovleniia Pskova." *Stroitel'stvo i arkhitektury Leningrada* (November 1946): 42–48.

Nechaev, Petr. *Prakticheskoe rukovodstvo dlia sviashchennosluzhitelei.* 5th ed. St. Petersburg: Tip. I. N. Skorokhodova, 1893.

Nekrasov, V. "Po obe storony okeana." *Novyi Mir* 11 (1962): 118–32.

Oleinits, F. F. "Vosstanovlenie Pavlovskogo dvortsa." *Stroitel'stvo i arkhitektury Leningrada* (November 1946): 36–39.

"O nachal'nykh meropriiatiiakh po preobrazovaniiu i razvitiiu Leningrada v obraztsovyi sovetskii i podlinno sotsialisticheskii gorod" (signed V. Molotov), *Izvestiia*, December 4, 1931; reprinted in *Vestnik Leningradskogo Oblispolkoma i Leningradskogo Soveta* 161 (1931): 1.

Oporkov, M. "Proektirovanie i zhizn'—pokonchit' s raspyleniem sil i sredstv pri novoi zastroike." *Leningradskaia pravda*, September 1, 1960, 2.

O religii i tserkvi: sbornik dokumentov, ed. F. I. Garkavenko. Moscow: Izdanie Politicheskaia literatura, 1965.

Orlov, M. A. *Leningrad: Putevoditel'.* 2nd ed. 2 vols. Moscow: OGIZ, 1933.

Panov, V. A. *Karlo Rossi 1775–1849.* Moscow, 1937.

Panteleev, L. [Aleksei Eremeev]. *L. Panteleev—L. Chukovskaia: Perepiska, 1929–1987.* Moscow: Novoe literaturnoe obozrenie, 2011.

"Paskhal'nye chastushi: Stikhi Nikolaia Semenova." *Iunyi proletarii* 7 (1925): 16.

Petrov, A. N., et al., eds. *Pamiatniki arkhitektury Leningrada.* Leningrad: Stroiizdat, 1958.

Piliavskii, V. I. *Natsional'nye osobennosti russkoi arkhitektury: Metodicheskoe posobie v pomoshch' lektoru.* Leningrad: Znanie, 1970.

———. *Zodchii Rossii.* Moscow: Gos. izd-vo arkhitektury i gradostroitel'stva, 1951.

———. *Zodchii Vasilii Petrovich Stasov (1769–1848).* Leningrad: Izdanie literatury po stroitel'stvu, 1970.

———. "Zodchii V. P. Stasov i ego tvorchestvo." *Stroitel'stvo i arkhitektury Leningrada* 10 (1949): 33–42.

Piliavskii, V. I., et al., eds. *Arkhitekturnyi putevoditel' po Leningradu.* Leningrad: Izdanie literatury po stroitel'stvu, 1971.

"Pod ploshchad'iu Mira." *Smena*, September 28, 1960, 2.

Pokrovskii, N. N., and S. G. Petrov, eds. *Arkhivy Kremlia. Politbiuro i tserkov', 1922–1925.* 2 vols. Moscow: ROSSPEN, 1997-1998.

Pope-Hennessy, Una. *The Closed City: Impressions of a Visit to Leningrad.* London: Hutchinson, 1938.

Popov, V. G. "Dmitrii Likhachev." *LitMir Elektronnaia Biblioteka*, http://www.litmir.co/br/?b=179777.

Preobrazhenskii, P. *Isaakievskii sobor: Istoriia postroiki khrama, ego sviatilishcha i khudozhestvennye dostoprimechatel'nosti (po povodu 75-letiia ego vozobnovleniia).* St. Petersburg: Izdanie tovarishchestva M. O. Vol'f, 1894.

Presidium of the Lenoblispolkom and Lensovet. "O poriadke sniatiia zontov nad vkhodnymi dver'mi, February 29, 1932." *Vestnik Leningradskogo Oblispolkoma i Leningradskogo Soveta* 20 (1932): 1.

"'Prikhod' ili kollektiv?," *Sobornyi razum* 3–4 [1918]: 1.

"Programma tserkovnykh reform, namechennykh gruppoi dukhovenstva i mirian v razvitii svoikh osnovnykh pozitsii, priniatykh na uchreditel'nom sobranii gruppy 16/29 maia 1922 g." *Zhivaia tserkov'* 10 (1922): 17.

Punin, Nikolai. *Mir svetel liubov'iu: Dnevniki, pis'ma*, edited by L. A. Zykova. Moscow: Slovo, 1998.

Ratiia, Sh. E., and P. N. Maksimov, eds. *Praktika restavratsionnykh rabot: Sbornik vtoroi.* Moscow: Akademiia stroitel'stv'a i arkhitektury, 1958.

Rotach, A. L. *Isaakievskii sobor, vydaiushchiisia pamiatnik russkoi arkhitektury*, edited by V. I. Piliavskii. Leningrad: Znanie, 1962.

Saki [H. H. Munro]. *The Complete Short Stories.* London: Penguin Books, 2000.

Samuel, Raphael. *Theatres of Memory*. 2 vols. London: Verso, 1994–1998.

Saunders, Matthew. "The Redundant Churches Fund Comes of Age" (1990), http://www.ihbc.org.uk/contextarchive/28/redundant.htm.

Savin, G. N., ed. *Peterburg-Leningrad: Al'bom*, text written by N. A. Bartenev. Leningrad: Lenizdat, 1967.

Shchukin, A. "Golubye kupola mecheti," *Leningradskaia panorama* 8 [1987]: 38–39.

Schulz, Gunther, et al., eds. *Bolschewistische Herrschaft und Orthodoxe Kirche in Russland: Das Landeskonzil 1917/1918; Quellen und Analysen*. Münster: Lit, 2005.

Serapina, N. M., ed. *Ermitazh, kotoryi my poteriali: Dokumenty 1920–1930 godov*. St. Petersburg: Zhurnal Neva, 2001.

Sevast'ianova, E. A. "Restavratsiia ubranstva inter'era Kazanskogo sobora," *Kazanskii sobor: Ofitsial'noe izdanie Kazanskogo kafedral'nogo sobora* 41, no. 5 (2009): 9.

Shkarovskii, M. V., *Russkaia pravoslavnaia tserkov' i Sovetskoe gosudarstvo v 1943–1964 godakh: Ot "peremiriia" k novoi voine*. St. Petersburg: Izdatel'skoe ob"edinenie DEAN + ADIA-M, 1995.

———, comp. *Pravoslavnye khramy Sankt-Peterburga, 1917–1945 gg.: Spravochnik*. St. Petersburg: BLITS, 1999.

———, comp. *Sankt-Peterburgskaia eparkhiia v dvadtsatom veke v svete arkhivnykh materialov*. St. Petersburg: Liki Rossii, 2000.

Shkarovskii, M. V., and N. Iu. Cherepnina. *Spravochnik po istorii pravoslavnykh monastyrei i soborov g. Sankt-Peterburga, 1917–1945 gg.: Po dokumentam TsGA-SPb*. St. Petersburg: Memorial, 1996.

60 slavnykh let, 1945–2005: Leningrad–Sankt-Peterburg; Spasennoe i sokhranennoe. St. Petersburg: GASU/Peterburgskii gosudarstvennyi universitet putei soobshcheniia, 2005.

Smirnov, I. P. *Deistvuiushchie litsa*. St. Petersburg: Petropolis, 2008.

Smirnov, V. V. "Skvernaia istoriia," *Neva* 3 (2004), http://magazines.russ.ru/neva/2004/3/smir19.html.

Sobranie opredelenii i postanovlenii Sviashchennogo Sobora Pravoslavnoi Rossiiskoi Tserkvi, 1917–1918 gg. 1918. Facsimile reprint, Moscow: Izdatel'stvo Novospasskogo monastyria, 1994.

Solofnenko, N. A. "Arkhitektura i zastroika Vyborga." *Arkhitektura Leningrada* 1–2 (1941): 57–60.

Soloukhin, Vladimir. *Slavianskaia tetrad'*. Moscow: Sovetskaia Rossiia, 1972.

Soobshcheniia nauchnoi chasti Gosudarstvennogo antireligioznogo muzei—byvshego Isaakievskogo sobora. Leningrad: Gosudarstvennyi antireligioznyi muzei, 1940.

Sorokin, Vladimir. "Interv'iu zhurnalu 'Gorod.'" December 2, 2002, http://www.vladimirskysobor.ru/klir/nastojatel/intervju-zhurnalu-gorod/.

———. "Leningradskii period." Unpublished typescript, undated.

———. "'Oni uzhe ne smeiutsia': Interv'ju." *Zhurnal Instituta Bogosloviia i filosofii* 9 (2000), 47–57

"Sovetskaia politika v religioznom voprose." *Revoliutsiia i tserkov'* 1 (1918): 1.

"Tat'iana Ivanovna Nikolaeva: Alleia slavy." http://www.srspb.ru/article.php?id=247.

Titlinov, Boris V. *Novaia tserkov'*. Petrograd: Tipografiia L. Ia. Ganzburg, 1923.

———. *Pravoslavie na sluzhbe samoderzhaviia v russkom gosudarstve*. Leningrad: Gosizdat, 1924.

Tolmacheva, N. Iu. *Isaakievskii sobor*. St. Petersburg: Paritet, 2003.

Trudy III-go S"ezda Russkikh Zodchikh v S-Peterburge. St. Petersburg: Ekonomicheskaia Tipo-Litografiia, 1905.

Trudy Vserossiiskogo s"ezda khudozhnikov, sostoiashchegosia pod Vysochaishim Pokrovitel'stvom Ego Imperatorskogo Velichestva Gosudaria NIKOLAIA ALEKSANDROVICHA i pochetnym predsedatel'stvom Ee Imperatorskogo Vysochestva Avgusteishego Prezidenta Imperatorskoi Akademii Khudozhestv Velikoi Kniagini Marii Pavlovny, Dekabr' 1911–Ianvar' 1912. 3 vols. St. Petersburg-Petrograd: Tipografiia P. Golike i A. Vil'borg, 1912–1914.

"Tsirkuliar NKP po Glavnauke vsem krai-, obl- i gubono i muzeinym p/otdelam pri nikh, No. 500/002/66 ot 17/1 1928 g." *Biulleten' Narkomprosa*, January 17, 1928, 2.

"Tsirkuliar po voprosu otdeleniia tserkvi ot gosudarstva," *Revoliutsiia i tserkov'* 1 (1919): 31.

Tyrkova-Williams, Ariadna. *Vospominaniia*. 1954. Reprint, Moscow: Slovo, 1998.

Ugolovnyi kodeks RSFSR, ofitsial'nyi tekst s izmeneniiami na 1 oktiabria 1953 g. Moscow: Gosudarstvennoe izdatel'stvo Iuridicheskoi literatury, 1953.

Ugolovnyi kodeks RSFSR: Priniat tret'ei sessiei Verkhovnogo soveta RSFSR piatogo sozyva. Moscow: Iuridicheskaia literatura, 1960.

Ugolovnyi kodeks RSFSR s izmeneniiami i dopolneniiami na 5 maia 1990 g. Moscow: Iuridicheskaia literatura, 1990.

Valentinov, A. A., ed. *Chernaia kniga: "Shturm nebes"; Sbornik dokumental'nykh dannykh, kharakter-izuiushchikh bor'bu sovetskoi kommunisticheskoi vlasti protiv vsiakoi religii, protiv vsekh ispove-danii i tserkvei.* Paris: Izd. Russkogo natsional'nogo studencheskogo ob"edineniia, 1925.

Vorob'ev, V., and N. A. Krivova, eds. *Sledstvennoe delo Patriarkha Tikhona: Sbornik dokumentov po materialam Tsentral'nogo arkhiva FSB RF.* Moscow: Pamiatniki istoricheskoi mysli, 2000.

Voronin, N., et al. "V zashchitu pamiatnikov proshlogo." *Literaturnaia gazeta,* August 23, 1956, 1.

Voronin, N., V. Kostochkin, and D. Likhachev. "Berezhno okhraniat' pamiatnikov stariny", *Sovetskaia Rossiia,* June 27, 1957.

"Vozvrashchenie Kazanskogo sobora: beseda s istorikom Mikhailom Shkarovskim", Pravoslavie.ru, September 19, 2011, http://www.pravoslavie.ru/48725.html.

Wright, Patrick. *A Journey through Ruins: The Last Days of London.* Oxford: Oxford University Press, 2009.

Zand, Arie. *Political Jokes of Leningrad.* Austin, TX: Silvergirl Paperbacks, 1982.

"Zapiska Otdela propagandy i agitatsii TsK KPSS po soiuznym respublikam 'O nedostatkakh naucho-ateisticheskoi propagandy.'" September 12, 1958, RGANI f. 4, op. 16, d. 554, ll. 5–13. http://www.rusoir.ru.

Zelinskaia, E. K., O. N. Ansberg, and A. D. Margolis, eds. *Obshchestvennaia zhizn' v Leningrade v gody perestroiki, 1985–1991.* St. Petersburg: Serebrianyi vek, 2009.

Zemtsov, S. M. "Rekonstruktsiia Sennoi i Obukhovskoi ploshchadei." *Arkhitektura Leningrada* 3 (1939): 47–48.

Secondary Sources

Andrews, James T. *Science for the Masses: The Bolshevik State, Public Science, and the Popular Imagination in Soviet Russia, 1917–1934.* College Station, TX: Texas A&M University Press, 2003.

Andrews, James T., and Asif A. Siddiqi, eds. *Into the Cosmos: Space Exploration and Soviet Culture.* Pittsburgh, PA: University of Pittsburgh Press, 2011.

"The Apogee of the Soviet Experience: Culture and Society in the Brezhnev Years." *Cahiers du monde russe* 54, nos. 1–2, 3–4 (2013).

Appadurai, Arjun, ed. *The Social Life of Things: Commodities in Cultural Perspective.* New York: Cambridge University Press, 1986.

Arnold, Victoria. 'The Experience of Sacred Place in Post-Soviet Russia: A Geography of Orthodoxy and Islam in Perm' Krai." DPhil thesis, University of Oxford, 2012.

Asad, Talal. *Formations of the Secular: Christianity, Islam, Modernity.* Stanford, CA: Stanford University Press, 2003.

Avgustin (Nikitin). *Tserkov' plenennaia: Mitropolit Nikodim (1929–1978) i ego epokha.* St. Petersburg: Izdatel'stvo Sankt-Peterburgskogo universiteta, 2008.

Bacon, Edwin, and Mark Sandle, eds. *Brezhnev Reconsidered.* Basingstoke: Palgrave, 2002.

Baiburin, Albert. "The Wrong Nationality: Ascribed Identity in the 1930s Soviet Union." In *Russian Cultural Anthropology since the Collapse of Communism,* edited by Albert Baiburin, Catriona Kelly, and Nikolai Vakhtin, 59–76. London: Routledge, 2012.

Barskova, Polina. "The Spectacle of the Besieged City: Repurposing Cultural Memory in Leningrad." *Slavic Review* 69, no. 2 (2010): 327–54.

———. *Zhivye kartiny: Leningradskaia blokada v litsakh.* St. Petersburg: Limbus, 2014.

Bass, Vadim. *Peterburgskaia neoklassicheskaia arkhitektura 1900–1910-kh godov v zerkale konkursov: Slovo i forma.* St. Petersburg: Evropeiskii universitet, 2010.

――――. *Peterburgskaia neoklassika 1900–1910-kh gg.: Arkhitekturnye konkursy; Zodchii, tsekh, gorod.* St. Petersburg: NP-Print, 2005.

Bassin, Mark, Christopher Ely, and Melissa T. Stockdale, eds. *Space, Place, and Power in Modern Russia: Essays in the New Spatial History.* DeKalb, IL: Northern Illinois University Press, 2010.

Bassin, Mark, and Catriona Kelly. *Soviet and Post-Soviet Identities.* Cambridge: Cambridge University Press, 2012.

Batorevich, N. I., and T. D. Kozhitseva, *Khramy-pamiatniki Sankt-Peterburga: Vo slavu i pamiat' rossiiskogo voinstva.* St. Petersburg: Dmitrii Bulanin, 2008.

Beglov, A. L. *V poiskakh "bezgreshnykh katakomb": Tserkovnoe podpol'e v SSSR.* Moscow: Izdatel'skii sovet Russkoi Pravoslavnoi Tserkvi, 2008.

Berger, Peter, ed. *The Desecularization of the World: Resurgent Religion and World Politics.* Washington DC: Ethics and Public Policy Center, 1999.

Binner, Rolf, Bernd Bonwetsch, and Marc Junge, eds. *Stalinismus in der sowjetischen Provinz 1937–1938: Die Massenaktion aufgrund des operativen Befehls no. 00447.* Berlin: Akademie Verlag, 2010.

Bittner, Stephen. *The Many Lives of Khrushchev's Thaw: Experience and Memory in Moscow's Arbat.* Ithaca, NY: Cornell University Press, 2008.

Bluestone, Daniel. "Academics in Tennis Shoes: Historic Preservation and the Academy." *The Journal of the Society of Architectural Historians* 58, no. 3 (1999): 300–307.

Bodewig, Herbert. *Die russische Patriarchatskirche: Beiträge zur äusseren Bedrückung und inneren Lage 1958–1979.* Munich: E. Wewel, 1988.

Bokareva, L. S. "Reforma pravoslavnogo prikhoda 1914–1917 gg.: Sinodal'noe vedomstvo." *Vestnik Leningradskogo gosudarstvennogo universiteta im. A. S. Pushkina* 4 (2012): 133–42.

Borkenau, Franz. *The Spanish Cockpit: An Eye-Witness Account of the Political and Social Conflicts of the Spanish Civil War.* London: Faber and Faber, 1937.

Bourdeaux, Michael. *Aida of Leningrad: The Story of Aida Skripnikova.* London: Mowbrays, 1976.

――――. *Opium of the People: the Christian Religion in the USSR.* London: Faber and Faber, 1965.

Boym, Svetlana. *The Future of Nostalgia.* New York: Basic Books, 2001.

Brandenberger, David. *National Bolshevism: Stalinist Mass Culture and the Formation of Modern Russian National Identity, 1931–1956.* Cambridge, MA: Harvard University Press, 2002.

Brandenberger, David, and Kevin Platt. *Epic Revisionism: Russian History and Literature as Stalinist Propaganda.* Madison: University of Wisconsin Press, 2006.

Brown, Kate. *Plutopia: Nuclear Families, Atomic Cities, and the Great Soviet and American Plutonium Disasters.* New York: Oxford University Press, 2013.

Bruce, Steve. *God Is Dead: Secularization in the West.* Oxford: Blackwell, 2002.

Brudny, Yitzhak M. *Reinventing Russia: Russian Nationalism and the Soviet State, 1953–1991.* Cambridge, MA: Harvard University Press, 1998.

Bruhat, Jean. "Anticléricalisme et mouvement ouvrier en France avant 1914." *Mouvement social* 57 (1966): 61–100.

Brumfield, William. *A History of Russian Architecture.* Cambridge: Cambridge University Press, 1993.

Buchli, Victor. *An Anthropology of Architecture.* London: Bloomsbury Academic, 2013.

Burmistrov, Dionisii. "Leningradskaia eparkhiia v usloviiakh antitserkovnykh gonenii v 1929–1939 gg. (po materialam arkhivov Sankt-Peterburga i Leningradskoi oblasti)," c. 2008, http://www.religare.ru/2_65553.html.

Busyreva, E. P. *Lev Il'in.* St. Petersburg: Muzei istorii Sankt-Peterburga, 2008.

Bychkov, Sergei. *Bol'sheviki protiv russkoi tserkvi.* Moscow: Tetis Pablishn, 2006.

Capéran, Louis. *La Crise du 16 mai et la revanche républicaine.* Vol. 1 of *Histoire contemporaine de la laïcité française.* Paris: Marcel Rivière, 1957.

――――. *La Laïcité en Marche.* Vol 3. of *Histoire contemporaine de la laïcité française.* Paris: Nouvelles éditions latines, 1961.

――――. *La Révolution scolaire.* Vol. 2 of *Histoire contemporaine de la laïcité française.* Paris: Marcel Rivière, 1959.

Chumachenko, Tatiana A. *Church and State in Soviet Russia: Russian Orthodoxy from World War II to the Khrushchev Years.* Edited by Edward E. Roslof. Armonk, NY: M. E. Sharpe, 2002.

———. "Pravovaia baza gosudarstvenno-tserkovnykh otnoshenii v 1940-e–pervoi polovine 1960-kh godov: Soderzhanie, praktika, primeneniia, evoliutsiia," *Vestnik Cheliabinskogo gosudarstvennogo universiteta* 15 (2008): 138–56.

"City Culture, Urban Culture." (Round Table.) *Forum for Anthropology and Culture* 7 (2011): 8–187.

Clark, Jonathan C. D. "Secularization and Modernization: The Failure of a 'Grand Narrative.'" *The Historical Journal* 55 (2012): 161–94.

Clark, Katerina. *Moscow, the Fourth Rome: Stalinism, Cosmopolitanism, and the Evolution of Soviet Culture, 1931–1941.* Cambridge, MA: Harvard University Press, 2011.

———. *Petersburg, Crucible of Cultural Revolution.* Cambridge, MA: Harvard University Press, 1995.

Colton, Timothy. *Moscow: Governing the Socialist Metropolis.* Cambridge, MA: Belknap Press, 1995.

Cooke, Catherine. *Russian Avant-Garde: Theories of Art, Architecture, and the City.* London: Academy Editions, 1995.

Crowley, David, and Susan E. Reid, eds. *Socialist Spaces: Sites of Everyday Life in the Eastern Bloc.* Oxford: Berg, 2002.

Cunningham, James W. *The Gates of Hell: The Great Sobor of the Russian Orthodox Church, 1917–1918.* Minneapolis: University of Minnesota Press, 2002.

Curtiss, John S. *The Russian Church and the Soviet State, 1917–1950.* Boston: Little, Brown and Company, 1953.

Dalgatov, Artur G. *"Oppozitsionnaia religioznost'" v sovetskoi Rossii (oktiabr' 1917 g.–konets 1930-kh gg.* St. Petersburg: Petropolis, 2002.

Daly, Jonathan. "'Storming the Last Citadel': The Bolshevik Assault on the Church, 1922." In *The Bolsheviks in Russian Society: The Revolution and the Civil Wars,* edited by Vladimir N. Brovkin, 236–59. New Haven, CT: Yale University Press, 1997.

Davis, Nathaniel. *A Long Walk to Church: A Contemporary History of Russian Orthodoxy.* Boulder, CO: Westview Press, 1995.

———. "The Number of Orthodox Churches before and after the Khrushchev Antireligious Drive." *Slavic Review* 50, no. 3 (1991): 612–20.

DeHaan, Heather D. *Stalinist City Planning: Professionals, Performance, and Power.* Toronto: University of Toronto Press, 2013.

Dement'eva, V. A., O. V. Taratynova, and B. M. Kirikov, eds. *Okhrana pamiatnikov Sankt-Peterburga: K 90-letiiu Komiteta po gosudarstvennomu kontroliu, ispol'zovaniiu i okhrane pamiatnikov istorii i kul'tury Sankt-Peterburga.* St. Petersburg: Propilei, 2008.

Desan, Suzanne. *Reclaiming the Sacred: Lay Religion and Popular Politics in Revolutionary France.* Ithaca, NY: Cornell University Press, 1990.

Dixon, Simon. "The 'Mad Monk' Iliodor in Tsaritsyn." *The Slavonic and East European Review* 88, nos. 1–2 (2010): 377–415.

———. "The Orthodox Church and the Workers of St. Petersburg, 1880–1890." In *European Religion in the Age of Great Cities, 1830–1930,* edited by Hugh McLeod, 117–39. London: Routledge, 2005.

Dluzhnevskaia, G. *Utrachennye khramy Peterburga.* St Petersburg: Izdatel'skii dom "Litera," 2003.

Dobrenko, Evgeny. *The Making of the State Reader: Social and Aesthetic Origins of Soviet Literary Culture.* Translated by Jesse Savage. Stanford, CA: Stanford University Press, 2001.

Dobrenko, Evgeny, and Eric Naiman, eds. *The Landscape of Stalinism: The Art and Ideology of Soviet Space.* Seattle: University of Washington Press, 2003.

Donovan, Victoria. *"Nestolichnaya kul'tura*: Regional and National Identity in Post-1961 Russian Culture." DPhil thesis, University of Oxford, 2011.

Duffy, Eamon. *The Stripping of the Altars: Traditional Religion in England, c. 1400–c. 1580.* New Haven, CT: Yale University Press, 1992.

Dunlop, John B. *The Faces of Contemporary Russian Nationalism*. Princeton, NJ: Princeton University Press, 1983.

———. *The New Russian Nationalism*. New York: Praeger, 1985.

———. *The Rise of Russia and the Fall of the Soviet Empire*. Princeton, NJ: Princeton University Press, 1993.

Edele, Mark. *Soviet Veterans of the Second World War: A Popular Movement in an Authoritarian Society, 1941–1991*. Oxford: Oxford University Press, 2008.

Elfimov, Alexei. *Russian Intellectual Culture in Transition: The Future in the Past*. Münster: Lit, 2004.

Engelstein, Laura. "Holy Russia in Modern Times: An Essay on Orthodoxy and Cultural Change." *Past and Present* 173 (2001): 129–56.

Erofeev, Konstantin. *Tserkov' i obshchestvo*. St. Petersburg: Izdatel'stvo Khristianskogo bibleiskogo bratstva sv. Apostola Pavla, 2007.

Ezrahi, Christina. *Swans of the Kremlin: Ballet and Power in Soviet Russia*. Pittsburgh, PA: University of Pittsburgh Press, 2012.

Fedotov, Aleksei. "Pervyi etap antireligioznykh reform N. S. Khrushcheva (1958–1961 gg.)." *Bogoslov. ru*, December 26, 2013, http://www.bogoslov.ru/text/3698574.html.

Figes, Orlando, and Boris Kolonitskii. *Interpreting the Russian Revolution: The Language and Symbols of 1917*. New Haven, CT: Yale University Press, 1999.

Filatov, S., and R. Lunken. "Statistics on Religion in Russian Reality." *Religion, State and Society* 34 (2006): 33–49.

Firsov, Boris. *Raznomyslie v SSSR: 1940-e–1960-e gody; Istoriia, teoriia i praktika*. St. Petersburg: Evropeiskii dom, 2008.

Fitzpatrick, Sheila. *The Commissariat of Enlightenment: Soviet Organization of Education and the Arts under Lunacharsky (October 1917–1921)*. Cambridge: Cambridge University Press, 1970.

———. *The Cultural Front: Power and Culture in Revolutionary Russia*. Ithaca, NY: Cornell University Press, 1992.

Formozov, A. A. "Rol' N. N. Voronina v zashchite pamiatnikov kul'tury Rossii." *Rossiiskaia arkheologiia* 2 (2004): 173–80.

Freeze, Gregory L. "All Power to the Parish? The Problem and Politics of Church Reform in Late Imperial Russia." In *Social Identities in Revolutionary Russia*, edited by Madhavan K. Palat, 174–208. London: Macmillan, 2001.

———. "Counter-Reformation in Russian Orthodoxy: Popular Response to Religious Innovation, 1922–1925." *Slavic Review* 54, no. 2 (1995): 305–39.

———. "From Dechristianization to Laicization: State, Church, and Believers in Russia." *Canadian Slavonic Papers* 57, nos. 1–2 (2015): 6–34.

———. "The Stalinist Assault on the Parish, 1929–1941." In *Stalinismus vor dem Zweiten Weltkrieg: Neue Wege der Forschung*, edited by Manfred Hildermeier, 209–32. Munich: Oldenburg Verlag, 1998.

———. "Subversive Piety: Religion and the Political Crisis in Late Imperial Russia." *Journal of Modern History* 68, no. 2 (1996): 308–50.

French, R. A., and F. E. Ian Hamilton, eds. *The Socialist City: Spatial Structure and Urban Policy*. New York: Wiley, 1979.

Fritzsche, Peter. "Specters of History: On Nostalgia, Exile, and Modernity." *American Historical Review* 5 (2001): 1587–1618.

Froese, Paul. *The Plot to Kill God: Findings from the Soviet Experiment in Secularization*. Berkeley: University of California Press, 2008.

Froggatt, Michael. "Science in Propaganda and Popular Culture in the USSR under Khrushchëv (1953–1964)." DPhil thesis, University of Oxford, 2006.

Frolov, V. A., ed. *Ot Muzeia Starogo Peterburga k Gosudarstvennomu muzeiu istorii Sankt-Peterburga: Issledovaniia i materialy*. St. Petersburg: GMI-SPb, 1997.

Frolova-Walker, Marina, *Stalin's Music Prize*. New Haven, CT: Yale University Press, 2016.

Gladarev, Boris. "Rozhdenie obshchestvennosti iz dukha goroda." In *Ot obshchestvennogo k publichnomu*, edited by Oleg Kharkhordin, 70–304. Res Publica 5. St. Petersburg: Izdatel'stvo Evropeiskogo universiteta, 2011.

Gorelova, S. A. "Pervaia Vserossiiskaia restavratsionnaia konferentsiia 1921 goda." *Khudozhestvennoe nasledie* 21, no. 51 (2004), http://art-con.ru/node/1193.

Gorham, Michael. "Tongue-Tied Writers: The *Rabsel'kor* Movement and the Voice of the New Intelligentsia." *Russian Review* 55, no. 3 (1996): 412–29.

Gorlizki, Yoram. "Too Much Trust: Regional Party Leaders and Local Political Networks under Brezhnev." *Slavic Review* 69, no. 3 (2010): 676–700.

Gorski, Philip S., and Ateş Altinordu. "After Secularization?" *Annual Review of Sociology* 34 (2008): 55–85.

Goscilo, Helena, and Steven Norris, eds. *Preserving Petersburg: History, Memory, Nostalgia*. Bloomington: Indiana University Press, 2008.

Grant, Bruce. "The Edifice Complex: Architecture and the Political Life of Surplus in the New Baku." *Public Culture* 26, no. 3 (2014): 501–28.

Greene, Robert. *Bodies Like Bright Stars: Saints and Relics in Orthodox Russia*. DeKalb: Northern Illinois University Press, 2010.

Gusarov, A. Iu. *Pamiatniki voinskoi slavy Peterburga*. St. Petersburg: Paritet, 2010.

Hagenloh, Paul. *Stalin's Police: Public Order and Mass Repression in the USSR, 1926–1941*. Washington, DC: Woodrow Wilson Center, 2009.

Halfin, Igal. *Stalinist Confessions: Messianism and Terror at the Leningrad Communist University*. Pittsburgh, PA: University of Pittsburgh Press, 2009.

Hatherley, Owen. *Landscapes of Communism: A History through Buildings*. London: Allen Lane, 2015.

Hellbeck, Jochen. *Revolution on My Mind: Writing a Diary under Stalin*. Cambridge, MA: Harvard University Press, 2006.

Hellberg-Hirn, Elena. *Imperial Imprints: Post-Soviet St. Petersburg*. Helsinki: SKS, Finnish Literature Society, 2003.

Hernandez, Richard J. "Sacred Sound and Sacred Substance: Bells and the Auditory Culture of Russian Villages during the Bolshevik *Velikii perelom*." *The American Historical Review* 109, no. 5 (2004): 1475–1504.

Hervieu-Léger, Danièle. *Religion as a Chain of Memory*. Translated by Simon Lee. Cambridge: Polity Press, 2000. Originally published as *La Religion pour mémoire* (Paris: Editions du Cerf, 1993).

Herzfeld, Michael. *Cultural Intimacy: Social Poetics in the Nation-State*. New York: Routledge, 1997.

Hoffmann, David L. *Peasant Metropolis: Social Identities in Moscow, 1929–1941*. Ithaca, NY: Cornell University Press, 1994.

———. *Stalinist Values: The Cultural Norms of Soviet Modernity, 1917–1941*. Ithaca, NY: Cornell University Press, 2003.

Holmes, Larry E. *Stalin's School: Moscow's Model School no. 25, 1931–1937*. Pittsburgh, PA: University of Pittsburgh Press, 1999.

Holquist, Peter. *Making War, Forging Revolution: Russia's Continuum of Crisis*. Cambridge, MA: Harvard University Press, 2002.

Hosking, Geoffrey. *The Awakening of the Soviet Union*. Cambridge, MA: Harvard University Press, 1990.

———. *A History of the Soviet Union*. London: Fontana, 1985.

Hudson, Hugh. *Blueprints and Blood: The Stalinization of Soviet Architecture, 1917–1927*. Princeton, NJ: Princeton University Press, 1994.

Huhn, Ulrike. *Glaube und Eigensinn: Volksfrömmigkeit zwischen orthodoxer Kirche und Sowjetischem Staat, 1941 bis 1960*. Wiesbaden: Harrassowitz, 2014.

Humphrey, Caroline. "The 'Creative Bureaucrat': Conflicts in the Production of Communist Party Discourse." *Inner Asia* 10, no. 1 (2008): 5–35.

_____. *The Unmaking of Soviet Life: Everyday Economies after Socialism*. Ithaca, NY: Cornell University Press, 2002.

Husband, William B. *"Godless Communists": Atheism and Society in Soviet Russia, 1917–1932*. DeKalb: Northern Illinois University Press, 2000.

Iarov, Sergei. *Konformizm v sovetskoi Rossii: Petrograd 1917–1920-kh godov*. St. Petersburg: Evropeiskii Dom, 2006.

Ioann (Snychev), ed. *Ocherki istorii Sankt-Peterburgskoi eparkhii*. St. Petersburg: Andreev i synov'ia, 1994.

Iurkova, Zoia. *Sennaia ploshchad': Vchera, segodnia, zavtra*. Moscow: Tsentropoligraf, 2011, http://lib.rus.ec/b/375320/read.

Johnson, Emily. *How St. Petersburg Learned to Study Itself: The Russian Idea of Kraevedenie*. University Park: Pennsylvania State University Press, 2006.

Jolles, Adam. "Stalin's Talking Museums." *Oxford Art Journal* 28, no. 3 (2005): 49–55.

Jones, Polly. *Myth, Memory, Trauma: Rethinking the Stalinist Past in the Soviet Union, 1953–70*. New Haven, CT: Yale University Press, 2013.

Kashevarov, A. N. *Gosudarstvo i tserkov': Iz istorii vzaimootnoshenii sovetskoi vlasti i russkoi pravoslavnoi tserkvi, 1917–1946 gg*. St. Petersburg: Sankt-Peterburgskii gosudarstvennyi tekhnicheskii universitet, 1995.

———. *Pravoslavnaia rossiiskaia tserkov' i sovetskoe gosudarstvo 1917–1922*. Moscow: Izdatel'stvo Krutitskogo podvor'ia, 2005.

Kaulen, M. E. *Muzei-khramy i muzei-monastyri v pervoe desiatiletie Sovetskoi vlasti*. Moscow: Luch, 2001.

Kedrinskii, A. A., M. G. Kolotov, L. A. Mederskii, and A. G. Raskin. *Letopis' vozrozhdeniia: Vosstanovlenie pamiatnikov arkhitektury Leningrada i prigorodov, razrushennykh v gody Velikoi Otechestvennoi Voiny nemetsko-fashistskimi zakhvatchikami*. Leningrad: Lenizdat, 1971.

Kedrinskii, A. A., M. G. Kolotov, B. N. Ometov, and A. G. Raskin. *Vosstanovlenie pamiatnikov arkhitektury Leningrada*. Leningrad: Lenizdat, 1983.

Kelly, Catriona.."The Bolshevik Reformation: February 1922", in *Historically Inevitable?* Edited by Tony Brenton. London: Profile Books, 2016, 244-62.

———. "Competing Orthodoxies: Identity and Religious Belief in Soviet and Post-Soviet Russia," in Mark Bassin and Catriona Kelly (eds.), *National Identity in Soviet and Post-Soviet Culture*. Cambridge, UK: Cambridge University Press, 2012, 299-320.

———. *Children's World: Growing Up in Russia, 1890–1991*. New Haven, CT: Yale University Press, 2008.

———."'A Dissonant Note on the Neva': Historical Memory and Local Identity in Russia's Second City during the Post-Stalin Era." *Journal of Eurasian Studies* 1, no. 1 (2010): 72–83.

_____. "'Ispravliat' li istoriiu?' Spory ob okhrane pamiatnikov v Leningrade 1960-kh–1980-kh godov," *Neprikosnovennyi zapas* 2 (2009), https://www.academia.edu/2001169/

———. "The Leningrad Affair: Remembering the 'Communist Alternative' in the Second Capital." *Slavonica* 17, no. 2 (2011): 103–22.

———. "Religion and *nauka*: Churches as Architectural Heritage in Soviet Leningrad." In *Science, Religion and Communism during the Cold War*. Edited by Paul Betts and Stephen A. Smith. Basingstoke: Palgrave, 2016, forthcoming.

———. *Remembering St. Petersburg*. Oxford: Triton Press, 2014. https://oxford.academia.edu/CatrionaKelly.

———. *St. Petersburg: Shadows of the Past*. New Haven, CT: Yale University Press, 2014.

———. "'Scientific Reconstruction' or 'New Oldbuild'? The Dilemmas of Restoration in Post-Soviet St. Petersburg." *Revue des études slaves* 1 (2015): 17–39.

———. "Socialist Churches: Heritage Preservation and 'Cultic Buildings' in Leningrad, 1924–1940." *Slavic Review* 71, no. 4 (2012): 792–823.

———. "The Traditions of Our History': 'Tradition' as Framework for National Identity in Late Soviet and Post-Soviet Russia." In *Loyalties, Solidarities and Identities in Russian Society, History and*

Culture, edited by Philip Ross Bullock et al., 141–60. London: School of Slavonic and East European Studies, 2013.

Kenworthy, Scott M. *The Heart of Russia: Trinity-Sergius, Monasticism, and Society after 1825*. New York: Oxford University Press, 2010.

———. "To Save the World or to Renounce It: Modes of Moral Action in Russian Orthodoxy." In *Religion, Morality, and Community in Post-Soviet Societies*, ed. Mark D. Steinberg and Catherine Wanner (Bloomington: Indiana University Press, 2008), 21–53.

Khan-Magomedov, S. O. *INCHUK i rannii konstruktivizm*. Moscow: Arkhitektura, 1994.

Kharshak, A. A. "Petr Evgen'evich Kornilov (1896–1981): Tvorcheskii put', sluzhenie." *Noveishaia istoriia Rossii* 1 (2013): 208–41.

Khlevniuk, Oleg, et al., eds. *Regional'naia politika N. S. Khrushcheva: TsK KPSS i mestnye partiinye komitety 1953–1964 gg.* Moscow: Rosspen, 2009.

Khodakovskaia, O. I., ed. "Blokadnyi khram: Religioznaia zhizn' blokadnogo Leningrada." http://blokada.mrezha.ru/duhov.htm.

Khodakovskaia, O. I., and A. A. Bovkalo. *Leningradskaia (Sankt-Peterburgskaia) dukhovnaia akademii: Professora i prepodavateli*. St. Petersburg: Divnyi ostrov, 2011.

Kirschenbaum, Lisa A. *The Legacy of the Siege of Leningrad, 1941–1995: Myth, Memories, and Monuments*. Cambridge: Cambridge University Press, 2006.

———. "Place, Memory and the Politics of Identity: Historical Buildings and Street Names in Leningrad-St. Petersburg." In Bassin, Ely, and Stockdale, *Space, Place, and Power*, 243–59.

Kizenko, Nadieszda. *A Prodigal Saint: Father John of Kronstadt and the Russian People.* University Park: Pennsylvania State University Press, 2000.

Kline, George L. *Religious and Anti-Religious Thought in Russia*. Chicago, IL: University of Chicago Press, 1968.

Koposov, Nikolai. *Pamiat' strogogo rezhima: Istoriia i politika v Rossii*. Moscow: Novoe literaturnoe obozrenie, 2011.

Kopp, Anatole. *Town and Revolution: Soviet Architecture and City Planning, 1917–1935*. London: Thames and Hudson, 1970.

Kormina, Jeanne [Zhanna]. "Ispolkomy i prikhody: Religioznaia zhizn' Pskovskoi oblasti v pervuiu poslevoennuiu piatiletku." *Neprikosnovennyi zapas* 59, no. 3 (2008), http://magazines.russ.ru/nz/2008/3/ko11.html.

Kormina, Jeanne [Zhanna], and Sergei Shtyrkov. "'Eto nashe iskonno russkoe, i nikuda nam ot etogo ne det'sia': Predystoriia postsovetskoi desekuliarizatsii." In *Izobretenie religii: Desekuliarizatsiia v postsovetskom kontekste*, edited by Jeanne Kormina, Alexander Panchenko, and Sergei Shtyrkov, 7–45. St. Petersburg: Evropeiskii universitet v Sankt-Peterburge, 2015.

Kotkin, Stephen. *Magnetic Mountain: Stalinism as a Civilization*. Berkeley: University of California Press, 1995.

Kozlov, Denis. "The Historical Turn in Late Soviet Culture: Retrospectivism, Factography, Doubt, 1953–91." *Kritika* 2, no. 3 (2001): 577–600.

———. *The Readers of Novyi Mir: Coming to Terms with the Stalinist Past*. Cambridge, MA: Harvard University Press, 2013.

Krasnov-Levitin, Anatolii. *Likhie gody, 1925–1941*. Paris: YMCA, 1977.

Krasnov-Levitin, Anatolii, with Vadim Shavrov. *Ocherki po istorii russkoi tserkovnoi smuty*. 2 vols. Moscow: Krutitskoe patriarshee podvor'e, 1996.

Krasnova, A. "Traditsii vsegda sovremenny." *Leningradskaia panorama* 3 (1984): 20.

Krivova, N. A. *Vlast' i tserkov' v 1922–1925 gg.* *Makhaon* 1 (1999), http://krotov.info/history/20/krivova/kriv01.html.

Krylova, L. N. "I. E. Grabar' i okhrana pamiatnikov: Chetyre etapa ego zhizni." *Grabarevskie chteniia* 5 (2004). Also online at http://art-con.ru/node/1765.

Kunin, M. E., ed. *Leningrad: Vidy goroda*. Designed by G. D. Elifanov. Photographs by M. A. Velichko, S. P. Ivanov, and M. A. Mitskevich. Moscow: Gosudarstvennoe izdatel'stvo izobrazitel'nogo iskusstva, 1954.

Kupriyanov, Pavel, and Sadovnikova, Larisa. "Historical Zaryadye as Remembered by Locals: Cultural Meanings of City Spaces." In *Russian Cultural Anthropology since the Collapse of Communism*, edited by Albert Baiburin, Catriona Kelly, and Nikolai Vakhtin, 220–53. Abingdon: Routledge, 2012.

Kuti, Csongor. *Post-Communist Restitution and the Rule of Law.* Budapest: Central European University Press, 2009.

Kynaston, David. *A World to Build: Austerity Britain, 1945–48.* London: Bloomsbury Publishing, 2007.

Kyzlasova, I. L. *Aleksandr Ivanovich Anisimov (1877–1937).* Moscow: Izd. Moskovskogo Gosudarstvennogo Gornogo universiteta, 2000.

Larkin, Maurice. *Church and State after the Dreyfus Affair: The Separation Issue in France.* London, Macmillan, 1974.

Lebina, N. B. "Deiatel'nost' 'voinstvuiushchikh bezbozhnikov' i ikh sud'ba." *Voprosy istorii* 5–6 (1996): 154–57.

Lebina, N. B., and V. S. Izmozik. *Peterburg sovetskii: "Novyi chelovek" v starom prostranstve; Sotsial'no-arkhitekturnoe mikroistoricheskoe issledovanie.* St. Petersburg: Kriga, 2010.

Lenoe, Matthew. *Closer to the Masses: Stalinist Culture, Social Revolution, and Soviet Newspapers.* Cambridge, MA: Harvard University Press, 2004.

Levinson, N. R. "Okhrana vnemuzeinykh pamiatnikov." *Sovetskii muzei* 6 (1932): 52–57.

Lidak, Ia. "Bol'she vnimaniia pamiatnikam stariny," *Sovetskii muzei* 5 (1932): 116–17.

———. "Zabota o pamiatnikakh proshlogo." *Sovetskii muzei* 5 (1938): 20–23.

Lincoln, W. Bruce. "Notes toward a Theory of Religion and Revolution." In *Religion, Rebellion, Revolution: An Interdisciplinary and Cross-Cultural Collection of Essays*, 266–92. London: Macmillan, 1985.

Lobanov, V. V. *Patriarkh Tikhon i sovetskaia vlast' (1917–1925 gg.).* Moscow: Panorama, 2008.

Lodder, C. "Lenin's Plan for Monumental Propaganda." In *Art of the Soviets: Painting, Sculpture, and Architecture in a One-Party State*, edited by Matthew Cullerne Bown and Brandon Taylor, 16–32. Manchester: Manchester University Press, 1993.

Lomagin, Nikita. *Neizvestnaia Blokada.* 2 vols. St. Petersburg: Neva, 2001–2002.

Luehrmann, Sonja [S. Lurman]. "Chto my mozhem znat' o religioznoi zhizni sovetskogo perioda? Sopostavlenie arkhivnykh i ustnykh istochnikov." *Gosudarstvo, religiia, tserkov'*, nos. 3–4 (2012): 485–504.

———. *Secularism Soviet Style: Teaching Atheism and Religion in a Volga Republic.* Bloomington: Indiana University Press, 2011.

Lur'e, Lev, and Aleksandr Kobak. "Rozhdenie i gibel' peterburgskoi idei." *Muzei i gorod*, special issue of the journal *Petersburg ars* (1993): 25–31.

Luukkanen, Arto. *The Party of Unbelief: The Religious Policy of the Bolshevik Party, 1917–1929.* Helsinki: Suomen Historiallinen Seura, 1994.

———. *The Religious Policy of the Stalinist State: A Case Study; The Central Standing Committee on Religious Questions, 1929–1938.* Helsinki: Suomen Historiallinen Seura, 1998.

Maddox, Steven. "Healing the Wounds: Commemorations, Myths, and the Restoration of Leningrad's Imperial Heritage, 1941-1950". Ph.D Thesis, University of Toronto, 2008.

_____. *Saving Stalin's Imperial City: Historic Preservation in Leningrad, 1930–1950.* Bloomington: Indiana University Press, 2015.

Mandelstam Balzer, Marjorie, ed. *Religion and Politics in Russia: A Reader.* Armonk, NY: M. E. Sharpe, 2010.

Maslova, Irina. "Deiatel'nost' Soveta po delam religii pri Sovete Ministrov SSSR v 1965–1985 gg.: 'Politika sderzhivaniia,'" *Religiia i pravo: Informatsionno-analiticheskii zhurnal* 1 (2005): 17–23.

_____. "Russkaia pravoslavnaia tserkov' i KGB," *Voprosy istorii*, no. 12 (2005), 86–96.

Maurer, Eva, Julia Richers, Monica Rüthers, and Carmen Scheide, eds. *Soviet Space Culture: Cosmic Enthusiasm in Socialist Societies.* Basingstoke: Palgrave, 2011.

McDannell, Colleen. *Material Christianity: Religion and Popular Culture in America.* New Haven, CT: Yale University Press, 1995.

McLeod, Hugh. *The Religious Crisis of the 1960s*. Oxford: Oxford University Press, 2007.

McLeod, Hugh, and Werner Ustorf, eds. *The Decline of Christendom in Western Europe, 1750-2000*. Cambridge: Cambridge University Press, 2003.

McManners, John. *Church and State in France, 1870-1914*. New York: Harper and Row, 1972.

Medvedeva, Mariia V. "Izuchenie i okhrana pamiatnikov arkheologii i arkhitektury epokhi srednevekov'ia Severo-Zapada Rossii v deiatel'nosti Imperatorskoi Arkheologicheskoi Komissii" (Avtoreferat diss., Institut istorii material'noi kul'tury RAN, 2007).

Merridale, Catherine. *Red Fortress: The Secret Heart of Russia's History*. London: Allen Lane, 2013.

Miller, Daniel, ed. *Anthropology and the Individual: A Material Culture Perspective*. Oxford: Berg, 2009.

Minkina, E. V. "P. P. Veiner: Muzeinyi rabotnik." In Frolov, *Ot Muzeia Starogo Peterburga*, 25-35.

Mitrokhin, Nikolai. "Bolezn' pod nazvaniem 'fond upolnomochennogo' ili neskol'ko stranits ob aktual'nykh problemakh izucheniia religioznosti v SSSR." *Gosudarstvo, religiia, tserkov'* 30, nos. 3-4 (2012): 505-11.

———. "Religioznost' v SSSR v 1954-1965 godakh glazami apparata TsK KPSS." *Neprikosnovennyi zapas* 73, no. 5 (2010), http://magazines.russ.ru/nz/2010/5/re8.html.

———. *Russkaia partiia: Dvizhenie russkikh natsionalistov v SSSR, 1953-1985 gody*. Moscow: Novoe literaturnoe obozrenie, 2003.

———. *Russkaia pravoslavnaia tserkov': Sovremennoe sostoianie i aktual'nye problemy*. Moscow: Novoe literaturnoe obozrenie, 2004.

Nash, David. "Reconnecting Religion with Social and Cultural History: Secularization's Failure as a Master Narrative." *Cultural and Social History* 3 (2004): 302-25.

Nikol'skaia, T. M. "Okhrana pamiatnikov iskusstva: Istoriia i perspektivy razvitiia." *Analitika kul'turologii* 17 (2010), http://cyberleninka.ru/article/n/ohrana-pamyatnikov-iskusstva-istoriya-i-perspektivy-razvitiya.

Nora, Pierre, ed. *Les Lieux de mémoire*. 3 vols. Paris: Gallimard, 1984-1992.

Norman, Geraldine. *The Hermitage: The Biography of a Great Museum*. London: Jonathan Cape, 1997.

Norris, Pippa, and Ronald Inglehart. *Sacred and Secular: Religion and Politics Worldwide*. Cambridge: Cambridge University Press, 2004.

Novikov, Feliks, and Vladimir Belogolovskii. *Sovetskii modernizm, 1955-1985: Antologiia*. Ekaterinburg: Tatlin, 2010.

Obertreis, Julia. *Tränen des Sozialismus: Wohnen in Leningrad zwischen Alltag und Utopie, 1917-1937*. Cologne: Böhlau, 2004.

Odintsov, M. I., ed. *Russkaia Pravoslavnaia Tserkov' nakanune i v epokhu stalinskogo sotsializma 1917-1953 gg*. Moscow: ROSSPEN, 2014.

———. *Russkie patriarkhi XX veka: Sud'by Otechestva i Tserkvi na stranitsakh arkhivnykh dokumentov*. Moscow: Izd. RAGS, 1999.

———, *Vlast' i religiia v gody voiny: Gosudarstvo i religioznye organizatsii v SSSR v gody Velikoi Otechestvennoi voiny, 1941-1945*. Moscow: Rossiiskoe ob"edinenie issledovatelei religii, 2005.

———. *Vlast' i tserkov' v SSSR i stranakh Vostochnoi Evropy, 1939-1958: Diskussionnye aspekty*. Moscow: Institut slavianovedeniia RAN, 2003.

Odom, Anne, and Wendy R. Salmond, eds. *Treasures into Tractors: The Selling of Russia's Cultural Heritage, 1918-1938*. Washington, DC: Hillwood Estate, 2009.

Ol', G. A. *Aleksandr Nikol'skii*. Leningrad: Lenizdat, 1980.

Orsi, Robert A. *Between Heaven and Earth: The Religious Worlds People Make and the Scholars Who Study Them*. Princeton, NJ: Princeton University Press, 2005.

Paert, Irina. "Demystifying the Heavens: Women, Religion, and Khrushchev's Anti-Religious Campaign, 1954-64." In *Women in the Khrushchev Era*, edited by Melanie Ilic, Susan E. Reid, and Lynne Attwood, 203-21. Basingstoke: Palgrave, 2004.

Paine, Crispin, ed. *Godly Things: Museums, Objects, and Religion*. Leicester: Leicester University Press, 2000.

———. *Religious Objects in Museums: Private Lives and Public Duties*. London: Bloomsbury, 2013.

Panchenko. Alexander. *Ivan i Iakov—neobychnye sviatye iz bolotistoi mestnosti.* Moscow: Novoe literaturnoe obozrenie, 2012.

———. "Popular Orthodoxy in Twentieth-Century Russia: Ideology, Consumption, and Competition." In Bassin and Kelly, *Soviet and Post-Soviet Identities,* 321–40.

Papernyi, Vladimir. *Kul'tura "dva."* Ann Arbor: Ardis, 1985.

Pare, Richard. *The Lost Vanguard: Russian Modernist Architecture, 1922–1932.* New York: The Monacelli Press, 2007.

Peris, Daniel. *Storming the Heavens: The Soviet League of the Militant Godless.* Ithaca, NY: Cornell University Press, 1998.

Petrone, Karen. *Life Has Become More Joyous, Comrades: Celebrations in the Time of Stalin.* Bloomington: Indiana University Press, 2000.

Petrov, Kristian. "Construction, Reconstruction, Deconstruction: The Fall of the Soviet Union from the Point of View of Conceptual History," *Studies in East European Thought* 60, no. 3 (2008): 179–205.

Petrov, S. G. *Russkaia pravoslavnaia tserkov' vremeni patriarkha Tikhona.* Novosibirsk: Izdatel'stvo Sibirskogo otdeleniia Rossiiskoi Akademii nauk, 2013.

Pipes, Richard. *Russia under the Bolshevik Regime, 1919–1924.* New York: Vintage, 1995.

Pivovarova, N. V. "Khristianskie drevnosti v Sankt-Peterburge: Iz istorii sobraniia i muzeefikatsii pamiatnikov tserkovnoi stariny." *Voprosy muzeologii* 1, no. 3 (2011): 57–66.

Plamper, Jan, *The Stalin Cult: A Study in the Alchemy of Power.* New Haven: Yale University Press, 2012.

Pogrebskaia, A. A. "Ob ispol'zovanii tserkvei Leningrada, zakrytykh v 1930-e gody", *Trudy Istoricheskogo fakul'teta Sankt-Peterburgskogo universiteta* 2 (2010), 317-326.

Poliakova, M. A., *Okhrana kul'turnogo naslediia Rossii: Uchebnoe posobie dlia vuzov.* Moscow: Drofa, 2005.

Pollard, John F. *Money and the Rise of the Modern Papacy: Financing the Vatican, 1850–1950.* Cambridge: Cambridge University Press, 2005.

Popov, A. P. *Khramy Sankt-Peterburga: Khudozhestvenno-istoricheskii ocherk.* St Petersburg: Lenizdat, 1995.

Popova, G. A. "L. A. Il'in: Pervyi director Muzeia Goroda." In Frolov, *Ot Muzeia Starogo Peterburga,* 48–56.

———. *Muzei Goroda v Anichkovom dvortse: Sobytiia, sud'by, kollektsii.* St. Petersburg: Almaz, 1998.

Pospielovsky, Dimitry. *A History of Soviet Atheism in Theory and Practice, and the Believer.* 2 vols. Basingstoke: Macmillan, 1987–1988.

———. "Kak Stalin tserkov' vozrozhdal." *Vesna* 2 (2005), http://ricolor.org/journal/s2005/13/.

———. "Na puti k sobornosti." *Kontinent* 121 (2004), http://magazines.russ.ru/continent/2004/121/po10.html.

———. *The Russian Church under the Soviet Regime, 1917–1982.* 2 vols. Crestwood, NY: St. Vladimir's Seminary Press, 1984.

———. *Russkaia pravoslavnaia tserkov' v XX veke.* Moscow: Respublika, 1995.

Powell, David. *Antireligious Propaganda in the Soviet Union: A Study of Mass Persuasion.* Cambridge, MA: MIT Press, 1975.

———. "The Effectiveness of Soviet Anti-Religious Propaganda." *The Public Opinion Quarterly* 31, no. 3 (1967): 366–80.

Pravilova, Ekaterina. "Les res publicae russes: Discours sur la propriété publique à la fin de l'empire." *Annales: Histoire, Sciences Sociales* 3 (2009): 579–609.

———. *A Public Empire: Property and the Quest for the Common Good in Imperial Russia.* Princeton, NJ: Princeton University Press, 2014.

Priestland, David. *Stalinism and the Politics of Mobilization: Ideas, Power, and Terror in Inter-War Russia.* Oxford: Oxford University Press, 2007.

Qualls, Karl D. *From Ruins to Reconstruction: Urban Identity in Soviet Sevastopol after World War II.* Ithaca, NY: Cornell University Press, 2009.

Rabinowitch, Alexander. *The Bolsheviks in Power: The First Years of Soviet Rule in Petrograd*. Bloomington: Indiana University Press, 2007.

Raskin, A. G., and T. V. Uvarova. "Vozvrashchenie imeni: Nikolai Il'ich Arkhipov." *Pskov: Nauchno-prakticheskii, istoriko-kraevedcheskii zhurnal* 33 (2010), 129–143.

Raskin, A. G., and N. N. Vesnina. *Okhrana i restavratsiia pamiatnikov arkhitektury Leningrada*. Leningrad: Stroiizdat, 1981.

Religioznye praktiki v sovremennoi Rossii, ed. Kathy Rousselet and Aleksandr Agadzhanian. Moscow: Novoe izdatel'stvo, 2006.

Rogers, Douglas. "Old Belief between 'Society' and 'Culture': Remaking Moral Communities and Inequalities on a Former State Farm," in *Religion, Morality, and Community in Post-Soviet Societies*, ed. Mark D. Steinberg and Catherine Wanner. Bloomington: Indiana University Press, 2008, 118–24.

———. *The Old Faith and the Russian Land: A Historical Ethnography of Ethics in the Urals*. Ithaca, NY: Cornell University Press, 2009.

Rogozianskii, A. B. *Strasti po moshcham*. St. Petersburg: Obshchestvo sviatitelia Vasiliia Velikogo, 1998.

Rogoznyi, Pavel. *Tserkovnaia revoliutsiia 1917 goda: Vysshee dukhovenstvo Rossiiskoi Tserkvi v bor'be za vlast' v eparkhiiakh posle Fevral'skoi revoliutsii*. St. Petersburg: Liki Rossii, 2008.

Roslavskii, V. M. *Stanovlenie uchrezhdenii okhrany i restavratsii pamiatnikov iskusstva i stariny v RSFSR 1917–1921 gg.: Igor' Grabar' i restavratsiia*. Moscow: Polimag, 2004.

Roslof, Edward E. *Red Priests: Renovationism, Russian Orthodoxy, and Revolution, 1905–1946*. Bloomington: Indiana University Press, 2002.

Ruble, Blair. *Leningrad: Shaping a Soviet City*. Berkeley, CA: University of California Press, 1990.

Ryan, James. "Cleansing NEP Russia: State Violence against the Russian Orthodox Church in 1922." *Europe-Asia Studies* 65, no. 9 (2013): 1807–26.

Sanchez-Sibony, Oscar. "Depression Stalinism: The Great Break Reconsidered." *Kritika* 15, no. 1 (2014): 23–50.

Sandomirskaja, Irina. "Catastrophe, Restoration, and Kunstwollen: Igor Grabar, Cultural Heritage, and Soviet Reuses of the Past," *Ab Imperio* 20, no. 2 (2015), 339–62.

Semenova, N. Iu., and N. V. Iljine, eds. *Selling Russia's Treasures: The Soviet Trade in Nationalized Art, 1917–1938*. Paris: The M. T. Abraham Center for the Arts Foundation, 2013.

Sharp, Neil. "The Wrong Twigs for an Eagle's Nest? Architecture, Nationalism, and Sir Hugh Lane's Scheme for a Gallery of Modern Art, Dublin, 1904–13." In *The Architecture of the Museum: Symbolic Structures, Urban Contexts*, edited by Michaela Giebelhausen, 32–53. Manchester: Manchester University Press, 2003.

Shchenkov, A. S., ed. *Pamiatniki arkhitektury v dorevoliutsionnoi Rossii: Ocherki istorii arkhitekturnoi restavratsii*. Moscow: Terra-Knizhnyi klub, 2002.

———, ed. *Pamiatniki arkhitektury v Sovetskom Soiuze: Ocherki istorii arkhitekturnoi restavratsii*. Moscow: Pamiatniki istoricheskoi mysli, 2004.

Shcherba, A. N. *Voennaia promyshlennost' Leningrada v 20–30-e gody*. St. Petersburg: Nestor, 1999.

Shearer, David. *Policing Stalin's Socialism: Repression and Social Order in the Soviet Union, 1924–1953*. New Haven, CT: Yale University Press, 2009.

Sheppard, Francis. *The Treasury of London's Past: An Historical Account of the Museum of London and Its Predecessors, the Guildhall Museum and the London Museum*. London: HMSO Publications, 1991.

Sherry, Samantha. *Discourses of Regulation and Resistance: Censoring Translation in the Stalin and Khrushchev Era Soviet Union*. Edinburgh: Edinburgh University Press, 2015.

Shkarovskii, M. V. *Iosiflianstvo: Techenie v Russkoi Pravoslavnoi Tserkvi*. St. Petersburg: Memorial, 1999.

———. *Obnovlencheskoe dvizheniie v Russkoi Pravoslavnoi Tserkvi XX veka*. St. Petersburg: Nestor, 1999.

———. *Peterburgskaia eparkhiia v gody gonenii i utrat, 1917–1945*. St. Petersburg: Liki Rossii, 1995.

———. *Russkaia pravoslavnaia tserkov' pri Staline i Khrushcheve: Gosudarstvenno-tserkovnye otnosh-eniia v SSSR v 1939–1964 godakh*. Moscow: Krutitskoe Patriarshee Podvor'e, 1999.

———. *Russkaia Pravoslavnaia Tserkov' v XX veke*. Moscow: Veche, 2010.

———. "Sankt-Peterburgskie dukhovnye shkoly vo 2-i polovine XX–nachale XXI veka" (Part 1). *Vestnik dukhovnoi istorii* 12, no. 4 (2008): 171–210.

———. "Sankt-Peterburgskie dukhovnye shkoly vo 2-i polovine XX–nachale XXI veka" (Part 2). *Vestnik dukhovnoi istorii* 13, no. 1 (2009): 259–66.

———. *Tserkov' zovet k zashchite Rodiny: Religioznaia zhizn' Leningrada i Severo-Zapada v gody Velikoi Otechestvennoi voiny*. St. Petersburg: Satis-Derzhava 2005.

Shlapentokh, Vladimir. *Public and Private Life of the Soviet People: Changing Values in Post-Stalin Russia*. New York: Oxford University Press, 1989.

Shlikhta, Natalia. "'Orthodox' and 'Soviet': On the Issue of the Identity of Christian Soviet Citizens (1940s–early 1970s)." *Forum for Anthropology and Culture* 11 (2015), 140–64.

Shternshis, Anna. *Soviet and Kosher: Jewish Popular Culture in the Soviet Union, 1923–1939*. Bloomington: Indiana University Press, 2006.

Shtyrkov, Sergei. "'V gorode otkryt Dvorets schast'ia': Bor'ba za novuiu sovetskuiu obriadnost' vremen Khrushcheva." In *Topografiia schast'ia: Etnograficheskie karty moderna; Sbornik statei*, edited by Nikolai Ssorin-Chaikov, 261–75. Moscow: Novoe literaturnoe obozrenie, 2013.

Shun'gina, Elena V. "Politika Sovetskogo gosudarstva v otnoshenii Russkoi pravoslavnoi tserkvi v 1940–1950-kh gg.: Vozvrashchenie kul'tovykh zdanii tserkvi (po materialam Leningrada)." Candidate diss., St. Petersburg Institute of History of the Russian Academy of Sciences, 2009.

Shvidkovskii, O. A. *Building in the USSR, 1917–1932*. London: Studio Vista, 1971.

Siegelbaum, Lewis, ed. *Borders of Socialism: Private Spheres of Soviet Russia*. Basingstoke: Macmillan, 2006.

———. *Cars for Comrades: The Life of the Soviet Automobile*. Ithaca, NY: Cornell University Press, 2008.

Smith, Mark B. *Property of Communists: The Urban Housing Program from Stalin to Khrushchev*. DeKalb: Northern Illinois University Press, 2010.

Smith, Stephen A. "Bones of Contention: Bolsheviks and the Exposure of Saints' Relics, 1918–30." *Past and Present* 204, no. 1 (2009): 155–94.

———. "Contentious Heritage: The Preservation of Churches and Temples in Communist and Post-Communist Russia and China." In *Heritage in the Modern World: Historical Preservation in Global Perspective*, edited by Paul Betts and Corey Ross, 178–213. Past and Present Supplement 10. Oxford: Oxford University Press, 2015.

———. "The First Soviet Generation: Children and Religious Belief in Soviet Russia, 1917–41." In *Generations in Twentieth-Century Europe*, edited by Stephen Lovell, 79–100. Basingstoke: Palgrave, 2007.

Smith, Susan N. "The Accidental Museum: Expropriating and Appropriating the Past." *Russian Review* 67, no. 3 (2008): 438–53.

Smolkin-Rothrock, Victoria. "'Sviato mesto pusto ne byvaet': Ateisticheskoe vospitanie v Sovetskom Soiuze, 1964–1968." *Neprikosnovennyi zapas* 65, no. 3 (2009), http://magazines.russ.ru/nz/2009/3/sm5.html.

———. "The Ticket to the Soviet Soul: Science, Religion, and the Spiritual Crisis of Late Soviet Atheism." *Russian Review* 73, no. 2 (2014): 171–97.

Sobchak, Anatolii. *Iz Leningrada v Peterburg: Puteshestvie vo vremeni i prostranstve*. St. Petersburg: Kontrfors, 1999.

Steinberg, Mark D., and Catherine Wanner, eds. *Religion, Morality, and Community in Post-Soviet Societies*. Bloomington: Indiana University Press, 2008.

Steindorff, Ludwig, and Günther Schulz. *Partei und Kirchen im frühen Sowjetstaat: Die Protokolle der Antireligiösen Kommission beim Zentralkomitee der Russischen Kommunistischen Partei (Bol'ševiki) 1922–1929*. Münster: LIT, 2007.

Stone, Andrew B. "'Overcoming Peasant Backwardness': The Khrushchev Antireligious Campaign and the Rural Soviet Union." *Russian Review* 67, no. 2 (2008): 297–320.

Strickland, John. *The Making of Holy Russia: The Orthodox Church and Russian Nationalism before the Revolution.* Jordanville, NY: Holy Trinity Publications, 2013.

Swenson, Astrid. *The Rise of Heritage: Preserving the Past in France, Germany, and England, 1789–1914.* Cambridge: Cambridge University Press, 2013.

Swenson, Astrid, and Peter Mandler, eds. *From Plunder to Preservation: Britain and the Heritage of Empire, c. 1800–1940.* Oxford: Oxford University Press, 2013.

———. "Preservation Policies and Nationalism in Britain." In *Heritage Preservation in Europe, 1800–2015,* edited by Mark Thatcher. Special issue of *Nations and Nationalism.* Forthcoming.

Takahashi, Sanami. "Church or Museum? The Role of State Museums in Conserving Church Buildings, 1965–85." *Journal of Church and State* 51, no. 3 (2009): 502–17.

Tarkhanov, Alexei and Sergei Kavtaradze, *Stalinist Architecture.* London: Laurence King, 1992.

Taubman, William, *Khrushchev: The Man and His Era.* New York: W. W. Norton, 2003.

Thompson, Michael. *Rubbish Theory: The Creation and Destruction of Value.* Oxford: Oxford University Press, 1979.

Toporov, V. N. "Peterburg i 'Peterburgskii tekst' russkoi literatury" (1971, 1993). In *Peterburgskii tekst russkoi literatury: Izbrannye trudy,* 7–118. St. Petersburg: Iskusstvo-Sankt-Peterburga, 2003.

Uhl, Katharina Barbara. "Building Communism: The Young Communist League during the Soviet Thaw Period, 1953–1964." DPhil thesis, University of Oxford, 2014.

Urban, Felix. "Recovering Essence through Demolition: The 'Organic' City in Post-War Berlin." *Journal of the Society of Architectural Historians* 3 (2004): 354–69.

Vail', Petr, and Aleksandr Genis. *60-e: Mir sovetskogo cheloveka.* Ann Arbor: Ardis, 1988.

Vakhtin, Nikolai, and Boris Firsov, eds. *Public Debate in Russia: Matters of (Dis)order.* Edinburgh: Edinburgh University Press, 2015.

van den Bercken, Willem. *Ideology and Atheism in the Soviet Union.* Berlin: Walter de Gruyter, 1988.

Verdery, Katherine. *The Political Lives of Dead Bodies: Reburial and Post-Socialist Change.* New York: Columbia University Press, 1999.

"V nasledstvo budushchim pokoleniiam: Nekotorye stranitsy istorii restavratsii Peterburga." http://www.d-c.spb.ru/archiv/29/34-37/34-37.htm.

Volkov, Solomon. *St. Petersburg: A Cultural History.* New York: Free Press, 1995.

Voronina, Olga G. "Pussy Riot Steal the Stage in the Moscow Cathedral of Christ the Saviour: Punk Prayer on Trial Online and in Court." *Digital Icons: Studies in Russian, Eurasian and Central European New Media* 9 (2013): 69–85.

Walker, R. Stephen. "Work in Progress: Towards a New Paradigm for the Sociological Study of Religion in the United States." *American Journal of Sociology* 98, no. 5 (1993): 1044–55.

Wanner, Catherine, ed. *State Secularism and Lived Religion in Soviet Russia and Ukraine.* New York: Oxford University Press, 2012.

Weiner, Amir, ed. *Landscaping the Human Garden: Twentieth-Century Population Management in a Comparative Perspective.* Stanford, CA: Stanford University Press, 2003.

———. *Making Sense of War: The Second World War and the Fate of the Bolshevik Revolution.* Princeton, NJ: Princeton University Press, 2001.

Whitehead, Amy. *Religious Statues and Personhood: Testing the Role of Materiality.* London: Bloomsbury, 2013.

Whyte, William. "How Do Buildings Mean? Some Issues of Interpretation in the History of Architecture." *History and Theory* 45, no. 2 (May 2006): 153–77.

Widdis, Emma, *Visions of a New Land: Soviet Film from the Revolution to the Second World War.* New Haven, CT: Yale University Press, 2003.

Willimott, Andy. *Living the Revolution: Urban Communes and Soviet Socialism, 1917–1932.* Oxford: Oxford University Press, 2016.

Wilson, Bryan. *Religion in Sociological Perspective.* Oxford University Press, 1982.

Wortman, Richard. *Scenarios of Power: Myth and Ceremony in Russian Monarchy.* 2 vols. Princeton, NJ: Princeton University Press, 1995–2000.

Wynot, Jennifer. *Keeping the Faith: Russian Orthodox Monasticism in the Soviet Union, 1917–1939.* College Station, TX: Texas A&M University Press, 2004.

Young, Glennys. *Power and the Sacred in Revolutionary Russia: Religious Activists in the Village.* University Park: Pennsylvania State University Press, 1997.

Yurchak, Alexei. *Everything Was Forever, Until It Was No More: The Last Soviet Generation.* Princeton, NJ: Princeton University Press, 2006.

Zhirkov, G. V. "Istoriia sovetskoi tsenzury perioda komissaroderzhaviia (1917–1919 gg.)." *Vestnik Sankt-Peterburgskogo universiteta, 2nd ser.* 1 (1994): 82–92.

Zhiromskaia, V. B., "Religioznost' naroda v 1937 godu," *Istoricheskii vestnik* 1 (2000), http://krotov. info/history/20/1930/1937_zher.htm.

Zhukov, Iu. N. *Stalin: Operatsiia Ermitazh.* Moscow: Vagrius, 2005.

Zitzewitz, Josephine von. "The 'Religious Renaissance' of the 1970s and Its Repercussions on the Soviet Literary Process." DPhil thesis, University of Oxford, 2009.

Zubkova, Elena. *Russia after the War: Hopes, Illusions, and Disappointments, 1945–1957.* Armonk, NY: M. E. Sharpe, 1998.

Zubok, Vladislav. *Zhivago's Children: The Last Russian Intelligentsia.* Cambridge, MA: Harvard University Press, 2009.

Index

A

Academy of Sciences,
    founder of Museum of the History of
        Religion, 125
    in pre-revolutionary Russia, 5, 9
    involvement in Soviet preservation policy,
        91–92, 169, 196
    see also Museum of the History of Religion
        and Atheism (Kazan' Cathedral)
All-Russian Local Church Council (Vserossiiskii
    Pomestnyi Sobor) (1917–1918), 23–24, 31,
    33–34, 35, 263 291n78, 302n53, 303n67
All-Russian Museums Congress, first (1930),
    123, 125
All-Russian Society for the Protection of Monu-
    ments of History and Culture, *see* VOOPIiK
Andreev, B. S., 227
Anisimov, Aleksandr, 76, 110, 307n107
ansambli, architectural, 305n85, 364n40
    churches as integral part of, 118–119, 206,
        256–257
    churches as unwelcome interruptions to, 80,
        112–113, 139, 233–234
    in city planning, 73, 93, 112–113, 139, 152,
        163–164, 231, 247–249, 251, 256–257
    difficulty of preserving, 69, 93–94, 118–119,
        206
    as historic feature of Leningrad, 93, 107, 138–
        139, 163–164, 202, 247–249, 256–257
    individual buildings and interiors as, 39,
        47, 54, 69, 76–79, 83, 93–94, 125, 206,
        245–246, 314n196, 320n90
    see also Haymarket (Leningrad)
anthropology, 20
antimins, 3, 182, 312n167

antireligious campaigns,
    following October Revolution, 22, 24–25, 30,
        44–54, 60–65, 66–67, 68–69, 79–81, 150
    under Stalin, 87, 94, 95–100, 113–114,
        123–126, 128–133, 136–138
    risk of counterproductive effects, 24–25, 30,
        35, 101, 124, 191, 334–335n160
    under Khrushchev, 190–194, 195, 198, 200,
        210, 217, 220–224, 238
    until end of Soviet power, 236–239, 252–254
    see also Decree on Religious Organizations
        (April 8, 1929); League of the Militant
        Godless; Museum of Dying Cult; Museum
        of the History of Religion and Atheism;
        relics, exposure of; "scientific atheism"
Antsiferov, Nikolai, 316 n 31
Aplaksin, Aleksandr,
    St. Anna of Kashin, Bol'shoi Sampsonievskii
        prospect, 317n44
Architecture of Leningrad (journal), 108, 132,
    143, 333n144
Arkhitektura v SSSR (journal), 107
Asaf'ev, Boris, 72
atheism, *see* antireligious campaigns; "scientific
    atheism"

B

Babel, Isaak, "At St. Walenty's," 1–3, 6, 61, 285n21
Baptists, 236
Baranov, Nikolai, 100, 142–143, 162, 163, 164–
    165, 328n68, 355–356n56, 359n114, 363n20
baroque architecture, 69, 77, 78, 144, 195, 241

Church of the Twelve Apostles, Main Post
Office, 39, 45–46

R

Rabinowitch, Alexander 19, 297n2
Rabkrin (Worker and Peasant Inspectorate),
305n91, 311n149
Rastrelli, Bartolomeo, 168, 289
Gostinyi dvor, Nevsky Prospect, 106
Smol'nyi Cathedral, 65, 78, 92, 245, 272
Trinity Cathedral, Trinity-St. Sergius Monastery, 214
Winter Palace, 80, 154, 166
Razodeev, B. A., 247
Red Gates (Moscow), demolition of, 90–92
Red Putilov Factory (later Kirov Factory), 69,
100, 374n25
see also Kirov Factory
regional studies, revival under Khrushchev, 199
registration of religious groups, 27, 53, 60, 67,
193, 236, 237, 253
relics, of St. Alexander Nevsky, 52, 207
exposure of, 30, 36, 44, 52, 64, 302n54,
304n82
religious believers,
administrative treatment of, 52–53,
87, 95–96, 100, 129, 179, 190, 224,
306n106
attitudes towards wider Church, 186
and church demolitions, 13–14, 137–138,
147, 203–204, 212, 239, 242–243
as objects of propaganda, 12, 15, 51–52, 61
popular harassment of, 180, 190, 224
as portrayed in Khrushchev-era discourse,
191–192
reaction against antireligious campaigns,
24–25, 30, 35, 101, 124, 191, 334–
335n160
worshipping in private, 140, 186
see also dvadsatki; petitions
Renovationist Church, see Church of Renovation
Restoration Commission, 26–27, 68
see also State Restoration Workshops
(Central); State Restoration Workshops
(Leningrad)
Restoration Workshops, see Restoration
Commission; State Restoration Workshops
(Central); State Restoration Workshops
(Leningrad)

Revolution and the Church (journal), 24–25, 29,
30, 35–36, 45
Rogov, Mikhail, 90, 323n119
Roman Catholics, attitudes towards sacred
space, 290–291n72
in Poland, 253
see also places of worship (non-Orthodox)
Romanov, Grigorii, 226
Romanov, Konstantin K.,
advocate of "church museums," 320n86,
321n101
attitude to religion and religious architecture, 44, 343n79
availability of information about, 17
career, 43, 72, 110, 138, 307n107, 314n197,
316n31, 329n80, 329–330n83
his criticism of aspects of Soviet policy,
54–55, 312n180, 314n197, 329–330n83
heritage preservation work of, 44, 54–55, 57,
77, 301n46, 309n129, 343n79
personal archive of, 279, 301n46, 307n107
Rossi, Carlo, 73, 108, 289n59, 328n71
General Staff Building, 233–234, 240
Pushkin (Aleksandrinskii) Theater, 107
Russian Orthodox Church, wartime name-
change to, 146
Russian revivalism (architecture), see style russe
Russification policies, 149–150

S

Saki, see H. H. Munro
Sautov, I. P., 241, 346n135, 370–371n139
Science and Religion (journal), 191–192
"scientific atheism," 61, 63, 190–191, 197, 200,
351n9
Second World War, see Great Patriotic War
secularization, models of, 13–16
Sedova-Trotskaia, Natal'ia, 47, 89, 90, 310n137,
310n138, 312n175, 313n183, 315n11
Sergii (Stratogorodskii), Metropolitan, 87, 146,
322n115
Sheremet'ev Palace, 80, 177, 319n80, 321n97,
348n173, 348–349n174
Shkarovskii, Mikhail, 148
Shul'ts, A. A., 74
Sorokin, Father Vladimir, 200, 273, 315n20,
375n36
Sovetskii muzei (journal), 123–124, 126
"Soviet traditions," 200
stagnation, in Gorbachev's terminology, 226